INDIA AND MALAYSIA

India and Malaysia
Intertwined Strands

VEENA SIKRI

MANOHAR
2014

First published 2013
Reprinted 2014

ISBN 978-93-5098-016-3

Published by
Ajay Kumar Jain *for*
Manohar Publishers & Distributors
4753/23 Ansari Road, Daryaganj,
New Delhi 110 002

Printed at
Salasar Imaging Systems
Delhi 110 035

To
my late parents
Krishna and Shiri Patti Datta
They gave me the gift of love.
They remain my inspiration.

Contents

Maps and Diagram

MAPS

DIAGRAM

Preface

I am grateful to Ambassador Kesavapany, former Director of ISEAS (Institute of Southeast Asian Studies), Singapore, for his support for the three-year project (November 2008 to November 2011) that has resulted in this book. During this period I was Visiting Senior Research Fellow at ISEAS.

The three years I spent as India's High Commissioner to Malaysia (September 2000 to December 2003) were among the most memorable years of my career with the Indian Foreign Service. The urge to research and work on this book came from the growing realization of the minimal awareness about the rich history of interaction between our two nations and peoples.

When this interaction began more than two millennia ago, there were no demarcated national boundaries. The interaction was really between the people of South Asia and Southeast Asia, driven by trade, religion, and culture. Friendship and understanding, equality and mutual benefit were its leitmotifs. Perhaps it is this absence of conquest and conflict that has led most historians and political analysts to underplay the strength of the pre-colonial interaction between South and Southeast Asia.

During colonial rule, certainly in the British-controlled areas of colonized Asia, popular memory of the pre-colonial interaction was submerged and suppressed. In the early decades of the twentieth century, Rabindranath Tagore rediscovered India's historical linkages with the East through the work of Dutch scholars. Jawaharlal Nehru took this forward by organizing, in March 1947, the first Asian Relations Conference. India's 'Look East' policy is not a creation of the twentieth century, but the resurrection of what was the considered and accepted way of life for South and Southeast Asia for over two millennia.

While tracing the contours of this interaction and its myriad strands along the vast canvas of time, I have sought to focus on the most significant moments and periods of interaction between India and Malaysia, analysing each in context, from the point of view of the people of India, Malaysia and, during the colonial period, even the British. I have tried to be as inclusive as possible in this analysis. Inevitably, however, some aspects and events have received more detailed attention than others. Some, due to constraints of space and time, may have been omitted.

By and large, I have been chronological in elucidating events and happenings. The two exceptions have been Chapter 12 on Rabindranath Tagore's visit to Malaya, and Chapter 15 on the Asian Relations Conference. Tagore's visit to Malaya, Singapore and Indonesia in 1927 signified, for India, the rediscovery of her pre-colonial cultural and trade links with the nations of the East. The memory of these interactions had been all but obliterated under colonial rule. Tagore's seminal role in the revival of these relationships is often underestimated. Tagore wrote to Jawaharlal Nehru, conveying his enthusiasm for the Asian renaissance, urging Nehru to 'give strength to the historic forces of Asian unity'. Nehru conceptualized the Asian Relations Conference as part of his own vision for the future of Asia. Malaya was an active participant in this Conference. The contemporary relevance of this Conference is the reason why I felt it deserved a separate chapter.

It is my hope that my endeavour in writing this book will generate interest in this under-researched area of political and socio-economic history, that it will encourage further scholarship on both past and contemporary aspects of relations between South and Southeast Asia.

I express my grateful appreciation for the extensive and unstinting assistance I received in my research from the directorial staff at several libraries. The library at ISEAS, Singapore, the library at the India International Centre (IIC), New Delhi and the library at the Nehru Memorial Museum & Library (NMML), New Delhi, are just three in a long list. They deserve special mention because of the unfailing cooperation and courtesies I received from them.

My friend, philosopher and soulmate, my bedrock of support in completing this book, has been my husband, Rajiv. His own direct involvement in the evolution of India's 'Look East' Policy, and his incisive appreciation of the situation in both India and Southeast Asia, have guided me at all stages.

Certainly, I accept sole responsibility for any errors of omission or commmision.

13 January 2013
New Delhi

VEENA SIKRI

Prologue

> You cannot deal with the future unless you come to terms with the past.
>
> RICHARD HOLBROOKE[1]

The genetic origins of Asian populations have been traced in a recent pan-Asian study, the findings of which were first published online on 10 December 2009 in a report in *Science*. This investigative study, the first of its kind on Asian populations, is titled 'Mapping Human Genetic Diversity in Asia: The HUGO Pan-Asian SNP Consortium'.[2] Over 80 scientists from 40 leading scientific institutions in ten Asian countries came together in the Human Genome Organization's (HUGO's) Pan-Asian SNP[3] Consortium to map the range of genetic diversity in Asia and trace the genetic origins of Asian populations.

Professor Edison Liu, executive director at the Genome Institute of Singapore (GIS) and president of HUGO, initiated and co-ordinated this research. The ten participating countries were India, China, Singapore, Philippines, Malaysia, Thailand, Indonesia, Japan, South Korea and Taiwan, covering the regions of South Asia, Southeast Asia and East Asia. Institutions in Malaysia included the Human Genome Centre, School of Medical Sciences, Universiti Sains Malaysia (Kubang Kerian, Kelantan) and the Department of Molecular Medicine, University of Malaya (Kuala Lumpur). The principal institution in India was the Institute of Genomics and Integrative Biology, Council for Scientific and Industrial Research (CSIR), New Delhi.

The study spanned five years. DNA samples from 1903 unrelated individuals representing 71 populations from these ten countries were collected and genotyped. The primary clusters corresponded overwhelmingly to the following language families or ethnic groups: the Altaic cluster, the Tai-Kadai/Sino-Tibetan cluster, the Hmong-Mien cluster, the Austro-Asiatic cluster, the Negrito-W cluster (characterizing the two Malaysian Negrito populations), the Negrito-E cluster (found mainly among Philippine Negrito populations), the Papuan cluster (characterizing mainly Papuan and east Indonesian populations), the Austronesian cluster, the Dravidian cluster (Indian populations speaking mainly Dravidian languages), and the Indo-European cluster (Indian populations speaking mainly Indo-European languages). Four clusters corresponded to single populations, namely the Bidayuh population of Malaysia, the proto-Malay Temuan population, the Mlabri inhabiting Thailand, and the African cluster.[4]

The analysis of molecular variance (AMOVA) and the genetic mapping conducted by scientists and institutions involved in this project support the 'one-wave' hypothesis. That is, the majority of the gene pool in Asia (the part that gave rise to all modern East Asian and Southeast Asian populations) was derived from a single initial entry of modern humans into the subcontinent.[5]

Edison Liu elaborated on these conclusions:

> We have redefined the genetic history of Asian migration. . . . Previously it was thought—because of archaeological, anthropological, and limited genetic data—that Asia was populated by two waves of migration. One wave was from Southeast Asia, called the Southern route, and the second from Central Asia, called the Northern route. . . . The HUGO Pan-Asian SNP Consortium findings point to a single wave of migration. . . . The reconstruction is out of Africa to India.[6]

The movement of people from Africa to India continued on to Thailand, Malaysia, Indonesia, the Philippines and beyond. From Southeast Asia, settlers migrated to other parts of Asia, including China. '. . . Dravidians (in Southern India) and Chinese had common ancestors. . . . What we are seeing is the transit of our ancestors in their travels out of Africa through India and into Southeast Asia and North Asia. . . . Along the way, they deposited progeny that later expanded, or contracted'.[7] For Edison Liu this movement of people is estimated to have started 100,000 years or 5,000 generations ago, essentially along the coastal route.

Professor Edison Liu further said:

> This study was a milestone not only in the science that emerged, but the consortium that was formed. Ten Asian countries came together in the spirit of solidarity to understand how we were related as a people and we finished with a truly Asian scientific community. We overcame shortage of funds and diverse operational constraints through partnerships, good will, and cultural sensitivity.[8]

In essence, the study has used modern scientific tools of analysis to show that the people of South, Southeast and East Asia are linked by a unifying genetic thread. The people of India and Malaysia, too, are intertwined with these genetic strands.

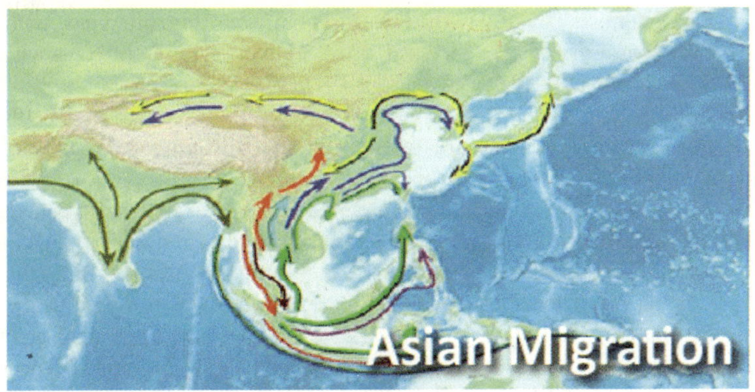

Map 1: Putative Prehistoric Migrations Across South and Southeast Asia
(© The HUGO Pan-Asian SNP Consortium)[9]

> According to . . . the Pan-Asian SNP Initiative, the most recent common ancestors of Asians arrived first in India (aqua green). Later, some of them migrated to Thailand and South to the lands known today as Malaysia, Indonesia and the Philippines. The first group of settlers must have gone very far south before they settled successfully. These included the Malay Negritos (brown), Philippine Negritos (purple), the East Indonesians, and early settlers of the Pacific Islands (dark green). Thereafter, one or several groups of people migrated North, mixed with previous settlers there and finally formed various populations we now refer to as Austronesian (light green), Austro-Asiatic (red), Tai-Kadai (a dark blue), Hmong-Mien (light blue), and Altaic (yellow), etc.

NOTES

1. Statement made in Jakarta, quoted in the *Jakarta Post* on 22 November 1999, accessed at http://images.thejakartapost.com/news/1999/11/22/rights-body-summon-top-brass.html on 29 June 2011.
2. www.sciencemag.org/cgi/content/full/326/5959/1541/DC1 published 11 December 2009, Science 326, 1541(2009) DOI: 10.1126/science.1177074.
3. A short DNA sequence, Single Nucleotide Polymorphism or SNP (pronounced snip).
4. 'Mapping Human Genetic Diversity in Asia', pp. 16-17 (access details at n. 2 above).
5. Ibid., pp. 40-1.
6. *Asia Times Online*, 19 December 2009, 'India is "Thailand" to Asia, Say Scientists' by Raja Murthy (Mumbai), quoting interview with Professor Edison Liu, accessed on 4 March 2011 at http://www.atimes.com/atimes/South_Asia/KL19Df03.html, pp. 1-2.
7. Ibid., p. 2.
8. Edison Liu, Press Release of the Genome Institute of Singapore, December 2009.
9. A map reconstructing human migration across Asia over the course of ancient history. The genetic data, which were paired with linguistic groupings, suggest that South Asia and Southeast Asia served as the starting point for subsequent population movement throughout the continent.

PART I

TRADE, RELIGION AND CULTURE: THE PRE-COLONIAL CENTURIES

1

The Ancient Beginnings

The earliest migrations into India and into Southeast Asia were by the land route, along the coast. Movement was tortuous and slow. Early settlements led to localized specializations in products and the consequent interest in trade through exchange of goods with other settlements. This soon brought about the development of coastal navigation in canoes and dugouts. The length of India's coastline, over 4,000 km and the abundance of her forests and rivers made riverine and coastal waterways a vital and essential means of communication.

Knowledge about the monsoon winds set the tone for more direct interactions between South and Southeast Asia. Seasonal winds powered sailing vessels setting out from ports along the east coast of India towards the present-day Myanmar, Malaysia, Indonesia, Thailand and beyond. Klaudios Ptolemaios, popularly known as Ptolemy, the Egyptian geographer who lived in the second century CE, has described Paloura (probably near Gopalpur-on-sea in present-day Odisha) as the *apheterion* (or *apheterium*), the point of departure on India's eastern seaboard, whence ships would strike out to the open seas in their journey to the Chryse or the Golden Chersonese (Malay Peninsula). The ships that sailed across the Bay of Bengal from Paloura would find their first landfall near the town of Syriam just south of Rangoon (Yangon) in Myanmar.

The memory of these legendary voyages from India to Southeast Asia is kept alive even today through the celebrations of *Bali Yatra* (journey to Bali) in the state of Odisha. The *Bali Yatra* festival is held each year on the full-moon day of the month of Karttika in the lunar calendar (November-December). The lyrics recited include the words *aa-ka-ma-bai, pana-gua-thoi. Aa-ka-ma-bai* are the first syllables of the four lunar months that guide the travel to and from Bali. These months are Asadha (July-August), Karttika, Magha (February-March) and Baisakha (April-May). Reminiscing the glorious sea-voyages to Southeast Asia, masses of people from all communities and creeds throng the coast, and those living inland throng river banks or even ponds and tanks to set afloat tiny boats made of paper, solapith (a herb like water-plant) or banana leaves. In these boats are placed small lamps (*deepa*), betel leaf (*paan*), and betel-nut (*gua*). The lamps are lit to the joyous chants of *aa-ka-ma-bai, pana-gua-thoi* and the boats are pushed out in the direction of Bali.

There were no nation states then, thousands of years ago. There were kingdoms, intrepid travellers, traders, and an insatiable demand for luxury goods and spices from Rome to China. Puranic[1] texts contain poetic Sanskrit place-names for different regions of Southeast Asia. These reflect the spread of the trade and the most sought-after commodities: gold from Suvarnadvipa (Sumatra and the Malay Peninsula) and Suvarnabhumi (Burma or Myanmar), camphor from Karpuradvipa (Borneo), cardamom from Takkola (an island along the north-west of the Malay Peninsula, perhaps present-day Phuket). Southeast Asia provided multiple destinations for traders to procure goods in great demand not only in India, but also across the Arab world, as well as in Europe and in China.

India was well positioned, midway between Europe and China. The Malay Peninsula and the islands of Sumatra and Java lay at the centre of the oceanic trade routes between India and China, uniquely positioned on both sides of the Straits of Malacca, providing key vantage points that have been successfully leveraged throughout history. These lands offered the most convenient locations for settlements, ports, and emporia where ships could land, merchandize could be stored and transhipped, and the myriad requirements of merchants, sailors, and other participants in the trade, serviced.

There is archaeological evidence to back up the conclusions reached by the HUGO SNP Consortium about the antiquity of human migration routes out of India into Southeast Asia and beyond. This evidence establishes such migratory movements going back to at least the early Iron Age, i.e. around 1200 BCE. In the years 1926-30, Professor H. Otley Beyer conducted a series of excavations in the Philippines. Subsequently, R.B. Dixon visited the Philippines to examine the objects unearthed in these excavations, and described his findings as follows:

> It is from finds in the Iron Age strata which overlie the neolithic deposits that immediate conclusions can legitimately be drawn. . . . Iron implements and weapons (include) knives, axes, daggers and spear-points; . . . (there are) glass beads and bangles, both green and blue, and finally beads of semi-precious stones such as agate, cornelian, amethyst and rock-crystal. . . . Now both the iron and glass objects are similar to and in some cases identical with the prehistoric glass and iron finds in the south of India. These occur in the dolmen tombs and urn burials which are found by hundreds and thousands, and which certainly antedate the historic Chera, Chola and Pandyan kingdoms, whose history goes back to the beginning of the Christian era or before. As finds of similar glass beads and bangles have recently been made in the Malay Peninsula, in dolmen tombs in Java, and in North Borneo, the inference is inescapable that we have clear evidence of a trade contact between the northern Philippines and southern India running way back into the first millennium BC. . . . In Chinese historical sources there are a few references to maritime traders bringing typical Indian products to China as far back as the 7th century BC. These accounts have generally been regarded with incredulity or strong suspicion at least. In view of this evidence from the Philippines the probability of these accounts is greatly increased.[2]

Over time, the migratory process accelerated due to advances in navigational skills and ship building prowess across the Indian subcontinent. This facilitated the emergence of trans-oceanic maritime routes across the Indian Ocean and across the Bay of Bengal. The migratory process also became much more interactive, with people and goods moving freely across the seas. Trade, religion, and culture were the leitmotifs of the process, technological prowess the mainstay. Interactivity and learning from others was the secret of its success. Political conquest through wars or coercion, subjugation through a colonial relationship, subversion of local cultures and identities, economic exploitation of overseas populations, these were conspicuous only in their absence.

MARITIME SKILLS: THE BASIS FOR THE ANCIENT INTERACTION BETWEEN SOUTH AND SOUTHEAST ASIA

Ancient texts are replete with references to India's maritime achievements. Radha Kumud Mookerji has described how 'for full thirty centuries India stood out as the very heart of the Old World, and maintained her position as one of the foremost maritime countries'.[3] It is the advent into Asia of European colonialism that brought about the weakening and virtual demise of India's ship building industry. Johann Georg Buhler (1837-98), renowned German scholar of ancient Indian texts and law, concluded, after studying references in ancient Indian texts, that these 'prove the early existence of a complete navigation of the Indian ocean, and of the trading voyages of Indians'.[4] The perusal of important textual references combined, wherever available, with archaeological evidence testify to the strength and longevity of India's maritime past.

Perhaps the oldest evidence on record is contained in the *Rigveda*, the ancient collection of sacred Indian hymns in the Sanskrit language. Some of its verses, notably the *Gayatri Mantra*, are still recited as prayers by Hindus, making the *Rigveda* among the world's oldest religious texts in continued use. German scholar Thomas Oberlies has used philological and linguistic markers to establish that the *Rigveda* was composed in the north-western region of the Indian subcontinent somewhere between 1700 and 1100 BCE, on an average more than 3500 years ago. The *Rigveda* contains several references to sea voyages, including those undertaken for commercial purposes. One passage (I.25.7) describes Varuna (credited with being the Lord of the Oceans) as having full knowledge of the ocean routes along which vessels sail. A second passage (I.56.2) describes merchants whose field of activity knows no bounds, who go everywhere in pursuit of gain, and frequent every part of the sea. A third passage (I.116.3) speaks of a naval expedition on which Tugra, the rishi king, sends his son Bhujyu to fight against enemies in distant islands. Bhujyu's vessel is shipwrecked by a storm on the high seas, and he is rescued by the twin brothers, the Asvins, in their 'hundred-oared galley'.

Among the many invocations in the *Rigveda* are several to Agni, the Lord of Fire: 'Do thou whose countenance is turned to all sides send off our adversaries as if in a ship to the opposite shore; do thou convey us in a ship across the sea for our welfare'.[5]

The *Ramayana* of Valmiki describes the life of Rama who, according to A.L. Basham, lived in the eighth or seventh century BCE.[6] The *Ramayana* contains several references to the maritime interactions between India and distant lands across the sea. In the Kishkindha Kandam of the *Ramayana*, Sugriva, the Lord of the Monkeys, while giving directions to his clansmen in their search for Sita, gives a discourse on all the possible places where she could have been concealed. Sugriva directs them to go to the cities and mountains in the islands of the sea, including Yavadvipa (the island of Java) and Suvarnadvipa (Sumatra and the Malay Peninsula). The land of Koshakarsa is also indicated as a likely place for Sita's concealment. This is none other than China 'the land where grows the worm which yields the threads of silken clothes'.[7] Yet another passage in this section refers to the Lohita Sagara or the Red Sea. In the Ayodhya Kandam of the *Ramayana*, a verse speaks about preparations for a naval battle when it says 'Let hundreds of Kaivarta young men lie in wait in five hundred ships (to obstruct the enemy's passage)'.[8]

The epic *Mahabharata*, composed by the sage Vyasa, chronicles the war traditionally dated to 3102 BCE.[9] The Adi Parva of the *Mahabharata* refers to the escape of the Pandava brothers (from the destruction planned for them) in a ship that was secretly and especially constructed under orders of the kindhearted Vidura. The ship is described as being of a large size, provided with machinery and all kinds of weapons of war, and able to defy storms and waves.[10]

The *Manusamhita* or *Manusmriti*, codified by Manu somewhere between 200 BCE and CE 200, includes descriptions of maritime warfare. It prescribes detailed laws for the shipping industry, including for marine insurance! One *shloka* (verse) says that the rate of interest on bottomry should be fixed by men well acquainted with sea voyages. The rates for boat-hire should be different for river journeys and for sea voyages. The rules regarding what can only be described as marine insurance prescribe, *inter alia*, that sailors are collectively responsible for the damage caused by their fault to the goods they carry, while absolving them of all responsibility if the damage is caused by an accident beyond human control.[11] The *Manusamhita* enjoins that those entrusted with the business of conducting trade with other countries must familiarize themselves with the production requirements and other relevant details of purchase or sale, including learning the languages and dialects of the countries involved.

The *Yajnavalkya Samhita*, part of the *Yajurveda*, contains a *shloka* which indicates that Hindus of all castes were in the habit of making adventurous journey by sea in pursuit of profit and gain.[12] At the same time, the *Manusamhita* and some of the oldest Dharmasutras (containing rules of conduct and rites as they were practised in various Vedic schools) forbade sea-voyages by orthodox Brahmins. Severe penance is prescribed if this rule is not obeyed, including loss of caste. Those Brahmins who have gone to sea, says the *Manusmriti*, cannot participate in certain religious ceremonies. Some Dharmasutras, accepting that transgressions of these restrictions were frequent and quite common, prescribe the duties payable by ship-owners to the king.

The *Vayu Purana* states that the Puranas were originally recited by the great god Brahma, and that one has to understand the Puranas if one is to appreciate the Vedas and the Upanishads. The Puranas have numerous references to merchants engaged in seaborne trade, about shipwrecks, about merchants embarking on sea-voyages in quest of pearls accompanied by people who knew all about pearl-fishing, and the parable about the dangerous plight of the man sailing on the great ocean in a ship overtaken by a whirlwind.[13]

The *Niryamaksutras* (training manuals) were put to good use in many coastal Indian towns to train persons so that they could participate in sea journeys. The *jalaniryamakas*, guides who could predict the behaviour of waters, and the *navikas* (pilots or navigators) were highly regarded members of the crew. A *mahanava* (big ship) would have a *sasaka* (captain), *kammakaras* (sailors who worked the sails on the open sea where the coast was no longer visible), and many others. There was a specific term, *jalapathakammikena*, for those who earned their living on the sea. The specialized terminology used in ancient Indian texts to describe seafaring activities is indicative of the extensive study, precise knowledge and high importance accorded to this field.

There are equally varied references to travel and trade by sea-borne vessels in ancient secular literature. Around the fourth or fifth century, Kalidas gave vivid descriptions about oceans as highways of commerce, about adventurous sea-voyages and naval fights, in *Raghuvamsa* and *Shakuntala*. The *Kathasaritsagara* (or Ocean of the Streams of Stories), the famous eleventh-century collection of Indian legends, fairy tales and folk tales retold by Somadeva who hailed from Kashmir, is full of references to interactions with distant countries through sea journeys, including specific mention of trade and commerce with Suvarnadvipa, the Malay Peninsula.

Ancient Buddhist chronicles and literature corroborate the conclusion that 'the ocean was freely used by the Indians in ancient times as the great highway of international commerce'.[14] Buddhist texts, too, highlight the extensive development of India's maritime shipbuilding and navigational skills and the ways in which these were put to good use for creating networks of commerce and culture across the high seas. The *Mahavamsa* or the Great Chronicle describes the life and times of the people of Ceylon (now Sri Lanka) from the coming of Prince Vijaya in 543 BCE to the reign of King Mahasena in the fourth century. The *Rajavaliya*, a historical narrative of Sinhalese kings, covers the island's history from its legendary beginnings up to the accession of King Vimaladharmasurya II in 1687, just prior to the commencement of colonial rule by the British.

The *Mahavamsa* and the *Rajavaliya* are replete with references to sea-voyages and sea-borne trade with India and beyond. The *Rajavaliya* describes a ship in which King Simhaba (also known as King Simhavahu) of Bengal sent Prince Vijaya away: it accommodated 700 passengers. Prince Vijaya landed on the southern shores of Ceylon on the day the Buddha attained *nirvana*, and founded the Great Dynasty of Ceylon. The Ajanta cave paintings (between say 100 BCE and CE 500) include one depicting Prince Vijaya's landing in Ceylon. The *Mahavamsa* says that the ship in which Prince Vijaya's Pandyan bride was brought from India to Ceylon carried 800 passengers. Voyages to Ceylon starting from the city of Morapura on the Ganga are described as taking twelve days.

The *Niddesa* is a Buddhist scripture, part of the Pali canon of Theravada Buddhism, believed to have been composed not later than the first century BCE. The *Niddesa* enumerates a number of Sanskritized place-names. Scholars like Sylvain Lévi have identified many of these with localities in the Malay Peninsula and other parts of Southeast Asia.

There was regular and ceaseless traffic between the port of Tamralipti (later known as Tamluk) in Bengal and the island of Ceylon. The legend about the Sacred Relic of the Tooth of Lord Buddha, as related in the *Dathadhatuwanso*, describes how, in the fourth century, 800 years after the death of Buddha, the Sacred Tooth Relic was carried from Dantapura (now Puri) in Odisha by Prince Dantha and his wife Hemamali to the port of Tamralipti, whence they travelled by the regular shipping service, and brought the Tooth Relic to Ceylon, landing in Lankapattana (now Ilankeiturei).[15]

The Jatakas, a vast and voluminous body of literature, relate to the previous births of Lord Buddha. It is considered that the Jatakas were composed over a 1,000-year period, beginning around 500 BCE. They contain specific descriptions of ships, sea-journeys and commerce across the high seas. The *Supparaka Jataka* describes the ship in which Buddha, the master mariner in his Supparaka Bodhisatta incarnation, made his voyages from Bharukachchha, the marsh of Bharu (present-day Bharuch). The ship in which he journeyed to the 'sea of seven gems' is described as carrying 700 merchants.

The *Samudda Vanija Jataka* describes a ship that accommodated 1,000 carpenters. The carpenters, all from the same village near Varanasi, built the ship secretly and used it to emigrate overseas to an island in order to avoid paying up the large debt they had incurred![16] The *Mahajanaka Jataka* recounts the adventures of a prince who, together with other traders, set out from Champa (present-day Bhagalpur in Bihar) with goods for trade and export to Suvarnabhumi.[17] Through these Jatakas we learn that the Ganga was in that epoch navigable by sea-worthy ships right up to Varanasi and Champa. Suvarnabhumi could here refer to either

Burma (now Myanmar), or the Golden Chersonese (present-day Malaysia).

The various Nikaya collections of the Buddhists contain specific references to sea-voyages that last for six months or more, made in ships which could be drawn upon shore in the winter. These were not just coastal sailings but sea voyages made out of sight of land. The *Digha Nikaya* describes how

> merchants carrying on sea-borne trade would take with them in their sea-going vessels certain birds of strong wing which, when the vessels were out of sight of land, would be let loose and used to indicate in which direction the land lay. If the shore were not near or within easy reach, the birds would return to the ships (after flying in all directions to get to land), but if there were land within a few miles the birds would not return.[18]

Thomas Williams Rhys Davids, the pioneering British scholar of Pali, places the Nikayas in the fifth century BCE. He considers this reference in the *Digha Nikaya* to be among 'the earliest in Indian books to ocean-going ships out of sight of land'.[19]

The move away from coastal shipping to traversing the high seas could not have succeeded without the simultaneous accumulation of two skills. The first was building sea-worthy vessels that could withstand adverse weather and sailing conditions, and could stay away from land without the necessity of berthing and replenishing supplies for increasingly long periods of time. The second set of skills relates to navigational techniques and the scientific understanding of monsoon winds and other related climatic conditions on the high seas in order to be able to determine the right season and direction of travel for each journey.

There are several references to the use of the earliest mariner's compass on Indian ships. The *Bombay Gazetteer* carries a report that

> the early Hindu astrologers are said to have used the magnet as they still use the modern compass, in fixing the North and East, in laying foundations, and other religious ceremonies. The Hindu compass was an iron fish that floated in a vessel of oil and pointed to the North. The fact of this older Hindu compass seems placed beyond doubt by the Sanskrit word *maccha-yantra*, or fish machine, which Molesworth gives as a name for the mariner's compass.[20]

Ancient Indian literature is replete with references to sea voyages beyond the western, eastern and southern shores of India, to trade and commerce across the oceans and to powerful seagoing vessels that were capable of undertaking such strenuous and hazardous journeys. These references are contextual and almost completely devoid of any hagiography. They occur in Hindu and Buddhist scriptures and in secular writings by authors from all walks of life. The strength and frequency of these references support the conclusion that naval prowess and mastery over sea travel were accepted as an integral part of life and living conditions in ancient India, well before the beginning of the common era.

There are very few direct references in ancient Indian literature to the ways in which ships were built or to the main centres of the shipbuilding industry. It was only a little over 100 years ago, that two ancient Sanskrit manuscripts, hitherto unknown, were discovered. Both provide invaluable insights into the economic history of ancient India. One of these, Kautilya's *Arthashastra*, has been translated and is widely read and appreciated. The other, the *Yukti Kalpataru*, which has not been translated in full, remains little known except to students of maritime history and technology. It finds mention in Aufrecht's *Catalogue of Sanskrit Manuscripts*.

The *Yukti Kalpataru* is considered to have been written in the eleventh century by King Sri Bhojaraja of Dhara (Dhar in today's Madhya Pradesh), a prolific writer who ruled from 1005 to 1055. The title of this work translates as 'The Wishing Tree (Kalpataru) of Artifice (Workmanship)'.[21] King Bhoja is known in history and literature as an erudite scholar. He is the author of several works such as the *Samarangana Sutradhara*, a treatise on architecture. The *Yukti Kalpataru* is a descriptive treatise covering diverse entities like jewels and ornaments, swords and ships.

Two chapters in this book deal in elaborate detail with every aspect of ship-building, a concise summation of the knowledge in this field that had accumulated with Indian ship-builders over the previous millennium and more. These chapters are respectively titled '*Nispadayanoddesa*' or 'Then comes the un-wheeled vehicle' and '*Jaghanya Jalayanani*' or 'Despicable water-vessels'.

The chapter on the 'un-wheeled vehicle' scientifically classifies every aspect of the ship-building industry. It describes the varieties of wood best suited for the construction of ships. The author concludes that the best wood for ship-building is that which is 'light, hard and cannot be joined'. The ship built with such wood is 'capable of passing through troubled waters' and brings 'wealth and happiness' to its owner. On the other hand, 'ships made of two different kinds of wood bring neither good nor comfort. They do not last for long, (the planks) rot, split and sink in the water'.[22] The author prescribes that no iron be used in holding or joining together the planks to be used for the bottoms of sea-going vessels, since such use of iron will inevitably expose the ships to the influence of magnetic rocks in the sea, or bring them within a magnetic field.[23]

The *Yukti Kalpataru* classifies ships according to whether they are river-going or ordinary (*samanya*), and sea-going or special (*visesa*). Within each group, vessels are categorized according to their length, breadth and depth or height. The book specifies which set of dimensions make a vessel steady and balanced in the water, and hence brings good-luck to the owner. Sea-going ships are classified by *dirgha* (according to length) and *unnata* (according to height), with specific indications of the groups (categorized according to dimensions) that bring ill-fortune or gain and profit to their owner.

The *Yukti Kalpataru* provides elaborate and detailed accounts about how ships are to be decorated and furnished. The colour that a ship is painted depends on the number of masts: white for a vessel with four masts, red for one with three masts, yellow for a two-mast vessel and blue for a single-mast ship. The prow of a ship must be beautifully shaped, with specific suggestions for the forms and figures to be used for decorative and auspicious purposes.

Three classes of ships are identified according to the length and positioning of the cabin. Ships with cabins extending from one end to the other are called *sarvamandira*, and are used for general transport. Ships with cabins in the middle, described as *madhyamandira*, are suitable for the rainy season and for pleasure trips. Ships with cabin(s) in the front are called *agramandira*. These are convenient in the dry season, for long voyages and for use in naval warfare. A ship with cabin(s) less than half of its length is swift. The *agramandira* ships are the ones alluded to in the *Ramayana*, the *Mahabharata*, and in Kalidasa's *Raghuvamsa*.

The chapter on the 'un-wheeled vehicle' concludes with the advice that 'lightness, hardness, mobility, hollowness and good proportion' are recommended attributes of ships. 'The king who builds his ships after considering all these, enjoys happiness throughout his life and gains victory in war. The king who builds his ships otherwise out of his ignorance, his reputation, strength, force and wealth are all destroyed.'[24]

Substantial archaeological evidence has been uncovered to establish the antiquity of India's involvement in sea-borne trade and ship-building. In the 1950s, the ancient port-city of Lothal was excavated, situated at the Gulf of Khambhat. This city dates back 4,500 years (2500-1900 BCE), with strong architectural and allied similarities to the Indus Valley civilization cities of Harappa and Mohenjodaro. Lothal has one of the world's oldest sea-faring harbours discovered so far. There is a dockyard, a warehouse, and a dry dock with a complex and sophisticated lock-gate system. The dockyard is constructed of fine bricks and is most scientifically designed to carry out the water flow, and to withstand even tidal-force currents. Over sixty-five Indus Valley seals were found in Lothal, with impressions of bamboo, rope and other packing materials, indicating the centrality of trade to the economy of the city. Other artefacts found here include pottery, semi-precious stones, and beads of gold. The town of Lothal is said to have been destroyed by frequent floods that occurred around 1900 BCE. It was completely abandoned by 1700 BCE.

Greek writers (Lucius Flavius Arrianus, Quintus Curtius and others) describing Alexander's campaigns in India in the fourth century BCE provide important details about economic activities. These accounts reveal that ship-building was a flourishing industry and major source of employment, with active demand for both river and ocean-going vessels. Arrianus describes dockyards, and the construction and supply by the tribe called Xathroi of transport vessels and galleys with thirty oars.[25]

With the end of Alexander's Indian campaigns, the Maurya dynasty consolidated its hold over large parts of India. Megasthenes, the Greek ethnographer, travelling in India in the third century BCE, provides further details about the ship-building industry and its prolific output. He confirms the existence of a class of ship-builders among the artisans, but says they worked for the state and not for any private person. 'These ships built in the royal shipyards were, however, let out on hire'.[26]

Kautilya's *Arthashastra* is a treatise on the science of politics and administration, composed towards the end of the fourth century BCE during the reign of Chandragupta Maurya. It is considered to be among the world's oldest treatises on the economic and social administration of a state. Kautilya has compiled the *Arthashastra* by bringing together all treatises on this subject written by earlier teachers.[27]

Kautilya's *Arthashastra* provides invaluable information about the conditions of the shipping industry, navigation and sea-borne trade prevailing at that time. The organizational structures described in this treatise had evidently been in place for long years, improved upon from one ruler to the next.

The administrative structures (relating to shipping and sea-borne trade) described in the *Arthashastra* include the *navadhyaksa* as one of the 40 key heads of departments throughout the country.[28] The *navadhyaksa* combines in one post the roles of the Admiral of the Fleet, the head of the Coast Guard, the head of the Merchant Navy, and the officer overseeing the administration of the inland waterways system. The word *navadhyaksa* has been variously translated as Controller of Shipping or Superintendent of Shipping.

The *navadhyaksa* is tasked with looking after 'activities concerning sea voyages and ferries at the mouths of rivers, as well as ferries over natural lakes, artificial lakes and rivers, in the *sthaniya* and other towns'. He has to manage the sea-borne trade, including sending off ships from the port at times suitable for voyage, and demanding 'duty from ships sailing on the sea when they come within the domain (territorial waters)' or call at the port. At the same time he must also 'destroy vessels that cause harm, also those coming over from the enemy's territory and those violating the regulations of the port'. The *navadhyaksa* is tasked with collecting boat-rentals from fishermen, ship-fares from sea-voyagers and duty on goods from traders. He must 'observe the regulations in a port town as fixed by the Commissioner of Ports'. He must also 'rescue boats that have gone out of their course or are tossed about by a gale'. These onerous and comprehensive responsibilities of the *navadhyaksa* indicate the central role of shipping and sea-borne trade in the life and economy of India 2,500 years ago.

Several representations of ships and boats in ancient Indian sculptures and paintings, even on ancient Indian coins, conform to the descriptions contained in the *Yukti Kalpataru*. At Sanchi in Madhya Pradesh the Buddhist *stupas*, which date back to the second century BCE, have numerous sculptures depicting boats and ships. The prows and other details of these vessels conform to what is prescribed in the *Yukti Kalpataru*. Scholars like Mookerji estimate that King Bhojaraja, author of the *Yukti Kalpataru*, may have compiled his treatise from works at least as old as the monuments in Sanchi.

The renowned frescoes of the Buddhist cave temples at Ajanta near Aurangabad in Maharashtra are known to have been executed over a period of almost 1,000 years beginning with the second century BCE and going up to about CE 800. The depictions of ships and boats are mostly in Cave 2, dated between 525 and 650. Distinct depictions of the *agramandira* and *madhyamandira* types of vessel can be identified.

Foreign or non-Indian sources, too, include significant literary references to Indian ship-building capacities and sculptural depictions of Indian ships. Among the most well known are the magnificent sculptures at Borobudur in Java, dating to the seventh century. These have splendid bas-relief depictions of Indian ships in full sail arriving at the port. 'The Javanese chronicles relate that about 603 a ruler of Gujarat, forewarned of the coming destruction of his kingdom, started his son with 5,000 followers, among whom were cultivators, artisans, warriors, physicians, and writers, in 6 large and 100 small vessels, for Java'.[29] The Philadelphia Museum (USA) exhibits a model of these 'outrigger ships' that voyaged from India to Java. They are described as being 60 ft long and 15 ft wide, built as 'a cage-work of timber above a great log answering for a keel, the hold of the vessel being formed by planking inside the timbers; and the whole being so top-heavy as to make an outrigger essential for safety'.[30] The scholars at the Philadelphia Museum attribute the great migration in the early years of the seventh century 'from Gujarat in ancient India near the mouth of the Indus to the island of Java . . . to the devastation of Upper India by Scythian tribes and to the drying up of the country.'[31]

This migration from Gujarat was part of the continuous two-way movement of goods and people between India and the Malay Archipelago. In the early years of the fifth century the Chinese pilgrim Fa-hien had arrived in Java on a similar ship, sailing from Tamralipti in India via Ceylon. Fa-hien's ship, with over 200 passengers on board, arrived in Java after more than three months of continuous sailing from Ceylon. Descriptions of this ship note that 'astern of the great ship was a smaller one as a provision in case of the larger vessel being injured or wrecked during the voyage'.[32]

The first century Roman author Gaius Plinius Secundus (better known as Pliny the Elder) in his *Natural History* published in CE 75, describes the sea between India and the island of Taprobane (Ceylon) as

> full of shallows not more than six paces in depth, but in some channels so deep that no anchors can find the bottom. For this reason ships are built with prows at each end to obviate the necessity of their turning about in channels of extreme narrowness. The tonnage of these vessels is 3000 amphorae (75 tons).[33]

Ancient Indian texts, literary references, numismatic and sculptural depictions, as well as works by foreign scholars and travellers contain abundant evidence of India's naval prowess, her mastery of the oceans that lay beyond her western and eastern shores, her ability to build ships of high tonnage that were strong enough to cross the seas. Trade and commerce may have been the motivating factors but the success achieved was the result of the coming together of organized statecraft, skilful artisans and scientific knowledge. The state supervised the ship-building industry, took responsibility for the quality of the vessels, and then fully supported private enterprise in the conduct of sea-borne trade. In return the entrepreneurs yielded huge wealth to the sovereign in duties, taxes and gifts. All in all a good example of public-private partnership!

India's shipping prowess played the determining role in ensuring a dominant position for India in the world of commerce. Indian goods travelling in non-Indian bottoms could never have yielded the leverage and wealth that accrued to India through the use of her own ships. India's strength came from her ability to be the emporium for trade with countries ranging from Rome, Greece and Egypt in the west to the Malay Archipelago and China in the east. Merchants and traders on Indian ships handled Indian goods sourced from different regions of the country, as well as non-Indian goods brought in from the West and the East. Goods sourced from the Chryse or the Golden Chersonese (present-day Malaysia) were a significant part of this trade.

INDIA'S TRADE WITH EUROPE ON THE EVE OF THE COMMON ERA

A huge stimulus to India's trade with the occident came when Emperor Augustus took control of the Roman Empire in 27 BCE. Prior to this, India's trade with the West had been conducted primarily through Egypt. The King of Egypt, Ptolemy Philadelphos (285-247 BCE) was among those who had received the envoys of Ashoka the Great, referred to in Ashoka's rock edicts as 'conquest by Dhamma'.[34] King Ptolemy founded the city of Alexandria, which soon became the principal emporium for trade between India and the West. The Greeks were the carriers in this extensive trade through Alexandria. The name *Yavana* by which Western merchants were known in India, whether in Sanskrit or in Tamil, is derived from the Greek word Iaones, the name of the Greeks in their own language.

From Alexandria the two sea-ports on the Egyptian coast used for the trade with India were Berenice and Myos Hormos. Sailings from these ports to and from India took place along the coasts of Arabia and Persia. This was gradually replaced by direct sailings across the Arabian Sea, making full use of the monsoon winds. The open-sea route had the advantage of being quicker and avoiding most (though not all) of the pirate-infested coastal route. The sea-route soon overtook, even eclipsed, the traditional overland routes of commerce in terms of volume and value of goods traded.[35]

Hippalus, the Egyptian pilot working for the Romans, is often credited with the discovery of the monsoon winds that led to the use of the direct route for sailing across the Arabian Sea. However,

Indian scholars are of the view that Indian sailors must have known about the monsoon winds much earlier than *c.* CE 45, the date normally referred to for Hippalus' 'discovery'.[36] Hippalus is said to have learnt about sailing with the monsoon winds from an Indian sailor, once again indicating that Indians had prior knowledge about the monsoons. In all likelihood, it was the pressure of burgeoning demand from the Roman Empire under Augustus for luxury goods from India and the Far East that led Roman ships to experiment with direct sailings across the Arabian Sea, using the monsoon winds in preference to the coastal route hitherto used, which had become heavily pirate infested.

Even in the fourth century BCE, the seafaring Axumite Kingdom located on the Red Sea in what is present-day Eritrea and northern Ethiopia, had developed trading relations with both India and Egypt. The first use of the monsoon winds in direct sailings across the Indian Ocean is said to have been between ports in India and Axum. Even after the Roman Empire took direct control of the trade with India from the European/African end, they often used Axum carriers for this trade. Braddell says,

> . . . the inhabitants of the Tamil coastal districts have been called from early times *paradavar* or sailors. They must early have discovered the periodicity of the monsoons since it is impossible to live on the coasts of southern India without noticing that phenomenon and the possibilities for sailing-craft which it offers. They kept the secret closely guarded from competitors so that it only became known in Europe when it was ascertained by Hippalus. . . .[37]

The monsoon route between India and Africa meant that sailings by the same ship could be completed within a year. The south-west monsoon was key for the voyage from the West to India. Ships would leave the eastern coast of Africa in July in order to catch these winds that would bring them safely into an Indian port within 40 days in the month of September. If the ship left earlier in June it would run the risk of arriving on India's west coast in August at which time conditions are very hazardous due to the ongoing monsoons. And the return voyage would start three months later with the north-east monsoon winds, with departure normally timed for December/January.

The Periplus of the Erythraean Sea[38] is the record of an experienced though anonymous merchant-sailor who navigated all around the Indian Ocean, including the east coast of Africa, the Red Sea, the Persian Gulf, the Malabar and Coromandel coasts of India and beyond to the mouth of the river Ganga and the Chryse farther east. W.H. Schoff has estimated the date of the text as CE 60 and the author to be an Egyptian Greek, a Roman subject who lived during the reign of Tiberius Claudius Balbilus.

The Periplus contains details about the ports involved in the trade on both sides of the Indian Ocean, the goods exchanged and the kinds of ships used, particularly along the Indian coast. There is mention of the Axumite port of Adulis and the island of Dioscorida (contemporary Socotra) where the inhabitants are described as 'foreigners, a mixture of Arabs, Indians and Greeks, who have emigrated to carry on trade there'. Mookerji concluded that 'in the age of the *Periplus*, the merchants of the country around Barygaza (west coast of India) traded to Arabia for gums and incense, to the coast of Africa for gold, and to Malabar and Ceylon for pepper and cinnamon, and thus completed the navigation of the entire Indian Ocean'.[39]

By the first century, in place of the port of Lothal that was no longer in use, new ports had been developed along the west coast of India. The port of Barygaza or Bharukachchha (present-day Bharuch in Broach district) on the river Narmada in Gujarat emerged as the most important sea-port servicing imports and exports for the entire north, north-western and central regions of the Indian subcontinent, including Kamboja (Afghanistan), Gandhara and Kashmir. This is the old Kamboj Dvaravati trade route, culminating in Barygaza. Goods arrived in Barygaza from the interior towns of Ozene (Ujjain), Paithan and Tagara (modern Dharur). *The Periplus* provides graphic and intricate details about the navigational skills of Indian sailors as they entered the very difficult port of Barygaza.

> This gulf is very narrow to Barygaza and very hard to navigate for those coming from the ocean. . . . Because of this, native fishermen in the King's service, stationed at the very entrance in well-manned large boats called *tappaga* and *cotymba*, go up the coast as far as Syrastrene (Surat), from where they pilot vessels to Barygaza.[40]

The Periplus describes several port-towns and market-towns along the Malabar and Coromandel coastlines of India. Moving south from Barygaza into the Dachinabades (Deccan) region, these include Souppara (modern Supara), Calliena (modern Kalyan) and Semylla (modern Chembur perhaps). In southern India these include the three great emporia along Limyrike (more or less the equivalent of the Malabar coast), namely Muziris (Pattanam in Kerala's Ernakulam district), Tyndis (said to be just north of Muziris) and Nelcynda (present-day Niranam in the central Travancore region of Kerala). The exports from these ports included pepper, spices, pearl, ivory, fine silks, and precious stones such as rubies, diamonds and amethysts.

Along the Coromandel coast (India's south-eastern coastal area, the name Coromandel being derived from the word *cholamandalam*, or the region ruled by the Chola kings), ports like Poduca (present-day Pondicherry or Puducherry), Sopatma (at the confluence of the sea and the Palar River, this served as the port for the great mart of Kancheepuram, and is estimated to be present-day Chennai), and Arikamedu (a few kilometers south of Puducherry) are described. Those living along the Coromandel coast used their own ships to trade with those living on the Malabar coast. At the major ports along the Coromandel coast

> . . . are found the native vessels which make coasting voyages to Limyrike—the monoxyla of the largest sort called *sangara*, and others styled *colandiophonta*, which are vessels of great bulk and adapted to the voyages made to the Ganges and the Golden Chersonese. . . .
>
> . . . the monoxyla are still in use, not canoes, as they are improperly rendered; but with their foundation formed of a single timber, hollowed, and then raised with tiers of planking till they will contain 100 or 150 men. Vessels of this sort are employed in the intercourse between the two coasts; but the *colandiophonta*, built for the trade to Malacca, perhaps to China, were exceedingly large and stout, resembling probably those described by Marco Polo and Nicolo di Conti. Varthema likewise mentions vessels of this sort at Tarnasari (Masulipatnam) that were of 1000 tons burthen [*sic*] designed for this very trade to Malacca.[41]

It is estimated that the first references to Southeast Asia in European writings were by the Latin geographer Pomponius Mela. He referred to the Chryse (island of gold), generally taken to mean the Malay Peninsula, in his *De Chorographia*, written around CE 45. Then comes the reference to Chryse in *The Periplus*. *The Periplus* describes the Chryse as 'the region beyond the Ganges', indicating that goods are sourced from this region by Indian merchants travelling on Indian vessels, and that beyond this region, there is China. Tortoise shell from the Chryse is described as 'the best . . . of all the places on the Erythraean Sea'. From China raw silk, silk yarn and silk cloth 'are exported to Damirica (South India) by way of the river Ganges'.

In the second century the Greek mathematician and astronomer Claudius Ptolemy, who worked in Alexandria, used the name Chryse Chersonesos (Golden Peninsula or Island) to refer to the area identified with the Malay Peninsula and the island of Sumatra.[42] He was perhaps following the long-established practice of references in Indian literature and texts to Suvarnadvipa (island of gold).

Numismatic evidence highlights that India's trade with Rome was at its height for a period of eighty years beginning with Augustus and to the reign of Nero (CE 68). With the Roman Empire at the height of its power in the first century, there was an almost insatiable demand among wealthy Roman citizens for the luxuries of the East. The principal components of this demand were for spices and perfumes, precious stones and pearls, and fabrics such as silks, muslins and cotton, together with dyestuffs and food items like rice. These goods were either sourced in India or obtained from countries further east through their trade with India. Indian merchants and traders also supplied European goods to India and beyond, right up to China. India's success in coordinating the supply-chain of goods that were in demand from Europe to China, including India, was greatly facilitated through the use of Indian bottoms to transport these goods. This bought tremendous prosperity to India.

Most of these goods were exchanged for gold. India's imports from Rome, the European goods her merchants purchased, were nowhere near the value of goods sold to Rome. Roman gold was flowing into India in payment for the silks and spices, the gems and the muslins. Roman coins dating to this period have been found in profusion throughout India, particularly in the south. In north India, much of this gold was melted and fresh gold coins minted with the local king's insignia. In any case, the main centre of the trade and commercial activity between India and Rome was in southern India, with the focus on the Andhra kings and those of present-day Tamil Nadu. The Andhra period (200 BCE to CE 250) was one of considerable prosperity where this region traded, over land and by sea, with western Asia, Greece, Rome and Egypt, as well as with China in the east. The southern kings did not melt the Roman gold coins that came in, but used them as currency, just as, many centuries later, English gold sovereigns were used as currency in India and other countries. Large quantities of Roman gold coins dating to the first century have been found in and near the present-day Coimbatore, and at Madurai and Cananore.

The Greek words for rice (*oryza*), ginger (*zingiber*) and cinnamon (*karpion*) correspond closely with their Tamil equivalents, *arisi, inchiver* and *karava*. This corroborates the view that it was through Tamil merchants or through trade based in the Tamil-speaking regions of India that Greek merchants purchased and later introduced these articles to Greece. Arab traders, too, were very active in India and in Europe. West of India, her merchants and shippers faced serious competition from Arab ships and traders. East of India, however, her ships and merchants held sway over Arab and European counterparts.

Silk, muslin and cotton were sold at fabulously high prices. Silk is said to have been exchanged by weight against gold when traded in the Persian and Roman Empires. Aromatics were in great demand for use in large quantities at every religious and funerary occasion. Nero is reported to have burnt at the funeral of his second wife, Poppaea (Augusta), 'fully a year's produce of cinnamon and cassia'.[43] Pliny in his *Natural History* has said that pepper and ginger from India fetched enormous prices in the markets of Europe, where they were purchased by weight against gold and silver. In the first century pepper was grown primarily in the regions adjoining the Malabar coast. In Roman times, pepper was exported from the three major ports along this coast. Large ships frequented these ports because of the bulk in which pepper, betel and other spices were exported.

There was equally great demand in Roman markets for precious stones, pearls and minerals. Among the most highly prized stones was the beryl. The beryl mined in the Padiyur mines (Coimbatore district) and the Vaniyambadi mines (Salem district), both in present-day Tamil Nadu, were believed to be among the purest and best in the world. In ancient times there were no other known sources of beryl. It is in the neighbourhood of these mines that the largest number of Roman gold coins have been found. The pearl fisheries, too, were located along the southern shores of India. The southern kings were fortunate in having within their jurisdiction three precious commodities that were in great demand in Rome: pepper, pearls and beryls.

Tamil kings are said to have maintained powerful navies, with large ships that voyaged to the east and west of India. Foreign merchants from many lands visited this region frequently. In Sanskrit and Tamil writings the word *yavana* is used to describe these merchants.[44] These are the Greeks from Egypt, mentioned in *The Periplus* and other literature as the ones who brought wine, brass, lead and glass for sale at Indian ports, and who paid in gold for pepper, betel, ivory, pearls and fine muslins. Roman soldiers were enlisted in the service of the Pandyas and other Tamil kings. Roman commercial agents (modern-day 'buyers') took up residence in more than one of the capital cities and market towns of south India.

> There is good reason to believe that considerable colonies of Roman subjects engaged in trade were settled in Southern India during the first two centuries of our era, and that European soldiers, described as powerful *Yavanas*, and dumb *Mlechchhas* (barbarians) clad in complete armour, acted as bodyguards to Tamil kings. . . .[45]

There are further descriptions of the foreign (*yavana*) colony at 'Kaviripaddanam', or 'Pukar', a busy port situated on the eastern coast at the mouth of the northern branch of the Kaveri River. Both town and harbour now lie buried under vast mounds of sand. Tamil poems tell of the importation of *yavana* wines, lamps, and vases. This testimony is confirmed by the discovery in the Nilgiri megalithic tombs of numerous bronze vessels similar to those known to have been produced in Europe during the early centuries of the Common Era, and by statements in *The Periplus*.[46] Kaviripaddanam is described as Kamara in *The Periplus* and as Khaberis by Ptolemy. The Tamil epics *Silappadikaram* and *Paddinappalai* describe the trading structures in place in this prosperous city, the state warehouses and godowns where goods received were stamped with the Tiger Stamp (the emblem of the Chola kings) after customs duty had been paid, and then handed over to individual merchants. The *Paddinappalai* describes the goods traded in the markets of Kaviripaddinam:

> Horses were brought from distant lands beyond the seas; pepper was brought in ships; gold and precious stones came from the northern mountains; sandal and aghil came from the mountains towards the west; pearls from the Southern seas, and coral from the eastern seas. The produce of the regions watered by the Ganges; all that is grown on the banks of the Kaveri; articles of food from Elam or Ceylon and the manufacturers of Kalakam (in Burma). . . .[47]

In addition to the strong economic links with the Roman Empire, there were burgeoning political links as well. Strabo's *Geography* refers to a mission or embassy sent to Augustus Caesar in 20 BCE by the Indian King Pandion (the king of the Pandyas) of south India. As for north India:

> from the time of Mark Antony to the time of Justinian, ie from 30 BCE to 550 . . ., their political importance as allies against the Parthians and Sassanians and their commercial importance as controllers of one of the main trade routes between the East and the West, made the friendship of the Kusans or Sakas, who held the Indus Valley and Baktria, a matter of the highest importance to Rome.[48]

These valuable insights into maritime trade routes elucidate India's pivotal role in world trade at that time. This was the combined result of her maritime capabilities, her ability to coordinate product supply chains across Asia and her strength as the source of some of the most precious commodities in demand at the time. The prosperity that resulted from India's participation in global commodity exchanges was shared throughout the Indian subcontinent and her neighbouring regions, from the north and north-western states, through the regions bordering the Ganga, Indus, Narmada and Kaveri rivers, along the western and eastern coastal belts of India and throughout the southern regions, right up to Sri Lanka and Myanmar.

India's chief imports were tin, lead, glass, amber, steel for arms, some coral and medicinal drugs, and frankincense from Arabia for her temples. India's exports were enormous. North and north-west India exported to Europe the finest sheep's wool and furs, semi-precious stones like onyx, lapis lazuli and jasper, asafoetida, musk and resinous gums, carpets and embroidered woollen fabrics. Among India's most valuable exports were silk and cotton textiles. Silk fabric was woven in India and also brought in from China for re-export. India's exports of cotton ranged from coarse canvas and calicoes to the finest muslins. Other exports included oils, brassware, indigo and other dyes, salt, drugs, sugar cane-based preparations, ornaments and aromatics. India held monopoly in her exports of pepper, cinnamon and other edible spices which were in great demand throughout Europe.

In the early centuries of the Common Era, the demand for luxury goods stepped up sharply in China. At the same time the evergrowing demand for edible spices made Indian traders seek fresh sources of supply for these products from the nations to the east.

The demand for gold and precious metals in India was insatiable. Gold possessions have traditionally been the strongest symbol of wealth in India. Before the Common Era, Indian traders had satisfied the demand for gold through their trade across the Indian ocean, with the Sumerians, the Persians, the Egyptians and with the Roman empire. So heavy was the flow or 'drain' of gold into India from the Roman Empire that already in the first century, Pliny the Elder in his encyclopedic *Natural History* laments that 'in no year does India absorb less than fifty million sesterces of our Empire's wealth'.[49] Other authors have estimated that each year the trade with India drained the Roman Empire of a hundred million sesterces, valued in the year 1909 at one million British pounds 'of which six hundred thousand pounds went to Arabia and four hundred thousand pounds to India'.[50] In the first century Emperor Vespasian banned the export of gold coins to India, considering such exports to be a grave threat to the Roman economy.

After the first century, the demand for luxury goods in Rome declined for some time, although the demand for spices and many other goods remained high. As a result, on two counts, the inflows of Roman gold into India fell sharply. The second principal source for gold imports into India had been from Siberia, through caravans that crossed Bactria, trading gold and silver for silks, cinnamon and other spices. In the last two centuries before the Common Era there had been large and unsettling movements among the peoples of Central Asia. There had been invasions into India through this very Bactrian route. This disrupted the trading routes and deprived India of an important source of gold.

All this led Indian merchants and traders to 'look east' and seek fresh supplies of gold from the fabled lands of Suvarnabhumi and Suvarnadvipa in Burma and the Malay Archipelago. By this time India's shipbuilding capabilities were well advanced. Strong seaworthy ships capable of transporting 600 to 700 passengers together with heavy cargoes were in use. As a result, what had in earlier millennia been a moderate interaction between South and Southeast Asia, now expanded manifold.

NOTES

1. Adjective, from the *Puranas*, ancient Sanskrit texts containing legends and folklore of varying dates and origins.
2. K.A. Nilakanta Sastri, *South Indian Influences in the Far East*, pp. 5-7.
3. Radha Kumud Mookerji, 1962 (1912), *Indian Shipping: A History of the Sea-Borne Trade and Maritime Activity of the Indians from the Earliest Times*, p. 3.
4. Ibid., p. 37, quoting Buhler.
5. Ibid., pp. 37-8.
6. A.L. Basham, *The Wonder That Was India*, 1956, p. 303.
7. Mookerji, op. cit., pp. 38-9, n. 3.
8. Ibid., p. 40, n. 1.
9. Romila Thapar, *A History of India*, vol. 1, p. 28, Penguin Books, 1990 (first published by Pelican Books, 1966).
10. Ibid., p. 41.
11. Mookerji, op. cit., p. 43.
12. Ibid.
13. Ibid., p. 44.
14. Ibid., p. 48.
15. Ibid., p. 50.
16. Ibid., pp. 51-2.
17. Ibid., pp. 52-3.
18. Ibid., p. 51.
19. Ibid., p. 72 (n. 5), quoting from *Journal of the Royal Asiatic Society* (April 1899, p. 432).
20. Ibid., p. 33 (n. 1).
21. Mamata Chaudhuri, 'Ship Building in the *Yukti Kalpataru* and *Samarangana Sutradhara*', paper submitted to the India National

Science Academy, Kolkata, 20 November 1975. http://www.new.dli.ernet.in/rawdataupload/upload/insa/INSA_1/20005af4_137.pdf accessed on 28 December 2009.

22. Ibid., in translation from the original text of *Yukti Kalpataru.*
23. Mookerji , op. cit., p. 14.
24. Chaudhuri, op. cit.
25. Mookerji, op. cit., p. 72.
26. Ibid., quoting Strabo (*The Geography of Strabo*, tr. H.C. Hamilton and W. Falconer, London, 1892-3).
27. Kangle, *The Kautilya Arthashastra*, translated and critiqued, 1965, part 3, pp. 1, 40, 59.
28. Ibid., part 2, pp. 162-5
29. Mookerji, op. cit., p. 34, n. 1.
30. Ibid., p. 34, quoting the signage in the Philadelphia Museum.
31. Ibid., p. 34.
32. Ibid., p. 32, quoting Beal, *Buddhist Records*, vol. II, p. 269.
33. Quoted in K.A. Nilakanta Sastri, 1939, *Foreign Notices of South India*, p. 49.
34. Rock Edict 13 says, *inter alia*, that conquest by Dhamma 'has been won here, on the borders, even 600 yojanas away, where the Greek King Antiochos rules, beyond there where the four kings named Ptolemy, Antigonos, Magas and Alexander rule, likewise in the south among the Cholas, the Pandyas, and as far as Tamraparni'. *The Edicts of King Ashoka*, an English rendering by the Venerable S. Dhammika, published in 1993 by the Buddhist Publication Society, Kandy, Sri Lanka, DharmaNet edition, 1994.
35. The overland routes included those across Central Asia along the Oxus to the Caspian and the Black Seas, through Persia to Asia Minor, or via the Persian Gulf and the Euphrates through Damascus and Palmyra to the Levant.
36. Nilakanta Sastri, p. 58.
37. Roland Braddell, 'An Introduction to the Study of Ancient Times in the Malay Peninsula', *JMBRAS*, vol. XIII, pt. II, 1935, p. 101.
38. *The Periplus of the Erythraean Sea: Travel and Trade in the Indian Ocean by a Merchant of the First Century*, tr. & ed. W.H. Schoff (London, Bombay and Calcutta, 1912).
39. Mookerji, op. cit., p. 93, quoting Dr. Vincent (*Commerce of the Ancients*).
40. *The Periplus of the Erythraean Sea'*, paras 43 and 44, pp. 39-40, accessed through openlibrary.org
41. Mookerji, op. cit., p. 93.
42. J.W. McCrindle, *Ancient India as described by Ptolemy,* pp. 197-203.
43. Mookerji, op. cit., p. 87.

44. Thapar, op. cit., p. 102 (n.) '*Yavana* and *Yona* in Indian sources referred to the Greeks, and by extension, to foreigners from Western Asia. The word was derived from Ionia'.
45. Mookerji, op. cit., p. 89, quoting Vincent A. Smith, *The Early History of India*, Oxford University Press, 1924, pp. 400-1.
46. Ibid., p. 90.
47. Ibid., p. 95, quoting from the *Paddinappalai*.
48. Ibid., p. 97, quoting the *Bombay Gazetteer* (vol. I, pt. i, p. 490).
49. Pliny: *Natural History* 6.96-111 (On India) accessed at http://www.fordham.edu/halsall/ancient/pliny-india.html on 14 April 2010.
50. Mookerji, op. cit., p. 86.

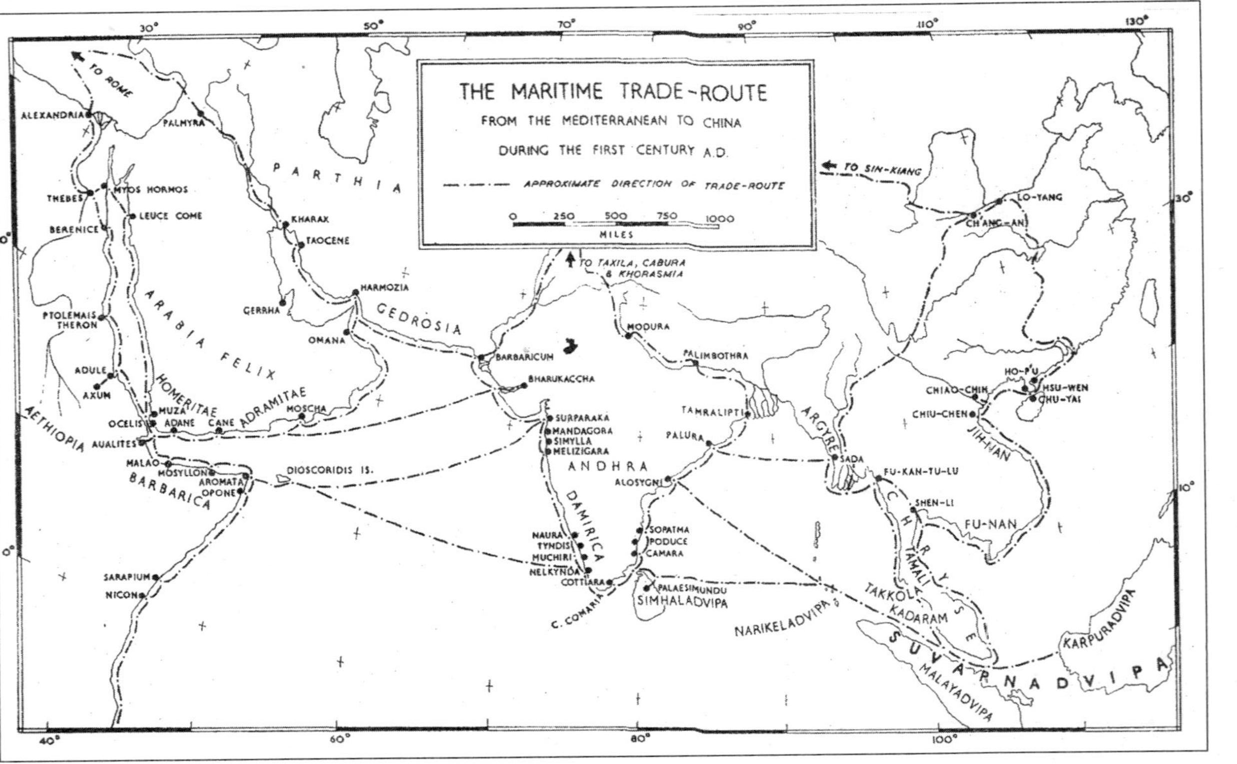

Map 2: The Maritime Trade Route from the Mediterranean to China during the First Century CE

2

Trading with the East

Trade provided the crucial impetus to the expansion and development of India's interactions with her eastern neighbours. The earliest trade routes between South and Southeast Asia were overland, but these were soon supplemented, even supplanted, by the maritime route.

Trade between China and India by the land route can be traced back to at least the first millennium BCE. There were three major overland routes for this connectivity. The first went across Afghanistan over the passes of the Hindu Kush mountains through Bactria and Central Asia to the western borders of China. The second traversed the Karakoram Pass to Leh in the Ladakh region of Jammu & Kashmir, and Kashgar in Xinjiang province. The third passed through Assam in north-east India through Myanmar to the province of Yunnan in south-west China. Some of these routes retained their importance and relevance for several centuries. Others lost out soon after the maritime routes emerged.

There are several instances of combined land-cum-maritime routes from India to China. These well-traversed routes included one that used the Isthmus of Kra for transhipment of goods bought and sold in China. For many centuries, Indian shippers used this route to avoid the pirate-infested Straits of Malacca. Alternatively, after sailing from Amaravati (the Andhra Pradesh coast) across the Bay of Bengal to Arakan and the Burmese deltas, two passes allowed comparatively easy access into the interiors of peninsular Southeast Asia, and thence to China. The third land-cum-maritime route to China, once again avoiding the Straits of Malacca, ran

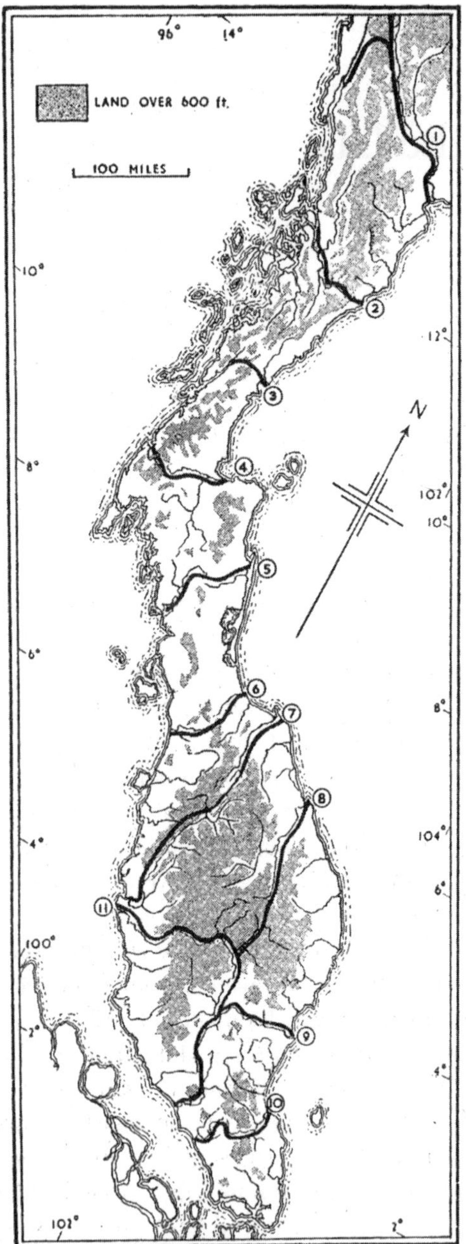

The rivers of the Malay Peninsula and the main trans-peninsular routeways: (1) the Three Pagodas and the Three Cedis routes; (2) the Tenasserim River route; (3) Kra Isthmus route; (4) Takuapa River route; (5) Trang River route; (6) Kedah-Patani route; (7) Perak-Patani route; (8) Kelantan-Malacca route by way of the Panarikan; (9) Pahang-Malacca route by way of the Panarikan; (10) the Sembrong route; (11) the Bernam-Pahang route

Map 3: Major River-cum-Land Routes across the Malay Peninsula

from Kedah in north-west Malaysia overland to Patani in present-day south-east Thailand. Map 3 highlights the major river-cum-land routes across the Malay Peninsula.

There are references in Kautilya's *Arthashastra* to China as the source of silk: 'By that are explained the silk and silk-cloth from the land of Cina'. Scholars have debated whether 'Cina' here refers to China or to Shina, the Gilgit tribe, which still carries on silk manufacture. Even if it is a reference to the Shina tribe, this does not preclude the import of silk from China by the land route.

The land route through Bengal, north-east India and Myanmar into the Malay Peninsula and beyond was the original route of human migration. It is tedious and impracticable because of several mighty rivers flowing in the north-south direction: the Irrawaddy, the Salween, the Menam and the Mekong, among others, combined with dense tropical vegetation and the rugged, mountainous and inhospitable terrain. It was soon supplanted by coastal sailing and later by sailing across the open seas. The maritime route has played the most significant role in the expansion of the linkages between India and Southeast Asia, beginning with the early years of the Common Era. The people of southern India have participated intensively in this movement, perhaps more so than those from any other part of the Indian subcontinent. Before the advent of colonial rule brought in artificial barriers to cut-off millennia old natural movements, intermingling was the way of life for the people of South Asia and Southeast Asia. Studies of this region based on prehistoric archaeology have concluded that 'diversity is the only hard fact that emerges, for any attempt to relate a particular culture to a particular ethnic group too often enters the realm of pure speculation'.[1]

The emissaries sent by Emperor Ashoka to Ceylon, Suvarnabhumi (Myanmar) and farther east used the maritime route in their travels. Ashoka's son, Mahindra, and daughter, Sanghamitra, were sent to Ceylon. Sanghamitra established there the Order of Priestesses or Nuns (*Bhikuni Sasana*), that later spread to Burma, Thailand, and China, primarily along the maritime route. Ashoka's missionaries Sona and Uttara are believed by the people of Myanmar to have been the founders of Buddhism in their country.

Pelliot has analysed the references in *Ts'ien Han Chou* written by Pan Kou, a Chinese writer who lived not later than the first century CE.[2] Pan Kou describes the year-long journey from Je-nan (Upper Annam in the Gulf of Tonkin) by boat along the coast and across the sea to *Houang-tche*, taken to be Kanchi (present-day Kanchipuram near Chennai). It takes almost ten months of travel, by the coastal route, across the open sea and by land, to reach the kingdom of *Fou-kan-tou-lou* (Pagan in Myanmar). From here it takes more than two months by boat to reach the kingdom of *Houang-tche* (Kanchipuram). Pan Kou writes that each of the nations he traverses have been trading with China (sending tribute) since the days of Emperor Wou (140-86 BCE).

Pan Kou writes that the Chinese were dependent for their transport on foreign ships. Experts have assessed that around 100 BCE Chinese vessels had not yet begun to sail to India. This began much later. However, by this time Indian goods had already begun reaching China by sea, with most of the trade with China conducted through the ports of southern India.

Pan Kou describes the kingdom of *Houang-tche* where 'there are official interpreters who belong to the administration of the palace'. The people 'go by sea to buy shining pearls, glass, rare stones and strange products, giving gold and silks in exchange'. The kingdom and the people of *Houang-tche* have friendly and good trading relations with other kingdoms, since 'in the lands to which they go, the people supply them with food and join them in their repast. The merchant ships of the foreigners take them to their destination by turns.' Pan Kou adds that in the period of Yuan-che (CE 1-6), the Emperor P'ing 'sent rich presents to the King of *Houang-tche* and asked him to send an embassy bringing a live rhinoceros as tribute'.[3]

On the return journey from the kingdom of *Houang-tche*, after travelling by boat for about eight months, they reach P'i-tsong (Pulau Pisang, an island off the coast of Johore in south-west Malaysia). Another two-month long journey by sea brings them back to Jenan. This vivid description of an ancient journey speaks powerfully about the dynamic relationship between India and China more than 2,000 years ago.

INTERMINGLING OF RACE, LANGUAGE AND CULTURE ACROSS SOUTH AND SOUTHEAST ASIA

Linguistic affinities are important indicators of migratory trends, identities and also cultural unity. Such affinities manifest themselves throughout South Asia and Southeast Asia. The Mon-Khmer languages comprise the autochthonous language family of Southeast Asia. These, together with the Munda languages of India, are considered to be the two primary branches of the Austroasiatic family of languages. The Mon-Khmer languages are spoken in Vietnam, Cambodia, Laos, Northeast Thailand, the upper Salween and lower Salween regions of Myanmar, by the Orang Asli or the Aslian (Jahaic, Senoic and Semelaic) in peninsular Malaysia, by the Nicobarese on the Nicobar islands in India, and by the Khasis in the north-eastern state of Meghalaya in India. The Munda languages are spoken by the Munda people who live across the eastern states of India (Jharkand, Bihar, West Bengal, Chhattisgarh, Odisha and Assam), and in parts of Bangladesh. The Munda languages are distantly related to Vietnamese and Khmer. The Tai languages include standard Thai, the national language of Thailand, Laotian, the national language of Laos, the Shan language of Myanmar, the Zhuang language from the southern Chinese province of Guangxi, and the Ahom language spoken in ancient Assam.

Long before the results of the HUGO Pan-Asian SNP Consortium were released in December 2009, anthropologists and archaeologists had supported the diffusionist theory of race, culture and language moving from South Asia across Southeast Asia right up to Australia. The Malay Peninsula has played a seminal role in this process of diffusion, situated as it is at a crucial vantage point in this trans-continental journey. In 2009, conclusions were reached on the basis of the comparatively new yet scientifically proven process of DNA testing. The strikingly similar conclusions reached by earlier researchers were based on archaeological findings and empirical evidence of apparently inexplicable similarities in race, culture, and language across regions that were at great geographical distances from one another.

Thus, linguists have concluded that there is a marked affinity between the Australoid and Munda languages. As though in confirmation, in 1920, in the region of Varanasi petroglyphs were discovered that were identical with Australian ones.[4] Similarly, most experts agree on 'the kinship between the Indus scripts and those of Easter Island . . . that there can be no doubt concerning their identity.'[5] Indeed, even a cursory comparison of the Easter Island and Indus Valley scripts offers rather convincing visual evidence that they are related.

Anthropologists too confirm the intermingling of the people of South Asia and Southeast Asia. In 1930 British anthropologist, Sir Grafton Elliot Smith wrote,

> People with the same physical characteristics as the Australian race are found in the South of India and Ceylon, and, mixed with other races, in Northeastern India, especially in Chota Nagpur. Others, again, are found in the Malay Peninsula (i.e. Sakai), Eastern Sumatra, Borneo and some islands in the Philippines; . . . there was a north to south migration . . . from Chota Nagpur eastward and southward through the Malay Peninsula.[6]

About *Orang Asli* tribes in the Malay Peninsula, American anthropologist A.L. Kroeber said in 1923:

> The *Sakai* or *Senoi* resemble a series of hill tribes scattered from India to the East Indies; the Vedda of Ceylon, the Irula and other tribes of southern India, and the Toala of Celebes. Perhaps the Kolarians or Munda-Kol of Central India, the Moi and other groups of Indo-China, the Nicobar islanders, and certain nationalities of Sumatra are also to be reckoned as partial representatives of the same type. This race, if it is such, is generalized with certain Caucasian and Negroid but few Mongoloid resemblances. It is perhaps to be classed as Australoid and has been named Indo-Australoid.[7]

Given the direction of the population drift to the south and south-east, the groups that have moved farthest in these directions are most likely to have lived the longest in their respective habitats. And the more isolated and remote the region where they now live, the more likely it is for these groups to have successfully preserved their identity, language and customs going back almost to the point in time when they left their original habitats. For example, the people of Easter Island, with their petroglyphs closely resembling the Indus Valley hieroglyphic script, give us an indication of the timespan, at least 5,000 years, when they started their journey from the north-west of India across 'monsoon Asia'. Similarly, the linguistic affinities between the Aslian or *Orang Asli* of Malaysia, those living in other parts of Southeast Asia speaking the Mon-Khmer group of languages and the Khasis of Meghalaya in north-east India, are significantly informative about migratory trends and the origins of communities.

This movement of people has not necessarily been uni-directional. Those who left the shores of India could and did return and interact. Trade, religion and culture remained the leitmotif of this interaction. The relationship between those who moved into newer areas and their kin in different parts of India remained one of equality and mutual respect. Societies grew and developed as independent entities, learning from each other and absorbing each other's political and social organizational experiences and practices.

The free movement of people across monsoon Asia continued right up to the advent of colonial rule, a process that began with the arrival of the Europeans in Asia in the very early years of the sixteenth century. Gradually, the territories of South and Southeast Asia were divided into areas of influence, ruled by one or the other European power. The movement of people became restricted. Trade and allied services like shipping were tightly controlled in order that all benefit may accrue solely to the colonial power. This led to the complete debilitation of India's maritime capabilities. Over time, as new and much narrower identities were created by colonial powers for the people under their control, even memories of pre-colonial interactions were sought to be erased. This was particularly true for Malaysia, which came under Britain's colonial control. British anthropologist Elliot Smith said:

> When we recognise the greatness of the achievement of Dutch archaeologists in the East Indies, the Americans in the Philippines, the French in Indochina . . .it is particularly humiliating to us as Englishman that so little is being done in Malaya to complete the links in the chains which this great jumping-off place in Asia and cultural exchange alone can supply.[8]

The results of the HUGO pan-Asian SNP Consortium study, and empirical evidence about the movement of peoples and their linguistic affinities, lead to the conclusion that the people living in what is picturesquely described by Jules Sion as 'monsoon Asia', essentially share the same roots. The shared roots among the people of South and Southeast Asia include ethnicity, language, and culture. Each of these aspects are important components of an individual's and a nation's identity. In practice, however, it is often impossible to separate or compartmentalize these three influences. It is equally difficult to define these factors within narrow geographic or national borders that may be of comparatively recent origin, or may have been imposed by colonial powers to suit their convenience a century or two ago.

For the anthropologist, a race is a biological group, based on a community of physical characters. As explained by German anthropologist A.L. Kroeber, '. . . it may seem of little moment whether the word race is restricted to its strict biological sense or used more loosely. In fact, however, untold loose reasoning has resulted from the loose terminology.'[9] Dato' Roland Braddell, in his pathbreaking *Study of Ancient Times in the Malay Peninsula*, gives two examples to illustrate the point made by A.L. Kroeber. The first of these pertains to India and the second to Malaysia. The term 'Aryan race', he says, is a meaningless expression, since Aryan is a purely linguistic term, indicating the Indo-European family of languages and the speakers of those languages. Yet, the term 'Aryan race' is repeatedly used as though it actually indicated a separate race.[10] The same holds true for 'Malay race', 'Dravidian race', or for that matter, the 'Anglo-Saxon race' or 'Latin race'. 'There is, strictly speaking, no such thing as the Malay race; there are the Malay people, the Malay culture and the Malay language, etc.'[11]

It is worth looking at Dato' Roland Braddell's references to India and Malaya in greater detail.

The theory about the Aryan 'race', about the 'Aryans' conquering north India around 1500 BCE, and destroying the earlier, more advanced, Indus Valley civilization was popularized by Max Müller (the renowned Indologist from Germany) and others in the mid-nineteenth century. The exact provenance of the Aryans remained undetermined (it still does), other than their being a nomadic group with their original home outside India. Some say that this theory emerged around the time when it became known that Sanskrit and other north Indian languages were related to the languages of Europe (hence the nomenclature of Indo-European languages). The theory of the Aryan invasion would make it seem that Europeans (or at least the non-Indian Aryans) brought their language(s) to India. By 1888 Max Müller had himself unequivocally refuted the concept of an 'Aryan race', saying that by referring to Aryans he means 'simply those who speak an Aryan language . . . to me an ethnologist who speaks of Aryan race is as great a sinner as a linguist who speaks of a dolichocephalic dictionary or a brachycephalic grammar.'[12]

New archaeological findings in north India have considerably added to the information about the ancient past that first came to light in the 1920s with the discovery of the buried townships of Harappa and Mohenjo-Daro, located along the Ravi and Indus rivers respectively. Since then numerous other settlements, numbering over 2,500, have been identified over a vast area stretching from Baluchistan to the shores of the Ganga and southwards to the valley of the Tapti River. Data from satellite photographs reveal that about 75 per cent of these settlements are concentrated not along the Indus River or even along the Ganga, but along the now dried up Saraswati River. Extensive research by scholars like Dr. Wakankar has shown that the Saraswati River went completely dry around 1900 BCE, and that, well before 3000 BCE, the Saraswati had stopped being a perennial river. This mighty river flowed from the Himalayas to the ocean across the present-day states of Punjab, Rajasthan and Gujarat.

In the *Rigveda* it is the Saraswati and not the Ganga that is described as the holiest river. The Ganga is mentioned only once, while the Saraswati is mentioned more than 60 times in the *Rigveda*. The vastness and beauty of the Saraswati are repeatedly praised and glorified. This places the *Rigveda* as having been composed in a period prior to 3000 BCE, much earlier than the dates estimated by Western scholars. In the *Mahabharata*, which was composed much later than the *Rigveda*, the Saraswati is referred to as a dying river.

The drying up of the Saraswati River was a catastrophic natural calamity, with serious consequences. The peoples living along this river had to migrate in massive numbers, and in several directions. During this period, there were repeated floods alternating with prolonged droughts along the Indus River and its tributaries. This added to the number of those migrating away from the Indus Valley. The Indus and Saraswati Valley civilizations dispersed slowly but continuously, over decades and centuries, spreading Vedic culture in whichever direction they went. The principal migration was towards the west and the north-west, including towards Europe. Thus, beginning as far back as 3000 BCE, it was Indians migrating to the West who transferred knowledge about Sanskrit and Indian culture to the people of Europe.

'For the next thousand years and more (after 2000 BCE), dynasties and rulers with Indian names appear and disappear all over West Asia, confirming the migration of people from East towards West.'[13] The Boghaz Keui inscription discovered in 1907 by the German archeologist, Hugo Winckler, established that in, 1400 BCE, in Cappadocia (eastern Anatolia in present-day Turkey), the Hittites and the Mittani, while concluding a treaty, had invoked the Vedic Gods Indra, Mitra and Varuna.[14] During 1500-1300 BCE, Mittani was a Hurrian-speaking state in present-day northern Syria. Around 1350 BCE, Mittani was considered to be a major international power. Some theonyms, proper names and other terminology exhibit the strong influence of Sanskrit language and Sanskrit speakers in Mittani matters of state. The reference to Vedic deities in the treaty concluded with the Hittites is one such example. In Mittani, the terminology for numericals bears close resemblance to Sanskrit (*aika* or *eka* for one, *panza* or *pancha* for five, *satta* or *sapta* for seven), much more than to Iranian or Indo-Iranian terms, which has *aiva* for one. Sanskrit-based interpretations of Mittani royal names make them easily understandable. Thus *priyamazda* is *priyamedha* 'whose wisdom is dear'; *citrarata* is *citraratha* 'whose chariot is shining', and *subandhu* is 'having good relatives'.

The Lithuanian language, considered to be the most conservative living Indo-European language, retains so many Sanskrit roots that any pedagogical study of Lithuanian can only be done by those who have knowledge of Sanskrit.

The close historical interlinkages between the people of north and south India are legion. The Dravidian people are considered to be descendants of the Vedic *rishi* Agastya. The kings of south India, such as the Chola and Pandya dynasties, trace their lineages back to

Manu, the author of the *Manusmriti*. The *Matsya Purana* describes Manu as originally being a south Indian king, Satyavrata. Vedic culture and traditions are the heritage equally of north and south India. 'The two cultures (north and south India) are so intimately related. . . . Any differences between them appear to be secondary, and nothing like the great racial divide that the Aryan-Dravidian idea has promoted.'[15]

The Dravidian people are those who speak the Dravidian languages. There is no such thing as a Dravidian race, as the following example pointedly illustrates. The Brahui people live in the Baluchistan province of Pakistan, with a population of over 1.5 million spread throughout the Kalat region of this province, distributed from the Bolan pass through the Brahui hills to Cape Muari on the Arabian Sea. The Brahui language is a member of the Dravidian family of languages. Physically the Brahui people resemble their Baluch and Pashtun neighbours. 'They are Muslim by creed and Sunnite by sect, though the Muslim rites overlie essentially Indian social customs. Women are not strictly secluded.'[16] They are considered to be Dravidian because of the language they speak.

A pathbreaking study has been conducted by scientists at the Centre for Cellular and Molecular Biology (CCMB) in Hyderabad, India, in collaboration with researchers at Harvard University (Harvard Medical School, Harvard School of Public Health and the Broad Institute of Harvard and MIT), the results of which were released in September 2009. This study has concluded that the proverbial Aryan-Dravidian race divide is a myth.[17] The result of the study shows that there is a genetic relationship among all Indians.

The study analysed 5,00,000 genetic markers across the genomes of 132 individuals from 25 diverse groups from 13 states. All the individuals were from six language families, covering all castes and communities as well as tribal groups. The study concludes that around 65,000 years ago initial settlements began in the Andaman Islands and ancient south India. Twenty-five thousand years later the ancient north Indians emerged. Eventually, the populations of the north and south mixed, giving rise to the present-day Indians, who are a mix of north and south, with genomic strains from two distinct ancestors: the Ancestral North Indian (ANI) and the Ancestral South Indian (ASI). The indigenous Andaman Islanders are unique in being ASI-related groups without ANI ancestry. The tribes in the Andaman Islands are the descendants of the first humans moving out of Africa. 'The genetics proves that castes grew directly out of tribe-like organizations during the formation of Indian society', the study said. The traditional Indian habit of marrying within one's caste or community leads to genetic mutations, thus explaining why certain diseases are concentrated only in a particular pocket of the Indian population.

The ANI is genetically close to Middle Easterners, Central Asians and Europeans. The ASI have a distinct genetic pattern, quite different from any other. The next stage of research now being planned is to ascertain whether Europeans and Eurasians descended from ANI.

Southern India is the region south of the Vindhya range of mountains, where the Deccan plateau is an important geographical feature. The word Deccan (vernacular *Dakkan*) is derived from the Sanskrit word *dakshina* or south, which literally translates as 'the right-hand country', because ancient Indians faced the rising sun in naming the points of the compass. Beyond the Deccan plateau the area was known as *tamilakam* or *tamilagam*, the land of the Tamils. The earliest statement of the territorial limits of *tamilakam* is by Tolkapiyyar, an ancient grammarian who lived around the fourth century BCE. He described *tamilakam* as the region that 'extended east to west from sea to sea, and north to south from the hills of sacred Tirupati to Cape Comorin'.[18] Over time, the people of the west coast, in what is today the state of Kerala, developed a distinct language of their own, Malayalam, with a strong Prakritic-Sanskrit base.

Southern India was munificently endowed for maritime activity: a long coastline with several natural harbours and river estuaries, dense forests with abundant timber admirably suited for ship-building, fishing, sailing and sea-faring as ways of life and economic activity. The inhabitants of the coastal districts of *tamilakam* have long been referred to as *paradavars* or sailors. The kingdoms of southern India provide the key for unraveling the long saga of

India's interaction with the peoples of Southeast Asia. The Pallavas and Cholas in *tamilakam*, the Andhra kings, the Kalingas and later the kingdoms of Bengal have been the fulcrum for the eastward movement of traders and merchants towards the Malay Peninsula and beyond. The history of south India is as central to the study and understanding of Indian history, as it is to that of Malaysia and Southeast Asia. In both cases the significance of this centrality has been insufficiently appreciated.

'What a tremendous part India has played in the history and in the cultures of Malaysia and south-eastern Asia generally . . . the nexus with India began in remote ages past so that the Indians who came in historical times were only following a well-known and long used track,'[19] is the conclusion arrived at by Dato' Roland Braddell. And Sir Charles Elliott has written that 'the destiny of south-eastern Asia with its islands depends on the fact that the tide of trade and conquest, whether Hindu, Muslim or European, flowed from India or Ceylon to the Malay Peninsula and Java and thence north to China with a reflux west in Champa and Camboja'.[20]

The term *Suvarnadvipa* used in ancient Indian texts refers to the Malay Peninsula and the Indonesian island of Sumatra. Sumatra almost joins the Malay Peninsula at the Straits of Malacca, and 'may have been actually continuous with it even in proto-historic times'.[21] Sumatra is often described as the 'original home' of the Malay, inasmuch as 'it is the home of Malay culture and the country where the earliest written specimens of the Malay language have been found'.[22]

Orang Asli is the term used in the Malay language, *Bahasa Melayu*, to describe the indigenous peoples in peninsular Malaysia. The literal meaning of *Orang Asli* is 'original people' or 'aboriginal people'. Today, the *Orang Asli* comprise less than 1 per cent of Malaysia's total population. The three main groups among the *Orang Asli* population are the Negrito, the Senoi and the Proto Malay, each with several sub-groups. The Senoics are the largest group, with about 54 per cent of the total *Orang Asli* population. The language they speak belongs to the Mon-Khmer group of languages, also spoken by the Khasis of Meghalaya in India. Among the Negritos, too, the language spoken by the second largest sub-group is from the Mon-Khmer group. The proto-Malays form 43 per cent of the *Orang Asli* population. Among the proto-Malays, too, the language of some sub-groups such as the Semelais is from the Mon-Khmer group.

The Jakuns, the largest group among the proto-Malays, are common to Malaysia and Indonesia. They are believed to have lived in Malaysia and Indonesia for at least 7,000 years. They are known to be people of the interior, living in remote areas, sometimes described as *Orang Hulu*, or upriver people. In Malaysia, they live primarily in the southern parts of the peninsula, concentrated today in the states of Pahang and Johor. They are the traditional hunter-gatherers: they hunt game, catch fish and gather fruit and forest products for bartering. Jules Sion, writing in *L'Asie des Moussons* says

> The Indonesians were the proto-Malays, whose sojourn in the interior of the large islands permitted them to better conserve their racial purity. . . . The Malays were simply Indonesians of the coasts, who became much less pure racially because of very diverse cross-breeding . . .; it is a mixed race, great in its diffusion and multiple in its varieties.[23]

The Sanskrit word for mixed is akin to *Melayu*. The Malays, essentially the people living in the coastal regions, were described by Indian sailors and travellers as *dvipantara*, and by Chinese seamen as *kun-lun*. The people so described included the Malays of Sumatra, the Sundanese, the Javanese and the Madurese of Java and the Balinese. G. Coedes describes them as 'the principal agents for the reception and diffusion of Indian culture in the archipelago'.[24] Through the process of intermarriage and close interaction, it was inevitable that the Malays who participated in the diffusion of Indian culture, themselves became part of the process of change that they helped to bring in.

'When the curtain lifts upon the history of the Malay Peninsula we shall find that it can only be understood as a part of the general history of south-eastern Asia or Farther India as it is called.'[25] The geographer Ptolemy first used the term 'Farther India' or 'India beyond the Ganges' in the second century. Subsequently, historians, anthropologists and social scientists adopted this terminology. They found it convenient on many grounds to group together all the people of south-eastern Asia within Farther India, including within its ambit Burma, Siam, French Indo-China, the Malay Peninsula, Indonesia, together with the Andaman & Nicobar Islands in the Bay of Bengal. This became the universally accepted practice, perhaps because it appropriately explained the historical process of interaction between South and Southeast Asia.

'Farther India' or 'India beyond the Ganges' does not convey any connotation of political conquest or colonial rule by the Indians. Beginning in the early years of the first century, a large number of Indianized kingdoms did emerge across Southeast Asia, covering the present-day territories of Cambodia, Vietnam (the kingdom of Champa), the small states of the Malay Peninsula, the kingdoms of Sumatra, Java and Bali; and parts of Burma and Thailand. At different points in time, some of these kingdoms/empires gained ascendancy over large parts of Southeast Asia. The empires of Funan and Srivijaya are just two examples. However, none of these kingdoms had any political ties with the mother country, India. 'Through reaction with the indigenous substratum . . . each of these states developed according to its own genius, although their cultures never lost the family resemblance that they owed to their common origin.'[26]

These sustained Indian influences in Southeast Asia were by no means the first contact, or a contact between strangers. Many of the early settlements 'were not always entirely new creations; in many cases (Oc Eo in Cochin China, Kuala Selinsing in Perak, Sempaga in Celebes, etc.), they were built on Neolithic sites that the seamen from India had frequented perhaps from time immemorial'.[27] The reasons for the larger settlements (beginning with the first century) were essentially trade related. The burgeoning Indian demand for gold was supplemented by the revived demand for luxury goods from the Roman Empire, as well as from the Seleucid Empire. Even the Sanskritized place-names in Southeast Asia identified specific trading interests, such as Takkola (market of cardamom), Karpuradvipa (Borneo-island of Camphor) and Narikeladvipa (Nicobar-island of coconut palms). Gold, spices, aromatic woods (sandalwood, eaglewood), and fragrant resins (camphor, benzoin) were the most sought-after commodities by the early Indian traders who settled across Southeast Asia.

THE EARLY SETTLEMENTS

The larger ships that India was now building facilitated bringing in larger cargoes. The use of bigger ships and more frequent sailings because of the increased demand for the goods being traded meant that larger numbers of people began travelling between India and the ports of Southeast Asia. These journeys were carefully timed to suit the monsoon winds, which invariably meant long waits of several months at each end. These sojourns were used by the ship's captain and crew for repairs of the ship. The merchants and traders travelling on board as owners, agents of owners or just passengers used these sojourns for accumulating the goods that would be taken on board for the return journey. Gradually, the system of storage and warehousing, described as emporium (or factory in British colonial times) came into being. Many of these became regional collection centres for goods. This is how settlements came up at crucial points across Southeast Asia along the maritime route from India to China.

The establishment of these settlements followed similar patterns and processes, no matter whether this happened in Aceh at the northern tip of Sumatra, along the western and eastern shores of the Isthmus of Kra, along the Java coastline, in Kedah and other coastal points of the Malay Peninsula, in Cambodia, the Celebes and Borneo. Two or three Indian vessels sailing together arrive at Aceh or Kedah or any other port of call. The newcomers establish relations with the chiefs of the region they are entering, earning favour with them by means of welcoming gifts, distribution of curative medicines for treatment of illnesses, and of amulets and other preventive charms against all dangers, real and imaginary. The newcomer either is or claims to be a rich man, a healer and a magician. Some may even claim to be nobility or of royal extraction.[28]

They are not unknown to each other, the Indian and the local chieftain. They, or their ancestors, have interacted before. Each is willing to benefit from the other, materially in exchange of goods and for improving their own systems. Perhaps that is why the process of acceptance and exchange is so peaceful. This is no *terra incognita* for the Indians. The Indians do not use interpreters. They learn the local language, no matter how different from their own. This gives them ready access to the community of people living there. They intermarry, the leaders with the daughters of the chiefs, and ordinary settlers with others. They are no longer strangers. They are now family.

A fifth-century Chinese text affirms this prevalence of intermarriage when it says that '. . . in the kingdom of Tun-sun there are more than a thousand Brahmins of India. The people of Tun-sun practice their doctrine and give them their daughters in marriage; consequently, many of these Brahmins do not go away.'[29] Scholars have located Tun-sun in the northern reaches of the Malay Peninsula, along the Isthmus of Kra, describing it as 'a trans-isthmian state through which travelers passed on their way from China to India'.[30]

There is epigraphic evidence across Southeast Asia revealing instances of intermarriage, and showing how kingdoms were led by individuals or families hailing either from India or Southeast Asia. Thus,

> the King Mulavarman, who left Sanskrit inscriptions in Borneo at the beginning of the fifth century, was the son of Asvavarman, whose name is purely Sanskrit, but his grandfather's name was Kundunga, which is certainly not. Sanjaya, founder of the Javanese dynasty of Mataram in the eighth century, was the nephew of a certain Sanna, whose name sounds like the Sanskritization of a Javanese name. . . . The genealogies of ancient Cambodia often present a curious mixture of Sanskrit and Khmer names. . . .[31]

Gradually, new communities come up in the coastal areas, an amalgam of the Indians and the local people they had first come into contact with. Given the size and permanence of these new settlements, the traders are soon joined by priests and scholars from India. These educated and learned individuals, leaving India for the first time, popularize the religions and arts of India, through the medium of the Sanskrit language. Over time, the locally spoken language is heavily infused with Sanskrit. The customs in these communities, particularly among the nobility and at court, mirror those in India. They now share a common religion with India, the Hindu-Buddhist heritage that is unique to vast regions throughout Southeast Asia. The people of these communities are the *Kun-lun* or the *Dvipantara*. In fact, according to the scholar G. Coedes 'the most ancient Sanskrit inscriptions of Farther India are not much later than the first Sanskrit inscriptions of India itself'.[32]

There is a general belief that the Hindus of India were debarred by their religion from travelling across the seas. Crossing the 'black waters' was said to be inauspicious, bringing defilement and pollution. Yet there are frequent references in Vedic literature and other religious texts to travel across the seas. There is a passage in the *Mrigendragama* 'which considers sea voyages for conquest or profit permissible and prescribes the use of a bright flame for rites involved'.[33]

The rapid spread of Buddhism within India and Ceylon in the last three centuries before the Common Era meant that the adherents of this faith had no constraints on crossing the 'black waters' either for commerce or for proselytizing their religion. This certainly provided fresh impetus for intensifying India's maritime contacts with the Malay Peninsula, the rest of Southeast Asia and beyond, right up to China. The active involvement of Buddhists in maritime activity can be seen from the large number of *Jataka* tales that deal with seafaring and maritime adventures. 'In many cases, the most ancient evidences of Indianization are the images of the Dipankara Buddha, who enjoyed great favour with the seamen frequenting the southern islands. The role of Buddhism is undeniable; it seems to have opened the way. . . .'[34]

The uniquely Hindu-Buddhist heritage of Southeast Asia combined elements of both religions with traditional beliefs of the original inhabitants. The Hindus, the Buddhists and the people in different parts of Southeast Asia amalgamated each other's traditions, evolving a unique harmonious blend acceptable to all. Throughout Southeast Asia, the role of the *brahmin* (priest) and the *kshatriya* (warrior) from India were considered central in the dissemination of the much sought after knowledge from the ancient Indian Sanskrit texts, in establishing systems of administration, and in bringing prosperity to the state. Their presence was seen as essential in augmenting the powers and prestige of the chief, whether Indian or Southeast Asian. It was with the help of the *brahmin* and the *kshatriya* that, over time, settlements in different parts of Southeast Asia were transformed into kingdoms. Rulers who were not from India were elevated 'to the level of *kshatriya* by means of the *vratyastoma*, the Brahmanic rite for admitting foreigners into the orthodox community'.[35] Sanskrit became popular across Southeast Asia because the local languages 'had no equivalent terms to use in transmitting these social, moral and religious innovations. It was, therefore, necessary to impose Indian terminology in all these domains, terminology that is still being used . . . after two thousand years.'[36]

G. Coedes has used the term 'Indianization' for the process described above. He makes it clear that there was no element of political domination in this process, nor did it involve any sustained large-scale migration or population transfers from India to Southeast Asia, other than the steady stream of merchants and traders, *brahmins* and *kshatriyas*. Essentially, this was a process of cultural assimilation throughout Southeast Asia, which meant bringing in 'an organized culture that was founded upon the Indian conception of royalty, was characterized by Hinduist or Buddhist cults, the mythology of the Puranas, and the observance of the Dharmasastras, and expressed itself in the Sanskrit language'.[37] Ancient Chinese sources 'tend to confirm the evidence . . . that the common traits of the countries of the Southern Seas are not those of colonies Indian in population but those of Indianised native societies.'[38]

In India, there are hardly any formal historical records or vernacular documents that can determine the provenance of those who travelled to Southeast Asia and collaborated in the establishment of trade-posts and kingdoms throughout this region. A reconstruction of the situation as it prevailed more than 2,000 years ago has been possible only through the painstaking work done by scholars, taking into account references in ancient Indian texts to these faraway lands, descriptions by European travellers and geographers, ancient Chinese texts and compilations by Chinese travellers, combined with archaeological findings, linguistic scripts, place names and cultural traditions throughout the Malay Peninsula and the rest of southeast Asia.

Southeast Asia's links with India evolved in multiple ways. Awareness about Southeast Asia and China is an intrinsic part of the traditional knowledge of people from every part of India. There were a large number of ports on the east and west coasts of India

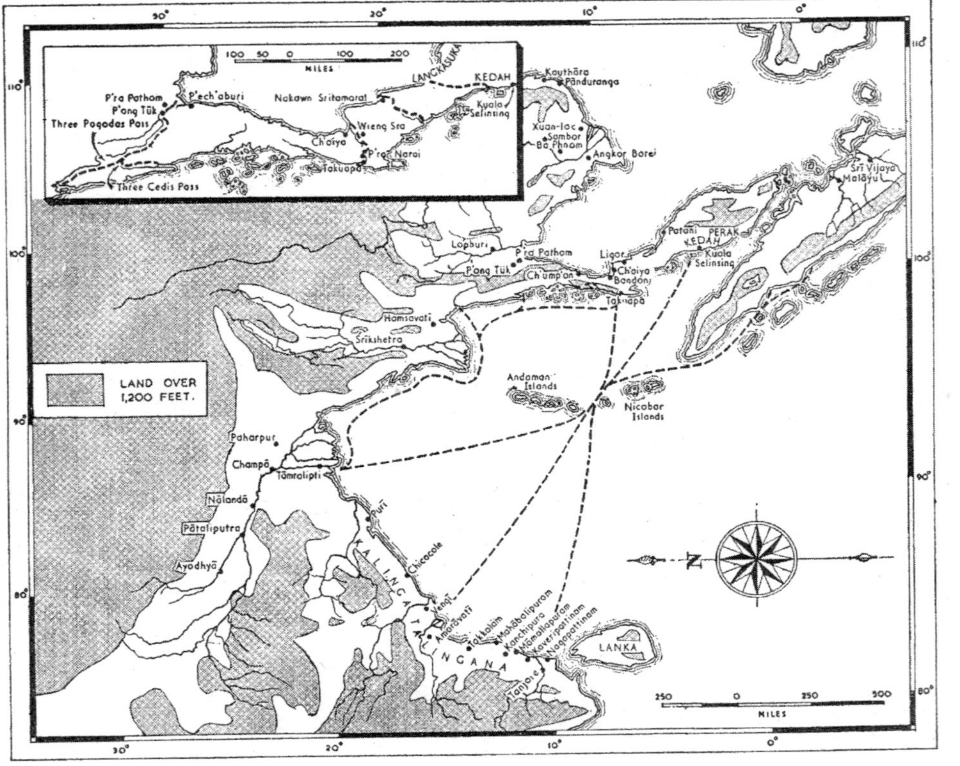

Map 4: Trade-cum-Migration Routes between India and Southeast Asia

involved in the maritime commerce with Southeast Asia and China. Tamralipti (Tamluk in the Midnapore district of present-day West Bengal), at the mouth of the river Ganga, was the starting point for merchants from the Gangetic towns of Varanasi (in present-day Uttar Pradesh) and Champa (in present-day Bihar), and even for those further west from the plains of north India. It was from Tamluk that the Chinese pilgrims Fa-hsien (early in the fifth century) and I-ching (towards the end of the seventh century) boarded Indian ships for their return journey to China. Further south along the eastern coast of India, there is Paloura, near Chicacole (Chilka lake) described by Ptolemy as the 'apheterion' or port of departure for the open-seas sailing to the Golden Chersonese and beyond. The *Periplus* has descriptions of the major ports along the eastern coast of South India that are involved in this trade, such as Kamara (Khabari for Ptolemy, Kaveripattinam in the Kaveri delta) and Podouke (perhaps present-day Puducherry or Pondicherry). Other major ports in south India were Nagapattinam and Masulipatnam, from where large vessels set sail to the Chryse, to other parts of Southeast Asia and to China. Along the west coast of India, there is evidence that the large ports of Bharukaccha (today's Broach), Surparaka (Sopara) and Muchiri (the Greek Muziris, today's Cranganore) were in trading contact with the Golden Chersonese or the Malay Peninsula.

Indian and foreign scholars have long debated the provenance of the Indians who, in ancient times, played the major role in fostering and nurturing the trade between India and Southeast Asia. 'All the eastern ports of India up to Tamralipti (Tamluk) contributed to this Indian expansion, but the South played the greatest role', concludes the scholar Louis de La Vallee-Poussin.[39] This conclusion seems appropriate, as it is borne out by comparisons of dynastic traditions, epigraphic evidence, architectural similarities and even place-names across Southeast Asia.

The very first Indianized kingdom in Southeast Asia was that of Funan, established in the first century, centred around the delta of the Mekong River. Scholars have concluded that

> . . . satisfactory comparison can be made between the dynastic tradition of the sovereigns of Funan and that of the Pallavas of Kanchi (Kanchipuram). Both the founder and the great Indianizer of Funan were of the Brahmanic

clan Kaundinya, a clan that originated in northern India, one branch of which exerted great influence over Mysore around the second century.[40]

The widespread popularity across Farther India of sage Agastya and his cult indicates the contribution of the Pandyas, who reigned in the region of present-day Tamil Nadu. Scholars like K.A. Nilakanta Sastri have concluded, upon examination of ancient scripts, that 'the alphabets of Farther India originated in southern India, with the influence of the script of the Pallavas predominating'.[41] In some cases, such as the Yupa inscriptions (seven inscriptions on stone pillars) of King Mulavarman from Kutai (East Borneo), which dates back to the fourth century, the script is not specifically Pallava, but resembles the script used by the Telugu-speaking Salankayanas, who ruled in the West Godavari region of present-day Andhra Pradesh till the middle of the fifth century. It was around this time that Telugu (and Kannada) languages began using separate scripts.

Scholars have drawn direct linkages between the Sailendras of Java and the Saila Bhaba dynasty that ruled Kalinga from the fifth to the eighth century. As far back as 300 BCE the Kalinga Empire was known for its wealth, military strength and maritime capabilities. In the third century BCE, the Greek Ambassador Megasthenes, while touring India had described the military strength of the Kalingas (an army of 1,00,000, with 1,700 horses and thousands of elephants). Emperor Ashoka invaded Kalinga in 261 BCE, and conquered it, but only after almost 1,00,000 soldiers lost their lives. After the death of Emperor Ashoka, his successor as Emperor of Kalinga, the Great Kharavela, adopted Jainism as his religion. One of the sacred texts of the Jains, the *Jaina Uttaradhyana Sutra,*[42] in the 21st Lecture titled 'Samudrapala' speaks of Pithunda port in Kalinga while relating the story of a merchant-trader who crossed the seas from this port to Champa, in present-day Vietnam. The renowned French orientalist Sylvain Levi discovered Pithunda port in district East Godavari in Andhra Pradesh, to the south of Pallur (Ptolemy's apheterion Paloura), near Chicacola and Kalingapatanam.

The glory of the Kalingas revived under the Saila Bhaba dynasty, a period often described as the golden age of the Kalingas. Maritime trade between Kalinga and the Malay Archipelago, which goes back more than 2,000 years, was renewed with great vigour under

Emperor Sailendra. The regional monicker Kalinga resembles Kling, the word used in Malaysia and Cambodia to refer to Indians. It is said, perhaps apocryphally, that Emperor Shailendra of Java gave the name Kalinga to the areas of the Malay Peninsula that were under his suzerainty. After the Saila Bhaba dynasty, under the Bhauma dynasty kings, the name Kalinga was replaced by Utkal. Udra was another part of the Kalinga empire. The name Ussa (Odra or Orissa) for Pegu (in Myanmar) and Srikshetra (Puri), the old name for Prome, also in Myanmar, shows their links with Odisha. The people of Myanmar use the word Talaing for the Mons, which corresponds closely with the Telengana region of contemporary Andhra Pradesh in India. In Sumatra, scholars have identified many names among the Karo Bataks that correspond to southern India, such as Chola, Pandya, Pallava and even Malayalam![43]

Among the lesser-known place-names, there is the kingdom of Taruma located in the region of Bandung, commanding the Sunda Strait, at the westernmost part of Java. Four stone Sanskrit inscriptions, dating to CE 450, have been found here. These are among the oldest evidence of Indianized kingdoms in Farther India, just a little later than the Kutai (East Borneo) inscriptions. They are certainly the oldest found in Java. Purnavarman, king of the land of Taruma, is the author of these inscriptions. There is a locality of the same name, Taruma, about 20 km north of Cape Comorin (Kanyakumari in Tamil Nadu).

> It is significant that these earliest records of Hindu settlement are found exactly in that part of the island where the Dutch traders first established their 'factories' and which became the centre from which the power of Holland has spread over the whole of the . . . Archipelago. The geographical position of the Batavian coast with regard to the continent of India and Sumatra and the special advantages its configuration offers to shipping and trade are circumstances which will easily account for a coincidence that is certainly not due to mere chance.[44]

In Sumatra, the oldest Indian archaeological find is an Amaravati statue of the Buddha. This was found in Palembang, near the hill Seguntang. It is made of granite, a stone unknown in Palembang. Amaravati, situated in coastal Andhra Pradesh, was the capital of the Satavahanas, the first great Andhra kings, who ruled from the second century BCE to the third century CE. Similarly, at Sempaga in the Celebes (Sulawesi in present-day Indonesia), a bronze image of Buddha of the Amaravati school was found. The bronze Buddha from South Djember and Sikendeng on the west coast of Celebes, and the colossal statue at Bukit are all in characteristic Amaravati style. It is quite likely that these images of the Buddha were brought here by early Buddhist sailors all the way from Andhra Pradesh, since there were sailings from south Indian ports to Sumatra at the time of the Satavahanas. The transport of the large stone Buddha of Palembang must have been more difficult.

Architecturally, it is perceived that the monolithic temples of Mamallapuram near Chennai (India), built early in the seventh century CE by the Pallava kings, share a close affinity with ancient monuments across Southeast Asia. However, there are monuments in Southeast Asia that reveal similarities with Gupta era monuments in the Gangetic plains and with other monuments of central India.

The interaction between South and Southeast Asia was a gradual process, one that has left deep imprints on every aspect of life, language, culture and development throughout the Malay Archipelago, Myanmar and Indo-China. This was a cumulative process, one that grew and intensified over the centuries, bringing together people from different regions of South and Southeast Asia. Trade was its most important motivation, not conquest or domination. There was no attempt at political control, or collection of revenues, or in any other way developing a hub-and-spoke relationship with the 'mother country'. As a result, the interaction seems to have remained largely peaceful, rather than one driven by the use of force or imposition of will.

This was not a one-way process where the Indians were givers and the Southeast Asians were passive recipients. This was a dynamic two-way exchange, with friendly and equal participation at every stage. The Indians could not obtain the unique goods they sought without the active cooperation of the upriver people and all others living across the Southeast Asian region. The Indian merchants were buyers and sellers. Their ships brought in goods from India and the West that were in great demand in Southeast Asia, right up to China.

The people across Southeast Asia were from the very outset an intrinsic part, first of the process of trade through exchange of goods, and later in the governance and management of the Indianized kingdoms. Through intermarriage, new lineages emerged, which only served to further strengthen the people-to-people links between South and Southeast Asia. Within a generation or two, there were no 'outsiders' or 'insiders', whether in society or in the trading process, in manning ships or in ruling kingdoms. The rulers of these kingdoms visited India, or sent embassies to visit Indian ports and to interact with Indian rulers and traders. This further reinforced the interest across Southeast Asia in the Indian systems of governance, in the Hindu-Buddhist traditions and in Indian culture.

SOUTH ASIA, SOUTHEAST ASIA AND CHINA

Scholars and analysts have tried to understand the dynamics of the entirely different interaction that evolved across this region in the pre-colonial period, between the people of India and Southeast Asia on the one hand, and India and China on the other. There were several reasons for this. Once again, trade, religion and culture provide the leitmotif to explain the difference.

India's geostrategic location and advanced (for the times) maritime capabilities allowed her to occupy centrestage in the conduct of trade between the West, India and the East. Right up to the seventh century CE, it was primarily Indian ships that sailed east of India. Their prime market was China, for sale of European and Indian goods, and for purchase of Chinese goods that would be sold in India and Europe. An equally important target was to access gold, spices and other high-value products from the Malay Peninsula, and other destinations in Southeast Asia. The settlements, and soon the kingdoms that came up across Southeast Asia in the early centuries of the first millennium, may have started as way-stations en route to China, or as gathering points for the valuable products of these regions, but soon enough, these were in themselves important markets and demand centres.

The location of the earliest settlements and kingdoms reveal both concerns: a direct trade-route to China, and access to the sought after products of Southeast Asia, such as gold and spices. The antiquity and type of artefacts that have been excavated at these sites reveal Indianized settlements dating back to the early centuries of the first millennium. It is not that these trade-routes were being traversed for the first time during this period. Archaeological excavations indicate the dates when enhanced numbers and greater frequency of movements across this region, combined with more intensive interactions with the peoples living here, led to the establishment of settlements, and the emergence of organized establishments, as compared to the earlier, seasonal visits. 'Regional markets in Southeast Asia can be identified from the third century BCE, and more or less regular maritime trade between India and Southeast Asia certainly existed by the first century BCE. This exchange grew rapidly in the first millennium CE with the emergence of intermediate ports-of-trade.'[45]

The maritime routes towards the east of India, be it to China, to the Malay Peninsula, the Golden Chersonese or other destinations in Southeast Asia, set off from the ports along India's east coast, or from Sri Lanka. Sailing east from the northern ports (of east India) brought the ship to the Arakan coast of Burma. Sailing from the southern ports (of East India) took the ship across the Bay of Bengal. Using the ten degree channel between the Andaman & Nicobar Islands would bring the sailing ships to the northern reaches of the Malay peninsula near Takuapa on the Isthmus of Kra. Alternatively, using the channel somewhat further south, between the Nicobar Islands and the Achin headland at the northernmost tip of the island of Sumatra would bring sailing ships to land near Kedah in present-day Malaysia. It can truly be said that Southeast Asia, particularly the Malay Peninsula, was 'strategically situated at the maritime chokepoint between India and China . . .'.[46]

Those who sailed to the Arakan coast travelled from Moulmein up the Ataran River to the Three Pagodas Pass at a height of around 800 ft. From this point travellers descended by way of the Me Nam Kwe Noi into the valley of the Mekong River and so to the plains of Lower Siam. A second, more difficult route, brought the traveller further south through Tavoy and the Three Cedis Pass to Lower Siam.

Where these routes converge and the traveller comes out into the composite delta of Lower Siam are the archaeological sites of Pong Tuk and Pra Pathom, attesting the use of one or both of these passes during the early years of the Christian era. . . . At Pong Tuk, . . . Professor Coedes excavated a settlement yielding Buddhist remains of the second to sixth century AD, while from Pra Pathom further down the valley have come finds attributable to the fifth or sixth centuries AD.[47]

Those who sailed to the Isthmus of Kra landed at the mouth of the Takuapa River. For centuries, they used the land route across the Isthmus of Kra from Takuapa to Bandon, Caiya or Ligor on the eastern shores of the Isthmus, from where the maritime journey towards the China-trade entrepôt of Funan would resume. Excavations conducted in this region have yielded rich results, even though the exact location of the legendary Takkola is by no means final.

In 1935 Dr Quaritch Wales investigated the site of a settlement on a small island off the mouth of the Takuapa River. The stratigraphy was greatly disturbed but 'the evidence of the potsherds alone confirmed that the place had flourished between the third and eighth centuries AD'. From this ancient settlement the Takuapa River leads up to a col at just under 2000 feet, from the far side of which the Khirirat River affords an easy descent into the coastal plain of Bandon. Dr Wales found traces of Indian penetration along this route, while on the plains beyond stand the remains of the city of Caiya and the smaller site of Wieng Sra, together with several other shrines and relics dating from the period under discussion.

Takuapa . . . seems to have retained its importance as a gateway to *Tambralinga* (Caiya district), for the Pra No Visnu found there is in the purest Pallava style, while a similar but locally modelled figure from Wieng Sra and three Brahmanic stone statues in the valley of the Takuapa River attest the continued use of the trans-peninsular route. With the statues was found a Tamil inscription of the ninth century AD, which places a tank constructed in the locality under the protection of the *Manigramam* (a powerful mercantile corporation) and the residents of a military camp (*senamukam*).

Similar Pallava style statues still in situ at Nakawn Sritamarat, whence came also two Sanskrit inscriptions of the sixth to eighth centuries, would seem to indicate that the Trang river afforded a route across the isthmus at this time.[48]

It is interesting to note that in the Isthmus of Kra, there is no evidence of such settlements at some of the shortest trans-peninsular routes, such as along the Tenasserim River from Mergui to Prachaub. This shows that, just as with other early settlements throughout the Malay Peninsula, these came up at sites that could support trading and agriculture, rather than just the physically most convenient or shortest transit to China. In other words, the Malay Peninsula 'was a local centre for the diffusion of Indian culture and not merely a barrier over which successive waves of migrants flowed on to found the great kingdoms of Indo-China and Indonesia'.[49]

Along the eastern shores of the Isthmus of Kra, going south to present-day Kelantan, large Indianized settlements came up, known as Tambralinga, Langkasuka, Ch'ih-Tu and Tan-Tan.

For most of the first millennium, Chinese shipping was confined to coastal sailings and a very large inland waterways network of barges and boats. The first Indianized settlement in Funan came up around the entrepôt which developed at the place of exchange of Chinese and non-Chinese goods. Chinese vessels came up to this point and offered their own products for sale in exchange for Indian, Southeast Asian and European goods.

Hitherto, China had depended almost exclusively on the land route for its trade with India and the West. In ancient China, at the beginning of the third century, the Han dynasty collapsed and was succeeded by the Three Kingdoms: the Wei, which comprised the central and northern provinces with its capital at Loyang; the Wu, which comprised the provinces south of the Yangtse River with its capital at Nanking; and the Shu, which included the western part of the empire with its capital at Chengdu. During this period, the southern kingdom of Wu found it impossible to use the traditional land route, the Silk Road, for its commercial relations with the West. This route passed through and was blocked (to the Wus) by the Wei kingdom. As a result, the Wu kingdom now sought to use the sea route to procure for itself the luxury goods it craved from the West.[50] For the first time, the ports on the south coast of China began to assume importance. First Tongking (also known as Tonquin or Tunkin), on the delta of the Red River in Annam district of present-day Vietnam, developed because of its proximity to Funan, followed soon thereafter by the growth of Canton (Guangzhou in Guangdong province of China) as a rival port.

After the Three Kingdoms there followed a period of considerable disturbances, rebellions and localized wars. It was only with the coming of the Sui period (CE 581-618) that the process of re-consolidation began, which continued with the glorious Tang period from CE 618 to 907.

Throughout this period, till the early years of the seventh century, Chinese shipping and maritime activities remained confined to the coastal regions. 'Chinese merchants seem not to have ventured very far afield and to have left chiefly to strangers the initiative in foreign trade, but outsiders found China a profitable country with which to deal.'[51] During the Song Dynasty (CE 960 to 1279), when the magnetic mariner's compass for navigation at sea was first introduced, this resulted in the rapid growth of China's merchant navy. Kuwabara, who was Commissioner of Merchant Shipping during the Song dynasty, says that 'Chinese trading ships before the Tang era were inferior in all respects to those of the South Sea countries'.[52]

This explains why Funan occupied a privileged position as the terminus of the single most important route of maritime commerce of that period. This route stretched all the way from the Mediterranean through the Red Sea and the Indian Ocean to India, and from India across the Bay of Bengal and the Malay Peninsula to Funan in Indochina.

NALANDA: 'INSATIABLE IN GIVING'

For 800 years, from the fifth or sixth century to the end of the twelfth century, the ancient University of Nalanda, located in the present-day state of Bihar in eastern India, was the most renowned and sought after centre of learning for religious (Buddhist) and secular studies. Scholars from Greece, Turkey and Persia, from Japan, Tibet, Mongolia, China, Korea, Indonesia and Sri Lanka and certainly from all across India congregated here in the oldest institution of learning known to mankind. The library at Nalanda, known as *Dharma Gunj* (Mountain of Truth) or *Dharmaganja* (Treasury of Truth) was so extensive that the collections of manuscripts housed therein burnt for several months when the campus was ransacked and set on fire by invaders.

Writings and descriptions by ancient scholars, travellers and learned men who visited and studied at the University of Nalanda attest to the academic and intellectual vibrancy of this institution, combined with the centrality of its role in nourishing and strengthening connectivities across Asia based on trade, religion and culture.

NOTES

1. G. Coedes, 1966, p. 11.
2. K.A. Nilakanta Sastri, *Foreign Notices of South India*, 1966, p. 44.
3. Ibid.
4. Braddell, *JMBRAS*, vol. XIII, pt. II, 1935, p. 81.
5. Ibid., p. 79.
6. Ibid., p. 82, quoting G. Elliot Smith.
7. Ibid., p. 83, quoting A.L. Kroeber.
8. Ibid., p. 70.
9. Ibid., p. 74.
10. Ibid.
11. Ibid., p. 75.
12. Max Mueller, *Biographies of Words and the Home of the Aryans*, 1888, p. 120, quoted in 'Demise of Aryan Invasion/Race Theory' by Dinesh Agrawal, Penn State University, USA, accessed at http://www.diehardindian.com/demogrph/moredemo/aryan.htm on 30 April 2010.
13. Ibid., p. 9.
14. Braddell, op. cit., p. 98.
15. 'The Aryan-Dravidian Controversy' by David Frawley, accessed at http://www.hindunet.org/hindu_history/ancient/aryan/aryan_frawley_1.html
16. *Encyclopaedia Britannica* accessed at http://www.britannica.com/EBchecked/topic/77226/Brahui on 1 May 2010.
17. Times News network (TNN) report dated 25 September 2009, accessed at http://articles.timesofindia.indiatimes.com/2009-09-25/india/281072053_1_incidence-of-genetic-diseases-indians-tribes on 12 March 2011.
18. Braddell, op. cit., p. 100, quoting Tolkapiyyar.
19. Braddell, op. cit., vol. XIII, p. 72.
20. Ibid., p. 98, quoting Sir Charles Elliott, *Hinduism and Buddhism* (1923), vol. III, p. 121.
21. Ibid., p. 93.

22. Bradell, op. cit., p. 86.
23. G. Coedes, *The Indianized States of Southeast Asia*, p. 12, quoting Jules Sion, *L'Asie des Moussons*, II, p. 483.
24. Coedes, op. cit., p. 12.
25. Braddell, op. cit., p. 89.
26. Coedes, op. cit., p. xvii (Introduction).
27. Ibid., p. 14.
28. Ibid., p. 22, quoting Gabriel Ferrand 'Le K'ouen-louen', *Journal Asiatique*, July-August 1919, p. 15.
29. Ibid., pp. 24-5.
30. Paul Wheatley, *The Golden Khersonese*, pp. 286-7.
31. Ibid., p. 24.
32. Ibid., p. 15.
33. Coedes, op. cit., p. 269, fn. 27, quoting N.R. Bhatt, *Mrigendragama*, (Publications de l'Institut Francais d'Indologie, 23, Pondicherry, 1962), p. 76.
34. Coedes, op. cit., p. 23.
35. Ibid., p. 24.
36. Ibid., p. 22, quoting Gabriel Ferrand, 'Le K'ouen-louen', pp. 15ff.
37. Ibid., p. 16.
38. Ibid., p. 25.
39. Coedes, op. cit., p. 29 (quoting Louis de La Vallee-Poussin *Dynasties et Histoire de l'Inde depuis Kanishka jusqu'aux invasions Musulmanes*, Paris, 1935).
40. Ibid., p. 30.
41. Ibid., p. 31.
42. *Jaina Sutras*, pt. II, by Hermann Jacobi, 'Sacred Books of the East', vol. 45, published in 1895. In the Introduction Hermann Jacobi writes that these were composed 'probably in the first centuries before our era, . . . additions or alterations may have been made till the first edition under Devardhigan in 454 AD'.
43. Coedes, op. cit., p. 30.
44. Ibid., p. 53, quoting the scholar Jean Philippe Vogel, who first deciphered and wrote about these inscriptions (fn. 65, p. 283).
45. Sebastian R. Prange, 'Like Banners on the Sea: Muslim Trade Networks and Islamization in Malabar and Maritime Southeast Asia', in Michael Feener and Terenjit Sevea (eds), *Islamic Connections: Muslim Societies in South and Southeast Asia*, Singapore: ISEAS, 2009, p. 27.
46. Ibid.
47. Paul Wheatley, *The Golden Khersonese*, pp. 195 and 10.
48. Ibid., pp. 195-6.
49. Ibid., p. 198.

50. Wang Gungwu, 'The Nanhai Trade', *JMBRAS*, vol. XXXI, pt. 2, 1959.
51. Roland Braddell, 'An Introduction to the Study of Ancient Times in the Malay Peninsula and the Straits of Malacca', *JMBRAS*, vol. XVII, pt. I, 1939, p. 156, quoting K.S. Latourette, *The Chinese, Their History and Culture*, 2nd edn. (2 volumes in one), 1934, p. 167.
52. Ibid., p. 156.

3

Indianized Kingdoms in the Malay Peninsula

In this chapter we follow the evolution of the Indianized kingdoms throughout Southeast Asia. The focus is on those kingdoms and areas that involved the Malay peninsula and present-day Malaysia. At each stage the corresponding situation in India is also highlighted.

Dato' Roland Braddell, during his extensive and intensive studies on the ancient history of the Malay Peninsula and the Straits of Malacca, concludes that 'No understanding of the ancient history of these regions can be obtained without . . . that of India, China and Farther India generally. Malaya is . . . a portion of a whole; it is in the main . . . a highway of migration and trade, a meeting-point of civilizations.'[1]

Over the millennia Malaysia and India evolved and developed in their respective milieu, unique in many ways, yet retaining a common thread of shared history and cultural values. The intertwined strands that caused these two civilizations to evolve in the way they have remain relevant to understanding key issues facing them today. Braddell aptly summed up the situation when he said 'history is geography set in motion . . . what today is a fact of geography becomes tomorrow a factor of history.'[2]

The two hundred years from 50 BCE to CE 150 witnessed a tremendous growth in trade and maritime activity by Indians throughout Southeast Asia. Sylvain Lévi and R.C. Majumdar described this period as the *terminus ante quem*, the latest possible date by which Indian settlements started coming up in the Malay Peninsula.[3] Expert opinion, taking into account early Chinese texts, agrees that the Indianized kingdom of Funan, ancient Kamboja, came up in the first century, and that of Champa not later than the second century.

During this period, along the Coromandel coast, the Chola king Kanta ruled from Campa (later called Kakandi) and from Puhar or Kaveripattinam. The similarity in nomenclature between Campa and Champa (in present-day Vietnam) is unmistakable. Nilakanta Sastri has described the Chola state as including the modern districts of Trichinopoly and Thanjavur and part of the Puddukottai state.

Puhar was counted among the few great cities of the time, a major emporium for trade, mentioned repeatedly in Sangam literature (the first three or four centuries). It was full of foreign merchants 'speaking different tongues, (who) had left their homes and come to reside (in Puhar) on terms of mutual friendship'. The goods traded included black pepper, gems, gold, sandal, and agil, 'the pearl of the southern sea', 'the coral of the western sea', 'food from Lanka' and 'goods from Kalagam'.[4] Kalagam is a reference to Malaysia, taken to be present-day Kedah. This was the emporium in Malaysia, corresponding to Puhar, from where goods were shipped to Tamilakam. These goods could have originated in the Malay Peninsula or could have been brought there from Funan, Champa or other parts of Southeast Asia either through the Straits of Malacca or by the land route across the Isthmus of Kra and north-east Malaysia. The Cholas were among the earliest to have systematically developed trade between India and Southeast Asia in the first two centuries CE.

In the third century, the Cholas gave way to the Pallavas, who ruled from Kanchi (present-day Kanchipuram) for the next 600 years till the ninth century, when they were overpowered by the later Cholas. The Pallavas have been dynamic participants in the interaction between India, the Malay peninsula, and beyond. The Pallavas ruled the northern Tamil Nadu region, together with Andhra Pradesh, and parts of Karnataka right up to the Arabian Sea coast. By the end of the sixth century they exercised control over the southern regions of Tamil Nadu as well. Originally Buddhist, most of them had become Saivas by the end of the sixth century, when Buddhism was in decline in the south.[5] Throughout their reign, however, the Pallavas were well known as patrons of Buddhism and Jainism. The Chinese monk Xuanzang (Hiuen Tsang) who visited Kanchipuram during the reign of Narasimhavarman I reported that there were 100 Buddhist monasteries and 80 temples in the city.

FUNAN, CHAMPA, THE SAILENDRA DYNASTY AND THE *SEJARAH MELAYU*

Funan probably began as a trading settlement at Oc Eo, where there was a port and an emporium to facilitate storage of goods. 'The nucleus of the civilization of Funan, out of which the whole of Khmer history was to develop, originated on the western coast of Indochina, at the landing point of Indian cultural influences'.[6] The capital of Funan, Vyadhapura (Sanskrit for 'city of hunters'), was about 200 km further north along the delta of the Mekong River, near the hill Ba Phnom and the village Banam, both located in the Cambodian province of Prei Veng.

The name Funan, taken from Chinese dynastic annals, is based on the old Khmer word *bnam*, the modern equivalent of which is *phnom* or mountain. This reflected the royal title used by the kings of Funan, which was in Khmer *kurung bnam*, and in Sanskrit *sailaraja* or 'king of the mountain'. This links up with the legend of the mythical Mount Meru, the sacred mountain in Hindu, Buddhist and Jaina cosmology, considered to be the centre of all the physical, metaphysical and spiritual universes. For the next 1,200 years and more, the legend of Mount Meru is the recurring theme throughout Indochina and the Malay Peninsula, reflected in the titles of ruling dynasties and in the monumental architecture at Angkor Vat, Borobudur, and other places. G. Coedes has described how well the legend of Mount Meru fits in with existing local beliefs across Indo-China and Southeast Asia:

> Indian-style kingdoms were formed by assembling many local groups—each possessing its guardian genie or god of the soil—under the authority of a single Indian or Indianised-native chief. Often this organisation was accompanied by the establishment, on a natural or artificial mountain, of the cult of an Indian divinity intimately associated with the royal person and symbolising the unity of the kingdom. This custom, associated with the original foundation of a kingdom or royal dynasty, is witnessed in all of the Indian kingdoms of the

Indochinese Peninsula. It reconciled their native cult of spirits on the heights with the Indian concept of royalty, and gave the population, assembled under one sovereign, a sort of national god, intimately associated with the monarchy. We have here a typical example of how India, in spreading her civilisation to the Indochinese Peninsula, knew how to make foreign beliefs and cults her own and assimilate them—an example that illustrates the relative parts played by Indian and native elements in the formation of the ancient Indochinese civilisations and the manner in which these two elements interacted.[7]

Information about Funan is available in Sanskrit inscriptions, including one found in the neighbouring kingdom of Champa, and in the Chinese annals after the visit to Funan by two Chinese envoys in the middle of the third century. The centre of Funan was located on the lower Mekong delta. The territory of Funan included, at different times, the regions known today as Cambodia, Laos, Siam (Thailand), Cochin China in southern Vietnam, and the Malay Peninsula.

Champa (*Nagara Campa* in Sanskrit) was a coastal state in what is today the Annam region in central Vietnam. The Cham people of Vietnam and other parts of Indochina draw their name from the Champa state of their ancestors. The word *campa* refers to the *champaka*, a tree that is as well known in Malaya as in India.

The kingdom of Champa, known as Lin-yi in Chinese records, was founded in the second century. Its links with India can be appreciated not only in the Sanskrit inscriptions found on its territory, but also the beautiful bronze Buddha dating back to this period, found in Dong-Duong, in the Amaravati region of Champa. The eponymous town of Amaravati in Andhra Pradesh was the capital of the Andhra kings, the Satavahanas. Amaravati (in India) is also the site of the famous Amareswara temple dedicated to Shiva, and the site of a great Buddhist *stupa* originally built during the reign of Ashoka:

When the Chams make their appearance in history they are already Indianised. Their royal dynasty descends from Siva and the title of 'Varman', which the Chinese transcribed as 'Fan', was used by them. The dominant religious cult was Sivaism, the god being worshipped under the names of Mahesvara and Paramesvara. At the end of the 4th century CE King Bhadravarman constructed the great Siva temple of Mi-son in Quang-nam . . . Buddhism was also practiced though perhaps to a less degree.[8]

Among the most significant shared traditions between the Pallava kings of south India and several regions of Southeast Asia is the legend about their respective foundation as dynasties. The Sanskrit inscription found in Champa records that the Brahman Kaundinya, recognized (even in the Chinese annals) as the founder of the kingdom of Funan, had received a javelin from the Brahman Asvatthaman, son of Drona.[9] Kaundinya threw this weapon to mark the location of his future capital, and then married Soma (daughter of the king of the Nagas[10]), who gave birth to the royal line. This mystical union was commemorated at the court of Angkor upto at least the thirteenth century, and modern Cambodian annals have preserved the memory of this commemoration.[11] This legend is identical to the belief about the origin of the Pallava kings. Similar legends exist about the origins of the kings in Champa, Pegu (in present-day Myanmar), Siam (Thailand), Sumatra, and in the annals of the *Sejarah Melayu*.

The Tamil classic, *Manimekhalai*, a poem about a Naga princess written in the early centuries of the first millenium, mentions a town named Nagapuram in Savaka-nadu and its two kings Bhumichandra and Punyaraja, who they say were descendants of Indra. Savaka-nadu in Tamil is the place where the Savakas live, and is taken by some as the name for the island of Java. Many scholars feel that the term 'Savaka or Javaka was generic for Malays',[12] without restricting this term to those living only in Java. This Naga legend is popular among the Pallavas of Kanchi. There are two inscriptions dating from the ninth century giving the genealogy of the Pallava kings. According to the first, Asvatthaman, son of Drona, married a Naga and their offspring was Skandasisya, the legendary ancestor of the Pallava kings.[13]

The origin of the Sailendra dynasty of Srivijaya, with its capital in Palembang (Sumatra), is also associated with the Naga tradition. In the *Chu-fan-chi* of Chao Ju-Koua, a twelfth-century work on Chinese trade, it is stated: 'They (the people of San-fo-tsi or Srivijaya) gave the title of long-tsing to their king'. Now the Chinese word, long-tsing, according to Pelliot, means 'the seed of the Naga'.[14]

The *Sejarah Melayu*, or the *Malay Annals*, too, contain references to the same Naga tradition, even though this is a much later text, dating to the sixteenth and seventeenth centuries. The Malay rulers of the Sultanate of Malacca are said to be descendants of the Sailendras. The traditional histories of Perak, Johore, Malacca and Singapore are concerned, *inter alia*, with tracing the descent of their rajas or kings back to the ancient Indian-Malay kingdom of Palembang, and also with tracing the descent of the kings of Palembang. Thus it becomes necessary to consider the *Sejarah Melayu* as analysed by scholars. The most detailed analysis has been given by Dato' Roland Braddell.[15] The Preface and Outline of the Malay Annals are contained in the *Journal of Malayan Branch of the Royal Asiatic Society*, vol. XVI, pt. III, 1938, pp. 1-41.

The *Sejarah Melayu* was re-written in 1612 from the original text brought back from Goa (India). 'The original nucleus from which (the) 1612 *Sejarah Melayu* is compiled, was written by a Malacca man in the court of Mahmud, the last Sultan of Malacca, a man who outlived the capture of the port by d'Albuquerque in 1511. . . . This Malacca author lived and wrote down to 1535'.[16] This manuscript was taken to Goa in 1536.

The author of the 1612 *Sejarah Melayu* is described as a civil servant,[17] working for the Bendahara Paduka Raja, Tun Sri Lanang, under the patronage of the then Sultan of Johore. The author says in the preface

> I happened to be present at an assembly of the learned and the noble, when one of the principal persons of the party observed to me that he has heard of a Malay story which had lately been brought by a nobleman from the land of Gua (Goa) and that it would be proper for some person to correct it according to the institutions of the Malays that it might be useful to posterity. On learning this I was firmly determined to attempt the work.[18]

The 1535 text is written in Malacca, but the 1612 text is written in Johore.

The *Malay Annals* were written and re-written after the advent of Islam to Southeast Asia, which probably accounts for the 'very Persian flavour of the genealogy of the Palembang kings'.[19] The *Sejarah Melayu* traces the descent of the ancient kings of Palembang to Alexander the Great, or Raja Iskandar. The last king of Singapore, who is the first king of Malacca, is called Iskandar Shah in the *Malay Annals*. Since

Sumatran folklore connected Alexander with Mahameru, the mountain of the Sailendra dynasty, and as the Malay rulers of Malacca claimed descent from these Sailendras, they also must have been connected with an Alexander who must have been the Macedonian conqueror! The end of the thirteenth century saw the coming of Islam; and according to Malay historians Alexander brought it; so tradition slipped an Iskandar into the Malacca genealogy at the most plausible place, the only possible place between the Hindu period and the historical rulers of Malacca.[20]

According to the *Sejarah Melayu*, is it Alexander the Great who was the progenitor of the Palembang dynasty and the one who brought Islam to this region? He could not have brought Islam to Malaya since he lived about 1,000 years before Prophet Muhammad. However, if the reference is to the descendants of Alexander the Great living in different parts of India, then certainly some among them could have been the ones to carry Islam to Malaya.

Dato' Roland Braddell concludes[21] that, given the 'strong connection of Indian ruling families in south-eastern Asia with the dynasties of southern India and particularly with the Pallava dynasty', Alexander the Great has been brought into the *Sejarah Melayu* as Iskandar, the founder of the Shailendra dynasty because the name Iskandar dates back to Skandasishya and Skandavarman, both of whom were early Pallava kings who ruled respectively in the third and fourth centuries CE. Skandasishya was born after his father, Virakurcha, seized the Pallava insignia of royalty and married the daughter of a Naga king.[22]

Iskandar is said to have dived into the sea, married the daughter of the king of the Oceans, and had three sons. In another section of the *Malay Annals*, it is Raja Suran 'who married the daughter of the Ocean King and had by her three sons'.[23] In the Menangkabau (Sumatra) version of the *Malay Annals*, it is Iskandar Zul Karnayn (Lord of the two horns, i.e. Alexander the Great) who begot three sons. In the fourth annal there is a reference to 'a raja of the land of Kling, named Adi Bernilam Raja Mudeliar, who was descended of Raja Suran'.[24] Thus, the *Sejarah Melayu* includes the reference to a southern Indian king who is a descendant of Raja Suran.

Dato Roland Braddell concludes that the repeated references to 'three sons' are probably references to the recognized royal houses of India, who traced their respective descent either from the *Chandra* (Moon, so *Chandravanshi* or Lunar descent), the *Surya* (Sun, so *Suryavanshi* or Solar descent) or the Agni-Kula (Fire, or descendants of the sage Jamadagni).[25] Raja Suran, from whom is traced the descent of the Palembang kings and the Malacca sultans,[26] was said to be of *Surya* descent. So were the Cholas. This is in keeping with the belief that, among Indian royalty, those who migrated to Southeast Asia were often the second sons or more distant relatives of the rulers, individuals who had little hope of ascending the throne, and so preferred to seek their fortunes elsewhere, without any further links to their mother-clan.

Raja Suran is depicted in the *Sejarah Melayu* as having three sons: Sang Sapurba, Sang Baniaka and Sang Nila Utama.[27] There are many versions of this legend in different declensions of the *Malay Annals*. Dato' Roland Braddell explains, quoting experts, that *Sang* is a title applied in Malay and Javanese to Gods and heroes of pre-Muhammadan times, probably of Sanskrit origin, derived from *swami*. *Purba* is the Sanskrit word *purva*, 'first'. *Sang Purba* may therefore be translated as 'first deity' or 'first chief'.[28] Sang Nila Uttama includes *nila*, the Sanskrit word for dark blue or sapphire, an epithet for Lord Shiva, and *Nila Uttama*, in Sanskrit, would mean 'the Sapphire-blue Chief or Supreme Being'. To complete the Shaivite references, some declensions of the *Malay Annals* depict Sang Sapurba riding a bull. Bat'h, the person depicted as arising from the vomit of the bull, gives Sang Sapurba the all-powerful title *Sri Tribhuvana Trimurti*. *Tribhuvana* means the three worlds—the heaven or sky, the earth and the lower regions. *Trimurti* signifies the trinity of three forms—Brahma, Vishnu and Shiva—encompassing respectively the powers of creation (the special attribute of Brahma), preservation (attribute of Visnu) and destruction (attribute of Shiva).

The three princes (sons of Raja Suran) are depicted as arriving at Mount Siguntang Mahameru in Palembang, Sumatra. Sang Sapurba becomes King of the Minangkabau where he slew the great serpent Saktimuna.[29] Sang Nila Uttama (shown in some declensions as the grandson, not the son, of Raja Suran) becomes King of Palembang, and goes on to become the founder of Singhapura (present-day Singapore) and the royal Malacca dynasty.

The legends of the *Malay Annals* highlight the ways in which the history and traditions of India are closely interwoven with those of the Malay Archipelago. The coming of the three princes to Mount Siguntang Mahameru is not just a Malay national legend. It is a quasi-historical description of the arrival of the Palembang dynasty (the Sailendra dynasty), which claim to be Sailendravamsa, or Family of the Lords of the Mountain. Many scholars describe the Sailendras as the rulers of the Srivijaya Empire. Bukit ('hill' in Malay) Seguntang exists. It is

> really a hummock on the banks of the Jambi River, the site of a later palace of the Sailendras. . . . Geographically it has nothing to do with Mahameru; but later tradition which knew of the legendary coming of the kings from the Mahameru foothills (Sailendras) and knew them also as Seguntang Kings identified the latter site with the foothills of the former.[30]

In this case, the tradition or legend has been confirmed by archaeology, because in 1920 a stone slab bearing an inscription in Pallava-grantha characters was discovered on the north-western side of the Seguntang hill. This is the oldest inscription ever found in the Malay language. It dates back to CE 683, and the language is a mixture of Sanskrit and Malay that is nowadays called Old Malay.[31]

It is significant to note that even today, the installation ceremonies of Malay Sultans follow the traditions described in the *Malay Annals*. The sultans of Perak, among others, continue to seek the blessings of the descendants of Bat'h for the strength and powers of *Sri Tribhuvana Trimurti*. In the words of Dato' Roland Braddell:

> The kingship which the Malay Annals record as having been founded in ancient Palembang was clearly an Indian one and has left many survivals in Malay law and custom. Thus the Sultans of Perak to this day are installed by the head of a family called the *Bangsa Muntah Lembu*[32] which claims descent from Bat'h and which avoids the flesh of the cow, as well as milk, butter, ghee, etc. and whose head is styled the *Sri Nara Diraja*; a Mohammedan family still clinging to ancient Brahminism. The *Sri Nara Diraja* whispers into the ear of the Sultan whom he is installing the *chiri* or installation formula which is in the *bahasa Jin*, or language of the genii, actually a very corrupt Sanskrit. . . . The Perak regalia are also interesting for the use of the *naga* or dragon in parts of it. . . .[33]

The cosmology of the famed Mount Meru continues to influence both ritual and political structure across the Malay Peninsula and across Southeast Asia. 'Preoccupation with the astrological numbers four, eight, sixteen and thirty-two, attributes of the fabulous Mount Meru, is one of the most persistent legacies of Hinduism in the ritual of Malay courts.'[34] The continuing practical importance of these numericals can be appreciated in a large number of countries across the region, where the state is organized as an image of the heavenly world of stars and gods. In the words of Richard Winstedt:

> In old Malacca, modern Perak, Kedah, Pahang and Negri Sembilan there was the same preoccupation with the astrological numbers 4, 8, 16 and 32 that has been traced in Burma, Siam and Cambodia. . . . At his enthronement a king of Siam or Cambodia is surrounded by eight Brahmins representing the Lokapalas who guard the eight points of the Brahmin cosmogony. In Kedah and Perak and Pahang there are 4 great chiefs and 8 major chiefs, and even the ground-plan of an old Perak palace shows pillars in four sets of 8, making 32 for each main section of the building. . . . In Negri Sembilan and in other states salutes numbered 8, 16 and 32. . . . Pegu in the 14th century had 32 provinces whose governors with the king made up the number of the gods in Indra's mountain paradise. . . . No Malay but a ruler may use a white or yellow umbrella, wear yellow raiment or have yellow house-furnishings or daggers mounted with bright gold or golden anklets.[35]

This long digression on the *Sejarah Melayu* and related issues at a point in history when the first Indianized kingdoms were coming up in the Malay Archipelago highlights the strength and longevity of the connectivities between India, Malaysia and the rest of Southeast Asia. The linkages that began in a sustained manner in the early years of the Christian era remain active and relevant in the twenty-first century.

In ethnolinguistic terms, Malayan influence is very prominent throughout Funan and Champa, particularly in the coastal areas. This includes the Indonesian influence. Today's Malay population is the product of frequent inter-marriages through the centuries with the Burmans, the Indians and much later, the Chinese and others. The Malays are dynamic, sea-faring people, who practised the Hindu and Buddhist religion for long, till the advent of Islam in the fourteenth century. Khmer influence in the languages of Malaysia and Indonesia is well-recognized, as is the Malayo-

Polynesian vocabulary in the Cham language. In today's Vietnam the Chams are considered to be part of the Malay ethnic group.

One can conclude that from the earliest times, the proto-Malays and later the Malays intermingled with the merchant traders coming from the Coromandel and Kalinga coasts of India. The resultant Indo-Malay communities, soon elevated to kingdoms, spread in Sumatra, Java, the Malay Peninsula and throughout Indo-China and other parts of Southeast Asia. These were the kingdoms based on strong Indian traditions of kingship, kinship and religion. However they were independent kingdoms in every way and soon developed their own mores and dynamics. Certainly, the people of the Malay Peninsula and Indo-China were full and active participants in the process of the growth, development and strengthening of these kingdoms. For example, in the latter half of the first millennium, when Indo-Malays from Java invaded Cambodia, the invaders were designated in Cambodian legend as the Chvea-Pream, i.e. Brahmanic Malays.[36]

THE INDO-MALAY KINGDOMS OF LANGKASUKA, KEDAH AND KELANTAN

Among the most intriguing early Indianized kingdoms is Langkasuka, in the north-east of the Malay Peninsula along the southern shores of the Gulf of Siam. The ancient Chinese text *Liang-shu* (*Liang Annals*), written in early seventh century, first describes the kingdom of Lang-ya-hsiu, now known to be Langkasuka. Subsequent Chinese texts mention Langkasuka right till the fourteenth century. The Liang Annals describe the kingdom as having been founded 400 years ago (i.e., early third century). It is described as a large and rich kingdom, where 'aloewood, barus, camphor and suchlike are especially abundant'.[37] It is estimated to have been situated 'astride the peninsula and have had access at the same time to the Gulf of Siam in the Pattani region and to the Bay of Bengal, north of Kedah',[38] thereby controlling one of the important land transportation routes between these two bodies of water. The *Liang-shu* speaks of King Bhagadutta, whose mother was an Indian princess, sending a tribute to the Emperor of China in 515.

There is important epigraphic evidence about the settlements and kingdoms in Funan, Champa and in the Malay Peninsula. The earliest of these is the Vo-Canh inscription dated paleographically to the second or third centuries CE. The inscription is in Sanskrit, thereby proving the presence of an Indianized or Indo-Malay Hindu kingdom in Vo-Canh, in the province of Khanh-Hoa, known in earlier times as the Kauthara province of the Champa kingdom.

Equally important are the inscriptions found on mainland Malaysia, south of the isthmus of Kra. The earliest of these was discovered by British Colonel James Low in the Malaysian province of Kedah, and in the British Malayan Province Wellesley, which is today the mainland portion of the state of Penang. These finds were made in the mid-nineteenth century, more than 150 years ago.

During his archaeological excavations in Kedah, Col. Low discovered an inscribed slate slab near Bukit Meriam beneath the floor of a ruined house. The inscription comprised two Buddhist verses written in Sanskrit in the oldest Pallava alphabet, ascribed by R.C. Majumdar to the fourth or fifth century CE.[39] The two stanzas of the inscription are the *ye-dharma* mantra and a verse:

ye dharma hetuprabhava hetum tesham tathagato hyavadat tesham cha yo nirodha evam vadi mahashramanah

Regarding dharmas that arise from a cause, the Tathagata taught their cause and also their cessation. Those were the words of the Great Mendicant.

ajnanacciyate karma janmanah karma karanam
jnananna kriyate karma karmmabhavanna jayate

Karma is accumulated through Ajnana; Karma is the cause of birth. Jnana leads to desistance from karma, and in the absence of karma there is no birth.[40]

The seven inscriptions found on the granite rock at Cherok Tekun in Province Wellesley are dated to the fourth century. R.C. Majumdar has described these inscriptions as being in Sanskrit, noting that the peculiar characteristics of south Indian alphabets are 'not very conspicuous in this record'.[41]

The most famous are the four inscriptions on a slate-stone slab found by Colonel James Low near the ruins of an old Buddhist temple in the northern part of Province Wellesley. This is now with the Indian Museum in Kolkata, India. This inscription dates back to the middle of the fifth century. The language is Sanskrit. This is recognized as a 'Pallava' inscription because of the Grantha-Pallava or Vengi characters used.[42] The characters used are very similar to those of Purnavarman's inscriptions in Java of the early fifth century. The slab has the outline of a *stupa* with seven *chattravali* (series of umbrellas) engraved on it. The text of the inscriptions include a Buddhist stanza and a prayer, a short prose passage of benediction wishing success in all ways and everywhere to the enterprises undertaken by the sea captain (*mahanavika*) Buddhagupta, hailing from Raktamrttika (Red-Earth land). The inscription contains the word *siddhayatra*, which is found in some early Indonesian inscriptions, where it refers to a pilgrimage to a holy place for the attainment of spiritual merit or potency leading to success.[43] It is interesting to see the north Indian name Gupta in this inscription. During this period Emperor Samudragupta's rule had, for a while, extended south to cover the Pallava regions as well.

There have been extensive research and discussions to determine the precise location of Raktamrttika. Paul Wheatley has quoted ancient Chinese texts describing an embassy sent to the country of Chih-t'u, or the Red-Earth Land. Chinese texts do not speak of Chih-t'u before CE 607, but by then this kingdom was already 150 years old. Based on the sailing route from Nanhai in China to Chih-t'u, and the length of the journey, Chih-t'u is located in north-eastern Malaya, in the region of today's Kelantan. The capital of Chih-t'u, known either as Seng-chih or Shih-tzu, was one month's journey inland, in the ulu of an east-coast river: . . . the Kelantan River springs immediately to mind. Not only is this river navigable by fair-sized boats, but also affords access to the gold fields of Ulu Pahang.[44]

These Chinese texts provide invaluable insights into the economic, social and political lifestyles of the kingdoms on the Malay peninsula in the first millennium CE. In the seventh century Chih-t'u and other kingdoms were part of Funan. There were more than one such kingdom and intermarriages were common amongst kingdoms. The king of Chih-t'u was Buddhist, though there were Brahmins at his court and Hindu rituals were followed. 'It is the custom to worship the Buddha but greater respect is paid to the Brahmins'.[45]

The Sui dynasty (CE 581 to 618) Emperor Yang-ti had 'called for men capable of opening up communications with far distant lands'. The two senior court officials who requested to be sent on an embassy to Chih-t'u were received with great honour by the king of Chih-t'u. Thirty ocean-going vessels were sent out by the king to welcome the visitors at the sea-port of the kingdom, and 'metal cables' were used to tow the visitors' vessels into port. There was tremendous pomp and pageantry at every stage, with the visitors receiving lavish gifts of gold. The Chinese texts note the similarity between the customs and material culture of Chih-t'u and other Indianized kingdoms, such as the ones at Dvaravati (in Siam), Ko-lo and Chen-la.

Ancient Chinese texts provide ample evidence about the wealthy lifestyles of the Indianized kingdoms, together with their practical knowledge of ship-building and allied technical skills. Since the preferred mode was to use the land-transhipment option through the isthmus of Kra rather than the pirate-infested Straits of Malacca, all the kingdoms along the north-western and north-eastern shores of the Malay Peninsula developed their own shipping fleets with ocean-going vessels.

Scholars have commented on the peaceful and harmonious coexistence of Hinduism and Buddhism in the kingdoms throughout Farther India. There is reference to this in the Cambodian texts.

> In ancient times there seems to have been the same religious tolerance in Farther India that is so marked a feature of life today. ... There was in Farther India none of the antagonism between Buddhism and Brahmanism, between Visnuism and Sivaism that led to so much bloodshed at various times and places in (India).[46]

B.R. Chatterji[47] points out that across South and Southeast Asia, a common pattern emerged, namely the combination of Mahayana Buddhist doctrines with the worship of Shiva. The author notes that this ancient Cambodian practice 'has its parallel in Champa, in Java under the Singasari and the Majapahit dynasties, and in Magadha and Bengal under the Pala dynasty'.

Equally important is the find known as the 'Pallava seal', an inscribed cornelian (part of a signet ring though the ring itself was not found), with an inscription in the Pallava script, engraved with the name of Sri Vishnuvarman. This was found at Tanjong Rawa in Kuala Selinsing in Perak. The writing appears to be earlier than the sixth century CE, comparable to that seen on some seals in Oc Eo.[48] This is indicative of the extent of the Funan empire's dominance over the Malay Peninsula (see Map 5).

The northern part of the Malay Peninsula, including Kedah and Kelantan provinces, and areas now in Siam (Thailand) such as the Isthmus of Kra, has played an important role in developing the trade and commercial relationship between India and China. This region faced peninsular India directly across the Bay of Bengal. The Indianized kingdoms in this region had a three-way role to play.

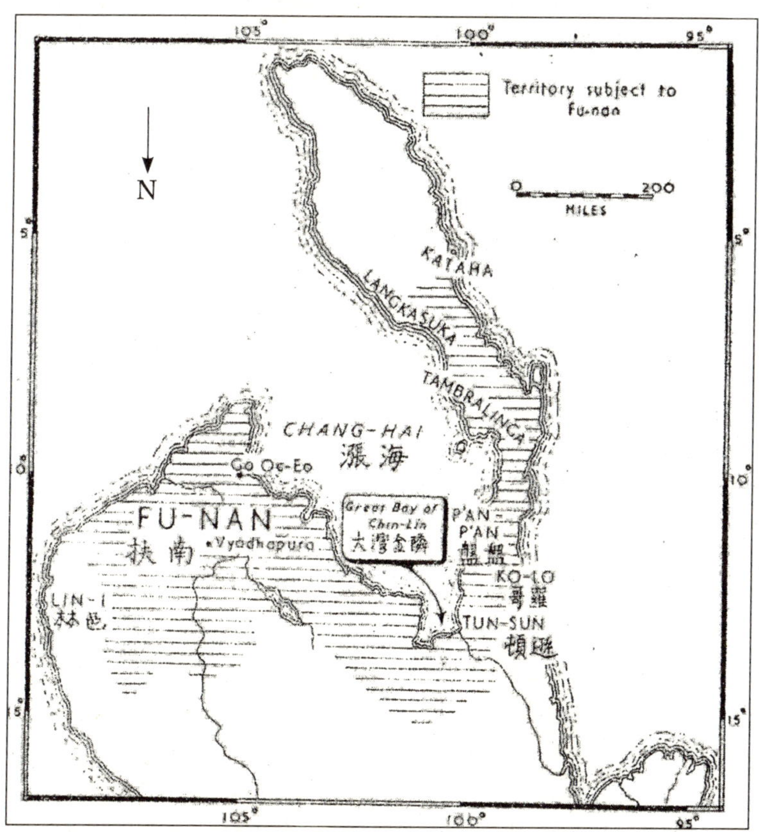

Map 5: The Extent of the Funan Kingdom

First, for ships coming from India, these kingdom(s) were the first port of call after crossing the Bay of Bengal, or for ships returning to India, these were the last ports of call before crossing the Bay of Bengal. This gave these ports a significant role in replenishment and stocking of provisions for ocean-going vessels, and accounted for the earliest trading settlements and later kingdoms that emerged in this region. Second, rather than being just way-stations, these kingdoms were themselves active participants in the trading process. They bought and sold goods from China and from India: luxury goods for the rulers and nobility and utilitarian goods for the rest of the population. Third, throughout most of the first millennium CE, given the intense problems of piracy in the Straits of Malacca, these northern kingdoms were important as transhipment and transit ports for the kingdom of Funan, either as the final destination or *en route* to China. They played a crucial role as emporia for storage of goods. There was an emporium, Sabana (Saba means eastern winds, the same as the province of Sabah in northern Borneo), at the southern tip of the Malay Peninsula, but this remained fairly unimportant because of the pirate-infested Straits of Malacca. There was a distinct preference for the overland route using the Isthmus of Kra.

The slate stone slab with the inscription praying for the success of Buddhagupta from Red-earth Land (identified above as being in the Kelantan region) was found very near to the Kedah region, in the estuary of the river Muda in the north of Province Wellesley. The inscription does not specify whether Buddhagupta was at the point of departure for his voyage or whether he had reached his destination. However, 'we can legitimately infer that the estuary of the Muda was either the resort of merchants or their home port during the fifth century CE'.[49]

EXCAVATIONS IN KEDAH AND PERAK BY QUARITCH WALES

In 1936, H.G. Quaritch Wales undertook major archaeological excavations at thirty sites in Kedah and Province Wellesley, five sites in Perak and three sites in Johore.[50] The detailed reports prepared by Quaritch Wales on his explorations and excavations, combined with his assessment and historical conclusions, cover the first millennium CE.

The Kedah region in north-west Malaysia lies at the entrance to the Straits of Malacca. This region provides the first sight of land for most ships crossing the Bay of Bengal, heading towards Southeast Asia. This factor, combined with the practical advantage of the excellent anchorage available in the estuary of the Merbok River, made Kedah the natural choice as port of call for traders and maritime travellers moving east from India. The first point of land normally sighted was the majestic *Gunung Jerai*, sometimes described as Kedah Peak. This added tremendous mystical appeal for travellers coming in from India. It was almost as if the gods themselves, from their abode in the mountains (reminiscent of Mount Meru), were welcoming travellers from India.

In the early years of the Common Era the final destination for most ships was port Oc Eo in Funan. From Kedah there was (and still is) an easy route to Ligor in the Langkasuka region along the south-east coast of the Gulf of Siam. In later centuries, a rail route was developed from Kedah to Ligor. The Takuapa route to the east coast (of the Gulf of Siam) is much shorter, so the choice of Kedah as one of the earliest Indianized settlements had much more to do with the availability of a good harbour in this region and the availability of suitable amounts of flat, fertile land. For centuries, Kedah remained the unrivalled leader among the settlements, and later the Indianized kingdoms in the Malay Peninsula. It was only much later, around the eighth century, with the growth of the Indian and Arab demand for tin that settlements in the tin-rich areas like Perak and Selangor became much larger and prosperous enough to suppress the perennial problem of piracy in the Straits of Malacca. This, along with the growth and prosperity of the Srivijaya Empire, encouraged the use of the Straits of Malacca as a shipping route for trade in preference to the transshipment route through Takuapa and Kedah to Bandon and Ligor.

In the course of the first millennium CE, as settlements grew in the estuary of the Merbok River, merchants and traders moved inland. They were now putting down roots, interacting and intermarrying with the people of Kedah. Temples and other structures came up along two rivers that separately fall into the Merbok estuary. The

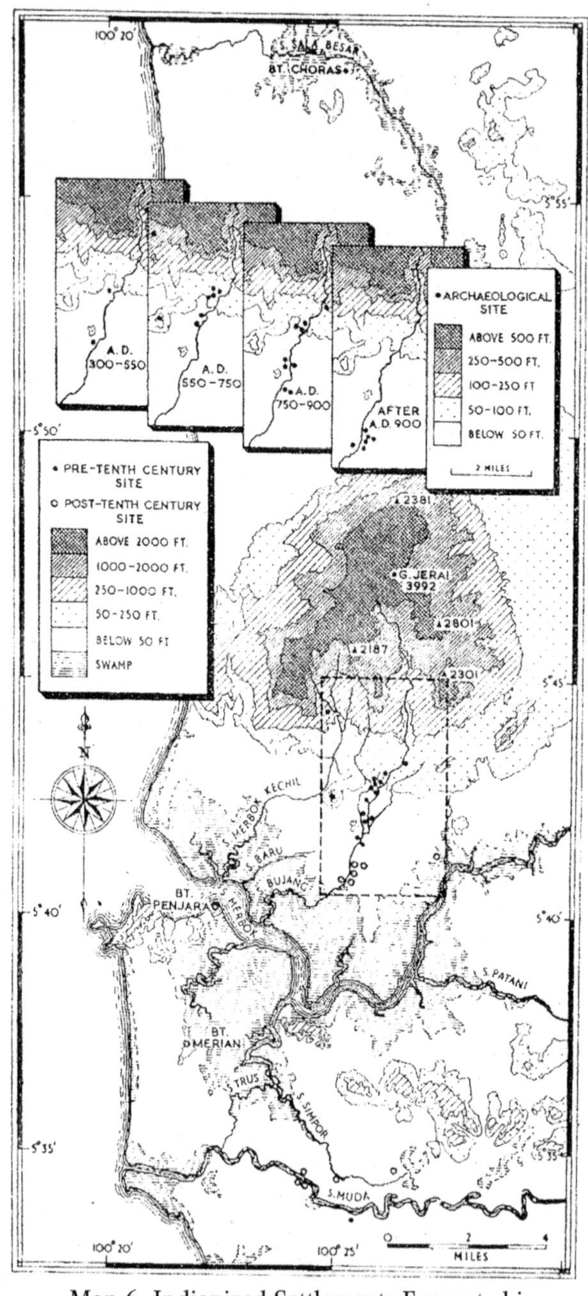

Map 6: Indianized Settlements Excavated in Kedah (north Malaysia)

first is the Sungai Merbok Kichil, and the second is the Sungai Bujang, a name based on the Sanskrit word *bhujanga*, which means serpent. In the course of his excavations, Quaritch Wales uncovered a well constructed Pallava temple near a waterfall along the Sungai Merbok Kichil. However, the largest number of structures he found are located in the Lembah Bujang, the valley of the Sungai Bujang. These date back from the fifth century right up to the twelfth century (see Map 6).

The earliest site excavated by Quaritch Wales, the only one north of Gunung Jerai, revealed the laterite base of a fourth-century Buddhist *stupa* located on the summit of Bukit Choras, an isolated, well-forested hill. This base is 3 ft high, measures 22.5 × 23.5 ft, and has laterite steps going up to it. Wales describes this as 'the earliest structure now known in Malaya, and it would be difficult to point to any older building anywhere in South Eastern Asia'.[51] The most important find here is a small inscribed slate stone found in the roots of a tree at the edge of the laterite platform. The inscription, four lines in all, contains in 'South Indian script . . . the Buddhist *credo*.'

Next in antiquity, are the laterite bases of two stupas found in the middle section of the Bujang Valley, dating to the fifth and sixth centuries CE. Here, Quaritch Wales found a sun-dried clay tablet inscribed in the Pallava-grantha script with a Mahayana Buddhist sutra from the Madhyamika school.[52] This inscription certainly predates the seventh-century Sumatran inscriptions which had hitherto been considered to be the earliest Mahayana Buddhist inscriptions in Southeast Asia. At Nalanda in India, the same *Pratityasamutpadasutra* has been found inscribed on bricks, which were then deposited in small *stupas*.

In this middle section of the Bujang Valley, Quaritch Wales excavated the foundations of 10 Hindu Saivite shrines, all dating from the mid-sixth century to the mid-eighth century. This includes the temple (site 9) at the very summit of Gunung Jerai. All these temples had been built on the right bank of the Sungai Bujang, in order that the main sanctuary (*vimana*) would face the east as is the rule for south Indian *linga* shrines. In those temples where the *snana-droni* (*yoni*) was found *in situ* and undisturbed, the spout (of the *yoni*) was to the right of anyone entering the shine. At one of these Shiva temples (site 4) the roof of a miniature bronze shrine was found, with 'close resemblance to the waggon-roofs of the Bhima and Ganesa raths at Mahabalipuram'.[53] Also found at this site, carved on a granite river boulder, was a representation of Ganesh, where, *inter alia*, the soles of the feet are touching each other. Hitherto, this attitude was considered to be exclusive to Javanese carvings of Ganesh. The Kedah Ganesh suggests, according to Quaritch Wales, that this attitude (in a Ganesh sculpture) is of Indian origin. Earlier excavations at this site had uncovered the fragment of the head of a granite Nandi and a bas-relief of Durga triumphing over the demon Mahishasura. The principal attributes of a Shiva temple are all in place at this site.

Among the interesting finds at this site are fragments of glass vessels, fine green glass, amber glass bases with pontil marks and a pink-tinted crenulated glass base, all believed to be of Middle Eastern origin and manufacture. This shows the presence of Arab traders in the midst of Indianized settlements and kingdoms.

The Saivite temples at site 8, belonging to a slightly later period (late seventh or eighth century), have the remains of a bronze Shiva statue rather than a *linga*. Foundation deposits have been recovered in the form of small silver capsules containing one small polished sapphire and one small polished pyrope (deep-red garnet) placed in each of the eight chief socles around the *vimana*. Also found are two nine-chambered reliquaries. These are quartzite receptacles with nine small cylindrical chambers cut in the floor of each. Very similar receptacles have been frequently found in Javanese *chandis*, which are really tomb-temples. The central compartment of the reliquary contains a part of the ashes of a cremated king; the others contain pieces of precious metals and semi-precious stones. The reliquary is buried beneath the posthumous statue of a king and queen, depicted in the form of Shiva and his consort Parvati. 'The King was represented in the form of that God into whom his soul returned after death.'[54] The bronze Shiva statue really represented the deceased king.

Many Java *chandis* can be closely dated because the charters of these tomb-temples have been found. No charter has been recovered for the Kedah *chandi*. However, Quaritch Wales is emphatic that the Kedah *chandi*, going by the relative plainness of the ornamentation, the early style of the bronze trident and other architectural details of this temple, pre-dates the Javanese *chandis*. According to him, the Kedah *chandi* is of Indian origin.

Two audience halls and two Buddhist (Mahayana) temples were excavated in the same section of Bujang valley, dated between CE 750 and 900. The tenth site foundation deposits include one gold and six silver discs, with Buddhist inscriptions in Sanskrit in the South Indian script. Once again Quaritch Wales emphasizes that these finds show no traces of Javanese or Sumatran influence. There is continuing evidence dating to this period about Arab traders frequenting this region. Two silver coins of the Abbasid Caliphate, one of which bears the date AH 234, corresponding to CE 848 have been found (at site 14).

During this period evidence begins to emerge about commercial contacts with China, though it is still not clear whether these were direct or through intermediaries.[55] Late Tang porcelain is found for the first time in excavations at site 11, dating from the eighth or ninth century. The scattered fragments of two Chinese mirrors dated to the Tang period were found at site 12.

Beginning around the tenth century, dating right up to the twelfth century, a large number of Hindu shrines were excavated. Most of these are brick structures. At Srokam (site 28) along the Sungai Muda, remnants of the fort of Srokam were found. Celadon fragments dating to the late Sung or Yuan periods were found. At Kota Aur (site 29) the outlines of the fort can be seen on the north bank of the Sungai Muda. At places where the river has eroded the area along the walls of the fort, foundations up to a depth of about 3 ft can be seen 'betokening a considerable duration and density of occupation'.[56] Celadon fragments found here include Ming blue and white dating from the fifteenth and sixteenth centuries. Opposite Kota Aur in Province Wellesley traces of brickwork were seen which appeared to be 'ruins of temples dedicated to the Buddhist and Hindu worship combined, although I suspect Siva was held the most honoured shrine'.[57]

The excavations conducted by Quaritch Wales in Perak were equally interesting. The geographic conditions in this region are quite different from those prevailing in Kedah, as the effects of flooding and frequent changes in the course of rapid rivers like the

Sungai Perak and the Sungai Dinding seem to have been disastrous for preserving the remains of any ancient cities situated on their banks. This factor, combined with the negative impact of tin-mining activities, particularly twentieth-century mining techniques, has made it difficult to conduct archaeological excavations in the province of Perak. The only region of Perak that has not been so ravaged by time is the district of Kuala Selinsing. Quaritch Wales concluded that:

> . . . it would be quite possible for large cities to have flourished on the Perak rivers and yet to have been completely destroyed. . . . Archaeological proof of such destruction is not lacking: ancient bronze images have been brought up by tin dredges or washed out of open-cast mines from beneath great depths of alluvium. The fact that they are found isolated and scattered shows how completely cities have been overwhelmed and their remains perhaps rooted up and disseminated over square miles of river basin. . . .[58]

At least six Buddhist bronzes are known to have been unearthed during mining operations in Perak. In 1931, at Pengkalen, near Ipoh in the Kinta Valley, an 18 inch bronze figure of Lord Buddha was dredged up, and given to the Perak Museum. It is ascribed to the Gupta school of art, dating to the fifth or sixth century, an early Hinayana bronze. A later Mahayana bronze (eighth to tenth centuries) was dredged up at Bidor and subsequently presented to the Perak Museum. It is a beautiful eight-armed Avalokiteshvara, 31 inches high. Two additional bronze Avalokiteshvaras were washed up during open-cast mining at Sungei Siput in Perak, hidden beneath 20 feet of alluvium.[59]

The *Malay Annals* contain descriptions of a pre-Malacca city, Gangga Nagara (city on the Ganga), located in the Dindings in north Perak, estimated to be near present-day Bruas. Archaeological finds to prove the location of Gangga Nagara have been difficult to come by. However, in Kuala Selinsing, two important objects have been excavated, the Pallava seal and a gold ring, with an image that could be Lord Vishnu mounted on his traditional *vahana*, the bird Garuda. Both objects are evidence that the people living here in early times were Hindus, though it is not clear whether they were from India, or Indonesians from the Majapahit empire centred in Java.

In Johor, 'the unchanging nature of the Johor River, with its scanty burden of alluvium and absence of flooding, make this one of the few localities in Malaya where (such) ancient remains might be expected to lie undisturbed where they were deposited, practically at present day ground level'.[60] In 1937, an important find was reported at Kota Tinggi on the Johor River, comprising around 600 beads. As much as 20 per cent of these beads were classed as belonging to the Roman Empire, dating to the first two or three centuries of the Common Era. About 7.5 per cent of the total were 'early Indian stone beads', and the remainder, over 70 per cent, were 'mostly of crude glass of no clearly assignable origin, either Arabic or later European'.[61] The comparatively high percentage of Roman beads suggests, according to Quaritch Wales, that they were brought to Johor soon after manufacture, indicating the great antiquity of the settlement at Kota Tinggi.[62] In addition to the beads, Ming blue-and-white porcelain was found, together with large quantities of potsherds decorated with stamped formal designs. The Ming blue and white has been dated to the sixteenth and seventeenth centuries, with some pieces from the early fifteenth century. The remaining porcelain pieces are of local manufacture, perhaps by Indonesians. The stamped herringbone design is seen in modern Perlis pottery and similar pieces were found by Quaritch Wales at some of the sites in Kedah.[63]

In Kota Tinggi, Quaritch Wales also excavated the lower portion of a small regularly oriented rectangular brick building, similar to the brick structures excavated in Pahang, said to be the remains of Buddhist or Hindu temples of perhaps the fourteenth century.

IMPORTANT CONCLUSIONS ON INDIA, MALAYA AND THE ORIGINS OF THE SAILENDRA EMPIRE

Quaritch Wales has drawn certain important conclusions from his excavations in the Malayan provinces of Kedah, Perak and Johor. According to him, there were four phases during which the trade movements between South and Southeast Asia, in particular between India and Malaya, were the most active. Indians, he says, came to Malaya primarily as traders, not settlers or colonizers. The settlements that came up as Indianized settlements were based on the interaction, intermarriage and intermingling of the people of South and Southeast Asia. This was a natural corollary of the primarily maritime trading process, conducted through sailing ships dependent on seasonal winds.

The first active phase of this trade is placed between the first and third centuries. The Ptolemaic town of Palanda is identified with Kota Tinggi in Johor. 'The carriers of the Roman beads are likely to have been Indians, the merchants from South India who brought their priests with them and about this time began to settle in the more suitable valleys—amongst which the Johore was probably not numbered'.[64] The people the Indians encountered in the Malayan coastal regions were essentially Indonesian. They were already exploiting the gold mines in Selinsing (Pahang), and readily interacted with the newly-arrived settlers at Kuala Selinsing (Perak).

The second active phase is between the fourth and sixth centuries. 'During this period Kedah was strongly Buddhist, Mahayana Buddhism flourishing side by side with the Hinayana at least during the latter part of the period.'[65] Kedah was probably part of the kingdom of Langkasuka situated at Ligor, which in turn was almost certainly under the suzerainty of the Funan Empire. The archaeological finds in the valley of the Sungai Kinta in Perak are evidence of an Indianized settlement, as early as the sixth century.

The third phase of interaction between India and Malaya dates from around 550 to 750. This phase is characterized by the extensive trading and cultural activities of the Hindu Pallava rulers of south India. The archaeological finds in Kedah bear testimony to this region's central role in the dissemination of this culture across Southeast Asia. The dissemination towards the east took place through the overland route from Takuapa and Kedah to Caiya and Ligor on the east coast. According to Quaritch Wales, these religious and cultural influences 'did not penetrate in unmodified form beyond the Peninsula'. Archaeological finds of this period combine 'certain Indian characteristics with a Malay cast of features', illustrating 'the process by which Pallava Hindu influences after modification in the Peninsula passed on to Sumatra and Java'.[66] The Straits of Malacca were little used during this period, and the dissemination, over time, to Java took place, in all probability, via the sea-route, using Peninsular Malaysia's eastern ports in present-day Kelantan and further north along the Bay of Bandon.

Quaritch Wales accepts the view of scholars like Moens, Schlegel and Gerini, that the term *Ho-ling* used in Chinese texts refers to Kalinga, and that the people from Kalinga (the present-day coast of Odisha) arrived first in Kedah, rather than in Java, as is often conjectured. The Chinese scholar I-Tsing used the term *Ho-ling* (a corruption of Kalinga) in the seventh century. 'Now we have no archaeological evidence for such a direct influx into Java in the seventh century whereas we most certainly have in Kedah.'[67] This direct influence of Kedah and Ligor on the early Java kings seems to have been insufficiently appreciated. The eighth-century Javanese king Sanjaya probably had his antecedents in Kedah (and Ligor), rather than directly in India. The *linga* temples excavated in Kedah, together with the nine-chambered reliquaries for royal relics found there 'were evidently the prototypes of the Javanese forms', inclusive of the *linga* temple founded by King Sanjaya in Gunong Wukir (Java).[68]

The fourth phase of Indian traders and settlers coming to the Malay Archipelago covers the period from around 750 to 900. The travellers were primarily from east and south India, with the Pala dynasty of Bengal, the Pallavas and later the Cholas of the south leading the interaction. Significantly, Quaritch Wales makes two important conclusions about this phase. First, he concludes that there were two separate Srivijaya entities. In other words, he dis-tinguishes between 'the Sumatran state of Srivijaya on the one hand and a peninsular state of Srivijaya (modern Caiya) on the other'.[69] Hitherto, the Ligor inscription of 775, which mentions Srivijaya, has always been taken to mean the Sumatran state of Srivijaya, and to indicate the overlordship of this state over the Malay Peninsula. Quaritch Wales points out the Ligor inscription is in good Sanskrit, while all the inscriptions found in Palembang and Bangka (Sumatra) are already by the seventh century written in Old Malay. Furthermore, there is no evidence of Sumatran sculptural influences in the Malay Peninsula, while excavations in

Bangka (a fragmentary four-armed figure attributed to the seventh century) 'shows signs of modification from a more nearly Indian form evolved in the Peninsula'.[70]

The fourth phase of interaction between India and the Malay Peninsula brought in strong influences of Mahayana Buddhism. This was the result of direct interaction with the Pala dynasty of Bengal, as is evidenced by the Nalanda copper plate of about 850. However, according to Quaritch Wales, archaeological and related finds reveal that the Buddhist influences of this period in Kedah and Perak 'indicate their predominantly Indian nature . . . which, incidentally, negative(s) any idea that Javanese or Sumatran reflux influence was a powerful factor in the culture of the Peninsula during this period. . . .'[71] Among the finds of this period at Kedah, the fragmentary earthenware jar, the bronze casket, the miniature weapons contained in the casket, the miniature *damaru* (drum), the dagger hilt and other finds all reveal their direct provenance from Indian designs, rather than those found in Java and Sumatra during this period. Quaritch Wales concludes that:

> . . . nowhere in Kedah, among remains of any period, have any sculptural, architectural or decorative motifs been recovered that are essentially Javanese or Sumatran in character. The same statement seems to hold good throughout Malaya. In Kelantan of course there is plenty of evidence of Javanese influence in the living culture of the people, but it is late in character and may be attributed to contacts in the Majapahit period.[72]

The second set of conclusions, which arise from the first, is that the Sailendra dynasty did not originate from either Java or Sumatra, but from Kalinga in India, and that the headquarters of the Sailendra Empire were located in Peninsular Malaya rather than in Java/Sumatra. Quaritch Wales feels that the 'distinctive and virile nature' of Javanese and Sumatran cultures is such that, had it held sway over the Malay Peninsula, it would definitely have left its epigraphic and archaeological imprint on this land. The Mahayanist founder of the Sailendra Empire 'was most probably a recent arrival from India in the VIIIth century (who) built up his empire at the expense of numerous smaller Hindu states'.[73]

There has been extensive debate about the exact location, whether on the Malay Peninsula or in Sumatra, of the Sailendra Empire's headquarters. Insufficient archaeological excavations during British colonial rule, and an even greater slackening of interest after Malaya achieved independence, has not helped in bringing closure to this debate. Quaritch Wales has marshalled evidence to show that the Sailendra Empire was centred around Kadaram (Tamil Kataha), rather than Sumatran Srivijaya. The location of Kadaram has traditionally been taken as Kedah, with its commanding position over the Straits of Malacca. Quaritch Wales shows that, rather than in Kedah, Kadaram could easily have been located in the Kinta Valley in Perak, 'somewhere near Sungai Siput where two of the Mahayanist bronzes came to light'.[74] Furthermore, the Visnuvarman of the Kuala Selinsing Seal (also found in Perak) could be the same as the Sailendra emperor Visnu mentioned in the Ligor inscription.[75]

Indian historian R.C. Majumdar has quoted from Chola inscriptions to show that the Sailendra Empire was headquartered in the Malay Peninsula, in Kadaram, and not in Sumatran Srivijaya. He says:

> On examining the Cola records it appears that the two kings (Culamanivarman and Sri-Mara-Vijayotunggavarman of the Sailendra dynasty) were regarded rather as kings of Kadara (or Kataha) also ruling over Srivijaya, than kings of Srivijaya. In all records, save one, they are referred to simply as rulers of Kataha, Kadara or Kidara. Even in the one exceptional case, viz., the Lar Lgereiden Grant, the Tamil portion refers to Cudamanivarman (=Culamanivarman) as king of Kadara, while the Sanskrit portion refers to Sri-Mara-Vijayotunggavarman as lord of Srivijaya, and extending the suzerainty of Kataha. This last phrase leaves hardly any doubt that the Colas regarded them (the Sailendra kings) primarily as rulers of Kataha who had extended their suzerainty over Srivijaya.[76]

This conclusion is further confirmed by Arab scholars (Abu Zayd Hasan, *c.* 916), who draw a distinction between Zabag, the capital of the Sailendra Empire, and Sribuza, or Srivijaya. According to Arab writings, this kingdom of Zabag, which already existed in the ninth century, is centred in Perak. The Moroccan scholar Edrisi (*c.* 1154) has stated that the ruler of the Malay Peninsula lived in Kalah (generally equated with Kataha).[77] Scholars have located Kadaram (known as *San-fo-tsi* in Chinese texts after 904), the capital of the Sailendra Empire, at differing points in the Malay Peninsula, ranging all the way from Kedah in the north, to the Kinta Valley in Perak, to the southernmost state of Johore.

The *Malay Annals* describe the attack by Raja Suran, a prince from India, identified as the Chola king Rajendrachola I, on the ruler of Gangga Nagara, located on the river Dinding in Perak. This is followed by a description of the attack by Raja Suran on Raja Chulan, who is ruling at Glangkui (or Gelanggi). Gelanggi is identified with Johore for it possessed 'a fort of black stone up the river Johore'.[78] The *Malay Annals* refer to the Chola king (Raja Suran) defeating the ruler of Gangga Nagara, and Raja Chulan, the ruler of Lenggui (Kota Gelanggi). The reference to Raja Chulan (as ruler of Gelanggi) in the *Malay Annals* has caused some confusion, since this name has conventionally been taken as that of a Chola king. Quaritch Wales asserts that name Chulan in the *Malay Annals* was probably a 'Malay corruption of the name of the Sailendra Emperor Culamanivarman who we know was reigning at the beginning of the eleventh century'.[79]

Significantly similar information is available from the Tanjore Tamil inscription of CE 1030 about King Rajendra Chola I's expedition to Southeast Asia. The Tanjore (present-day Thanjavur) inscription has detailed references to the successful outcome of Chola king Rajendra's expedition. This expedition, which took

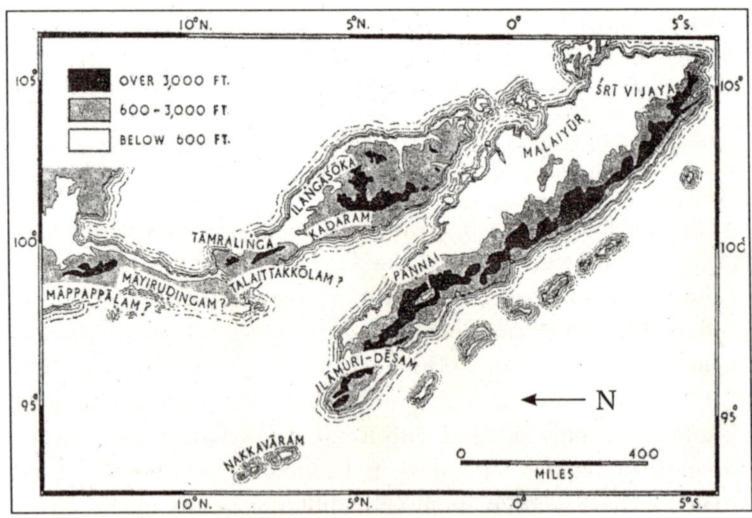

Map 7: Rajendra Chola I's Campaign in the eleventh century CE: Southeast Asian place names from the Thanjavur Inscription

place in 1025, could have been preceded by others, said to have taken place in 1007, under King Rajaraja I, and in 1017, under King Rajendra Chola I. The inscription refers to King Rajendra Chola I's victories across Southeast Asia, including Aceh, Palembang (Srivijaya), Pannai (facing Malacca) and Malaiyur (Jambi or Malayu), all in Sumatra, Valaippanduru (perhaps Panduranga in Champa, in today's Vietnam), and several regions of the Malay Peninsula, including Langkasuka (Ligor and Kedah), Takkola, Tambralinga and Kadaram (in the Perak region, according to Quaritch Wales).[80]

The Rajendra Chola I expedition, as well as the two that preceded it, seem to have had more to do with trade-disputes, and the forced payment of tribute (to kingdoms in Sumatra and the Malay Peninsula) for ships moving through and beyond the Straits of Malacca, *en route* to China. The element of territorial aggrandisement through conquest was conspicuous by its absence, since the Chola king(s) returned to south India without establishing their reign in either Sumatra or the Malay Peninsula. The scholar Paul Wheatley accepts that 'there is no evidence whatever' of 'a permanent subordination' to the Cholas by any of the kingdoms in Sumatra and the Malay Peninsula.[81]

In 2005, satellite maps seemed to confirm the existence of the famed 'Lost City of Kota Gelanggi' in the southern state of Johore. Aerial photography done in 2004 by Canberra based independent

The Lost City of Kota Gelanggi? Satellite photographs taken by MACRES which seem to match the aerial photographs taken by the Canberra photographer

researcher, Raimy Che-Ross, and remote sensing satellite images (confirmed by MACRES, the Malaysian Centre for Remote Sensing in 2005),[82] both show man-made structures that could be the 'fort of black stone up the river Johore' referred to in the *Malay Annals*. The information so far yielded by the remote sensing satellite images could match with this description of Kota Gelanggi, although further exploration is needed to establish this.

The narration of events in the *Malay Annals*, the Tanjore Tamil inscriptions of CE 1030, and the remote sensing satellite images of Johore (2005) revealing the remains of what looks like a fort: all three taken together are a strong indicator of the Sailendra Empire's location in the southern regions of the Malay Peninsula. The capital of the Sailendra Empire could be at either one of two locations, in Perak or in Johore. Further archaeological research is needed to make a final call on this issue.

The CE 1025 expedition by king Rajendra Chola I seriously weakened the Sailendra Empire. For some years, trade, religious and cultural links with India continued, before the ascendancy of the Thai kingdoms on the one hand, and the Javanese kingdoms on the other, disrupted the direct linkages between India and the Malay Peninsula. 'About the year 1090, at the request of the Sailendra king, Kulottunga I renewed the charter (*tamrasasanam pannittaravendum enru*) of the *Sri Sailendra-Cudamanivarma-vihara* established at Negapatam nearly a century earlier. . .',[83] indicating a continuation in the normal linkages.

By the twelfth century, however, in Perak/Johor, 'anarchy had probably followed the fall of Kadaram'.[84] Shortly thereafter, the Empire started disintegrating and new entities emerged in Sumatra, Java and the Malay Peninsula. The old Srivijaya kingdom (over which the Sailendras had established suzerainty) disintegrated, with the kingdoms of Malayu (south-east Sumatra) and Java gaining ascendancy. In the northern portions of the Sailendra Empire, there is evidence that, by the end of the twelfth century, Langkasuka (Ligor and Kedah) had broken away from the Sailendra Empire. In the words of Quaritch Wales:

> The Caiya inscription, dated 1230 CE, certainly gives the impression that King Chandrabhanu of Ligor was then an independent ruler. . . . As Candrabhanu would have required a port on the West coast as a base for his attack on

Ceylon (recorded in the *Mahavamsa*), he presumably controlled . . . Kedah. The resemblance between the Sung and the provincial Sung Chinese porcelain found at both Caiya and Kedah suggests thriving overland trade in the XIIth and XIIIth centuries and the remains at Kedah Sites 19-23 suggest prosperity. . . . (F)rom this time Langkasuka, as is indicated by the Pandya inscriptions, usurped the name Kadaram from the moribund capital of the Sailendras, a name which in the form of Kedah is still borne by the modern Malay state.[85]

By the early years of the fourteenth century, the Sukhotai kingdom of Siam had established its authority over the northern part of the Malay Peninsula. Friction developed between Ligor and Kedah

which prevented them from working harmoniously together for the promotion of overland trade as they had done for the benefit of both until they had ceased to form part of the Sailendra Empire. At that time Mahayanism declined in the Peninsula, and Ligor became a strong centre of Hinayana Buddhism as a result of contacts with Ceylon and Sukhotai. . . . On the other hand Kedah remained purely Malay and favoured Hinduism and Tantrism, until its conversion to Islam further accentuated the cultural gulf between it and Ligor.[86]

The Javanese empire of Majapahit (which declined in the early decades of the sixteenth century) held sway over large regions in the east and south of the Malay Peninsula. The culture of the modern Kelantan Malays bears testimony to this direct influence. However, 'there is certainly no shred of archaeological or cultural evidence of actual occupation of the west coast of the Peninsula by Javanese. . .'.[87]

The series of invasions faced by India, beginning with the Turks and the Afghans in the twelfth and thirteenth centuries, right up to the establishment of the Mughal Empire in India by Emperor Babur in 1526, brought in major disruptions to the established links between South and Southeast Asia. None the less, the people of the two regions remained in contact with each other. Trade, religious and cultural linkages continued to prosper and evolve in myriad ways.

The *Malay Annals* describe the thirteenth-century dynasty that emerged in the kingdom of Palembang (Sumatra) as claiming descent from the Chola Raja Suran. It is this dynasty that was the founder of Singapura and the Malacca dynasty.[88] Quaritch Wales concludes that 'the *Malay Annals* are chronologically right in the order in which they deal with the Chola invasion and the foundation of the (new) Palembang State'.[89]

NOTES

1. Roland Braddell, 'An Introduction to the Study of Ancient Times in the Malay Peninsula and the Straits of Malacca', *Journal Malayan Branch Royal Asiatic Society* (*JMBRAS*), vol. XVII, pt. I, 1939, p. 151.
2. Ibid., vol. XIII, pt. II, 1935, p. 100.
3. Majumdar, 1937, pp. 69-70.
4. Braddell, op. cit., pp. 152-3, quoting K.A. Nilakanta Sastri.
5. Ibid., p. 153.
6. Coedes, *The Indianised States of Southeast Asia*, p. 37, fn. 7 quoting Pierre Gourou ('Civilisations et geographie humaine en Asie des moussons', *Bulletin de l'Ecole Francaise d'Extreme Orient*, XLIV (1954), p. 469).
7. Coedes, op. cit., pp. 26-7, quoting from his own book *Les Peuples de la Peninsule Indochinoise*, p. 57.
8. Braddell, *JMBRAS*, vol. XVII, pt. I, 1939, pp. 161-2.
9. In the *Mahabharata*, Drona or Dronacharya is the royal *guru* or teacher to the Kauravas and the Pandavas. He was a master of advanced military arts, including the *devastras* (most powerful weapons of the gods). Arjuna was his favourite student. Drona's love for Arjuna was second only to his love for his son Asvatthaman.
10. C.S. Srinivasachari, 1927, has written about the strong connection between the Cholas and the Nagas, with Kaveripattinam, the ancient Chola capital being recorded as the capital of the Nagas. Other scholars (Jayaswal, 1933), says that by the third century the dominion of the Nagas, who were the early rulers of India, extended through Nagpur and Bastar up to the land of the Andhras.
11. Coedes, op. cit., p. 38.
12. Braddell, *JMBRAS*, vol. XVII, pt. I, 1939, p. 155.
13. Ibid., vol. XIV, pt. III, 1936, p. 49, quoting B.R. Chatterji ('Indian Cultural Influence in Cambodia', 1928, pp. 4-5).
14. Ibid., p. 49, quoting B.R. Chatterji, 'Indian Cultural Influence in Cambodia', 1928.
15. Ibid., vol. XIV, pt. III, pp. 39-59.
16. *JMBRAS*, vol. XIV, pt. III, 1938, p. 27.
17. R.J. Wilkinson 'Papers on Malay Subjects, Malay Literature', pt. I, 1907 and R.O. Winstedt, 'A History of Malaya', *JRAS(MB)*, 1935, vol. XIII, pt. I, pp. 1-270, quoted in Braddell, ibid., pp. 39-59.
18. 'An Outline of the Malay Annals', *JMBRAS*, vol. XVI, pt. III, pp. 38-9.

19. Braddell, *JMBRAS*, vol. XIV, part III, 1936, p. 40.
20. Sir Richard Winstedt 'History of Malaya', *JRAS(MB)*, 1935, vol. XIII, pt. I, pp. 34-5, quoted in Braddell, ibid., pp. 40-1.
21. Braddell, *JMBRAS*, vol. XIV, pt. III, 1936, pp. 42-3.
22. K.A. Nilakanta Sastri, *A History of South India*, pp. 101-2.
23. Braddell, op. cit., p. 44.
24. Ibid.
25. Ibid.
26. Ibid., p. 43.
27. Ibid., p. 52.
28. Ibid., p. 53, quoting Sir William Maxwell ('Aryan Mythology in Malay Traditions, *Journal of the Royal Asiatic Society* (NS), 1881, vol. XII, p. 403).
29. Ibid., p. 54.
30. Ibid., pp. 54-5.
31. Ibid., pp. 56-7.
32. Family of the Cow's Vomit.
33. Ibid., p. 57.
34. Wheatley, op. cit., p. 51, fn. 5.
35. Richard Winstedt, *The Malays: A Cultural History*, pp. 68-9.
36. Rene Morizon 'Monographie du Cambodge', 1931, pp. 11-13, quoted in Braddell, *JMBRAS*, vol. XVII, pt. I, 1939, p. 163.
37. Wheatley, op. cit., p. 253.
38. Coedes, *The Indianised States of Southeast Asia*, p. 39.
39. Wheatley, op. cit., p. 273.
40. Sastri, *South Indian Influences in the Far East*, p. 82.
41. Braddell, *JMBRAS*, vol. XVII, pt. I, 1939, p. 166.
42. Ibid., p. 167.
43. Sastri, op. cit., p. 83
44. Paul Wheatley, *The Golden Khersonese*, Chapter III, p. 36. Information about Chih-t'u first appeared in the *Chih-t'u Kuo Chi*. This text is no longer extant, but the substance of its narrative is preserved in parallel passages in the *Sui-Shu*, the *Pei-Shih*, the *T'ai-P'ing Yu Lan*, and the *Wen-Hsien T'ung-K'ao*.
45. Ibid., p. 28, quoting from the cited Chinese texts.
46. Braddell, *JMBRAS*, vol. XVII, pt. I, p. 176.
47. Ibid., quoting B.R. Chatterji (*Indian Cultural Influence in Cambodia*, 1928, p. 241).
48. Coedes, op. cit., p. 51.
49. Wheatley, op. cit., p. 274.
50. H.G. Quaritch Wales 'Archaeological Researches on Ancient Indian Colonization in Malaya', conducted by the Greater-India Research Committee representing the Royal Asiatic Society, India Society, and

School of Oriental and African Studies, under the patronage of the Governments of Kedah, Perak, and Johore (1937-9), as well as Mrs. C.N. Wrentmore (1935-6) and H.H. the late Maharaja Gaekwad of Baroda (1934-5), published in the *JMBRAS*, vol. XVIII, pt. I, 1940.

51. Ibid., p. 7.
52. Ibid., p. 9.
53. Ibid., p. 14.
54. Ibid., p. 20, quoting W.F. Stutterheim's catalogue on the Jogjakarta Museum in Indonesia.
55. Wheatley, op. cit., p. 277.
56. Wales, op. cit., p. 44.
57. Ibid., p. 45, quoting Col. James Low, *Kedah Annals*, p. 107.
58. Ibid., pp. 49-50.
59. Ibid., pp. 50-2.
60. Ibid., p. 61.
61. Ibid., p. 60.
62. Ibid., p. 61.
63. Ibid., p. 62.
64. Ibid., p. 68.
65. Ibid.
66. Ibid., p. 71.
67. Ibid.
68. Ibid., p. 72.
69. Ibid.
70. Ibid., p. 73.
71. Ibid.
72. Ibid., p. 74. The powerful Majapahit Empire, based in eastern Java from the thirteenth to the sixteenth centuries, is often described as the last Indianized kingdom in Indonesia.
73. Ibid., p. 74.
74. Ibid., p. 79.
75. Ibid., p. 77.
76. Ibid., pp. 74-5, quotng from R.C. Majumdar (*Suvarnadvipa*, p. 208).
77. Ibid., p. 76.
78. Ibid., p. 77.
79. Ibid., p. 78.
80. Coedes, op. cit., pp. 142-3.
81. Wheatley, *The Golden Khersonese*, p. 203.
82. 'Satellite Confirms Structures of Kota Gelanggi', Saturday 19 February 2005, published in *The Star*, Kuala Lumpur, accessed on 26 March 2011 at http://www.malaysiagis.com/index.php/local-gis/news/41-gmu-news/274-satellite-confirms-structures-of-kota-gelanggi.
83. Wheatley, op. cit., p. 203.

84. Wales, op. cit., p. 83.
85. Ibid., pp. 80-1.
86. Ibid., p. 84.
87. Ibid.
88. Ibid., p. 80.
89. Ibid.

4

The Malacca Sultanate and the Coming of Islam to Malaya

Islam came to the Malay world the same way as Hinduism and Buddhism had: through merchants and traders from south India. Even after the advent of Islam in the Malay archipelago in the thirteenth century, the connectivities and interaction that had hitherto characterized the relationship between South and Southeast Asia continued almost unchanged, right uptil the commencement of the colonial era. The scholar R.O. Winstedt summarizes this process when he says:

> In time, a few (of the Indians) married into leading Indonesian families and brought Hindu ideas of kingship, just as more than a thousand years later the Muslim Tamils married into the families of the Sultans and Bendaharas of Malacca. The coming of the Hindu appears to have been very similar to the later arrival of the Muslim from India and the Hadramaut, the Brahmin and the Kshatriya taking the place to be usurped by the Sayid.[1]

Historical changes, and new political dispensations in the thirteenth century in both South Asia and Southeast Asia, has led many chroniclers to assume that cultural contacts between these two regions snapped once Islam arrived in the Malay Archipelago. The coming of Islam to South and Southeast Asia is assumed to be the factor that led to a seeming hiatus in the contacts between these two regions. In reality, despite far-reaching political changes in both South Asia and Southeast Asia, the situation remained largely unchanged after the advent of Islam.

In India, Muhammad of Ghor began a process of conquest that led to the establishment of the Delhi Sultanate, ushering in a period of rule by Turkic and Afghan dynasties. In Southeast Asia there was the gradual decline of the large Indo-Malay kingdoms centred at different times in Indo-China, Indonesia and Malaysia. Mercantile and maritime trade routes became increasingly Muslim-dominated both in the Indian Ocean and in maritime Southeast Asia. The advent of Islam to this region began with the kingdoms in the northern tip of Sumatra, followed by the establishment of the Malacca Sultanate.

ARAB TRADERS IN SOUTHEAST ASIA AND CHINA

Maritime trade between Persia, the Arab kingdoms, India, Southeast Asia and China existed even in ancient times. Arabic, Indian and Chinese literature do have references to Arab and Persian settlements and commerce throughout this region at different periods. The Greek writer, Cosmas Indicopleustes, writing early in the sixth century CE, accepts that Persian traders were already much in evidence in Ceylon. However, his view is that the Persians only went as far as Ceylon and exchanged goods there with merchants who came 'from the remotest countries' including China and perhaps Malaya and the Ganges area.[2] The Chinese notices of the Persians under the name Po-se date back to CE 455 during the Wei dynasty. However, there is some confusion because Chinese texts show the same name being given to another group of people from the Malay Archipelago. Scholars accept that 'only from the Mohammedan period did Persian ships really appear in the Far East'.[3] I-Tsing, writing in CE 692, says that for his travels to the south, he sailed from Canton on a Persian ship which took him to Srivijaya, indicating indirectly that Chinese ships were still not venturing beyond coastal sailings.

Chinese texts describe the first Arab (Ta-shih) embassy to the Chinese court as taking place in CE 651. In CE 748 the Chinese priest Kanshin wrote about Persian, Arabic and Sinhalese ships in Canton. 'The last reference to Po-se in Chinese literature is in CE 758 when, with the Ta-shih (Arabs), they formed a colony at Kuang-chou (Canton) strong enough to sack and burn the city'.[4] Foreign trade does not seem to have revived again at Canton till CE 792.[5]

Prolific and rich Arabic literature is among the important sources of information and knowledge about the early history of the Malay Peninsula. In the middle of the tenth century Abu Zaid, native of the port Siraf on the Persian coast, edited what is perhaps the earliest surviving Arabic work on India, Southeast Asia and China, titled *Akhbar as-Sin wa'l-Hind* (Tales of China and India), a compilation of accounts provided by several travellers, one of whom was Sulaiman. The date of this compilation is uncertain. It could be CE 850 or even earlier. There have been numerous writers who followed this tradition of providing detailed travelogues, including Ibn Khurdadhbih, Ibn Rustih and Ya'qubi. Contemporaries of Abu Zaid, geographers, travellers and writers, were Mas'udi, Abu Dulaf, and Buzurg b. Shahriyar of Ramhurmuz (he wrote the famous book *Ajaib al-Hind* or *The Wonders of India*). Later writers included Al Biruni in the eleventh century, Idrisi in the middle of the twelfth century, and Yaqut in the beginning of the thirteenth century.

Most of these writers provide extensive descriptions about maritime trade routes, trading experiences and descriptions of the lands beyond India. Abu Zaid tells of the massacre of foreign merchants in Canton in CE 878, when the rebel Huang Ch'ao besieged and sacked the city.[6] As a result, all direct trade between China and the Middle East virtually stopped.

The place described as Kalah in Arabic literature, now became the entrepôt for the China trade as well as that with the Malay archipelago. Abu Zaid describes Kalah as 'the centre of commerce for aloeswood, camphor, sandalwood, ivory, tin, ebony, baquamwood (brazilwood), spices of all kinds and a host of objects too numerous to count'.[7] Mas'udi says about Kalah 'today this place is the general rendezvous of the Muslim vessels from Siraf and Oman, who meet here with the boats from China'. He also attributes 'mines of gold and silver' to Kalah and Sribuza. Other writers have described Kalah as a prosperous city, inhabited by Muslims, Hindus and Persians.[8] This is cited as one of the few reports about Muslim trading colonies in Southeast Asia. A similar indication about Arab merchants living in Java can be gleaned from Yaqut's writings where he says about China 'we have not seen anyone who has been there and penetrated the interior. The merchants only reach the border which is a place known under the name of Jawa, situated on the edge of the sea and which resembles India. From here is exported aloes, camphor, nard, cloves, mace, medicinal plants of China and Chinese vases'.[9]

Kalah and Qaqullah are two place-names relating to the Malay Peninsula mentioned frequently in Arabic literature. Kalah has conventionally been assumed to refer to Kedah. However, Paul Wheatley, after much study, has concluded that for Kalah, the Tenasserim coast, in present-day Myanmar, is a much more plausible location. The largest island off the mouth of the Tenasserim River is even today called Kala.[10] Kalah is described as being part of the kingdom belonging to al-Zabaj, i.e., Srivijaya, indicating the extensiveness of this kingdom. It is also likely that Kalah was part of the kingdom of Kedah. Paul Wheatley estimates that Qaqullah referred to a place north-west of Kalah, also along the Tenasserim coast. Both Kalah and Qaqullah are described as prosperous and rich, walled cities, with numerous gardens and abundant springs. Abu Dulaf describes Kalah with a tin mine 'such as does not exist in any other part of the world', and 'they forge the Qala'i swords, which are the true Indian swords'.[11] Abu Dulaf adds that the people 'have a system of justice, prison and fines'. They also seem to have an interest in democracy because, according to Abu Dulaf 'the people . . . put themselves in a state of defence against their king when they wish to make him respect their interests'.

For almost a century there is no record or literary mention of any foreign trade in Canton, but from CE 970 onwards, trade was revived and continued uninterrupted throughout the Sung and Yuan dynasties into Ming times. Scholars have noted that during this period the incoming Ta-Shih (Arab) merchants normally changed ships in the Malay Archipelago, since they seemed to prefer Chinese ships for the journey into Canton.[12] An authoritative account of Arab and Chinese trade in the twelfth and thirteenth centuries has been provided by Chau Ju-kua, who was inspector of foreign trade in Ch'uan-chou.[13] He describes how, for the Ta-Shih merchants leaving China, their first stop after 40 days sailing was at Lamuri, at the north-western tip of Sumatra. They spent some months here, trading. This was the beginning of Arab settlement in Southeast Asia in Lamuri. In Sumatra, too, in Sribuza, the capital of the kingdom of al-Zabaj (Srivijaya), another Ta-shih community was established for trading purposes.

However, it is difficult to estimate the number of Ta-shih merchants involved in foreign trade in Canton and among other communities in Southeast Asia. 'The Chinese term P'u, which appears in front of so many names connected with the Arab trade, has often been taken by scholars to indicate an Arab.'[14] The Chinese, however, used the term P'u for both the Arab Abu and the Cham Po (also the Sumatran title Po which was originally Cham and was used in Acheh in the sense of prince). Some of the Chams were Muslim, too.

The Ta-shih merchants prospered wherever they lived. They were leading members of the community in Canton, where foreigners were treated very leniently as part of the policy to encourage foreign trade. In the empire of the Maharaja (al-Sribuz or the Srivijaya empire), too, they enjoyed considerable freedom. One among them, Sindbad, was appointed inspector of ports and bays and registrar of shipping by the Maharaja.[15] The P'u traders, whether they were Arab or not, involved themselves in intraregional trade in Southeast Asia as much as in the foreign trade with their respective home countries. While based in Canton, they travelled between Borneo, Sumatra and the Malay Peninsula, where the local princes deployed some of these merchants as envoys to the Chinese emperor.

Several conclusions can be drawn from this brief survey of the extensive Arab and Persian trading interests, combined with their commercial and maritime activities in Southeast Asia and China. These activities spanned close to a millennium, beginning in the seventh century and tapering off only after the arrival of European colonialists in Asia. Ports along the Malabar and Coromandel coasts in India and in Ceylon were important destinations for merchants sailing from Arabia and Persia. These ports were their take-off points, from where they set sail for destinations in Southeast Asia and China.

Detailed accounts provided through their writings

> indicate clearly . . . that the Arabs were intimately acquainted only with the northwestern coasts of the (Malay) Peninsula in the vicinity of Kalah (and) Qaqullah. . . . From the lack of material . . . about the southern stretches of

the Peninsula we may conclude that, apart from its role as a barrier, it played a negligible part in the trade of Southeast Asia.[16]

Along the eastern coast of the Malay Peninsula references are made only to Pulau Tioman, the island situated off the southeast coast, as a stopover and a source for fresh food and drinking water, and to the Pahang region. The French National Library (Bibliothèque Nationale) has in its possession several Arabic navigational tracts compiled by master navigators between CE 1450 and 1550. Two of these contain directions for mariners travelling along the Malay Peninsula. These, too,

make it clear that the Arab pilots were better acquainted with the West coast of the Malay Peninsula than with its eastern seaboard. The interior was unknown apart from a vague belief in the existence of "tin mountains". . . . Settlements are comparatively few and several that might have been expected to appear, such as Muar, Selangor, Bernam, Bruas and Perak, are omitted.[17]

It could be that the route the Arabs took lay along the shores of Sumatra. Lamuri (part of present-day Aceh) at the north-western tip of Sumatra was well known to the Arabs, since it has been described as their first landfall after leaving China. Arab writings frequently mention the Srivijaya empire. 'The earliest Muslim monument in the (Malay) archipelago is said to be a grave at Leran (Gresik) in eastern Java dated 1082 CE, commemorating a Muslim woman, presumably the wife of a merchant.'[18]

In the final analysis, it does seem that the Arabs remained totally preoccupied with their trading and mercantile activities in Southeast Asia and China. They were prosperous and successful businessmen. They intermingled and adapted successfully with each community they chose to settle in with. There is little or no evidence of the Arabs or Persians being active proselytizers in this region, at least up to the fifteenth and early sixteenth centuries:

The colonies or settlements, set up at quite a few important places in Southeast Asia, were the general result of this commercial activity. They were semi-permanent settlements for the roving merchant population. Many individuals stayed in them only for a winter or while they gathered their cargo, while others, acting as agents, stayed for periods often as long as 10 years. These settlements were established solely for commercial reasons and it is doubtful if any Muslim missionary work was carried on. The rapid conversion of

Southeast Asia during the 14th century was thought to be the work of zealous Indian converts, although there can be no doubt that the existence of Muslim settlements, some of two or three centuries standing, did much to influence local populations and prepare the way for later proselytizing.[19]

INDIA'S MUSLIM TRADING COMMUNITIES

In India, too, Islamic trading communities have a long history, particularly in Gujarat and in the southern coastal regions, respectively along the Malabar and Coromandel coasts. Beginning with the eighth-century Arab and Persian traders settled in these areas. 'Their communities grew chiefly through intermarriage with the local women.'[20] Over the centuries they prospered and acquired great wealth and influence. They enjoyed the protection of local rulers, particularly because they did not proselytize or interfere in local politics. Many members of such communities would have been among the P'u traders in Chinese cities like Canton as well as at Lamuri in the north-western tip of Sumatra, and other places in Southeast Asia. The descendants of these communities are well known even today: the Moplahs of Malabar in the south Indian state of Kerala and the Maracayars of the Coromandel coast in the south Indian state of Tamil Nadu, among others. Their interests in mercantile and maritime activities continue unabated.

By the thirteenth century, Islam was the religion of choice for increasing numbers of the south Indian-led mercantile and maritime networks across South and Southeast Asia. Already in the eleventh century one learns about Sayid Nathar Shah, among the most famous missionaries in the Tamil-speaking areas. He travelled in Arabia, Persia and north India before settling in Trichinopoly, which was renamed Natharnagar.

It is a natural corollary and inherently logical that the Moplahs, Maracayars and others should bring their religion with them to the Indo-Malay kingdoms of Southeast Asia, in the same way as their sea-faring and intrepid ancestors had brought Hinduism and Buddhism to this region. 'From the thirteenth century onwards, many Muslim traders and religious leaders active in southeast Asia hailed from India rather than the traditional Arab heartland.'[21] Sufi scholars now replaced Brahmin priests. These Sufi scholars played a significant and successful role in explaining Islam to the rulers of the Indo-Malay kingdoms, as had the Brahmin priests in the previous millennium. The Sufi scholars were as successful in incorporating several highly esteemed existing practices into the idiom of Islam as the Buddhists and Brahmin priests had been with existing local customs over the previous thousand years. As a result, beginning with the fourteenth century, the Pasai and Malacca Sultanates were able to make a unique contribution to the progress and development of Islamic traditions in Southeast Asia.

Several historical events coincided to make the late thirteenth century a significant period for the advent of Islam in Southeast Asia. In southern India the Muslim communities had attained such stature and wealth that most contemporary travellers now referred to the Coromandel Coast by the Arabic name Ma'abar. Historical records maintained in the court of Kublai Khan reveal that in 1281 Kublai Khan sent an embassy to the Pandyan king of Ma'abar, in which he referred to an earlier Ma'abar embassy to China which had been led by a Muslim envoy Chamaliting (Jamaluddin). In Ma'abar the king's Chamberlain was also a Muslim named Puali (Abu Ali).[22] In the following year the Chinese envoy visited Quilon (Kollam, in present-day Kerala), where the king's minister was one Muhammad. Here the Chinese envoy met an envoy from Sumuta, which is identified with Samudra at the northern tip of the island of Sumatra. The Chinese envoy visited Sumuta on his return journey.[23] This provides confirmation of Samudra's close dealings with the kingdoms of south India in the last quarter of the thirteenth century.

The strength and proximity of these contacts can be discerned from the description of the embassy or the joint mission sent in CE 1286 to the court of the Chinese Emperor. 'The largest mission which had yet visited the Mongol court from the countries of the South was that which arrived in 1286. It had in it representatives of 10 states, all of them members of the reigning families.'[24] These included representatives of Ma'abar, Mangalore (or some place near it), Cranganore (Kayankulam), Lambri and Samudra, both on the northern tip of the island of Sumatra.

Soon thereafter, in the early years of the fourteenth century, the Delhi Sultanate extended its power to southern India. By CE 1330 Madura, capital of the Pandyan dynasty, was made a province of the Delhi Sultanate. From CE 1335 to 1378 Madura was ruled by a dynasty of independent Muslim sovereigns.

ISLAM COMES TO THE MALAY ARCHIPELAGO

It is exactly around this period that foreign travellers describe the advent of Islam in the Malay Peninsula and archipelago. In CE 1292 Marco Polo visited the kingdoms around the northern tip of Sumatra. By this time Kedah had declined in importance as the main trading port, and Pasai (in northern Sumatra) had taken its place. Marco Polo relates how he met Muhammadans in the port of Perlak, but not in Samudra or Pasai. In 1346, however, the traveller Ibn Batuta 'found the king of Samudra an ardent Moslem'.[25] There are many historical references to the kingdom of Samudra-Pasai, although some mention just Samudra (derived from the Sanskrit word for ocean) or just Pasai. In years to come the language of Pasai, an early form of Malay written in the Jawi alphabet, became the lingua franca across the area later known as Indonesia and Malaysia.

The detailed account of the advent of Islam to the Malay Archipelago is contained in the *Hikayat Raja-Raja Pasai* or the *Chronicles of Pasai*. They are the oldest among the Malay chronicles and, according to R.O. Winstedt, 'they served as a model for the *Sejarah Melayu*, whose author has paraphrased and quoted them and imitated their contents'.[26]

The Chronicles of Pasai start with King Merah Silu of Pasai taking the title Sultan Malik al-Saleh on his conversion to Islam. Sultan Malik's gravestone, beautifully inscribed and imported from Cambay in Gujarat (India) gives CE 1297 as the year of his death. The Chronicles then describe the reigns of the next two Sultans and end with Majapahit's conquest of Pasai in CE 1350.

Sultan Malik al-Saleh's gravestone being from Cambay has led many scholars to believe that it was the Gujarati Muslim traders who were instrumental in bringing Islam to the kingdom of Pasai. However, both the Chronicles of Pasai and the *Sejarah Melayu* are specific in pointing to Ma'abar as the source-land for Islam in Pasai (Sumatra) and the Malay Peninsula.

The Arabic word Ma'abar refers to a crossing point or fording place. Originally, it referred to the south Indian districts of Madura and Tanjore, since they were on the straits opposite the island of Ceylon. Over time the word Ma'abar came to be used for the entire Coromandel Coast. After the fourteenth century, the word Ma'abar dropped out of usage altogether, and was completely forgotten. The *Sejarah Melayu* and the Chronicles of Pasai seem to have used different words for Ma'abar: Ma'abri, M'atabar, Mengiri. However, G.E. Marrison has shown that in the Jawi script, all three are very similar, and refer to Ma'abar.[27]

The *Sejarah Melayu* has the following to say about how Islam first arrived in the Malay Peninsula:[28]

> The Prophet said to his companions, 'In the time to come there will arise a state in the east called Samudra. When you hear of it, go there and convert the people to Islam, for many saints will arise in that country; but there is an ascetic (fakir) in Ma'abri whom you are to take with you'. Sometime after the pronouncement of the Prophet, the name of Samudra became known to all the people of Mecca.
>
> Then a ship set sail and called at Ma'abri, where the King was Sultan Muhammad, descendant of Abu Bakar. When the sailors told him they were making the voyage on the instructions of the Prophet, Sultan Muhammad left his palace and his kingdom. He boarded the ship as an ascetic and set sail for Samudra.
>
> After some time at sea they reached Fansuri (Barus) . . . and then Lamiri (Acheh) . . . and then Haru (Deli) . . . and then Perlak. At each place the people were converted to Islam. Since no-one was able to read the Quran, the ascetic knew this was not Samudra, and he sailed on.
>
> When they reached Samudra, the ascetic met King Merah Silu and converted him to Islam. That night while Merah Silu was asleep, he dreamt he was in the presence of the Prophet, who blessed him. The next morning the ascetic came ashore with his Quran and desired Merah Silu to read it; which Merah Silu did. And the ascetic said 'This is the Samudra which the Prophet spoke of'. Merah Silu was then installed as king with title of Malik al-Saleh.

Samudra-Pasai was the first kingdom in Southeast Asia where the ruler was converted to Islam and the mission to Sumatra that achieved this, set out from the Coromandel Coast of India. The significant detail, that the Ma'bari Sultan is said to have been a descendant of Abu Bakr, finds resonance and parallels in contemporary Tamil tradition. The town of Kayalpattinam along the Coromandel Coast in Tuticorin (Toothukudi) district in Tamil Nadu maintains its Sufi traditions with active followers of the Qadiriyya and Shadhiliyya *tariqas* among its residents. It is said that Kayalpattinam was founded by a descendant of Abu Bakr, a certain Muhmmad Khalji from Cairo (al-Qahira).

> That this legend was current in Kayalpattinam in the 15th and 16th centuries can be gauged from the many individuals with the nisba al-Qahiri (and, in one case, al-Khalji) mentioned on Kayalpattinam epitaphs of the period, and from the practice of referring to Kayalpattinam as 'Kakir' (Qahir) in Islamic Tamil literature, first documented in a poem dated to 1590.[29]

Two important Tamil scholars of the seventeenth century also claimed descent from Abu Bakr (Abd al-Qadir of Adirampattinam and Sulayman b. Sadaq). Thus, 'claims to descent from Abu Bakr were common among the Ma'bari religious elites of the 15th to 17th centuries—exactly the period in which the legend of the Ma'bari Sultan was recorded in Malay chronicles'.[30]

Scholars have also noted how 'the Malay story of the Sultan of Ma'abri who left his kingdom to preach Islam in Sumatra, looks very much like an adaptation of the tradition of the immortal Perumal of Cranganagore related in the *Tohfat ul-Mujahidin*'.[31] The *Tohfat ul-Mujahidin*, or *Tribute to the Strugglers* is among the earliest extant historical treatises about the Indian state of Kerala. The author is the renowned sixteenth-century Islamic scholar and member of the Qadri order of Sufism, Shaikh Zainuddin Makhdum, who hailed from Ponnani on the Malabar Coast. He describes how Islam's first contact with India took place along the coast of Malabar. He writes about the harmonious and friendly relations among Hindus and Muslims in Kerala, and their joint struggle against Portuguese colonialists after Vasco da Gama arrived in Kerala in 1498.

In the *Tohfat ul-Mujahidin* the last Perumal was As-Samuri, a Malayalam word meaning 'sea-king', which, in the form of Zamorin, is familiar in later years as the title of the ruler of Calicut. The word *samuri* corresponds to the Sanskrit *samudra*, the very name adopted by the Sumatra kingdom of Pasai. Furthermore, the Chronicles of Pasai mention that the full title of the later Sultan Malik al-Zahir includes the south Indian title Perumudal Perumal. The Chronicles of Pasai are replete with references to south India, including details about the Tamil merchant who informs Sultan

Malik al-Saleh of the presence of gold in his kingdom, and the performances in Pasai by Tamil jugglers.[32]

It is significant that in southern India (Kerala and today's Tamil Nadu) and in most of Southeast Asia, particularly Indonesia, the followers of Islam adhere to the Shafi'i school of the Sunni sect. When Ibn Battuta visited Samudra in CE 1345, he describes the then Sultan Malik al-Zahir as following the Shafi'i school and 'taking a lively interest in the legal discussions of his theologians'.[33] On the other hand, the Muslims of Gujarat are either Shias or belong to the Hanafi sect among the Sunnis. The influence of Gujarat on Malay literature and Islam in Southeast Asia came much later, in the seventeenth century, when Shaikh Nur al-Din al-Raniri published his *Sirat al-Mustakim* (1628) and the *Bustan as-Salatin* (1638).

The coming of Islam, first to South Asia and later to Southeast Asia, was a gradual process. At the popular level, the process of conversion to Islam was largely driven by the activities of Sufi orders and individual holy men. 'Sufism and its mystical traditions facilitated the incorporation of existing south Indian and Southeast Asian customs into the new faith'.[34]

In India, for example, along the Malabar coast in the state of Kerala, new converts to Islam continued with the matriarchal system that had been a distinctive social practice in the pre-Islamic period. In Java the absorption and adoption of Islam was a slow process. There are several instances in Java and other parts of Indonesia where the forms of Islamic prayer, and the legends associated with Islam, were adapted to accommodate local spiritual practices. The resulting amalgam is often described as 'syncretic'. The reality is that until recently, Javanese Islam developed within the context of a multi-ethnic Islam (Malays, Bugis, Banjars, Minangkabau and Acehnese, among others) in a multireligious state.

Stephen Headley encapsulates this process when he says:

> For almost four centuries before the appearance of a Wahabite reform movement in the late eighteen hundreds, there was a long and gradual accommodation of Islam to Javanese culture itself. The following example of this mode of acculturation is taken from the village of Krendawahana. . . . In a nineteenth century Javanese poem, the *Suluk Nala Kirdha*, we read of a wandering Muslim scholar, by the same name, who seeks wisdom from five successive teachers in

order to understand the meaning of Allah's name. His fifth and final teacher is not a Muslim, but the goddess Durga. She has a traditional sanctuary, an altogether different kind of mosque, an invisible kingdom in a sacred forest. Nonetheless she knows more about the meaning of Allah's name than the four Islamic teachers Nala Kirdha has consulted previously. The figure of the goddess Durga who can penetrate the meaning of the name of Allah shows the extent to which Java took possession of Islam on her own terms. This feature of the inversion of values–Islam being higher *vis-à-vis* the outside world and Javanese tradition being superior *vis-à-vis* the insular world—is what is meant by the deliberately paradoxical title given to this volume, Durga's Mosque.[35]

In other words, throughout the Indian Ocean region, this gradual process was more akin to the 'acceptance of Islamic practices into pre-Islamic cosmology and customs rather than conversion to a new orthodoxy'.[36]

For a prolonged period Hindu-Buddhist and Islamic practices co-existed peacefully throughout Southeast Asia and China. In Java, for example, there are inscribed gravestones from Tralaya near the site of the Majapahit court indicating that by 1368, there were already several practising Muslims among the high-ranking members of the court.[37] At the same Majapahit court, during the fifteenth century, 'a new Bhakti Saivite cult that had its origins in the contemporary South Indian Vijayanagara court became popular'.[38] There is evidence in Balinese texts that the Majapahit court was linked in a regular religious dialogue with the kingdom of Vijayanagara. Balinese religious leaders 'interfaced with South Indian religious scholars at Majapahit's religious centres'. It is only in the sixteenth century, after Majapahit's 'demise' that Bali initiated its own direct discourse with south India.[39] Among the renowned Javanese epic poems or *kakawin* is the fifteenth-century *Siwaratrikalpa*, a narrative intertwined with instructions for the worship of the *linga* on Shivaratri or 'Night of Lord Shiva', an occasion still celebrated with great fervour throughout India.

The Sufi orders or *tariqas* (brotherhoods) moved along the Indian Ocean trade networks, side-by-side with the Muslim merchants, in their quest for spreading the message of Islam. Indeed, in a successful blending of roles as scholars and merchants, many Sufis were themselves active participants in the trading networks. The Shafi'i school or *madhab* was particularly prominent among the Muslim communities involved in the trading networks along the

Indian ocean littoral. This had an important practical advantage, in that adherence to the same school of law was a useful and relevant facilitator in the adjudication of disputes. The family of the thirteenth century Shafi'i scholar and mystic, Masud al-Jawi, is said to have been involved in the spice trade between India and Southeast Asia. Masud al-Jawi himself is linked to the Qadri Sufi order, which also played an influential role in the development of Islam in Southeast Asia.

The Hadhramaut region in Yemen has been prominently associated with mercantile and religious activities along the Malabar Coast in India as well as in the Malay Peninsula. Members of the Hadhrami *sharif* or *sayyid* clan (who claim direct descent from the Prophet) migrated to South and Southeast Asia, where they were renowned for their skills in commerce and their knowledge of the *shari'ah*. They were active as Sufi scholars, teachers, judges as well as in the government. Their presence in almost every Muslim community across South and Southeast Asia provided an important thread of connectivity and continuity in these societies.

THE KINGDOM OF MALACCA

Professor Wang Gungwu has shown that Raja Parameswara visited China as the Raja of Malacca before he converted to Islam and became Iskandar Shah, the first Sultan of Malacca.[40] Wang Gungwu has also shown that after Sultan Iskandar Shah died in 1413 or 1414, his son Megat Iskandar Shah became the second ruler of Malacca. After him, the third ruler of Malacca was Sri Maharaja, who converted to Islam only much later in life, whereupon he became Sultan Muhammad Shah. This seems to confirm that the coming of Islam to the Malay Peninsula was a slow and gradual process.

The first three kings of Malacca had excellent relations with China.

> All three kings of Malacca were transported to China in Chinese ships following some of the Cheng Ho expeditions. Malacca needed help against Siam and China needed a base for fleets to the Indian Ocean. This was a sound basis for 30 years of close relations between Malacca and China. After 1434, the Chinese decided to withdraw from active involvement in overseas affairs.

No Chinese fleet thereafter sailed to Malacca and no other kings of Malacca ever visited China again. Sri Maharaja was the last king to make the visit and it was an extended one because no Chinese shipping was available to send him and his entourage home. He must have seen clearly the change in Chinese policy and realised that Malacca must now fend for itself against Siam and other potential enemies. But after 30 years of Chinese protection, Malacca was obviously ready to look after itself and it did so with increasing confidence and success for the remainder of the century.[41]

The *Sejarah Melayu* has numerous references to show that Malacca was a centre for religious studies in addition to being a centre for trade. In the early years after their conversion to Islam, the Sultans of Malacca would send an embassy to Samudra-Pasai in northern Sumatra to discuss the finer points of the religion, and to learn the views of the scholars there. 'As early as the first half of the 15th century Sultan Mansur of Malacca was interested in the problems of esoteric religion, and sent an embassy to Pasai in North Sumatra to discuss whether or not the dammed and the blessed were in their respective places for all eternity.'[42] Sultan Mahmud was the ruler of Malacca when it was captured by the Portuguese in 1511. The *Sejarah Melayu* describes Sultan Mahmud 'sending to Pasai for the answer to a problem that was a matter of discussion between Irak, Khorassan and what the chronicle refers to as the land beyond the river'.[43] Pilgrims came to Malacca from other parts of the Malay Archipelago to study Islam. This was a matter of considerable pride for the people of Malacca. Sultan Mahmud is recorded as trying to dissuade his father from making the pilgrimage to Mecca on the grounds that 'Malacca was the right Mecca'.[44]

As in Islamic theology, so in trade, too, Malacca could hold to its own in comparison with any of the great port-cities of the world at that time. In the middle of the fifteenth century CE, under Sultan Muzaffar Shah, Malacca acquired control over Dinding (Perak) and Selangor, places that supplied Malacca with both foodstuffs and tin. Soon thereafter, Sultan Muzaffar Shah imposed control over both shores of the Straits of Malacca, thereby safeguarding the flow of gold from the Minangkabau (Sumatra) hinterland. Despite determined opposition from Siam, he was successful in establishing authority over Singapore and Bentan, which were at

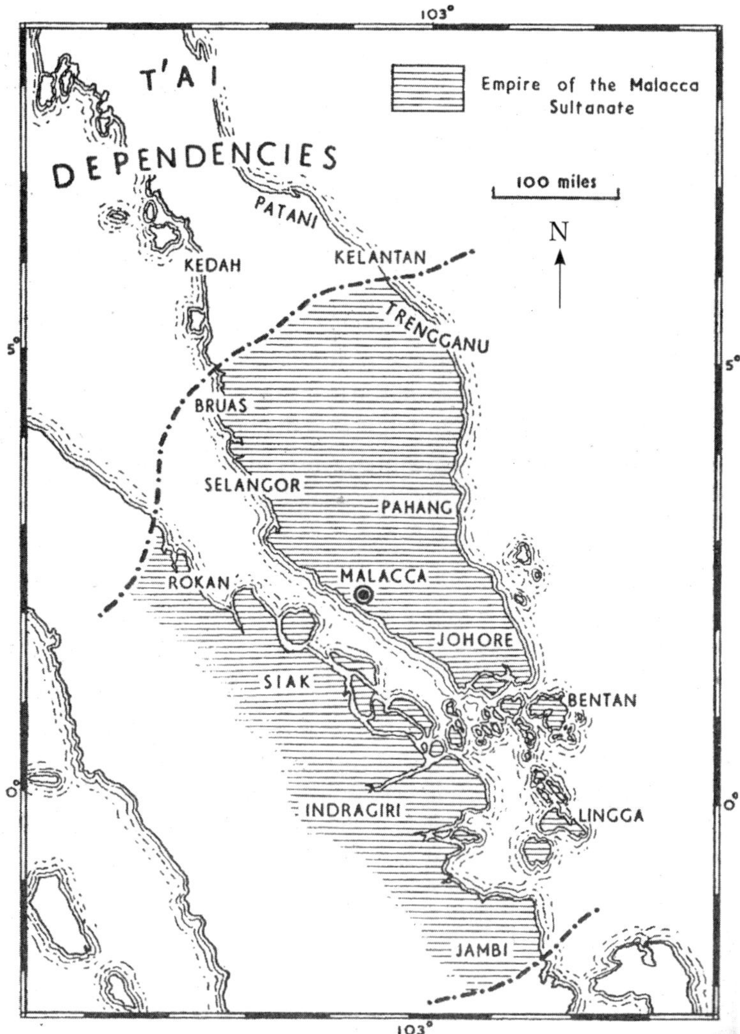

Map 8: The Malacca Sultanate at its Greatest Extent.

the time 'pirate lairs at the strategic meeting point of the China and Java Seas'.[45]

Under Sultans Mansur Shah and Sultan Alauddin, increasing areas of the Malay Peninsula and of Sumatra came under the Malacca Empire, including Perak, parts of Kedah, Pahang,

Trengganu, and Johor, and in Sumatra, Rupat, Jambi, Siak and Bengkalis, together with the Karimun islands and Lingga. When the Portuguese arrived in 1511 'Malacca controlled all the northern shore of the Strait, the most important part of the southern shore, the archipelagoes athwart its eastern approaches and sundry other island bases which had formerly harboured pirate fleets preying on the commerce of these seas'.[46]

It is this absolute control of the Straits that enabled the Sultanate of Malacca to emerge as an important fulcrum in the functioning of the global trade networks from Venice through India to China and the Moluccas. Malacca's pivotal position lay at the junction of the Indian, China and Java Seas, at the heart of 'monsoon Asia', where the seasonal reversals of wind direction made it (Malacca) the most advantageous choice for a regional entrepôt for the collection and transshipment of cargoes. By the second decade of the fourteenth century, Malacca had become:

> . . . the collecting centre for produce of the Archipelago and the distributing point for Indian textiles. Of comparatively minor importance was the third element in the web of South-East Asian commerce, the China trade. . . .
>
> The fundamental basis of Malaccan trade was an exchange of the staple products of the Archipelago for the staple manufactures of India. Malacca was in effect a collecting centre for the spices of the Bandas and the Moluccas and a distributing centre for the textiles of Gujarat, Coromandel, Malabar and Bengal. In addition to the not inconsiderable quantity of cloves and nutmegs brought to Malacca by traders of the Archipelago, every year eight ships sailed from that port directly to the Moluccas where they bartered coarse Cambay cloth and the tails of white Bengal cattle for a total of five or six thousand *bahars* of cloves. From Malacca these were shipped westwards, mostly in Indian bottoms, together with a rich variety of island products such as nutmegs, mace, Borneo camphor, sandalwood, lignum aloes, benzoin, musk, seed-pearls, batiks, carpets, Javanese krises and bird-plumes. From her own Peninsular territories Malacca contributed consignments of tin.
>
> For her trade relations with the West, Malacca was dependent on the intermediacy of the entrepôt of Cambay. 'Malacca', says Tome Pires, 'cannot live without Cambay, nor Cambay without Malacca'. . . .
>
> Merchants from the rest of the Indian littoral formed their companies either at Calicut or Pulicat or in Bengal. Yearly three or four vessels voyaged to Malacca from the Coromandel coast, together with another one or two from Pulicat, bringing 'rich cloths of great value'. While the Gujaratis monopolised the cream of the Malaccan trade, the merchants from Coromandel handled the greater part by bulk.[47]

Chinese junks regularly visited Malacca, where they bartered large quantities of textiles (silks, satins, taffetas and others), seed-pearls, musk, camphor, copper and iron-ware, alum, saltpetre, sulphur in exchange for pepper and other spices, tin, red beads and carnelians, aromatics and drugs, and very large amounts of ebony wood from Singapore.

Most ports had just one *shahbandar* (literally, ruler of the port) to handle all the ships coming into the port. Malacca had four *shahbandars*.

> The most important was the one who dealt with the ships from Gujarat. Another was in charge of merchants from the Coromandel Coast, Bengal, the Mon Kingdom of Lower Burma, and Pasai in North Sumatra; a third in charge of those from Palembang, Java, the Moluccas and the Bandas, Borneo and the Philippines; and a fourth in charge of the Chinese and merchants from the eastern ports of the Indo-Chinese Peninsula.[48]

The Sultanate of Malacca's rapid rise to the pinnacle of commercial success and prosperity by the early years of the sixteenth century is an excellent example of the well-managed collaboration and cooperation between Indian and Arab merchants and traders on the one hand, and the skilful administration and leadership of the Sultan on the other. Gujarat's central role in this trade came about because its chief port, Cambay, was the main meeting point for merchants and ships travelling to Malacca from the western ports of Cairo, Aden, Mecca (the port of Jeddah), and from the Persian Gulf. For these merchants, too, their principal purchase in India was cotton textiles and piece-goods for sale in Malacca. In this, they were following the trading pattern established by Indian merchants who traded extensively in piece-goods with Malacca.

Malacca's rise to the status of an international emporium or entrepôt resulted from its skill and success in bringing together products from across the Malay Archipelago and even from China, for sale to Indian and Arab merchants. Malacca was just a fishing village at the start of the fifteenth century. This is affirmed through the account given by Tome Pires, the Portuguese apothecary and traveller who spent 2½ years in Malacca at the beginning of the sixteenth century.[49] *Nagarakretagama*, the renowned Javanese *kakawin* (also known as *kawi*) or long narrative poem written in 1365 by Mpu Prapanca does not include Malacca among the places on the Malay Peninsula that are listed and described.

In a remarkably short period of time Malacca became an established trading centre with close links to the Sumatran ports across the Straits, as well as with Bengal, the Coromandel Coast, and Gujarat in India. Old Chinese texts provide valuable descriptions of Malacca. The *Ying-Yai Sheng-Lan* written by Ma-Huan in 1451 describes the visit to Malacca in 1409 by the eunuch Cheng-Ho as an envoy of the Chinese emperor. He 'conveyed the commands of the Emperor. . . . He raised the place to the status of a city, since when it has been known as the Kingdom of Malacca.'[50]

Malacca's prosperity depended on the volume of trade passing through the Straits. In order to enforce their control over the Straits, successive Sultans of Malacca were able to impose their authority over extensive regions of the Malay Peninsula. These included Johore, Singapore and Bentan to the south, and Selangor, Pahang and Trengganu to the north and east. Across the Straits along the eastern shores of Sumatra, the regions of Jambi, Indragiri, Siak and Rokan, too, came under Malacca's control. Intermarriage between the ruling families of this region became the conduit through which Islam, which had come to Malacca from India through Pasai in north Sumatra, now spread throughout the Malay Peninsula.

As Malacca grew in importance as an entrepôt for trade, so did the numbers of foreign merchants resident there. Traders from Sumatra 'were quickly joined by Bengalis, and then by Gujaratis, Klings, Parsis and merchants from as far afield as Arabia'.[51] Tome Pires 'estimates the number of foreign merchants in the city in 1509 to be about 4,000, of whom 1,000 were Gujaratis. . . . Pires makes no mention of Chinese residents in Malacca.'[52] Muslim merchants from the Coromandel Coast had established family links with the Sultans of Malacca. There are several prominent examples of intermarriage between the families of Coromandel Muslims and the Malacca Sultans. The third Sultan of Malacca, Sultan Muzaffar Shah's mother was the daughter of a rich Tamil merchant from Pase in Sumatra.

The entrepôt at Cambay (and other ports in India), too, were dependent on Malacca for a handsome proportion of the goods they traded with the West. Venice was the penultimate destination for these goods, from where they travelled overland to the major European cities, including London. Tome Pires' oft-quoted conclusion was that 'Whoever is lord of Malacca has his hand on the throat of Venice'.[53]

After the Portuguese overran Malacca, the Southeast Asian end of the Muslim dominated Indian Ocean trade networks, hitherto centred on Malacca, now made Acheh (in North Sumatra) the focus of their activities. Religious and political supremacy, too, moved to Acheh from Malacca. The kingdom of Acheh mounted a struggle against Portuguese colonialists, for which they received support from some states of India (notably Gujarat) as well as from Abbysinia, Arabia and Turkey.[54] This aptly illustrates the close connectivities among the peoples living along the littorals of the Indian Ocean trading networks. The predominant religion among these peoples had changed from Hinduism and Buddhism of the pre-fourteenth century period to Islam. None the less, their commercial and trading partnerships, based on camaraderie, friendship and mutual respect, remained as strong as ever.

MALAY LANGUAGE AND LITERATURE

The active roles played by Malacca and Acheh as centres for study and discussion of Islamic theology and mysticism had a galvanizing impact on Malay language and literature. Malay became one of the important cultural languages of the Muslim world. Histories, legends and fables were translated into Malay. During this period, the prolificacy of Malay language writers and scholars brought about what has been described as 'literary emancipation'.[55]

The Malay language has traditionally been expressive and internally resilient. Its willingness to absorb new words and ideas from the languages of peoples with whom they (the Malay speakers) were interacting has further strengthened and enriched the Malay language. Long before the written script appeared, spoken Malay was considered to be a language of great precision with a 'flexible syntax enabling the emphatic word or phrase to be placed in its just position of prominence in the sentence'.[56] Sanskrit words were added to the Malay lexicon over time, beginning with the commencement of the Common Era. Classical Sanskrit became the language of prayers, rituals and ceremonies. Several early inscriptions found throughout the Malay Peninsula, including in Sumatra, are in Sanskrit in the Tamil script. However, at court and for the common man, the *lingua franca* was Sanskritic Malay rather than Prakrit, the colloquial form of Sanskrit.

In the eighth and ninth centuries the Malay Peninsula's interaction with India intensified yet again, this time with Bengal under the Pala dynasty. This time Sanskrit came in the Nagari script, together with the Mahayana form of Buddhism. Several Buddhist tablets have been unearthed in Kedah, in Trang and Jaiya, in the Sanskrit language and the Nagari script.

At the same time, around the eighth century in Java, there evolved from the Pallava alphabet of South India the Kawi script, an old form of Javanese. Before the Kawi script faded out (by CE 1400), there was a prose summary made of the renowned Indian epic, the *Mahabharata*. This was done in CE 1000, and followed up in CE 1157 by a poetical version in Kawi script, done by Mepu Sedah, of one section of this epic, the *Bharatayuddha*. The Malay version of the *Bharatayuddha*, namely the *Hikayat Perang Pandawa Jaya*, can be traced back to its Kawi original. Similarly, the Malay version of the story of Bhauma, son of Bhumi the earth, namely the *Hikayat Sang Boma* (or *Sang Samba*), can be traced back to the old Javanese *Bhaumakavya*.

'The presence of every Indian influence that has ever reached the Malay archipelago and peninsula is to be found in the Malay version of the *Ramayana*, namely the *Hikayat Seri Rama*, which critical scholarship has proved to contain elements from the south, the north and the east of India.'[57] Essentially, as in India, so in Malaya, the source for the *Hikayat Seri Rama* remained the oral tradition. And the oral version of the *Ramayana* in Malaya was an amalgam of all the influences that had flown into it from different parts of India.

In Java, near Yogyakarta, the earliest depiction of the legend of Rama can be seen in the beautiful reliefs sculptured late in the ninth century or early in the tenth century on Chandi Lara Jonggrang, one of the Prambanan group of temples. Around CE 925 a poet named Yogiswara did a Kawi rendering of the *Ramayana*. Hundreds of years later, when Kawi was no longer understood, versions of the

Ramayana were written in new Javanese, in recensions known as the *Serat Kanda* and the *Rama Kling*.

The Malay classical redaction of the *Ramayana* is known from two texts, one of which has, since 1633, been in the Bodleian Library at Oxford. According to Sir Richard Winstedt, the version of the *Ramayana* in one of these editions was completed after the twelfth century, and the version in the edition with the Bodleian library 'must have existed for some time before that'.[58] None the less, since the Bodleian text of the *Hikayat Seri Rama* was printed after the advent of Islam, the impact is evident in several places. In the Bodleian text 'the Prophet Adam visits Ravana at the time of his ascetic practices and gets Allah to give him sovereignty on earth and in heaven, in the sea and under the ground . . .'.[59] Sir Richard Winstedt concludes that

> it would appear as if the Bodleian text was written down for a Muslim court, like that of Malacca, which still recognized the *kshatria* caste of princes and warriors and was still conservative enough to like the old tales of the Hindu period, provided they were presented in a form which Muslim pundits could condone. The preface states it is a story famous among all *kshatria*, a term that in Malaya fell into disuse with the fall of Malacca.[60]

The *Malay Annals* or the *Sejarah Melayu* relates how, by the middle of the fifteenth century, the story of Rama had gained widespread popularity and acceptance throughout the Malacca region. The folk hero Hang Tuah talked about Rama's brother, Laksamana, and so 'got a nickname which the Sultan turned into a title'.[61] In the Malacca Sultanate the Laksamana was the Admiral of the Fleet, responsible for security in the Straits of Malacca, the critical maritime chokepoint in the all-important India-Southeast Asia-China trade route. The *Hikayat Hang Tuah,* a Malayo-Javanese romance modelled upon the Panji tales, was written down in its present form in the sixteenth century. 'It is notable as the only original romance in Malay literature, and like its Panji models it purports to have a historical basis.'[62] Legends about the swashbuckling young hero, Hang Tuah, had evolved in the Javanese and Tamil quarters of Malacca. Hang Tuah lived in the second half of the fifteenth century. The sixteenth century narrator/writer of these legends must have worked from the oral tradition that had grown up around Hang Tuah, most of it dating to the pre-Islamic period.

There are reminiscences of the *Ramayana*, episodes relating to south India and visits to Kalinga and China.

After the fourteenth century, with the advent of Islam to the Malay Peninsula, more and more Arabic and Persian words were added to the Malay language. The earliest inscription in Jawi, or Malay written in the Perso-Arabic script, can be seen on the Terengganu stone bearing the date 1326 or 1386, recording the Islamic penalties for various offences that were required to be enforced by the Muslim Raja Mandulikas. 'The inscription is in Malay but contains a large number of Sanskrit words and translates *Allah taala* by the Sanskrit words *Dewata Mulia Raya*. . . .'[63] The influence of Indian Muslims present in large numbers in the ports of Malacca and Samudra-Pasai is evident in several Malay literary texts written after the advent of Islam. In the *Sejarah Melayu*, for example, the Arabic title *makhdum* is used when referring to religious teachers. This is done 'in India but never in Arabia and seldom in Persia'.[64]

The Malay *Hikayat Iskandar Dhu'l-Karnain* or *The Romance of Alexander the Great* is estimated to have been 'derived from a Perso-Arabic source in British India. It was because of the epithet *Dhu'l-Karnain* or Two-Horned that *al-Iskandar* was identified by the Arabs with a prophet mentioned in the Quran (XVIII 82) and turned into a champion of Islam.'[65] In the eleventh century the Arabs learnt that the *Shahnama* of Firdausi describes Alexander as the founder of the throne of Iran. It is this legend that is followed in the Malay text on Alexander the Great. Malay etymologists have taken Alexander's conquest of Andalusia (Spain) as a reference to Andelas, an old name for Sumatra. 'Accordingly, from Alexander's marriage with the daughter of Kaid, the Indian ruler, they found a pedigree for the kings of Palembang, and their descendants the rulers of Singapore, Malacca and Perak.'[66] The Indian context, which fits in most naturally in this legend, is consistent with the legend contained in the *Sejarah Melayu* about the advent of Islam to Samudra-Pasai from India's Coromandel coast.

The *Hikayat Kalila dan Damina* is essentially the Malay translation from the Arabic version of the *Panchatantra*, Sanskrit for Five Principles. The *Panchatantra* is a collection of Indian animal fables in verse and prose, written by Pandit Vishnu Sharma around the second or third centuries BCE, based on even older oral traditions. The earliest translation of these fables into a non-Indian language was done in CE 570 into Pahlavi, followed by a translation into Syriac, and later into Arabic in CE 750 under the title *Kalilah wa Dimnah*. The *Panchatantra* is well known in the Malay Archipelago. 'One of the tales is illustrated on the ninth century Chandi Mendut in Java. . . . There is a version of the book in Middle Javanese, two versions in New Javanese and two in Madurese.'[67] The Malay recension, *Hikayat Kalila dan Damina* dates to the seventeenth century. It differs from the Arabic and Persian translations. According to R.O. Winstedt, it may have been translated from a south Indian edition, based on several recensions, and the translation may have been done in the Dutch East Indies. More than 150 years later the renowned Malayan writer, Munshi Abdullah, completed (in 1835) his translation of the *Panchatantra* into Malay. His work, the *Hikayat Pancha Tanderan*, is based on the Tamil version, one of the oldest recensions of the *Panchatantra*, and is qute different from the *Hikayat Kalila dan Damina*.

The impact of the *Ramayana* and other Indian epics can be seen in the vast Malayo-Javanese body of literature contained in the Panji tales, and in Malay works of later periods. However, the influence of Indian epics on Malay literature does not detract from the creativity and style of writers in the Malay language. The context, ethos and literary genius of Malay writers are unique and irreplaceable, firmly rooted in their own history and traditions. Classical Malay literature is quintessentially syncretic and composite in origin and style, a blend of Hindu, Buddhist and Islamic influences.

Alongside classical Malay literature, there developed an equally rich heritage of religious literature in the Malay language. The body of religious literature that developed after the advent of Islam infused the Malay language with new intellectual strength and vigour. Malay became the cultural language of Islam, with a literature particularly rich in mystical writing.

The two noteworthy points here are first, that the centre of Islamic theology had shifted to Acheh in North Sumatra after the Portuguese captured Malacca in 1511, and second, that the interaction with India, this time with its Islamic theologists and mystics in addition to the merchants and traders, remained intense throughout the period of Islamization in Southeast Asia.

Scholars have compared the works of four important mystical authors writing in Malay around the beginning of the seventeenth century.[68] Three of the writers were Malay, one was from India. All of them flourished in Acheh. They were great scholars, travellers, and finally, preachers who had many followers throughout the Malay Archipelago. They were active participants in the then ongoing debate about the role of Sufism and mysticism in Islam, not just passive recipients of knowledge about stated positions. Through their activities in Arabia, in India and in Sumatra, there is yet another outstanding example of the linkages between trade, religion and culture as it evolved in South and Southeast Asia in the sixteenth and seventeenth centuries.

Hamzah Fansuri hailed from Fansur (Barus) on Sumatra's west coast. He died early in the seventeenth century. He expressed sophisticated mystical ideas in prose and poetry, and may have been the first to develop, in Malay, the Indian (now South Asian) poetic form known as the *sha'ir* (quatrains with a fixed number of syllables and a fixed rhyme pattern).[69] Hamzah was well-travelled. His poems refer to his visits to Mecca, Jerusalem, Baghdad (where he visited the tomb of Abdul-Qadir Gilani, founder of the Qadiriyya order or *tariqa*), and the capital of Siam, Ayuthia, where he attributes his profoundest mystical insights to his interaction with the substantial Persian community there. Several passages in his poems appear to imply that he was affiliated with, and possibly even a *khalifa* of, the Qadiriyya order.[70] The Qadiriyya order is popular among the Muslims of south India.

The second renowned mystic, Shamsu'l Din (he died in 1630), was Hamzah's disciple, and formulated similar metaphysical doctrines. He wrote in Arabic and in Malay. He was the first person from the Malay archipelago to put forward the doctrine of the 'seven stages', *martabat tujuh*, based on the work of the Gujarati author, Muhammad b. Fadl Allah Burhanpuri (completed in 1590), which was titled *Al-Tuhfa al-Mursala ila Ruh al-Nabi*. This text by Muhammad b. Fadl Allah Burhanpuri soon became popular among

Muslims in India, Indonesia and the Malay archipelago. It outlines a system of seven grades or manifestations of Being, a theosophical system that, while based on the same concept of the unity of being as that espoused by Hamzah, and earlier by the thirteenth century thinker, Ibn al-Arabi, expresses it in a different formal structure.[71] Muhammad b. Fadl Allah Burhanpuri was affiliated with the Shattariyya order, founded by Abdullah al-Shattar (died 1415) who hailed from Jaunpur, India. The Shattariyya order, which was popularized in Bengal by Qazan Shattari, soon developed a large following in Iran, Turkey, Indonesia, and several other countries.

Shamsu'l Din, as religious adviser or *Shaykh al-Islam* to the then Sultan of Acheh, Sultan Iskandar Muda (1607-36), brought about the investiture of the ruler into his Sufi *tariqa*. Shamsu'l Din also had a political role as foreign minister and on occasion, as Viceregent. 'This combination in a single individual of the roles of Sufi adept, *murshid* to the ruler, and holder of two senior positions of state is striking.'[72]

The third scholar and author was Nur al-Din al-Raniri, who hailed from Ranir (now known as Rander) in Gujarat, India. He died in 1658. He was a prolific writer in Malay, and lived in Acheh from 1637 to 1644. Some biographers have suggested that 'he may have studied Malay with the significant Malay community resident in Gujarat'.[73] It is also possible that he spent time in Malaya, probably in Pahang, judging from the detailed knowledge of the kings of Pahang reflected in his book, *Bustan al-Salatin*, and his closeness to Sultan Iskandar Thani of Acheh, who originated from Pahang. He became politically very powerful after his appointment as adviser, or *Shaykh al-Islam*, to the Sultan of Acheh. In a significant reflection on the importance of Sufi thought in the kingdom of Acheh at that period, Nur al-Din al-Raniri has written that his uncle, one Muhammad Jilani Raniri, had come to Acheh to teach the law 'but was forced to engage in debate on Sufi doctrines; he had to go to Mecca to acquire the requisite learning and only after his return as a Sufi teacher did he make many disciples in Acheh'.[74]

The Dutch author, Martin van Bruinessen, has this to say about Nur al-Din al-Raniri:

Raniri himself adhered to a more moderate variety of *wahdat al-wujud*, according to which the world has no real existence and is but an illusory mirror image of Reality. He was an adept of the Rifa'iyya order, and the *silsila* he gives in one of his books shows that the branch to which he belonged had been present in Gujarat for several generations, with the Hadrami Arabs of the Al-Aydarus family as its shaikhs. In the 19th century, the Rifa'iyya was still present in Acheh but it remains unclear whether this was due to Raniri's teaching or to a later incursion of the same order.[75]

In Acheh, Nur al-Din al-Raniri was known for his fierce polemics. His position remained secure as long as Sultan Iskander Thani was on the throne. Less than three years after the Sultan's death, al-Raniri was replaced as *Shaykh al-Islam* by a Minangkabau scholar named Sayf al-Rijal 'who had himself received much of his educational training in India, at Surat, and who adhered to the *wujudiyya* teachings of Raniri's predecessors'.[76]

The fourth mystic writer and Sufi scholar was Abdurrauf of Singkel, considered to be the last of the great Achehnese Sufis. He died around 1690. He lived in Mecca for nineteen years, studying Islamic law and Sufi doctrines under one of the *khalifas* of the Shattariyya order. With their permission he founded a branch of this order in Acheh, from where his disciples carried his message across the Malay peninsula, including to the rural areas.

In Mecca and Medina, in Gujarat and along the Coromandel coast, and in the Malay archipelago, Indian and Malay experiences remained intertwined throughout the process of Islamization. 'The strains and stresses between orthodoxy and heterodoxy in the Mughal Empire found an echo in Acheh.'[77] The flowering of heterodoxy seen during the reigns of Mughal Emperors Akbar (1573-1605) and Jahangir (1605-27) was matched in Acheh by the fullest development of heterodox mysticism under Sultan Iskandar Muda. Just as the movement towards orthodoxy strengthened considerably under Emperor Aurangzeb (1658-81), so, too, in Acheh, after the death of Sultan Iskandar Muda, orthodox views prevailed. Hamzah and Shamsu'l Din were heterodox, while al-Raniri and Abdurrauf were orthodox.

Throughout this period up to the eighteenth century, the evolution of Sufi theology, and the emergence of new Sufi *tariqas* continued apace with the study and discussion of Islamic law and jurisprudence, both in Delhi and Acheh. Indeed, the majority of the *ulema* or Islamic scholars who were instrumental in bringing Islam to South and Southeast Asia themselves had Sufi affiliations with one or the other *tariqa*. The Sufi Shaikhs were not necessarily considered as a group separate from the *ulema*. The Sufi movement continues to represent an important dimension of Islam in South and Southeast Asia, an important reason for the large number of adherents it attracted. Whenever society tended to become more orthodox and compartmentalized, it only weakened the resolve and ability of the people to resist external challenges. This is what happened in South and Southeast Asia in the eighteenth century, when neither region could stand up to the forces which led to the colonial conquest of both regions.

European colonialists took over the governance of South and Southeast Asia. The colonial powers then proceeded to carve up these regions among themselves. The people of South and Southeast Asia were now separate and divided after an uninterrupted association and interaction of over 2000 years.

NOTES

1. G. Coedes, *The Indianized States of Southeast Asia*, p. 22, quoting from R.O. Winstedt ('History of Malaya', *Journal Malayan Branch Royal Asiatic Society*, XIII (1935), p. 18, and 'Indian Influence in the Malay World', *Journal of the Royal Asiatic Society* (1944), p. 186).
2. G.R. Tibbetts 'Early Muslim Traders in South-East Asia', *JMBRAS*, vol. XXX, pt. I, 1957, pp. 6-7, quoting J.W. McCrindle, *The Christian Topography of Cosmas: An Egyptian Monk*, Haklyut Society, London, 1897, pp. 365-6.
3. Ibid., p. 8, quoting B. Laufer, *Sino-Iranica*, Field Museum, Chicago, 1919, pp. 468-87.
4. Ibid., p. 9.
5. Ibid., p. 27.
6. Ibid., p. 19.
7. Wheatley, op. cit., p. 217.
8. Tibbetts, op. cit., p. 22, quoting from the tenth-century work by Muhallabi, an Egyptian.
9. Ibid., p. 24.
10. Wheatley, op. cit., p. 224.
11. Ibid., p. 217.

12. Ibid., p. 28.
13. Ibid., p. 29.
14. Ibid., p. 30.
15. Ibid., p. 41.
16. Wheatley, op. cit., p. 232.
17. Ibid., pp. 242-3 in Chapter XV 'The Master Navigators: 1450-1550'.
18. G.E. Marrison, 'The Coming of Islam to the East Indies', *JMBRAS*, vol. XXIV, pt. I, 1951, p. 28.
19. Tibbetts, op. cit., p. 44
20. Marrison, op. cit., p. 34.
21. Sebastian R. Prange, op. cit., p. 38. Snouck Hurgronje in *The Acehnese* (two volumes, translated by A.W.S. O'Sullivan, Leiden: E.J. Brill, 1906) first put forward the view that the sources of Southeast Asian Islam lie in India as much as the Middle East.
22. Marrison, op. cit., p. 35, and K.A. Nilakanta Sastri, *Foreign Notices of South India*, p. 155.
23. Marrison, op. cit., and quoting E.H. Parker ('The Island of Sumatra', *Asiatic Quarterly Review*, 3rd Series, vol. 9, no. 17, 1900, pp. 127-44.
24. Sastri, ibid., p. 155.
25. R.O. Winstedt, 'The Advent of Muhammadanism in the Malay Peninsula and Archipelago', *Journal Straits Branch Royal Asiatic Society*, no. 77, April 1917, p. 171.
26. R.O. Winstedt, 'The Chronicles of Pasai', *JMBRAS*, vol. XVI, part II, 1938, p. 24
27. Marrison, op. cit., pp. 30-1.
28. Marrison, op. cit., pp. 29-30, quoting *Sejarah Melayu*, ed. Sir Richard Winstedt, *JMBRAS*, vol. XVI, pt. III, 1938. (The quote from the *Sejarah Melayu* has been paraphrased.)
29. Torsten Tschacher 'Circulating Islam: Understanding Convergence and Divergence in the Islamic Traditions of Ma'bar and Nusantara', in Michael Feener and Terenjit Sevea, eds., *Islamic Connections*, p. 51.
30. Ibid., pp. 51-2.
31. Marrison, op. cit., p. 36.
32. Ibid., quoting 'Hikayat Raja-Raja Pasai' (ed. J. Mead, *Journal Straits Branch of the Royal Asiatic Society*, no. 66, 1914).
33. Ibid., p. 36.
34. Prange, op. cit., p. 36.
35. Stephen C. Headley, *Durga's Mosque: Cosmology, Conversion and Community in Central Javanese Islam*, Institute of South East Asian Studies, Singapore, 2004, p. 12.
36. Prange, op. cit., p. 37, quoting David Parkin ('Inside and Outside the Mosque: A Master Trope', in D. Parkin and S.C. Headley, eds., *Islamic Prayer*, p. 3).

37. Hall, op. cit., pp. 228-9.
38. Ibid., p. 220.
39. Ibid., p. 220, fn. 8.
40. Wang Gungwu 'The First Three Rulers of Malacca', *JMBRAS*, vol. 41, pt. I, 1968, pp. 11-22.
41. Ibid., pp. 21-2.
42. A. Johns, 'Aspects of Sufi Thought in India and Indonesia in the First Half of the Seventeenth Century', *JMBRAS*, vol. XXVIII, pt. I, 1955, p. 70, quoting from the *Sejarah Melayu*, (ed. Winstedt, *JMBRAS*, vol. 16, pt. 3, 1938, pp. 127-8).
43. Johns, op. cit., pp. 70-1, quoting *Sejarah Melayu*, p. 178.
44. Johns, op. cit., p. 71, quoting R.O. Winstedt ('A History of Malaya', *JMBRAS*, vol. 13, pt. 1, 1935, p. 52).
45. Wheatley, op. cit., p. 309.
46. Ibid.
47. Ibid., pp. 313-15, quoting, as indicated, from Tome Pires (vol. I, pp. 45 and 212-14).
48. D.G.E. Hall, 'A History of South-East Asia', p. 228.
49. Armando Cortesao, *The Suma Oriental of Tome Pires: An Account of the East, from the Red Sea to Japan, Written in Malacca and India in 1512-15*, Hakluyt Society, London, 1944, vol. II, book 6 (quoted in Wheatley, op. cit., p. 307).
50. Wheatley, op. cit., p. 321.
51. Ibid., p. 312.
52. Ibid., fn. 8.
53. Cortesao, op. cit., vol. II, p. 287, quoted in Wheatley, op. cit., fn. 1 on p. 313.
54. Winstedt, op. cit., p. 80.
55. Johns, op. cit., p. 71.
56. Richard Olaf Winstedt, *A History of Malay Literature*, 1939, p. 1.
57. Ibid., p. 26.
58. Ibid., p. 27.
59. Ibid., p. 28.
60. Ibid.
61. Ibid., p. 29.
62. Ibid., p. 44.
63. Ibid., p. 1.
64. Ibid., p. 58.
65. Ibid., p. 64.
66. Ibid., p. 59.
67. Ibid., pp. 81-2
68. Johns, op. cit., pp. 71-7.

69. Martin van Bruinessen 'Origins and Development of the Sufi orders (*tarekat*) in Southeast Asia', *Studia Islamika* (Jakarta), vol. I, no. 1, (1994), p. 4.
70. Ibid.
71. Anthony H. Johns, 'Islamization in Southeast Asia: Reflections and Reconsiderations with Special Reference to the Role of Sufism', *Journal of Southeast Asian Studies*, vol. 31, no. 1, June 1993, p. 52.
72. Ibid.
73. Peter G. Riddell, 'Shari'a-Mindedness In the Malay World and the Indian Connection', in Michael Feener and Terenjit Sevea (eds), op. cit., p. 176.
74. Bruinessen, op. cit., p. 5.
75. Ibid., p. 6.
76. Riddell, op. cit., p. 177.
77. Johns, op. cit., p. 73.

5

Indian Ocean Trading Networks

It is important to encapsulate the situation in South and Southeast Asia on the eve of the European colonialists' arrival in this region. The people of South and Southeast Asia had been interacting with each other, intermarrying and living in amity for over 2,000 years. There were myriad intertwined strands in this relationship: shared economic prosperity through trade, shared cultural and literary traditions, and shared religions, whether Hinduism, Buddhism or Islam. They even shared legends about the founding of the Hindu Buddhist kingdoms across Southeast Asia, beginning with the legend about Kaundinya relating to the founding of the Funan Empire.

The Indians did not come as colonialists, neither were the Southeast Asian communities just passive participants in the very successful infrastructure of multilateral trade that developed. The Indo-Malay people, living in what may have been originally envisaged as staging posts *en route* to or on the way back from China, soon became active stakeholders and participants in the trading process.

The prosperity of the Indo-Malay kingdoms derived from several factors. First, their organizational abilities in handling the complex requirements of multilateral and multinational trade and shipping at each of the ports, including keeping track of incoming and outgoing ships and cargos, providing berthing, warehousing and other facilities, levying of duties and looking after traders, shippers and crew from myriad destinations. Second, each Indo-Malay kingdom was a contributor to and active participant in the trading process. Each of them had unique products to supply that were in demand either in India, in China or in the Middle East and Europe.

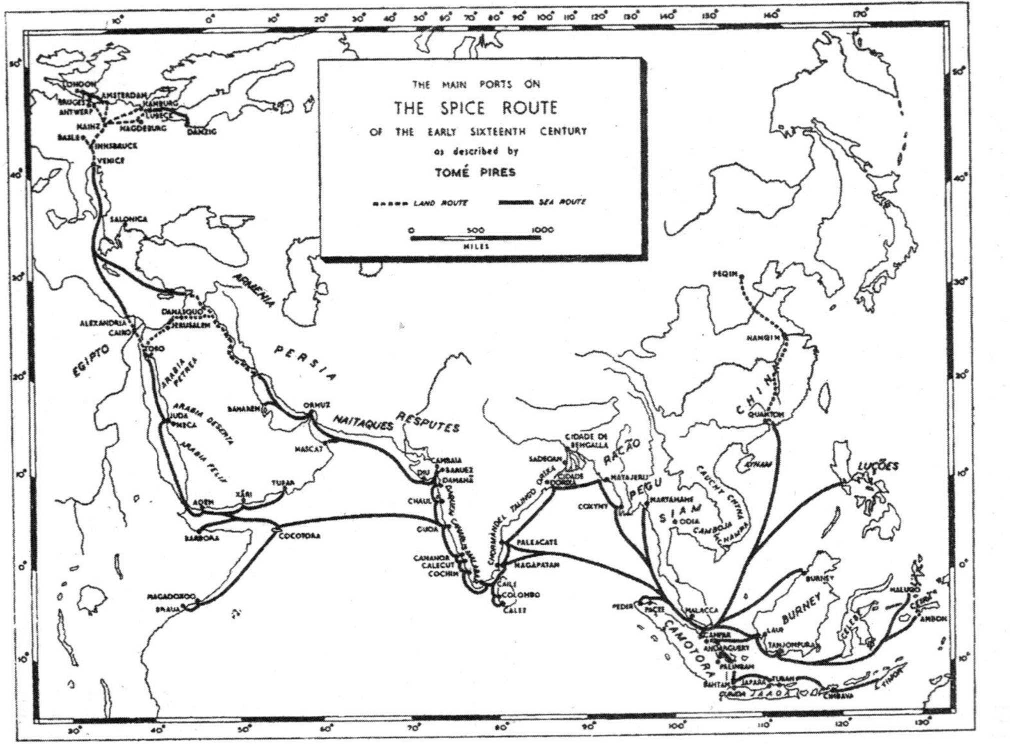

Map 9: The Main Ports on the Spice Route between Europe and Asia in

These kingdoms were also buyers of some of the products brought to their shores. Finally, the success achieved by the Indo-Malay kingdoms was the result of the successful partnership between the communities. The communities intermarried, particularly among the ruling elite, shared their prosperity and lived as one. Intermarriages also took place among the ruling families of these kingdoms located in different regions of the Malay Archipelago, thereby strengthening relationships and cementing political alliances. In the words of Kenneth Hall:

> The point is that Indian Ocean networks were based in economic and cultural dialogue rather than in dominance, and it is the subtlety of this point that has been overlooked in the most recent research by non-Southeast Asia specialists, who see Southeast Asia's populations as intermediary and/or peripheral to the major markets and cultural centres in the Middle East, South Asia, and China.[1]

The coming of Islam to the Malay Peninsula coincided with the period of Mughal rule in India. The gradual process by which Islam came to the Malay Peninsula did not alter or substantially change the mutual respect and regard which the people of India and the Malay Peninsula had for each other. Trade with and through India continued unabated. The Sultans were religious, deeply interested in discourse and in improving their knowledge about Islam, as well as in strengthening their hold on the levers of state power. International trade was the mainstay of their wealth and prosperity. This required open-mindedness and a cosmopolitan approach in dealing with the large number of foreigners who thronged their ports and courts.

Trade, religion and culture have been intrinsically intertwined throughout the Malay Archipelago, during both the Hindu-Buddhist and Islamic periods. The foreign merchant was considered to be the source of continuing prosperity and wealth for the ruling elite and the people. In turn the foreign merchant, too, prayed for the continued well-being of the community he traded with in order to maintain his own prosperity.

Among the earliest references to trading structures and foreign merchants in Southeast Asia are contained in the Srivijaya stone inscriptions found at various places on the island of Sumatra, dating to the seventh century CE. These are in the Tamil Grantha script, the earliest known to Southeast Asia. The Telaga Batu inscription refers to the *puhawang*, the Malay, not Sanskrit, word used in the context of a shipowner with valuable cargos, and *vaniyaga*, or long-distance, seafaring merchants. The Kedukan Bukit inscription associates the *puhawang* with 'a royal quest for magical powers'.[2] The *puhawang*, also an expert in shipbuilding, provides the ships that facilitate the sovereign's voyages to acquire the spiritual power (*siddhayatra* in Sanskrit) considered necessary to legitimize his authority. A fifth century Malay Peninsula inscription also uses this word to describe how the sovereign acquired *siddhayatra* on a journey accompanied by a local 'great sea-captain'.[3] And there are legendary references to the Srivijayan monarch who daily offered the tribute of a gold bar thrown into his kingdom's river estuary as 'a symbol of his indebtedness to the maritime trade'.[4] The monarch realized that the wealth of his kingdom would soon dissipate if the *vaniyaga* or foreign merchants left the Srivijaya port.

The ninth century (833) Kalirungun Sanskrit inscription found in Kedu in central Java is the earliest in Southeast Asia that lists the foreign traders (*vanigrama* or *banigrama*) residing there. This list is entirely restricted to the regions of South and Southeast Asia. The foreign merchants are described as being from Champa (present-day Vietnam), Remman (Ramanyadesa in the Mon region of Myanmar), Kmira (Cambodia), Kling (Kalinga on India's east coast), Aryya (Ayyavole, a south Indian merchants' guild from Aihole, Karnataka), Pandikara (Karnataka), and Singhala (Sri Lanka). Later inscriptions carry similar lists. The eleventh century (1021) inscription found in Cane in the Brantas River delta adds Drawidas (Cholas). Inscriptions from the 1040s and 1050s change Drawida to Cholika, replace Pandikira with Karnataka, and add Malyala (the Malabar Coast in present-day Kerala).[5] The inclusion of Chola kingdom representatives in this list so soon after the Chola trade wars of 1024-5 highlights the continuity in the trading interests and trading pattern of this south Indian kingdom with the region of Southeast Asia.

It is only in the fourteenth century, in the 1305 Balawi inscription, that for the first time there is mention of merchants from Cina (China) in addition to the now repetitive list of other foreign merchants. This particular inscription indicates for the first time that the rulers of Java were, by this time, using foreign merchants as revenue agents or tax collectors.

If the Indo-Malay kingdoms throughout the Malay Archipelago needed the foreign merchants, the prosperity of these merchants, too, depended on the facilitation and goodwill of the rulers. Several Tamil inscriptions (from the tenth to the fourteenth centuries) have been found in west Sumatra, north Sumatra, the Malay Peninsula, Myanmar and even in China, where the south India-based merchants' guilds have offered grants, and have endowed Hindu temples for their own well-being and that of the rulers in the various kingdoms. These are seen as illustrative of their commitment to the cities and regions where they are earning profits through their trading activities.

The CE 1088 Tamil inscription found in Barus, then a major camphor-exporting port in northern Sumatra, gives the south Indian merchant guild's name (*Nanadesa-Tiaiyayirattu Ainnurruvar*), details about their activities, and offers a grant to the *nagar senapati*, the local armed guards who accompanied the merchants. In the late thirteenth century there were at least two Hindu temples in the foreign merchants' sector in Guangzhou (Canton) port, both in the south Indian style. In the Shiva temple there is a Tamil and Chinese inscription dated 1281, dedicating the temple 'for the welfare of the illustrious body of the illustrious Chekachai Khan'.[6]

The presence and active participation of south Indian merchants and traders in the economic life of the Malay Archipelago continued well into the colonial era in Southeast Asia. After the end of the Chola era, the Vijayanagara kingdom in south-east India continued taking a keen interest in international trade. Their socio-political contacts with the Majapahits and other kingdoms continued. The demand for south India's textiles in Southeast Asian markets continued to rise up to the seventeenth century. Malay literature (the fifteenth-century *Sejarah Melayu* or the *Malay Annals*) and writings by foreign travelers (Tome Pires early in the sixteenth century) continued to have prominent references to Kalinga merchants, this term now being used collectively for all merchants based in south India.

Within this broad spectrum, significant changes are discernible in the pattern of trade and socio-economic interaction between South

Asia and Southeast Asia after the coming of European colonialists. The coming of Islam did not materially alter the pattern of contacts and trade. The arrival of the colonialists did.

SITUATION IN INDIA ON THE EVE OF THE COLONIAL ERA

Nicolo de Conti, the Italian merchant and explorer from Venice, travelled to India and Southeast Asia in the first quarter of the fifteenth century. He avers that

> the natives of India build some ships larger than ours, capable of containing 2000 butts, and with five sails and as many masts. The lower part is constructed with triple planks, in order to withstand the force of the tempests to which they are much exposed. But some ships are so built in compartments that should one part be shattered, the other portion remaining entire may accomplish the voyage.[7]

About the merchants of South India Nicolo de Conti notes that 'they are very rich, so much so that some will carry on their business in forty of their own ships, each of which is valued at 15,000 gold pieces'.[8]

Before the arrival of the Portuguese, the Sultans of Ahmedabad were known as 'lords of the sea'.[9] In the sixteenth century, well after the Portuguese had made their presence felt in India, Bassein (Vasai, north of Mumbai) and Agashi (district Thane in the Indian state of Maharashtra) were the great timber-producing (Bassein) and timber-trading areas with a large dockyard where ships were built (Agashi). The *Bombay Gazetteer* records 'the equality on which these places stood with Portugal in the art of shipbuilding. . . . One of the Surat ships stopped by Sir H. Middleton on its voyage to the Red Sea in 1612 was 153 feet long, 42 beam, 31 deep, and said to be of 1,500 tons burden.'[10] Similarly, it has been recorded around the same time that one of the Dabhol (the principal port in the south Konkan region along the west coast of India) ships stopped by Captain Saris in the Red Sea was '153 feet from stem to stern, breadth 42, height 31, burden 1200 tons, the mainmast 108 feet, the mainyard 132. The English ships of that age (1611) were 300 or 350 tons at most'.[11]

The Italian traveller Ludovico di Varthema, who visited Calicut (Kerala) in the early years of the sixteenth century, has provided detailed accounts of the shipbuilding industry in this port-city, including the types of ships constructed there.[12]

The Mughal Emperor Akbar (1556-1605) established and maintained an imperial naval establishment centred in the provinces of Bengal and Sindh. The seventeenth-century English traveller, Thomas Bowery has left behind for posterity intricate descriptions of his travels around the Bay of Bengal, covering the Coromandel Coast, the Golconda Coast (in present-day Andhra Pradesh), the states of Odisha and Bengal, right up to Kedah in the Malay Peninsula and Achin in Sumatra.[13] He has described the ports, the impressive mercantile fleets, the goods imported and exported, the foreign ships present in each port, and the wealth of the local merchants. He writes about ships and boats that are 'among the best of the kind for this period'. According to Thomas Bowery, one of the ships belonging to the King of Golconda and built for trade with Mocha in the Red Sea 'could not be, in my judgement, less than 1000 tons in burden'.[14]

Across India, large cross-secions of society were involved in the maritime trade between India and the Malay Archipelago, covering almost all communities and religions. There were the weavers and growers, the merchants and traders, the financiers, and the shipowners, maritime officials and sailors. Very often there were overlapping responsibilities, with the same group of people performing more than one function.

Throughout India, merchants from all communities: Bania (Hindu), Jain and Muslim, were active participants in the trade with Southeast Asia. The Parsis, Persians, Arabs and Armenians were involved as well, though in smaller numbers. In north India, the Marwaris and Khatris were prominent participants, while in the south the Telugu speaking Chettis of the Balija and Komatti communities were the leading Hindu merchant communities.

> The maritime merchants of Coromandel were in good measure Muslim, a few of Arab origin, but mainly members of the Muslim communities of coastal southeastern India, known as Marakkayars in Coromandel and as Chulias in parts of southeast Asia to which many had migrated on a permanent or

semipermanent basis. The migrants also included some Chetty merchants. The overall numbers involved were fairly large....[15]

Merchant communities from the south-west coast of India, too, were actively involved in the trade with Malacca and the eastern littoral of the Bay of Bengal. The Muslim Mappila merchants from the Malabar Coast played a predominant role in controlling this trade.

From the east coast of India, the traditional involvement of the Hindu merchants of Kalinga (Odisha) in the trade with the Malay Archipelago continued even after the advent of the Europeans. They operated from the ports of Balasore and Pipli in present-day Odisha. By the seventeenth century the dominant group among these merchants were the Shahs, who had migrated to this region from Gujarat, together with a large number of Bengali Hindu families who were smaller stakeholders in this trade. Persian merchants settled at the port of Chittagong were heavily involved with the pepper trade with Pasai and other ports in the Malay Archipelago.

A reconstruction of the shipowning maritime trading community of Bengal has been possible based on information from the archives of the Dutch East India Company. Archival information reveals that 'a major component of the maritime trading community of Bengal was that of state officials, mostly Muslim, at both senior and junior levels, engaged in maritime trade on the side and taking full advantage of their official position to maximize returns from their investment'.[16] Throughout the seventeenth century those involved included Prince Shah Shuja, Nawab Shaista Khan, Nawab Inoriya Muhammad of Odisha, Diwan Malik Beg of Odisha, Faujdar Ahmed Beg of Hughli and Faujdar Nawazish Khan of Rajmahal. This closely mirrors the pattern of the English country trader that was widely prevalent by the end of the seventeenth century. It is probable that the rising clout of the East India Company (EIC) with the Mughals in Delhi and rulers of Bengal forced this group of state officials out of business. What is certain is that 'once these officials withdrew from participation in maritime trade towards the end of the seventeenth century, the Bengal-Southeast Asia trade virtually collapsed'.[17]

Along the Coromandel Coast, too, a fair number of officials were 'substantially' involved in the coastal and trans-Bay of Bengal trade with the Malay Archipelago. Prominent among them was the Persian, Mir Muhammad Sayyid Ardestani, who was appointed to a high post in the Sultanate of Golconda, and in the 1660s, held the office of Subedar of the Bengal province under the Mughals.[18]

In Gujarat, however, the situation was quite different. Under the Mughals, members of royalty were involved only with the shipping service for hajj pilgrims to Saudi Arabia, even though these vessels also carried large amounts of freight cargo in either direction. Other than this, there was no substantive role for officials in the maritime trade conducted through the ports of Gujarat. In the port-town of Surat, described as India's chief commercial city under the Mughals 'the Bohras, of both Sunni and Shia faiths and who claimed no foreign lineage, were the most numerous among the Muslim merchants'.[19] In addition, there were the Arabs, the Persians and the settled Turkish communities. Hindu merchants and shipowners, too, played a prominent role in the economic life of Surat. In late seventeenth-century Surat, the Bohra Mulla Abdul Ghafur was among the richest merchants in the region. He owned 'as many as seventeen sea-going ships with a total dead-weight carrying capacity of well over 5000 tons. The overall size of the Surat mercantile marine at this time was slightly above one hundred ships'.[20]

Large shipowners like Mulla Abdul Ghafur rarely travelled on their ships. Trading the goods on board, purchase of the return cargo and management of the sea-voyage was in the hands of the *nakhuda* or the ship's captain. The *nakhuda* worked closely with the shipowner's appointed agent in each foreign port. In Malacca and other ports in the Malay Archipelago, most of these agents were 'Kelings', a term originally derived from Kalinga, and most often used as a generic description for those who had come from south India. These trade and shipping agents, or Kelings lived in these ports on a permanent or semi-permanent basis. It was the Kelings who dominated the management of the trade between India and the Malay Archipelago.

Along the Coromandel Coast, too, there were fairly large ship-owners, who owned up to ten ships each. However, the majority of shipowning maritime merchants across Indian ports owned just one or two ships. They almost invariably travelled on their own ships as *nakhudas*, combining all the onerous duties that this entailed. The third, and very large category of Indian maritime merchants was the one where the merchant was not a shipowner, but conducted his trade by renting freight space, and passenger space for himself on board others' vessels. There was intense competition among shipowners, including the Europeans in the sixteenth and seventeenth centuries, to secure this freight and passenger business, since these revenues contributed handsomely to the profits of each journey.

All these three categories of maritime merchants involved in coastal and high-seas trade needed the services of the *sarraf* or the merchant specializing in money transactions and transfers, and the intermediary merchant or the broker who facilitated supply of goods for export or disposal of goods brought in on the return journey. The Hindu Bania community dominated the establishments providing both these services. The *sarraf* establishments were to be found primarily in urban areas. Under the Mughals, the *sarraf* merchants were entrusted with remitting large sums of money from one part of the empire to the other, even to areas outside the empire but within the Indian subcontinent.

By far the most important *sarraf* establishment in the empire was that of the Jagat Seth family operating from its headquarters in Murshidabad in Bengal. In addition to its other extensive activities, this house handled the remittance of the central revenues from Bengal to Delhi amounting to over ten million rupees per annum.[21]

For the maritime merchant the services of the *sarraf* were particularly useful in handling the trade in bullion, coming in either from the west or the east.

The services of the *sarraf* and the intermediary merchant were in great demand with nobles and officials of the Mughal Empire. These nobles and officials 'played an essentially passive role in the conduct of their business operations leaving the decision making in most areas to their agents and brokers'.[22] European trading enterprises and private traders, too, depended on the services of the intermediary merchants 'both for the procurement of the export goods and the sale of the import goods, generally to a much greater extent than the Indian merchants engaged in coastal and overseas trade were obliged to do'.[23] The pattern that emerges reveals the integrated, interdependent and cohesive society that prevailed in India in the early sixteenth century, where people from all communities and religions worked together for their individual and common prosperity.

There are hardly any statistical records relating to the pre-Portuguese period about volumes and values of trade between India and the Malay Archipelago. However, some useful estimates on this account have been made by the Portuguese traveller Tome Pires, who visited Malacca around 1515, soon after the Portuguese conquest of this city in 1511.[24] Tome Pires has estimated that, just before the Portuguese conquest of Malacca, Indian cloth was imported into this entrepôt from Gujarat (five vessels a year, one large carrying 70,000-80,000 cruzados worth of cloth, the other four being smaller vessels bringing in 15,000-30,000 cruzados worth), from the Malabar Coast (three or four ships a year each bringing in 12,000-15,000 cruzados worth of cloth), from Pulicat (one or two ships a year, each valued at 80,000-90,000 cruzados), and from Bengal (one or two junks a year, each bringing in 80,000-90,000 cruzados worth of cloth). Anthony Reid (citation in footnote) estimates that the total figure for Malacca's annual imports of cloth in the pre-Portuguese period comes to 460,000 cruzados, equivalent to 19.3 tonnes of silver.

Most of the Indian cloth coming in to Malacca was sold in exchange for spices, gold, camphor, tin, sandalwood, alum and pearls. Some of the cloth was re-exported outside the region of Southeast Asia, notably to China and Ryukyu (Japan). Chinese goods purchased in Malacca against Indian cloth included porcelain, musk, silk, quicksilver, copper, and vermilion. There were also additional exports of Indian cloth that arrived at Malay Archipelago ports other than Malacca, such as Pasai and Kedah. It has been estimated that, for Indian textiles and piece-goods, 'net Southeast Asian imports may therefore have been in the region of 25 tonnes equivalent of silver. Assuming Pires was referring to their value in Malacca, the purchase price in India would have been closer to 15 tonnes of silver'.[25]

After more than a millennia of direct trade between India and the Malay Archipelago, the market for Indian textiles and piece goods in Southeast Asia had become highly specialized and territory-specific, with an enormous variety of products and materials being traded. Different types of Indian cloth, categorized by texture, weave, design, colour and dimension (for piece-goods) were shipped from one or the other Indian port, for supply to specific areas and regions throughout Southeast Asia. The variables in this complex matrix included type of textile product (or piece-good), place of production in India, port of shipment, port of discharge in Southeast Asia, final destination or source of demand, and finally, value of the product, or the quantity of spices for which it could be exchanged.

Merchants and traders had to be very careful to avoid losses because goods that were in high demand in Sumatra, for example, were likely to be unsaleable in Bantam (Java) or in Johor because of the region-specific popularity of each product. Even the description and names of the textile products were often a combination of their Indian and Malayan names. 'Dutch and English records of the seventeenth century mention more than 150 varieties of Indian textiles exported to Southeast Asia'.[26] The more expensive textile products were the finer muslins (from Bengal and the Deccan region) and calicos (from Calicut or Kozhikode in Kerala and also from Gujarat). These were popular throughout Southeast Asia, but were supplied in different categories, depending on the specific destination. These could be printed, or patterned (in the weaving), or transformed (i.e. cut to proper size and dyed), or made into specific articles such as '*Ickatt Pingon* (Malay for girdle), *Chawdor Pintados* (painted *chadar* or sheet), *Tappe Anacke* (children's skirt), *Tappe chintz* (a skirt of chintz), *Dragma Malaya* (a dragon in the Malayan fashion)'.[27] Also included in this list were the *patola* weaves exported from Surat (Gujarat) and other *ikat* weaves from Kalinga.

The less expensive or plain goods were woven all over India, along the Coromandel Coast (longcloth, dungarees, percales), in Gujarat and Sind (*baftas* and *duttees*), in north India (*semianos* from Samana in Patiala, *mercoolees* from Hardoi and Unnao, *ambertees* from Patna, among others), from Bengal (*mulmuls* and *cassas* made in Malda and Dhaka, *sologessees* and *ginghams*), and from the Deccan (*oringalls* or material for veils, from Warrangal, which were supplied in many varieties, depending on the destination).

Essentially, the success and longevity of this intra-Asian trade as it evolved over two millennia resulted from the complementarity rather than competitiveness of the goods that were traded between India and the Malay Archipelago. Each participant in the trading process benefitted financially from his transactions, whether as a supplier or purchaser of goods, or as a financier. This was a well-balanced trading process, based on mutual benefit rather than domination through conquest or subjugation.

India's well-developed sea-faring capabilities provided the foundational underpinning that sustained and facilitated India's dominant position in this trade. India's control over the Indian Ocean trading networks weakened only when these shipbuilding capabilities were snuffed out under British colonial rule.

NOTES

1. Kenneth R. Hall, 'Local and International Trade and Traders in the Straits of Melaka Region: 600-1500', *Journal of the Economic and Social History of the Orient*, vol. 47, no. 2 (2004), p. 214.
2. Ibid, p. 223.
3. Ibid.
4. Ibid., pp. 222-3.
5. Ibid., p. 224.
6. Chekachai Khan was the ruling Mongol/Yuan monarch. Hall, op. cit., p. 227.
7. Radha Kumud Mookerji, *Indian Shipping*, p. 142, quoting *India in the Fifteenth Century*, Hakluyt Society's Publication, II, p. 10.
8. Ibid., p. 142, quoting ibid., p. 27.
9. Ibid., p. 143.
10. Ibid., pp. 144-5, quoting *Bombay Gazetteer*, Bombay Government Press, Bombay, 1896, vol. I, pt. II, pp. 34-6.
11. Ibid., p. 145, quoting Vincents' *Commerce of the Ancients*, vol. II, p. 38.
12. *Travels of Ludivico di Varthema*, tr. into English and published by the Hakluyt Society of London, 1863.
13. Thomas Bowery, *A Geographical Account of Countries Round the Bay of Bengal, 1669 to 1679*, ed. Sir Richard Carnac Temple, Hakluyt Society, London, 1905.

14. Mukherjee, op. cit., p. 165.
15. Om Prakash 'The Indian Maritime Merchant, 1500-1800', *Journal of the Economic and Social History of the Orient*, vol. 47, no. 3, p. 449.
16. Ibid., p. 451.
17. Ibid.
18. Ibid., p. 450.
19. Ibid., p. 441.
20. Ibid., p. 444.
21. Ibid., p. 437.
22. Ibid.
23. Ibid.
24. Tome Pires, 1515, *The Suma Oriental of Tome Pires*, tr. Armando Cortesao, Hakluyt Society, 1944, pp. 269-72, quoted by Anthony Reid, op. cit., pp. 21-4.
25. Reid, op. cit., p. 22.
26. Sen, op. cit., p. 100.
27. Ibid., p. 101.

PART II

ASIA IS DIVIDED: THE COLONIAL PERIOD

6

The Colonialists Arrive

By the end of the fifteenth century the Portuguese were the leading naval power in Europe. Their ability to construct strong and large ships, capable of carrying crew and cargo over long distances, placed them ahead of other European nations of the day. Their navigation and military skills, and their success in maritime trade and exploration led them further afield to seek supremacy over the Arabs in the Indian Ocean. Economic and commercial motives were paramount in the Portuguese effort to wrest control of the Indian Ocean trading networks. At this point in time, the Ottoman Empire derived an important part of its revenues from its monopolistic control of the spice trade in Europe through Venetian markets.

Vasco da Gama rounded the Cape of *Bona Esperanza*, better known as the Cape of Good Hope, in November 1497. Six months later in May 1498, he sailed to Calicut on India's Malabar coast. From this point on, it became the declared intention of the Portuguese to create a new Asian spice route using the Cape of Good Hope. The first Portuguese settlement was established in Cochin, now Kochi, the historical centre of the Indian Ocean pepper trade. The Portuguese soon realized that control of trading centres along the Malabar coast, even the capture of Goa in 1510, was not enough to secure mastery of the Indian Ocean trading networks. Indian and Arab traders were still able to collect all the spices, textiles and luxury goods they wanted, from other ports in India, and from the great emporium in Malacca, where the produce of Siam, Burma, China, Sumatra and the Spice Islands, was traded.

The Portuguese conquest of Malacca in 1511 was vital for their dominance of the Indian Ocean. It was as significant as the capture of Goa (India) in 1510 and of Hormuz, at the mouth of the Persian Gulf, in 1515. These were important plumes in the cap of Don Afonso de Albuquerque, based in Goa as the second Portuguese Viceroy. Well into the first half of the seventeenth century, Portuguese Malacca continued to prosper. Trade expanded enormously, yielding vast profits for the colonial masters. After 1545 the Portuguese were successful in obtaining a share in the trade of Bantam, located in the north-west of the island of Java. Bantam, by then the principal port for the supply of pepper to both India and China, had an annual trade (just in pepper) amounting to 3.5 million pounds, or 1.6 million kg.

Politically, however, the situation in the Malay Archipelago remained unsettled and disturbed. Sultan Mahmud Shah of Malacca, who had escaped when the city fell, moved to the island of Bintang in the Straits of Singapore with his flotilla of ships more or less intact. He made every effort to cut Malacca off from its supply of goods. The Portuguese themselves were none too successful in establishing direct trading relationships with the Moluccas and other sources of the spice trade. Acheh became the focal point of the opposition to Portuguese overlordship. Between 1529 and 1587 there were repeated attempts by the then Sultan of Acheh to dislodge the Portuguese from Malacca.

This was a period of rapidly shifting alignments throughout the Malay Archipelago. Sultan Mahmud Shah's new headquarters in Bintang was destroyed by the Portuguese in 1526. His younger son, Sultan Alauddin Riayat Shah established his royal residence at Pekan Tua along the Johor River, thereby establishing the kingdom of Johor. His elder son Sultan Muzaffar Shah moved to Perak, where he founded the dynasty that still reigns there. Since the 1460s, Pahang was being ruled by a scion of the Malacca dynasty. For several decades after 1526, Johor, Perak and Pahang remained on friendly terms with the Portuguese, primarily because of their apprehensions and concerns about this rapidly rising power, combined with the aggressive intentions of the Sultan of Acheh *vis-à-vis* the states of the Malay Peninsula.

The kingdom of Acheh had, by now, consolidated its hold over the neighbouring principalities of Pedir and Pasai, both renowned as 'pepper ports . . . and was carrying on a rich trade with Gujerat and China'.[1] The Portuguese as well as the Malay peninsula kingdoms of Johor, Perak and Pahang needed each other to resist Acheh's determined and well-coordinated attacks. In the 1560s, the then Sultan of Acheh 'built up a league of states against the Portuguese, obtained gunners, guns and ammunition from Turkey, and amassed a bigger fighting force than ever before. Before striking at Malacca he dealt a staggering blow to his rival, the Sultan of Johore'.[2] Each time the Portuguese were successful in resisting the attacks by the Sultan of Acheh.

By 1584, however, the Portuguese fell out with their erstwhile ally, Johor, over matters relating to the trade monopoly. So much so that Johor now sought the help of Acheh in its siege of Malacca. By the end of the sixteenth century the tables had turned once again. Johor had reorganized and recouped its strength to such an extent that it was able to seriously threaten Acheh. It was now Acheh's turn to send an embassy to Malacca seeking Portuguese help.

Early in the seventeenth century, under Sultan Iskandar Muda (1607-36), Acheh regained its vigour and determination to oust the Portuguese and tighten its control over kingdoms in the Malay Peninsula. Already, since 1575, when Acheh attacked Perak, it was successful in establishing a loose form of suzerainty over this state. By this time Perak's vast deposits of tin were yielding increasing profits, given the rising demand for tin among European traders coming to Southeast Asia around the Cape of Good Hope.

Indian traders were active participants in the buying and selling of tin. 'Tin was not only sent back to Europe but also used as a medium of exchange for the inter-Asian trade.'[3] Indians and Europeans (Portuguese, Dutch, English and French) began going directly to Perak to buy the substantial amounts of tin being mined along the Perak River and its tributaries.

Perak earned the ire of Acheh when it agreed, early in the seventeenth century, to allow the Portuguese to establish a factory in Perak, thereby giving it direct access to tin supplies. Under Sultan Iskandar Muda (Acheh), there were differences between Acheh and the Portuguese on issues concerning the states on the Malay Peninsula. Taking advantage of the declining Portuguese power, Sultan Iskandar Muda tried once again in 1616, this time together with Johor, to dislodge the Portuguese from Malacca. The Portuguese successfully fended off this joint attack. Despite this, the Sultan of Acheh was able to extend his control both over coastal areas on the island of Sumatra, and over the peninsular states of Pahang (1618), Kedah (1619), and once again over Perak (1620).

It is around this time that the increasingly visible presence of other European powers is felt throughout Southeast Asia. The Portuguese had hardly been popular as the first European colonial power in this region. Their policy of seeking to dominate, even crush, local rulers is often cited as an important cause for their downfall. 'They behaved as conquerors rather than merchants, and when internal disorganization and lack of discipline began to appear, as they did before the middle of the sixteenth century, general corruption resulted.'[4]

Throughout the sixteenth century, the Netherlands and England had been building up their maritime and armaments skills to match the Portuguese. The English defeat of the Spanish Armada in 1588 was a significant indication of the turning tide. The English and the Dutch also acquired the geographical and practical knowledge so essential to navigate their way to India and Southeast Asia, whether through the Magellan Straits or around the Cape of Good Hope. In this regard, the publication of Jan Huyghens van Linschoten's *Reysgeschrift van de Navigatien der Portugaloysers in Orienten* in 1595, followed by *Itinerario, Voyagie ofte Shcipvaertvan Jan Huygen van Linschoten naar Oost ofte Portugaels Indien* in 1596, revealing top-secret Portuguese navigation charts combined with nautical data about currents, deeps, islands and sandbanks, was particularly timely and helpful.

In 1595, the first Dutch trade expedition set out to the East Indies via the Cape of Good Hope. Over the next five years, before the end of 1601, the Dutch sent out 15 fleets, comprising 65 ships, in their very determined effort to capture the spice trade from the Portuguese. These forays were considered highly successful. The ships travelled extensively, visiting Java, Sumatra, the Malay Peninsula, Borneo, the Moluccas, the Banda islands, Siam, Canton and Japan. They were able to secure trading rights, establish factories, and achieve handsome profits. The Portuguese found themselves at a great disadvantage, unsuccessful in driving the Dutch out of the Malay Archipelago, or in preventing the rulers across the area from granting trading rights to their European rivals.

THE EAST INDIA COMPANY

The merchants of London favoured an independent effort via the Cape to secure their participation in the spice trade. Their petition to the Queen to set up a joint-stock company for this purpose was granted and on 31 December 1600, the *Governor and Company of Merchants of London Trading into the East Indies* came into being, commonly known as the East India Company or the English East India Company. The Dutch followed suit soon thereafter, with the formation of the United East India Company or the VOC (*Vereenigde Oostindische Compagnie*) on 20 March 1602.

The English East India Company (EIC) sent out its first fleet in 1601. They were successful in establishing their first factory in Bantam in northwest Java, and received active assistance from the Sultan of Acheh. Bantam remained the Asian headquarters for the EIC till 1682. The kingdom of Bantam covered most of western Java and southern Sumatra. Bantam was a flourishing centre of trade and commerce in the Malay Archipelago, and Chinese ships came here for their pepper purchases. For the first twenty years imports of pepper from Java remained the staple item in the trade portfolio of the EIC.

The English soon realized the extent of the resistance they faced from the Dutch and the Portuguese in their efforts to break into this lucrative spice trade. They also realized that they had nothing to sell that was of any interest to the spice traders of Southeast Asia. England's major surplus product, woollen cloth, evinced no interest in the tropical climes of Southeast Asia. Instead of expending silver bullion on the purchase of spices, the EIC turned to India for purchase of textiles and cotton piece-goods which could be profitably exchanged for spices in Southeast Asia. Opium became another important product that the EIC took from India for sale in China and throughout the Malay Archipelago. Thus, England's initial interest in India grew out of its concern to stem the outflow of silver bullion, and to improve its terms of trade with Southeast Asia.

The English first arrived in India in 1608, landing at Surat, situated at the mouth of the river Tapti on the Gujarat coast, on 24 August. Surat was then the most important port for the overseas trade of the Mughal Empire. It was also the centre for the flourishing textile manufacturers of Gujarat. The Portuguese were well entrenched in Surat when the British arrived. They had secured their trading arrangements with the Mughal authorities, ensuring a virtual monopoly over trade with India, and were confident about their supremacy of the seas.

Captain William Hawkins, who led this first voyage of the EIC to India, was carrying a personal letter addressed to Mughal Emperor Jahangir by King James I of England, seeking trade concessions. Despite Captain Hawkins' persistent efforts for over two years, he had to return home empty-handed. It was only on the EIC's tenth voyage, which landed in Surat on 5 September 1612, that the English were successful in their efforts. It was perhaps the English victory in their naval skirmish with the Portuguese in November 1612 at Suvali (a small town 20 km north of Surat), described as the Battle of Swally, that convinced the Governor of Gujarat, and subsequently Emperor Nuruddin Salim Jahangir (1605-27), to grant to the English the trading concessions they sought.

In his letter to King James I, sent in 1617 through Sir Thomas Roe, Emperor Jahangir wrote:

> Upon which assurance of your royal love I have given my general command to all the kingdoms and ports of my dominions to receive all the merchants of the English nation as the subjects of my friend; that in what place soever they choose to live, they may have free liberty without any restraint; and at what port soever they shall arrive, that neither Portugal nor any other shall dare to molest their quiet; and in what city soever they shall have residence, I have commanded all my governors and captains to give them freedom answerable to their own desires; to sell, buy, and to transport into their country at their pleasure.[5]

The EIC derived great benefit from the patronage of the Mughal Emperors. They soon eclipsed the Portuguese, who had established just three bases, respectively at Goa, Chittagong and Bombay. Bombay was later ceded to England as part of the dowry of Catherine de Braganza. The EIC established its factory at Surat in 1612. Already in 1611 the EIC had set up base at Masulipatnam on India's Coromandel coast. Surat (India) and Bantam (Java) were now the EIC's two principal establishments, both designated as Presidencies. In less than two decades, by 1628, 'Bantam was now a station of inferior importance to Surat, the government of Bantam was reduced to an agency, dependent on the Presidency of Surat, which became the chief seat of the Company's government in India'.[6]

By 1639 the EIC had a trading post in Madras (known then as Fort St. George), and by 1647 the EIC had 23 factories in different parts of India, including Calicut, Cranganore, Patna and Agra. The one in Bombay came up in 1668 and the one in Calcutta (known as Fort William) in 1690. Fort St. George (Madras) developed rapidly to become the most important centre for the EIC's trading activity in South and Southeast Asia. In 1682 Fort St. George replaced Surat (and Bantam) as the EIC headquarters for the eastern trade.

The concept of a factory was an interesting one.

> Each factory consisted of a compound containing living quarters, public rooms, warehouses and open yards, the whole surrounded by a fence or wall as security against fire or thieves . . . the English factory at Hirado in Japan had a wharf fronting the harbour and, as well as the usual buildings, there was a garden with a pond for koi carp and a dovecote, an orchard, a vegetable patch, and a Japanese o-furo or hot bath, which friends and neighbours were often invited to share.[7]

Factories were run by a chief factor and a council of factors. A group of factories in the same area was known as a settlement, governed by an agent and a council. A group of settlements in the same region were described as presidencies, administered by an agent.

The EIC made every effort to expand its activities in the Malay Archipelago. By 1623 the EIC had established factories in Sumatra at Acheh, Tiku and Priaman (both in west Sumatra), in Java at Bantam and Batavia (Jakarta), in Borneo at Sukadana (west Kalimantan) and Banjarmasin (south Kalimantan) and at Patani on the east coast of the Malay Peninsula. The EIC achieved considerable success, but were persistently hemmed in by the Dutch who, having arrived on the scene just ahead of the English, had concluded successful trading arrangements with most of the sultans and rulers in the region.

The Dutch zealously and effectively guarded their trading rights, firmly resisting any interference or what they perceived as an attempted poaching in the areas under their influence. As a result, in the all-important spice trade, while the EIC had liberal access to supplies of pepper through their factories in Sumatra and Java, they were excluded from access to supplies of cinnamon, cloves, nutmeg and other fine spices. These were produced in the Moluccas (also known as the Spice islands), the Banda islands and the Ambon island, all of which are today part of Indonesia, and in the seventeenth century were under the control of the Dutch VOC.

This is where the EIC's trading strategy, of exchanging Indian textiles for spices in the Malay Archipelago, proved very useful. It yielded large profits, since the fame and popularity of Indian textiles allowed them considerable leverage in accessing the goods they wanted, if not directly, then indirectly. The EIC was following the millennia-old trading pattern set by Indian merchants in their interaction with the Malay Archipelago and other parts of South-east Asia.

In 1641, the Dutch drove the Portuguese out of Malacca. The fortunes of Malacca never recovered after this. For the Dutch, Malacca became just one of a number of archipelago ports. The VOC decided to make Batavia (now Jakarta) the headquarters of its entire Asian trading network. Malacca lost its role as an international emporium, and became just a 'guardpost protecting shipping through the Straits'.[8] Immediately after securing Malacca, the Dutch moved towards gaining control over the tin-producing states of the Malay Peninsula. 'Tin was their main interest in the Peninsula; it was of prime importance to them in their commercial dealings with both India and the Chinese.'[9] For long years, the Sultans of Acheh and the northern Malay States (primarily Kedah and Perak) resisted the Dutch. However, by 1663 Acheh had gone into decline and the Dutch, through an agreement known as the Painan Contract, were able to bring practically the entire west coast of Sumatra under their supervision and control.

The Malay state of Johor was the most direct beneficiary of the decline of Malacca and the ascendency of the Dutch. For most of the sixteenth century Johor had suffered hostile attacks from Portuguese Malacca and from the Sultan of Acheh. In 1641 the Sultan of Johor allied with the VOC in the Dutch assault on Malacca. In acknowledgement of their support, the Dutch granted Johor special trading privileges, more than those given to any other Malay kingdom in the region. This was part of Dutch policy to divert trade away from Malacca. The Dutch also mediated a peace treaty between Johor and Acheh in 1641. Despite the grave setback to its fortunes after the regicide against their Sultan in 1699, Johor continued to strengthen its political and economic domination of the Malay Peninsula well into the eighteenth century.

By the middle of the fourteenth century, the kingdom of Ayudhya, by now the dominant Thai power, began to exercise control over many Malay states, particularly the northern ones. They were able to do this through the kingdom of Ligor, which was by now a major maritime outlet for the Thais. Early in the eighteenth century, in the face of threats from the kingdom of Siam (Thailand), the capital of Johor moved further south, away from the Johor River to the island of Riau. The strategic location of Riau at the southern tip of the Malay Peninsula, the crossroads for maritime traffic, combined with longstanding Johor expertise and skills in managing international trade, ensured a welcoming environment for traders from east and west. Riau was soon a thriving entrepôt. Indian traders arrived there in large numbers. Like Malacca and Acheh before it, Riau, too, 'became an important Islamic centre, with scholars from Gujarat and the Arab world expounding religious precepts to the faithful'.[10]

Several Malay states maintained their traditional links with India well after the European colonial powers had arrived in South-east Asia. In Kedah, Sultan Muhammad Jiwa (he died in 1779) is remembered for his ability to retain his independence of action despite Dutch pressure to enter into a commercial contract with them. He preferred to maintain an open port. Kedah's direct trading links with India yielded good revenues, which allowed the economy of this state to thrive, supported by the pepper trade and Kedah's rice exports to the rest of the Malay Peninsula. Sultan Muhammad Jiwa had, in his youth, travelled to India, Palembang and Java. In Acheh, in Malacca, in Kedah and in Johor, traders from India continued to form the single largest community.

By the eighteenth-century European colonialists had entrenched themselves throughout Southeast Asia and in parts of India. In the Malay Peninsula the Portuguese had been replaced by the Dutch who, in turn, were soon to be replaced by the English. The Europeans used their settlements in India to buy Indian goods for trading in Southeast Asia against their requirements of spices and other products. They were imitating the pattern of trade that Indian merchants had followed with great success for close to two millennia.

NOTES

1. D.G.E. Hall, *A History of South-East Asia*, p. 367.
2. Ibid.
3. Barbara Watson Andaya and Leonard Y. Andaya, *A History of Malaysia*, p. 60.
4. Hall, op. cit., p. 271.
5. *Indian History Sourcebook: England, India, and the East Indies, 1617* CE, sourced at http://www.fordham.edu/halsall/india/1617englandindies.html on 25 June 2010.
6. James Mill, *The History of British India* in 6 vols, 3rd edn., published in 1826 by Baldwin,Craddock and Joy, London; vol. I, chapter II, accessed online on 26 June 2010 at http://oll.libertyfund.org/option=com_staticxt&staticfile=show.php%3Ftitle=840&chapter=79889&layout=html<emid=27, p. 16.
7. Anthony Farrington writing in *Trading Places: The East India Company and Asia, 1600-1834* (The British Library, 2002) accessed from EAST INDIA COMPANY FACTORY RECORDS, sources from the British Library, London, Part I: China and Japan, on 22 June 2010, at http://www.ampltd.co.uk/collections_az/eic-factory-1/highlights.aspx
8. Andaya and Andaya, op. cit., p. 70.
9. Hall, op. cit., p. 370.
10. Ibid., p. 79.

7

India's Trade with the Malay Archipelago in the Age of Colonialism (Sixteenth and Seventeenth Centuries)

The 300 years from the fifteenth to seventeenth centuries have been described as the 'age of commerce' in Southeast Asia.[1] This period was characterized by the coming of Islam, the advent of European colonialists, the strengthening of the state, expansion of urban areas and above all, extensive involvement of this region in transoceanic trade and commerce.

The Portuguese, followed by the Dutch and the British, came to India and to Southeast Asia to participate in the fabled spice trade. Their objective was to control and monopolize this trade in order to maximize profits. They soon realized that the quantum of profits from the spice trade was closely linked to exports of textiles and cotton piece goods from India to Southeast Asia. The development of ports and allied urban areas, together with the codification of laws and strengthening of the state's administrative capacities were closely linked to the requirements of commerce.

Strenuous efforts by European colonialists to wrest control of this trade adversely affected the relationship between India and Southeast Asia. The Portuguese, for example, introduced the requirement of a *carte de passage* to restrict the hitherto free movements of ships across the Indian Ocean and the the Bay of Bengal. Despite such efforts, India remained intertwined with the kingdoms of Southeast Asia in trade, religion and culture, a continuation of its age-old commercial, cultural and religious links with this region.

India could do this as long as she retained control over her shipbuilding capacities and capabilities.

RISING DEMAND FOR SPICES IN EUROPE

The treaty concluded by Venice in 1345 with the Mamluke rulers of Egypt established a stranglehold for Venice over the spice trade in Europe. The Mamlukes had consolidated their hold over the land routes serving Beirut and Damascus, ensuring safe progress for the caravans carrying spices from India to the Mediterranean through the Red Sea and Persian Gulf ports. However, after the fourteenth-century collapse of the Central Asian overland 'Silk Route' due to the breakdown of *Pax Mongolica*, the latter half of this century witnessed a sharp rise in the use of the Indian Ocean maritime trade routes between Egypt, India, Southeast Asia and China. The demand for spices in Europe was on the upswing, with further exponential increases after Vasco da Gama's discovery in 1497 of the maritime route to India via the Cape of Good Hope.

This upswing in European demand for spices coincided with an upsurge in demand for spices and other luxury goods from China. The Italian traveller Marco Polo, during his visit to China in the late thirteenth and early fourteenth centuries, has described the Chinese demand for spices as being 100 times that of Europe. The end of the fourteenth century saw the start of two centuries of prosperity and population growth in China. From 1405 to 1433 seven naval expeditions from China travelled across Southeast Asia and the Indian Ocean, led by Admiral Zheng He under the patronage of the Ming Emperor. Each expedition returned home with enormous amounts of pepper, spices and other products from India and the Malay Archipelago, further stimulating the demand across China for these items.

Interestingly, the item for which there was the largest demand, *Piper nigrum*, popularly known as black or round pepper, is native to Kerala, along the Malabar Coast of India. 'Pepper was not mentioned among the products of Sri Vijaya, nor as growing in Sumatra at the time of the visits of Marco Polo (1292) or Ibn Battuta (1355).'[2] However, records of the first Zheng He (Cheng Ho) expedition mention pepper growing in northern Sumatra, indicating that it must have been introduced there from India in the late fourteenth century. Pepper crops were so abundant in Sumatra and the Malay Peninsula (Kedah, Pahang, Patani, Songkhla) that already by 1500 the Portuguese estimated, as recorded by the traveller Tome Pires, that 'these new Southeast Asian pepper fields produced nearly 2500 tonnes, against 3600 for Malabar'.[3] By the year 1600 the eastern coast of India was importing pepper from Sumatra. It has been calculated on the basis of ship movements that the entire Malacca Straits region must have exported about 4,650 tonnes of pepper in the year 1600 and 6,500 tonnes of pepper in 1630.[4] The Dutch and the English entered the fray in 1596, seeking their own supplies of pepper and other spices. This pushed up demand and led to even higher prices and volumes of export.

Similarly for the other major spices, namely cloves, nutmeg and mace (the covering of the nutmeg seed), shipments into Europe started rising sharply towards the end of the fourteenth century. 'An annual average of 9 tonnes of cloves and two of nutmeg may have been brought to Europe in the years 1394-97, rising sharply to 32 and 10 tonnes respectively in 1399-1405.'[5] These spices, native to the Moluccas (Maluku) and the Banda islands, have been high value components of the Indian ocean trade since ancient times. By the end of the fifteenth-century Venice alone was importing annually 52 tonnes of cloves, 26 tonnes of nutmeg and 12 tonnes of mace. A hundred years later, by the end of the sixteenth century, these figures had doubled despite the disruptions caused by Portuguese efforts to impose sole buying rights (for themselves) on the island-producers of these spices. In the first quarter of the seventeenth century, amidst intense competition between the Portuguese, the Dutch and the English, European consumption rose to an all-time high of over 200 tonnes of cloves, 200 tonnes nutmeg and 70-80 tonnes of mace.[6]

THE PORTUGUESE (AND LATER THE DUTCH) SEEK CONTROL OF THE SEAS AND THE SPICE TRADE

The Portuguese did their utmost to monopolize shipping and trading rights over the pepper and other spices going from India and Southeast Asia to Europe. In the early years of the sixteenth century, particularly after their conquest of Malacca in 1511, the Portuguese introduced the system of the *cartaz* or passport. This obliged any Indian or other Asian ship, under threat of seizure on the high seas in the event of non-compliance, to seek permission of the *Estado da India* if they wished to operate in the Indian Ocean, the Bay of Bengal, the Straits of Malacca or any Asian waters.[7] In subsequent years the Dutch VOC and the English East India Company also adopted the same system. This marked the first time ever that external constraints were imposed seeking to curtail the hitherto unqualified right of free navigation on the high seas for Asian maritime travellers, be they merchants or voyaging on orders of their sovereign.

Initially, the Portuguese conquest of Malacca and their subsequent attempts to monopolize the Bay of Bengal trade did create problems for Indian merchants operating from the Coromandel Coast. Private Portuguese trading groups began settling down at Pulicat and the neighbouring port of Sao Tome de Mylapore. Another important Portuguese settlement came up at Nagapattinam along the south Coromandel Coast in the 1530s. Despite this, Indian ship owners and merchants kept up their trade volumes with Malacca till the middle of the sixteenth century. Soon, however, once the Portuguese insisted on allowing only concession voyages on a reserved-route basis between Pulicat and Malacca, Indian merchants found themselves almost completely excluded from this run. They were required to hire freight space aboard the concession holders' ships, rather than ply their own vessels. The rise in import duties at Malacca, together with the increase in freight charges added to the costs of Indian and Southeast Asian traders on this route.

Indian and Southeast Asian merchants, keen to avoid any major debilitating impact of these new regulations on their trade turnover, responded in two ways. At the Indian end, by the late sixteenth century, Masulipatnam, situated further north along the Coromandel Coast in the region now under the Golconda Sultanate, developed as the major port of choice for Indian and Southeast Asian traders. In the Malay Peninsula, traders and shippers moved away from Malacca to ports in Perak and Kedah.

Acheh (in north Sumatra) emerged as an important alternative centre for this Bay of Bengal trade, the successor entrepôt to Malacca and a strong focus within the region for the opposition to the Portuguese presence. Nagapattinam, too, traded extensively with Acheh during this period. New sea-lanes were used, via the Maldives, to reach traditional destinations in the Persian Gulf and the Red Sea without being challenged by the Portuguese.

The traditional partners in the intra-Asian trade, whose linkages went back in time to the early years of the first millennium, came together to protect their collective commercial interests in the face of the Portuguese intrusion. The Sultan of Acheh attacked Portuguese Malacca fourteen times. 'They commissioned large ships to be built in India, obtained guns from the Turks and cast their own.'[8] In the seventeenth century the shipbuilding capacities at Surat, Cochin and along the east coast of India were renowned throughout Asia. 'Ships carrying thirty or forty cannons were being built at Surat. . . . Ships of 600 tons were said to be operating from Masulipatnam on the Coromandel Coast.'[9] The Surat shipbuilders supplied the Gulf States as well. 'The Omanis built up a navy in the European sense of specialized fighting ships. One of their ships built at Surat was thought to be "above a thousand tun", carrying "at least a hundred guns".'[10]

Early in the sixteenth century the Portuguese proved their supremacy in naval battles, thus establishing a string of bases around the Indian Ocean, in the Bay of Bengal, the Straits of Malacca and beyond. None the less, their presence did not remain uncontested. Indians and the Sultanates throughout the Malay Archipelago made every effort to strengthen their defences by building bigger and better ships and artillery weapons. Johor and Acheh in the Straits of Malacca, the Mughals, the Marathas, the Zamorin (*Samoothiri*) of Kozhikode, and the rulers of the Vijayanagara Empire in India all fought back. In 1735 the Marathas captured the *Derby*, a large merchant ship categorized as an English East Indiaman. On land, Maratha armies were successful in reducing the area under Portuguese control. In south India, European control over pepper production along the Malabar Coast was weakened. In 1741 the Dutch were defeated in Travancore and by the 1760s, Mysore emerged as a dominant power. In Sumatra and Java the Dutch hold was weakening, and in the Malay Peninsula their position in Malacca was being besieged.

> Thus, by the middle of the eighteenth century the Europeans were facing increasingly effective military opposition throughout Asia. The Portuguese had lost much territory; Dutch influence was contracting; and the richest English settlement in the East, Calcutta, passed briefly into Asian hands in 1756. Military weakness did not necessarily mean commercial decline.[11]

This comment brings out that, despite the fighting spirit and military-cum-naval preparedness of the states of India and Southeast Asia, as well as their close coordination with each other, it was the commercial policies and practices of the European powers that impoverished the people of India and the Malay Archipelago, ousted their participation in the trading process, and finally subjugated them to colonial rule.

In the 1620s, when European consumption of cloves, nutmeg and mace had reached an all time high, the Dutch VOC succeeded in establishing its monopoly over the production of nutmeg and mace in the Banda Islands. Immediately, the VOC policy directives seem to have been to drastically reduce, even halve, the quantities reaching the European market. As expected, the prices of nutmeg and mace went up correspondingly. By 1642, the VOC achieved a similar monopoly over the supply of cloves from the Moluccas. In their effort to reduce the production of cloves, the VOC went about 'destroying all clove trees outside the areas of the closest Dutch control in southern Amboina and the Lease Islands'.[12] As a result, the selling price of cloves is said to have doubled in Europe and tripled in India. These unnaturally high prices led to the permanent reduction of European clove consumption, with the introduction of a cheaper alternative, Brazilian 'clove-wood'. When the VOC once again raised the production of cloves, there was a glut in European markets and prices crashed. The VOC incurred commercial losses. However, no matter whether the VOC made a profit or incurred a loss, 'once the monopoly was established, the export of Moluccan spices no longer contributed to the wealth of Asian cities and traders, but to the VOC and its enclave entrepôts'.[13] Eventually, this led to the impoverishment of the growers, merchants and traders of India and Southeast Asia.

THE ROLE OF INDIA'S TEXTILE EXPORTS

Almost as soon as the Europeans arrived in Malacca and other parts of Southeast Asia, they discovered the importance of India's textile exports to this region. They found that there was an enormous demand for Indian textiles of various qualities and varieties, which was already being met through the active system of intra-Asian trade that had evolved between India and the Malay Archipelago. Indeed, Indian textiles 'constituted the principal medium of exchange for the trade of Southeast Asia with the outside world'.[14] The Europeans, particularly the Dutch and the English, quickly adopted this traditional pattern of intra-Asian trade, thereby saving themselves the cumbersome and difficult requirement of importing large amounts of silver bullion to pay for their purchases of pepper, cloves, nutmeg and mace. Their success in manipulating this exchange of Indian textiles for spices brought them enormous wealth in the sixteenth and seventeenth centuries, which provided a strong base for the political power they sought in the eighteenth century. In other words,

> the poor Indian weavers shaped the course of world history by unconsciously laying the foundation of British and Dutch colonial empires. . . . The importance of Indian textiles as the principle medium of exchange in Southeast Asia will be evident from some of the treaties concluded by the Dutch and the English with local rulers, which fixed the prices of spices in terms of Indian piece-goods. Sometimes even the customs duties and presents to the rulers and their officers for trading concessions were payable in Indian piece-goods . . . the Dutch sometimes paid their soldiers in the Spice Islands in Indian textiles, which they bartered for spices, selling the spices again to the Company.[15]

VOC documents contain records of several contracts reflecting this reality. The 1649 VOC contract with the Queen of Acheh specifies the package of Indian textiles to be handed over for every *bahar* (360 Dutch pounds) of pepper. The package indicates the exact number of piece-goods to be included of each variety, such as broad *baftas* (with or without border), *percales*, longcloth (also called guineacloth), *oringalls* (also called *betilles*). Two 1660 contracts with the *Panglima* (ruler) of Padang (west Sumatra) similarly indicate the package of piece-goods per *bahar* of pepper, although the specific contents of the package are quite different from the one chosen by the Queen of Acheh. The second 1660 VOC contract is also with the *Panglima* of Padang, this time specifying the amounts, in Indian textiles, to be paid for the trading concession in Padang. These amounts are to be paid to the *Panglima*, to each of two *Orang Kayas* (noblemen), to each of two judges, and to each of four *mantris* (ministers).[16]

The collation of VOC records provides some perspective on the scale of profits earned by the Dutch through this exchange of Indian textiles for Malay Archipelago spices.[17] In the early years of the seventeenth century, with purchase prices of Indian textiles quoted for Masulipatnam, and sale prices in the Malay Archipelago (for pepper and spice equivalents), the trade yielded handsome profits, varying from an average of 400 per cent to a high of 900 per cent and more. *Serassa Gober* (sheets made of serassa cloth) were purchased in India for 2.67 rials and sold for 12 to 15 rials. The highly valued *cassas* of Bengal were purchased for 1.27 rials (*cassa-poutta*) and 2.33 rials (*cassa-mera*) and sold for 11 to 12 rials each. The list goes on and on.

These levels of profit are usuriously higher than the comparatively modest levels of profit that prevailed in the pre-Portuguese period. In those days, 15 tonnes of silver worth of Indian textiles were sold for the equivalent of 25 tonnes of silver in the Malay Archipelago, yielding a profit of 60 per cent (details on page 139).

INDIA AND SOUTHEAST ASIA WORK TOGETHER TO RESIST EUROPEAN COLONIALISTS

With the advent of the Portuguese, the already substantial pre-Portuguese levels of exports of Indian textiles to the Malay Archipelago are estimated to have doubled by the end of the sixteenth century. During the travels of Sir James Lancaster to the Malay Archipelago 'he seized a single Portuguese ship in 1602 carrying a cargo valued at 300,000 cruzados, mostly in cloth, from Coromandel to Melaka'.[18] This was more than three times the size of the largest ship sailing from India to the Malay Archipelago. However, in the Acheh harbour, Sir James Lancaster records seeing sixteen to eighteen ships from India, indicating that Indian merchants and traders were still active in their trade with Southeast

Asia. Roughly half of these ships were probably from Gujarat, since Dutch records show that in 1608, eight 'large junks' from Gujarat visited Acheh.[19]

The records maintained by English and Dutch travellers to the Malay Archipelago in the first quarter of the seventeenth-century highlight certain important conclusions. First, despite early efforts by the Portuguese to dominate the intra-Asian trade between India and the Malay Archipelago and channel it exclusively through Malacca, the merchants and shippers from Gujarat, the Malabar Coast and all across the Bay of Bengal from the Coromandel Coast to Sumatra, were more than able to hold on to their own and maintain the levels of trade throughout the sixteenth century. Shipments from Indian ports continued at the same levels as in the pre-Portuguese period, while large volumes of additional shipments took place from the Indian ports dominated by the Portuguese such as Nagapattinam, Cochin, Goa, Porto Novo (south of Cuddalore on the Coromandel Coast) and San Thome (now a part of Chennai). As a result, overall trade figures doubled in the sixteenth century.

Second, with the arrival of the Portuguese in Malacca, the Chulias (Muslim merchants from south India), the Bengalis and the Gujaratis diverted their ships to Acheh and to the northern Javanese ports of Banten, Japara and Gresik. It is from these ports that Islam came to Java around 1530, signaling the end of the Majapahit kingdom.

Third, in Malacca, the Portuguese relied extensively on the community of Indian traders who had been living there for generations. They were not sea-farers, but were active as brokers. They were in regular interaction with the Malays and the Minangkabaus, living upstream, and would prepare the package of goods needed by individual shipowners and merchants calling at Malacca. The Dutch, too, after they conquered Malacca in 1641, found the services of this group of well-assimilated Indians quite indispensable.

> They (the Indians) had their factors in the interior and had contacts with the Menangkabau who came from the highlands with their gold and pepper. In fact the Dutch could not procure gold except through them. To the Menangkabau they sold cloth in exchange for gold. These Klings or Indians were also the lessees of whatever gold fields there was to be found in the suburbs of Malacca.[20]

At this time

> most Malay states had a growing Indian population, many of whom were Moslem traders from the Coromandel Coast. . . . Some of these traders were incorporated into Malay courts, taking up influential intermediary positions such as scribe or interpreter and thus serving to reinforce the key role of Indians in Malay commerce.[21]

In each of the Malay states, whether it be Kedah, Perak, Malacca, Pahang or Johor, merchants and traders from India integrated through intermarriage. This was particularly true for those who stayed on for long tenures in Malayan cities, as the buyers of local products to be exported to India. This had, after all, become the norm and practice during the millennia and more of intra-Asian trade that preceded the arrival of the Portuguese.

Some of these intermarriages are recorded. A genealogy of Maharaja Perba of Pahang, stated to have been recorded around 1884, says that the Sultan of Johor granted Pahang to

> the Four Persons, firstly Seri Maharaja Perba, secondly Maharaja Indera Putera, thirdly Maharaja Indera Putera Pahlawan, and fourthly, Shahbandar . . . Seri Maharaja Perba came from Menangkabau. . . . The Shahbandar is descended from a southern Indian on one side and a white Chinese on the other.[22]

The Chinese had started coming to the Malacca Sultanate in small numbers as merchants and traders. They had intermarried and settled down there, their descendants popularly known as the *Baba Nyonya*.

The burgeoning trade-driven prosperity in the Malay Peninsula in the seventeenth century attracted the Minangkabau from their homeland in Sumatra. The Minangkabau, who followed the matrilineal system of descent, had traditionally travelled to the Malay Peninsula to live in what is today the Negri Sembilan state. They were active in gold and tin mining and soon became a politically powerful group. Similarly the Bugis, originally from the Celebes, and other south Sulawesi groups, soon became a strong force in the Riau Archipelago and in the area that is today the state of Selangor. They were renowned as skilled mariners and powerful merchants.

There was intense rivalry, even conflict, between the Malays, the Minangkabau and the Bugis. Over time, however, the ruling families of these groups intermarried and settled their differences. Malay became their common language, even though each group retained its own traditional centre of influence and activity.

In the first quarter of the seventeenth century the Dutch and the English entered the fray for dominance of the spice trade in the Malay Archipelago. The competition became intense, often leading to an over-supply or glut of Indian textiles on the market. After 1641, the Dutch began stringently implementing very specific policies, aimed at establishing their monopolistic control over the spice trade in the Malay Archipelago. They wanted to dictate prices on key products, whether bought or sold, and in order to achieve this, they worked towards the elimination of all other merchants and middlemen from the trading process. 'Thus Schouten, the Dutch Commissioner sent to study and make proposals on the Malacca trade, recommended that the Dutch hold a monopoly of pepper, spices, sandalwood, tin and the principal varieties of cloth.'[23]

The Dutch also wanted to strengthen the role of Malacca as the most important entrepôt in the Malay Archipelago, visited by all merchants and shippers coming to this region. It was felt that this would enhance Dutch leverage in manipulating trade volumes and prices to their benefit. 'Orders were sent to Dutch factors in India that passes to Indian vessels were to be given only to Malacca, and only from there could they be permitted to proceed to any other port of the Peninsula.'[24] In July 1641, as an income-enhancing measure, the Dutch raised import and export duties on goods moving into and out of Malacca to levels higher than the Portuguese had levied. This proved to be an unpopular move, which backfired. Malacca began to rapidly lose favour as the emporium of choice in this region.

The Dutch then sought to secure exclusive contracts with the rulers of the states in the Malay Peninsula in order to strengthen their monopolistic control of commodity-trade. Tin was the most important among these commodities. The first such contract or treaty was signed with the Sultan of Kedah in June 1642, whereby half of all the tin produced by or imported into Kedah was required to be sold to the Dutch at a fixed price. Payment for this could be made either in cash or in equivalent amounts of cotton piecegoods.

Ships from Surat, Bengal, the Coromandel Coast or any Indian port could trade in Kedah only after obtaining written permission from the Governor of Malacca. This permission was given only if the ships from India had called at Malacca and paid their tolls there. Similar treaties were signed with Junk Ceylon (present-day Phuket) in 1643 and with the Governor of Bangery in 1645.

The results of these treaties were not at all satisfactory from the Dutch point of view. Indian traders moved all their business to Acheh. Here they could sell their textile products and in exchange buy pepper, spices, tin and other products assembled for them by the traders of Acheh who had no restrictions on trading with the ports of Sumatra and Malaya. This seriously hurt the interests of Malacca and

> in 1646 almost no tin could be obtained by the Dutch from the Malay Peninsula and there was no peppper export from Malacca. He (Governor of Malacca) proposed the use of force against these Indian merchants: 'Only if these entire people are driven from the sea for all time can the fruits of Malacca be properly enjoyed, otherwise the trade will decline increasingly from time to time.[25]

Gujarati merchants, among the most successful in India's trade with the Malay Archipelago, had hitherto been quite lax in heeding restrictions imposed by the European colonialists. After July 1647, this became much more difficult because the Council of India at Batavia (now Jakarta) decided to ban all Indian ships from trading with Acheh and the tin-producing areas of the Malay Peninsula. At the Indian end, in Surat, simmering tension between Dutch officials and the Gujarat administration erupted in April 1648. The Dutch factory and storehouse at Surat was attacked. In retaliation, the Indian Ocean based Dutch fleet moved in towards Surat and 'seized two large ships belonging to the Moghul Emperor with a rich cargo to the value of 1.5 million guilders'.[26] In September 1649, the Mughal Governor of Surat and the Dutch signed a treaty accepting, *inter alia*, that the merchants of Surat would henceforth 'abandon their sea-traffic to Achin, Perak, Kedah, Junk Ceylon, Malacca and other places. . . .'[27]

Simultaneously, the Dutch blockaded the Perak River and

stopped the tin trade until the Queen of Acheh, who held suzerainty over Perak, directed the Sultan of Perak to sign a treaty with the Dutch (this was done in August 1650), pledging that 'the entire trade of Perak was to be shared by the Dutch and the Achinese to the exclusion of all other nations, European or Indian'.[28] Serious differences arose in the implementation of this treaty, as a result of which a second treaty was signed in June 1659, this time directly between the Dutch and the Queen of Acheh. This treaty decided that the tin of Perak would be divided equally between the Dutch and the Achinese, and that 'the traders from Surat, Coromandel, Bengal, Malabar, Arakkan, Pegu as well as the English and the Danes were to trade only at Achin and not go to any of the ports on the Malay Peninsula'.[29]

The objective of these treaties was to ensure the largest share for the Dutch in the tin and cloth trade of the Malay Peninsula, and to prevent any direct participation by the Indians and other Europeans in this trade. To some extent this was easier said than done. The Dutch had to be mindful that in several Indian states they had been given permission to establish factories together with freedom of trade and special privileges. The Indian traders in these states quite naturally expected reciprocal privileges in the Dutch-controlled territories in Southeast Asia. The rulers of powerful Indian states, particularly in southern India, even threatened reprisals against Dutch interests. In the Malay Peninsula, too, individual Malay States were fairly lax in observing the treaties concluded by them with the Dutch. The Sultan of Kedah is said to have continued his trade with the Coromandel Coast, despite the Dutch repeatedly denying permission for his ships to go to India. The Portuguese and the English liberally issued passes for Indian ships to travel to Malacca and Acheh. The Dutch often felt obliged to honour these passes, especially during periods of entente with their European rivals. Thus, after 1667, when the Second Anglo-Dutch War ended, English ships were openly trading with Malacca, Kedah and Perak, and the Dutch could do nothing about it. 'Indian merchants began to hire English vessels and carry on their trade in these ports under the protection of the English flag.'[30]

DRAWING DOWN OF DIRECT INTERACTION BETWEEN INDIA AND SOUTHEAST ASIA

There is little doubt, however, that by the end of the seventeenth century the era of intensive and free interaction between South and Southeast Asia was drawing to a close. The cracks in this millennia old friendship that first developed with the Portuguese conquest of Malacca in 1511, deepened after the formation of the EIC and the VOC, especially after the Dutch takeover of Malacca in 1641:

> In view of the importance of the textile trade, the Dutch and the English were determined to dominate it. By force of arms, intimidation of local rulers and economic pressure, like denial of shipping facilities, creating a glut in the market and resorting to drastic price cutting, they practically drove away Indian merchants from the trade. As the European traders themselves commented, the Indian merchants were superior in commercial shrewdness and knowledge of the local market, and wherever conditions were free they could outbid other competitors.[31]

The people of India and the Malay Archipelago did not give up easily. They kept their direct trade linkages going as long as feasible. After the English East India Company wrested political power from the Mughals in 1757, the combination of forces working against this direct trade and interaction became too strong to be opposed.

The early signs of this decline in the traditional direct trade were visible soon after the first quarter of the seventeenth century. Cloth cargos from Gujarat to Acheh declined to just three ships a year in the 1630s, 'and by the 1690s they had ceased coming at all'.[32] However, exports from the Coromandel Coast to Malacca, Acheh and other destinations in Southeast Asia continued to grow for another four decades, peaking in the 1670s before they started to decline. 'The Dutch estimated in 1675 that the whole Coromandel Coast had exports worth 10 to 12 million guilders, equivalent to 100-120 tonnes of silver. The majority of this was cloth, and its major destination had been Southeast Asia until Europe began to take over in the 1650s.'[33] Coromandel shipowners carried most of this cloth in their own vessels to Southeast Asia, persisting with a tradition that went back more than 1500 years. Ships belonging to the Sultans of Kedah, Acheh and other Malay states also called at ports along the Coromandel Coast, bringing their own goods, and buying textiles and cotton piece goods in exchange. This explains the continued closeness and empathy, cemented through intermarriage, between the peoples of the Coromandel Coast and the Malay Archipelago.

The combined textile exports (Gujarat, Coromandel and all other sources) from India to Southeast Asia probably peaked in the 1650s 'at a value of about 60 tonnes silver equivalent per year, roughly four times what it had been in 1510. This would represent almost two million pieces of cloth a year (the VOC alone brought a million pieces to Batavia in 1652, of which 314,000 for the Indonesian market), for a total Southeast Asian population of barely 25 million'.[34] Although Coromandel cloth exports to Southeast Asia kept growing for several more decades, by the 1680s this overall figure of VOC purchases of Indian piece goods for export to Southeast Asia had probably halved.

One significant reason for the collapse of India's textile exports to Southeast Asia was the impoverishment of the end-users, the people throughout the Malay Archipelago. Before the advent of the Europeans, Indian merchants traded through direct interaction with the growers or miners in the case of tin. There were sizeable communities of people from India who lived throughout the Malay Archipelago, intermarried and brought up families. They were familiar with conditions and products obtainable in the fertile and rich interiors of each region. They were perceived as friends and family, not as outsiders.

The principle source of wealth and purchasing power for the people of Southeast Asia was the income they derived from their direct participation in the spice and other trades. Throughout the sixteenth century and for most of the seventeenth century the tremendous boom in European demand for pepper, spices and other products translated into the correspondingly high demand for Indian textiles across the Malay Archipelago. It was the VOC's monopolistic trade policies, aimed at garnering profits and wealth for the Company by excluding the growers and suppliers, that led to a sharp reduction in the financial capabilities of large sections of the people throughout the Malay Archipelago.

The Dutch and British records from the 1630s onwards contain repeated complaints that the people of island Southeast Asia were so impoverished by the loss of their export trade that they could no longer buy Indian cloth as before. After two decades of Dutch blockades and interruptions of its pepper trade, the population of Banten 'formerly so opulent and prodigal in its daily clothing, now made a very impoverished and desolate impression', and had been obliged to weave its own cloth.[35]

In the 1670s and 1680s the VOC subdued Makassar in the Celebes, now the South Sulawesi province of modern Indonesia. As a result, the Bugis and the people of Makassar, who lost control over their hitherto lucrative spice trade, are reported to have 'resumed their former weaving because they could no longer afford to buy Indian cloth'.[36] In the 1690s, the people of Jambi (Sumatra) too, started weaving their own cloth or buying it from Java. By the end of the seventeenth-century Dutch officials reported 'the impossibility of preventing the Javanese from growing their own cotton and weaving their own cloth rather than buying from the Dutch'.[37] This resistance to buying from the Dutch was a combination of several factors. In part it was helplessness that resulted from impoverishment. It was also an expression of resistance to colonial exploitation. It was an expression of solidarity among the traditional trading partners of South and Southeast Asia, a vote of confidence in the friendship between the peoples of India and the Malay Archipelago, a friendship that pre-dated by millennia the arrival of the colonial powers. The artisans of South and Southeast Asia exchanged experiences and learnt from each other the skills and techniques of weaving. Today the woven *ikats* and other fabrics of Southeast Asia are renowned worldwide for their beauty and artistic elegance.

The declining exports of Indian textiles to the Malay Archipelago towards the end of the seventeenth century was matched by the rise of India's textile exports to England and Europe. Throughout the seventeenth century, the English lagged behind the Dutch in their participation in the spice trade and the export of Indian textiles to the Malay Archipelago. In the 1630s the English were sending substantial amounts of Indian textiles to Makassar (South Sulawesi) for exchange against spices, but after the 1660s, when the VOC established its control over this region, the English sent just one shipload of cloth each year from south India to Banten (Java), with an average value of 10,000 English pounds, or one tonne of silver.[38]

During this period, however, the English did open up a whole new market for Indian textile products by pioneering the sale of these goods in Europe. By the 1650s Indian textiles 'had replaced pepper as the premier item of England's Asian trade. Pepper formed less than 10 per cent of English homeward cargoes in the 1680s, and other Southeast Asian produce was scarcely significant.'[39] For the Dutch, too, by the end of the seventeenth century, pepper constituted only 11 per cent of the invoice value of homeward cargoes (as against 56 per cent around 1620), while Indian textiles imports into Europe by the Dutch now accounted for more than half of Dutch homeward cargoes.[40]

The VOC's mercantilist policies imposing monopolistic contracts on Sultans and rulers throughout the Malay Archipelago had severely curtailed the unrestricted free trade regimes that had hitherto prevailed between India and the Malay Archipelago. This had stirred up a fair degree of resentment by the end of the seventeenth century. Artificial quantitative controls placed by the Dutch on the farmers and growers impoverished them to such an extent that they could no longer afford to buy Indian textiles and other products. New and expanding markets in Europe for Indian textiles meant that before the end of the seventeenth century, Indian traders, too, had started looking to the west as the source of their income and prosperity.

The 'age of commerce' in the Malay Archipelago began winding down by the end of the seventeenth century. This marked the end of an era, the era of trade with India that stretched back in time to at least the early centuries of the first millennium CE. The seamless unity of the Indian Ocean trading system as it had evolved over this period now stood disrupted. Prior to the advent of the Europeans, the intra-Asian trade among the Indian Ocean littorals had been essentially a democratic and participatory process, with the benefits shared among all participants. The reasons for this were neither altruistic nor philanthropic. Each participant in the trading process realistically recognized the interdependent nature of this process. Success was assured only if all participants received due and fair returns: domination and/or subservience would only result in resistance which could disrupt the entire process. Even on occasions when differences of perception arose over trade policy, leading, for example to the eleventh century Chola 'raids', these were not aimed at perpetuating control or imposition of political will.

As against this, the Europeans, when they arrived on the scene in the sixteenth century, sought financial benefit for themselves and their people. This could only be extracted at the cost of one or the other erstwhile participants, thereby impoverishing them.

Another 'age of commerce' would revive in a new *avatar* some 200 years later. This time, too, the colonial powers would derive maximum benefit from the frenzied demand for tin, rubber and other products to meet the needs of the industrial revolution in the West.

Naval supremacy, more specifically, domination of the high seas or 'blue-water' supremacy, had been a key determinant in the changing fortunes of European powers in India and the rest of Asia. In the sixteenth century it was the Portuguese who had the command of the seas. The very existence of the Portuguese empire in Asia depended on this. They had a few naval bases, notably at Goa and Malacca. They maintained garrisons at these bases and at a few other places such as Amboina and Tidore in the East Indies. The Portuguese empire 'was merely a widely extended chain of trading centres to which the Portuguese compelled the trade of the East to resort . . . it could not possibly survive the loss of the command of the sea.'[41] Early in the seventeenth century the Portuguese received a major setback when their fleet of 26 ships lost a naval battle in 1606, off the coast of Malacca, where they were defeated by the Dutch fleet which had just eleven ships. After this the Dutch and the English successfully wrested away from the Portuguese most of their major territories in Persia, India and the Malay Archipelago, capped by the loss of Malacca to the Dutch in 1641.

The command of the seas passed from the Portuguese to the Dutch. This was a period of bitter rivalry, even hostility, between the Dutch and the English. As a result the English East India Company was unable to maintain its early acquisitions in the Malay Peninsula. The VOC, with the full support of the Netherlands government, 'began to turn their factories into fortresses and to build up a strong army and navy'.[42] The English East India

Company preferred to sacrifice its trade in the Malay Archipelago and focus on its trade with India rather than burden itself with extra costs on defence and armaments. 'This unwillingness to diminish dividends for the sake of security was characteristic of the (EIC) Directors' policy throughout the greater part of the (seventeenth) century.'[43] In 1622, for example, the Dutch had eighty three ships in the East, the English only twenty-eight.[44] After the Amboyna massacre of 1623 the EIC abandoned several of its factories in the Malay Archipelago. This region was no longer regarded as the principal area of the EIC's operations in the East, and attention was concentrated more and more on the trade with India.

In India, too, for most of the seventeenth century, the Dutch were 'much more powerful than the English. Their fortresses were more numerous and much wealthier and in 1649 they imposed terms on the Great Mogul himself. Without sea power he had to choose between submission and the destruction of his trade'.[45] Indeed, for a while it seemed that the Dutch would succeed in combining their supremacy in the Malay Archipelago and in India. The VOC was overtly hostile to the presence of the English in the Malay Archipelago, and had a strong role in ensuring that the English moved out of Bantam (Java) by 1683. However, the Dutch seemed to regard their trade in India as being comparatively less significant. As a result, the VOC did not attach as much importance to achieving full control, including monopolistic rights in the Indian market, and so did not take quite so hostile a position against the English in India. Soon after the British victory in the Battle of Plassey in 1757, when the Dutch finally comprehended the significance of the Indian trade and what the events of 1757 meant in terms of strengthening the position of the English in India, it was already too late for them to do anything about it.

NOTES

1. Anthony Reid, *An 'Age of Commerce' in Southeast Asian History*, p. 2.
2. Ibid., p. 17.
3. Ibid.
4. Ibid., pp. 18-19.
5. Ibid., p. 12.

6. Ibid., p. 14.
7. Om Prakash, 'The Indian Maritime Merchant, 1500-1800', *Journal of the Economic and Social History of the Orient*, vol. 47, no. 3 (2004), p. 453.
8. P.J. Marshall, 'Western Arms in Maritime Asia in the Early Phases of Expansion', *Modern Asian Studies*, vol. 14, no. 1 (1990), p. 19.
9. Ibid., pp 20-1.
10. Ibid., p. 22, quoting J. Ovington, *A Voyage to Suratt in the Year 1689* (London, 1696), p. 208).
11. Ibid., pp. 23-4.
12. Anthony Reid, op. cit., p. 14.
13. Ibid.
14. S.P. Sen, 'The Role of Indian Textiles in Southeast Asian Trade in the Seventeenth Century', *Journal of Southeast Asian History*, vol. 3, no. 2, September 1962, p. 92.
15. Ibid., p. 94.
16. Ibid., pp. 105-7, quoting Pieter van Dam '*Beschryvinge van de Oostindische Compagnie*', *Boek* II, *Deel* I, p. 262 (for the 1649 contract) and p. 290 (for the 1660 contract), and *Boek* II, *Deel* III, pp. 291-2 for the trading concession contract.
17. Ibid., p. 107, with figures taken from Pieter van Dam (ibid), *Boek* II, *Deel* I, p. 19.
18. Anthony Reid, op. cit., p. 22, quoting from James Lancaster, 1603, *The Voyage of Sir James Lancaster to Brazil and the East Indies, 1591-1603*, ed. Sir William Foster, London, Hakluyt Society, 1940.
19. Ibid., p. 22, quoting Pieter Verhoeff, 1611, *De Reis van de vloot van Pieter Willemsz Verhoff naar Azie 1607-1612*, ed. M.E. van Opstall, vol. I, The Hague, Nijhoff for Linschoten-Vereeniging, 1972.
20. S. Arasaratnam, 'Some Notes on the Dutch in Malacca and the Indo-Malayan Trade 1641-1670', *Journal of Southeast Asian History*, vol. 10, no. 3, special issue on International Trade and Politics in Southeast Asia 1500-1800 (December 1969), p. 484.
21. Andaya and Andaya, op. cit., p. 93.
22. W. Linehan 'A History of Pahang', *Journal of the Malayan Branch, Royal Asiatic Society*, vol. XIV, pt. II, 1936, p. 203.
23. S. Arasaratnam, op. cit., p. 481, quoting 'Schouten's Report of his visit to Malacca, 7 September 1641', *JMBRAS*, vol. 14, p. 60.
24. S. Arasaratnam, op. cit., p. 484.
25. Ibid., p. 486, quoting *Corpus Diplomaticum Neerlando-Indicum*, I, p. 520.
26. Ibid., p. 487, quoting ibid., I, pp. 521-2.
27. Ibid., p. 487.
28. Ibid., p. 487, quoting ibid., I, pp. 538-9.

29. Ibid., p. 488, quoting ibid., II, p. 152.
30. Ibid., p. 489, quoting 'Orders reproduced in Report of Governor Balthasar Bort on Malacca', 1678, *JMBRAS*, vol. V (1927), pp. 157ff.
31. S.P. Sen, op. cit., pp. 94-5.
32. Anthony Reid, op. cit., p. 22, quoting S. Arasaratnam, *Merchants, Companies and Commerce on the Coromandel Coast 1650-1740*, New Delhi: Oxford University Press, 1986, p. 126.
33. Ibid., p. 22, quoting S Arasaratnam, ibid., p. 96.
34. Ibid., p. 23, quoting Ruurdje Laarhoven 'Textile Trade out of Batavia during the VOC Period', paper presented to the 7th National Conference of the Asian Studies Association of Australia, 1988.
35. Anthony Reid, op. cit., pp. 23-4, including quote from M.A.P. Meilink-Roelofsz *Asian Trade and European Influence in the Indonesian Archipelago between 1500 and about 1630*, The Hague: Martinus Nijhoff, 1969, p. 258 (quoting Philip Lucasz, 1634)
36. Ibid., p. 24, quoting W.Ph. Coolhaas (ed), *Generale Missiven van Gouverneurs-Generaal en Raden aan heren XVII der VOC*, 7 vols, The Hague: Nijhoff, 1960-85.
37. Ibid., p. 24.
38. Ibid., p. 23
39. Ibid., p. 17, quoting K.N. Chaudhuri, *The Trading World of Asia and the English East India Company, 1660-1760*, Cambridge: Cambridge University Press, 1978, p. 529, and K.N. Chaudhuri, 'Foreign Trade', in *The Cambridge Economic History of India*, vol. I: *c.1200-c. 1750*, Cambridge: Cambridge University Press, 1982, pp. 382-407.
40. Ibid., p. 17, quoting Kristof Glamann, *Dutch-Asiatic Trade 1620-1740*, The Hague: Martinus Nijhoff, 2nd edn., 1981, pp. 14-15.
41. Lennox Mills, 'Brtish Malaya (Part I)', *JMBRAS*, vol. I, pt. II, 1925, p. 2.
42. Ibid., p. 5.
43. Ibid., p. 6.
44. Ibid., p. 5.
45. Ibid., p. 12.

8

The Eclipse of Direct Trade between India and the Malay Peninsula in the Eighteenth Century

The eighteenth century was a turbulent one, with far-reaching changes in India, the Malay Archipelago and throughout the world. In 1707, the Kingdom of Great Britain came into being through the political union of England and Scotland. In India, after the Battle of Plassey in 1757, the EIC wrested the political initiative in Bengal. This was followed-up with similar successes in other states, particularly in south India. In 1773, the British parliament granted regulatory control over the EIC to the British government, and established the post of Governor-General of India with Warren Hastings as the first incumbent. In 1776, with the decisive outcome of the American War of Independence, Britain lost her American colonies. The establishment of the British settlement in Penang in 1786 marked the first formal entry of Britain in the Malay Peninsula. In the mid-eighteenth century, the Seven Years War in Europe seriously exacerbated Anglo-French rivalry in Southeast Asia. Each of these events directly or indirectly influenced the interaction between India and the Malay Archipelago.

The British were now increasingly aware that even with a purely mercantilist doctrine 'commercial success necessarily depended upon political control or influence'.[1] The eighteenth century in Asia was an era of intense political rivalry among the Europeans, with the British, the French and the Dutch, not to mention the Portuguese and the Danes, all seeking influence for commercial gain. Naval strength, strategy and supremacy were key determinants in ensuring control in an area that stretched from the Cape of Good Hope in the west to Canton in the east. The tables turned in favour of the British primarily because, by the early years of the eighteenth century, the British Royal Navy was a strong institution, with purpose-built state-owned warships and a professional officer corps. Successfully executed naval strategy helped the British 'to forestall competitors from annexing strategically located islands and harbours along the trade routes to India and China (which) led in time to the acquisition of a network of island bases and naval stations around the littoral of the Indian Ocean'.[2]

INDIA'S SHIPBUILDING INDUSTRY IN THE EIGHTEENTH CENTURY

India, too, had continued to build upon her ancient skills and expertise in ship-building to develop maritime skills of formidable repute. In the seventeenth and eighteenth centuries the Maratha Empire, founded in 1674 in south-west India by Chatrapati Shivaji, made tremendous contributions to Indian shipping and maritime skills and enterprise. Colaba (in Mumbai) was the headquarters of the formidable naval fleet built-up under the leadership of Chatrapati Shivaji. In 1698 Kanhoji Angray took over the command of the Maratha navy with the title of *Dariya Saranga*. In November 1721 Angray successfully defeated the attack against the Maratha navy by the combined fleet of the Portuguese and the British, which included 600 soldiers and at least four men-of-war ships. For most of the eighteenth century, the Maratha naval fleet engaged, often with dramatic success, ships belonging to the Portuguese, the Dutch, the French and in particular, the English. It was only in 1818 that the British finally held sway over the Marathas.

At first, the Indian shipping industry continued its growth impetus under the British EIC. The English naval establishment in India was put on a permanent footing in 1615, first in Surat, and later as the Bombay Marine after it moved base. Indian shipbuilders were appointed as master-builders, including among them, scions of several well-known Parsi families. Many great ships were built at the Bombay dockyards. 'It boasts such a dry dock as is, perhaps, not to be seen in any part of Europe, either for size or convenient situation.'[3]

The teakwood ships built in Bombay were considered to be vastly superior to the oakwood vessels built in England on two crucial counts: durability and cost of construction. Lt. Colonel A. Walker, writing in 1811, assessed the difference as follows:

It is calculated that every ship in the navy of Great Britain is renewed every twelve years. It is well known that teak-wood built ships last fifty years and upwards. Many ships Bombay-built after running 14 or 15 years have been brought into the Navy and were considered as strong as ever. The *Sir Edward Hughes* performed, I believe, eight voyages as an Indiaman before she was purchased for the Navy. No Europe-built Indiaman is capable of going more than six voyages with safety.[4]

Lt. Colonel Walker notes that 'ships built at Bombay also are executed by one-fourth cheaper than in the docks of England, so that for the English-built ships requiring to be renewed every twelve years, the expense is quadruple'.[5]

The EIC also developed the Bengal Marine, headquartered in Calcutta (now Kolkata). The first ship built at the Calcutta dockyards was launched in 1781. The 'Register of Ships built on the Hugli from 1781-1839 (including Calcutta, Howrah, Sulkea, Cosipore, Tittaghar, Kidderpore and Fort Gloucester)' shows that the total number of ships built during this period was 376.[6] Between 1801 and 1821 (both years inclusive) the 237 ships built on the Hugli totalled 1,05,693 tons. This figure 'reckoned at an average cost of 200 rupees per ton, makes the enormous sum of two crores of rupees and upwards; a considerable part of which sum was absorbed in the payment of wages to native artificers and labourers, to the great benefit of the country'.[7]

There are two tributes to Indian shipbuilders and the ship building industry, from widely different sources, that are eminently worth quoting. The first, in 1800, was by Lord Wellesley, the then Governor General of India. While describing the potential of Calcutta as a shipping centre, he said:

The port of Calcutta contains about 10,000 tons of shipping, built in India, of a description calculated for the conveyance of cargoes. From the quantity of private tonnage now at command in the port of Calcutta, from the state of perfection which the art of shipbuilding has already attained in the state of Bengal (promising a still more rapid progress and supported by abundant and increasing supply of timbers), it is certain that this port will always be able to to furnish tonnage to whatever extent may be required for conveying to the Port of London the trade of the private British merchants of Bengal.[8]

The second tribute is by the Flemish artist, F. Balthazar Solvyns, who lived in Calcutta from 1791 to 1803. During this period he created a remarkable series of etchings portraying the life and culture of the people of Bengal. In the introduction to the third volume of his etchings, *Les Hindous*, he remarks:

In ancient times the Indians excelled in the art of constructing vessels, and the present Hindus can in this respect still offer models to Europe—so much so that the English, attentive to everything which relates to naval architecture, have borrowed from the Hindus many improvements which they have adapted with success to their own shipping. . . . The Indian vessels unite elegance and utility, and are models of patience and fine workmanship.[9]

The decade of the 1840s saw the Indian shipbuilding industry go into decline. Henceforth no large ships were built in India. In 1858, the year after the First War of Independence in 1857 (also known as the Sepoy Mutiny or the Great Rebellion), the rule of the British EIC was transferred to the Crown in the person of Queen Victoria, who was proclaimed Empress of India in 1876.

The policies now adopted by the British led to the emasculation of the Indian economy, bringing it to the point of vassalage of the colonial power. India moved from being among the world's largest exporters of manufactured goods to being a supplier of raw materials for British industry, and a market for consumption of the manufactured products produced therein. Every Indian industry that could pose an obstacle to British domination of India and of the regions to the east of India, were curbed to the point of elimination. India's thriving shipbuilding industry, the pride of India for two millennia and more, is among the most notable sectors to have suffered this fate. From the peaks of success attained by Indian shipbuilders in the first quarter of the nineteenth century, this industry went into a precipitate decline such that after 1840, no large ships were built in India till after India attained independence in 1947.

India's shipbuilding industry

was discouraged through arbitrary tariffs or restrictive legislative measures. The arrival in London of Indian-owned, Indian-captained and Indian-manned ships aroused much hostility on the part of the British shipping interests. They feared ruin through the competition of these eastern 'intruders'. The British government's response to pressures to safeguard and encourage British shipping was a resort to arbitrary legislation. On 25 July 1814 an Act (54. GeorgeIII, c.134) was passed by Parliament severely restricting Indian shipping and ships employing Indian sailors. The Act stipulated that ships entering English waters whose crews were not at least 75 per cent British were liable to forfeiture, while the captain in all cases had to be a white Briton. Finally, even the use of Indian-built ships was prohibited in the Indo-British trade from 1814 onwards, although this was evaded for many years afterwards. In India itself local shipping was also discouraged by discriminatory tariffs. In the Madras Presidency, for instance, the general import duty on goods bought in by Indian ships was raised to 15 per cent in 1872 compared with 7½ per cent in the case of British ships. Even other foreign ships were given preference over local ships. These measures dealt an effective blow to the Indian shipping industry and, combined with the technical progress of Western shipping, reduced it to insignificance by 1840, after which no large ships appear to have been built in India until comparatively recent times. A corollary to these changes was the fact that Indians ceased to play any major role in the external sea-borne trade of India. This role had already considerably declined in the days of the (British) East India Company's monopoly; the eclipse of Indian Ocean shipping simply served to effect the *coup de grace*.[10]

The decline of India's shipbuilding industry had a deleterious impact on the almost two millennia old interaction between South and Southeast Asia. It was the proverbial last straw. By the end of the seventeenth century the hitherto free trade exchanges among the Indian Ocean littorals had already been seriously disrupted. The shipping restrictions introduced first by the Portuguese early in the sixteenth century were avidly adhered to, even strengthened by the Dutch and the English. The reduced purchasing power among the people of the Malay Archipelago that resulted from the artificially imposed quantitative controls (over the spice-production process) brought in by the Dutch, destroyed the free market exchanges that had provided the platform for trade, cultural and religious interaction for close to 2,000 years.

The maritime merchants of the Coromandel Coast persisted with their trade and cultural exchanges with the Malay Archipelago as long as they could. They were the last to give up, when in addition to all other impediments, conditions of production had deteriorated significantly for the textile weaver in southern India. Ships were still being built, but were reserved exclusively for the use of the EIC. It became unviable and financially impossible for Indian merchants to support voyages to the Malay Archipelago.

India's mercantile fleet has traditionally had blue-water capacities. India's merchant ships could hold their own in terms of quality and durability of construction, tonnage and cargo facilities against the best ships of the day, built anywhere in Europe. However, this remained primarily a mercantile fleet, without the weaponry and other 'teeth' needed to engage in naval battles on the high seas. The Indian Ocean trading system as it evolved before the sixteenth century was much more cultural and interactive rather than bitterly fractious and competitive, constantly seeking one-upmanship. The nations participating in this network preferred to accommodate each other in the interests of collective prosperity, rather than strive for dominance at every turn. Battles for supremacy (particularly in India) were fought on land, and along the riverine and coastal areas, rarely on the high seas.

The Indian Ocean littoral nations and their mercantile fleets were constantly honing mechanisms to deal with the challenges posed by piracy, a perennial and serious problem in Asian waters. Here, too, efforts to tackle this problem focused on the pirate-infested waters along the coastlines and river estuaries rather than on the high seas. The naval capacities developed by India and other littorals along the Bay of Bengal and the Malay Archipelago were efficient and effective along the coastal and near-coastal areas. Right up to the late eighteenth and early nineteenth centuries, the European navies found their hold over these coastal areas under constant threat. India and many states of the Malay Archipelago had successfully built-up capacities for what is often described as 'brown-water navies'. The Maratha navy was an apt example of this. The Mughals, too, had a very large number of riverine and coastal vessels, but not enough naval attack vessels with adequate fire-power to engage in battles on the high seas.

These inadequacies became evident when India, and soon thereafter the states of the Malay Archipelago, were confronted with large

European naval ships as they came sailing into the Indian Ocean around the Cape of Good Hope beginning with the Portuguese in the early years of the sixteenth century. The large ships in the Portuguese fleet could be matched by size with those in the merchant fleets of several Indian states. However, the vessels in the Indian mercantile fleet were not armed sailing ships or men-of-war geared for naval battles. In the eighteenth and nineteenth centuries, when naval supremacy became the *sine qua non* for political and economic control in Asia, India and other Indian Ocean littoral nations lost out.

THE SEARCH (BY THE BRITISH) FOR AN EASTERN NAVAL BASE

The bitter Anglo-French global rivalry of the eighteenth century found its reflection in the events leading up to the establishment of the British base at Penang in 1786. In 1778, the war over the rebellion in North America became international, spreading to Europe and to European colonies in India and the Malay Archipelago. The Dutch joined the French in opposing the British. The security of British sea-lanes to India and China was severely impaired by the French occupation of the Cape of Good Hope and Trincomalee (in Ceylon), and by the Dutch control over the Straits of Malacca and the Sunda Straits.

Bombay was the only natural harbour with the British along this entire route. 'Between Calcutta and Canton, there was not a single British port except the isolated station of Bencoolen (west Sumatra).'[11] During the north-east (winter) monsoon in India, the British fleet in the Bay of Bengal and the Malay Archipelago was forced to take shelter in Bombay. Any damaged or disabled ships from the fleet had to go all the way to Bombay for repairs and refitting. This is when the Madras and the Bengal Presidencies became vulnerable to attack by the French (from their bases in Trincomalee and Mauritius) and by the Dutch (from their bases in the East Indies). This vulnerability adversely impacted the highly lucrative textile exports from these regions, as well as the equally profitable opium and tea trade that had developed with China. In the winter of 1782 the French Admiral Pierre-Andre de Suffren was successful in almost completely blockading Calcutta. Clearly, the centre of gravity of British power and interests in India had shifted from the west coast to the east coast of India.

Thus it was strategic-cum-mercantile considerations that hastened British efforts to establish a commercial entrepôt and naval base in the Bay of Bengal or in the Malay Archipelago, *en route* from India to China. '. . . Orders were given to search for a harbour in the Eastern Archipelago as early as 1763.'[12] The Court of Directors and the Calcutta Council of the EIC sent envoys and sought reports on the suitability and availability of several sites. The search began with the Indian side of the Bay of Bengal, where New Harbour in the Hughli River was considered 'too unhealthy' for a naval base. The Andaman and Nicobar Islands, too, were ruled out as being unsuitable. Acheh proved to be unattainable, as did the Rhio Island in the Straits of Malacca. No suitable site could be found in the Straits of Sunda or south of these Straits.

The search now focused on the northern areas of the Malay Peninsula. The Madras Council of the EIC had received the proposal sent to them by a Madras-based private British merchant company who had for some years been trading with Acheh and the Straits of Malacca. Francis Light was then the agent in charge of the Kedah factory of this company. The Kedah region was particularly well known to traders from the Coromandel Coast. In the 1770s Kedah was free from its earlier tributary status with Siam (Thailand), but was under attack from the Sultan of Selangor. 'The Sultan of Kedah was too weak to retaliate, and he therefore offered to Light the port and fortress of Kedah town if his employers would assist him.'[13]

Francis Light urged upon his employers that the offer of the Sultan of Kedah be accepted, particularly because if it were turned down the Sultan of Kedah would make the same offer to the Dutch. If the Dutch were to accept such an offer, they would be in a position to prevent any British vessels from passing through the Straits of Malacca. In 1771, Francis Light wrote to his employers about Penang, an island off the main coast of Kedah, as being the most suitable site for a British settlement since 'it possessed an excellent harbour, and facilities for refitting all ships bound for China; and it could also become a trading centre from which they would be supplied with tin, pepper, rattans, etc.'[14] The British, however, were extremely reluctant to involve themselves in internecine quarrels among the Malay Sultans. As a result the negotiations with the Sultan of Kedah were unsuccessful, and the offer lapsed.

The Dutch continued with their efforts to exclude the British from all trading activity in the Malay Peninsula. They held possession of almost all the strategic points on both sides of the Straits of Malacca with the exception of Acheh, Junk Ceylon and Kedah. Francis Light moved his trading activities to the island of Ujong Salang (earlier known as Junk Ceylon, presently as Phuket). In 1780 Light met Governor-General Warren Hastings in Calcutta with a message from the Governor of Ujong Salang offering the British a settlement there. Finally, in July 1786, the EIC decided to establish a factory at Penang (named the Prince of Wales Island) with Francis Light as its superintendent. Penang was just one week or ten days' sailing time from the Coromandel Coast.

This was a new intertwining in the age-old relationship between the people of India and the Malay Peninsula: for the next 90 years (after 1786) it was first the EIC and much later the British Indian government that was responsible for protecting British interests in Malaya. British strategic-cum-commercial interests in Penang were best expressed in the letter that the then Acting Governor-General of India wrote to Francis Light in January 1787, where he said that Penang was founded mainly

> to secure a port of refreshment and repair for the King's, the Company's and the Country's ships, and we must leave it to time and to your good management to establish it as a port of commerce. . . . We desire you will refrain from levying any kind of duties or tax on goods landed or vessels importing at Prince of Wales Island, and it is our wish to make the port free to all nations.[15]

The British had been absent from the Malay Peninsula for more than 150 years. The Company's initial presence through factories in Patani (in present-day south Thailand) and in Kedah had been withdrawn within the first few decades of the seventeenth century. After this, it was the English country trader who had maintained close social and economic linkages with the Malay Sultanates.

Francis Light was one such country trader. He had resigned his commission as a lieutenant in the British Navy in order to seek his fortune in India. He became the captain of a country ship, defined as a ship owned in India and engaged in trade and commerce across the Indian Ocean. Country trade was intra-Asian trade, conducted east of the Cape of Good Hope, as distinguished from the 'Europe' trade between Europe and the East via the Cape. The English EIC was involved in 'Company country trade'. In addition there were a large number of 'private' country traders, such as the Madras merchant firm of Jourdan, Sullivan and de Souza, who had first received the suggestions about Kedah and Penang from their agent in Kedah, Francis Light.

'The links between the English East India Company and the British private country traders were especially close. During the eighteenth century British private country traders outnumbered all others from Europe, and by the end of that period their activities had become professionally organized and financed.'[16] Writing to his minister in May 1787, the French Admiral d'Entrecasteaux (commander of the Indian station of the French Navy) conveyed his amazement at the ubiquity of British country traders when he said 'the more one sails in these seas, Monseigneur, the more one is astonished by the enormous power of the English in these vast and fertile countries'.[17]

In essence, the English country trader aimed at supplanting and substituting himself for the Indian trader who was so closely acquainted with every aspect of trade, religion and culture throughout the Malay Achipelago. Over the course of the eighteenth century, the Company and the private country traders substantially and substantively took over the role of the Indian merchant who had been plying this route for at least 2000 years.

This was particularly true of the Malay Peninsula:

> At a time when official English interest in the Malay world was minimal, these men (country traders) had formed close associations with Malay courts. They sometimes acted as advisers on political and military matters and were often on intimate terms with the ruler. Speaking fluent Malay . . . the influence of such traders was considerable. Although Malays still viewed the Netherlands as the most powerful European state, they were becoming conscious of England's mounting prestige.[18]

The English country trader, on his part, was constantly on the lookout for regular supplies of tin, a product much in demand in Europe at the time. The Dutch emphasis was on 'persuading' the Malay Sultans to pledge all tin supplies to the Dutch. The English country trader's interest was in reaching out to those Sultans who had resisted such pledges, and were able to assure him (the country trader) regular supplies of tin. In this way the English country trader was able to maintain the interests of the English EIC without provoking any direct confrontation between the English and the Dutch.

There were several reasons for the English country trader's success in inveigling himself into favour with Malay Sultans at the expense of the similar longstanding access hitherto enjoyed by Indian merchants, and after 1641, by the Dutch. Most of these related to the dominating position in trade and commerce that the English had attained throughout the Malay Archipelago by the end of the eighteenth century.

WRESTING CONTROL OF THE TEXTILE TRADE IN INDIA

For the English, their most significant commercial success in India was the increasing degree of control they were able to impose in the course of the eighteenth century on the textile weaving and trading sectors. This enabled the British to squeeze out and almost eliminate the Indian trader from the all-important supply of textile piece goods to the Malay Archipelago. The initial incentive for establishing such control arose as a result of the burgeoning demand for Indian textiles in England, in addition to the traditional market for these goods throughout the Malay Archipelago and in Africa. The Coromandel Coast was one of the main areas for procurement of these goods.[19]

During the seventeenth and eighteenth centuries, expanding trade opportunities, particularly in textiles, led the English to substantially enhance their presence along the Coromandel Coast, with the establishment of Fort St. George (in present-day Chennai) in 1639, and Fort St. David (at Cuddalore, 160 km south of Chennai) in 1690, together with residencies at important ports like Vishakhapatnam. The principal exports all along the Coromandel Coast were cotton goods, that were woven, dyed and printed in innumerable hinterland villages across the length and breadth of the area that falls in the modern states of Andhra Pradesh and Tamil Nadu.

The English demand for textile piece goods closely followed the pattern set by the Indian merchants who had preceded them in this trade: quantitatively very large orders, with very precise specifications in terms of measurement, weave and print for each market, combined with specific delivery and shipping schedules. EIC officials sought the help of Indian textile merchants, who for centuries had been successfully performing the onerous task of coordinating and organizing such requirements. The Company imported large amounts of bullion and specie into India for making advance payments to these merchants (and ultimately to the weaver). This created a flourishing mint market in Madras (now Chennai). A significant number of Madras merchants drawn into the Company's textile trade belonged to the Hindu Chetty community. The Chulias or Tamil Muslim merchants of south Coromandel stayed away from such involvement. Their trade with the Malay Peninsula and other parts of Southeast Asia carried on uninterrupted till the end of the eighteenth century, conducted through the smaller ports that were still independent of the English. In the 1780s, when many Indian merchants and weavers suffered because of the Company's changed policies, the uninterrupted trading activity of the Chulias ensured the prosperity of large numbers of weavers and trading communities who were associated with them, like the Coimbatore Chetties.

The early years of the Company's textile trade out of India coincided with increasing monopolistic controls enforced by the VOC in large areas of the Malay Archipelago. Indian textile merchants were denied access to their traditional markets in Sumatra, Java, Malacca and other parts of the Malay Peninsula. As a means of overcoming these restrictions, Indian overseas trading activities were increasingly conducted in partnership with the English, on Company ships to avoid Dutch attacks. Over time this reduced the role of Indian shipping in the trade with the Malay Archipelago, and allowed British shipping to dominate. British owned Indian shipyards built some of the largest ships of the day, but the Indian owned shipbuilding industry suffered. In the second half of the nineteenth century, British owned Indian shipyards, too, stopped constructing East Indiamen.

The initial decades of the Company's textile trade were ones of great prosperity for the Indian textile merchants who chose to partner the English. They were given the coveted status of 'Company Merchants', which conferred special perquisites and fiscal privileges, including secure transfer of money through the facility of drawing Bills of Exchange from one settlement to another. At the same time these merchants (and the weavers) were not bound to deal exclusively with the English. 'Up to the 1670s, the wealthy and influential coast merchants strove for dominance both in the hinterland states as well as in the European enclaves.'[20] These merchants worked on the basis of substantial advances of up to 50 per cent of the total value of orders. They also lent money to English private traders and to a large number of Company officials who conducted their own private trade. Often the Indian merchants were partners in the trading ventures undertaken both by English private traders and by Company officials.[21]

The Indian textile merchant became an important intermediary between Company officials and English private traders on the one hand, and local society on the other. There were other intermediaries who worked directly with Company officials as their private staff. There was the *dubash*, who organized the payment of commission from merchants when contracts were sealed, and kept private accounts for his boss. At lower levels there was the *gumastah* and the *kanakapillai*, employed by the Company as well as by English and Indian merchants, who worked in warehouses, customs posts, the mint and in clerical positions on the staff of senior officers.

This system, essentially based on the principles of free trade and the rules of the marketplace, underwent a sea change after 1757 'during the transition from trade without political power to trade with political power'.[22] The Anglo-French Wars (the 1749-54 War is known in India as the Second Carnatic War), with naval battles raging up and down the Coromandel Coast, completely disrupted trading patterns and schedules between India and the Malay Archipelago. 'For many successive years . . . trade was at a standstill. When the English had reasserted their supremacy, there was a desperate shortage of cash to place orders.'[23] The crippling expenses incurred on these Wars meant that the earlier liberal imports of British bullion into India became, for some years, a thing of the past. This had a disastrous impact on the production side of the textile trade since the southern (Carnatic) states were known to have 'a notoriously gold-consuming economy. . . . There was a chain of extended credit down to the weaving village, mainly kept going by the money put in by European companies'.[24] With neither cash-flow nor the continuous stream of fresh orders, the large merchant trader at the top of the chain and the weaver at the lowest rung both found themselves facing arrears and heavy, unrepayable debts.

The situation was further compounded by the growing demand, throughout the eighteenth century, for bullion to finance Britain's burgeoning trade with China, now centred around the purchase of tea. Tea was an increasingly popular social beverage in Europe, with a seemingly insatiable demand. Company officials in India and English private traders attached the highest priority to the China trade with regard to allocation of funds and shipping. They remitted the profits of their Indian and intra-Asian trading operations through China (for purchase of tea) to Europe. From the 1760s there was a brisk export of Madras Pagodas[25] to China. The export of Pagodas by the Company was legal. English private traders exported Pagodas as cargo both to China and to London, in breach of existing regulations. This fairly substantial drain of bullion from India seriously aggravated the availability of liquidity for investments in the weaving and manufacture of textile piece goods.

The Peace of Paris concluded in 1763 signalled the end of the Anglo-French wars. The Company now sought to rehabilitate the textile trade in the Carnatic region. The manner in which they went about this indicated the fundamental change that had taken place in British-Indian equations and relationship. The Company now tried to eliminate altogether the intermediary role of the Indian merchant trader. First in Cuddalore, and then in Madras, the Company acquired weaving villages as *jagir* villages, to be kept exclusively for the Company's textile trade. In these villages, weavers' looms that were used to serve any other trade would now be taxed. These new practices were similar to the Calcutta model of investment adopted in 1753. The Madras Council of the Company decided in May 1771 to 'take the investment into our hands by standing ourselves in place of merchants and employing agents or *gumastahs* to make advances to weavers and superintend looms'.[26]

In effect the Company brought in their own officers and Indian officials, who had no prior knowledge or experience of the textile trade, as substitutes for the entire gamut of merchants, their agents, brokers (*nattavars*), and head weavers at the village level who had been in this trade for generations and centuries. Perhaps predictably, major problems arose, in no small measure due to resistance and opposition from the large cross-section of the village and urban population that had hitherto been actively involved in one or the other aspects of this trade. The weavers themselves were greatly impoverished by the Company's monopolistic restrictions preventing them from working for the Dutch, the French or any other employer. The Company's decision to give out weavers' advances partly in yarn (to be used for the weaving) instead of wholly in cash enormously increased their (the weavers') debt burden. As a result the weavers ran up to huge arrears with the Company. 'Disaffection spread, the weavers refused to work, deserted their villages and dispersed to neighbouring districts and some to Dutch and French enclaves, refusing to return. . . .'[27]

By 1784 the Company's financial problems were so serious that they could no longer continue the practice (started in 1771) of employing weavers directly. The Company then 'decided to go back to the contract method in many areas and publicly advertised for tenders for the supply of piece-goods'.[28] The erstwhile Indian merchant-middleman who had been thrown into debt and disarray by the sudden change in Company policy in 1771, was now in no position to compete seriously for these tenders. The conditions of these tenders were such, with cash advances reduced to a minimum, two-thirds of the advance payment to be made in copper, and the final payment to be accepted in Bills of Exchange drawn on London, as to be financially ruinous and therefore unacceptable to most Indian merchants. It was the British private trader and a few European merchants who benefited enormously by securing this business. They displaced the Indian merchant, who finally lost control of the trade he had conducted for generations. The condition of the Indian weaver did not improve either. The British private trader went to the weaving villages and placed orders with the weavers. However, he 'was able to use the *Zamindars*' (landholders') coercive power as a sanction against the weavers'.[29]

Sinappah Arasaratnam has explained this succinctly when he says:

> In the long history of commerce on the southern Indian coast, there have been periods of fundamental change in the flow of this external commerce to which internally basic social and economic adjustments have been made. The decline of Roman and Western trade, the rise of Southeast Asian trade, the growth and decline of the big mercantile corporations, the Chola/Srivijaya conflict, the Arab thrust and the Islamization of some trading communities, were various phases and incidents in that continuing process. The impact of the events of the second half of the eighteenth century far outweighed any of these in their intensity and in the disruptive nature of their consequences'.[30]

The Company

> (does) not want any more the intervention of Indian merchants with whom they are in active and unequal competition. They require subordinate bureaucratic functionaries relating to trade and agriculture. . . . The era of Company trade fostered the Indian merchant. The era of Company raj was to foster the *gumastah*.[31]

The Company's success in wresting control over the cloth-producing process away from the Indian merchant allowed the English country trader direct access to the piece-goods trade. This gave the English country trader, with his now assured and steady supplies of Indian textiles, much more preference in the courts of the Malay Sultans. This success was achieved at the expense of the Indian merchant, who could no longer guarantee assured supplies of textiles.

THE OPIUM TRADE AND THE ARMS TRADE

During the eighteenth century, two additional aspects of India's trade with the Malay Archipelago decisively militated against the continuation of the Indian merchant in the pole position that he had hitherto enjoyed. These two issues, which also served to considerably strengthen the position of the British EIC in the Malay

Archipelago *vis-à-vis* the Dutch VOC, were the Company's policies regarding export of opium, and their involvement in the arms trade in the Malay Archipelago.

The Dutch began importing opium from India to the Malay Archipelago in the seventeenth century, soon after they took over Malacca. These imports increased rapidly as the local population grew addicted to smoking tobacco mixed with opium.

> A hundred years later their consumption had reached such heights that the Governor of Malacca could tell his superiors that 'the people of Rembau, Selangor and Perak, like other natives, cannot live without opium', while Chinese accounts show that east coast Malays were equally addicted.[32]

The sale of opium became an important attraction at the British entrepôts in the Malay Peninsula, which encouraged visits by local merchants. So much so that 'in 1786 Francis Light was to recommend the import of large quantities of the drug to Penang specifically to attract merchants'.[33]

For the British EIC, China was the principal target country for sale of opium, a spectacularly lucrative trade that saw exponential growth after British victory in the Battle of Plassey in 1757. One hundred years later, in 1858-9, the profits earned by the Company's Opium Agency constituted as much as 17 per cent of government revenues. In 1913 the British government announced the end of the opium trade to China. British opium trade in India went through four phases. The first phase, after 1757, saw private participation by Company officials, whose control of the market grew with the Company's domination over India. The second phase began after 1765 with the formal declaration of a monopoly controlled privately by these officials. In the third phase, from 1773, this monopoly was run by and on behalf of the Company, using the Contract System. And in the fourth phase, from 1797 onwards, the Company set up its own monopoly through the Opium Agency.[34]

The Opium Agency's monopoly for procurement of opium was centred in Patna (Bihar) and Benares (present-day Varanasi in Uttar Pradesh). Private cultivation of poppy and sale of opium were banned. There were reports that peasants were forced to grow poppy, especially when the Opium Agency was trying to quickly increase output. Reports prepared respectively in 1820 and in 1832 point out that 'the peasants hardly got anything from poppy, almost the whole amount having been misappropriated by *zillahdars* (intermediaries)' and that 'two principle circumstances form the chief obstacles to an extensive poppy cultivation . . . viz., the inadequate price the cultivators receive for their opium and the oppression to which they are subjected from the *gumastahs* (employed agents)'.[35]

There is a fair degree of similarity between the monopolistic systems of contracting used by the Company in India for procuring exportable goods in the textile and opium sectors. The weaver and the opium grower were impoverished and oppressed. The Indian merchant was eventually (in the case of textiles) and right from the start (in the case of opium) completely excluded from participation in the export trade. In the case of opium there is, in addition, the strong opprobrium of the Company's close association with the evils inflicted by opium consumption on the people in China, the Malay Archipelago and in India. In the words of the then Archbishop of Canterbury

> the true principle of morals is to have nothing whatever to do with that which is shown to be necessarily productive of evil. The English nation caused the opium evil in China, and we are responsible for that evil. I also protest against the principle of raising revenue by temptations to evil. It might be right for a government to pause before interfering with private trade; but in this case we ourselves are carrying on the evil trade. Such a thing on the part of a great government is, I think, without a parallel in the whole extent of the world.[36]

In the seventeenth century the VOC had strictly forbidden sale of arms within the Malay Archipelago. In the eighteenth century the English and the French had few compunctions about allowing such sales. British country traders not only sold armaments, they 'were also willing to trade their knowledge of the manufacture of gunpowder and cannon'.[37] It is said that when a French crew went ashore to trade in Terengganu in 1763, they took with them 'two cases of muskets, two cases of opium, and some knives'.[38]

By the end of the eighteenth century the Coromandel merchant had been ousted from the Indian textile trade by the British private trader backed by the political might of the Company. For almost 2,000 years the Coromandel merchant had been the mainstay of trade, religious and cultural contacts between India and the Malay Archipelago. His exit from the Indian textile trade brought an end to this era of mutually beneficial trade, economic and people-to-people interaction. During the ensuing colonial era it seems that even the memories of such interaction either faded away or were obliterated. So much so that the interaction between India and the Malay Archipelago during the colonial era is often looked upon as a new process, with little or no reference to the antiquity and rich history of the past. Contemporary history books (writing about this ancient period) do not adequately reflect the reality and strength of the pre-colonial interaction between South and Southeast Asia. This needs rectification.

Appreciating the intensity and essential egalitaranism of the interaction between India and the Malay Archipelago before the arrival of the European colonialists is crucial for overcoming prejudices and misperceptions that have crept into contemporary relationships between and within nations across this region. We tend to overlook the fact that, in South and Southeast Asia, all of us, to a greater or lesser degree, are direct descendants of the pre-colonial traders, entrepreneurs, religious leaders or ordinary seamen, who thronged each other's shores and thrived on the all-round prosperity that resulted from such exchanges.

NOTES

1. B.E. Kennedy 'Anglo-French Rivalry in Southeast Asia 1763-93: Some Repercussions', *Journal of Southeast Asian Studies*, vol. 4, no. 2 (September 1973), p. 199.
2. Ibid., p. 199.
3. Radha Kumud Mookerji, *Indian Shipping*, p. 179, quoting Sir Cyprian Bridge on 'India and the Navy' in the *London Spectator* of 9 April 1910.
4. Ibid., p. 180 quoting Lt. Colonel A. Walker, 'Considerations on the Affairs of India' written in 1811, *Records of the Bombay Government* (1856).
5. Ibid., p. 180.
6. Ibid., p. 182.
7. Ibid., p. 181, quoting John Phipps, 'Papers Relative to Shipping in India', Scott, Calcutta, 1840.

8. Ibid., p. 182.
9. Ibid., p. 183. The author found this rare work in the splendid library of the renowned Bengali artist, Abanindranath Tagore.
10. K.S. Sandhu, *Indians in Malaya*, p. 33.
11. Lennox Mills, 'British Malaya Part I', *JMBRAS* vol. I, pt. II, 1925, p. 22.
12. Ibid., p. 21.
13. Ibid., p. 24.
14. Ibid., p. 25.
15. Ibid., p. 27.
16. Andaya and Andaya, op. cit., p. 313, fn. 16.
17. B.E. Kennedy, op. cit., p. 207, letter quoted from *Francaises Nouvelles Acquisitions*, vol. 9373, p. 87.
18. Andaya and Andaya, op. cit., p. 100.
19. S. Arasaratnam, 'Trade and Political Dominion in South India, 1750-1790: Changing British-Indian Relationships', *Modern Asian Studies*, vol. 13, no. 1 (1979), pp. 19-40, provides an excellent case study of this process of establishing control.
20. Ibid., p. 21.
21. Ibid., p. 22, quoting the detailed accounts of a prominent Indian merchant (Cashia Chittee Andeapa) who lived in the first three decades of eighteenth century. These have survived among the private papers of Governor Benyon (1735-44).
22. Ibid., p. 27.
23. Ibid.
24. Ibid.
25. Pagoda was a unit of currency, a coin made of gold or half gold minted by Indian dynasties as well as by the British, the French and the Dutch. The British EIC had issued in Madras a coin described as the Star Pagoda, worth approximately 8 shillings.
26. Arasaratnam, op. cit., p. 30.
27. Ibid., p. 34.
28. Ibid., p. 38, and fn. 52.
29. Ibid., p. 38, with fn. 54.
30. Ibid., p. 40.
31. Ibid.
32. Andaya and Andaya, op. cit., p. 100.
33. Ibid.
34. Rachel E. Kranton and Anand V. Swamy, 'Contracts, Hold-Up, and Exports: Textiles and Opium in Colonial India', published in December 2006, accessed on 12 July 2010 at http://www.williams.edu/Economics/wp/swamytextileopiumdecember2006final.pdf, pp. 20-1, with fn. 46.

35. Ibid., p. 21.
36. J.P. Jones, 'British Rule in India: II', *The North American Review*, vol. 168, no. 509 (April 1899), p. 467.
37. Andaya and Andaya, op. cit., p. 101.
38. Ibid.

9

The Nineteenth Century: Division of the Malay World and Consolidation of British Colonial Rule

In the nineteenth century British commercial interests, combined with the consolidation of her political control as the predominant colonial power in India and the Malay Peninsula, succeeded in excluding the Indian merchant from prominent participation in his traditional sphere of mercantile activity in Southeast Asia. After close to two millennia of uninhibited mingling and mutually beneficial trade and people to people interaction, the colonial period brought in much more segmented and controlled exchanges between the people of India and the Malay Peninsula. Indentured labour and convicts, overseers and foremen, railway workers and members of the police force: these are the categories that served the interests of the colonial power.

The growing commercial and political strength of the British presence in both South and Southeast Asia shut most large Indian merchant traders out of their hitherto dynamic and lucrative linkages with the Malay Archipelago. In the nineteenth and twentieth centuries, there was continued brisk interaction between India and the Malay Peninsula, but the nature and pattern of such interaction was quite different from the mutually beneficial free-trade mould of the pre-colonial era. The context and subtext were totally different. This time around the colonial power, Great Britain, was the controlling and deciding authority both in India and in the Malay Peninsula. It was Great Britain's perceived needs and primarily commercial considerations that drove the interaction between India and Malaya. Smaller traders and builders, artisans and *munshis*, indentured labour and convict labour arrived from different corners of India in large numbers. They made an invaluable contribution to the economic growth and prosperity of Malaya.

MUNSHI ABDULLAH AND THE PERANAKAN KLING

The memories of earlier pre-colonial interaction remain embedded in the DNA of the people of India and the Malay Peninsula. The life and ancestry of Munshi Abdullah, described by R.O. Winstedt as 'the greatest innovator in Malay letters',[1] aptly illustrates this. In the words of R.O. Winstedt:

> Abdullah bin Abdul Kadir came of stock and surroundings that had for centuries produced Malay writers. His great-grandfather was an Arab from Yemen, a teacher of Arabic and religion, who migrated to Nagore (Nagapattinam district in Tamil Nadu, India) and married a Tamil woman. Of their sons, one settled in Amboina, two in Java, and the fourth, Abdullah's grandfather, went to Malacca and married a lady of his own mixed blood, who was head teacher in its Tamil settlement, Kampong Pali, where two hundred children, boys and girls, studied the Koran, and, if they wished, learnt to read and write Malay. The sons of the marriage grew up linguists, conversant with Malay, Tamil and some Arabic. One of them, Abdul Kadir, the father of Abdullah, combined trading and teaching, taught Malay to William Marsden the lexicographer. . . . After that, he got a job with the Dutch harbour-master at Malacca and in 1785 married a Malacca-born Muslim, grand-daughter of a Hindu from Kedah.[2]

There is nothing unusual about Munshi Abdullah's family tree. There were scores of thousands like him, living across the Malay Archipelago as well as in India: in Gujarat and all along the Coromandel and Malabar Coasts. They were and are symbols of the traditional interactive relationship between the people of India and Malaysia where, over the centuries, friendships and business dealings had evolved, through intermarriage, into close family ties.

Born in 1796, Munshi Abdullah's life-experiences were in themselves illustrative and typical of the composite society that has traditionally been characteristic throughout the Malay Peninsula:

> Having mastered the Koran and Arabic . . . Abdullah devoted two and a half years to learning Tamil, then three or four years to studying Hindustani with sepoys in the British forces in Malacca, and finally some years to

> acquiring Malay. At that time there were only a few men in the port expert at writing Malay, four of them of foreign extraction and four Malays, while of the younger generation the only student of the language was Abdullah. . . . (H)e assisted his father in his business of writing letters and contracts. In 1811 Raffles, afterwards founder of Singapore, came to Malacca . . . in addition to a Malay clerk of Tamil blood, whom he had brought from Penang, he employed Abdullah . . . to write letters to native rulers, copy and collect Malay manuscripts and write articles on Malay idioms and poetry. . . . A Protestant clergyman, Mr Milne, came to Malacca, and Abdullah became *munshi* to him and other missionaries, learning from them English and from their Chinese teacher some Cantonese. . . . In 1835 in collaboration with a Tamil friend he translated the *Panchatanderan* or Tamil version of the *Panchatantra* into Malay under the title of *Hikayat Galilah dan Daminah*. His autobiography (*Hikayat Abdullah)*, the best record of Malayan events of his period, was finished in 1843 and lithographed in 1849. . . . Abdullah is the greatest master of an easy colloquial Malay who has ever lived, taking as his model the conversational passages in the *Sejarah Melayu*, which he edited.[3]

Abdullah Munshi belonged to the large community of Jawi Peranakan or Jawi Pekan families, the result of intermarriage between Malays and Indian Muslims living in the Straits Settlement areas of Penang, Malacca and Singapore. *Jawi* is the Arabic word for the Malay Archipelago and *peranakan* is a Malay word meaning 'born of'. *Pekan* is the Malay word for 'town'. Jawi Peranakan was the term popularly used in Singapore, Jawi Pekan in Penang. In Malacca Peranakan Kling (born of Indians) was the term for this community popularized by Abdullah Munshi himself.[4]

This does show that, at least till the end of the nineteenth century, the term *kling* was not used in any perjorative sense for members of the Indian community. The Malay word *kling* is recognized as a derivative from Kalinga, the region comprising the modern state of Odisha in eastern India. In ancient times the port on the Kalinga coast near present-day Gopalpur-on-Sea was the *apheterion* or point of departure for ships sailing to the Malay Archipelago. So all those arriving on these ships were given the generic name *kling*, meaning from Kalinga. Similarly, many centuries later, all those arriving in the Malay Peninsula on ships sailing from ports in Bengal were known as Bengalis, even though most of them were from other north Indian states, including the Punjab, rather than just from Bengal.

The emperor of China is said to have referred to Rajendra Chola as *Raja Kling*. The *Sejarah Melayu* uses the term *kling* as a generic reference to India rather than just to Kalinga or south India, when it describes Hang Nadim's visit to *Benua Kling*. The *Hikayat Hang Tuah* also has a chapter describing Hang Tuah's visit to *Benua Kling*. The Dutch 'Dagregister' referred to Malacca's Indian inhabitants as *Clings* or *Klingers*. British writers during the colonial period use the term *kling* as a generic reference for people from India, following the pattern of usage of the Dutch and Portuguese colonialists in the Malay Archipelago. Nicholas Belfield Denny in 'A Descriptive Dictionary of British Malaya' (1894) defined *kling* as 'a general term for all the people of Hindustan, and for the country itself'. Scareboeus is quoted in the 16 September 1887 issue of *The Penang Gazette* as stating that 'the word *kling* is a most interesting one and points to a connection between the Straits and India reaching nearly as far back as the time of Alexander the Great, the only trace of which remains in its continued application to the natives of southern India'.[5]

Intermarriage between Indians and Malays has been an intrinsic, natural and fully integrated part of the social structure throughout the Malay Archipelago from the early years of the first millennium CE. In the pre-colonial period such marriages between Indian Muslims and members of the nobility and royalty had taken place in several Malay Sultanates, including Johor and Kedah. Going further back in time to the pre-Islamic period, legends about kingdoms and dynasties throughout the Malay Archipelago are replete with instances where the foundational event was the royal marriage between an Indian and a Malay. During the Hindu Buddhist heritage period in the Malay Archipelago, from Borneo to Java to the Malay Peninsula, such Indo-Malay ruling families were unquestioningly accepted. When Islam came to this region, it spread peacefully through the conversion of these ruling families to the new religion. The ruling families and dynasties remained the same, as happened with the descendants of Raja Paramesvara in Malacca. Only their religion changed.

The process of intermarriage continued during and after the period of the Malacca Sultanate. The royal families of Kedah, Johor,

Perak and other regions of the Malay Peninsula adopted Islam, but continued with their earlier social rituals, including coronation practices. Trade, religion and culture retained their centrality as the driving forces of the continuing interaction between India and the Malay Archipelago. Indian Muslim traders and Sufi *pirs* were important figures at the courts of the Malay Sultans. By most accounts, towards the end of the eighteenth century when the British were moving in to Penang, 'there were still some Indians remaining in positions of considerable influence in the Malay courts as the Sultans' merchants, general advisers and financiers'.[6] Their presence was substantial enough for Francis Light to regard it as a 'serious obstacle' to the expansion of British trade and commerce in this region, especially because, in his assessment, 'the Chulias . . . seem resolved if possible to exclude the English from any connection in the places where they trade. . . .'[7]

The British, it would seem, saw their commercial and political success in the Malay Archipelago as intrinsically linked to the alienation of the traditional Indian presence and influence at Malay courts. This became possible when British domination of the sea-lanes east of India and the precipitate decline of India's shipbuilding industry by the middle of the nineteenth century gave the English the all-important control they sought over India's trade with the Malay Archipelago. This enabled the British to subjugate the Indian influence at Malay courts, and replace it with their own. 'The subservience of the Malay courts (to the British) meant that the Indians lost a significant avenue of investment, income and prestige.'[8] What is worse, according to scholars who have studied the British Colonial Office's Straits Settlements original correspondence '. . . steps were taken (by the British) to prevent any return to these positions (by the Indians) in the future.'[9]

Despite this, Indians continued to arrive in Penang and parts of the Straits Settlements after 1786. Indian Muslims from the Coromandel and Malabar Coasts were the largest group among the arriving Indians. Many of them married Malay women, thereby creating the Jawi Peranakan or the Straits Malays. The colonialists often described this group by the perjorative term of 'half-breeds'.[10] This may well be the reason why, during the colonial period, the term *kling* acquired a pejorative connotation. A much truer and more accurate description comes from Professor Ghulam-Sarwar Yousof when he says:

> One of the greatest manifestations of the fusion of the culture of the Indian peninsula and local Malays, has been the birth of the *Jawi Peranakan* community—a community of mixed Tamil (or Malayalee) Muslims and Malays—that has played an important role in Malaysia's economic, social and political life. In this case it was not a mere borrowing, but a total fusion between the heritage of Tamil and Malayalee Muslims and that of the indigenous Malays.[11]

Malay culture has traditionally been diverse and encompassing, rather than exclusive. It has absorbed and integrated all the influences that, over the millennia, have combined to create this composite culture. From the Orang Asli to the Straits Malays, the Jawi Peranakan and the Jawi Pekan, to the Kelantanese and the Minangkabau, each strand has its own unique heritage that is today subsumed within Malay culture. *Boria* theatre from India used to be performed when *Awal Muharram* was observed. The popular Malay folk dance, the *joget* was performed at cultural festivals and weddings. Interestingly, the *joget* has Portuguese roots, and uses the Western violin, the Arab *rebana*, Southeast Asian gongs and Kelantanese singing style. The *zapin* dance, popular in Johor and brought there by Arab missionaries, is traditionally accompanied by Islamic devotional chanting, and is meant to spread knowledge about the history of Islamic civilization. The *Malay Mak Yong* from the Patani region of Southern Thailand, the entrancing *silat* martial art tradition, and the beautiful *Kuda Kepang* dance brought to Johor by Javanese immigrants, dramatising tales about victorious Islamic holy wars: each reflects different facets of the composite culture of all the Malays, not just those in the urban areas or the former Straits Settlements.

Unfortunately, many of these traditions are no longer part of the daily lives and celebrations of the Malays. As a result, the separate identities of the different ethnic groups that brought these traditions into the fold of the Malays have also blurred, even disappeared. The scholar Abdur-Razzaq Lubis, himself of Mandailing descent (north-west Sumatra), has attributed this to efforts to localize the history of Malaysia, which have resulted in the narrow interpretation of an exclusive 'Malay identity'. He feels that by 'reducing the rich human diversity of the Peninsula into three races—Malays, Chinese and Indians—many historical ethnic cultures were lost'.[12]

During the colonial period in Malaya, the hitherto free and easy intermingling among all ethnic and religious communities became much more straitjacketed. As a result, a greatly heightened consciousness about race and religion emerged all across the nation. Possible reasons for such trends and tendencies will be analysed in subsequent chapters. Before doing so, let us see how the interaction between India and Malaya evolved during the nineteenth century, together with related developments in the Malay Peninsula, as the process of European colonization gathered strength and momentum.

PENANG AND INDIA: CHANGED BUT CONTINUING INTERACTION

The 150 years after Francis Light took possession of Penang in 1786, right until Malaya's independence in 1957, saw a fresh wave of interactivity between India and Malaya. The Company (East India Company) was now, for the first time, a territorial power in the Malay Peninsula. The Company held sway till 1876, after which the British Indian government took over the responsibility for managing British interests in the Malay Peninsula.

In 1786, Kedah was still a major centre for trade, cultural and religious interaction between India and the Malay Peninsula. The Chulias, or Indian (primarily Tamil) Muslim traders from the Coromandel Coast, were now a prominent community in Kedah. Ever since the Portuguese took over Malacca in 1511 the Chulias had preferred to make Kedah the centre of their trading activities in the Malay Peninsula. Francis Light had worked for the Company in Kedah and in Phuket (Junk Ceylon), where he had interacted with Indian traders and merchants from the Coromandel Coast and other parts of India. It is hardly surprising then, that soon after Francis Light arrived in Penang, among the earliest non-Malay groups referred to as residents of Penang are the Chulias. Among them 'one Alauddin bin Meerah Hussein Lebai is mentioned as the founder of the Ariffin mosque in Mesjid Kongsi. He is said to have arrived in Penang with Light himself'.[13]

According to the account written by an Englishman who visited Penang in 1763-4, there was already at that time a shrine or *keramat* (tomb of Sufi saint or *pir*) on the island. This was known as *Keramat Tuah* in Datuk Keramat, said to be the tomb of Sangli Peerappa, also known as Fakir Melana from the Malabar coastal region of India.[14] The Penang City Council records show that in 1789, just three years after becoming a British trading post, there was a fire in the city's Malabar Street, indicating a significant enough presence of migrants from Malabar to have a street named after them.[15] Some years later Malabar Street was extended to include areas of Chulia influence and renamed Chulia Street. The early immigrants to Penang from India's Malabar Coast also lived in Kampong (village) Malabar, as well as Kampong Kaka and near the *Keramat Dato Koya*, dedicated to the Malabari saint, Syed Mustapha Idris. Muslims and non-Muslims alike continue to worship at this shrine, paying their respects to this remarkable mystic. The British granted land for building the shrine, and even named the adjacent road after him. The terms Kaka (and Mappla) are still used to refer to Muslims from Kerala (Malayalee-speaking), and Koya is a well-recognized Malayalee Muslim surname.

In a letter written to the Company Representative in Calcutta in 1793, just seven years after the establishment of Penang, Francis Light notes the presence of 1,000 Chulias as being among the largest non-Malay communities.[16] This would have included both Tamil and Malayalee-speaking Indian Muslims, since the Indian state of Kerala (where the Malayalee language is spoken) was formed only in 1956, many years after India attained independence. Malabaris in Penang had close historical associations with Tamil Muslims from the village of Kadayanallur, in Tirulnelveli district of Tamil Nadu, who came to Penang in large numbers in the 1880s. Malabari Muslims, fleeing Portuguese persecution in India in the sixteenth century, had brought Islam to Kadayanallur. The friendship and cooperation between these two communities continued in Penang in the nineteenth century.

The first *Kapitan Kling* (head of the Tamil Muslims) in Penang was Kader Mohideen, who in 1802 built the beautiful *Kapitan Kling* mosque on land granted by the then Lt. Governor of Penang. Among his most prominent successors as *Kapitan Kling* was Mohammed Merican Noordin, a Tamil Muslim who arrived in Penang around 1820. He endowed one of the first schools for the Indian Muslim community 'for the learning of English, Hindoostanee, Malay, Tamil, Malabar and the Alkoran'.[17] This illustrates the diverse origins of the Indian community in Penang, and their interest in integrating with the Malay and English-speaking communities, while keeping alive their traditional linguistic and cultural heritage.

Almost simultaneously with the decision to acquire Penang, the Company sent 30 *lascars* (sailors) to Penang from Bengal. This group (together with most subsequent arrivals from north India, who sailed to Malaya from the ports of Bengal) is described as Bengali, although they are likely to have been Punjabis or Pathans. Soon enough, the British and other Europeans 'referred to all South Indians as Klings and North Indians as Bengalis'.[18]

Indian Muslims built several additional mosques throughout Penang, including the Bengali Mesjid in 1803 and the Alimsah Mesjid on Chulia Street in 1811. The Chulias arrived in Penang in large numbers in keeping with their long history of trade, cultural and religious interaction with the Malay Peninsula. Over the years, the Chulias assimilated into the Penang population through marriage 'to form the core of the Malays in Georgetown or the Jawi Pekan'.[19]

Even though the Tamil Muslims (Chulias) formed the largest group, Indians arriving in Penang from 1786 onwards represented a mosaic of all religions, including Hindus, Sikhs, Christians and Parsis. 'The fact that by the year 1833, the Mariamman Temple in Queen Street had already been founded, gives clear indication of the presence of a reasonable number of Tamil Hindus in Penang.'[20] By 1835 land had already been acquired and a Trust created for building and managing the north Indian Hindu temple now known as the Sri Kunj Bihari Temple.[21] The earliest Sikhs to arrive in Penang were political prisoners from the Punjab, officers and men of the army defeated by the British when they annexed Punjab in 1848.

The Company had high hopes for and expectations from Penang. In the Company's evaluation, Penang would develop as the long-sought after naval base east of India, it would emerge as the largest trading-hub in the Far East, and it would develop its own indigenous agricultural production and manufacturing strengths. In 1805, based on these expectations, the Directors of the EIC raised Penang from being a dependency of Bengal to the rank of a Presidency, known as the Eastern Presidency. This was now the fourth Presidency of India, on par with the Presidencies of Madras, Calcutta and Bombay.

As a result, Penang became a very natural point of intensified contact between India and the Malay Peninsula, a continuation in many ways of the millennia old traditional links between India and the region of Kedah in the Malay Peninsula. Given its location to the east of the Bay of Bengal

> Penang always belonged more closely to the Indian world than Melaka or Singapore. Indian soldiers, sailors and servants accompanied the landing party on the very first day of Penang's occupation, and other Indians quickly followed, first from Kedah, then the neighbouring states and later from India itself.[22]

Penang took over the role played by Kedah in earlier centuries as the first port of call for Indians arriving in the Malay Peninsula. As with Kedah, Penang too, came to be described as an 'Indian port'[23] and an 'Indo Malay settlement'.[24] For most of the nineteenth century these epithets were a reflection of Penang's commercial prosperity as an entrepôt, where the trade continued to depend largely on the sale of Indian manufactures and textile piece goods in exchange for goods from the neighbouring regions of North Sumatra, Northwest Malaya, Southwest Thailand and Burma's Tenasserim coast. Over time, many Penang Indian families moved out to Singapore and other regions of the Malay Peninsula, depending on their involvement in business, trade, agriculture or other activities.

As soon as it was declared a Presidency, Penang witnessed a great infusion of senior British officials and bureaucrats, together with the expected paraphernalia associated with such an important new establishment. This entailed heavy, fixed and recurring expenses which made the entire exercise an unremunerative one. The great expectations for Penang were never fully realized. Despite this, the areas of Penang and Province Wellesley (on the mainland opposite Penang, acquired from the Sultan of Kedah in 1800), together with the much more successful experiment with Singapore after 1819, continued to flourish and prosper as entrepôts, extending their network of contacts with the interior regions of the Malay Peninsula on the one hand, and with the outside world on the other.

In 1826 the Straits Settlements came into being, when Malacca and Singapore were transferred from Bengal to the control of Penang. Soon thereafter, however, in 1830, the Eastern Presidency was abolished. The Straits Settlements now became a Residency under the EIC, with its capital located in Singapore after 1832. Essentially, at this point in time, the EIC's firm position was 'unalterably opposed to extending its empire in the Straits' as a result of which 'it was impossible for trade with the Peninsula to develop as it did after Great Britain began to bring the Malay States under her control in 1874'.[25]

Before 1874, the British were so absorbed with their interests in Europe and India that they had little energy left to expend on the Malay Archipelago. Even the terms on which Penang and Province Wellesley were ceded to the British by the Sultan of Kedah became the subject of a long and bitter controversy, centred around whether the Company was bound to defend the Sultan against Siam. At the Congress of Vienna in 1815, the British allowed the Dutch to regain all their possessions in the Malay Archipelago because 'British statesmen failed to realize the immense value of the Archipelago. It was not considered worth keeping, when weighed in the balance against the importance of Dutch friendship in Europe.'[26] Malacca, which had been with the British since 1795, was given back to the Dutch.

In 1818 the renowned British administrator Sir Stamford Raffles was instructed not to move ahead with his plans for setting up a British outpost on the island of Rhio (not too far from Singapore) 'if the Dutch advanced claims, even of the slenderest. . . .'[27] And when Stamford Raffles left Calcutta for Penang/Singapore in December 1818 after discussions with Governor-General Lord Hastings, the latter directed him in a despatch to '"desist from every attempt to form a British establishment in the Eastern Archipelago". Fortunately, however, Raffles carried out his mission so quickly that Singapore was occupied before the letter reached him.'[28]

The natural advantages of Singapore were soon self-evident, with its excellent harbour and commanding position at the southern entrance to the Straits of Malacca. From the outset Singapore was a free port completely devoid of any customs and port duties. This policy yielded early and rich dividends. Trade and shipping through Penang suffered serious reversals after the establishment of the British outpost in Singapore in 1819, with Malacca being even more severely affected. In 1827, Penang and Malacca, too, were declared free ports. Even though Singapore was able to secure large portions of the entrepôt trade with Siam and China, including the opium trade, Penang retained its trade with India, Burma, northern Sumatra and large parts of the Malay Peninsula. Manufactured goods from Great Britain and India, large quantities of silk and other goods from China were traded in Penang for 'Straits Produce', namely pepper, spices, tin, camphor, ebony, antimony, birds' nests, tortoise-shell, rattan, gold-dust, pearls and sandal-wood. Trade in the Straits Settlements increased phenomenally between 1825 and 1864, from 4 million British pounds to 18.6 million British pounds. Imports and exports through Penang more than quadrupled, from 1.1 million British pounds in 1825 to 4.5 million British pounds in 1864. The trade through Singapore went up five times from 2.6 million British pounds in 1825 to 13.25 million British pounds in 1864. Trade through Malacca remained low, growing from 0.32 million pounds in 1825 to 0.82 million British pounds in 1864.[29]

THE ANGLO-DUTCH TREATY OF 1824

Perhaps the most significant event in Southeast Asia in the nineteenth century was the signing of the Anglo-Dutch Treaty in 1824. The British perceived this as the logical culmination of the work begun by them at the Congress of Vienna, given the importance they continued to attach to Holland's friendship and support in Europe. The establishment of Singapore in 1819 had greatly angered the Dutch. At the same time, the retrocession of Dutch possessions in the Malay Archipelago at the Congress of Vienna had reignited and exacerbated tensions between the British and the Dutch throughout this region, especially after the Dutch reasserted their suzerainty over Malacca, Negri Sembilan, Selangor and Perak (in the Malay Peninsula) and reintroduced their monopolistic policies. The British government felt it best to settle all disputes by dividing the English and the Dutch spheres of influence throughout this region.

Under the terms of the Anglo-Dutch Treaty of 1824, the Netherlands ceded all its establishments on the Indian subcontinent (known as Dutch India since 1605) together with all its interests on the Malay Peninsula. The British, on their part, ceded their factory in Bencoolen (Bengkulu) and all other interests on the island of Sumatra to the Netherlands, confirmed the return of Java to the Netherlands, and agreed not to establish any presence south of the Straits of Singapore, or to enter into any treaties with the rulers of these regions.

The Anglo-Dutch Treaty may have been occasioned by Great Britain's geo-strategic concerns in Europe and Asia. Its most immediate impact was the effective division of the Malay world into two: Malaya came under British control, and the area known as the Dutch East Indies was colonized by the Netherlands. This division of the Malay world persists to the present day, with the 1824 line dividing the British and Dutch spheres of influence now representing the international border(s) between Malaysia, Indonesia and Singapore.Within the Malay Peninsula, the 1824 Anglo-Dutch Treaty divided the kingdom of Johor, with the Rhio-Lingga Archipelago situated south of Singapore going to the Dutch. To quote British scholar Lennox Mills: 'In the history of British Malaya few events have been of more momentous importance than the Anglo-Dutch treaty of 1824, and few have been decided with so little attention to the importance of the local interests involved.'[30]

Abdur-Razzaq Lubis has described the political divisions imposed by the 1824 Anglo-Dutch Treaty as 'arbitrary, artificial and culturally illogical' because this Treaty 'severed the ancient ties that linked the (Malay) peninsula culturally to Sumatra and the Riau-Lingga archipelago'.[31] In a separate analysis he adds that 'this is an enduring colonialist legacy which had been defended by a narrow, nationalistic interpretation of the Malay race. The prejudicial identity of the "pure Malay" brought about an administrative ethnic cleansing which extinguished the history of other non-Malay inhabitants of the land.'[32]

This 'narrow nationalistic interpretation of the Malay race' was an important part of the process initiated by the British to create an aura of exclusivity around the Malay Sultans and rulers. The pre-colonial diversity of interaction with Indians and myriad other ethnicities from across the Malay Archipelago was restricted to the point of obliteration of even the memory of such interactions. This certainly helped the British to maximize their commercial and economic interests in Malaya for the next 130 years and more. However, the unfortunate legacy of distinctions on grounds of 'race' that such policies left in their wake are still around to haunt and hamper the post-colonial realization of the full socio-political and economic potential of Malaysia, including its relations with India.

NOTES

1. R.O. Winstedt, *A History of Malay Literature*, 1939, p. 117.
2. Ibid.
3. Ibid., pp. 117-19.
4. Naidu Ratnala Thulaja 'Jawi Peranakan', written on 14 July 2003 for the National Library Board Singapore. Accessed on 9 August 2010 at http://infopedia.nl.sg/articles/SIP_356_2005-01-13.html.
5. Sabrizain, 'A Historical Perspective on the Word Keling' accessed on 11 August 2010 at http://www.sabrizain.org/malaya/keling.htm.
6. K.S. Sandhu, *Indians in Malaya*, 1969, Cambridge University Press, p. 43.
7. Sandhu, ibid., p. 43, *inter alia*, quoting H.P. Clodd, *Malaya's First Pioneer*, London, 1948.
8. Ibid., p. 43, brackets mine.
9. Ibid.
10. Andaya and Andaya, op. cit., p. 180.
11. Prof. Ghulam-Sarwar Yousof, 'The South Asian Cultural Impact Upon Penang', Keynote Address at the Colloquium on 'Indians in Penang: A Historical Perspective' organized by the Penang Heritage Trust in September 2001, p. 5.
12. Ong Ju Lynn 'The Mandailings in Peninsular Malaysia: Roots of Penang Malay', p. 3, quoting paper on 'The Indonesians in Penang' presented by Abdur Razzaq Lubis at the Malay Colloquium held in Penang on 25 August 2001. Accessed on 9 August 2010 at http://

www.mandailing.org/Eng/rootsofpenmal.html

13. Yousof, op. cit., p. 3.
14. Ibid.
15. Suresh Narayanan (Universiti Sains Malaysia) 'From Malabaris to Malaysians: The Untold Story of Malayalees in Penang', paper presented at September 2001 Colloquium in Penang on 'Indians in Penang—A Historical Perspective', pp. 2-3.
16. Ibid., op. cit., p. 2.
17. Ibid., p. 3, quoting Su Khin Khoo, *Streets of Georgetown Penang* (1993, Janus Print and Resources), p. 73. Suresh Narayanan indicates that the reference to 'Malabar' is presumably to the Malayalam language or to Malayalam written in Arabic script, which was popular among Muslims from Malabar.
18. Ibid., p. 4, quoting from C.M. Turnbull, *The Straits Settlements, 1826-1867* (1972, University of London, The Athlone Press), p. 8.
19. Ibid., p. 2, quoting Salleh Hussain, *A History of Early Penang, 1786-1867* (1990, Penang, Malaysia German Society).
20. Yousof, op. cit., p. 3.
21. Satish K. Shukla 'Origins and History of Sri Kunj Bihari Temple and Some Other Temples', paper presented at Colloquium on 'Indians in Penang: A Historical Perspective' held in Penang on 22 September 2001.
22. C.M. Turnbull, 'Penang's Changing Role in the Straits Settlements, 1826-1946', p. 5, paper presented at International Conference on 'The Penang Story', held in Penang in April 2002 (http://penangstory.net.my/main-conference.html, accessed on 9 August 2010).
23. K.G. Tregonning, *The British in Malaya: The First Forty Years*, 1965, Arizona, p. 165.
24. Suresh Narayanan, op. cit., p. 4, quoting C.M. Turnbull, *The Straits Settlements, 1826-67*, University of London: The Athlone Press, p. 8.
25. Lennox Mills, 'British Malaya Part I', *JMBRAS*, vol. I, pt. II, 1925, p. 47.
26. Ibid., p. 52.
27. Ibid., p. 55.
28. Ibid.
29. Lennox Mills, 'British Malaya Part II', *JMBRAS*, vol. III, pt. II, 1925, p. 192.
30. Lennox Mills, 'British Malaya Part I', p. 71.
31. Abdur-Razzaq Lubis, 'Perceptions of Penang: Views from Across the Straits', paper presented at 'The Penang Story: International Conference 2002' held on 18-21 April 2002 in Penang, p. 2. Accessed on http://penangstory.net.my/main-conference.html on 9 August 2010.
32. Ong Ju Lynn, op. cit., p. 3, quoting Abdur-Razzaq Lubis.

10

Interaction between British India and British Malaya: The Indentured Labour Issue

The establishment of Penang as a British settlement in 1786 marked a turning point in the relationship between India and Malaya. Before 1786 the people of India and the Malay Archipelago had been spontaneous and free in their interaction. Trade, religion and culture had been the leitmotifs of this interaction. After 1786 the British, following up on their growing political and economic control in India, turned towards consolidating their position in the Malay Archipelago and the Far East. The EIC's motivations were primarily economic and commercial, combined with the strategic backup provided by its naval base in Singapore.

Essentially, the EIC sought to emulate the success of India's merchants and traders in the mutually beneficial patterns of trade and commerce they had evolved with this region over the past millennia and more. Gradually, the Company was successful in gaining control over the export production centres (textiles, opium) in India and the shipping lanes between India and the Malay Peninsula. British 'country traders' were equally successful in securing for themselves key advisory positions with the Malay Sultans, very often dislodging or replacing Indian merchants in the process. Nevertheless 'Indian traders were . . . still to be seen, at times in highly influential positions, at the Malay ports and courts at the time of Francis Light's landing at Penang'.[1]

After 1786 Penang, rather than mainland Kedah as hitherto, became the major centre for trade and commercial interaction between India and the Malay Peninsula. Several Indian merchants shifted their business to Penang, not only from Kedah, but from other Malay states such as Perlis and Selangor, even from Acheh (Sumatra) and Borneo. Even after 1819 when the lion's share of the trade moved to Singapore, Penang remained the first port of call for ships arriving from India, and the final port of call for ships leaving for India from Singapore, Malacca and Penang itself. As a result Penang soon became the single largest port of immigration/ emigration from and to India.

Merchants, traders and financiers from India began to use Penang as their base almost from the moment of its inception as a British Settlement. Francis Light has himself described how, before the end of the 1780s, Chulia (Tamil Muslim) vessels from Nagore, Nagapattinam, Porto Novo and Pondicherry were a common sight in the Penang waters.[2] The Straits Settlements Factory Records (SSFR) for this period (1769-95) reveal that by the early 1790s, Penang's links with the Bengal ports had been firmly established. According to the SSFR (10 April 1789) the first shop-house to be built in Penang by an Indian trader was in 1788, by a Bengali trader from Calcutta. And by early 1794, according to SSFR (1 August 1794), this movement of merchants and others from India to Penang had reached '1300 to 2000 men per year'.[3]

Indians were active in every profession, as traders and shop-keepers, as builders and foremen, in the police force and the security services, as construction and agricultural labour and as coolies. Initially their presence and activities were limited to the Straits Settlements (Penang, Malacca and Singapore), but by the end of the nineteenth century Indians were rapidly extending their activities throughout the Federated Malay States (FMS), which came into being in July 1896. In many ways this represented the continuation of the interactive immigration and emigration between India and the Malay Peninsula that had been the hallmark of the first millennium.

This time, however, the British had the upper hand *vis-à-vis* the Indians, both as regards proximity to the Malay Sultans and direct participation in the processes of trade between India and the Malay Peninsula. Quite expectedly, the British did their best to consolidate this advantage. The British were none too encouraging in allowing Indians to rise to prominent positions. As the British extended their colonial control over Malaya, they ensured that all major financial, shipping and commercial activities remained with European entities. Employment for Indians in these entities was restricted to subordinate positions. Land policy favoured for the most part Malay or European ownership.

More than one-third of the post-1786 (after the establishment of Penang as a British Settlement) migration from India to Malaya comprised commercial, cultural, professional or other categories of non-labour immigrants. K.S. Sandhu has provided the break-up, showing that of the total estimated arrivals in Malaya from India between 1786 and 1957, approximately 4.25 million Indians, 65.3 per cent were labourers, and 34.7 per cent were non-labourers.[4] Sandhu has estimated that an overwhelming 99.2 per cent of the Indian immigrants into Malaya (sample years from 1844-1941) were from south India, with the Tamil-speaking immigrants comprising 85.2 per cent, the Telugu speaking immigrants 6.8 per cent and the Malayalam speaking immigrants 6.4 per cent.[5]

Prominent members of the Jawi Peranakan and the south Indian Muslim communities joined hands to launch the first ever Malay language newspaper in 1876. The first editor of this newspaper was Munsyi Mohamed Said bin Dada Mohiddin, a south Indian Muslim, who remained the editor for 12 long years till 1888.

In the process of consolidating their political hold and administrative control over the Straits Settlements and the FMS, the British faced an acute shortage of engineers, contractors, planters, agency houses, bankers, doctors, educationists, English-speaking school teachers, clerical and administrative staff. The first teacher-training institution in Malaya opened as late as 1907, the first technical school opened in 1906 and did not assume college status until 1942. The first medical school opened in 1904, and was given university status only after the Japanese occupation.[6] European companies filled the entrepreneurial niche. For the posts of teachers, technical assistants and clerks, it was the English-educated Indians and Ceylonese who responded in large numbers, attracted by the prospects of pensionable government jobs with salaries that were substantially higher than those prevalent in India and Ceylon. They found jobs on plantations and in the railways, road-building and land survey sectors as supervisors, foremen, technicians and office assistants, invaluable intermediaries between Indian labour and the primarily British employers. In the words of K.S. Sandhu: 'Just as South Indians proved to be invaluable in the clerical and technical services, similarly Northern Indians, particularly the tall, sturdy Sikhs, were much sought after for such employment as soldiers, policemen, watchmen and caretakers.'[7] Providing adequate internal security was proving to be a difficult task for the British in Malaya, given the diverse and widely dispersed population. Chinese secret societies were considered as posing a special problem, both as a source of crime and public disorder and as a 'political threat, to the extent that if not controlled they might take possession of the country'.[8]

In their effort to establish an efficient police force for meeting the needs of internal law and order, the British considered recruiting Malays, other Southeast Asians (Javanese, Filipinos, Bugis), Chinese, Jawi Pekans, South Indians and Europeans. Each was considered 'unavailable, impracticable or unsuitable'.[9] Finally the British in Malaya decided to follow the successful experience of their compatriots in Hong Kong who had (beginning 1867) recruited Sikhs in large numbers for induction into the police force. Even before the Straits Settlements could receive its first batch of Sikh policemen in 1881, a Malay chief in Larut, Perak had commissioned a retired British police officer in 1873 'to go to Northern India and enlist a force of fighting men to help him save his tin mines from the depredations of Chinese insurgents'. As a result 'ninety-five men, mainly Sikhs, Pathans and Punjabi Muslims . . . (arrived) to put down the disorders caused by feuding Chinese clans.'[10] When the British took control of Perak after the Pangkor Treaty of 1874, these men formed the nucleus of the new Perak Armed Police. Many more Northern Indians followed. They joined the police forces in other Malay States and in the Malay States Guides, a military regiment created in 1896.

Across Malaya, among the most prominent and commercially active groups from India were the Chettiars, a renowned Tamil Hindu community of businessmen and financiers with roots in the Ramnad and Puddukottai districts of the Madras Presidency. The Chettiar sub-group most prominent in Malaya was the Nattukottai

Chettiars, known for their wealth and prosperity. In the Madras Presidency they owned extensive properties both in the countryside and in the cities (hence they were also known as Nagarathars). The Chettiars started arriving in the Straits Settlements in the first half of the nineteenth century. Most scholars would agree with S. Arasaratnam that:

> Among the Indian commercial groups (in Malaya) the Chettiar had the widest impact on the country because of the nature and range of their activities. They came to Malaya primarily as money-lenders. Their money-lending activities brought them in contact with the economy of the country and, as in Burma, released a process of change affecting many classes of people. They provided credit to people of various groups—European entrepreneurs, Chinese speculators, Indian hawkers and peddlers, and Malay royalty and peasants. The (British) Government was aware of the function they were performing, and the Chief Secretary made favourable references to the Chettiar and defended them against criticism in the Federal Council in 1923.[11]

The (British) Malayan government considered that the Chettiars' role in providing credit across the board to individuals in different social groups had a positive influence on the economy. The Chettiars operated extensively in rural areas across the FMS and among the Unfederated Malay States, in Kedah and Johor, giving loans with deposit of land titles or a mortgage as security. Over time the Chettiars began to acquire land throughout Malaya, much of it as a result of forfeiture of such mortgages. The Great Depression of 1929 brought this issue into sharp focus, when, as a result of declining exports and incomes, there was a sudden spurt in the sale of secured land by peasant proprietors and small-holders.

Already in 1913, the British Malayan government had passed the first Malay Reservations Act, restricting sale of Malay-owned lands. Rising landlessness among the Malay peasants became a particularly sensitive issue in Perak, and at the instance of the Sultan, several legislative measures were enacted in the FMS, primarily the Small Holdings (Restriction of Sale) Bill of 1931, and the Malay Reservations Act of 1933. In 1935, the Money-Lenders' Ordinance was adopted by the Straits Settlements Legislature.

The Chettiars were well-organized, even though they preferred to have their own exclusive groupings rather than join hands with the rest of the Indian immigrant community. During legislative discussions they received support from the Chinese and the Europeans rather than from Indian members. They established their own Chettiars' Chambers of Commerce all across the Malay Peninsula, in Singapore, in Penang and in Malacca, as well as a separate one for the FMS. By 1938, Indian ownership of the rubber estates stood at close to 88,000 acres, representing 4 per cent of the total acreage under rubber in Malaya, most of it with the Chettiar community.[12] The Proceedings of the Federal Council for 1939 reveal that the landholdings owned and/or mortgaged by Indians amounted (in 1938) to over 98,000 acres in Perak, 50,000 acres in Selangor, 38,000 acres in Negri Sembilan and 31,000 acres in Pahang.[13]

When the Chettiars' Chambers of Commerce came together to submit a joint petition to the V.S.S. Sastri delegation (when it visited Malaya in 1937), it was stated therein that 'the Chettiar community in Malaya have played a very big part in financing the development of the country and it is estimated that at the present time they have about $ 300 million invested in Malaya'.[14] Professor Khoo Kay Kim placed the figure of Chettiar investment in Malaya by 1930 at Rs. 500 million (citing a one-to-one equivalence between the Indian rupee and the Malayan ringgit/Straits dollar).[15] In another analysis Professor Khoo Kay Kim has said:

> It is difficult to document private Malay feelings towards Indians. But there is some evidence to indicate that in the Malay states, even at the time when the Malay Reservation Act was first introduced in 1913, there was no hostile feeling towards the Chettiars (Indian money-lenders). The Malay Reservation Act owed its origin to the initiative of British officers who felt that the Malays were rapidly losing their lands to the Indian moneylenders through foreclosures. But, it has been said that many Malays tended to think of the Chettiars as good-hearted (*baik hati*) persons. It was believed that those who managed to establish close relations with the Chettiars would be able to borrow small sums without collateral.[16]

The earliest Parsee association with Penang dates to the 1880s, and is linked to visits by the renowned Parsee Theatre from Bombay. Parsee merchants in Bombay patronized this form of theatre, which originated in the lavish entertainment first performed in the palace of Nawab Wajid Ali Shah of Oudh (Awadh region in present-day Uttar Pradesh in north India). Subsequently, prominent businessmen in Penang patronized local troupes, and the genre of theatre that developed acquired the name *Bangsawan*. *Bangsawan*'s early repertoire included the traditional Indian plays performed in Hindustani by the Parsee Theatre such as *Raja Harishchandra* and *Gul Bakawali*. The language was changed to Malay, and the repertoire expanded to include Indonesian, Thai and Chinese plays. These were performed in Penang and in other cities across Malaya as well as in Singapore, Brunei and Indonesia. 'Troupes involved multiracial casts, production crews as well as professional managers and owners of theatre companies.'[17]

A small number of Parsee families did put down roots in Penang, Taiping and other parts of the Malay Peninsula. Notable among these is Manecksha Mistry who lived in Penang in the early years of the twentieth century, but later moved to Taiping where he owned rubber estates, and has a road named after him. Another Parsee, Dr Homi Mehta, renowned for his work combating leprosy and malaria, served in different positions across the Malay Peninsula beginning 1915, including in Penang for 30 years. He passed away in 1963 at the age of 77.

IMPACT OF THE SEPOY MUTINY

The Sepoy Mutiny of 1857 (also described as India's First War of Independence) caused the British Crown to assume direct administration of India. The EIC itself was finally dissolved on 1 June 1874. Before this, in 1867, the responsibility for the Straits Settlements was transferred from the India Office to the Colonial Office. Nonetheless uptil 1873 the British government strictly adhered to its policy of non-intervention in the Malay states, despite strong lobbying from the mercantile communities in the Straits Settlements. The British were still hampered by their concerns about Dutch reactions to any interventionist moves by them.

From the middle of the eighteenth century, tin mining had emerged as an increasingly remunerative and profit-yielding activity across the Malay Peninsula, centred particularly in the states of Perak, Selangor, Negri Sembilan and Pahang. However, the law and order situation in these states had almost completely collapsed as a result of internecine feuds among the Malay Sultans, combined with heavy and continuous hostilities between the several secret societies that had sprung up among the thousands of Chinese tin miners who had taken up residence in this region. After the Anglo-Dutch Treaty (1824) gave the British a free hand in the Malay Peninsula, they moved ahead to consolidate their control over these four tin-rich Malay States. Finally, under the terms of the Pangkor Engagement, beginning with Perak and Selangor in 1874, Pahang in 1888 and the newly-formed Negri Sembilan (confederation of nine small Minangkabau states) in 1895, each of these states 'accepted' a British Resident to advise the Sultan on all matters except Malay religion and custom.

The British Residents introduced administrative mechanisms that had already been tried out in India, such as the State Council (on the model of the Indian Councils created by the Act of 1861) and the Penal Code of the Straits, adapted from the Indian Penal Code. In 1896 the FMS was formed with Kuala Lumpur as its capital. The position of the British Resident General stationed in Kuala Lumpur was a powerful one, with substantially complete administrative and political control vested in him. It was perhaps the result of this perception that in 1909, when the Anglo Siamese Treaty ceded the four northern states of Perlis, Kedah, Kelantan and Trengganu to the British, the Sultans of these States refused to join the FMS. They accepted British Advisers, but retained their financial autonomy. The state of Johor, too, refused to join the FMS, and accepted a British Adviser in 1914. These five states together were known as the Unfederated Malay States.

This composite political structure, comprising the Straits Settlements (a British Colony, covering Singapore, Penang and Province Wellesley, and Malacca, including Naning); the FMS (Perak, Negri Sembilan, Selangor and Pahang); and the Unfederated Malay States (Kedah, Perlis, Kelantan, Trengganu and Johor), remained in place till the Japanese occupation of Malaya in 1941.

The development of this three-way political structure seems cumbersome, even patchy. It was introduced in haste, geared primarily towards ensuring British political and administrative control so that they could derive maximum economic benefit from burgeoning world demand, first for tin towards the end of the nineteenth century, and subsequently for rubber in the early years of the twentieth century. Immigrant labour from India and China were part of this pattern, filling an urgent need in the face of acute local scarcity, and facilitating maximization of profits.

The British were eminently successful in meeting their objectives. In the years following the conclusion of the Pangkor Engagement of 1874, Malaya's exports of tin rose to 26,000 tons in 1889; 51,733 tons in 1904, and just under 70,000 tons in 1929. By the early years of the twentieth century, Malaya's output of tin was over 50 per cent of the total world output.[18] The tin industry in Malaya was dominated by the Chinese.

In the case of rubber, the boom in production and exports was even more dramatic. Rubber had been introduced to Malaya in 1877 as an experimental plant, at a time when world production was dominated by jungle rubber. Twenty years later, by 1897, only 345 acres were under rubber in Malaya. In 1905, the acreage under rubber had increased to 50,000, but Malayan exports of rubber were a meagre 200 tons, compared to the world production of 62,145 tons of jungle rubber. Just eight years later, by 1914, rubber produced on Malayan plantations was delivered in New York at a price lower than that of jungle rubber from South America. And by 1920, Malaya exported 196,000 tons of rubber, or 53 per cent of total world production.[19] This was the miracle achieved through the back-breaking toil of impoverished immigrant labour brought in from India in ever-increasing numbers.

Before the Second World War there was no political enfranchisement in Malaya. There were legislative councils with official and nominated members. Although Malays and Chinese were routinely appointed to these councils, Indians were excluded right till the 1920s. In 1922 an Indian was first nominated to the Straits Settlements Legislative Council, followed in 1928 by the nomination of an Indian to the Federal Council of the FMS. The gathering momentum of India's freedom movement and struggle for independence made the British increasingly wary about the resonance that this could elicit among the oppressed and poorly paid Indian labour in Malaya, especially because this very question of the political and economic status of the Indian community in

Malaya continued to be the cause of serious consternation and concern in India.

Indian intelligentsia living and working in Malaya were subject to the closest scrutiny by the British Malayan government. According to the scholar, Professor K.S. Sandhu:

> Partly, it appears, for this purpose a governmental political organization, the Special Branch, was created in 1919 and two Indians from the Indian police force were seconded to it as supernumerary officers. One of the functions of this organization was to keep a 'local suspect list' of 'subversive' Indians—that is Indians who evinced an interest in such matters as conditions of labour or political questions in general—and harass them if necessary. . . . Perhaps even more drastic steps were taken to prevent, as far as possible, the entry into Malaya, henceforth, of Indians capable of leadership or political agitation.[20]

IMMIGRANT LABOUR

In sharp contrast, immigration into Malaya by Indian labour 'was not only welcomed but openly solicited'.[21] Just three months after the Penang settlement became operational, Francis Light had written to the Governor-General in Council, India, requesting a 'supply of one hundred coolies, as the price of labour in Penang was enormous'. This request was turned down, but the Straits Settlements factory records (SSFR) reveal that a second request, this time for artificers (skilled craftsmen), was accepted and a group of twenty five Bombay artificers landed in Penang in July 1787.[22]

The demand for labour increased exponentially in the nineteenth century, almost invariably exceeding the available supply. In 1800 the Company acquired Province Wellesley (Seberang Prai) on the Kedah mainland, followed by the establishment of Singapore in 1819 and the return of Malacca after the Anglo-Dutch Treaty was signed in 1824. In addition to the labour requirements for the construction and development of these urban areas, a huge demand for labour arose for commercial agriculture. The investments began with the cultivation of spices and pepper in the 1790s, moving on to sugar in the 1830s, coffee in the 1870s, the 'rubber rush' in the early decades of the twentieth century with everyone pursuing the acquisition of 'white gold' (latex), followed soon thereafter by the cultivation of palm oil and tea. In the mining sector the mid-nineteenth century witnessed the 'tin rush', where Chinese labour met most of the extensive requirements. Added to this was the demand for labour to build roads and lay railway tracks, hacking through jungles, swamps or highlands. The nature of the demand was essentially for low paid, unskilled and 'manageable' labour.

The relevant British authorities did explore several options before they decided to bring in the substantial labour from India. The Malays were most reluctant to work as wage labour. They were few in number, and were themselves landowners, by and large self-sufficient in all their requirements. By the end of the nineteenth century, the authorities preferred the Malays to remain in their *kampongs* (villages), particularly if these were in the *padi* or rice growing areas.

> In Kedah/Perlis in 1920, for example, applicants for rubber plantation land were prohibited from employing local Malay labour, and were required to satisfy the government that they were in a position to import sufficient immigrant labour for development and maintenance purposes before their applications could be approved.[23]

White labour or European labour was considered unaffordable because of the 'decent wage standards' that would need to be observed, combined with appropriate facilities for housing, medical treatment and the like. It would also be difficult to resist demands by European labour for formation of trade unions. Above all, the employment of white labour was considered inappropriate and not in keeping with 'the prestige of the Europeans'.[24]

In the 1780s, the British experimented with using African slave labour, as had been done on the plantations in the West Indies. This effort proved to be short-lived, since the slave trade was prohibited in British territories by the early years of the nineteenth century, and slavery was legally abolished in August 1838. After this, African labour was unwilling to come across to Malaya even as free immigrants.

In Asia itself, according to Colonial Office documents, records maintained on sugar estates and rubber plantations, parliamentary proceedings in the British parliament and reports prepared by various commissions appointed (in the late nineteenth and early twentieth centuries) to enquire into the conditions of indentured labour and the question of Indian immigration,[25] several options were explored for importing the much-needed labour for working on plantations and railways. In Korea and Japan, the respective governments were opposed to sending their nationals as low-wage labour. Labour from Java, who would have been easier to assimilate, proved difficult to import 'largely because of the emigration restrictions imposed by the Dutch government' combined with contractual terms that made the 'cost of importing such labour . . . almost prohibitive, being two or three times that of an Indian of the same category.'[26]

The Chinese were acknowledged across the board to be excellent workers. By the early years of the nineteenth century they were already present in substantial numbers throughout the Straits Settlements. They were beginning to move into the FMS for tin and gold mining, and other lucrative activities. The principle issues mitigating against using Chinese labour on the plantations and for infrastructure projects were: first, that they were considered as 'inclined to be disorderly, cost more in police and supervision and (gave) more trouble',[27] relating principally to their membership of rival secret societies. Secondly, Chinese labour was aggressively ambitious and upwardly mobile, reluctant to work for anyone other than his own countrymen, and quite unlikely to stay on for any length of time in low-paid, physically arduous work. The Chinese government did not encourage emigration, and the entire process of recruiting Chinese labour from mainland China had been monopolized by a few labour brokers, described as 'coolie rings'. It proved impossible for European planters to break this monopoly. Finally, the then Governor of the Straits Settlements reflected the prevailing political assessment when he said in 1887

> I am . . . anxious for political reasons that the great preponderance of the Chinese over any other race in these Settlements, and to a less marked degree in some of the Native States under our administration, should be counterbalanced as much as possible by the influx of Indian and other nationalities. . . .[28]

The British even used convict labour from India to meet the perceived shortfall in labour supply. 'Convicts transported from South Asia to Southeast Asia in the late eighteenth and early nineteenth centuries were part of a global system of forced migration.'[29] Scholars, who describe this group as 'convict workers' rather than 'professional or habitual criminals', have estimated that:

> After 1820 a quarter of a million convicts were shipped across the world's oceans to colonise Australia, New Caledonia, Singapore and French Guiana, and to meet labour demand in Gibraltar, Bermuda, Penang, Malacca and Mauritius. . . . Transportation, like the recruitment of slaves and contracting of bonded workers, was complementary to the international migration of free European peoples before 1914. Convictism was a labour system existing in many countries of the world in the nineteenth century.[30]

The convict workers were 'members of a labour force that was recruited and organised to service the projects of the emerging British Empire in the region. . . .'[31] The movement of convicts from South Asia to Southeast Asia was much smaller than the numbers transported from Britain to Australia and North America. British India:

> dispatched 4000-6000 convicts to Bengkulen between 1787 and 1825, and 15,000 to the Straits Settlements between 1790 and 1860. Another 1000-1500 were transported from Ceylon to Malacca in the Straits Settlements between 1849 and 1873, and several thousand more were sent to Burma and to areas outside of Southeast Asia, principally Mauritius between 1815 and 1837 and the Andaman Islands after 1857.[32]

Interestingly, there was also the reverse movement of 'convict workers' from Southeast Asia to South Asia, and 'natives of the Malay countries' were transferred to India, Chinese from Singapore and Hong Kong were exiled to India and from Hong Kong also briefly to the Straits Settlements, and convicts from Ceylon and Burma were dispatched to these venues as well'.[33] By all accounts, both in South Asia and Southeast Asia, convict workers mingled freely with the local population, even intermarried and settled down in the land to which they had been 'exiled'. 'An estimate for Singapore suggests that in 1838 only 60 per cent of the convicts returned to India, a number that fell considerably by the 1860s when "only very few returned".'[34]

All this changed after the 1857 First War of Independence (the British described it as the Sepoy Mutiny) in India. This time, when the British Indian government wanted to send 'huge numbers of mutineers and rebels' to the Straits Settlements, 'the response from Singapore was swift and emphatically negative'.[35] In short, 'this dynamic worked well for both parties as long as convicts seemed malleable and valuable as workers. But as soon as the government in India threatened to dump its mutineers and rebels on the Straits Settlements in the aftermath of the Mutiny/Rebellion of 1857, the local administrations in the penal colonies were no longer willing to host any more transportees.'[36]

INDENTURED LABOUR FROM INDIA BEGINS TO ARRIVE IN MALAYA

All this while, the British Malayan authorities had been turning to India for increasingly large-scale recruitment of the labour they needed for Malaya. The British Indian government had its own concerns, and was restrictive about the regions from which labour could be recruited for Malaya. The north Indian states were excluded because Britain's distant colonies like Fiji, West Indies and Mauritius drew most of their labour requirements from this region. The north Indians, principally the Punjabis, Rajputs, Pathans and Marathas were also the main source of recruitment for the British Indian defence and police services.

At the same time, a fair number of European planters, government officials and contractors with the public works and railways departments moved to Malaya from Ceylon, where they had been working with south Indian labour, largely from present-day Tamil Nadu. Several of these planters and government officials or their English-speaking subordinates even knew Tamil. All of them were comfortable working with south Indian labour, described by the planters as their 'mainstay', and by the contractors as being eminently suitable for working on road and railway construction projects.

In the then Madras Presidency, it was decided to focus on the poorest and most deprived sections of society as the recruiting base for labour emigrants to Malaya. This group was 'considered the most satisfactory type of labourer, especially for light, simple, repetitive tasks'.[37] The subtext seems to have been that this group was 'malleable, worked well under supervision and was easily manageable'.[38] The expectation was that they would willingly accept low fixed wages, would not object to strenuous manual labour, and were most unlikely to resort to collective bargaining, unionism or strikes. All this 'made them almost the ideal labouring material for the furtherance of capitalist endeavours in Malaya'.[39] It is difficult not to cringe at the cynicism of such sentiments.

The British Indian government had serious reservations about the conditions of service for Indian labour going to Malaya, as a result of which restrictions and controls had been imposed on sending Indian labour to Malaya. No such controls were imposed on Indian labour going to Fiji, West Indies, Mauritius, Ceylon (now Sri Lanka) or Burma (now Myanmar), since these destinations 'offered generally higher wages, better conditions of service and a lower cost of living, than did Malaya'.[40] In 1890, for example, wages for Indian immigrant labourers were Rs. 10 per month in Burma, as against Rs. 4 or 5 per month in the Straits Settlements for the same category.[41] 'Moreover, while every Indian in Burma and Ceylon landed a free man, many of his countrymen venturing to Malaya did so as indentured labourers'.[42] Living conditions, too, were considered unattractive in Malaya, with poor housing and inadequate medical attention resulting in a heavy death toll from tropical diseases like malaria and beri-beri.

Most of these ills were associated with the infamous system of indentured migration, euphemistically described as 'assisted labour migration', that was the principle form of labour migration from India to Malaya till it was abolished in 1910. The British introduced indentured emigration from India in the nineteenth century after slavery was abolished in the British territories in 1833-4. The indenture or contract, assumed to have been signed voluntarily, in effect bargained away the labourer's personal freedom for an extended period. All he got in exchange were abysmally low wages, indescribably hard work, and appalling living conditions, without any recourse to or means of redressal.

In most British colonies indentured labour migration was strictly regulated. Indentured labour was recruited by the respective colonial governments and then made available to employers, primarily on sugar estates. In Malaya, the system of indentured labour migration evolved differently, as a result of which indentured labour was 'far less liberally treated'.[43] Indentured labour moving from India to most British colonies were given free passages, while those moving to Malaya 'had to pay back all advances received and the cost of his passage'.[44] Worse still, written contracts for indentured labour going to Malaya imposed on the labourers 'a criminal liability for the most trivial breaches of the contracts in place of the civil liability which usually attached to such lapses'.[45]

> In Malaya . . . recruitment was by speculators or employers themselves or through their own private agents in India. The Malayan government's function was merely to watch over the fulfillment of the contract between the individual employer and the immigrant. In practice even this was seldom done.[46]

The speculators were mostly shipowners, who would advance money to a head *maistry* (recruiting agent). The head *maistry* would send his subordinate *maistries*

> to villages and persuade coolies to emigrate . . . by representing, in bright colours, prospects of enrichment and advance. . . . The *maistries* get ten rupees a head for every adult coolie they bring, all contingent expenses being paid. . . .They (the coolies) are then shipped on the shipowner's vessel and accompanied by the head *maistry* to the port of destination. . . . Each man (coolie) fetches about five pounds; and all expenses of maintenance, passage money, etc., are discharged by the purchaser. The ship-owner and head *maistry* divide the profits. . . .[47]

Most of this indentured labour landed in Penang, from where they were sent to Province Wellesley (Seberang Prai) and to the state of Perak for the sugar plantations. This activity was so profitable that all manner of 'persuasion', including kidnapping, was resorted to. It has been estimated that more than a third of the indentureds, both legal and illegal (verbal contract, they traveled as regular passengers) were not agricultural labourers at all, being mainly weavers, oil-millers, washermen and cooks.[48] This contributed to the already high mortality rates among Indian indentured labour in Malaya. Ships moving to Malaya were so overcrowded that the Indian Passenger Acts of 1857 and 1859 were passed to check this malpractice, unfortunately to little or to no avail.

Most of the Indians going to Malaya as indentured labour were from south India, with 'only a few hundred recruits from the Bengal areas of the Ganges valley'.[49] Since most of the legal or supervised emigration of indentured labour took place through the port of Nagapattinam, the recruitment areas remained primarily in the nearby districts of Tanjore, Trichinopoly, Madras, and sometimes Salem and Coimbatore. The illegal or unsupervised emigration of indentured labour used other ports such as Karaikal, Pondicherry, Cuddalore, Porto Novo and Nagore. In the early years it was Indian-owned sailing ships that carried the indentured labour to Malaya. However, as the era of steamships dawned and the Indian shipping industry went into decline, and government supervision increased, European shipping took over the movement of indentured labour to Malaya.

The movement of indentured labour from India to Malaya is estimated to have started in 1844.[50] Statistical records are available only from 1866. Till the early years of the twentieth century, the flow of labour from India to Malaya disappointed the British authorities, who had expected large supplies of cheap labour, absolutely essential for development and prosperity in Malaya. During the decade 1880-9, for example, Ceylon and Burma remained much more attractive destinations. During this period Indian immigrants moving to Ceylon numbered almost 5,00,000, while those going to Burma were close to 1,65,000, with those going to Malaya remaining at just under 1,40,000.[51]

The British authorities (in Malaya) then initiated special efforts to 'sell' Malaya as an attractive destination for Indian labour by projecting an improvement in the terms and conditions of service. After receiving the report of a fact-finding mission sent to Malaya, the British Indian government finally withdrew, in 1897, all restrictions on emigration of Indian labour to Malaya. In 1900, according to the India Office documents on 'Emigration Proceedings of the Government of India', agreement was reached to facilitate the free flow of emigration to Malaya, with the caveat that this emigration was to be only from South India.[52] The system of indentured labour was abolished in 1910 and wages of the now free labourers were raised to levels above those prevailing at the time in Ceylon and Burma. In 1907 the Indian Immigration Committee was established. Very soon, through its Indian Immigration Fund, this Committee took over responsibility for 'virtually all expenses connected with *kangany* recruitment'.[53] From 1909 onwards, the estate owners could no longer deduct from the labourers' wages any costs they may have incurred in the process of his/her emigration.

An important indicator of the keenness of the Malay States to secure Indian labour in large numbers was the decision in 1887 to initiate 'a steamship subsidy . . . to stimulate immigration.'[54] The Straits Settlements, Perak, Selangor and Johor came together to contribute towards an annual subsidy of $30,000 (Straits dollars), which would enable a substantial reduction in the price of a single journey steamship fare (from Rs. 15 to Rs. 8) from Nagapattinam (on the Coromandel Coast) to Penang. Initially this was a fortnightly service. Soon enough, the remaining Malay States joined in, the annual subsidy was increased to $250,000, the frequency of services was increased, and the British India Steamship Navigation Company now sailed between a larger number of south Indian and Malayan ports.

Large depots were set up at Nagapattinam and several other towns in the Madras province (Avadi, Papakovil, Melpakkam), with government officers being assigned to each of these depots to 'supervise and generally encourage the movement of Indian labour to Malaya'.[55] Similarly in Malaya there were three quarantine and immigration depots at Penang, Singapore and Port Swettenham to accommodate the labour immigrants as they arrived and to facilitate their movement to the estates in the interior.

By using retroactively the average figure for annual arrivals of indentured labour in Malaya from 1866-1910, 2,700 per annum, combined with the estimated 1,700 per year that arrived on verbal contract, the total figure for indentured labour movement from India to Malaya is 2,50,000, a quarter of a million people![56] Their living and working conditions were so deplorable that desertions were frequent, even though the penalties, if caught, were severe. There is one example for the year 1895 on the Gula estate in Perak, where there were 610 desertions out of a total labour force of 1,026 indentured immigrant labour.[57] There are estimates that in some years, the death rate could have been as high as 80 to 90 per cent among newly arrived indentured labour.[58]

In India there was mounting public outrage against the system of indentured labour, and the indignities it was inflicting on unsuspecting Indians. The leaders of India's freedom movement vigorously championed this cause. The gathering momentum of the struggle for Indian independence ensured that this issue received the prominence and attention it deserved, including a ready public platform and staunch support from every corner of the country. In 1910 Mazharul Haque, speaking in the Council of the Governor General of India, summed up matters vividly when he said:

> . . . the whole system of indentured labour is vicious in principle; it brutalises the employer; it demoralises the employed. It perpetrates the worst form of slavery in the guise of legal contract; it is bad in its inception, inhuman in its working and mischievous in its results, and ought to be done away with without any further delay.[59]

Finally in 1910, thanks to the unrelenting efforts of the Anti-Slavery Society in the UK, information about the high mortality rates among indentured labourers in Malaya was released in the British House of Commons. The criticism and opprobrium that this caused ensured that the system of recruiting indentured labour was finally scrapped. This was replaced by the *kangany* system of recruiting labour, said to be 'free', but not quite so in practice.

The *kangany* system of recruiting free labour was already in use by coffee and rubber planters in Malaya in preference to the indentured labour recruited for the sugar estates. According to the *Government of Madras Proceedings in the Public Department* for the year 1870, this system began functioning around the 1860s.[60] This system is named after the *kangany* or headman of the estate, who was deputed by his employer or association of employers to visit India for recruiting labour. In practice the *kangany* was not necessarily the headman or foreman, but the most trusted among the coolies already working on the estate. It was his responsibility to select workers who would be appropriate for the tasks awaiting them on that particular estate or group of estates. He normally recruited labour from among his relatives, neighbours and friends in his home village or taluk (cluster of villages, forming an administrative unit) in India. This was preferred in the interests of homogeneity and good working relationships on the estate, as well as encouraging entire families to move to Malaya. On each estate there could be one head *kangany* and many *cinna kanganys* (deputy or minor *kanganys*) who were answerable to the head *kangany*.

The *kangany* carried with him to India the *kangany* licence issued in his name and registered with the Deputy Controller of Labour in Penang. This licence specified the maximum number of labourers to be recruited (twenty, with the upper limit extended to 50 men for subsequent recruitment), the wage rates each labourer would receive, and the *kangany's* commission, paid to him by his employer per head of labour recruited (the legally permitted commission was as high as Rs. 26 per head before 1909, when it was reduced to just Rs. 10 per head. The employer frequently topped this up unofficially). After 1923, when the government of India appointed an Agent in Malaya, the *kangany* had to have his licence endorsed by this Agent as well prior to his departure for India.[61] After arriving in India the *kangany* needed to have his licence endorsed by the Malayan Emigration Agent (later designated Commissioner) or his assistants based at the main Malayan emigration depots at Avadi and Nagapattinam (earlier known as Negapatam). Finally, before proceeding to his village to start the recruiting process, the *kangany* obtained financial advances to defray his travel and recruiting expenses from one of the European firms (Messrs Binny and Company or Messrs Madura Company) who were the financial agents of his employers, the estate owners in Malaya. These very same companies had earlier dealt with indentured labour, and were now also the agents for the British India Steam Navigation Company, the sole carriers (since the 1890s) for all 'assisted' migrants between India and Malaya.[62]

The *kangany* had to offer several incentives to 'persuade' labour to emigrate to Malaya. Any outstanding debts of the prospective emigrant were settled, 'gifts' were given to his family members being left behind, and a lavish 'farewell party' arranged. The next step was to visit the village *munsif*. The village *munsif* (local magistrate), after satisfying himself that there were no objections to the individuals' emigrating, would sign against each emigrant's name, now entered on the back of the *kangany*'s licence. The emigrant's journey to Malaya could now begin, first by train to one of the Malayan emigration depots, where there were some more inspections and signatures required, followed by the sea-journey to Penang.

The *kangany* system of labour recritment became the mainstay of the labour emigration from India to Malaya. From 1898, the year from which regular statistical records were maintained, to 1938, the year that the *kangany* system was scrapped, more than 1.15 million *kangany* recruits came from India to Malaya. Extrapolating for the earlier years based on the *kangany* system having started in the 1860s, and the number of recruits under this system working on the coffee plantations in Malaya, the total arrivals in Malaya under the *kangany* system are estimated at 1.19 million between 1865 and 1938. 'This total represents more than 62 per cent of the total assisted labour migration, nearly 44 per cent of all labour (migration) and almost 28 per cent of the total Indian immigration into Malaya up to the end of 1957.'[63]

There are several significant aspects that emerge from this analysis of the *kangany* system, responsible for bringing in the largest number of labour recruits from India to Malaya. The numbers recruited under this system were driven by demand from the estate and plantation owners in Malaya rather than supply or availability of labour in India. The controlling factor was the number of *kangany* licences issued by the Deputy Controller of Labour in Penang. The recruitment of *kangany* labour was almost entirely from the Tamil speaking areas of south India, with small percentages from the Telugu (present-day Andhra Pradesh) and Malayalee (Malabar Coast of present-day Kerala) speaking regions of India. The overwhelming majority of *kangany* labour was recruited for the rubber plantations of Selangor and Perak. The *kangany* recruits going to Malaya were overwhelmingly male, with very few women or children, despite legislation passed by the government of India (Indian Emigration Act, 1922 and the Indian Emigration Rules, 1923) which, *inter alia*, stipulated that 'there should be at least one female emigrant for every 1.5 males assisted to emigrate as labourers'.[64] These provisions were never seriously enforced. In any case, the general impression and conviction among the male *kangany* recruits was that they were going abroad for a limited period, and would soon return home.

The *kangany* system served its purpose by providing much-needed labour for the plantations of Malaya. However, this system came under increasing criticism within India and Malaya, among

Indian nationalists and public interest groups, primarily targeting the misuse and abuse of the system. The Madras Annual Report on Emigration and Immigration, in 1926, described some of these shortcomings:

> Sharp recruiting practices on the part of the *kanganys* included purchasing recruits from professional recruiters or hotel keepers; forging signatures of village *munsifs*; exploiting family quarrels to get some member of the family to emigrate; promising young men that they would find wives in Malaya if they went there; catching recruits at village 'shandies', not unlike the practice of shanghaiing on the China coast; matching strangers in order to circumvent the rule that minors and women must be accompanied by a parent or relatives; misrepresentation of work and wages; substituting unfit persons for ones already passed as healthy; recruiting for estates other than their own; and, finally, not being *kanganys* at all but professional recruiters posing as *kanganys*.[65]

Technically, the labourers recruited under the *kangany* system were 'free', unlike those recruited earlier (before 1910) as indentured labour. Labourers recruited under the *kangany* system were not required to enter into contracts, and the law allowed them to leave their job after giving thirty days' notice. In practice, however, *kangany* labourers remained in thrall to the *kangany* who had recruited them. The *kangany* was their sole point of contact for all service matters, and they could interact with their employers only through the *kangany*. 'In disputes between the *kangany* and labourers, the *kangany* usually had the support of the managers.'[66] And the *kangany* would hardly ever allow a labourer to leave the estate, since he (the *kangany*) received from his employers in addition to his wages, a fixed amount as 'head money' per labourer per working day.[67]

By the 1920s, the *kangany* system of recruitment, the conditions under which emigration and transportation of the recruited labour were taking place, and the terms of employment were increasingly perceived within India and Malaya as being iniquitous and humiliating, not much different from the system of indentured labour. In the surge of nationalist sentiment in India amidst the mounting demand for independence from colonial rule, the maltreatment of Indian labour recruited by British and European commercial entities for working on overseas plantations became a potent symbol of the indignities Indians were suffering at home and abroad at the hands of the colonial power. Mahatma Gandhi's seminal work in South Africa during this period, supporting the rights of indentured labour and resisting racial discrimination had a huge impact back in India. The clarion call was for equal rights with the British, at home and abroad. The treatment of Indian labour working overseas became an issue that was debated at almost every annual session of the Indian National Congress. Resolutions were adopted calling for the immediate amelioration of the situation being faced by Indians in Malaya and other British overseas territories.

By the second decade of the twentieth century the media across India had taken up this campaign. Established newspapers like the *Amrita Bazar Patrika* published from Calcutta, *The Hindu* and the *Indian Emigrant*, both published from Madras, the *Servant of India* (published by the Servants of India Society, Poona), *Young India* (the weekly journal in English published by Mahatma Gandhi from 1919 to 1932), *Swarajya* and a host of others were unrelenting in their criticism of Indian emigration to Malaya and other destinations. In 1918, writing in the *Servant of India*, Mohandas Karamchand Gandhi, Henry Polak and C.F. Andrews had this to say in condemnation of assisted emigration of Indian labour and the treatment of Indians abroad:

> . . . the India Office and the Government of India . . . have not stood up for the rights of the labourers or the honour of Indians to the same extent as they are bound to do. Even the Government of (a) tiny (British colony) seems to prevail in a dispute with the Indian Government. . . . In being asked to give her labour under any terms to outside agency, India suffers a humiliation almost unexampled in the world. . . . In fine, India neither needs nor countenances the idea of assisted emigration. . . .[68]

The influential Madras daily, *The Hindu*, writing in 1937, strongly criticized the governments of India and Malaya on their policies regarding migration of Indian labour between the two countries:

> . . . The Indian in Malaya today is discriminated against on every side. His status is . . . far below that of other communities in the country. The public services are closed to him; under cover of protecting native interests arable land is denied to him; in the professions his existence is barely tolerated. . . .

> Even the Malaya-born Indian, who does not know India, is treated as an alien in the land of his birth! To permit emigration of Indians to a country where they are treated with such little consideration seems consistent neither with the self-respect of India, nor with the best interests of prospective emigrants. . . .[69]

In Malaya, too, concerted and unremitting efforts were made by all segments of society to highlight the plight of plantation labour from India. The *Malay Mail*, published in Kuala Lumpur, carried details of the travails faced by Indian labour immigrants in their issue of 30 January 1913.[70] Members of the Indian intelligentsia in Malaya were seriously concerned about the situation, and often spoke out even at the risk of being charged with sedition by the British Malayan government. In 1922, for example, the *Tamilaham*, a Kuala Lumpur Tamil weekly, published an article 'urging the Indians not to come to Malaya to work on rubber plantations'.[71] Other Indian-owned publications, too, took up this issue, including the *Tamil Nesan*, *Indian Pioneer*, *Indian*, *Indo-Malayan Review* and *Indian Association (Penang) Bulletin.*

The Indian (a weekly published every Saturday from Kuala Lumpur), in an article carried on 4 April 1936, recalls that:

> . . . the early settlers (from India and Ceylon) went to Malaya at the express invitation of the Native Rulers supported by the British Government. For instance, the Sultan of Selangor issued a proclamation inviting outsiders to help in the development of the country, and the Colonial Secretary of the Straits Settlements issued the following notification dated the 25th January 1875: 'we fully approve of the proclamation, and our above-mentioned officers will assist all good men who will go to Selangor and provinces either to settle or trade there'.[72]

A few months later, in a hard-hitting front-page article carried on 12 December 1936 and titled 'The Indian Labour Problem in Malaya', the author N. Raghavan, Barrister-at-law, described the existing system of emigration from India to Malaya as 'unfair, unscrupulous and intolerable', adding that 'once they (Indian immigrant labour) become domiciled here . . . do not hold out to them a third class citizenship imprinting on them the badge of inferiority.'[73]

At the time he wrote this article, N. Raghavan was President of the Indian Association, Penang. Several such associations representing the Indian community had been formed throughout

Malaya and Singapore, bringing together professionals and business entrepreneurs. There was, for example, the Selangor Indian Association (Kuala Lumpur), the Singapore Indian Association, the Kinta Indian Association (Ipoh), the Kedah Indian Association, the Butterworth Indian Association (Province Wellesley), and the Coastal Indian Association (Klang), among others. These Associations represented the 30 per cent non-labour component of the contemporary Indian migration to Malaya, which began with the establishment of Penang in 1786. The leaders of these associations were sensitive to the plight of plantation labour and were increasingly concerned about the iniquity and inequity of the treatment meted out to the Indians coming to Malaya to work on the plantations. They were keenly aware of the political furore in India over this issue.

It is not as if the Indians (in India and Malaya) were the only ones concerned about the abysmal conditions of Indian immigrant labour. In 1933 Sir Samuel Wilson, the then Permanent Under Secretary of State for the Colonies in the British Colonial Office, visited Malaya as part of his mandate to report on the administrative problems of the colonies. In Chapter VII of his Report, he said:

> No one will deny the important part that the non-Malays, who have made Malaya their home, have played in its development, and the share they are destined to take in helping its future progress, and I think that for this reason alone they are entitled to an assurance that their interests will not be allowed to suffer as a result of effect being given to a policy of decentralization. Moreover, subject to a policy of preferential employment of qualified Malays in the Government Services, and the reservation of sufficient lands for Malay needs, I take the view that the persons born in the Malay states of non-Malay parents (although only British protected persons) should be treated in those states in exactly the same way as persons born in the Colony of non-Malay parents (who are British subjects) and should have the same professional and business opportunities as European British subjects.[74]

This can be pinpointed as the crux of the issue, namely the substantially inferior treatment given to Malaya-born non-Malays, who had no other place to call home. In highlighting this issue, Sir Samuel Wilson was in effect recalling the decisions taken at the Imperial Conference held in London in 1921. (These Conferences, called Colonial Conferences before 1911, were periodic gatherings of government leaders from the self-governing colonies and dominons of the British Empire, held between 1887 and 1937, before the establishment of regular meetings of Commonwealth Prime Ministers in 1944.) The 1921 Imperial Conference, *inter alia,* resolved that, while every dominion (of the British Commonwealth) had the right to determine the composition and character of its population, at the same time 'the existence of political and other disabilities upon any part of British subjects settled in a dominion, or allowed to settle in a dominion, was an anomaly which must be removed'.[75] Not surprisingly, the only dissenting voice (after the adoption of this resolution) came from General Jan Smuts, the then Prime Minister of South Africa.

The British administration in Malaya did announce some steps, which they hoped would ameliorate the plight of Indian immigrant labour, but these were of little avail in the face of the strong control exercised by plantation owners. In the late 1920s, an Indian representative was appointed to the Federal Council in Malaya, as well as to the Indian Immigration Committee. Such steps played only a limited role in bringing India's concerns to the table in these official forums where matters of direct relevance to Indian immigrants, including plantation labour were discussed. The Indian Immigration Committee remained primarily an employers' body, with just two Indians in a group of 5 officials and 11 non-officials. In several of the FMS, seats set apart for Indians were often filled with members of other communities. The Agent of the British Indian government in Malaya drew pointed attention to this in some of his annual reports. Indian representation was notable by its absence in most local boards, including the Railway Board, the Standing Labour Sub-Committee of the FMS Railways, the Singapore and Penang Harbour Boards, most of which had representation from the Chinese community. 'Rural Boards like that of Province Wellesley (where Indians form some of the oldest settlers in Malaya, and where they constitute a very important section of the community) have no Indian members on them at all.'[76]

In response to mounting negative domestic public opinion about the condition of Indian labour in Malaya, the British Indian government sent a high-level delegation led by V.S. Srinivasa Sastri to Malaya in December 1936. The mandate of this delegation was to comprehensively investigate and study the conditions of the Indian immigrant community in Malaya, particularly Indian labour: the rates and payment of wages, the hours of work, provision for residence, medical treatment, education of the children of estate labourers, opportunities for subsidiary occupations, sex ratio and, finally, their political and social status. The Indian associations in diverse towns of Malaya and Singapore had been trying to form a central body to coordinate the efforts of individual associations. In anticipation of the Sastri visit, these efforts were accelerated in order that the views placed before the Sastri delegation could be the united expression of shared concerns and objectives.

The Central Indian Association of Malaya (CIAM) was the association formed to bring together individual Indian associations. During the nine years of its existence (it was voluntarily disbanded at the end of the Second World War), CIAM strongly championed the cause of Indian immigrant labour in Malaya. In India, too, CIAM kept the media and the public abreast of developments on all issues concerning Indian immigrant labour. CIAM repeatedly petitioned the Indian National Congress and the Madras Legislative Assembly to ban the emigration of Indian labour to Malaya.

The constituent organizations of CIAM prepared a detailed memorandum for presentation to V.S. Srinivasa Sastri's delegation. However, the formalities of registering CIAM could not be completed. Consequently, N. Raghavan, President of the Indian Association, Penang, presented the memorandum to V.S. Srinivasa Sastri. This memorandum is a pithy summary of the legitimate aspirations of all sections of the Indian immigrant community in Malaya, combining their analysis of the causes for the present difficulties facing them with a statement of the requests they were putting forward and the positive support they were anticipating from the British Indian government for these requests. There are several significant features of this memorandum that deserve to be highlighted.

First among these is the recognition by the leaders of Indian associations across Malaya (who participated in preparing this memorandum) that their interests were closely intertwined with the 70 per cent of the Indian immigrant community that were plantation labourers. The memorandum stated:

> It has been customary in the past . . . to regard Indian immigrants and settlers as nothing more than a large labour force. Indian questions here (in Malaya), we admit, have been to a very large extent labour questions, but questions of political status generally speaking affect not only the 70 per cent, but the whole Indian community. They are so interconnected that the solution of the one without the solution of the other will only result in an undesirable patchwork. . . . We do desire the solution of (a) those economic questions affecting Indian labour and (b) political questions affecting Indians generally. . . . The whole future of the Indian connection with Malaya depends on a satisfactory solution of both these questions.[77]

This willingness among the 30 per cent Indian immigrants, who were much better off in economic terms than those working on plantations or as labour on public projects, to make common cause with their impoverished brethren, is significant. This expression of unity among all Malayan Indians, regardless of occupation or profession, disturbed the British administration in Malaya. Did the British administration in Malaya put in special efforts to ensure that soon after this resolution was passed, this resolve for unity among many leaders of the Indian community suddenly weakened? In 1936, this unity of purpose also meant that the CIAM memorandum received much more careful attention in India from nationalist leaders. The British Indian government and the British administration in Malaya remained slow in their response to the fervent appeal contained in this resolution.

Second, the memorandum is unequivocal in blaming the British Administration in Malaya for the prevailing confusion in the enunciation and implementation of policies regarding the rights of those living in Malaya, whether in the Straits Settlements, the FMS or the Unfederated Malay States. For example, according to the memorandum, the declared policy had stated that 'the aim of the government is to provide primary education free of cost in the Malay language to all boys and girls of parents domiciled in the Malay peninsula' with the avowed purpose of 'building up a Malayan citizenship among all races whose home is Malaya'. In practice, however, implementation of such policies varied in different parts of the peninsula, as did the treatment accorded to Indians. The memorandum regrets that 'no adequate efforts have been made by the Home Government to elicit a satisfactory declaration of policy from the local governments as regards Indians in Malaya, and to get Indian claims for equality of citizenship and opportunity established beyond the predilections of individual administrators'. The memorandum stated:

What we ask for is a common policy both in the Colony and in the other parts. If the Government is striving for a Malayan citizenship as was announced in the past, the very worst thing that they can do to further it and nurture it is to identify it with a Malay one. It is, to quote one of our soundest jurists, our object 'to insist on clear thought and clear expression by His Majesty's Government' and to point out that the absence of this clear thought and clear expression has given rise to all manner of misunderstanding and has disturbed very violently the extraordinarily happy relations that subsisted in the country before Malayanisation came into our politics.[78]

Finally, the memorandum spells out the areas in which the Indian immigrant community in Malaya were seeking equal opportunity. The memorandum sought a reconciliation between the unending efforts of the British administration to bring in more plantation labour from India (improvement in the conditions of recruitment, wages and other terms of service for labour were specified), their policy of encouraging this labour to settle in Malaya with the persistent refusal of the same British administration to confer on these settlers equality of status with other communities living there. The memorandum clearly said:

Indians in the Federated Malay States have never attempted to make any inroads into the legitimate rights and demands of any other community. They have always advocated a policy of 'live and let live'. There is therefore acute disappointment that those Indians who are born and domiciled in the States will forever have to satisfy themselves with a decidedly secondary status. To tell persons who have been here for years, who know of no country other than this, whose affection and attachment are more towards this land than to any other, that they can at no time in their existence expect to receive equality of treatment with the other British subjects or subjects of the Sultans is perhaps the high watermark of political injustice.[79]

The V.S. Srinivasa Sastri delegation submitted its report soon after its return to India. When this was discussed in the Standing

Emigration Committee of the British Indian government, 'the (Indian National) Congress members of the Committee, it is understood, expressed profound dissatisfaction with the Report, particularly with regard to the recommendations in connection with toddy shops, sex ratio, political status and admission of Indians into the administrative service'.[80] The Foreign Department of the All India Congress Committee (AICC) issued a statement from Allahabad on 31 March 1937 where it recognized that 'Indians in Malaya have received the Sastri Report with some disappointment. They are unable to agree with some of the recommendations in the report and feel that a few of their problems have not been touched at all.'[81]

On the all-important issue of labourers' wages, the AICC statement emphasizes and supports the demand for adequate wages placed before the Sastri delegation by the Indian Associations in Malaya. The statement points out that on 20 March 1937, Chinese estate labourers secured 'without any delegation but by direct action' an increase in wage standardized at 75 cents per day for tappers, 55 cents for male and 50 cents for female unskilled labour. As against this, the Sastri Report had recommended that the Government of India press for the introduction of standard rates of 1928, namely 50 cents per day for men and 40 cents for women'. The AICC Foreign Department's statement enunciates clearly that 'unless the wages of Indian labour were standardized at the rate similar to Chinese wages, they would remain inadequate and the Indian labourer would continue in his present state of poverty and degradation'.[82]

V.S. Srinivasa Sastri prepared an additional report covering 'General Indian Problems'.[83] In the section on 'Appointments in Public Services' V.S. Srinivasa Sastri recounted the adverse criticism by the Indians in Malaya at the exclusion of Indians born and domiciled in Malaya from joining the recently constituted Special Service in the FMS. 'To this service only members of the British and Malay races are admitted', said V.S. Srinivasa Sastri in his additional report, adding that 'in recent years a pro-Malay policy has been in operation in the peninsula' and that this policy 'represents and fulfils the wishes of their Highnesses the Sultans and may not be modified except with their full consent. . . . It appears that not even in the third or fourth generation can a non-Malay attain to the status of a subject of the Sultans.'[84] This statement in the Report further increased the angst and consternation in India.

According to *The Hindu* newspaper, V.S. Srinivasa Sastri 'sets forth the explanations which the (British) Malayan government have offered and their view that these grievances are not occasioned by any racial bias'. *The Hindu* adds:

> Taking the question of citizenship rights, we are told that the reason why these rights have been withheld from Indians is that the Sultans of the States forming the Federated Malay States are against the grant of such rights. If that is so, they have only to be told that unless they agree to the grant of such rights, emigration of Indian labour to their States will not be permitted.[85]

The Indian public, it would seem, was no longer ready to accept the British explanation that wanted ever larger numbers of Indian emigrant labour for the plantations and public works in Malaya, while simultaneously denying to the progeny of this labour and of all Indians in Malaya, basic civil, economic and social rights on the grounds that the Sultans were against the same. The British sought to project Malay and Indian/Chinese rights as a zero-sum game, which it was (and is) not. The terms of the Pangkor Engagement or the Pangkor Treaty of January 1874 obliged the Sultans (it really applied just to the Sultan of Perak, but was used as the template for all the FMS) to act upon the advice of the British Resident 'in all questions other than those touching Malay religion and custom' (Clause 6). Clause 10 provided 'That the collection and control of all revenues and the general administration of the country be regulated under the advice of these Residents'.[86] These clauses provided the British a free hand and almost complete administrative control over the FMS. Yet they invoked the name of the Sultans whenever inconvenient questions were raised.

Scholars[87] have concluded that:

> . . . the British fostered the belief that Chinese (and Indians) really did not belong to local society—regardless of length of residence—and only Malay aristocrats and their colonial advisors should be allowed full participation in political or administrative roles. The origin of the British colour bar against non-Malay Asians is critically reported by George Maxwell (a former high-ranking colonial civil servant): 'With thirty-five years service in Malaya, and with intimate friendship with Rulers over two generations, I can say that I

never heard one of them say anything that would tend to support such an idea [exclusion of non-Malays from administrative appointments]. From the very earliest days of British protection, the Rulers have welcomed the leaders of the Chinese communites as members of their State Councils, and have paid the greatest deference to their opinions and advice. Other non-Malayans [non-Malays] are now members of the State Councils. The policy of keeping non-Malayans out of the administration owes its inception to British officials, and not to the Rulers.'[88]

Malayan Indians received the Sastri Report with consternation and dismay. N Raghavan, writing in *The Indian* on 13 March 1937, described the Sastri Report as 'apologetic in tone . . . weak in conception, and as a study of our situation, shallow beyond compare.' The Report rejected most of the suggestions and views put before the delegation during their four weeks' stay in Malaya: those pertaining to the economic and social interests of plantation labour, as well as others relating to the political status and general well-being of the entire Indian immigrant community in Malaya. Among the very few positive recommendations in the Report was one to restore or reinstate the 1928 wage rates for plantation labour, which had been slashed during the years of the Great Depression. This, too, was poorly received as being inadequate. 'What we want-and it was made quite plain to the Delegation' said N. Raghavan in his 13 March 1937 article in *The Indian* 'is not merely a restoration of cuts, but *adequate* wages. We want not merely a starvation wage but sufficient wage, if not to compensate for our coming all the way from India to this country, at least to satisfy some very elementary human needs'.

The Hindu, after its scathing criticism of the Sastri Report, concluded:

The Indian in Malaya today is discriminated against on every side. His status is that of a helot and far below that of other communities in the country. The public services are closed to him; under cover of protecting native interests, arable land is denied to him; in the professions, his existence is barely tolerated. Whereas the British, the Malay and even the Chinese are admitted into the volunteer corps, the Indian is excluded from it. Even the Malaya-born Indian, who does not know India, is treated as an alien in the land of his birth! To permit the emigration of Indians to a country where they are treated with such little consideration seems consistent neither with the self-respect of India, nor with the best interests of prospective emigrants. We trust that the Government of India and the Assembly will consider these aspects of the problem before they take any final decision on the question (of non-recruited assisted emigration).[89]

NOTES

1. K.S. Sandhu, *Indians in Malaya*, p. 118.
2. Ibid.
3. Ibid.
4. Ibid., p. 159, Table 5a.
5. Ibid., p. 159, Table 5b.
6. Ibid., pp. 67-8.
7. Ibid., p. 69.
8. Ibid., p. 70.
9. Ibid., p. 72.
10. Ibid., p. 73, fn. 3.
11. S. Arasaratnam, *Indians in Malaysia and Singapore*, pp. 92-3, quoting (in the last sentence) the 1923 Proceedings of the Federal Council of the Federated Malay States.
12. Ibid., p. 96, quoting the Malayan Year Book for 1930.
13. Ibid, p. 96.
14. *The Indian*, 6 February 1937, p. 4, under the title 'Malayan Chettiars' Joint Memorial'.
15. Professor Khoo Kay Kim, *Sunday Star*, 26 January 1996, accessed on 30 September 2010 at http://nagarathar.tripod.com/contributions_chettiars_malaya.htm.
16. Professor Khoo Kay Kim, 'Malay Attitudes Towards Indians', in K.S. Sandhu and A. Mani (eds), *Indian Communities in Southeast Asia*, pp. 270-1. Professor Khoo Kay Kim is quoting Ahmad Nazri bin Abdullah, '*Undang-undang Tanah Simpanan Melayu*' (The Malay Reservation Act), in *Sejarah Masyarakat Melayu Moden* (A History of Modern Malay Society), ed. Khoo Kay Kim (Kuala Lumpur, Persatuan Muzium Malaysia, 1984), p. 106.
17. Yousof, op. cit., p. 9.
18. D.G.E. Hall, *A History of South-East Asia*, p. 606.
19. Ibid.
20. Sandhu, op. cit., p. 45.
21. Ibid.
22. Ibid., p. 47, quoting from the SSFR.
23. Ibid., p. 52, fn. 5.
24. Ibid., p. 53.
25. Ibid., documents quoted at various points, pp. 52-67.

26. Ibid., p. 56.
27. Ibid., p. 54, quoting the Report of the Commissioners appointed to enquire into the State of Labour in the Straits Settlements and Protected Native States (1890), p. 66.
28. Ibid., p. 58, quoting Sir Frederick Weld, Governor of the Straits Settlements in 1887, from the Colonial Office records.
29. Anand A. Yang, 'Indian Convict Workers in Southeast Asia in the Late Eighteenth and Early Nineteenth Centuries', *Journal of World History* (University of Hawai'i Press), vol. 14, no. 2 (June 2003), p. 179.
30. Ibid., p. 179, quoting Stephen Nicholas and Peter R. Shergold 'Unshackling the Past', in *Convict Workers: Reinterpreting Australia's Past,* ed. Stephen Nicholas, Cambridge, 1988, p. 7).
31. Ibid., pp. 180-1.
32. Ibid., p. 180.
33. Ibid., p. 181, quoting the Bengal Public Consultations (October 1808 and June-July 1830) and India Criminal Judicial Consultations (July-December 1845 and June-September 1856).
34. Ibid., p. 204, quoting K.S. Sandhu (from Sharon Siddique and Nirmala Puru Shotam, *Singapore's Little India: Past, Present and Future*, p. 9, Singapore, 1982).
35. Ibid., p. 205.
36. Ibid., p. 208.
37. Sandhu, op. cit., p. 56, quoting the 'National Archives of India: Emigration Proceedings of the Government of India', January 1884, B proc 7-14.
38. Ibid., p. 56, quoting D.W. Figart, *The Plantation Rubber Industry in the Middle East*, Washington, 1925, p. 174.
39. Ibid., p. 57, quoting The Fabian Society, *Labour in the Colonies*, London, 1942, pp. 1-30.
40. Ibid., p. 60.
41. Ibid.
42. Ibid.
43. Ibid., p. 76, quoting 'Straits Settlements Government Gazette', Singapore, 1882, p. 490.
44. Ibid., p. 77.
45. Ibid., p. 85.
46. Ibid., p. 76.
47. Ibid., p. 79, quoting H.J. Stokes, Acting Sub-Collector, Tanjore in the 'Government of Madras Proceedings in the Public Department', 1870, pp. 40-4 (13 September 1870).
48. Ibid., pp. 81-2, quoting Report of the Commissioners appointed to enquire into the state of labour in the Straits Settlements and Protected Native States, 1890 (Singapore), pp. 36-45, Appendix A & L.

49. Ibid., p. 82.
50. Ibid., p. 78.
51. Ibid., p. 61, quoting figures from the Report of the Commissioners appointed to enquire into the state of labour in the Straits Settlements and Protected Native States, 1890, Singapore.
52. Ibid., p. 62.
53. Ibid., p. 91.
54. Ibid., p. 61.
55. Ibid., p. 64, quoting the Planters' Association of Malaya, 'Papers on Tamil Immigration presented at 12th annual meeting of the Planters' Association of Malaya, April 30, 1919', Kuala Lumpur, pp. 1 ff.
56. Ibid., p. 81.
57. Ibid., p. 85.
58. Ibid.
59. Ibid., quoting the 'Proceedings of the Council of the Governor General of India', 1911-12, L, 378.
60. Ibid., p. 89, with fn. 4.
61. Ibid., p. 92, including fns. 2, 3 and 4.
62. Ibid., pp 92-3.
63. Ibid., p. 96.
64. Ibid., p. 98.
65. Ibid., p. 100, quoting MAREI (Madras Annual Report on Emigration and Immigration), 1926, pp. 5-6; MAREI, 1930, p. 6, Annual Report of the Agent of the Government of India in British Malaya (ARAGIBM), 1926 pp. 5-11, 23; *The Straits Times*, 3 March 1912.
66. Ibid., p. 100.
67. Ibid., p. 101, quoting the *Amrita Bazar Patrika*, daily newspaper published from Calcutta, in its issue of 15 January 1913.
68. Ibid., pp. 108-9, quoting from *The Servant of India*, 1918, I, viii, pp. 88-9.
69. Ibid., p. 109, quoting from *The Hindu* of 6 March 1937.
70. Ibid., p. 101.
71. Ibid., p. 110.
72. *The Indian*, 4 April 1936, article on p. 10 entitled 'Malaya and the Foreigners', quoting the *Ceylon Spectator.*
73. *The Indian*, 12 December 1936, pp. 1 and 15.
74. Quotation from the Sir Samuel Wilson Report reproduced from the Memorandum submitted in November 1936 in Kuala Lumpur to the Indian delgation led by V.S. Srinivasa Sastri by N. Raghavan, President of the Indian Association, Penang, as carried by *The Indian*, 30 January, 1937, p. 2.
75. Quote from V.S. Srinivasa Sastri's public lecture on 'Indians Abroad', organized by the Indian Association Singapore in the Victoria

Memorial Hall, delivered before an audience of 2,700 persons of all nationalities, as reported in *The Indian* of 23 January 1937, pp. 4-5.

76. Extract from text of memorandum submitted to V.S. Srinivasa Sastri's delegation by N. Raghavan, President of the Indian Association, Penang, as carried in *The Indian*, 23 January 1937, p. 14.
77. Ibid., p. 2.
78. Ibid.
79. Ibid., pp. 2 and 14.
80. *The Indian*, 24 April 1937, p. 1.
81. *The Indian*, 10 April 1937, p. 13, reproducing the text of the statement of the Foreign Department of the All India Congress Committee on the Sastri Report.
82. Ibid.
83. Full text of V.S. Srinivasa Sastri's additional report has been carried by *The Indian* in its issue of 6 March 1937, p. 11, following the Official Summary of the Delegation's Recommendations and Conclusions, carried in the same issue on pp. 1, 6 and 11.
84. Ibid., p. 11.
85. *The Indian*, 20 March 1937, quoting *The Hindu*, Madras.
86. D.G.E. Hall, *A History of South-east Asia*, p. 595.
87. Charles Hirschman, 'The Making of Race in Colonial Malaya: Political Economy and Racial Ideology', *Sociological Forum*, vol. 1, no. 2 (Spring, 1986) p. 353.
88. Ibid., quoting George Maxwell, 'The Mixed Communities of Malaya', *British Malaya*, February 1943, p. 118.
89. *The Indian*, 20 March 1937, p. 9, quoting *The Hindu*.

11

Jawaharlal Nehru Visits Malaya

The intense emotions aroused in India over the difficulties faced by Indian emigrants to Malaya, particularly those working as plantation labour and on public works projects, had led to the visit of the V.S. Srinivasa Sastri delegation, followed by the publication of his report. The Sastri Report, unfortunately, had served only to further inflame passions and had fuelled anger, both in India and Malaya. It is no surprise, then, that within weeks of the report's publication, the news broke that Pandit Jawaharlal Nehru, who was then President of the Indian National Congress, would visit Malaya after his visit to Burma. Pandit Nehru arrived in Penang on 23 May 1937 from Rangoon (now Yangon) by the *S.S. Karoa* for a fortnight's stay in Malaya, accompanied by his daughter, Indira Priyadarshini Nehru and his private secretary.

Formally, it was stated that Pandit Nehru 'has kindly accepted the invitation of the management of *The Indian* to visit Malaya for a short while, mainly for the purpose of enjoying a much-needed rest after his recent illness'.[1] However, as a result of intense public interest in meeting and interacting with him, Pandit Nehru had a hectic programme of meetings and public lectures in Penang, Taiping, Ipoh, Rawang, Batu Caves, Kuala Lumpur, Singapore, Johore Bahru, Batu Pahat, Muar, Malacca, Kuala Kubu, Port Dickson (where he rested for four days), Seremban, Semenyih, Kajang, Klang, Port Swettenham, Fraser's Hill, Bentong and Butterworth. He left Penang on 5 June 1937, by the *S.S. Karagola*, sailing for Rangoon, from where he transferred to an Indian liner owned by the Scindias. Pandit Nehru arrived in Calcutta on 13 June via Akyab and Chittagong.

This was Pandit Jawaharlal Nehru's first visit to Malaya. He was by this time a leader of national and international fame and standing. People from all communities and races evinced keen interest in his visit. It was a private visit, but British officials from the Labour Department met him, anxious to explain the situation regarding Indian labour on the estates. They invited him to visit any area or estate. He met Malay officials on the estates and at various gatherings. Prominent Chinese community leaders and entrepreneurs hosted him on several occasions. In Singapore he was 'officially received' at the Naval Base and the new Air Base.[2] In his 'Farewell to Malaya' statement to the press given at Butterworth on 4 June 1937, Pandit Nehru said:

> I carry back many treasures with me—the memory of this beautiful country so richly endowed by nature, and (the) far more precious memory of the love and affection that have been showered upon me in such abundant measure. To my own countrymen here of all classes, from the labourer in the field to the merchant or professional person, I find it difficult to express my gratitude. . . . But the welcome that I received from others also, from the people of the country, the Malayans, and the people of China who live here in such large numbers, and from the Ceylonese who are so near akin to us. To them all I am most grateful.[3]

The Indian immigrant community in Malaya gave Pandit Nehru a rapturous welcome wherever he went. Crowds of up to 15,000, some of the largest ever seen in Malaya, were present at several of his public meetings, at every railway station, at every stop on his road journeys.[4] Pandit Nehru spoke at length about the situation in India, the arduous struggle for independence and the role of the Indian Natonal Congress. There were the inevitable stream of questions and petitions about the adverse conditions and difficulties faced by Indian immigrant labour, including comments on the V.S. Srinivasa Sastri Report.

The mainstream media (largely British-owned) provided their own assessments, referring to 'agitators' and saying that Pandit Nehru is 'talking politics and not praising sufficiently the British Government and the British Empire'.[5] Pandit Nehru pointed to these references, and answered these critics by saying unequivocally 'I have been shown every courtesy by all I have come into contact with, the government officials included, but that does not mean that when I meet my own countrymen, I must not speak on subjects which are of common interest to us.'[6] Similarly, in his address in Kuala Lumpur on 25 May 1937, Pandit Nehru said 'A Malayan daily has suggested that apparently there is some secret motive behind my visit to this country. I want to state that I do not act secretly or furtively and I have given expression to whatever I have had in my mind.'[7]

Pandit Nehru's views and advice as conveyed to the Indian immigrant community in Malaya, in 1937, showed great perspicacity and prescience. Much of what he said remains relevant today, more than 65 years later. Pandit Nehru was deeply aware of the close historical links between Malaya and India, and attached great significance to maintaining and developing the ties of friendship between the two countries. Addressing the Indian immigrant community in Ipoh on 24 May 1937, he said:

> The country of Malaya had contacts with India a thousand years ago and here a large number of Indians came and settled down . . . and for hundreds of years brought contacts of one kind or other. But our new relationship with Malaya should be one of friendship. You must make friends with the people and try to help them as far as possible.[8]

The very next day, speaking in Kuala Lumpur (Selangor) he added:

> I want you to remember this: whether we (the people of India) can do much for you or not, we have not forgotten the Indians who have gone abroad. I want Indians to go abroad and to be on friendly terms with other people and not to think of their advantage at the cost of the people of the country where they are settled.[9]

He despaired of India's colonially subservient position, but spoke with great conviction about the important roles India and China were destined to play in world affairs. Speaking in Singapore on 26 May 1937 he said:

> You who live here in Malaya may be largely acquainted with the Indian 'coolie' as he is called with some contempt. It is true perhaps because India herself has sunk to the coolie ranks among nations, and perhaps that contempt is justified, but remember that if India has gone down, she has also the vitality to rise again and is going to play a big role in the history of Asia and in the history of the world. . . . You may think that China is a weak nation today, and not strong

enough to combat or face aggression from outside. But do not think that a great nation like China, which has been carrying on for several thousands of years with many ups and downs, is going to collapse because some foreign power has attacked her territories. China will rise again and play an important role in world affairs. And similar will be the position of India.[10]

It hurt Pandit Nehru deeply that in Malaya 'the Indian community . . . is very backward, specially so in politics. A comparison with the Chinese in almost every department of life and business is very much to the disadvantage of the Indians.'[11] This was his assessment conveyed privately in a letter written from Port Dickson on 29 May 1937, addressed to Rajendra Prasad, senior leader of the Indian National Congress and future president of India. A few days later Pandit Nehru made his concerns public. In his article titled 'The Indian Labour Problem in Malaya' published in *The Indian* on 5 June 1937, Pandit Nehru said:

I fail to see entirely why Indian labour should be paid less than Chinese or other labour. Apart from other and vital considerations which affect the Indian labourer and his present relatively low standard of living, there are national aspects of this question, and India must claim equality of status and wage with others.[12]

Through this article carried in *The Indian* on 5 June 1937, Pandit Nehru stated his views on the problems facing Indian labour in Malaya, and how the situation could be ameliorated. He explained that while he had not visited any estates, he had read the V.S. Srinivasa Sastri Report and the memorandum prepared by the group of Indian Associations, and had held several discussions with officers of the Labour department of the (British) Malayan government, as well as with Indian labourers.

Pandit Nehru's first observation was that:

At present, as far as I know, there is little in the nature of labour organization in Malaya. I was told, however, and I was glad to hear it, that the labour department would welcome the formation of trade unions. . . . When we speak of trade unions we think invariably of workers' unions. But chambers of commerce and planters' associations and other employers' organisations are as much trade unions as any labourers' union. . . . Unorganised workers are helpless before them.[13]

Pandit Nehru queried further:

. . . what exactly are we driving at when we talk of labour and its future? Is it just to maintain a large force of labour, with a certain minimum degree of security and comfort, ever supplying larger dividends to industry, but with no other vital change in their condition? Or do we think in terms of raising them educationally, culturally and economically ever to higher levels, and making them citizens of the country they live in and of the larger world? Surely, only the second alternative is worth working for, and it is the only possible way if one takes a long view. . . . In Malaya probably the labour population is never thought of as consumers. To some extent this is true owing to the nature of Malaya's principal industries and a lack of other industries. But a closer analysis would demonstrate that the wealth and prosperity of Malaya would increase greatly if the purchasing power of the masses was continually raised. Fortunately for Malaya, nature has blessed the country to an unusual degree and it has not suffered so far from the ills that afflict the world. Why should it not utilize this natural wealth to raise all the people who live here to ever higher standards, educationally, culturally and in other ways? Every investment of this kind pays itself back hundred-fold in the human material that it produces.[14]

Pandit Nehru addressed the vexatious issue of toddy-shops when he said:

It is our desire and settled policy in India to put an end to the drink evil. We are told, however, that the revenue from excise cannot easily be dispensed with and this excuse serves to continue a policy which saps the energy and vitality of the worker and impairs his efficiency. In Malaya at least this should be no reason for continuing toddy shops. The fear that *samsu*[15] brewing may spread may have some basis, but surely this is no reason why a present evil should be allowed to continue.[16]

The conclusions Pandit Nehru drew from his analysis were specific and clear. 'Therefore,' he said, 'I think that wages should be kept at as high a level as possible. A maintenance level is not enough. Labour is at least as important, if not more so, as capital in the development of industry, and labour should share in the prosperity of the industry, as it is made to suffer when industry languishes.' He also suggested that 'it is eminently desirable to reduce the working day to eight hours in Malaya'. And he expressed his entire agreement with the V.S. Srinivasa Sastri Report that 'the *kangany* system of recruiting labour should go. I have heard much against it and nothing in its favour.'[17]

On the importance of education, Pandit Nehru said that 'if it is our purpose to raise the human material in the labour areas to higher levels, then education becomes a vital necessity. I feel that there is tremendous room for improvement in this respect and the fullest opportunities not only for primary but secondary education should be provided for.' In a separate message written on the eve of his departure from Malaya, Pandit Nehru expanded further on the theme of education when he said:

It is the business of the state to provide free education and medical facilities for all. In a rich country like Malaya this is easily possible but none the less conditions being what they are we must help ourselves where the state fails to perform its functions. For education is a vital matter for the community and all its future depends on the human material it produces and trains. In this matter the Chinese in Malaya have set a fine example by putting up innumerable up-to-date schools. Why should not the Indians follow?[18]

At the end of his first visit to Malaya Pandit Nehru advised the Malayan Indians that

their duty to Malaya is to live in friendship and fullest co-operation with the children of the soil, with the Chinese, and with all others who live here. They must consider the interests of Malaya as their own, for Malaya has become their land by birth or adoption, and must work for the progress of this country in every way. The people of the soil must feel that we come to co-operate with them and not to injure their interests in any way.[19]

In an earlier statement to the press in Singapore made on 2 June 1937, Pandit Nehru had said:

In regard to the children of the soil, it is right that their interests should have precedence over others. But if Indians or others are born here and have made Malaya their permanent home, why should they not be considered also as children of the soil?[20]

Finally, Pandit Nehru described the Malayan Indian community's

duty to themselves. My first reaction here was not a very favourable one. I found too many small Indian groups functioning separately. There was no conflict between these groups but nevertheless, they weakened the community. Strength requires a larger unity comprising all these groups. . . . A larger number of Indians here belong to the labouring class and our future in Malaya is thus closely bound up with the future of Indian labour here. It is necessary therefore that middle-class Indians should seek to serve the labouring masses in every way and remain in close touch with them, so that they may know their needs and wants and might help them in their struggle.[21]

Pandit Nehru touched a raw nerve here, zeroing in on one of the most sensitive issues within the Malayan Indian community. There had been moves afoot since the early 1920s to bring together the small and disparate Indian associations into a single united organization. *The Indian* had carried an article in December 1925, prophetically calling for the establishment of a Malayan Indian Congress.[22] A beginning was made in 1928 by convening annual conferences of Indian associations, with the objective of discussing and passing resolutions on matters of interest to all sections of Indians, including labour issues (wages, repatriation, land settlement, toddy control), social issues (education for the Indians in Malaya, representation on Councils and public bodies, registration of Hindu marriages) and measures to promote unity.

'British official attitude' did not really encourage such meetings. At the fourth annual conference of Indian associations held in Ipoh in April 1931, the president 'made a radical speech condemning the way in which Indian labour was being treated', alleging that 'labour was being grossly exploited by the European capitalist'. This speech set off a strong reaction in British official and capitalist circles. The influential *Straits Times* 'condemned the speech as contrary to the tradition of Malayan politics, which were characterized by moderation and restraint' and expressed the hope that 'the extremism and polemics which . . . were the features of nationalist politics in India . . . would not be imported into this country (Malaya) and mar the good relations that existed between communities and individuals.'[23] The annual conference of Indian associations did not meet again after this. It is only in 1936-7, in anticipation of the visit of the delegation led by V.S. Srinivasa Sastri, followed by the visit of Pandit Jawaharlal Nehru, that steps were initiated for the formation of CIAM.

Even after his return to India Pandit Nehru continued to follow, with great interest, developments concerning the Indian immigrant community in Malaya. In 1938 the *kangany* system of recruitment was formally abolished when the (British) Indian government placed a ban on all assisted labour emigration. According to the records of the Debates of the Legislative Assembly of India (1939) and the Planters' Association of Malaya Circulars (1946), the British Malayan government approached the government of

India in 1939, 1940, 1941 and also after the Japanese occupation had ended, seeking a resumption of assisted labour emigration to Malaya. Each time the request was declined.[24]

Malayan planters tried to sidestep the ban on *kangany* recruitment from India by bringing out larger numbers under the then permissible category of non-assisted labour emigration. As a result, in September 1938, the Legislative Assembly in India amended the Indian Emigration Act of 1922, authorizing the Indian government to control unassisted labour emigration as well. It is reflective of Pandit Jawaharlal Nehru's continuing interest in developments affecting Indian labour in Malaya that in December 1938, eighteen months after he had sailed from Penang on 5 June 1937, he said in a message sent to *The Indian*:

> The memory of my visit to the beautiful and pleasant land of Malaya is fresh in my mind, but, above all, I think of the lot of the thousands of the Indian workers there.
>
> I have come to know of the heavy reductions which were made by planters in the wages of Indian labourers without any reference to India. I am glad that the Central Indian Association of Malaya resisted this and that the government in India banned all recruitment of south Indian labour to Malaya. Subsequently it appears that undercover of 'voluntary emigration' labour recruitment continued in illicit form. But in September last the central assembly passed an amending bill regulating this form of labour emigration also.
>
> Efforts are now being made by vested interests in Malaya to open out a fresh source of cheap labour from India which they can exploit at their will. We have to be vigilant to prevent any such opportunity being given to them. India cannot and will not permit the exploitation of her children in this way and we must insist that no Indian worker is allowed to be lured away abroad unless decent wages and conditions of livelihood are assured for him. Therefore all emigration to Malaya must stop till such time as guarantees are forthcoming of proper treatment of our workers.
>
> It is the business of all Indians in Malaya to support the cause of Indian labour there.[25]

The importance of Malayan Indians coming together to ameliorate the difficulties being faced by Indian labour remained in the forefront of Pandit Nehru's thoughts. Despite its limited longevity, CIAM, formally founded in 1937-8, did succeed in playing this unifying role among the diverse groups that comprised the Malayan Indian community. CIAM effectively took up cudgels to defend the interests of Indian labour in Malaya. They kept the Indian Legislative Assembly and the Indian National Congress informed about the adverse developments concerning Indian labour, sending them petitions and representations with information, advice and suggested policy recommendations. In Malaya they took up issues relating to wages and toddy shops with the planters and the Indian Agent. CIAM was the first Indian organization which carried on political activity as one of its declared aims, and should thus be regarded as the first political party of Malayan Indians.[26]

This was a difficult and sensitive juncture for the Malayan Indian community. Their numbers were large, with the 1931 census in Malaya placing the Indians at 6,21,847 compared to just 44,000 in 1881, an exponential, almost 15-fold increase in just 50 years.[27] The labour component of this immigration, close to 70 per cent of the total figure, had been socially engineered by the plantation owners and the British Malayan government, drawn from the deprived and dispossessed sections of society, predominantly from a few districts of the Madras Presidency. They were Hindu and primarily male. In the 1891 census in Malaya, there were just 18 females per 1,000 Indian males. It is only very gradually that the sex ratio ameliorated, with 171 females per 1,000 Indian males in the 1901 census, 308 in 1911, 482 in 1931, going up to 692 at the time of Malaya's independence in 1957.[28]

Over the years, the ameliorating sex ratio and even the growing numbers of Indians in Malaya were increasingly due to Indians born in Malaya, to parents who were in large measure naturalized Malayans due to their long stay there. Indeed, after 1938, when all labour immigration from India was banned, the local-born Malayan Indians remained the sole cause for the growing numbers of the Malayan Indian community in each successive census. The number of Malayan-born Indians were estimated to be just 12 per cent of the Malayan Indian community in the 1911 census, but this figure rose to 21.1 per cent in the 1931 census, and to 49.8 per cent in the 1947 census. In the 1957 census, at the time of Malaya's independence, about two-thirds of Malayan Indians were born in Malaya.[29] Among these Indians, there was the growing consciousness of being Straits-born or Malayan-born. They had considerably fewer contacts with India than their parents' generation. Yet, right up to the Japanese occupation of Malaya and other parts of Southeast Asia, Indians and Chinese born in Malaya were denied the right to citizenship of Malaya.

RACE, ETHNICITY AND COMMUNALISM IN COLONIAL MALAYA

Scholars have concluded that 'communalism lay at the very basis of public policy in (British) Malaya'.[30] During the period of British colonial rule in Malaya, ethnic communities were physically and socially segregated from each other. This could be ensured because of the striking coincidence between ethnic groupings and occupational specialization: the Chinese in the mines, the Indians on the plantations and the Malays in agriculture. As a result, 'the economic division between peasant cultivation and the export sector also marked the ethnic division between Malays and non-Malays'.[31] Moreover,

> land policies tended to discourage Chinese and Indians from entering subsistence agriculture. Malays were encouraged to remain in their rural villages. Even in towns where there was the potential for inter-ethnic contact, residential areas, marketplaces, and recreational space were typically segregated along ethnic lines. Although there may have been traditional preferences for socializing within one's own community, colonial policies did nothing to encourage movement toward an integrated society. . . . It was only in schools and in some professional organizations that there was a possibility for structured inter-ethnic interaction. Except for the English language schools in urban areas, the overwhelming majority of children attended vernacular schools that were ethnically homogeneous.[32]

In Malaya, the division of society on the basis of ethnicity facilitated control by the colonial power through the practice of 'divide and rule'. This ethnic or racial compartmentalization blended with the policy of white-race superiority practised by most European colonialists, including the British, throughout Asia and Africa in the nineteenth and twentieth centuries. 'The important point is that modern racism is not a prehistoric residue; it was a "new" theory that accompanied the rise of European technological superiority and expansion.'[33] Thus,

> racial ideology legitimated the vast inequality in economic terms between Europeans and Asians. . . . The gaps in economic standards between Europeans and Asians in the civil service also served to maintain the social distance that froze relationships in a vertical plane between superiors and inferiors. Racism—the ideology of inherent differences—provided a theory of entitlement for unjust rewards which could not otherwise be justified.[34]

Britain depended on retaining, even widening economic disparities, for their profits, with the help of the Malay Sultans. Hence, while the immigrant communities' difficulties grew,

> for the Malay aristocracy. . .colonialism had a number of beneficial elements. The sultans and their families received fabulous allowances and were given appropriate status deference by colonial officials anxious to maintain the fiction of Malay sovereignty. The children of the Malay aristocracy were allowed to join the junior ranks of the elite colonial service.[35]

None of the other races was allowed this privilege. The British carefully fostered this feeling among the Malay aristocracy about the need to retain the exclusivity of their privileges, rather than sharing these with the immigrant communities in recognition of the latter's immense contribution to the prosperity of Malaya. Over time, particularly by the end of Second World War, the Malay aristocracy perceived their colonial masters as their allies in what was now seen as a 'struggle' for resisting the grant of equal rights to the immigrant communities (Chinese and Indian).

The perspective is somewhat similar regarding the Malay Reservation Enactments which, for the Federated Malay States, were first adopted in 1913 and subsequently in 1933. Beginning in 1930 with Kelantan, separate Malay Reservation Enactments were passed for each of the Unfederated Malay States thus making this law applicable to all states in Peninsular Malaya, except Penang, Malacca and Singapore. The Malay Reservation, or 'red-ink grants' as they are commomly described, is a special category of notified land that can only be owned, dealt with or transferred to Malays, natives of the state where the land is located, and to certain specified bodies, statutorily recognized as Malay. 'This is to protect and preserve the Malay race by prohibiting all kinds of transactions involving Malay reservation land with non-Malays' and to ensure that the Malays remain 'permanent settlers on agricultural land'.[36]

This paternalistic approach by the British towards the Malays was projected in 1910 as being necessary to free them 'from the clutches of those people who now remit to India the large sums of money which they bleed from the (Malay) people'.[37] This is an unmistakable reference to the Chettiars from the Madras Presidency who, by this time, were well established as financiers and money-lenders throughout Peninsular Malaya. Just as in the eighteenth and nineteenth centuries the British had effectively curtailed the activities of Indian merchants and traders in the Malay Peninsula, it was now the turn of the Indian financiers to face British ire.

British colonial civil servants felt that the Malay was 'prodigally and improvidently divesting himself of his birth-right and inheritance' and that 'unless a better judgement is exercised on their behalf the result will be extinction of the Malay yeoman-peasant'.[38] In the same year, 1910, the British established a Committee 'to inquire into and report on the question of the alienation of hereditary rights in land by Malays and the desirability or otherwise of preventive or remedial action being taken'. This Committee recommended that to prevent the Malays from becoming 'dispossessed wanderers', suitable areas of land should be notified 'for alienation to persons of the Malay race and religion only'. This is said to be the first time that the British were equating or associating the Malay race with religion. Moreover, to keep the price of this notified land low (which would discourage non-Malays from buying the land), it was suggested that the Malays should not be allowed to plant rubber or more than a limited number of fruit trees on their land.[39]

Under the terms of the first Malay Reservation Enactment passed in December 1913, 'no rubber trees could be planted on the Malay reservation land although the Malays were eager to open vast areas for rubber plantation. Thus, the British deliberately denied the Malays their opportunity to share the prosperity of the country, which rubber had brought.'[40]

The 1913 Malay Reservation Enactment did not achieve its stated purpose of stopping the Malays from selling their land to non-Malays. J.M. Gullick says 'there was no attempt made by the (British) Residents to consult Malay rulers on the policy and implementation of the new land tenure in the Malay States'.[41] In short, the Residents arrogated wide and undefined administrative powers to themselves. The Residential system was most effective in mobilizing the Malay rulers to open up the Malay States for the attainment of British economic interests. This was what Emerson characterized as Indirect Rule, namely to lawfully rule and exploit the economy and the country 'by using the Rulers to bolster their (British) own position'.[42]

In 1933, a much more drastic Malay Reservation Enactment was brought in. 'It was designed to make it "as unhealthy as possible" for Malay proprietors to deal or negotiate with their land titles'. The British were hailed as the ones 'who have the welfare of the Malays really at heart' and the 'Malay's best friends'.[43] Realistically, in 1933, it was the Chinese who were the chief source of concern for the British. The Chinese had become 'very powerful economically, socially . . . and posed a threat to British rule. . . . The objective of the Malay reservation policy was designed to prevent the Chinese from owning new land.'[44] In the ultimate analysis

> the British . . . used the Malay Reservation Enactment to hold land not so much for the interest of the Malays but rather for the disposal of the British companies. By 1938 the British owned more than 43 per cent of alienated land in the Malay States. The actual beneficiaries of the Malay Reservation policy owned only 27 per cent (paddy land), and the Chinese and Indians merely 23 per cent.[45]

The Malaysian scholar concludes that 'the "love" the British expressed for their Malay subjects was in fact a political ruse to protect their own supremacy in the Malay States. The British wanted the Malays to remain economically undeveloped and in need of protection.'[46]

The American scholar, Charles Hirschman, has concluded that 'the "racial divisions" among the multi-ethnic population of Peninsula Malaysia are largely a product of colonial practices and European ideology in the decades following the "forward movement" in the 1870s'.[47] The Indians and the Malays have known and understood each other, lived and worked together over the centuries, pre-dating the colonial period in the Malay Peninsula. The Chinese, too, have been active in this region at least since the days of the Malacca Sultanate. Any 'cultural barriers' or differences were accommodated and overcome, and there was a gradual process of 'acculturation', which included intermarriage.

When the British colonialists decided to meet the enormous economic potential for the export of rubber and tin through immigrant labour, it led to 'a wave of Chinese and Indian immigrants, on an historically unprecedented scale' to the states of the Malay Peninsula. Instead of meeting the demographic challenges caused by this situation through a natural process of 'ethnic accommodation and adjustment', the British saw their twin interests of retaining control and profit maximization best served through a policy of segregation.

> The new immigrants . . . were not thrown into contact with Malays but were segregated geographically, economically and socially from the local population. The colonial government 'managed' the plural society by trying to maintain the Malay feudal social structure in the countryside and a 'temporary' immigrant population working in the mines, plantations, and cities.[48]

Interaction removes misconceptions, segregation reinforces preconceived notions about racial stereotypes. Not unexpectedly, the three major communities, the Malays, the Indians and the Chinese

> tended to accept the unfounded generalizations of innate racial differences about other communities. Once established, ideas have a life of their own. Moreover, racial ideologies tended to legitimate [*sic*] actions by Malay and non-Malay leaders in both colonial and post-colonial society. More than rubber and tin, the legacy of colonialism was racial ideology.[49]

SITUATION ON THE EVE OF THE JAPANESE OCCUPATION

During and in the aftermath of the First World War, the impact and influence of Indian nationalism and the struggle for independence made itself felt among Malayan Indians. The Ghadar and Khilafat movements received strong resonance and support respectively from Sikhs and Punjabi Hindus, and from Indian Muslims living in Malaya. In December 1914, Punjabis of the Malay States Guides, influenced by the Ghadar movement, refused to go to East Africa, and in February 1915, the Fifth Native Light Infantry mutinied, killing a number of Europeans and releasing German and Austrian prisoners-of-war. After conducting a Court of Inquiry, the British concluded: 'The town and settlement of Singapore together with the neighbouring States enjoy a widespread and unenviable notoriety as being a focus of Indian seditionists. . . . It is also well known to harbour rank seditionists of Indian nationality among its residents.'[50]

From now on, the British made every effort to insulate Malayan Indians from the influences of Indian nationalism. British Malaya was frequently described as an oasis of 'apolitical tranquility'. In fact, however, 'the influence of three separate Asian nationalisms—Chinese, Indian and Indonesian—was itself a source of increasing internal tension'.[51] The British colonial administration in Malaya managed these tensions through the communalization of society, and encouraging the emergence of 'competitive communal nationalisms'. The seemingly plural society was in actual practice deeply divided along communal lines. The British effort and strategy was to ensure that the most intense conflicts and tensions remained within the confines of each communal group, or between the communities. Under no circumstances were the communal groups allowed to unite and collectively face the colonial regime. The scholar Michael Stenson has described as 'schizoid' the policies followed by the British in Malaya to achieve these ends.

For example, by the 1930s, the British were actively encouraging the creation of a substantial and permanent Indian labour force in Malaya, believing this to be the only way to prevent the infiltration of nationalist ideologies from India, while simultaneously hedging their bets against a ban by the Indian government on labour-emigration to Malaya. The rubber industry's high productivity and profits were dependent on Indian labour, yet the British maintained the myth (in their public pronouncements) that the Indian labour force was alien and transitory, and consequently could not be accorded either full political rights, or any social security and education for their children, or even a fair wage for their backbreaking physical contribution to the production of rubber.

Right from 1913, when Malay Reservations (for land) were first enacted,

> the Malay peasantry were discouraged from entering the rubber export economy as smallholders and instead were encouraged to produce rice in order to complement rather than compete with the interests of British capital.

Their function was to provide both a stable political base and cheap food for Chinese and Indian labour. . . . As their labour was needed for the plantations and mines, access to land was also effectively closed to Chinese and Indian labourers by the 1930s.[52]

Similarly,

non-Malay challenges were also warded off by the systematic exploitation of their many old and new divisions. Straits-born Chinese were wooed in preference to the politically aroused China-born. Ceylon Tamils were appointed in the 1930s to official councils as representatives of 'Hindu' interests, in order to deny recognition to Indian communal and nationalist sentiment. Malayan-born Indians were urged to split from the nationalistic Indian-born and to identify with the land of their birth. Separatist Dravidian subnationalists and Muslim League supporters were favoured with benign indulgence while the more aggressively nationalistic Central Indian Association of Malaya (CIAM) was pointedly ignored or openly criticized.[53]

By the 1920s, several Indian associations had become active. The earliest Indian association was the Ipoh Indian Association founded in 1904. Most of these associations were established by the English-educated Indian elite, including merchants, administrative and clerical staff, doctors and lawyers. The formation of these associations was contemporaneous with the establishment of the *Kesatuan Melayu*, or Malay associations led by the English-educated Malay elite. In the early years after the Indian associations started, their focus was on social and sports activities. Gradually, these associations took up charitable welfare work, including setting up of free dispensaries and schools, even an unemployment fund. The impact of the Great Depression of 1929, which brought into sharp focus the discriminatory treatment against Malayan Indian labourers who now faced massive retrenchment and deportation, was an eye-opener for the English-educated Indian elite in Malaya.

Indian nationalist leaders were carefully following the fate of the by now very large community of Malayan Indians. It was the task of the newly-appointed agent of the Government of India in Malaya to report on the problems being faced by the Indians living in Malaya, as well as to liaise with government departments there. Among his first major tasks, and successes, was to gain recognition for Indians as a group (rather than sub-divided by region and religion, as hitherto). The Indians were now recognized as the third major Asian community for purposes of representation on official councils and committees.

From now on, there were systematic efforts to form pan-Malayan Indian associations, including Chambers of Commerce, culminating in September 1936 in the formation of CIAM. The visits to Malaya by Nobel Laureate Rabindranath Tagore (1927) and Indian National Congress leader Pandit Jawaharlal Nehru (1937) infused the idea of remaining united and its importance for Malayan Indians. In the Malayan context, CIAM was perceived as a communal organization, representing the interests of the Malayan Indians. The leadership of CIAM realized the importance of representing the community as a whole, including the dispossessed estate labour. At one of its earliest annual general meetings, in 1937, the then President of CIAM emphasized that 'raising the status of Indian labour was the key to a higher status for the community as a whole'.[54]

Despite some initial successes by CIAM, the plight of Indian estate labour remained abysmal. By the late 1930s, particularly after Pandit Nehru's visit to Malaya in 1937, it was a matter of utmost concern for the Indian leadership as they continued their struggle for independence from colonial rule. Several books and articles analysing the situation in Malaya were published in India and Kuala Lumpur. One Indian journalist was perhaps reflecting the mood of the times when he wrote:

> The pro-Malay policy pursued in recent years and the policy of discrimination showed against Indians by the Governments here have created suspicion in the minds of the Indian public men, that in the course of time the history of Indians in South Africa will be re-enacted here too.[55]

In August 1938, K.A. Neelakandha Aiyer, the then Secretary of CIAM, wrote a book on the situation confronting Malayan Indians. This book was noticed and widely read in India, in political circles and by the general public. Michael Stenson sums up K.A. Neelakandha Aiyer's views as follows:

> Like some other CIAM leaders, he was imbued with the ideal of emancipated Indian labourers possessing full civil rights, regarded as the social equal of the Chinese and Malay labourers and able to rise by their own abilities out of

the labouring class. Thus Neelakandha Aiyer demanded not merely restrictions upon the supply of labour and the granting of full citizenship rights in Malaya but also the abolition of the economic and social restrictions that effectively bound the Indian labourers to the estates. All forms of protective legislation had been tried and found wanting. If they were to emancipate themselves from the bondage of a landless plantation proletariat, the Indian labourers had to be granted land of their own: not just vegetable plots on the estates, designed to keep the wolf from the door during depression, but land for independent peasant agriculture. They needed also to receive proper education in government schools, rather than the child-minding that went on in the estate Tamil schools.[56]

These were the views of an Indian living and working in Malaya. Later the same year (1938), when Pandit Kunzru from India toured Malaya to study all aspects of this issue, he accepted CIAM's position in its entirety. Equality of status for the Malayan Indian (and other permanent immigrants) was recognized as the essential prerequisite for full integration into Malayan society. During this period, the British press in Malaya often advocated that Indians living in Malaya stay away from Indian nationalists (seeking freedom from colonial rule). This position was difficult to sustain in a situation where large numbers of Indian labourers continued to arrive in Malaya at the behest of the plantation owners, and with the support of the colonial authority, only to discover the dire straits being suffered by their compatriots. It was quite natural for Malayan Indians to seek amelioration by discussions within Malaya and equally, particularly for the more recent arrivals, to consult with their compatriots in India.

Despite CIAM's best intentions of making the interests of the Malayan Indian unskilled labourer the central focus of its activities, actual results fell far short of expectations. CIAM did achieve some success in raising wages and improving working conditions for the Indian labourer. The 1938 ban on further emigration of Indian labour to Malaya was also the result of CIAM's efforts. CIAM's urban-oriented, English-educated, primarily Malayalee-speaking leadership tried its best to connect with and motivate the vast majority of Tamil and Telugu-speaking labourers, largely located on remote rural plantations, to join hands with CIAM. Across Malaya, between 1938 and 1941, a large number of new Indian associations were formed, which then nominated representatives to CIAM. However, CIAM and its member associations could never become a mass movement, primarily because of the non-involvement of grass-roots activisits and the labourers. 'However keenly an upper organization might watch over their interests, the ultimate workers for the labourers' welfare must be the labourers themselves. . . . Our vested interest is the indispensable labourer. We must build it up, strengthen it and thereby strengthen ourselves as a community.'[57]

The Second World War was a time of great stress and deprivation for the Malayan Indian plantation labourer. Before the Japanese occupation, CIAM and its constituent associations continued to cooperate with the colonial power, hoping to secure concessions for the estate workers. 'Instead of following the line of the Indian National Congress, which made support for the imperial war effort dependent upon the promise of early independence, Indian leaders in Malaya pledged loyalty to the High Commissioner and co-operation in prosecuting the war in Europe. . . .'[58] Individual Indian associations, such as those in Selangor and Singapore, raised thousands of dollars as contribution towards the war effort.

The sole response to this sympathetic approach was the intensified exploitation of Malayan Indian plantation workers. Rubber production was declared an 'essential service', with production, prices and profits to the plantation owners going up enormously in the first two years of the war. Despite this, the Indian plantation worker was forced to work at pre-war wages, with considerable evidence of systematic intensification of labour extracted by estates during this period through longer hours and enhanced employment of women and children. 'The publication of a report by a European medical officer pointing to the long hours worked on estates by Indian women, the increase in malnutrition and the high rates of infant mortality, together with other reports of *santoshavellai* or "voluntary" unpaid labour being extracted on estates, aroused extreme indignation.'[59] The then British High Commissioner for the FMS himself queried whether 'there was any justification for the great difference between the rate of 85 cents for Chinese labourers and 55 cents for Indians',[60] of course, without actually doing anything much about it. The then

President of CIAM (speaking at the annual general meeting in January 1941) expressed his distress over the sufferings of Malayan Indian workers, recognizing that 'no amount of patient pleading was able to make any breach in the grim defences of the citadel of conservative capitalism'. None the less, he remained hopeful that 'conditions are heading for a betterment'.[61]

Notwithstanding CIAM's approach of cautious optimism, intermittent strikes by Indian estate labourers demanding equality with Chinese labourers had been reported since December 1939, culminating in widespread, serious strikes in the first half of 1941 on the Klang rubber estates and at the Batu Arang coal mines, to name just two sites. Strike committees were formed on each estate. The petition drawn up presenting the strikers' common demands included issues such as parity in the remunerations for Indian and Chinese labourers, the provision of 'proper' education for children and proper medical facilities, the closing of toddy shops, freedom of speech and assembly, abolition of 10 to 12 hour working days, free access to the estates for relations and friends, permission for labourers to mount bicycles in front of European managers and Asian staff, and permission to the labourers to form associations.[62] The substance of these demands tragically highlight the miserable, discriminatory conditions under which Malayan Indian estate labour lived and worked.

By May 1941, when some of those charged with 'instigating' the strikes were arrested, the call for going on strike spread beyond Selangor to the state of Negri Sembilan as well. About 20,000 Malayan Indian estate workers were involved. The strikes were brutally suppressed, even though a small five cents increase in wages/allowances was conceded. (Wages for Chinese estate workers rose even further in response to demand.) Several workers died, there were large-scale arrests, deportations and repatriations.

The British administration, in Malaya and in London, was seriously concerned that 'a politicized Indian population in Malaya might adopt the Indian National Congress policy of non-cooperation with the war effort'.[63] The rubber industry, and consequently the Indian labourers who were indispensable for its productivity and continued growth, were crucial to the war effort, both as a strategic raw material and for the income it yielded to the exchequer. According to the then Secretary of State for the Colonies:

> Malaya is a vital area for the point of view of defence in present circumstances, in fact almost an eastern wall for India itself. Apart from its strategic significance in that respect, the maintenance of its rubber output to the economic war effort and to our dollar exchange resources is of the greatest possible importance, and it is accordingly more necessary to act strictly there against disturbing agitation than in areas less directly affected by our war needs.[64]

The strong and unwarranted action by the British Malayan government in suppression of the Malayan Indian estate workers caused deep consternation in India. The Government of India took up the matter strongly with the British Colonial Office. 'Sir Shenton Thomas[65] thought that he would be obliged to hold an open inquiry into the "disturbances", but on the urging of the UPAM[66] and with the implicit support of the Colonial Office, he was able to resist pressure from the Government of India to do so.'[67] The British authorities succumbed to the pressures exerted by large corporate houses and plantation owners through UPAM and RGA (Rubber Growers' Association), despite being fully aware of the pitiable condition of Malayan Indian labourers working on rubber estates, and their ruthless exploitation by the estate owners. Instead of moving towards ameliorating the conditions under which these labourers lived and worked, blame for the disturbances was placed at the door of the colonial official (Controller of Labour) who had 'committed the cardinal sin of asking CIAM to negotiate on the view that wage rates were a matter of bargaining within the framework of the laws of demand and supply'.[68] Chinese labour had successfully negotiated several rounds of wage increases through the same office, so there was nothing unusual about what the official had done. Besides, as pointed out by this official in his own defence, 'industrial unrest was inevitable if reports of huge profits continued to appear. . . .'[69] Another colonial official (Resident of Selangor) was blamed for not arresting the key leader(s) who, according to the authorities, had been subverting and inciting Malayan Indian labourers to revolt.

The agitation and unrest among Malayan Indian plantation labour in 1941 highlights several important issues which are crucial for understanding subsequent political, economic and social developments in Malaya, and the interlinkages between India and Malaya. The ability of the British to bring the dangerously volatile situation under control in 1941 was greatly facilitated by the segregation or 'islandisation' of Malayan society that the British had engineered over the decades. 'Race' and religion were the perceived fault-lines for this segregation, which has resulted in the almost irreversible communalization of society across Malaya. In 1941, the segregated deployment of Chinese and Indian labour weakened their ability to interact and coordinate negotiating positions. This, combined with the British policy of separate communal negotiations on wages and allowances, ensured the timely containment and control of the agitating Malayan Indian plantation labour. Indeed, it was reported that the Chinese-dominated Malayan Communist Party (MCP) 'was severely rebuked by its headquarters for losing the opportunity of extending influence during the strikes'.[70]

The primary concern of the plantation owners, and through them of the British authorities, was to retain, during and after the War, this core of docile, pliable and low-cost labour from India. For this reason, any and all proposals for the economic and social emancipation of this 'bonded' labour group were staunchly resisted. During the 1941 agitation and strikes, the initial decision by the Controller of Labour to invite CIAM to negotiate on behalf of Malayan Indian estate labour could have been a game-changer. CIAM would certainly have been effective in ensuring more equitable terms and conditions for estate labour. CIAM's involvement would have been invaluable in bringing the Malayan Indian community closer as a group, overcoming the differences of class and community that had kept them apart. It is easy to understand why UPAM and RGA were aghast at this prospect and had the Controller of Labour's decision reversed no sooner it was announced.

The imperious manner in which the 1941 Malayan Indian estate labour strikes were suppressed had significant long-term consequences, for both India and Malaya. For Malayan Indian estate labour it was a traumatic and distressing experience, which 'tended to create a feeling of suppressed anger among Indians'.[71] Collective opinion among them turned irrevocably against the colonial power, Britain. Consequently, they were unstinting in their enthusiasm and support for Netaji Subhas Chandra Bose's campaign for freeing India from British colonial rule. After the War, Malayan Indians were equally strong supporters of *Merdeka* or independence for Malaya.

In the early years after its formation, CIAM leaders had been unequivocal about their unity of interests with Malayan Indian estate labour. However, given their overall position of support for the British war effort, CIAM's support for the Klang strikes was considered 'half-hearted'. This had already disappointed the Malayan Indian estate labour. The communal organization, CIAM, was perceived as no longer prioritizing the interests of the poor in their group. When CIAM was no longer allowed to negotiate on their behalf, the estate labour found themselves essentially on their own. After the War, many among the Malayan Indian estate labour moved away from communal organizations to class-based or issue-based groupings. Workers' solidarity became more relevant for them than communal solidarity. In effect, the communally divided polity that the British ordained for Malaya contributed to the marginalization of the Malayan Indian community as a whole. The largest and poorest component of the Malayan Indian community, the Malayan Indian estate labour, was unable to find succour either through their largest communal grouping, first CIAM and later the Malayan Indian Congress (MIC), or through the several non-communal, multi-racial or class-interest based parties that had come up before and after *Merdeka*.

The issue is primarily one of prioritizing the cause of Malayan Indian estate labour, whether by CIAM/MIC or by any other group. In Malaya, as in India, the development of pan-Indian community groupings (CIAM, MIC, Indian National Congress) proceeded apace with the emergence of sub-communal groupings, and the development of sub-communal nationalisms. This is quite natural given the diversity of the Indian populace, and the natural inclination to preserve the linguistic and cultural heritage of one's region of origin. There need be no mutual contradiction between these two trends, which often develop apace. There can be instances of the same individual assuming membership of both the national (or communal) group, and the sub-communal group as well.

Thus, beginning with the 1930s, several groupings emerged in Malaya, such as the All-Malayan Tamil Association and the Tamil Reform Associations (inspired by the Self Respect Movement developed by E.V. Ramasamy Naicker in Madras state in the 1920s, commonly known as the Dravidian movement). Several Tamil newspapers came up to rival the oldest Tamil newspaper, the *Tamil Nesan*, such as the *Munnetram* (Progress or Uplift) begun in 1929, *Desa Maru* in 1930, *Seerthirutham* (Reform) in 1931, and *Tamil Murasu* in 1935. And then there were the Ceylon Tamil Associations, the Chettiar Chambers of Commerce, and the Malayan Indian Association (MIA) founded in 1935 to give 'organizational expression to the view that the future of Indians in Malaya lay in full identification with Malayan Society and co-operation with the colonial government'.[72] There were also several North Indian cultural and religious associations.

Right up to the 1920s 'British reports indicate that Muslims were the most nationalistic of the Indian communal groups'.[73] Several eminent merchants and professionals among them headed Indian associations in Singapore, Penang and other cities. By the late 1920s, however, the rise of the Muslim League in India made its impact felt in Malaya. 'By 1935 support for the Muslim League was undoubtedly growing and many Indian Muslims were being led on a divergent political path from the Congress and Dravidian mainstreams of Indian nationalism in Malaya.'[74] As in India, so in Malaya, too, the colonial ruler common to both nations cleverly exploited, even exacerbated these differences. Doubts began to emerge and rifts developed among the leaders of several important Indian associations across Malaya.

By the 1940s, as the debate over Malay privileges began gathering momentum, the Jawi Peranakan community (Indian Muslim merchants who had intermarried among the Malays) increasingly threw in their lot with the Malays, at least partly in anticipation of the special privileges being assured to this group by the colonial administrators. Since the advent of Islam in Malaya, Indian Muslim merchants had enjoyed traditionally close relations with Malay Sultans. The moving away of Indian Muslim merchants from the mainstream Malayan Indian groups broke this crucially important link between Malay rulers and Malayan Indians, that harked back deep into the pre-colonial past. The other strong link, between the Chettiars and Malay Sultans, had already been weakened through legislation brought in by the colonial administrators.

As against this, the strong relations between Malay rulers and Chinese merchants, which, too, dated back to the pre-colonial period, remained intact and flourished. Taken as a whole, the pre-Second World War colonial period in Malaya saw the heightened development of communal and sub-communal nationalisms. This was perhaps:

> an inevitable consequence of colonial policies that actively encouraged the creation of a permanent Chinese and Indian labour force while refusing to take any measure to promote its social or political integration. The facile excuse of the British obligation to protect a fearfully defensive Malay society from the fierce blast of competition from aggressive immigrants barely concealed the cynical calculation that the perpetuation of British rule and the promotion of British economic interest was best promoted by a policy of divide and rule. In its devotion to economic expansion based upon the systematic exploitation of cheap migrant labour, in its persistent opposition to the rise of political awareness amongst the Asian population, the colonial regime exposed the narrowly economic basis of its imperialism.[75]

NOTES

1. *The Indian*, 15 May 1937, p. 8.
2. Ibid., 12 June 1937, p. 6.
3. *Selected Works of Jawaharlal Nehru*, Series 1, vol. 8, p. 694.
4. *The Indian*, 5 June 1937, pp. 4 and 5 and 12 June 1937, pp. 6 and 11.
5. *Selected Works of Jawaharlal Nehru*, Series 1, vol. 8, p. 672 (address to Indians in Singapore).
6. Ibid., p. 674.
7. Ibid, p. 668, 'On His Visit to Malaya', speech at Kuala Lumpur (Selangor) on 25 May 1937, taken from *The Hindu* of 2 June 1937.
8. *Selected Works of Jawaharlal Nehru*, Series 1, vol. 8, p. 666, quoting *The Hindu* of 2 June 1937.
9. Ibid., p. 670.
10. Ibid., p. 673, quoting from *The Hindustan Times*, 13 June 1937.
11. Ibid., p. 677, quoting from Pandit Nehru's letter dated 29 May 1937, written from Port Dickson (Malaya), addressed to Rajendra Prasad (from the *Rajendra Prasad Papers*, National Archives of India).

12. Ibid., 'Indian Labour in Malaya', quoting *The Hindustan Times*, p. 683; also carried in *The Indian* 'The Indian Labour Problem in Malaya', 5 June 1937, p. 6.
13. Ibid., pp. 681 and 680.
14. Ibid., pp. 681-2.
15. Popularly known as Chinese spirit, distilled from rice or sorghum.
16. Ibid., p. 684.
17. Ibid., pp 682-4.
18. Ibid., pp. 683 and 691.
19. Ibid., p. 690, 'To Fellow Countrymen in Malaya', an article written on 4 June 1937, on the eve of Pandit Nehru's departure from Malaya, carried in *The Bombay Chronicle* on 15 June 1937, and in *The Indian* on 12 June 1937.
20. Ibid., pp. 688-9, carried in *The Hindustan Times* on 13 June 1937 and reprinted in *Eighteen months in India* (Allahabad, 1938), pp. 175-7.
21. Ibid., p. 690.
22. *The Indian* (vol. 1, no. 9, December 1925), quoted in Arasaratnam, op. cit., p. 97.
23. Arasaratnam, op. cit., pp. 97-8, *inter alia* quoting the *Straits Times* editorial of 6 October 1931.
24. K.S. Sandhu, *Indians in Malaya*, p. 115, with fn. 1.
25. *Selected Works of Jawaharlal Nehru*, Series 1, vol. 9, pp. 218-19, carried in the *National Herald* on 6 December 1938.
26. S. Arasaratnam, *Indians in Malaysia and Singapore*, p. 99.
27. Sandhu, op. cit., p. 183, Table 7.
28. Arasaratnam, op. cit., p. 32.
29. Ibid., pp. 32 and 45.
30. Ibid., p. 101.
31. Paul H. Kratoska, 'Ends That We Cannot Foresee: Malay Reservation in British Malaya', *Journal of Southeast Asian Studies*, 1983, Department of History, National University of Singapore.
32. Charles Hirschman, op. cit., p. 353.
33. Charles Hirschman, 'The Meaning and Measurement of Ethnicity in Malaysia: An Analysis of Census Classifications', *The Journal of Asian Studies*, vol. 46, no. 3 (August 1987), p. 568.
34. Charles Hirschman, 'The Making of Race in Colonial Malaya', p. 355.
35. Ibid.
36. Bashiran Begum Mobarak Ali, 'The Red-Ink Grant: Tracing Legitimacy in History', pp. 1 and 7 (see bibliography for access details).
37. Ibid., p. 8, quoting from the minute recorded by the British Resident in Perak on 7 September 1910.
38. Ibid., p. 10.
39. Ibid., pp. 9 and 10, including fn. 58 on p. 9.

40. Ibid., pp. 10-11.
41. Ibid., p. 12, quoting J.M. Gullick, *Rulers and Residents: Influence and Power in the Malay States 1870-1920*, Singapore: Oxford University Press, 1992, p. 198.
42. Ibid., p. 12, quoting R. Emerson, *Malaysia: A Study in Direct and Indirect Rule*, London: Macmillan, 1937 and C. Mary Turnbull, *A Short History of Malaysia, Singapore and Brunei*, Singapore: Grayham Bash, 1981, p. 13.
43. Ibid., pp. 11-12.
44. Ibid., p. 14, quoting R. Emerson, op. cit.
45. Ibid., p. 14.
46. Ibid.
47. Hirschman, 'The Making of Race in Colonial Malaya', p. 356.
48. Ibid.
49. Ibid., p. 357.
50. Michael Stenson, *Class, Race and Colonialism in West Malaysia*, pp. 39-40, quoting 'Report of the Court of Inquiry on the Mutiny of the Fifth Native Light Infantry and the Malay States Guides 1916', L/Mil/17/19/98, India Office Library and Records, London, p. 8.
51. Ibid., p. 35.
52. Ibid., p. 4.
53. Ibid., pp. 37-8.
54. Ibid., p. 48.
55. Ibid., pp. 43-4, quoting M.N. Nair, *Indians in Malaya*, Koduvayar: Koduvayar Press, 1937, pp. 47-8.
56. Ibid., pp. 50, taken from K.A. Neelakandha Aiyer (comp.), *Indian Problems in Malaya: A Brief Survey in Relation to Emigration*, Kuala Lumpur: Indian Office, 1938.
57. Ibid., pp. 54-5, quoting K.M. Kannampilly, member of the Singapore Indian Association, writing in *The Indian*, 24 August 1939.
58. Ibid., p. 59.
59. Ibid., p. 60.
60. Ibid., p. 63.
61. Ibid., p. 61.
62. Ibid., p. 64.
63. Ibid., p. 69.
64. Ibid., quoting the Selangor Estate Strike File, Colonial Office Records, draft telegram for Secretary of State for the Colonies to the India Office, August 1941.
65. British High Commissioner for the Federated Malay States.
66. United Planting Association of Malaya (UPAM).
67. Ibid., p. 67.
68. Ibid., pp. 67-8.

69. Ibid., p. 68.
70. Ibid., quoting Sir Shenton Thomas, British High Commissioner for the Federated Malay States, in his letter to the Secretary of State dated 28 August 1941, Selangor Estate Strike File, Colonial Office Records.
71. Ibid., p. 70, quoting from N. Raghavan, *India and Malaya: A Study*, Bombay, Longman, 1954, p. 68.
72. Ibid., p. 77.
73. Ibid., p. 75.
74. Ibid., p. 76.
75. Ibid., p. 84.

12

Rabindranath Tagore Visits Malaya

In 1927, ten years before Pandit Nehru's visit, Rabindranath Tagore had visited Malaya. This was his voyage of rediscovery. This was Tagore's, and through him, India's first reintroduction to the reality of the intense cultural and commercial linkages between South and Southeast Asia that had existed in the pre-colonial era. Under colonial rule, both nations' (India's and Malaya's) memories of these interactions had dimmed to the point of obliteration.

Tagore's interest in Malaya and Indonesia had been kindled during his vist to the Netherlands in 1920. In Holland he met Javanese noblemen, Raden Mas Noto Soeroto, grandson of the head of the autonomous principality of Jogjakarta, and Soeriosoeparto, who later became Mangkoenegoro VII of Surakarta and played host to Tagore and his party in Java in 1927.[1] Both these noblemen were intellectuals, familiar with Tagore's works. Noto Soeroto had even translated several of his works from Dutch into Javanese. Both were leading figures in Java's cultural renaissance movement, *Boedi Oetomo* (Beautiful Endeavour), and as such, these noblemen were keenly interested in Tagore visiting Java in order to meet fellow intellectuals and familiarize himself with the island's shared cultural affinities with India.

Tagore was tremendously excited to learn about the details of the pre-colonial interaction provided to him by Dutch and Javanese scholars. From then on, he wrote and spoke repeatedly about the need to rekindle the embers of these friendships (between South and Southeast Asia) that had been all but extinguished during the years of colonial rule in Asia. In 1924, during his first visit to Peking (now Beijing)

Tagore preached the virtues of close interaction among Asian cultures. . . . Young Chinese actors of the Crescent Moon Society performed his play *Chitra* in English on Tagore's birthday, May 8, 1924, at the Peking Normal University . . .some of Tagore's admirers even established an Asiatic Association in Shanghai to foster solidarity among all Asians.[2]

This (1927) was Rabindranath Tagore's third visit to the east. In 1916, Rabindranath Tagore had travelled by sea to Japan, stopping *en route* at Rangoon, Penang, Singapore and Hong Kong, before continuing onwards to North America. In 1924 Tagore visited China for the first time, preceding this with visits to Burma and Japan, and following it up with a visit to Latin America.

In 1927, Rabindranath Tagore sailed east for Singapore from Madras on the French ship *Amboise*. This fifteen-week visit, from 12 July to 27 October 1927, covered exclusively the Malay Peninsula, Java and Bali. Rabindranath Tagore travelled as an 'intellectual pilgrim' motivated by the hope that he could 'collect source materials there for the history of India and to establish a permanent arrangement for research in this field'.[3] In another letter written on 15 July 1927, Tagore said 'India's learning had once spread outside India . . . the people outside accepted it. . . . We have embarked on this pilgrimage to see the signs of the history of India's entry into the universal.'[4] Travelling with him were Suniti Kumar Chatterjee, Professor of Linguistics at Calcutta University, Surendranath Kar, artist and architect, and Dhirendra Krishna Deva Varman, painter and musician.

The 1927 voyage to Malaya, Java and Bali had several objectives. One among these was to explore 'the factors of a common Asiatic cultural unity'[5] and 'to discover the Asian cultural identity'.[6] Tagore wanted to familiarize himself with the remains of ancient Indian culture as well as present-day life and living arts in this region. He wanted to explain the concept and ideals that had motivated him to establish Visva Bharati, a world university that should be 'one nest for the world—*yatra visvam bhabatyeka nidam* (where the world makes its home in a single nest)'.[7] With this vision for international cooperation in the arts and in education, Tagore wanted to establish close cultural cooperation through exchange of scholars and artists between his university at Santiniketan and the people of Malaya, Java and Bali. Fund-raising for Visva Bharati was certainly among the objectives of his visit.

Rabindranath Tagore's vision for a better world was firmly based on his all-encompassing philosophy of education combined with strengthening international coexistence through people-to-people interaction across borders among artists, cultural personalities, intellectuals, academicians and educationists. While he vigorously opposed 'the monstrous features of European nationalism . . . Tagore's critique of nationalism . . . was perfectly compatible with his anti-colonialism and his patriotic poetry.'[8] Mahatma Gandhi described Tagore as the 'ardent nationalist' and as 'Gurudeva, the supreme teacher'.[9]

In Malaya and in Java, the initiative and invitation for Tagore's visit had come through eminent individuals and cultural organizations. The British Indian government, the British Malayan authorities and the Dutch Indonesian government facilitated the visit at every stage. On arrival in Singapore, Tagore was, for a few days, the guest of the British Governor, Sir Hugh Clifford. Later on he stayed with the eminent Namazie family (of Iranian origin, the family had lived in Madras before moving to Singapore). He received an overwhelming welcome from all communities and sections of society during his whirlwind tour of the Malay Peninsula. In addition to Singapore he visited Malacca, Seremban, Kuala Lumpur, Kajang, Klang, Ipoh, Teluk Anson, Taiping and Penang.[10]

There were innumerable receptions and speaking engagements, hosted by the Straits' Chinese business community, by Chinese schools and Chinese associations, by Indian Associations, by specially created multi-racial Committees. The Chinese were especially appreciative of Tagore's 'endeavours to make provision for the study of Chinese language and Chinese culture at the Visva Bharati'.[11] To the Muslims who came to meet him, 'Tagore was not only a poet of the highest calibre but . . . had also attained *tassawuf* or enlightenment of a Sufi mystic.'[12] Tagore delivered the inaugural address at the annual conference of the Malayan Teachers' Association. At this event, Suniti Kumar Chatterjee spoke at length about the importance of education in the mother tongue for all children, in addition to education in the English language.

The British authorities at the highest levels associated themselves with almost every event in honour of the poet-philosopher who had been awarded the Nobel Prize for Literature in 1913.

Members of the Indian community were present everywhere in large numbers. 'All the arrangements for Tagore's tour of the Malay Peninsula had been made by Ariam Williams (Aryanayakam), a Tamil Christian scholar of divinity who originally hailed from the Jaffna Peninsula of Ceylon.'[13] The interest and joy in welcoming Tagore touched people from all faiths and every walk of life, including Tamil Hindus and Muslims, Punjabi Hindus and Muslims, Sikhs and Pathans, Gujarati Hindus and Muslims, including the Khojas and Bohras, Kerala Hindus, Muslims and Christians. In 1927, Indian Muslims played a leading role in the community, and in several cities, such as Taiping, the President of the Indian Association was Muslim.[14]

The Indian diasporic entrepreneurs and merchants' associations, with their longstanding historical presence in the Malay Peninsula, were particularly supportive of Tagore's visit. They saw great potential for reviving ancient trade links through Tagore's proposals for stronger cultural and educational interaction between India and Malaya. In Malacca and in smaller towns across the Peninsula, Tagore also learnt about the dismal difficulties being faced by Indian immigrant labour working on the plantations. 'Some of the British rubber barons seemed unhappy with the Indian poet's "triumphal progress" through the Malay Peninsula.'[15] The local English language media sought to rake up, in garbled fashion, the 1924 article written by Tagore criticizing the British practice of using Indian troops overseas. Tagore was protesting against what he witnessed in China, 'the brutal use of Sikh armed police against the Chinese in Shanghai'.[16] The mischievous misquote in the Malayan media made it seem that Asian countries were preparing to target Europe, a reflection perhaps of serious disquiet over Tagore's exhortations for the nations of Asia to come together with the objective of rekindling historical linkages and friendship. The offensive editorial (in the *Malay Tribune* of 2 August 1927) was effectively rebutted through a strong rejoinder in the *Malayan Daily Express*.[17]

It is of great contemporary relevance that Rabindranath Tagore saw the essential commonality of all religions as a strong uniting factor. *The Straits Times* (Singapore) commented that 'it is remarkable that at his university, people of all religious beliefs actually meet in common worship—Christian, Hindu, Mohammedan, Buddhist—and Dr Tagore explained it in a few words: "Behind all the religions" he said, "we all bask in the same sunlight"'.[18] Elsewhere in the same interview, Rabindranath Tagore provided valuable insights, amazingly relevant today, on the ultimate goal of education, and the need for people from different races and religions to come together in understanding and friendship:

> Many people think that the University is merely an educational institution. But the education that is needed now is that which makes men fit to know each other.
>
> The different races in these modern days are brought in close contact, but we have not yet acquired the mentality to translate this great fact. What we need for the students of the present day is a universal outlook, to enable the great problem, the race problem, to be successfully grappled with and overcome.
>
> I have come to this country, which is very cosmopolitan. I find here a great mixture of races and hope that the atmosphere of mutual sympathy and cooperation in this Malay State will provide a proper soil for the idea which I represent.
>
> Each nation has its department of individual interest—like politics, commerce, etc. There it would be difficult to meet. But on the common ground of culture, of science, of religion, we can meet—and it is my hope that the University of Visva Bharati (will) provide a common meeting ground, a real meeting place for the individual cultures of each nation, which once established, we shall be able to know each other better.
>
> Then that feeling of estrangement could be diminished and it is my hope that in the future we shall be united in a proper spirit of spiritual cooperation—for that only is the link which will bind nation and nation.[19]

Two days later, on 23 July 1927, while speaking on 'The Unity of Man' at the Victoria Theatre in Singapore, Tagore emphasized the importance of teaching about the environment in promoting understanding among people:

> Learning then to love this beautiful earth, to love their fellow-beings and serve them, they (students) would go forth with that attitude of mind devoid of all racial prejudice. . . . For it was only by shedding racial individuality in its narrow prejudiced sense that individual man would find freedom in the world of man.[20]

Tagore's views on race relations, enunciated in Malaya almost 85 years ago, remain strikingly relevant today.

Tagore pursued with great vigour his views on the importance of improving relationships among Asian countries. In 1932, during a visit to Iran, he said:

> Each country of Asia will solve its own historical problems according to its strength, nature and need, but the lamp that they will each carry on their path to progress will converge to illuminate the common ray of knowledge . . . it is only when the light of the spirit glows that the bond of humanity becomes true.[21]

It was Tagore's ardent hope that this rediscovery of India's historical links with the East would form the bedrock for the revival and strengthening of India's linkages with all Asian countries. He visualized the need for Asian unity, and with this in mind, Rabindranath Tagore wrote to Jawaharlal Nehru in 1939:

> India's great awakening had crossed deserts and mountains, the overflow of her glorious epoch of culture touched far continents and left permanent deposits in distant shores of Asia. In my visits to China and Japan, and to Siam, Java and Bali, I felt profoundly moved to find how the communion of our culture had persisted even up to our own days and I cannot help hoping that as a messenger from India's youth you would give strength to the historic forces of Asiatic unity, bringing new urge of neighbourly understanding to our eastern people. India herself is passing through an eclipse when her own reality is lost to her in a haze of parochial politics, sectarianism, and domestic contention: contact with a greater world of eastern culture will, I fervently hope, help in removing her obsessions and enliven her whole national existence with a new humanity.[22]

Rabindranath Tagore's views on friendship and cooperation among Asian nations, as expressed through this letter to Jawaharlal Nehru and earlier during his visits to Iran, China and Malaya, would certainly have played their role in the crystallization of thoughts and ideas that led to the convening by Jawaharlal Nehru of the Asian Relations Conference in New Delhi in early 1947.

It is interesting that in his letter to Nehru, Tagore does not include Malaya in the list of countries/regions where Indian cultural influences have visibly 'persisted even up to our own days'. After 1786 (the establishment of Penang) the British were, in every province, seeking to displace Indian mercantile and commercial activity, to substitute Indian presence and influence at the courts of the Sultans with their own. It is not surprising, therefore, that in British Malaya, remarkably little attention was paid to preserving or excavating historical and archaeological evidence relating to India's age-old interactions with the Malay Peninsula. The inadequacy of archeological research in Malaya was highlighted somewhat graphically by Roland Braddell, when he quoted Sir Grafton Eliot Smith as saying:

> When we recognise the greatness of the achievement of Dutch archaeologists in the East Indies, the Americans in the Philippines, the French in Indo-China, the Japanese and Chinese, and such enthusiastic amateurs as Drs Heanley and Shellshear in Hong Kong, it is particularly humiliating to us as Englishmen that so little is being done in Malaya to complete the links in the chains which this great jumping-off place of Asia and cultural exchange alone can supply. Will not the India Society urge upon the Colonial Office and the Government of Singapore and the Federated Malay States the importance of this work and their duty to the world to make their proper contribution to a vital research?[23]

In Java, on the other hand, near Jogjakarta at the Prambanan temple complex (known as *Candi Loro Djonggrang*) Tagore was witness, in September 1927, to the unique, and successful collaborative efforts being undertaken to reconstruct and restore these Hindu temples. All the three major temples in this complex had their *shikars* or spires missing, with broken fragments lying scattered all over the temple grounds. 'Dutch historians were delving deep into the Indian *Silpasastras* to uncover the ancient Indian temple-building canons', while engineers 'were relying on the intuition of the Javanese craftsmen, who unerringly put the broken fragments together as in a giant jigsaw puzzle. It is a miracle story of cross-cultural collaboration, and full credit goes to the Netherlands East Indies government for sponsoring the scheme.'[24]

As he travelled through Java, visiting Batavia, Surabaya, Surakarta, Bandung and Jogjakarta, Rabindranath Tagore appreciated the intellectual depth and aesthetic beauty of Java's syncretic culture. The influence of the Indian epics, the *Ramayana* and the *Mahabharata*, is unmistakable, as these continue to be an inalienable part of Javanese culture. Yet, what is important to the Javanese is no longer the religious significance of these texts or the ceremonies of worship that continue to be performed whenever these epics are presented, but the fulfilment of

> their craving for aesthetic emotion (*rasam*). . . . That is to say, it is not meaning, but some inner satisfaction that they ask. . . . This may perhaps be explained by saying that they have within them their own idea of Beauty of Perfection, and any external performance that is attuned to it evokes a response from it and gives them joy—a joy that may surely be called spiritual.[25]

It is in this spirit that contemporary maestros like Ramli Ibrahim in Kuala Lumpur are keeping alive the history and traditions of cultural exchange between India and the Malay Archipelago.

In Jogjakarta, Rabindranath Tagore was invited by the *patih*, the chief minister of the Sultan, to a staging of the *Ramayana* where the performers were boys from his family and from the Sultan's family. Tagore recognized the indisputable affinity between Javanese and Indian dancing, and this delighted him, but he equally accepted that over time, 'Javanese dance and drama departed from the classical Indian model to develop their own distinctive style. . . . (T)he Indian visitors could not but recognize the originality of the art of Java.'[26] In Surakarta, Tagore was fascinated by the Javanese shadow-theatre, or *Wajang Poerwa*, performance that he was invited to at the house of Prince Koesoemajoedo. In a beautiful interpretation of the moving shadows on the lighted screen, Tagore said:

> We see the creation only when the Creator, who abides in the region of light, conceals himself behind it. He who knows that with the created forms the Creator is in constant connection knows the truth. He who sees the process of creation apart from the Creator, sees only Maya. There are seekers of truth who would tear away the screen and go over to the other side—that is to say they want to see the Creator apart from his creation—and nothing can be so empty as the Maya of their illusion. This is what I felt as I looked at this show.[27]

In Java, Tagore had the opportunity to meet leading intellectuals and educationists. In Jogjakarta, he was introduced to the Muhammidaya movement for Islamic reformist education (which seeks to combine Islamic identity with nationalism) through the Indian national from Bombay, Mirza Ali Baig, who was the link between Javanese and Indian Muslims. While in Bandung, Tagore visited the theosophical teacher-training centre in Lembang, where he attended a pan-religious prayer meeting with readings from the Koran and the Bible, and from the Jewish, Buddhist and Hindu scriptures.[28]

The highlight of Rabindranath Tagore's Bandung visit was his meeting with Soekarno (born Kusno Sosrodihardjo), who later became the first President of Indonesia after independence from Dutch colonial rule in 1947, and other nationalists. During this meeting, Tagore realized that 'young Indonesian nationalists were keeping a sharp eye on the Indian political scene. They knew a great deal about Gandhi, Chittaranjan Das, Motilal Nehru and Sarojini Naidu. The poet and his companions were much impressed by the charming young leader.'[29]

The people of Malaya and Singapore have treasured and kept alive the memories of Rabindranath Tagore's 1927 visit. At the initiative of the Tagore Society of Singapore, the Tagore Centenary Celebration Committee was established, which, in 1961, planned and executed a befitting commemoration of the poet's birth centenary. The celebrations were planned in the spirit of Tagore's ideals of universal brotherhood, reflecting his message that 'the more important things in cultural unity and universal brotherhood are those which make for unity and not which separate'.[30] As part of the celebrations Tagore's plays were staged in Malay, Chinese, Tamil and English. The Centenary Celebration Committee included representatives of diverse organizations, including the Malay Youth Literary Association, the Ministry of Culture, the China Society, Radio Singapore, the Malay Film Productions Ltd, the Chinese Chamber of Commerce, the Maha Bodhi Vehara, the Central Sikh Temple, the Nanyang University Students' Dramatic Society, the Adult Education Board, and a wide cross-section of Indian community associations.

Glowing tributes paid to Rabindranath Tagore by the leaders of Singapore and Malaya focussed on the continuing relevance of the poet's ideals in moving towards the socially and racially integrated society that was the shared objective of Malaya and Singapore. Singapore prime minister Lee Kuan Yew emphasized that Tagore's

> noble personality towered over the passions, hatreds and strife which disfigured civilization in his life-time, and continue to disfigure it today. . . . We would also do well . . . to remind ourselves of Tagore's message that the quality of our

lives and of our civilization depends more on the internal wealth that we can accumulate than on external possessions.[31]

Tunku Abdul Rahman Putra, Prime Minister of Malaya, in his message on the poet's birth centenary, said:

(T)he greatness of Tagore is not confined to India; today he belongs to Asia and the world.

The wide range of his thought, his emphasis on the dignity and soul of man, his understanding of human frailty had an influence which has reached far beyond the boundaries of his own lifetime, and is still an enriching source of inspiration to mankind.

Above all, Tagore was a man of peace, and I am sure that if he were alive today and contemplating the tensions of the modern world and its conflicts of power he would be urging always the cause of peace and goodwill. Let us honour his memory then by dedicating ourselves anew to follow the path of peace.[32]

Lin Wo-Chiang, President of the Singapore Tagore Society, who had for several years headed the China Bhavan at the Visva Bharati University in Santiniketan, expressed his satisfaction that 'an increasing number of Malayans in all walks of life patronize the Tagore Society, Singapore, to emulate and propagate the cherished aims of Gurudev'. He concluded his message with the following quote from Gurudev Rabindranath Tagore: 'He who is one, who is above all colour distinctions, who dispenses the inherent needs of men of all colours, who comprehends all things from their beginning to the end, let Him unite us to one another with wisdom which is the wisdom of goodness'.[33]

In 2011, the one hundred fiftieth birth anniversary of Rabindranath Tagore was observed with equal vigour and respect in Singapore. The Institute of South East Asian Studies (ISEAS) Singapore organized and took part in a series of four seminars commemorating this event, at Harvard University (USA), in Beijing, in Kolkata, and in Singapore.

Rabindranath Tagore's visits (in 1927) to Malaya and Java provide interesting contrasts and comparisons. It is a pity that the potential held forth by this journey for reviving the traditional historical linkages between India and the Malay Archipelago through cultural and educational exchanges could not be fully realized. Java and Bali were under Dutch colonial rule and India under British colonial rule. This made it inconvenient and difficult to facilitate exchanges. With Malaya, it should have been much easier, but British colonial policies of keeping the races apart and evincing minimal interest in higher education (in Malaya) meant that here, too, there was very little by way of follow-up. Nonetheless, Tagore's voyage of rediscovery in 1927 was in many ways the keystone of the twentieth century revival of the pre-colonial linkages and friendship between the people of South and Southeast Asia.

NOTES

1. Arun Das Gupta 'Rabindranath Tagore in Indonesia: An Experiment in Bridge-Building', in *Bijdragen tot de Taal-, Land-en Volkenkunde* 158 (2002), no. 3, Leiden, 451-77, p. 457, downloaded from http://www.kitlv-journals.nl on 7 October 2010.
2. Sugata Bose, *His Majesty's Opponent: Subhas Chandra Bose and India's Struggle Against Empire*, Delhi, 2011, p. 8.
3. Sugata Bose, 'Rabindranath Tagore and Asian Universalism', p. 8, quoting the letter from Tagore to Ramananda Chattopadhyaya (28 May 1927), cited in Prabhat Kumar Mukhopadhyay, *Rabindra-jibani*, p. 312, vol. 3, 3rd edn., Calcutta, 1991. Sugata Bose's article accessed on 6 October 2010 at http://www.iseas.edu.sg/nsc/documents/conferences/Rabindranath%20Tagore%20and%20Asian%20Universalism.pdf.
4. Ibid, p. 8, quoting the letter from Tagore to Nirmalkumari Mahalanobis, reproduced in Rabindranath Tagore, *Java Jatrir Patra* (Letters of a Traveller to Java) in *Rabindra Rachanabali*, vol. 19 (Calcutta, 1957).
5. Jayati Bhattacharya, 'Patriotism and Passion: Resonances of Tagore and Bose in Southeast Asia', paper presented at ISEAS, Singapore Conference on 'An Age in Motion: The Asian Voyages of Rabindranath Tagore', 11-13 May 2010 (under publicaton), p. 4, quoting 'Dr Suniti Kumar Chatterjee's Report of the Java Tour', in Swapna Majumdar (ed.), *Rabindrabiksha* (bilingual), no. 39, Rabindrabhavan, Visva Bharati, 7 August 2001.
6. Arun Das Gupta, op. cit., p. 456, quoting File Java, Rabindrabhavan Archives, Santiniketan, Tagore Archives.
7. Ibid., p. 458, quoting Tagore's writings in *Visva Bharati and its Institutions*, 1961, Santiniketan: Visva Bharati.
8. Sugata Bose, op. cit., p. 7.
9. Arun Das Gupta, op. cit., p. 454.
10. *The Straits Times* (Singapore), Thursday, 21 July 1927, p. 10, columns 1 and 2, 'A Cultural Unity: To Bridge Gulf Between East and West', Interview with R. Tagore.

11. Bhattacharya, op. cit., p. 5, quoting 'Dr Suniti Kumar Chatterjee's Report of the Java Tour'.
12. Bose, 'Rabindranath Tagore and Asian Universalism', p. 10.
13. Ibid.
14. The President of the Indian Association in Taiping in 1927 was Mohamed Ghows, taken from the Tagore Centenary Volume, 1961, published by the Singapore Tagore Centenary Celebration Committee, p. 27.
15. Bose, 'Rabindranath Tagore and Asian Universalism', p. 10.
16. Ibid.
17. Ibid.
18. *The Straits Times* (Singapore), 21 July 1927, Col. 2.
19. Ibid., column 1.
20. *The Straits Times* (Singapore), 23 July 1927, p. 9, 'Dr Tagore-Crowded Audience Listen to the Poet'.
21. Sugata Bose, *A Hundred Horizons: The Indian Ocean in the Age of Global Empire*, Delhi: Permanent Black, 2006, by exclusive arrangement with Harvard University Press, p. 265, quoting Rabindranath Tagore's *Parashye (in Persia)* in *Rabindra Rachanabali*, vol. 22, pp. 480-8 and 511-20.
22. Jayati Bhattacharya, op. cit., p. 17, quoting Tagore's letter to Jawaharlal Nehru dated 17 August 1939, written from Santiniketan, included in Krishna Dutta and Andrew Robinson (eds), *Selected Letters of Rabindranath Tagore*, Cambridge: Cambridge University Press, 1997, pp. 512-13.
23. Roland Braddell, 'An Introduction to the Study of Ancient Times in the Malay Peninsula and the Straits of Malacca', *JMBRAS*, vol. XIII, pt. II, 1935, p. 70.
24. Das Gupta, op. cit., p. 469.
25. Ibid., p. 471, quoting Rabindranath Tagore in *Visva Bharati Quarterly* 6: 277 = Tagore 1961: 104-7.
26. Ibid., pp. 468 and 470.
27. Ibid., p. 466, quoting *Visva Bharati Quarterly* 6: 178 = Tagore 1961: 96-7.
28. Ibid., p. 472.
29. Ibid., p. 473.
30. *Tagore Centenary Volume*, 1961, published by the Singapore Tagore Centenary Celebration Committee, p. 1, quoting from the Foreword written by Lee Siow Mong, Chairman of the Committee.
31. Ibid., pp. 4-5.
32. Ibid., p. 6.
33. Ibid., pp. 9-10.

13

India and Malaya during the Japanese Occupation: Netaji Subhas Chandra Bose

The first four decades of the twentieth century were among the most tumultuous and traumatic in the history of contemporary (i.e. colonial period) interaction between Malaya and India. The pre-colonial period was one of free and equal interaction between South Asia and Southeast Asia. The colonial period, particularly the first forty years of the twentieth century, witnessed huge waves of forced or quasi-forced migration, primarily from India to Malaya. The sheer numbers are staggering. According to K.S. Sandhu, around 4.25 million Indians moved to Malaya between 1786 (the establishment of Penang) and 1957, the year of Malaya's independence. The labour component of this migration was around 65 per cent. Almost three-fourths of this migration, 73.2 per cent to be precise, amounting to more than 3.1 million Indians moved to Malaya between 1900 and 1941, in a period of just four decades out of the total span of 171 years.[1]

Not all of them stayed on in Malaya. There were years, particularly in the early 1930s during and after the Great Depression, when there was a strong reverse flow, with many more Indians returning to India as compared to the numbers arriving in Malaya. The reverse flow was maximum in the first four decades of the twentieth century. Between 1900 and 1941, more than 2.1 million Indians returned to India. This was around 70 per cent of the total figure of 3.0 million Indians that returned to India from Malaya between 1786 and 1957.[2]

The net immigration into Malaya from India during this period (1786-1957) was 1.23 million. Once again, the first four decades (1900-41) of the twentieth century saw the greatest activity with around 1.0 million Indians migrating to Malaya during this period. Thus, over 80 per cent of the total migration from India to Malaya during the colonial period took place in the first forty one years of the twentieth century.

With this intensive and extensive movement back and forth between India and Malaya, it is not at all surprising that there remained keen awareness and interest on both sides of the Bay of Bengal about contemporary developments. The growing strength of the struggle for independence in India and mounting concerns about the condition of Indian immigrants in Malaya moved in tandem. Pandit Jawaharlal Nehru's visit to Malaya in 1937 amply demonstrated this.

THE JAPANESE OCCUPATION OF MALAYA AND SINGAPORE

The Japanese occupation of Malaya and Singapore from 1942 to 1945 was a traumatic experience for all inhabitants of this beautiful land. There is little doubt, however, that Malayan Indian labour working on plantations and public works suffered the most, largely as a result of the the highly vulnerable situation they were already in when the Second World War broke out, in 1939. Fifteen years after Rabindranath Tagore's visit to Malaya in 1927 and five years after Pandit Nehru's visit in 1937, it was Netaji Subhas Chandra Bose and the Indian National Army that became the focus of attention throughout South and Southeast Asia during the Japanese occupation.

CIAM, formed in 1937 had been vigorously seeking amelioration of the living and working conditions of immigrant Indian labour in Malaya. The leaders of CIAM, and the Indian immigrant community found themselves in a catch-22 situation. Every effort to seek redress for their problems within Malaya had proved unsuccessful. Long-term Indian residents and the growing percentage of the Indian community who were Malayan-born, had no assured rights to live as equal citizens of Malaya. Indian labour on the plantation and estates lived segregated and isolated lives. In these circumstances it is easy to understand the yearning of this community to maintain links with Indian nationalists and cultural figures, and to retain their Indian identity. Yet, the permanently settled Indian community's interest in doing so went against them.

Several scholars have discussed this painful contradiction. The scholar S. Arasaratnam concluded that for the Malayan Indian community, the

> communal separateness led to the preservation and strengthening of its Indian-ness and as long as this Indian-ness was preserved the connexions with India would be implicitly retained. In short, the aims of preserving the identity of the Indian community in Malaya and of cutting off all connexions with India were not compatible.[3]

In 1938, K.A. Neelakandha Aiyer, a prominent CIAM leader and opinion-maker among Malayan Indians wrote that 'until the local Indians cease to be aliens and gain the status of the Malayans, it is the duty of Indian nationalism to see that the settlers here continue to be true Indians and to counteract any attempts which seek to divide one section of Indians from another'.[4]

In the same year, 1938, Subhas Chandra Bose was elected President of the Indian National Congress at its session held in Haripura, near Kadod town in the Surat district of Gujarat. A powerful leader and a compelling orator, Netaji (respected leader, as he was popularly known) was a staunch advocate of *purna swaraj* (complete self-rule or independence) for India from British colonial rule. He had served as Mayor of Calcutta in 1930, but had also been imprisoned several times by the British, including for three years without trial in Mandalay (Burma), ending in 1927.

In early 1939, Subhas Chandra Bose was re-elected president of the Indian National Congress for a second term at the session held in Tripuri (near Jabalpur in the state of Madhya Pradesh). With some prescience, Netaji foresaw the imminent outbreak of war in Europe. He advocated non-cooperation with the British in their war effort, and a strong push for India's independence. Differences of opinion on these issues with Mahatma Gandhi and Jawaharlal Nehru forced Netaji's resignation as President of the Indian National Congress in April 1939. Within weeks, Netaji announced the formation of the Forward Bloc. In early 1940, Subhas Chandra Bose called upon the people

> not to help the Imperialist War with men, money or materials, and to resist by all means and at all costs the exploitation of Indian resources for the preservation of Empire. The Indian people, hungry for freedom, participated in their thousands in the struggle launched throughout the country by the Forward Bloc on April 6 (1940).[5]

Netaji was arrested by the British in July 1940, and later placed under house arrest. In January 1941, he escaped while under house arrest, slipping away to Berlin (via Peshawar, Kabul, Moscow and Rome) in order to 'supplement from outside the struggle going on at home'.[6] In Berlin, Subhas Chandra Bose 'was allowed the use of broadcasting facilities and inaugurated the *Azad Hind* (Independent India) Radio beamed to India'.[7] These broadcasts, which began in January 1942, were received with tremendous enthusiasm in India.

Very soon, the theatre of action and interest shifted to Asia. The Japanese army launched an amphibious assault on Malaya on 8 December 1941 on its eastern coast at Kota Bharu in the northern province of Kelantan. This was done in conjunction with the Japanese army moving south overland from Thailand to attack Malaya's western provinces. On 10 December, Japanese aircraft destroyed two British battleships, HMS *Prince of Wales* and HMS *Repulse*, that had arrived in the South China Sea just before the outbreak of hostilities. On 11 December the Allied troops which included Indian and Malayan soldiers, were defeated by the Japanese at Jitra (Kedah). Penang was subjected to heavy aerial bombardment by the Japanese right from 8 December, and on 17 December, the British abandoned Penang. Europeans were evacuated from Penang: all others were left behind. The negative psychological impact of this decision was huge, leading several historians to conclude that 'the moral collapse of British rule in Southeast Asia came not at Singapore, but at Penang'.[8]

The British and European withdrawal resulted in serious economic dislocation and administrative chaos. Some Indians, too, did leave, but 'the bulk of the Indian community remained behind to face Japanese occupation'.[9] Essentially, the wage economy disintegrated, which severely impacted Indian plantation and public works labourers, whose daily sustenance depended on their monthly incomes. During the Japanese occupation, workforce deployment on plantations was severely curtailed and all public works ceased. Erstwhile Indian plantation labourers faced food scarcity and a complete breakdown in health and sanitation services.

On 11 January 1942, the Japanese entered and occupied the capital city of Kuala Lumpur unopposed. By the middle of January they were in the southern state of Johor, and by 31 January, the Allied forces had formally left Malaya. The same evening, the Japanese army launched its invasion of Singapore from the north, through the recently occupied (by them) Malayan state of Johor. This move caught the British off guard, since they had all along planned the protection of Singapore against attacks by sea, from the south of the island. Singapore had been expected to hold out for at least six months against any attack: in actual fact, Singapore fell by 15 February, just one week after the Japanese started the aerial bombing of Singapore (on 8 February). The then British prime minister, Winston Churchill, described the fall of Singapore to the Japanese as the 'largest capitulation' in British history.[10]

The price that the Allied forces had to pay on losing the battle was 7,500 killed, 10,000 wounded, and about 1,20,000 captured for the entire Malayan campaign.[11] In Singapore alone, about 80,000 British, Australian and Indian troops became prisoners of war. In Malaya, about 40,000 Allied troops were captured by the Japanese, with another 10,000 either killed or wounded.[12] There are varying estimates about the number of Indian officers and soldiers captured by the Japanese in their Malaya and Singapore campaigns. One scholarly estimate places the figure of Indians captured by the Japanese in Singapore at 32,000, with the overall figure for Malaya and Singapore at over 40,000.[13]

Almost immediately after occupying Malaya and Singapore, the Japanese sought to put into effect their plans to unite Indian POWs (and other Indians living in Southeast Asia) against the British, by exploiting the Indians' deep interest in achieving independence from British colonial rule. Rash Behari Bose, an Indian national living in Tokyo since the 1920s, was working closely with the Japanese to bring these plans to fruition. On 17 February, two days after the fall of Singapore, the Indian POWs were brought to Farrer Park for being formally handed over to Japanese command and control. At this meeting, they were addressed by Captain Mohan Singh, who had fought the Japanese at Jitra with the 1/14th Punjab Regiment. Mohan Singh invited officers and soldiers to join the Indian National Army (INA), which was being formed to fight for Indian independence. Scholars have estimated that nearly half of those present at Farrer Park ultimately joined this, the first INA.[14]

By April 1942, the All-Malayan Indian Independence League (IIL) was formed, bringing together the leaders of various pre-war Indian associations in Malaya and Singapore, including CIAM, Chambers of Commerce and the Ramakrishna Mission. People from all communities and religions joined in, including Hindus, Muslims and Sikhs. 'The Indian Independence League had branches in cities and towns throughout Southeast Asia and functioned like a government within a government. They reunited families, providing food and shelter to the destitute, found jobs for the unemployed, gave medicine to the sick, settled disputes, and established ownership of property.'[15] The IIL made special efforts to look after, and improve the living conditions for the now jobless plantation labourers.

By May 1942, the formal process of recruitment to the INA began in Singapore. In June 1942 in the Bangkok Conference of all its branches, the IIL was recognized as the central civilian authority, with the INA subordinate to it. The 34-point resolution of this Conference conveyed very specific demands to the Japanese government on political issues, including recognition of India as an independent nation with the IIL as its representative, and respect for India's sovereignty and territorial integrity. The resolution 'requested the Japanese government to arrange for the transfer of Subhas Chandra Bose to East Asia. One thing the resolution demanded which Tokyo could not concede was the recognition of INA as an equal allied army'.[16] Without the leadership and charismatic presence of Subhas Chandra Bose, and in the absence of any meaningful response from the Japanese to the 34-point resolution, the IIL and the INA floundered. By December 1942, the first INA had been virtually disbanded, with many members reverting to their earlier status of POWs.

Finally, in January 1943, the Japanese accepted the IIL's request and invited Subhas Chandra Bose to lead the Indian nationalist movement in Southeast Asia. Netaji left Berlin in February, travelling first by a German submarine (up to Madagascar) and subsequently on a Japanese submarine (up to Indonesia). His perilous and dangerous journey culminated in Tokyo, where he met Japanese generals and the prime minister.

Netaji's arrival in Singapore on 2 July 1943 had an electrifying impact on the Indian community throughout the Malay Peninsula. The first INA had been primarily dependent on Indian POWs for its recruitment base. The second INA under Netaji drew in large numbers from the Malayan Indian community throughout the Malay Peninsula, infused now with a new sense of purpose and identity, combined with increasing anti-colonial fervour. On 4 July Subhas Chandra Bose assumed office as president of the IIL in East Asia, taking over the reins from Rash Behari Bose. Later the same day, in his rousing Presidential address to the IIL East Asia delegates' Conference, he called for 'military discipline as well as an unflinching loyalty to the cause'[17] of India's freedom from colonial rule. The very next day, on 5 July, in his speech delivered as the Supreme Commander of the INA, at a military review of the INA, Netaji gave the famous call *Chalo Dilli* or 'To Delhi, to Delhi!'

'A true soldier', Subhas Chandra Bose said,

> needs both military and spiritual training. You must–all of you—so train yourselves and your comrades that every soldier will have unbounded confidence in himself, will be conscious of being immensely superior to the enemy, will be fearless of death, and will have sufficient initiative to act on his own in any critical situation, should the need arise. . . . You are today the custodians of India's national honour and the embodiment of India's hopes and aspirations. So conduct yourselves that your countrymen may bless you and posterity may be proud of you.[18]

Hideki Tojo, Prime Minister of Japan, had travelled to Singapore to see the INA for himself,[19] and on 6 July the premier of Nippon and Netaji, standing side by side, reviewed the INA parade and marchpast. This 'was a rare experience and a wonderful tonic to the already high morale' of the INA.[20]

In his speech at the mass meeting held in Singapore on 9 July at the Padang in front of the Municipal Offices, Netaji explained that his 'object in leaving India was to supplement from outside the struggle going on at home', and that 'the time has come for three million Indians living in East Asia to mobilize all their available resources, including money and manpower' in support of India's struggle against colonial rule. He described the INA as the *Azad Hind Fauj* or India's Army of Liberation, and he announced his decision to establish 'a unit of brave Indian women to form a "Death-defying Regiment" who will wield the sword, which the brave Rani of Jhansi wielded in India's First War of Independence in 1857'.[21] Three days later on 12 July he addressed a meeting of Indian women held under the auspices of the women's section of the IIL (Singapore), where he exhorted them to play an active role in the do-or-die struggle for India's freedom.

For the next two years Netaji continued his indefatigable efforts throughout Southeast Asia, moving from Singapore to other parts of the Malay Peninsula, to Thailand, Burma and Indo-China, mobilizing men and women, and raising financial resources for the INA and the *Azad Hind* government in their relentless struggle for India's liberation from the bondage of colonial rule. His brilliant oratory, his meticulous planning and execution drew tremendous response and support from the Malayan Indian community, and inspired the admiration and respect of all those he came across. The success of Subhas Chandra Bose's efforts in generating awareness, interest and desire for self-rule across Southeast Asia was among the important contributory factors that made it impossible for the colonial powers to revert to the pre-war situation when they returned to this region in 1945.

Netaji's impact on the Indian immigrant community was transformational. Many of the civilians who joined the INA, including the Rani of Jhansi Regiment, were Malayan born. They had never been to India. Their response to Netaji's appeal was inspired by the nobility and importance of the cause he was championing: the cause of freedom, equality and independence, the determination not to submit anymore to injustice and exploitation. This touched a sensitive chord in the Indian immigrant community, given the record of discrimination and maltreatment suffered by plantation and public works labourers in Malaya in the pre-war years. Abid Hasan, who had earlier accompanied Netaji on the epic submarine journey from Germany, expressed these feelings succinctly when he said: 'We (now) had a purpose in life. We had something to live for and something to die for. We had acquired a self-respect not known to many of us before. He called us to greatness and we came.'[22]

The men and women who volunteered in the thousands to join the INA came from all walks of life, from all communities and religions, and from every corner of the Malay Peninsula. The genuinely secular, national character of the INA was truly remarkable. 'The greatest among its achievements was to gather together, under one banner, men from all religions and races of India, and to infuse in them the spirit of solidarity and oneness, to the utter exclusion of all parochial sentiment.'[23] Netaji referred to this in a radio broadcast on Bangkok Radio on 18 July 1943, when he said 'I can confidently assert that the Hindu-Muslim question is a British creation. This is proved by the fact that though the Indian National Army is mainly composed of Muslim soldiers, there is perfect harmony between them and their Hindu comrades.'[24] The total size of the INA is is estimated to have been around 45,000 officers and men, including Indian POWs and the civilians who enlisted after Subhas Chandra Bose's arrival in Southeast Asia.[25]

Among the thousands of young men from Malaya who volunteered for the INA the name of James Joseph Puthucheary stands out. His life is a fitting example of the foundational influence exerted by Subhas Chandra Bose and the INA on a whole generation of young men (and women) in Malaya and Singapore. As a young twenty year-old living in the southern state of Johor where Puthucheary's father was a government officer, 'Netaji's arrival in Malaya was a personal epiphany'.[26] He enlisted and saw action with the INA in the Imphal campaign. He was the only member of his platoon to survive the retreat to Mandalay. He was in Calcutta when India attained independence in August 1947. Inspired to support Malaya's struggle for independence, James Puthucheary returned to Singapore the same year, where he joined Raffles College. Here he formed the Malayan Students' Party with an agenda focused on 'the development of a Malayan consciousness, a Malayan culture and a Malayan nation. The party argued that Malayans should abandon their narrow racial identities and embrace a larger Malayan identity for the sake of national unity.'[27] Puthucheary was imprisoned by the British Singapore government in 1951 under the Internal Security Act. He was a founding member of Singapore's PAP (People's Action Party), but later broke away from them. When he was expelled from Singapore, he moved to Malaya, living there till his death in 2000. He acquired great renown as an eminent economist, a trade unionist and a lawyer.

Lakshmi Swaminadhan, a young medical doctor from Madras who had moved to Singapore in 1940, played a key role in the planning and realization of the activities of the women's wing of the IIL and the INA. Within three days of Netaji's address at the mass rally on 9 July, she was able, with the help of the INA, to motivate and train twenty women to present arms to Netaji in a formal all-women guard of honour. By October 1943, Lakshmi was appointed Commander of the Rani of Jhansi Regiment (RJR), head of the women's section of the IIL and head of the Women's Department in the cabinet of the provisional government of Free India, the *Azad Hind* government, that had just been formed. She toured the Malay Peninsula, meeting hundreds of educated women and women labourers from the plantations. Lakshmi was the pivot for the motivation and recruitment of women in both civilian and military capacities.

There are no exact figures for the size of the RJR. In the first phase, 500 women were recruited, though later this figure probably went up to 1,000 or even 1,500.[28] The largest proportion of these volunteers, perhaps as high as 80 per cent, were south Indian Tamils from the Malayan rubber estates. They did not have much education since 'Tamil schools on the estates were designed and kept ineffective with the goal in mind of keeping workers tied to the plantations'.[29] However, the years preceding the Japanese occupation had witnessed a heightened awareness among plantation labour about the need to collectively fight for their economic, social and political rights. 'The 1930s saw the beginning of collective resistance among Indian plantation workers. The most famous confrontation occurred in Klang in 1941 when thousands of workers struck during the period from 8 April to 7 May. In May 1941, some Indian labourers were shot by British estate owners for demanding higher wages.'[30] Most of the volunteers from the rubber estates were staunchly anti-British. The war years had only made matters worse, with severe impoverishment and deprivation to the point of starvation for large numbers on the estates.

In this situation Netaji's inspirational speeches found an almost instantaneous response. Young men and women besieged the recruiting offices, motivated by the fervour of adventure, patriotic idealism, and above all, a newfound self-respect. In the words of Lakshmi Swaminadhan (later Lakshmi Sahgal):

> Youth is a time of idealism and adventure. Indian youth in South-East Asia were living in a psychological vacuum, with no sense of identity. They could never identify themselves with a foreign colonial power, nor were they acceptable to the sons of the soil. Netaji brought a purpose and a sense of identity into their lives. . . . Being workers, they were potentially militant and subconsciously they were aware of being a subject race.[31]

In May 1945, Lakshmi was arrested in Burma by the British army. She was sent back to India in March 1946. The following year she married Col. Prem Kumar Sahgal of the INA.

The second-in-command of the RJR was Janaki Thevar (later Janaki Athi Nahappan), a convent-educated young girl of eighteen living with her family (a prominent Hindu business family) in Kuala Lumpur, when Subhas Chandra Bose arrived to speak at the Selangor Padang. Janaki's family had moved to Malaya at the turn of the century. Janaki had never been to India, but she was familiar with the dynamic role of women leaders like Sarojini Naidu in India's independence movement. Her response to the appeal for volunteers and donations made by Subhas Chandra Bose at the Selangor Padang meeting was instantaneous: she took off the gold earrings and necklace she was wearing and handed these over to Netaji. She wanted to volunteer for the RJR but this became possible only after Lakhsmi Swaminadhan spoke directly to Janaki's parents and convinced them to grant permission for both Janaki and her sister Papathi to do so. Janaki was among the first commissioned officers of the RJR, eventually reaching the rank of captain and second-in-command of the regiment.

Other early recruits from Malaya for RJR were Rasammah and her sister Ponnammah. They lived in Ipoh where their father, P.E. Navarednam, was President of the Malayan Teachers' Association.

It was in this capacity that he had, in 1927, received Rabindranath Tagore at the association's annual meeting. Theirs was a devout Christian family, hailing from Ceylon. They were fully aware of India's struggle for independence under the leadership of Mahatma Gandhi and Jawaharlal Nehru. Both sisters volunteered for the RJR immediately after listening to Subhas Chandra Bose's address in Ipoh, but once again, it was only after Lakshmi Swaminadhan's direct intercession with their mother that permission was granted for them to join the RJR. Rasammah has said about her life in the RJR 'I was with women from very different backgrounds, different economic situations and very deprived homes. . . . There was a sense of egalitarianism. . . . We knew some of us would die. . . . We wanted to die for India'.[32]

In June 1944 the first large batch of Ranis (the affectionate name given to members of the RJR) arrived in Rangoon under the command of Lt. Janaki Thevar. Another unit commanded by Lakshmi travelled north to Maymyo. The unit commanded by Janaki travelled on the infamous Siam Burma Death Railway, built with the forced labour of estate workers (primarily Indians from Malaya) and British, Australian and Indian POWs. The INA and RJR endured incredible hardships, including aerial bombardment and armed confrontations,[33] but rarely lost their motivation and spirit of camaraderie. Finally, they were forced to retreat in the face of reversals suffered by the Japanese army in the Imphal campaign. In Moirang, Manipur there is an INA memorial, which commemorates the place where the flag of *Azad Hind* was raised by INA Colonel Shaukat Hayat Malik.

On 8 July 1945 Subhas Chandra Bose laid the foundation stone for the INA War Memorial at the Esplanade Park in Singapore. The motto of the INA was inscribed on the Memorial—*ittefaq, itmad, qurbani* or unity, faith, sacrifice. In paying homage to the martyrs of the INA, Netaji said

> The future generations of Indians who will be born, not as slaves, but as free men, because of your colossal sacrifice, will bless your names and proudly proclaim to the world that you, their forbears, fought and suffered reverses in the Battle of Manipur, Assam and Burma, but through temporary failure you paved the way to ultimate success and glory.[34]

This memorial was destroyed by the British when they reoccupied Singapore. In 1995, however, the National Heritage Board of Singapore placed a large plaque at the site where the old memorial stood. This site, now called the Former Indian National Army Monument, is officially one of the historical sites of Singapore.

The RJR was in many ways a microcosm of the much larger INA. Yet it was unique in that the Ranis of the RJR were almost entirely recruited in Malaya, Singapore and Burma. The RJR did not have the strong component of Indian POW recruitment that was characteristic of the INA. The Ranis responded to Netaji's impassioned appeals based on their own belief and conviction about the importance of their lives in India's struggle for independence. Even today, many erstwhile members of the RJR, living in Kuala Lumpur and other cities and towns across Malaysia, continue to be active in public life subsequent to a full service career. Those who went back to the estates have had full working lives and have raised large families. In the words of Meenachi Perumal, who lives on an estate in Selangor.

> Netaji told us to keep the fire of freedom burning, but I really did not know whom to pass it on to. I pass the spirit on to my grandchildren by telling them of my experiences, hoping that they would never be cowards and be willing to stand up and die for the cause they truly believe in.[35]

Lakshmi Sahgal 'feels that the Rani of Jhansi Regiment was the most significant aspect of the INA'.[36] The Ranis felt (and feel) an enormous sense of pride and achievement in what they accomplished. The sacrifice and dedication of the Ranis and all other members of the INA, living (and dying) not just for themselves, but for the cause of Indian independence, brought in for them a whole new value system and set of beliefs. The Ranis have kept these alive by passing them on to future generations. The RJR 'promoted dramatic change in the post-war lives of its members' and 'launched feminist echoes that spread far beyond membership in the Regiment'. In India women had, for the first time, left their homes to participate in Mahatma Gandhi's *satyagraha* and *swadeshi* campaigns. In Malaya, by creating the RJR, Netaji exponentially expanded the horizons for women's participation as equals in every aspect of society's struggle.

The powerful legacy of Subhas Chandra Bose, the INA and the RJR endures equally in India and far beyond India's shores, in Malaya and Southeast Asia. In India after the war, when the British sought to put three of Netaji's most trusted officers on trial for treason at Red Fort—Shah Nawaz Khan, Prem Sahgal and Gurbakhsh Singh Dhillon—there was a spontaneous, nation-wide upsurge of protests. Every Indian cherished and valued the strongly patriotic contribution to the cause of India's independence made by Subhas Chandra Bose through the INA and the RJR. Mahatma Gandhi, the apostle of non-violence, wrote to the then Viceroy, Lord Wavell:

> Though I have nothing in common with any defence by force of arms, I am never blind to the valour and patriotism displayed by persons in arms. . . . India adores these men who are on trial. No doubt the Government has overwhelming might on their side. But it will be a misuse of that power, if it is used in the teeth of universal Indian opposition.[37]

The Indian National Congress and the Muslim League both made the release of the three detenus an important political issue in their ongoing freedom struggle against the British. The legal team for the Defence, which included Pandit Jawaharlal Nehru, provided evidence to establish the legality and validity of the INA, and focused on the inalienable right of an enslaved people to fight for their freedom. During the court-martial, which commenced in November 1945, protests amounting to mutiny broke out in several Royal Indian Navy establishments in Karachi, Bombay, Calcutta and Vishakhapatnam, and in Royal Indian Army establishments in Madras and Pune. These protests within the armed forces shook the confidence of the British about the continuing loyalty of the defence forces to the British Crown. This was no doubt an important factor which the British were forced to take into account, hastening their ongoing negotiations with Indian political parties for independence.

Quite expectedly, all three INA officers were found guilty and sentenced to deportation for life. However, in view of the mounting protests and public pressure, the British Commander-in-Chief of the Indian Army confirmed, but then rescinded the sentences. The INA officers were released amidst tremendous rejoicing, which extended throughout India and the Malay Peninsula.

In Malaya, Singapore and Burma, the erstwhile INA and RJR officers and soldiers, now back with their respective families, celebrated this victory as their own. They felt vindicated and proud that their efforts and sacrifice for the cause of freedom and independence had not been in vain. This infused them with a tremendous sense of confidence that enabled them to face with courage, equanimity and determination their own struggle in the run-up to independence in the Malay Peninsula. In the words of the scholar, P. Ramasamy:

> In Malaya and Singapore, the total involvement of Indians in the INA greatly influenced and guided the nature of their post-war political, social, economic and cultural developments. It is often remarked in Southeast Asian academic circles that without an adequate historical understanding of the INA phenomenon, it would be difficult to fathom the complex nature of Indian community's post-war developments.[38]

NOTES

1. K.S. Sandhu, *Indians in Malaya*, pp. 310-13, Appendix 3 on 'Total Indian arrivals in Malaya, 1786-1957', which has been compiled with reference to the Straits Settlements Factory Records, the Madras Annual Report on Emigration and Immigration, the Annual Report of the Agent of the Government of India in Malaya, Statistical Abstracts for British India, Minutes of the Meetings of the Indian Immigration Committee, and several other documents.
2. Ibid., pp. 316-17, Appendix 4 'Total Indian Departures from Malaya, 1786-1957'.
3. Arasaratnam, *Indians in Malaysia and Singapore*, p. 101.
4. Ibid., p. 102, quoting K.A. Neelakandha Aiyer, *Indian Problems in Malaya*, Kuala Lumpur, 1938, p. 89.
5. Hari Vishnu Kamath, 'Subhas Chandra Bose', accessed on 15 October 2010 at http://www.congresssandesh.com/AICC/history/presidents/subhas_chandra_bose.htm.
6. Ibid., p. 2, quoting Subhas Chandra Bose.
7. Joyce Chapman Lebra, *Women Against the Raj*, ISEAS, Singapore, 2008, p. 39.
8. Christopher Bayly and Tim Harper, *Forgotten Armies: Britain's Asian Empire and the War with Japan*, Penguin Books, London, 2005, p. 119, quoted in 'Battle of Malaya' on Wikipedia, p. 4 of 7, accessed on 13 October 2010 at http://en.wikipedia.org/wiki/Battle_of_Malaya.
9. Arasaratnam, op. cit., p. 103.

10. Winston Churchill, *The Hinge of Fate*, vol. 4, Houghton Mifflin Harcourt, 1986, p. 81, quoted in 'Battle of Singapore', accessed on Wikipedia on 13 October, 2010, p. 1 of 12, at http://en.wikipedia.org/wiki/Battle_of_Singapore.
11. Ibid. (Wikipedia website), p. 11 of 12, fn. 1.
12. Ibid. (Wikipedia web-site, p. 1 of 12.
13. Peter Stanley, 'Great in Adversity: Indian Prisoners of War in New Guinea', p. 1 (accessed on 15 October 2010 at http://www.awm.gov.au/journal/j37/indians.asp), quoting I.C.B. Dear (ed.), *The Oxford Companion to World War II*, p. 1010, New York: Oxford University Press, 1995.
14. Joyce C. Lebra, *Japanese Trained Armies in Southeast Asia*, New York: Columbia University Press, 1977, p. 25, quoted in 'First Indian National Army' accessed on 14 October, 2010 at http://en.wikipedia.org/wiki/First_Indian_National_Army.
15. Joyce Chapman Lebra, *Women Against the Raj*, p. 47, quoting John Thivy, 'The Struggle in East Asia', Netaji Research Bureau, Calcutta, 1971, p. 29.
16. Ibid., p. 47.
17. Sisir K. Bose and Sugata Bose (eds.), *Chalo Delhi: Writings and Speeches (1943-1945) by Subhas Chandra Bose*, Netaji Collected Works, vol. 12, Kolkata, Delhi: Netaji Research Bureau and Permanent Black, 2007, p. 39.
18. Ibid., pp. 47-8.
19. Lebra, op. cit., p. 48.
20. Bose and Bose (eds.), op. cit., p. 49.
21. Ibid., pp. 52-4.
22. Ibid., p. 48, quoting Abid Hasan Safrani *The Men from Imphal: The Struggle in East Asia*, Calcutta, Netaji Research Bureau, 1971.
23. Ibid., p. 56, quoting B.K. Ahluwalia and Shashi Ahluwalia, *Netaji and Gandhi*, New Delhi, Indian Academic Publishers, 1982.
24. Bose and Bose, op. cit., p. 68.
25. Peter W. Fay (1993), *The Forgotten Army: India's Armed Struggle for Independence, 1942-45*, Ann Arbor, University of Michigan Press, pp. 525-6 provides an estimate attributed to a British intelligence officer, which concludes by saying that in 1945, at the end of the INA, it consisted of about 40,000 soldiers, including 18,000 civilians who enlisted, quoted in 'Indian National Army' accessed on 15 October 2010 on http://en.wikipedia.org/wiki/Indian_National_Army.
26. Timothy Norman Harper, 'Revolt in Malaya: the Indian Connection', Sisir Kumar Bose Lecture 2007 delivered at the Netaji Research Bureau, Calcutta in January 2007, published in *The Oracle*, January 2008 issue, p. 33.

27. Lee, Hwee Hoon, 'James Joseph Puthucheary', National Library Board Singapore, accessed on 20 October 2010 at http://infopedia.nl.sg/articles/SIP_1471_2009-02-24.html.
28. Lebra, op. cit., p. 77.
29. Ibid., pp. 60-1, quoting T. Marimuthu, 'The Plantation School as an Agent of Social Reproduction', from *South Indian on the Plantation Frontier in Malaysia,* ed. Ravindra Jain, New Haven, CT, Yale University Press, 1970, pp. 465-6.
30. Ibid., p. 63, quoting P. Ramasamy, 'Labour Control and Labour Resistance in the Plantations of Colonial Malaysia', in *Plantations, Proletarians, and Peasants in Colonial Asia*, ed. E. Valentine Daniel, Henry Bernstein and Tom Brass, London: Frank Cass, 1992, pp. 97-100, and Usha Mahajani, *The Role of Indian Minorities in Burma and Malaya*, Bombay: Vora, 1960, p. 145.
31. Ibid., p. 78, quoting Lakshmi Sahgal, *The Oracle* II, 1980, Netaji Research Bureau, Calcutta, pp. 61-2.
32. Ibid., p. 81, quoting an interview with Ms. Rasammah Bhupalan conducted in Kuala Lumpur on 17 April 2007.
33. Ibid., pp. 64-5, interview by the author with a veteran of the RJR, corroborated by INA Major General Shah Nawaz Khan in *My Memories of INA and its Netaji*, Delhi: Rajkamal Publications, 1946.
34. Netaji Research Bureau, Calcutta.
35. Ibid., p. 65.
36. Lebra, op. cit., p. 105.
37. Letter from Mahatma Gandhi to the then Viceroy of India, Lord Wavell, quoted in *Footprints on the Sands of Time: Rasammah Bhupalan* by Aruna Gopinath, Arkib Negara Malaysia, 2007, p. 97.
38. Lebra, op. cit., Epilogue by P. Ramasamy, 'The Impact of INA on Post-War Malaya', p. 110.

PART III

THE POST-WAR AND POST-COLONIAL YEARS

14

India and Malaya in the Post-War Period

After the Second World War, the convincing defeat suffered by the Conservative Party in the July 1945 elections in Britain heralded the beginning of the end of British colonial rule in India. The British then sought to 'revive and re-centre their Asian empire on Southeast Asia. . . . For a time in 1945 and early 1946, the whole area from the borders of Bengal and Assam almost as far as the Australian Sea was united for the first and only time in a single, interconnected government. South East Asia Command had become the largest administrative apparatus on earth',[1] with Louis Mountbatten as the Supreme Allied Commander. The British brought in Indian troops as the mainstay of this Command, in support of the reoccupation of Burma, Malaya and Singapore, as well as to carry out the responsibilities that the British had undertaken on behalf of the French in Indochina and the Dutch in Indonesia. The British even sent an Indian Army contingent of 37,000 to occupied Japan.

Indian officers and soldiers were resentful and unhappy at being re-deployed in this manner, without a break after the end of the Second World War. Secret British intelligence reports describe abysmally low morale among the Indian forces in post-Second World War Southeast Asia, with several suicides and 'growing sympathy' for the INA.[2] Indian troops received direct appeals for support from Vietnamese and Indonesian nationalists. In the battle of Surabaya, where the British fought Indonesian nationalists, there were desertions with several Indians 'embedding' themselves with the Indonesians.

The Indian National Congress bitterly opposed the use of Indian troops abroad. The Congress supported the emerging republics of Vietnam and Indonesia. After the battle of Surabaya, Nehru demanded to visit Java to assess the situation. 'After Java, it was clear that further British action against national liberation movements with Indian soldiers would be impossible. This marked the end of the Indian Army as an instrument of British world power.'[3] By October 1945, the then Viceroy of India, Lord Wavell, urged the earliest possible withdrawal of Indian troops deployed in Southeast Asia.

By early 1946, the protests and mutinies that had begun in India against the court martial of the INA officers spread to Singapore, where 'more than four thousand men were involved in a strike'[4] at Seletar, deploring the use of Indian troops abroad. This caused the British in Malaya to intensify the action they had already initiated against the Indian community. In the words of the scholar and author, Timothy Harper:

> The British took vengeance on the entire community for its support for the INA. Even those Indian soldiers who had not joined the INA faced fatal hostility and neglect. . . . The shadow of the charge of 'adhering to the King's enemies' hung over the civilians who had supported Netaji. Within a week of reoccupation, many of them were arrested and detained in the notorious Pudu jail in Kuala Lumpur. But this backfired on the British. Local opinion—in all communities—was firm against these arrests. The full weight of Indian public opinion made itself felt in Malaya. . . . By early December 1945, this issue was causing so much difficulty in India, that it led Wavell to plead personally with Mountbatten to either try the men or release them. The witchhunt against Indian civilians in Southeast Asia rapidly lost all moral force and the prosecutions unraveled. But they cast a long shadow.[5]

Amongst the Malayans worst affected by the Second World War were the Indians working on rubber estates and other plantations, as well as public works labourers. More than 50,000 Indian immigrant labour are estimated to have lost their lives during the Japanese occupation of Malaya,[6] mostly as the result of their participation in Japanese forced labour schemes. It is estimated that, during the period of Japanese occupation, of the '72,200 labourers sent from Malaya to Burma and Thailand, over 29,000 were reported to have died and 24,000 "deserted"; many of this number were lost in jungle, or (were) disguised statistics of fatalities in the camps'.[7] The impact of these tragic deaths was traumatic and shattering at the micro-level of individual families and small communities of Indian immigrant labour isolated on various estates.

Indian plantation labour in British Malaya was 'subject to one of the strictest labour regimes on earth'.[8] Yet, when the British sought to reimpose this regime after their reoccupation of Malaya at the end of the Second World War, the hitherto 'docile' Indian labour was no longer so. The returning INA men altered the situation inexorably. As part of the effort to break out of their isolation and provide a participatory voice to the Indian community,

> more and more Indians joined communist-dominated organizations such as left-wing trade unions. For INA returnees, involvement in the activities of the left-wing organizations was not a contradiction. For the majority, the struggle against British imperialism was a continuation of the struggle first headed by the INA.[9]

The INA returnees instilled new confidence and pride among Indian plantation labour, leading them to question the harsh trespass laws and other conditions of work imposed upon them. In October 1947 there was concerted action by the plantation labour against the management, which 'for the first time—had managers fleeing their estate'.[10] The efforts of the INA returnees to usher in changes and reform in working conditions for plantation labour found ready resonance among Chinese estate workers. All communities now came together to form the pan-Malayan Federation of Trade Unions.

In many ways the impact and influence of Netaji Subhas Chandra Bose and the INA in Malaya extended far beyond the Indian community. For the Malays and the Chinese, as well as for the Indians in Malaya, Netaji's rallies held throughout Singapore and the Malay Peninsula, combined with his vibrant oratory, were the first political gatherings ever held on this mammoth scale. This represented 'the true dawn of mass politics in Malaya'.[11] The notable orator and Malay nationalist leader in the post-war era, Ahmad Boestamam, acknowledged Subhas Chandra Bose as 'his real inspiration'.[12] In the words of Timothy Harper:

> For all communities, the days of Japanese occupation had a millennial edge to them; the INA was a template for political action. . . . The INA was the first step in the internationalization of nationalism. With this came the vital sense of history being open, at a juncture when the people of colonial Asia could shape their own future as they had not been able to do within living memory.[13]

Even as the INA returnees were contributing positively towards getting the process of labour and social reforms underway, disturbing news about the dismal condition of Malayan Indians was causing consternation among all sections of society in India. On the one hand, Malayan Indian plantation labour and railway workers found themselves in abysmal economic straits. The situation was particularly serious for the families of the tens of thousands who did not return from the forced labour on the Siam Burma Death Railway that the Japanese had condemned them to endure. On the other hand, those who had joined the INA or the IIL, and who did return to their pre-war lives throughout Southeast Asia (Malaya, Singapore, Burma, Borneo and Siam) were confronted with politically motivated cases launched against them by the post-war British administration in Malaya.

JAWAHARLAL NEHRU'S SECOND VISIT TO MALAYA

All this led the Working Committee of the Indian National Congress to request Pandit Jawaharlal Nehru to visit Malaya and Singapore.[14] Pandit Nehru spent a little over one week in Malaya/Singapore, from 18 to 26 March 1946. Nehru visited Singapore, Johore Bahru, Malacca, Seremban, Kuala Lumpur, Ipoh, Taiping Butterworth, Penang and Alor Star.[15] This was his second visit to this region, nine years after his first visit in 1937.

This was a particularly sensitive assignment for Pandit Nehru. In India, he was fully involved with the ongoing negotiations with the British over the transfer of power in preparation for India's independence. In March 1946, the nation was anxiously awaiting the visit of the British Cabinet Mission. At the same time, Pandit Nehru and the Congress had been closely following the plight of the Malayan Indian all across the Malay Peninsula. By late 1945, Nehru had already applied for a passport and travel facilities to visit Malaya,[16] anticipating the important need for his presence there. The British authorities took several months to process the approvals, with the result that the dates for Nehru's visit to Malaya almost coincided with the key visit of the Cabinet Mission to India. Despite this, the visit to Malaya went ahead.

By January 1946, the Congress had a medical mission in readiness to go to Malaya, awaiting the permission to do so.[17] Around this time, following the pattern of the Red Fort trials against INA leaders, 'the Government of India sent a number of Indian lawyers to defend Indians accused of collaboration with the enemy in Malaya'.[18]

Pandit Nehru minced no words about the devastating economic plight of Indians in Malaya. Speaking at a Press Conference which coincided with his departure for Malaya, he said in response to a question that:

> I have received reports that Indian women in Malaya are going about wearing gunny bags as their dress. Urgent demands have been made for saris. Millowners in Bombay are prepared to gift immediately a hundred bales of cloth. I wrote to the Government of India a month ago for an export licence and transport facilities to despatch the cloth to Malaya, but the matter has not yet been decided.[19]

At the same press conference Jawaharlal Nehru spoke about being 'informed that a large number of Indians in Malaya are being pushed back into India. Many of them have no homes here, having been born and brought up in Malaya. I doubt the wisdom of sending all of these people back to Madras. . . .'[20] He was also disturbed to learn that 'a prominent Indian . . . has been court martialled and sentenced to seven years' imprisonment in Borneo, presumably because of his membership in the Indian Independence League.'[21]

The deep concerns expressed by Pandit Nehru were no doubt reflective of the views of broad cross-sections of society across India. Nehru and the Congress were determined to do whatever possible to ameliorate the condition of Malayan Indians. Yet, while conveying his solidarity with and support for them, Nehru remained sensitive to their status as Malayan Indians. Hence, he emphasized how important it was that 'Indians in Malaya should organize themselves into a committee to help themselves'.[22] He advised them on setting up the Indian Relief Committee to organize and channelize assistance to the most needy sections amongst them. He agreed to be the (absentee) Chairman of this Committee, and appointed respected members of the Malayan Indian community, including stalwarts of the INA like N. Raghavan, J. Thivy and Janaki Thevar to run the Committee. J. Thivy was later the first President of the Malayan Indian Congress (MIC).

Nehru was pained, even appalled, to witness the debilitating poverty being suffered by Indian labourers and their families, living on plantations and working on the railways. Nonetheless, Nehru was effusive in his praise of the resilience and inner strength of these very people. In his First Report on his Visit to Malaya, Pandit Nehru said:

> My dominant sensation during this visit to Malaya was one of exuberant vitality of the people there. Nine years ago I went to Malaya and found it politically speaking a placid place with practically no public life. . . . Now all this was changed. . . . (T)he Indian population . . . has changed considerably during this ordeal (Japanese occupation) and it was psychologically different. . . . They remembered the days when in a vague kind of way they functioned as members of a free government and they were proud of them. Even the half-clad and naked labourers held themselves up straighter than they used to. The INA and IIL had taught them discipline and everywhere groups of Indian men and women in tattered uniforms tried to function as disciplined soldiers and indeed functioned very satisfactorily. There were also the *Balsena* (boys' brigade) and the *Balikasena* (girls' brigade). It surprised me to see these Tamil workers of the rubber plantations transformed into these military groups. It surprised me still more to see the new spirit among the timid and gentle-faced Tamil women some of whom went about in uniform.[23]

An issue of some importance and concern for Pandit Nehru was the personal, social, economic and political relationships among the Indians, Malays and Chinese, particularly in the aftermath of the Japanese occupation. In his assessment and reports on his 1946 visit to Malaya, Nehru expressed his pleasure and satisfaction on this count. He said that, in the first place:

> Everywhere I was welcomed not only by the Indian population but by the Chinese and Malayans. The Chinese particularly played an important part in all these welcomes and gatherings. Others who took part were Indonesians, Eurasians, Ceylonese, etc. To give some idea of the universality of the welcome I might mention that in Ipoh 123 organisations joined in welcoming me. At

one of my meetings one of the Sultanas of the State, where I was having the meetings, attended. In another State, that of Keddah, I paid a short visit to the Sultan whom I found very interesting, and subsequently a formal Malayan feast was organized in my honour by the Sultan's brother. This was attended by people of all communities including British officers. Everywhere goodwill was expressed for India and for Indian freedom and it was emphasized that the whole of South East Asia looked up to the coming independence of India. Much interest was taken in the forthcoming negotiations with the members of the British Cabinet Mission.[24]

On the relationship between the communities, Pandit Nehru was precise and clear, even prescient:

I was interested and pleased to find that there was no conflict of any kind between the Indians and the Chinese or the Indians and the Malay(an)s. . . . While the Indians got on well with both the Chinese and the Malay(an)s, there was a sense of conflict between the Chinese and the Malay(an)s. Some people think that this conflict is likely to come to a head in the course of a year and there might even be big-scale trouble between them. They have already been a number of riots between these two communities.[25]

Pandit Nehru added:

I was interested in finding out how the activities of the INA affected the relations of Indians with the Chinese and the Malay(an)s. I was assured by all three communities that this had no bad effect. This was surprising because the Chinese, or some of them, had organized a regular resistance movement against the Japanese occupation while the INA was obviously in many ways cooperating with the Japanese. Nevertheless there was no sense of conflict between the INA and the Chinese resistance movement and they even had a number of secret contacts. The Chinese evidently realized that the INA was not so much cooperating with the Japanese as working for the freedom of India with which they sympathized. The position was undoubtedly a difficult one for all concerned, but the fact remains that it did not lead to any bad blood between the Indians and the Chinese and at present their relations are definitely good. My visit has undoubtedly led to an even greater improvement in all these inter-racial relations in Malaya.[26]

Pandit Nehru did however express some concern about the relations between the British and the Indians, referring, in this context, to the 'bitterness' that had crept in. In Nehru's words:

These English people, some army men but mostly planters and others, were Japanese prisoners or internees and they were treated very badly by the Japanese. . . . They were made to work hard on public works like roads etc., and generally they were degraded in many ways. . . . Many of them broke up completely and behaved in a manner which is distressing to think of. . . . Many of these persons are now officials of the BMA (British Military Administration) and it is natural that they should feel vengeful not only against the Japanese but also to some extent against Indians who held superior positions in those days.[27]

Among the extraordinary aspects of Pandit Nehru's visit to Malaya in 1946 was his interaction with Lord Louis Mountbatten, Supreme Commander of the Allied Forces in Southeast Asia, and Lady Edwina Mountbatten, both of whom he was meeting for the first time. In Nehru's words, the BMA and Lord Louis Mountbatten 'gave me every facility and indeed went out of their way to help me during my visit. I believe this was largely due to Lord Louis Mountbatten's initiative'.[28] According to the scholar Timothy Norman Harper, the then Viceroy of India, Lord Wavell, had conveyed to Lord Mountbatten that 'Nehru was to be treated as a future prime minister of India'.[29] Harper confirms Nehru's views and assessments when he says:

When the British could find no transport for him (Nehru), Mountbatten lent his own, and traveled with him. The sight of Nehru by Mountbatten's side was a political sensation. Nehru's first engagement was a visit to a welfare centre for Indian troops in Singapore in the company of the Mountbattens. They were mobbed together with Nehru and had to escape. It was, of course, a fateful meeting. But again, Nehru was feted by representatives of all communities. A crowd of 100,000 people gathered outside the Adelphi Hotel where he stayed. Chinese leaders feasted him at their 'millionaires' club, the Ee Hoe Hean Club. Wherever he stopped, the local Communists' representatives came to see him. . . . Nehru's visit was the high-water mark of India's influence on the freedom struggle in Southeast Asia.[30]

Pandit Nehru had enunciated that 'the object of my visit to Malaya was especially to find out about the ex-INA and the Indian Independence League people as well as to investigate, in so far as I could, the general conditions and living standards of the Indian workers'.[31] It came as a great relief to Pandit Nehru when Lord Louis Mountbatten told him 'at my very first meeting . . . that he was following the policy laid down in Delhi in regard to INA, i.e., he was not going to proceed against anyone for collaboration alone with the Japanese. . . . This meant that practically speaking all those in prison still would be discharged.'

Lord Louis Mountbatten did raise with Pandit Nehru the issue of 'tracing . . . the funds of the Indian Independence League or the Provisional Government of Azad Hind.'[32] Pandit Nehru took this matter very seriously, particularly because of its potential to become a divisive issue among the Malayan Indians. G.P. Hutheesing, who had travelled to Malaya with Pandit Nehru as his secretary, was instructed to stay behind to investigate this matter thouroughly. After receiving G.P. Hutheesing's report on his investigations, Pandit Nehru wrote a confidential letter on 16 April 1946 to Maulana Abul Kalam Azad, President of the Indian National Congress.[33] This was Nehru's third report on his visit to Malaya. In the first report on his visit to Malaya, Pandit Nehru had already conveyed to the President that a large sum of money belonging to the Provisional Government or the IIL 'amounting to about Rs 3,000,000 was, I believe, seized by the British Government from the Rangoon branch of the Azad Hind Bank'.[34]

In his third report Nehru conveyed further details about 'sums of money, notably 1,000,000 piastas ($ 500,000) which was seized by the BMG (British Military Government). The BMG also seized a large quantity of medical stores which had been given to the Ramakrishna Mission. There are also some blocked accounts of the IIL in Japanese currency which probably have no value now.'[35] Based on Hutheesing's findings, Nehru said in this third report that 'Shri Bose, before his departure, had directed that all funds should be used in two ways, first in giving immediate relief to the INA or IIL personnel, secondly to create a trust fund for the purpose of giving relief to Indians'.[36] This is the genesis of the Indian Relief Committee and the Trust Fund that Pandit Nehru was so successful in creating, during his eight-day stay in Malaya, in 1946.

Pandit Nehru did request Lord Louis Mountbatten 'to hand over to the trust fund we were creating the monies they (the British) had seized from the Provisional Government of Azad Hind and the IIL so that these might be used for relief work among Indians'.[37] Nehru received no commitment from Lord Mountbatten on this, leading him to conclude that 'I am continuing my efforts to get these funds transferred for relief work, but I am not by any means sure that this will be done'.[38] Nehru was successful in raising substantial additional funds for the Trust Fund, both through the purses given to him during his stay in Malaya ($85,000), and through recovering the gold bars that had originally belonged to the IIL ($60,000).[39]

Pandit Nehru was unequivocal in supporting the conclusions arrived at by Hutheesing regarding the IIL funds that 'there is no evidence of malfeasance', explaining that the extraordinary state of affairs caused by the interregnum between the Japanese surrender and the reoccupation of Malaya by the British may have led to confusion and inefficiencies. Nehru's deep interest in all issues concerning the overseas Indian community in Malaya, his sincere efforts at unravelling the tangles in order to raise the community's morale and bolster their self-confidence were unprecedented and most effective. His message to the Malayan Indian community was strong and clear: that they should remain united and organize themselves in a broad-based and inclusive manner, in order to support the weakest and poorest among them, while simultaneously playing a purposeful role in promoting friendship with others and contributing to the development and prosperity of Malaya. Soon after Nehru's return to India, Malayan Indians entered the mainstream of political activity in Malaya with the formation, in August 1946, of the Malayan Indian Congress (MIC).

Pandit Nehru left Malaya just five days before the British proposal for a Malayan Union came into force, on 1 April 1946. He was repeatedly queried in public interactions about his views on the Malayan Union proposal. He was guarded in his replies, since he did not want to enter into any controversy on internal Malayan politics. In Nehru's first report on his visit to Malaya, he commented:

> I did not express an opinion about the scheme of Malayan Union, . . . in any event I did not want to enter into Malayan politics. The scheme is agitating Malayans and Chinese alike. To the Indians I said that I had no doubt that some time or other they would have to choose their nationality in Malaya, in Burma and in Ceylon; they could not have the privileges and obligations of two nationalities at the same time. . . . The choice really was an individual matter. Indians who had been born in Malaya and have sometimes lived there for generations might well choose Malayan nationality. That did not mean, of course, a break with India in the cultural sense, but it did mean a certain political status; in any event Indians must cultivate the goodwill of the other people of Malaya. . . . The future of Indians in Burma, in Malaya and in Ceylon

lies in their co-operation with the people there and in the strength of a free Indian government behind them.[40]

THE MALAYAN UNION PROPOSAL

The proposal for a Malayan Union, put forward by the British government just weeks after their reoccupation of the Malayan Peninsula at the end of the Second World War, was the first ever to address the question of Malayan nationhood. It was the first effort to bring together the states on the Malayan Peninsula under one administration on a *de jure*, rather than just *de facto* basis. Prior to the Japanese occupation, the British had been administering three separate entities in Malaya: the Straits Settlements (a Crown Colony, comprising Singapore, Penang, Malacca and Province Wellesley), the Federated Malay States (Perak, Selangor, Negri Sembilan, and Pahang) and the Unfederated Malay States (Johor, Kedah, Kelantan, Terengganu, Perlis and Brunei, the last-named located on the island of Borneo). The senior British officer (whose advice the Sultans were treaty-bound to accept) was the Resident in each Federated State and the Adviser in each Unfederated State. They enjoyed considerable independence, although nominally (at least in the Federated Malay States), they reported to the Chief Secretary in Kuala Lumpur, who in turn was responsible to the Governor of the Straits Settlements, the *ex officio* head of government for the territory as a whole.

The rapid economic growth in Malaya in the first half of the twentieth century led to considerable centralization of administrative power with the Chief Secretary in Kuala Lumpur. This meant that the individual powers hitherto enjoyed by the Residents and Advisers gradually shifted towards the Chief Secretary in Kuala Lumpur. The proposal for a Malayan Union was meant to address and streamline such issues, and to lead the Malayan Peninsula towards self-rule as a united country.

The debate over the Malayan Union proposal raged between two streams of thought within the British administration. One school of thought

favoured political and administrative decentralization, and the broadening of existing Malay privileges such as a monopoly of land ownership in certain areas, a monopoly of posts in the Malay Administrative Service, special representation on the various federal and state councils, and so on. According to the rival school, the Malayan mainland was one country, created politically and economically during the half-century before 1930, and the Malays were only one of several nations or races composing it. The former was called the pro-Malay or devolutionist school; the latter was sometimes called the pan-Malayan school.[41]

According to the scholar P.T. Bauer:

For a variety of reasons most of the British administrators belonged to the pro-Malay school. . . . The majority of the British in the east have a decided preference for Malay manners and customs against those of the Chinese and Indians. . . . There was also a conscious or unconscious economic basis for the pro-Malay attitude. The Malays, unlike the Chinese, were not economic competitors of the British in Malaya. . . . (For) the business community . . . however . . . the advantages of centralized administration told in favor of the pan-Malayan school. When nationalist sentiment in China and India grew stronger in the 1920s and Kuomintang flags were flying from Chinese houses in Malaya and Congress flags from most Indian dwellings, the British administrators were especially reluctant to abandon the policy of strengthening the Malays through the granting of special privileges. The principal loyalty of the Chinese and Indians lay outside Malaya, they pointed out. It was true; but it was equally true that until the discrimination against the Chinese and the Indians was abandoned, these races could not be expected to consider Malaya their home.[42]

The 'discrimination' that P.T. Bauer describes was the result of the system of segregation and separation put in place by the British administration, not by the Malays. The uncertainty the Chinese and Indians felt about their future in Malaya was the result of these discriminatory policies. P.T. Bauer has also described how the British 'considered that their primary duty was to the Malays, whose ancestors (even if not the original settlers of the country) had been in Malaya well before the masses of the Chinese and Indian immigrants'.[43] What the British perhaps overlooked is that the ancestors of the Malays included the Indians who had been interacting with the people of the Malay Peninsula for close to two millennia, living in Malaya, intermarrying and playing an active role at the court of Malay Sultans, right up to the advent of the British in the last quarter of the eighteenth century.

In 1942, in the midst of the Second World War, the British Colonial Office in London established the Colonial Research Committee under Lord Hailey, tasked with investigating post-war arrangements in British colonies. On the situation in Malaya Lord Hailey said:

> It is obvious that there are many advantages in the existing system which is practically one of direct official rule, under the façade of advice to the Malayan rulers! . . . Sooner or later we will have to face squarely the question whether we are to allow the façade of Sultan-rule to persist, with all the difficulties which it presents to the attainment of any form of self-government, or to build up a constitution on the basis of realities.[44]

Lord Hailey's major concern was 'autocratic rule in the hands of the Sultans and their Malay advisers' and whether the system (in Malaya) would 'enable a suitable status to be given to those Chinese and Indian immigrants who may acquire a permanent interest in the country'.[45]

These were important concerns. However, during this very period, policy analysis within the British Colonial Office and the British Foreign Office was veering towards taking into account the 'legitimate fear of the Malays' *vis-à-vis* other people in the Peninsula.[46] By May 1943, the Colonial Office, while considering this 'ethnicity variable' in the post-war arrangements, was of the view that 'Malay interests must be recognized as paramount . . . but . . . other communities with permanent interests in the country must be given their due opportunity to share in an advance towards self-government.'[47] In May 1944, in the appendices to the War Cabinet Memorandum on Policy in regard to Malaya and Borneo, presented to British Prime Minister Clement Attlee, it was noted that 'self-government should not merely develop towards a system of autocratic rule by the Malay Rulers, but should provide for a growing participation in the Government by the people of all communities in Malaya, subject to a special recognition of the political, economic and social interests of the Malay race'.[48]

The one person who staunchly opposed incipient moves towards an ethnocratic post-war Malaya was Lord Louis Mountbatten, Supreme Commander of the Allied Forces in South East Asia, based at the time in Ceylon. It was the 'Colonial Office's desire to assign a special position to the Malays in the post-war administrative structure that drew most of his ire'.[49] In July 1944, Lord Mountbatten expressed his views unequivocally in his comments on a Colonial Office memo to the War Office, which had *inter alia* referred to a post-war structure in which 'participation in the Government by all the communities in Malaya is to be promoted, subject to a special recognition of the political, economic and social interests of the Malay race'. In his letter to the Mr. Stanley of the Colonial Office who had written this memo, Lord Mountbatten said:

> I cannot help feeling that in the long run nothing could perhaps do more to perpetuate sectional antagonisms, to the rise of which you pointedly refer in your letter, than the giving of special recognition to one race. . . . I feel that our objectives should be to break down racial sectionalism in every way open to us, politically, economically and socially, and to endeavour to substitute for it the idea of Malayan citizenship.[50]

In his reply to Lord Mountbatten, Stanley provided unique and direct insights into Colonial Office perceptions about the situation in Malaya. Stanley said:

> The Malays are, by general consent, not at present capable of competing on equal terms economically and educationally with the 'immigrant races'—Chinese and Indian. From the beginning of our relations with the States we have pursued in the Malay States the policy of taking positive measures to prevent the submergence of the Malays in the public services and in the ownership of land by the more energetic, competent and resourceful Chinese. The most damaging criticism of our new policy will be precisely on these grounds, since we are endeavouring to admit non-Malay communities to a political equality with the Malays in the State territories. We shall make certain of estranging the Malays unless we can assure them of measures not only in the political and social field, which will prevent such 'equality' inevitably resulting in their submergence, but also in such matters as the reservation of Malay lands, which otherwise will certainly pass into the hands of the ubiquitous Indian money-lender. . . . The social basis of Malayan society for some time to come cannot be expected to be other than communal, seeing that intermarriage is virtually non-existent, and religion, language and domestic customs must be potent factors in maintaining the present distinctions.[51]

Did the Colonial Office's statement on the compartmentalization or isolation of the three races from each other reflect the reality? Or, was it a presumption, derived perhaps, from British perceptions about the way they would like things to be. Empirically, there has been regular interaction and intermarriages between the Malays, the

Chinese and the Indians over the centuries. The families of Malay rulers were often in the vanguard of such cultural, social and trade interlinkages. There are, even in contemporary times, members of Malay royalty who do not hesitate to speak about this publicly. On 16 November 2010 in Kuala Lumpur, Raja Zarith Sofiah Sultan Idris Shah, the consort of the Sultan of Johor, delivering the keynote address at the Conference on 'Voices of Peace, Conscience and Reason', described 'her own ancestral background as a mix between Sumatran and Peranakan Chinese', adding that 'it was important to recognise the diversity of Malaysian society, brought about by centuries of interracial and interfaith marriages and communication'.[52]

Going back to the narrative of the Malayan Union proposal, Lord Mountbatten did not accept Stanley's assertions favouring the communal division of society in Malaya. Lord Mountbatten said in his letter to Stanley on 6 September 1944:

> I fully appreciate that the social basis of Malayan society cannot for some time be other than communal, and that the fostering (among) the three peoples of Malaya of the conception that they are in fact Malayans, will be an uphill business. . . . Since I wrote to you, I have received from the War Office copies of the Directives on Chinese policy, and on the Creation of Malayan Union Citizenship. It is essential that the Chinese and Indian elements should be legally assimilated, and should be made to feel committed to local responsibility, instead of being merely a group of exploiters, or a source of cheap labour.
>
> I am sorry to see from your letter that the Malays should by general consent be found incapable of competing on equal terms, 'economically and educationally' with the Chinese and Indians . . . one is inclined to fear that an opinion of the natives' qualities may become an *idée fixe*, which will militate against a proper appreciation of their potentialities under improved conditions.[53]

With this exchange of letters, the lines were clearly drawn between two distinct streams of British opinion. The Colonial Office supported a protected position for the Malays, while Lord Mountbatten led those who were equally convinced about the need for a general Malayan citizenship with equal rights and responsibilities for all. Lord Mountbatten's opinion held sway. One year later, soon after the British reoccupation of the Malay Peninsula at the end of the Second World War, a British emissary, Sir Harold MacMichael, spent close to three months in Malaya in the last quarter of 1945. His *Report on a Mission to Malaya*, published in February 1946, averred that 'although the special position of the indigenous Malays needed to be safeguarded, reforms were overdue in the system of representation in order to permit the claims of other races, Chinese and Indian for the most part . . . to receive reasonable satisfaction.'[54] The Malayan Union proposal was published as the official British White Paper of 1946 ('Malayan Union and Singapore'). This White Paper was based on the MacMichael Report. Sir Harold MacMichael obtained the written consent of all the Malay Sultans to his proposal.

The Malayan Union proposal sought to bring together the FMS, the Unfederated Malay States, Penang, Malacca and Province Wellesley, as a colonial protectorate. Singapore was to remain a Crown Colony. The proposal envisaged complete administrative centralization within the Malayan Union, including loss of the nominal sovereignty of the Malay Sultans. It also envisaged a Malayan Union citizenship, to be given to all persons born in the region covered by the Union or in Singapore, as also to those who had resided in this region for ten of the immediately preceding fifteen years. The Malayan Union proposal anticipated that in the future, citizenship could be acquired on five years' residence. Author and scholar Cheah Boon Kheng has noted that under this plan

> the British had intended to end Malay sovereignty, impose direct rule in Malaya and create an equal citizenship for both Malays and non-Malays. If this plan had been fully implemented, Malaya would have become more of a 'Malayan' nation-state than a 'Malay' nation-state.[55]

Momentarily, it seemed as if the pan-Malayan school of thought had prevailed. The Malayan Union proposal was implemented and took effect from April 1946. Technically, the Malayan Union did last for a little under two years. However, very soon after the Malayan Union came into force, British policy-makers brought in

> a 180-degree turn from a proposed polity with equal citizenship to one where Malays were dominant, privileged and power-brokers. Some of this story has been detailed . . . but many documents remain unreleased by the British. The full story of this reversal and the huge effects this had on the subsequent development of Malaysia remains to be written.[56]

Certainly, Lord Mountbatten's departure from Singapore just a few weeks after the Malayan Union came into force must have been an important factor that facilitated this reversal in British policy. His successor as Supreme Allied Commander of the South East Asia Command, Lieutenant General Montagu Stopford, joined his post in June 1946, and by November 1946, this Command was disbanded.

Equally important in bringing about this policy reversal was the establishment of UMNO (United Malays National Organisation), the political party founded by Dato' Onn bin Jaafar in March 1946. Resisting the introduction of the Malayan Union was UMNO's immediate objective, perhaps the central reason behind the formation of the party. Meetings were organized throughout the Malay Peninsula decrying 'the loss of status by the Malay Sultans and the loss of rights by the Malays as a whole'.[57] This was supplemented by vigorous lobbying in the House of Commons in London and in the British media by the influential 'pro-Malay' group, primarily former high-ranking British officials of the Malayan Civil Service. Several of these officials played a central role in the formation of UMNO, and continued for many years to occupy key advisory positions in the party.

The formation of UMNO came at a time of rising political consciousness and awareness among the Malays. However, this awareness was strongly centred in Malay elite circles, comprising the Malay Sultans, their extended families and senior court officials. Onn Jaafar himself was a member of the Johor political elite. The Malay elite had benefitted the most from British largesse, whether in terms of allowances and perks, education in elite schools, or jobs in the civil services and allied facilities.

The Malay Sultans, who had signed documents accepting the Malayan Union proposals, now said that this had been done under duress. The Sultans in the northern (unfederated) Malay states recalled their comparatively recent status of quasi-independence under nominal Siamese rule, and so fuelled the opposition to the Malayan Union proposal. The Malay Sultans in the Federated Malay States, too, strongly opposed the loss of status for the Malay Sultans that the Malayan Union proposal envisaged, even though each of them had individually signed treaties with the British, beginning as far back as January 1874, when the famous Pangkor Engagement was negotiated by the British with the Sultan of Perak. Under the terms of the Pangkor Engagement, the Sultan had agreed that he would ask for and act upon the advice of the British Resident 'in all questions other than those touching Malay religion and custom'.[58]

The Malayan Union provision for granting citizenship across-the-board to large numbers of Chinese and Indian immigrants was skilfully exploited to generate negative reactions and whip up opposition to the Malayan Union proposal. Traditionally, the Malay Sultans had never opposed the immigration and long-term residence of Chinese and Indians in Malaya. Historically, Indian, Chinese and European traders have been the mainstay for foreign interaction and the resultant prosperity of Malay Sultans.

There was a third factor that was assuming considerable importance in Malaya. After the Second World War, the continuing impoverishment and discriminatory policies against Chinese and Indian immigrant workers did see a rise in protests and civil disturbances. The erstwhile MPAJA (Malayan People's Anti-Japanese Army), which had received covert support from the British in the later stages of the Second World War, now partially regrouped as the MNLA (Malayan National Liberation Army), the military wing of the Malayan Communist Party (MCP). The British used the term Malayan Races Liberation Army (MRLA) to describe the MNLA. The MCP's increasing recourse to strikes and violence, particularly from 1946 onwards, culminated in what the British considered to be an 'armed revolt', which led to the declaration of a national emergency in June 1948.

Chinese and Indian residents of Malaya were active participants in the MCP and the MNLA, though not in very large numbers as far as the Indians were concerned. Outside the Malay elite, a fraction of Malays, too, were participants in these movements. As against this, Malays, Chinese and Indians employed with the police and allied agencies played an active role in countering the Communist insurgents and negating their influence. Yet, the antipathy and anger among the people against the violent tactics of the MNLA was often given a racial flavour, with the Malays (portrayed as staunch opponents of the communists) arrayed against the Chinese and the Indians. This, too, was used (before January 1948) to fuel Malay opposition to the Malayan Union proposals.

THE FEDERATION OF MALAYA AGREEMENT

In the light of the (orchestrated) opposition to the Malayan Union, the British initiated a fresh round of consultations through a Political Working Committee created in July 1946. This Committee, with the declared objective of recommending a new constitutional framework for the Malayan Union, consisted of six British officials, four royal delegates and two UMNO representatives. Scholar Geoff Wade has commented that:

> The question remains as to why it was decided that only Malay representatives were to negotiate the future of Malaya with the British. Was it simply the Colonial Office officials reasserting their paternalistic concern for Malay people, or was it an awareness of the growing power of the Left, represented predominantly by Chinese persons, which sparked this remarkable change? Regardless of the reasons, this decision must be seen as the most fateful and harmful decision in the British decolonization of Malaya.[59]

The new constitutional proposals, drafted essentially by the British Colonial Office, were released in December, 1946. Opposition to these proposals was spontaneous and instantaneous. Malayan, Chinese and Indian organizations joined hands to form the PMCJA (Pan-Malayan Council for Joint Action), which included trade unions and political parties across the spectrum of the Malayan Left and Right. In February 1947, a new coalition of Malay political and cultural organizations came up, the PUTERA (Pusat Tenaga Rakyat), organized as a counterweight to UMNO. In March 1947, the PMCJA and PUTERA formed an alliance to coordinate their efforts against the proposed Federation of Malaya constitution. Huge rallies were held in Kuala Lumpur, Malacca and other towns, urging and demanding that the new constitution provide for a united Malaya inclusive of Singapore, responsible self-government through a fully elected central legislature, equal citizenship rights for all who have made Malaya their home, constitutional Sultans who would govern through democratic state councils, and special measures for the uplift and advancement of the Malay people.

Neither these demonstrations and the demands put forth, nor the Consultative Committee convened by the British Malayan government to ascertain the views of the non-Malays (this included two Chinese and two Indians) made any significant difference to the final outcome. The Federation of Malaya Agreement, which came into effect in February 1948, abrogated key egalitarian elements of the Malayan Union proposals. The requirements for citizenship of the Federation were much more complicated and restrictive than those included in the Malayan Union proposal. The Malays were recognized as 'people of the country' without acknowledging that they, too, had migrated, and still continue to migrate to the peninsula from many other places in the archipelago and beyond. The Malays were themselves the progeny of interracial and intercommunity marriages. The Federation of Malaya constitution provided automatic citizenship for the Malay (defined as a person who 'habitually speaks the Malay language, professes the Muslim religion and conforms to Malay custom'), regardless of length of residence in the country. For all other communities, requirements of residence were imposed.

The Federation of Malaya constitution established the Conference of Rulers, together with a federal structure, with central and state legislatures. 'The Federation was something of a compromise, but weighted on the Malay side. Malay influence was preserved through the Sultans and predominant Malay representation in the State and Federation governments as well as by the citizenship clauses.'[60] Geoff Wade's assessment is that 'the constitution was thus a blueprint for Malay ethnocracy'.[61] This constitution formed the basis for the Federation of Malaya Constitution adopted at the time of Malayan independence in 1957.

The manner and process in which the Federation of Malaya Agreement was finalized, further entrenched the communal divisions in Malayan society, the hallmark British legacy in this country. The Federation of Malaya Agreement was an imposed solution, just as the Malayan Union proposal had been. Both proposals, drafted by the British, were drawn up after whatever consultations they deemed necessary, with selected representatives of the Malay, Chinese and Indian communities. Almost invariably, these consultations were held separately, with little effort to bring the Malays,

Chinese and Indians together to the same negotiating table, so that they could understand each other and solve any differences to mutual satisfaction. The MCA (Malayan Chinese Association) had not yet been formed; the MIC, strong supporters of the pan-Malayan proposal, decided to boycott the negotiations for the Federation of Malaya Agreement, and it soon became clear that opinion within UMNO was divided on the crucial issue of 'Malaya for the Malayans'.

There was serious discomfort and unhappiness among the Chinese and Indian communities, chiefly because insufficient attention had been given to their political status and to the need for equal rights among all citizens of Malaya. However, these communities were not united, either within or among themselves.

The MIC, formed in August 1946, after Pandit Nehru's visit to Malaya, did not enjoy the whole-hearted backing of Malayan Indian opinion in its decision to boycott the negotiations on the Federation of Malaya Agreement. The pro-Communist, left-wing groups, particularly Indian labour organized in trade-unions, supported the MIC's position, while the conservatives in the Indian leadership did not. The very positive PMCJA-PUTERA unity soon fractured. First, 'Malay leaders . . . broke away from it when on citizenship and representation differences between them and other communities widened. . . . The outbreak of communist guerilla activity and the declaration of emergency in June 1948 put an end to the united front.'[62]

In the early years after its formation, the MIC remained a marginalized organization, unable to garner the support or serve the interests of the multifarious Malayan Indian organizations and regional groupings. There were at least two other directly competing organizations, the Malayan Indian Association and the Federation of Indian Organizations. Then there was the divide between the north Indians and the south Indians, between the plantation labour and the urban professionals, between big business and small traders, even the religious divide that emerged in the early years after the war, when Indian Muslims and Sikhs sought separate representation on the legislative Council.[63] The MIC could not, during this period, fulfil its foundational ambition of serving as an umbrella organization for all Malayan Indians, along the lines of the Indian National Congress in India. The MIC did not take up labour issues, perhaps because the trade union organizations were actively involved with these issues in the immediate post-war period. The MIC did not have effective branch organizations in the smaller towns and rural areas. And in June 1948, the MIC announced a voluntary suspension of political activity until the end of the emergency.

The British Malayan government 'tended to encourage these trends towards factionalism among Malayan Indians by granting swift recognition to the various communal organizations that were revived or founded'[64] in the immediate post-war years. Indeed, the British Malayan government did not readily recognize any of the Malayan Indian organizations as representing or being capable of speaking on behalf of the Malayan Indian community. Rather than the representatives of community organizations, the British nominated eminent Malayan Indian lawyers and businessmen to speak on behalf of the Indians. This adversely affected the interests of the community as a whole, most particularly, those of the overwhelmingly large numbers of plantation labour from India.

During Pandit Jawaharlal Nehru's second visit to Malaya in 1946, as on his first visit in 1937, he emphasized the need for Malayan Indians to appreciate the sensitivity of the Malays, while at the same time to unhesitatingly speak up against injustice and discrimination. 'Nehru's advice of 1937, probably repeated in 1946, (was) that Indians should not appeal for rights over the heads of the indigenous Malay population.. . .'[65] The essential point Pandit Nehru is making is that this should not be a zero-sum game. Justice and non-discriminatory equality for the Indians (and Chinese) need not, and indeed should not, be perceived as detracting in any way from the constitutional position accorded to Malays in the 1957 Constitution. Differences of opinion and perception can be resolved to mutual satisfaction, without conflict and misunderstanding. The acceptability of this view was reflected in the following comment published in the *Malayan Daily News* on 4 March 1946:

> There are several points at which the interests of the Malays and those of the immigrant races clash and it remains to be seen whether the broadened basis of the constitution incorporating the Malayan Union will be able to smooth over

such conflicts. Neither the Chinese nor the Indians desire to see the Malays suffer in any way by this new constitutional dispensation. As a matter of fact, we think, they would be extremely sorry if there were any adverse effect on the Malays. What they desire is that their own interests should not be consistently ignored but that the recognition they receive should bear some proportion to the contribution they have made towards the building up of the country.[66]

In October 1946 a wide cross-section of groups joined hands in advocating that the new constitution be drafted by convening a constituent assembly (the MCP wanted a national association democratically elected by universal suffrage) representing all major races and the full range of political opinion. The supporters of this proposal included the newly formed MIC (Malayan Indian Congress), the Malayan Democratic Union, the Malay Nationalist Party and the AMCJA (All Malayan Council for Joint Action). This multi-racial support for convening a constituent assembly was a stong indication of the broad-based consensus on the need for a genuinely democratic structure after Malayan independence. This was certainly not a case of Malays versus the rest. There was a convergence of views on this subject among all races, with the exception of the conservative Malay elite who, in turn, had the support of a strong section of the colonial administration.

In the last quarter of 1947, PUTERA/AMCJA published *The People's Constitutional Proposals for Malaya* based on 'lengthy multi-racial discussion and representing the spirit of communal compromise'.[67] These were intended as an alternative to the Federation of Malaya proposals (also known as the Anglo-Malay proposals) that were currently under discussion. Under the People's Constitutional Proposals, the Malay rulers would be constitutional monarchs and citizenship would 'constitute a true nationality, termed 'Melayu' with the duty of allegiance to the nation. All other allegiances should be renounced. The insistence upon full nationality rather than mere citizenship was at the very core of the People's Proposals. . . .'[68] Today, 55 years after *Merdeka*, the People's Proposals seem prescient when they argue that under the Anglo-Malay proposals (which formed the basis for the 1957 Constitution of Malaya):

There will be no allegiance because allegiance is expressly divorced from citizenship; there will be no loyalty and no national unity, because there is no allegiance; there will be no political rights and no civic duties, because there will be no loyalty; there will be racial disharmony and class strife, because there will be no national unity, because there is no democracy.[69]

The People's Proposals envisaged a popularly elected Representative Assembly in which 55 per cent of seats would be allocated to Malays for the first three Assemblies. A Council of Races was proposed to scrutinize all legislation to prevent racial discrimination. Malay was proposed as the official language, although other languages could be used in the Assembly. 'The Muslim religion and Malay custom would be entirely in the hands of the Malays. By these means, the People's Constitution attempted to reconcile Malay fears of racial submergence with the desire for democratic advance and the development of a genuine national unity.'[70]

The People's Proposals did elicit positive appraisals across Malaya. Even the conservative *Straits Times*, known as the organ of British capital in Malaya,[71] accepted that:

It is a creative contribution to Malayan political thought, admirable as a study of the position of the non-Malay citizen in relation to the land of his birth and to his Malay fellow citizens, and convincing in its destructive analysis of the complicated compromise on Malayan citizenship, that was reached by the Anglo-Malay Working Committee. . . .[72]

Ultimately, it was the combined views of the conservative Malay elite and the colonial administration that prevailed. Anyone with different views was branded a communist. The strong initial impetus led by PUTERA/AMCJA for a powerful multi-racial nationalist movement withered away.

The British no doubt considered the possibility of involving conservative Chinese and Indian leaderships in negotiations, but the Malay elite demanded direct and exclusive negotiations and the British were acutely aware that the perpetuation of their authority rested upon the support of conservative Malay society. It was essential that it remain conservative.[73]

UMNO remained adamantly set against the round-table format of negotiations, simultaneously bringing together all groups and parties. And the British succumbed to their pressure. In the words of the then Police Adviser to the BMA (British Military Administration) 'I believe that if we uphold Malay sovereignty we stay happily in Malaya; if we achieve that we shall once more make the country great and prosperous; and we may well do much to retain Burma, and regain India for the Empire'.[74]

THE MIC, UMNO AND MCA: BRITISH PERSPECTIVES ON COMMUNAL POLITICS IN MALAYA

The MIC was closely involved in drawing up the People's Proposals. However, there were serious doubts about the extent to which the MIC represented the interests of the vast numbers of Malayan Indian labour. In the immediate aftermath of the war, when the returning British attempted to restore and re-impose the old pre-war rates of pay, the impoverished, under-nourished and distressed Indian labour turned to militant unionism. Several independent ILUs (Indian Labour Unions) were formed, notable among these being the ones in the Malayan states of Kedah, Perak and Negri Sembilan. Many of these ILUs incorporated in their activities, the serious work on social reform and self-respect movements that had been initiated on many estates by the *Thondar Padai* or Volunteer Corps. The ILUs took the lead not only in enforcing strikes but also in social reform activities like enforcing bans on toddy drinking, improving health and solving marital and other disputes. The ILUs also put forward strong demands for provision of education facilities for the children of estate workers, particularly through the establishment of Tamil schools.

Many of the ILUs became part of the Chinese-dominated GLUs (General Labour Unions), normally as an Indian section and under Indian leadership. Unfortunately however, the ILUs lost out on two counts, as a result of which major demands put forward by Malayan Indian labour remain unrealized even today. The historical baggage that came along with the British-imposed racial division of labour in Malaya ensured that the Indians and Chinese were never able to effectively coordinate their demands *vis-à-vis* their employers. In effect:

> Colonial divide-and-rule practices were nowhere so apparent and so effective as in the colonial employment structure where Indians and Chinese were employed on different tasks, in different manners, at different wage-rates, as a means of preventing united bargaining. . . . It was these problems inherent in

the fragmented structure of plural society that made it possible for European employers and officials to achieve some success in splitting Indian from Chinese labour.[75]

At the same time when the MIC tried to bring all Malayan Indians under one banner, it was singularly unsuccessful in bringing on board the Malayan Indian labour leaders from the GLUs/ILUs. The MIC wanted to set up a Labour Department to look after the interests of Indian labour on a pan-Malayan basis. The GLUs were vehemently opposed to this suggestion since it could lead to effective competition for leadership of Indian labour. At the first MIC meeting in August 1946, the labour unions were grossly under-represented both in terms of numbers of their members, and in terms of their political significance. The Indian representatives from the GLUs asked for representation in proportion to the number of their supporters. They also wanted the MIC's Labour Department to be abolished. When both requests were denied, they left the meeting.

Malayan Indian labour lost out on both counts. Their problems remain unredressed either by the class organizations, the trade unions, or by the Malayan Indian communal organization, the MIC. The MIC remained essentially an urban-based organization. In the early years its effectiveness was greatly diminished because of its inability to register all Malayan Indians as voters.

The MIC, as an integral constituent of the Alliance Party, was party to all the compromises that were reflected in the final version of Malaya's 1957 or *Merdeka* Constitution. It is quite likely that MIC leaders shared the view of Pandit Nehru and other Indian National Congress leaders that the MIC's presence as a member of the ruling Alliance government would be sufficient to safeguard the interests of Malayan Indians.

The same British Malayan administration that had, for over hundred years, been active as the facilitator in bringing across plantation labour from south India to Malaya, was now (after aborting the Malayan Union proposal) not interested in ensuring an equitable and fair representation for Indians in the constitutional bodies of the soon-to-be independent Malaya. In 1951, when the 'member system' was introduced into the then Malayan Federal government, 'unofficial members were appointed by the

Government as political heads, and spokesmen in the legislature for certain departments. Among those appointed were three Malays, one Chinese, one European and one Ceylonese. . . . Indians were excluded from a share of political power'.[76]

What were the reasons for the British Colonial Office's unseemly speed in concluding the new Federation of Malaya constitutiton, with terms so fundamentally different from those on which the Malayan Union was based? Perhaps this had more to do with Britain's geo-political and strategic calculations in the emerging Cold War scenario after the Second World War, rather than genuine concern for the welfare of the Malays. The British were deeply concerned about maintaining their post-war power in Asia, with Singapore as the new fulcrum after the loss of India and Burma. For this purpose, Singapore was to continue as a Crown Colony. The Malayan Union that was being discussed by the British Colonial and Foreign Office even in 1942, envisaged the inclusion, one way or the other, of territories controlled by the British on the island of Borneo, namely Sarawak, Brunei and North Borneo (now Sabah).[77]

The British were wary of China, particularly the mounting victories of the Soviet Union supported Communist Party of China, and the post-war leftist insurgencies that were gathering strength in the Malay Peninsula. The decision to exclude Singapore from the Malayan Union and maintain it separately as a Crown Colony, was motivated equally by the role envisaged for Singapore in protecting Britain's trade, maritime and defence interests in the region, and by concerns that Singapore's predominantly Chinese population would tilt the numerical balance in the peninsula in favour of the Chinese. At this point, the predominant British interest in the Malay Peninsula was to somehow prevent Chinese domination and to resist being overwhelmed by the communists. These were their paramount concerns, and the switch away from the much more egalitarian Malayan Union proposals towards a constitution favouring Malay domination and control could have been motivated by British apprehensions about Malaya being overrun by the communists.

Memories of the British eviction from the Malay Peninsula in 1942 by the Japanese, the wounded pride and the humiliation that this had entailed, were far too fresh in British minds. The British were not prepared under any circumstances to risk a repeat of such a scenario, this time at the hands of the communists. They preferred to prepone their departure, granting independence to Malaya in 1957. This was a good three years before the end, in 1960, of the emergency that had been declared by the British in 1948 throughout the Malay Peninsula as a result of the communist insurgency.

In the post-war period, the Malay rulers were recognized as the staunchest allies of the British in their efforts to prevent a Chinese dominated, communist Malay Peninsula. The communist insurgency brought about this paradigm shift in British perceptions and policy. As late as 1942, in the midst of Second World War, the British Colonial Office had strategized that although 'the Malay rulers have never been ready to recognize Chinese, however long established in their states, as being nationals of those states', nevertheless 'it is desirable, even at this stage, that the formal status of "British protected persons" should be given to those Chinese who are domiciled in the Malay States'.[78] The Malayan Union proposal was, *inter alia*, the outcome of these perceptions. As a result of the ongoing Cold War and the growing success of the communist insurgents, all this changed and the Federation of Malaya Agreement came into effect in February 1948.

The Malay elite strongly supported the Malay Sultans in opposing the leftists and the communist insurgency. Communist and socialist ideologies held no appeal for this group. Malay (and non-Malay) students in higher educational institutions across the Peninsula, too, primarily the progeny of the rich and influential, were apprehensive and afraid that communism would bring them the same fate as the propertied class in communist China. In the words of author and political commentator, Ahmad Mustapha Hassan:

> Psychological warfare skilfully utilized by the British against the communist insurgency put the fear of God into the Malays. The result was that communism as a militant ideology failed to make any inroad in Malay hearts and minds. There were a few who joined, but they were very insignificant as they could not influence the broad mass of the Malays to support them. Nationalism took root first, before any other ideology could influence the Malays. Socialism, and

the communist ideology, had become synonymous with the Chinese in the Malay mind. The British too portrayed communism as being anti-Islam. The British thought that this would, probably, prolong their stay in Malaya. They were wrong.[79]

Malay nationalism took root in 1946 with the formation of UMNO in the aftermath of the coming into force of the Malayan Union. Before this, despite British efforts to maintain a regime of social compartmentalization in Malaya, interaction, even intermarriage had been a normal and natural phenomenon across society. To quote Ahmad Mustapha Hassan:

> . . . the new Malays were a mixed breed, between the traditional Malay and the immigrant Indian Muslims. These new Malays were often in a very confused state of mind as regards their ethnic identity. To be known only as Malays would connote backwardness and being uncultured. To be identified as Indians would entail a loss of certain privileges that accrued to the Malays. . . . The decision to completely identify themselves as Malays came about when nascent Malay nationalism asserted itself in the immediate aftermath of the Second World War.[80]

The Indian Muslims and the Malays merged seamlessly to form the backbone of UMNO. This explains why the MIC, when it was formed in August 1946, was the party for the Indians who were non-Muslim. By nomenclature and by membership, the MIC was created as a communal organization, for the Malayans of Indian origin. However, its orientation and approach to issues of nation-building in Malaya was strongly non-communal. MIC's membership and leadership was drawn primarily from urban professionals—lawyers, teachers, doctors, journalists, junior government employees, and business community representatives. MIC, essentially the successor organization to CIAM, represented the second generation of Indian middle class political activists. They were greatly influenced by the Gandhian movement and the struggle for independence led by the Indian National Congress. At the same time 'most of them—being local-born—possessed a much firmer orientation towards Malaya as their permanent home'.[81]

In the early years of its existence, the MIC remained a marginalized organization. The vast majority of Malayan Indians were plantation workers, who faced the most abominable hardships and impoverishment in the aftermath of the war and Japanese occupation. Their interests in fighting for political emancipation, democratic rights and social justice were being vigorously represented by the communist-dominated trade unions. Even though the post-war trade union movement in Malaya was overwhelmingly Chinese, 'Indian radicals exercised a disproportionately influential role in its leadership'.[82]

There was massive labour unrest with violent confrontations throughout the Malay Peninsula. This, combined with apprehensions about the subversive activities of the MCP (Malayan Communist Party, officially known as the Communist Party of Malaya or CPM) aimed at supporting the insurgents, resulted in declaration of the Emergency in June 1948. Soon thereafter, throughout Malaya, communist-dominated trade unions were replaced by smaller unions, whose leadership was avowedly anti-communist. The largest among these new unions, the NUPW (National Union of Plantation Workers), now took on the task of defending the interests of its members. The MIC's early association with the radical left alienated large sections of the urban professionals, who had been the mainstay behind the formation of the MIC.

The MIC adopted the strategy of non-violent, non-cooperation, with the British Malayan government, which included the boycott of local colonial institutions. This strategy, based on Gandhian principles, had been most effective when applied universally in India. In Malaya this strategy could not yield dividends in a situation where UMNO and after 1949, the MCA (Malayan Chinese Association) were cooperating on most counts with the British.

The MIC's strong views on maintaining a non-communal approach clashed with the rapidly evolving British perspective on communal politics in Malaya. In the pre-war period, the British had encouraged a racially segregated society in Malaya. Realizing the inherent pitfalls in formalizing this social separation through political structures, the British, with the strong support of Lord Mountbatten, initially sought a non-communal political structure for Malaysia. The Malayan Union proposals prepared by the British were essentially non-communal. However, in their own assessment made in December 1951, the British Secretary of State for the Colonies, through a Memorandum prepared for the Cabinet, said that the creation of the Malayan Union 'met with such opposition from the Malays that it was rescinded (perhaps too readily) and replaced by the present Federation Agreement, under which the Malays have greater executive authority than before the war, at any rate in the former Federated States'.[83]

This Memorandum, which was marked 'Secret' at the time but has since been declassified, describes the salient features of the Federation of Malaya Agreement and then goes on to say:

> Thus, partly from the heterogeneous nature of the population, and partly because of the existence of Malay Rulers, a political pattern has been formed ill-adapted to the needs of a small country at any time, least of all at a time of political convulsion and emergency. . . . We cannot now reshuffle all the cards. Some, but not all, of the administrative tangle to which I shall refer in the course of this paper is due to these causes, but the administration, like the country, is covered with jungle.[84]

The Memorandum accepts that UMNO 'aims at "Malaya for the Malays" and has consistently stood for preservation of the "special position" of the Malays under the Federation Agreement. This position is reflected, for example, in the admission of all Malays to Federal Citizenship, whereas not more than one-third of the Chinese qualify for it'.[85] Well before the 1951 Memorandum, in the Colonial Office's political report for November 1948, British civil servants recognized some of the 'abuse' resulting from the recently introduced Federation of Malaya constitutional arrangements when they said that 'there is no doubt that UMNO is aiming at a form of government in which non-Malays will have little share. . . .'[86]

The British Secretary of State for the Colonies, not quite comfortable with this brand of UMNO politics, notes in his December 1951 Memorandum (indicating tacit support) that, in September 1951, the founding leader and hitherto President of UMNO Dato' Onn Jaafar had broken away from UMNO to form his own party, the (IMP) Independence of Malaya Party.

> IMP marks a clean break with the tradition of racial separation in Malayan politics, and has as its slogan 'Unity, Freedom, Independence and Equality for All'. . . . IMP has been strongly supported by the Chinese and Indians but has found little favour among the Malays. . . . Despite his loss of Malay support he (Dato Onn) is still a force in the land.'[87]

Dato' Onn Jaafar resigned as President of UMNO over the issue of allowing non-Malays to join UMNO. The MIC, together with the Indian Chambers of Commerce, the FIO (Federation of Indian Organisations) and the Ceylon Federation of Malaya, among others, immediately accepted Dato' Onn's invitation to become founder members of IMP. The MIC looked upon IMP as the Malayan version of the Indian National Congress, and instinctively preferred it to the ultra-communal UMNO. 'Despite its Sino-Malay leadership in the persons of Dato' Onn and Tan Cheng Lock, many people thought that the IMP was an Indian party, and indeed it subsisted largely on its Indian membership until it was dissolved two years later.'[88] It is interesting to note, as an aside, the rather dismissive opinion about the MIC held by the British. In his December 1951 Memorandum, the Secretary of State for the Colonies says: 'The role of the Indian parties, the Malayan Indian Congress and the Federation of Indian Organisations, has never been clearly defined, and internal dissensions have so far prevented the development of any effective Indian political policy.'[89]

Simultaneously, however, the forces favouring communal politics in Malaya were also gathering momentum. In February 1949, the MCA (Malayan Chinese Association) came into being with the implicit support of the British, as an alternative and also in opposition to the mainland China supported CPM (Communist Party of Malaya). The first President of the MCA was a prominent Straits Chinese businessman. Among the earliest to join the MCA were former members of the Kuomintang, including senior generals of the Kuomintang Army. Soon after the MCA came into being, UMNO and MCA formed an electoral alliance. In the 1952 Kuala Lumpur municipal elections this alliance was victorious. Dato' Onn Jaafar's IMP, which included the MIC, suffered a devastating defeat.

This effectively ended all serious efforts by the British to establish non-communal politics as the norm in Malaya. Perhaps, their efforts were not sincere enough, or were marked by a distinct difference of opinion between the Colonial Office mandarins in London and the Malay-speaking senior British civil servants in Malaya, many of whom took on key roles as advisers to UMNO. In the words of scholar Geoff Wade:

This was an opportunity for non-ethnicized politics which was completely bypassed by Malayans. Again this missed opportunity must be in part assigned to the earlier activities of Dato Onn himself but equally to the policies of the British in terms of their absolute enthusiasm for Malay dominated ethnicized politics in the peninsula.[90]

THE BRITISH ARE KEEN TO LEAVE MALAYA

By the early 1950s the British appeared to be in a hurry to leave Malaya. The only way they could do so was by giving self-rule or home-rule to the Malayans. The British government was well aware of the delicate and tenuous inter-racial situation prevailing at the time. The internal assessment, conveyed through the 6 April 1955 Memorandum on Malaya, sent to the Cabinet by the Secretary of State for the Colonies, said that 'it will be essential, if internal strife is to be avoided, to continue to affirm that we shall still not withdraw until a true partnership of communities has been established in Malaya'.[91] The 'true partnership of communities' should logically have been along non-communal lines. However, the sound defeat of the non-communal IMP by the UMNO-MCA Alliance in the Kuala Lumpur and other municipal elections held during 1952-3, as well as in the 1954 state elections (where the Alliance won 226 of the 268 seats nationwide), combined with Britain's own preference for and high comfort-levels in dealing with the UMNO leadership, led them to a different conclusion.

The British came to the ethnocratic conclusion that the 'true partnership of communities' could be represented by an alliance among the three major communal parties: UMNO, MCA and MIC. The MIC had broken away from IMP in September 1953, but took the decision to join the Alliance only in October 1954. Even at this point, there were strong feelings in the MIC against the communal approach to politics, and as a corollary, against joining the UMNO-MCA Alliance.

The decision to join the Alliance was taken by the All Malayan Indian Congress Committee in October 1954, by a narrow majority of one out of a total of 55 delegates, of whom 17 abstained and 10 who were present during the discussion absented themselves during the voting; the 55 delegates themselves represented only one-fifth of all the party's branches. Two members of the party resigned in protest and several others regarded the decision as null and void under the circumstances, but no one formally challenged it so that it was accepted as final. . . .[92]

The MIC formally became a full member of the Alliance in April 1955. In the first federal elections, held in Malaya in July 1955, the UMNO-MCA-MIC Alliance won 51 of the 52 seats available. This Alliance formed the first Malayan government, with Tunku Abdul Rahman as Chief Minister. The stamp of communal politics that began with the UMNO-MCA Alliance in January 1952, created to defeat IMP in the Kuala Lumpur municipal elections, was now a permanent feature of the Malayan (later Malaysian) political scene. The UMNO-MCA-MIC alliance was one based on convenience, an electorally successful combination, that ensured victory through cross-voting across party (synonymous here with communal) lines. Each party realized that their strength lay in unity across communities, not domination by any one community over the others. This key principle is today often pushed aside, leaving the political discourse dominated by race and religion, rather than unity in diversity.

Doubts have persisted about the extent to which the three components of the Alliance Party—UMNO, MCA and MIC—can be said to represent the interests and longings of the common man in Malaya. During the debate in the British Parliament on the Federation of Malaya Independence Bill on 12 July 1957, Fenner Brockway (MP from Eton and Slough) said:

One has the feeling that the Alliance Party, which has done magnificent work in bringing harmony between the races—and, obviously, has the overwhelming support of the people who elected 51 members of that party out of the 52—is divided by a considerable gulf from the people of Malaya. One has the feeling that that party consists of members of a professional class and of a traditional aristocracy. And then one thinks of the subsistence rice cultivators, who sometimes have to pay 50 per cent of the rice they produce as rent for their land. One thinks of the labourers on the rubber plantations; one thinks of the industrial workers in the tin mines and in the iron ore industry. One thinks of the workers in the shops and offices belonging to the Chinese and Indian population. Between them and the type of person who is a member of the Legislature and the Government there is a big gulf. Yet that Legislature will function effectively only if it serves the purpose of lifting the standard of life of the common people.[93]

On the eve of Malaya's independence the political space, as distinct from the social and economic space, was divided along ethnic lines. Yet, neither race nor religion were dominant factors in the public discourse at that time. Raja Petra Kamarudin has encapsulated the situation as follows:

> UMNO never 'fought' for independence or *Merdeka*. UMNO never 'took' Merdeka. Merdeka was handed to UMNO on a silver platter because the British could no longer afford the financial cost and loss of lives and assets in their war (called The Emergency) against the Communist Terrorists (CTs) of the Communist Party of Malaya (CPM). In short, it was not taken. It was given. And there is a big difference between the two. The British were fighting a war in Malaya. But they refused to call it a war. They called it an Emergency. If they called it a war then the insurance companies would not cover their losses in Malaya. And they were losing a lot to the CT saboteurs. So it was called an Emergency to prevent the insurance companies from wangling out from paying the insurance claims. . . . So *Merdeka* was offered. . . . The British wanted to deal only with the Alliance Party because most of its leaders were educated in England and had demonstrated . . . pro-British tendencies . . . *Merdeka* fitted the British agenda. And the agenda was to get rid of the problem in a peaceful manner before they got kicked out by the MCP and lost everything. And the manner in achieving this would be to ensure that those who took over would be those whom the British 'groomed' and who would not stab the British in the back once they were in charge. . . . But UMNO was told in very clear terms that it has to bring MCA and MIC on board. *Merdeka* is not for UMNO but for the Alliance Party. Unless MCA and MIC can come to terms with UMNO then *Merdeka* would not be given. The Alliance Party was a British idea. *Merdeka* was a British idea.[94]

The British 'idea' of *Merdeka* or independence for Malaya was driven by self-interest. The elements of self-interest are evident from a perusal of the Report of the Federation of Malaya Constitutional Conference that was held in London in January and February 1956.[95] This Report was approved by all participants in the Conference. The representation from Malaya in this Conference was twofold: four members representing the Sultans and four members representing the Alliance Government (UMNO, MCA and MIC) led by the then Chief Minister Tunku Abdul Rahman. The United Kingdom was represented by the Secretary of State for the Colonies and the British High Commissioner for the Federation of Malaya, along with a large team of Advisers and senior officials.

It was agreed at this Constitutional Conference that a self-governing or independent Malaya would remain within the British Commonwealth. This was a matter of serious interest to the British because it facilitated implementation of the agreement that UK and Malaya would negotiate a Treaty of Defence and Mutual Assistance (with Australia and New Zealand as observers). This Treaty would give UK 'the right to maintain in the Federation the forces necessary for the fulfillment of Commonwealth and international obligations', and an independent Malaya would provide to the UK the 'facilities needed in the Federation for the maintenance and support of these forces, which would include the Commonwealth Strategic Reserve'. In return, the UK 'will undertake to assist the Federation Government in the external defence of its territory'.[96] The Secretary of State for the Colonies adds his comment that this agreement 'meets in full the requirements that we have set ourselves beforehand'.[97]

Another key issue for the UK was to seek protection for the large investments made in Malaya during the colonial period by British and other foreign investors. This they secured through the 'repeated assurances' by the Malayan delegation regarding 'continuation of the present policy whereby the overseas investor could, after payment of local taxes and obligations, remit to his country within the framework of ordinary and reasonable exchange control requirements, funds for the payment of dividends and for the repatriation of his capital'.[98] The Malayan delegation also conveyed their intention of retaining their membership of the Sterling Area after attaining full self-government. This was important for the UK in the light of Malaya's contribution to the strength of the Sterling Area through the direct earnings of dollars from rubber and tin. During the five years prior to Malaya's independence (1950-5), Malaya contributed a surplus with the dollar area of about 500 million pounds, and sterling balances during this period increased by about 110 million pounds.[99] By any standards, this was a remarkably substantial contribution to the stability of the Sterling Area.

The British considered Malaya to be an important partner in the then on-going Cold War against the forces of communism. The Report on this 1956 Constitutional Conference recognizes fully

> the vitally important position of the Federation (of Malaya) in the world-wide struggle against communism. . . . For this reason, if the Emergency has not been brought to an end by the time that full self-government and independence within the Commonwealth is attained, Her Majesty's Government will still be prepared to consider with the Federation Government whether the financial needs of the Federation would justify special assistance from Her Majesty's Government towards meeting the cost of the Emergency over and above the substantial assistance which will continue to be given through the forces and services provided by the United Kingdom to sustain the fight against the Communist terrorists.[100]

Generous financial offers were made by the British 'to finance certain capital costs of expansion of the Federation Armed Forces'; 'to examine sympathetically with the Federation its borrowing needs on the London market in connection with its development plans' and 'to provide assistance, subject to the approval of Parliament, in the form of a loan to the Federation to enable it to finance its contribution to the Tin Buffer Stock'.[101]

The geo-strategic importance of Malaya for the British, combined with the self-interest and mutual benefit accruing to both nations is evident from the contents of this Report. However, it is most significant that there is little or no mention of either religion or race in this Report. All issues are discussed from Malaya's national perspective rather than from the point of view of any one group within the nation. There is agreement on the need for 'Malayanization' of the armed forces and all other public services, through setting up independent statutory bodies such as the Public Service Commission, Judicial Service Commission, Police Service Commission and the Federation Armed Forces Council. The Report discusses the need for recruiting 'suitably qualified' individuals for each service, but there is no mention about racial quotas or other categorization in the civil service. The focus was on providing to the people of Malaya a democratic, equitable system, which would combine political liberties with economic and social development as the strongest bulwark against communism.

THE REID COMMISSION AND ITS OUTCOME

The 1956 Constitutional Conference agreed on setting up a Constitutional Commission for finalising the constitution for an independent Malaya. This Commission was to be chaired by Lord Reid, with the participation of nominated representatives from Australia, Canada, India, Pakistan and UK. The terms of reference for this Commission included, *inter alia*, making recommendations for 'the safeguarding of the special position of the Malays and the legitimate interests of other communities'.[102] This is perhaps one of the very few references in the Report of the 1956 Constitutional Conference to Malays as a separate group, and even here safeguarding the 'special position of the Malays' is juxtaposed with safeguarding the 'legitimate interests of other communities'. This juxtaposition reflects recognition of the core reality that, for peace and harmonious progress in Malaya, both aspects needed to be considered as inalienable. Safeguarding the 'special position of the Malays' is as important as safeguarding the 'legitimate interests of other communities'. Any uneven focus on one without the other can lead only to dissension and disharmony.

The terms of reference for the Reid Commission, as it came to be known, were finalized 'in the light of the proposals submitted by the Malayan delegation' to the 1956 Constitutional Conference in London. The full terms of reference required preparing the constitution for a federal form of government in Malaya

> based on parliamentary democracy with a bi-cameral legislature, which would include provision for:
>
> (i) the establishment of a strong central government with the States and Settlements enjoying a measure of autonomy . . .;
> (ii) the safeguarding of the position and prestige of Their Highnesses as constitutional Rulers of their respective States;
> (iii) a constitutional Yang di-Pertuan Besar (Head of State) for the Federation to be chosen from among Their Highnesses the Rulers;
> (iv) a common nationality for the whole of the Federation;
> (v) the safeguarding of the special position of the Malays and the legitimate interests of other communities.[103]

These terms of reference, based on the wishes of the Malayan delegation to the 1956 Constitutional Conference, are eloquent about the egalitarian nature of the Constitution that the leaders of Malaya envisaged for themselves. The reference to 'common nationality for the whole of the Federation' in point (iv), and bringing in parity between the 'special position of the Malays' and the 'legitimate interests of other communities' in point (v) are important reflections of this concern for an inclusive and equal Malaya. Two of the five points in the terms of reference relate to the role, position and prestige of the Malay Sultans, rulers in their respective states. The opposition in Malaya to the Malayan Union proposals (1945-6) was more of concern about the loss of status and position of the Malay Sultans, rather than the proposed equality of status for all citizens of Malaya, regardless of race or religion.

The members of the Reid Commission were Lord William Reid, a Lord of Appeal in Ordinary, Sir Ivor Jennings, Master of Trinity Hall, Cambridge, Sir William McKell, a former Governor-General of Australia, B. Malik, a former Chief Justice of the Allahabad High Court (India) and Abdul Hamid, judge of the West Pakistan High Court. The member from Canada could not join because of illness. The Reid Commission drafted the Constitution between June 1956 and February 1957. The Commission held close to 120 meetings and received more than 130 memoranda from various individuals and organizations. The Conference of Rulers and the Alliance Party (UMNO, MCA and MIC), too, submitted memoranda containing their views on the future Constitution to the Reid Commission. The Reid Commission prepared the first draft of the Malayan Constitution by February 1957. This was then intensively discussed in a series of Working Party meetings held in Kuala Lumpur. The Working Party members included four representatives of the Malay Rulers, four representatives of the Alliance Party-led government, and senior British officials such as the High Commissioner, the Chief Secretary and the Attorney General. Finally, Constitutional talks were held in London in May 1957, with the participation of the Colonial Office.

In Malaya, the Alliance Government tabled a White Paper in Parliament in July 1957, to explain the changes made to the Reid Commission's draft Constitution by the Working Party and the subsequent Constitutional talks in London. The White Paper was debated in the Malayan Parliament on 10 July 1957. Later the same month, the Federation of Malaya Independence Bill was introduced in the British parliament, where it was discussed and passed as an Act. The Federal Constitution of Malaya was passed by the Federal Legislative Council in Kuala Lumpur on 15 August 1957 and on 31 August 1957, the Federation of Malaya became an independent sovereign country.

The iteration of these details and their sequencing is important. Fifty-five years later, the people of Malaysia remain divided in their interpretation of several key constitutional clauses and issues, even on the intentions of their founding fathers. Secondly, the fall-out of the decisions taken at the time of independence in 1956-7 have had a decisive inluence, equally on domestic politics and policies, and on Malaysia's foreign policy and bilateral relations with countries across the world, including India.

The 12 July 1957 debate in British parliament on the soon-to-be-adopted Constitution of Malaya brought out quite succintly the deep concerns of the Malayan Indians. Member of Parliament for Crosby, Graham Page said, during this debate:

> It is, perhaps, worth remembering that it was on our instigation and with our encouragement that the Indians came to Malaya. . . . At the end of the last century and the beginning of this century, the development of our plantation industry brought in Indian unskilled labour by means of the Indian Immigration Fund which was supported by the employers and the Governments of Malaya. Therefore, we bear a rather special obligation towards the Indians who have come and in a great many cases have settled in Malaya to produce the Indian community that is there now. Our obligation towards the Indians was increased by the Japanese occupation. The majority of those forced into Siam to build the Siam-Burma Railway were Indians, and it is estimated that as many as 60,000 Indians died in that way. The three years of Japanese occupation undoubtedly caused very great disruption to the life of the Indian community in Malaya.
>
> Bearing this in mind, one looks rather critically at the terms of the future constitution to see what protection it gives to that minority, the Malayan Indians. In the past, the Indian has contributed very substantially to the development of the country, and he can do so in future. In the past, it has been mainly the unskilled Indian labour, without whom the rubber plantations might never have been developed. Nevertheless, there is now the business and professional Indian who has now settled in Malaya, and these are the shopkeeper, the school master, the clerk, railway officials and so on, the majority of whom are drawn from the Indian community, a community which shows a very high rate of literacy compared with the Chinese and Malays.
>
> It appears that the Reid Commission took one single Indian party as speaking for the Indians as a whole, the Malayan Indian Congress, which had sunk its identity in the Alliance Party. I do not think the Malayan Indian

Congress spoke for all, or even perhaps a majority, of Indians, certainly not the business, professional and artisan class of Indian, in Malaya. There were many other Malayan Indian associations which gave evidence before the Commission, but the Commission did not seem to take account of the views, or to pay very much attention to them. . . . So, in the points I want to make, I think I am putting forward the views of the whole of the Indian community in Malaya.

The three points about which they were particularly concerned were, first, citizenship, secondly, the special privileges of the Malayans and, thirdly, religion. Of course, the point of citizenship has bedeviled the Constitution ever since the Malayan Union. . . . There will be many Indians who will have to take advantage of Article 17 registration, even Indians who were born in the Federation. In many cases they do not come under any of the previous provisions so as to make them citizens of Malaya, and they will have to resort to Article 17. There may well be a possibility of discrimination against them. One wonders whether this is a deliberate reservation for the purpose of discriminating. I hope not. The great importance of this point about citizenship is that so many other things depend upon it, the franchise, entry to the public service, the judiciary and so on. . . . I would have hoped that that decision, instead of being in the hands of the Minister, had been left in the hands of the Election Commission as the Reid Commission suggested.

Now with regard to the special privileges of the Malayans, these include the admission to the public services, the operation of business under licence and the grant of scholarships, bursaries and educational preferences, the Reid Commission Report seemed to perpetuate these special privileges of the Malayans, at least for fifteen years. I prefer the proposal of the new Constitution, which allows them to be reviewed at any time when the head of the Federation is advised that that may be necessary. . . . The land reservations, also, are far more controlled in the proposed Constitution than was recommended by the Commission. I feel that on these points in particular the Indian community might be satisfied.

On religion, the Reid Commission recommended . . . that there should be no mention of State religion in the Constitution. It is now inserted in Article 3, but is so watered down by the later Articles that I do not think there can be any real fear of a non-secular State being created.[104]

Graham Page accurately reflected the concerns of the Malayan Indians on the eve of independence in 1957, even though hindsight has shown that he was perhaps too sanguine about the ability of the safeguards built into the proposed Constitution to protect these concerns. Other British Members of Parliament voiced similar concerns. Ms Joan Vickers, MP from Plymouth, Devonport, said that her main concerns related to religion and citizenship. She quoted paragraph 169 of the Reid Commission Report which stated:

> It is Their Highnesses' considered view that it would not be desirable to insert some declaration such as has been suggested that the Muslim Faith or Islamic Faith be the established religion of the Federation. Their Highnesses are not in favour of such a declaration being inserted and that is a matter of specific instruction in which I myself have played very little part.[105]

Ms Joan Vickers enquired for what reasons Article 3 had now been introduced in the proposed Constitution, stating Islam to be the religion of the Federation. She expressed her concern that this would eventually lead to 'religious parties, as religion is tied up with race, . . . which . . . would be a very great mistake.'[106] The Under Secretary of State for Commonwealth Relations, while replying to this debate, gave the reason for this change as the Malay Rulers having 'altered their views' in the light of 'important and responsible representations which were made in this matter'.[107] Scholars have opined that the Reid Commission member from Pakistan had a major role to play in influencing opinion to bring about the insertion of Article 3 in the Constitution.

Ms Joan Vickers also expressed her disquietude about the requirements specified in Article 17 for citizenship for non-Malays born in the Federation, viz., that they should be more than 18 years of age, that they must have resided in the Federation for five of the preceding seven years, and they must be certified as bearing good character. She queried the discriminatory and subjective nature of these requirements, and enquired about the reasons for bringing these in, particularly since in 1953 and 1954, the Alliance Party's stated and published position on citizenship had been much more liberal, requiring all Malayan-born non-Malays to have resided in the Federation for just five years preceding the elections in order to make them eligible for citizenship and voting.[108]

Similar doubts were expressed by several Members of Parliament, participants in the debate in British parliament on 12 July 1957, on the Federation of Malaya Independence Bill. Arthur Creech Jones (Wakefield) supported Ms Joan Vickers for pinpointing a number of the doubts which have existed in our minds in regard to certain problems which the (Malayan) Constitution raises. The question of religion, the limitation on the official language, the problems associated with land, and the difficulties arising out of the matter of citizenship—all these things raised doubts and anxieties not only in Malaya itself but also in this country. We hope that, by tolerant administration and good will between the various races, our fears may be proved unjustified.[109]

G.B. Drayson (Skipton) recalled the debate on this Bill that had been held the previous day in the Parliament of Malaya. He said that during the course of this debate, which had gone on for twelve hours, 'very grave doubts were expressed by some members of the Malayan Parliament as to whether the difficulties had been properly overcome', adding that 'many of us are, naturally, apprehensive when we see in a White Paper, or in a Bill, what appears to us to be racial discrimination, depriving minorities of their lawful rights'.[110]

Gilbert Longden (Hertfordshire, South-West) queried 'why do Her Majesty's government reject the Reid Commission's proposal that the Chinese and Indian languages should be used in the legislature for at least ten years? . . . are there to be interpreters in the Legislative Assembly?'[111]

James Griffiths (Llanelly) encapsulated the situation when he said:

The Constitution is a whole series of checks and balances and a compromise to try to reconcile one interest with another. . . . I would say to everybody in Malaya on *Merdeka* that when I read the Constitution and think of it in operation, the Old Book is true: 'the letter killeth, but the spirit giveth life'. I hope, indeed, that the spirit which has made this day possible—a spirit of tolerance, good will and understanding of each other—will prevail, because it is upon that that the future depends.[112]

The 1957 debate in the British Parliament, on the Federation of Malaya Independence Bill, highlights the serious concerns of its members on a broad range of issues concerning the Constitution proposed for the soon-to-be independent Malaya. Prominent among these were issues relating to citizenship and nationality, religion, the official language, land reservation and ownership. It comes as no surprise that in India, too, there was intense concern and debate about the prospects and future of Malayan Indians, relating primarily to their social and economic upliftment and their ability to share freedom and equality with all in an independent Malaya. These concerns were vividly expressed at the national level as well as by various political, economic and social organizations in different parts of India.

The Indian Agent in Kuala Lumpur, who had been in place since the late 1920s, found resistance at all levels, including from the British, when he tried to forge unity among the multiple strands that made up the dynamic group of Malayan Indians. The reasons for this are that the pre-independence development of the Malayan economy, subservient as it was to British mercantile and colonial interests, remained rooted in the exploitation of cheap Indian and Chinese labour in order to maximise profits from the exports of rubber and tin. The British achieved this objective by controlling labour through the division of labour along racial and communal lines. Even within one community or race, sub-communal segregations were encouraged in order to hinder communal solidarity and unity. The scholar Michael Stenson has noted that:

> The social structure of this colonial 'plural' society, with its infinitely complex racial division of labour, was designed to prevent Asian unity and to maximize returns to metropolitan capital. The British monopolized political power through the Malayan Civil Services and dominated the heights of the economy through the mercantile agency houses that had interlocking investments in the rubber and tin industries. . . . The traditional Malay elite was co-opted into the British pattern of administration. Chinese *towkay* capitalists dominated the lower levels of the planting, mining and mercantile sectors of the economy. . . . Chinese, Indian and Ceylon Tamils predominated in the subordinate ranks of the Civil Service. . . . Sikhs and other Punjabis performed paramilitary roles in the police, the lower ranks of which were Malay. On the estates, there were European managers, Ceylon Tamil or Malayalee clerks and Tamil or Telugu labourers, while Malay peasants remained in a post-traditional economy of small-scale agriculture, fishing and collecting. Because of Muslim inheritance laws and the Malay Reservations enactments, most Malays were land-owners (if only on a small scale) and few became full-time paid labourers. The formation of capitalist and working classes amongst Malays was limited and delayed. Most Chinese were wage labourers, employed either by Chinese *towkays* or on a contract basis by European companies. Tamil labourers, on the other hand, were almost invariably employed on a permanent checkroll basis and were housed in company or government-owned 'lines' or barracks. One needs only to mention the Chettiar money-lenders, the Marakkayar shopkeepers or the

Punjabi milkmen and watchmen to appreciate the full complexity of this racial division of labour.

The interests of the Malay aristocrat administrator elite were identified with those of the British, in opposition to the Chinese *towkays*. Chinese labour was employed separately from and in competition with Indian labour. Punjabi and Malay police were employed to control the unruly Chinese. The British have often refuted the Asian allegation of 'divide-and-rule' tactics on the grounds that the peoples of modern Malaya were already divided, but it can hardly be denied that the diverse peoples of modern Malaya were brought together on British initiative in a carefully constructed system of Asian checks and balances.[113]

The highly compartmentalized migration and living conditions of the Indians who came to Malaya during the nineteenth and early twentieth centuries prevented, as it was meant to do, the emergence of a cohesive Indianness among them. The doctors, lawyers, teachers and other professionals who migrated independently from India to Malaya were much more influenced by the stirrings of Indian nationalism, but in the early years, they had little direct contact with Indians working in other sectors. The twin processes of economic exploitation and social fragmentation kept the Indians apart. British Malaya was a 'glorified commercial enterprise rather than a state dedicated to the welfare of its peoples'.[114]

The twelve post-war years before Malaya received independence in 1957, reveal the emergence of diverse, even conflicting pressures and streams of opinion within the British establishment, within India and among the peoples of Malaya. Immediately after the Second World War, once the British returned to Malaya and Singapore, mounting concern about discrimination against Indians who were erstwhile members of the INA, and about the abysmal condition of Indian plantation labour and railway workers in Malaya led to Jawaharlal Nehru's visit to this region in March 1946. Lord Mountbatten, too, strongly opposed 'racial sectionalism', but the Malayan Union proposal, bringing in a 'Malayan' nation state rather than a 'Malay' nation state, did not survive much beyond Lord Mountbatten's departure from his post as Supreme Allied Commander of the South East Asia Command.

The Federation of Malaya Agreement, successor to the Malayan Union proposal, was negotiated by the British almost entirely on communal lines. The committee that drafted these proposals was dubbed the 'Anglo-Malay' Working Committee. The People's Constitutional Proposals for Malaya, seeking a round-table, participatory format for these negotiations together with the convening of a Constituent Assembly in Malaya for drafting the new constitution, were given short shrift. The formation of UMNO (March 1946) set the trend for race-based parties, with the creation of MIC in August 1946 and MCA in February 1949. The Alliance Government (UMNO, MIC amd MCA) participated in the Federation of Malaya Constitutional Conference in London in early 1956, which, in turn, led to the establishment of the Reid Commission for drafting the Malayan Constitution. There were continuing concerns about several provisions of the Malayan Constitution, as highlighted in the July 1957 debate, in the British Parliament, on this subject.

In the ultimate analysis, the British Government was unable to move away from the consequences of the 'infinitely complex racial division of labour' they had instituted in Malaya. Neither did they really care. They were in a hurry to leave Malaya, apprehensive about the outcome of the mounting Communist insurgency. Their paramount concern was the protection of their long-term commercial interests in Malaya, and they were confident that the system they had devised for Malaya would be adequate for this.

NOTES

1. Harper, *Revolt in Malaya: The Indian Connection*, p. 34.
2. Ibid.
3. Ibid.
4. Ibid.
5. Ibid., p. 35.
6. Sandhu, *Indians in Malaya*, p. 171.
7. Harper, op. cit., p. 35.
8. Ibid., p. 36.
9. Lebra, *Women Against the Raj: The Rani of Jhansi Regiment*, p. 111 (Epilogue by P. Ramasamy) .
10. Harper, p. 36.
11. Ibid.
12. Ibid.
13. Ibid., pp. 36-7.

14. *Selected Works of Jawaharlal Nehru*, vol. 15, p. 56, First Report on his Visit to Malaya (a 13-page confidential letter dated 28 March 1946 sent to Congress President Maulana Abul Kalam Azad).
15. Ibid., pp. 58-9 (First Report on his Visit to Malaysia).
16. Ibid., p. 39, letter to N. Raghavan of Penang.
17. Ibid., p. 39.
18. Ibid., p. 61 (First Report on his Visit to Malaya).
19. Ibid., p. 112.
20. Ibid., p. 113.
21. Ibid., p. 112.
22. Ibid., p. 39.
23. Ibid., p. 62.
24. Ibid., p. 59.
25. Ibid., pp. 59-60.
26. Ibid., p. 60.
27. Ibid.
28. Ibid., p. 57.
29. Harper, op. cit., p. 37.
30. Ibid.
31. *Selected Works of Jawaharlal Nehru*, vol. 15, p. 61.
32. Ibid.
33. Ibid., pp. 79-82.
34. Ibid., p. 66.
35. Ibid., p. 80.
36. Ibid.
37. Ibid.
38. Ibid., p. 81.
39. Ibid., p. 66.
40. Ibid., pp. 67 and 69.
41. P.T. Bauer, 'Nationalism and Politics in Malaya', *Foreign Affairs*, vol. 25, no. 3, April 1947, p. 505.
42. Ibid., p. 506.
43. Ibid.
44. Geoff Wade, 'The Origins and Evolution of Ethnocracy in Malaysia', Asia Research Institute (National University of Singapore) Working Paper Series no. 112, April 2009, pp. 4-5, quoting A.J. Stockwell (ed.), *Malaya* (3 parts), British Documents on the End of Empire, London HMSO, 1995, pt. I, pp. 48 and 49.
45. Ibid., p. 5.
46. Ibid., p. 4, quoting a joint British Colonial Office-Foreign Office policy paper prepared in August 1942.
47. Ibid., p. 5, quoting Colonial Office memorandum CO 825/35/6 no. 14, dated 14 May 1943.

48. Ibid., p. 6, quoting the said Appendices: I 'Draft Directive on Policy in Malaya' and II 'Draft Directive on Policy in Borneo', CAB 66/50, WP (44) 258.
49. Ibid., p. 6.
50. Ibid.
51. Ibid., p. 7, quoting letter from Stanley to Mountbaten (CO 825/42/3 no. 27), dated 21 August 1944.
52. *New Straits Times*, 17 November 2010, accessed at http://www.nst.com.my/nst/articles/6sofia/Article/art_print accessed on 19 November 2010.
53. Wade, p. 7, quoting Mountbatten's letter to Stanley (CO 825/42/3 no. 28), dated 6 September 1944.
54. Bauer, op. cit., p. 509, quoting Sir Harold MacMichael, 'Report on a Mission to Malaya' Colonial no. 194, London, His Majesty's Stationery Office, February 1946.
55. Cheah Boon Kheng, *Malaysia: The Making of a Nation*, ISEAS, Singapore, 2002, quoted in Wade, p. 8.
56. Wade, p. 8.
57. J. Kennedy, *A History of Malaya:* AD *1400 to 1959*, Macmillan & Co Ltd, London, 1962, p. 267 .
58. Hall, *A History of South-East Asia*, p. 595.
59. Wade, op. cit., p. 9.
60. Hall, op. cit., p. 269.
61. Wade, op. cit, p. 9.
62. Arasaratnam, *Indians in Malaysia and Singapore*, pp. 118-19.
63. Ibid., p. 116.
64. Muzafar Desmond Tate, *The Malaysian Indians*, p. 78.
65. Ibid., p. 152.
66. Ibid., p. 159, fn. 49, quoting the *Malayan Daily News.*
67. Ibid., p. 121.
68. Ibid.
69. Ibid.
70. Ibid., p. 122.
71. Ibid., p. 116.
72. Ibid., p. 133, fn. 44, quoting the *Straits Times* of 15 October 1947.
73. Ibid., p. 116.
74. Ibid., p. 117, quoting letter from R.H. de S. Onraet, Police Adviser to BMA, to T.K. Lloyd, pt. I, file 50823/3/2, series 273, 675, Colonial Office Records.
75. Ibid., p. 138.
76. Arasaratnam, op cit, p. 119.
77. Wade, op. cit., p. 4.

78. Ibid.
79. Ahmad Mustapha Hassan, *The Unmaking of Malaysia*, SIRD, Malaysia, 2007, p. 137.
80. Ibid., p. 109.
81. Ibid., p. 83.
82. Ibid., p. 85.
83. Memorandum by the Secretary of State for the Colonies, dated 21 December 1951, p. 3, posted on the *Malaysia Today* website (http://www.malaysia-today.net/) on 1 November, 2010, by Raja Petra Kamarudin 'Why Onn Jaafar really left UMNO to form IMP (Part 10 of the series on the Social Contract)'.
84. Ibid., pp. 3-4.
85. Ibid., p. 4.
86. Wade, op. cit., p. 15, quoting Colonial Office document CO 5373/3746 Federation of Malaya—Political developments (1948).
87. *Malaysia Today* posting dated 1 November 2010 by Raja Petra Kamarudin, enclosing the Memorandum, p. 4.
88. Tate, op. cit., p. 208, fn. 130.
89. *Malaysia Today* posting dated 1 November 2010 by Raja Petra Kamarudin, enclosing the Memorandum, p. 4.
90. Wade, op. cit., p. 16.
91. Raja Petra Kamarudin, 'Was Merdeka Taken or Was It Given?', posted on *Malaysia Today* website on November 2010, on http://www.malaysia-today.net, enclosing photocopies of Memorandum by the Secretary of State for the Colonies to the Cabinet on 'Malaya: Review of the Situation', dated 6 April 1955, p. 2.
92. Tate, op. cit., pp. 208-9, fn. 131.
93. Hansard, Federation of Malaya Independence Bill, H.C. Deb 12 July 1957 vol. 573 cc633-715, accessed at http://hansard.millibanksystems.com/commons/1957.jul/12/federation-of-malaya-independence-bill on 18 December 2010, p. 33 (of 43).
94. Raja Petra Kamarudin, 'Was *Merdeka* taken or Was it Given?', posted on 8 November 2010 on www.malaysia-today.net , pp. 1-2.
95. Detailed extracts (photocopied) from this Report have been posted on www.malaysia-today.net by Raja Petra Kamarudin on 22 October 2010, 25 October 2010, 27 October 2010 and 28 October 2010.
96. Annex C (Notes on the Main Conclusions and Recommendations of the Conference) to the Memorandum dated 21 February 1956 on 'Federation of Malaya' sent to the Cabinet by the Secretary of State for the Colonies, p. 285, posted by Raja Petra Kamarudin on 28 October 2010.
97. Ibid., p. 285.

98. Ibid., p. 286.
99. Hansard, Federation of Malaya Independence Bill, H.C. Deb 12 July 1957, vol. 573 cc633-715, accessed at http://hansard.millibanksystems.com/commons/1957.jul/12/federation-of-malaya-independence-bill on 18 December 2010, statement by the Secretary of State for the Colonies, p. 7 (of 43).
100. *Malaysia Today* (see fns. 95 and 96 above), pp. 263(1) and 263 (2), posted on 22 October 2010.
101. Ibid., p. 263(2).
102. Ibid., posted on 28 October 2010, p. 281.
103. Ibid., Annex B 'Extract from the Report of the General Purpose Committee of the Conference: Constitutional Commission', posted on 28 October 2010, pp. 280-1.
104. Hansard, Federation of Malaya Independence Bill, H.C. Deb 12 July 1957, vol. 573 cc633-715, accessed at http://hansard.millibanksystems.com/commons/1957.jul/12/federation-of-malaya-independence-bill on 18 December 2010, statement by Graham Page, pp. 34-6 (of 43).
105. Hansard, Federation of Malaya Independence Bill, H.C. Deb 12 July 1957, vol. 573 cc633-715, accessed at http://hansard.millibanksystems.com/commons/1957.jul/12/federation-of-malaya-independence-bill on 18 December 2010, statement by Ms Joan Vickers, p. 31 (of 43).
106. Ibid., p. 31.
107. Ibid., p. 42 (of 43).
108. Ibid., p. 31 (of 43).
109. Ibid., p. 38 (of 43).
110. Ibid., pp. 24-5 (of 43).
111. Ibid., p. 18 (of 43).
112. Ibid., p. 9 (of 43).
113. Michael Stenson, *Class, Race & Colonialism in West Malaysia: The Indian Case*, University of Queensland Press, St Lucia, Queensland, Australia, 1980, pp. 6-7.
114. Ibid., p. 29, quoting Victor Purcell.

15

The Asian Relations Conference

In 1946, during his second visit to Malaya, Jawaharlal Nehru 'made twenty speeches in eight days to around 60,000 people'.[1] The significantly recurrent theme in these speeches was Nehru's perspective on post-colonial Asia. Pandit Nehru emphasized the need for Asian nations to reinvigorate their traditional, historical linkages that had been torn asunder by two centuries of colonial rule. Speaking in Singapore on 18 March 1946 Nehru said:

> If India aspires for freedom, it is in a free world and when India is free, every ounce of her energy shall be used for the freedom of all subject nations. This is true of Indonesia, Malaya or any other country in the world.[2]

The burgeoning thought in Nehru's mind was to convene an Asian Conference that could be helpful to the understanding of Asia's problems and to the promotion of cooperation among Asian peoples.[3] His travels in Asia had convinced him that colonial rule had left the peoples of Asia divided from and ignorant about each other. When Nehru returned to India after his visits to Malaya and Burma (March 1946), he added weight to this thought when he said that 'the desire for holding an Asian Conference had been expressed to him by General Aung San and others'.[4]

Soon after this, the ICWA (Indian Council of World Affairs) began its preparations for the ARC (Asian Relations Conference), which was eventually convened in New Delhi from 23 March to 2 April 1947. In his inaugural address at the ARC, Pandit Nehru coalesced the views of many when he said:

> It so happened that we in India convened this Conference, but the idea of such a Conference arose simultaneously in many minds and in many countries of Asia. There was a widespread urge and an awareness that the time had

come for us, people of Asia, to meet together, to hold together and to advance together.[5]

EVOLUTION OF IDEAS ON ASIAN UNITY

Many scholars have written about the concept of Asian unity. 'The idea of Asian unity evolved late in the nineteenth century conjointly with the emergence of Asian nationalist movements. Indeed, Pan-Asianism was basically the international expression of incipient domestic demands for freedom and of the growing consciousness of Eastern peoples of their intrinsic Asian identity.'[6] Late in the nineteenth century, India's Swami Vivekananda was among the earliest proponents of Asianism. He articulated his views on Asia through a series of articles carried in *Udbodhan*, the Bengali journal he started in January 1899 for the Ramakrishna Mission. Subsequently, these articles were published as a book, *The East and the West.*

The Japanese scholar and philosopher, Okakura Kakuzo, was introduced to Swami Vivekananda in Calcutta in December 1901 through the latter's American disciple, Josephine MacLeod. The Indian thinker and the Japanese philosopher travelled together to Bodh Gaya and Sarnath, key Buddhist pilgrimage sites in north India. They were intellectual soulmates. After Swami Vivekananda's passing away in July 1902, Okakura remained in close contact with the Tagore brothers, Surendranath and his younger brother, Rabindranath. It is said that Okakura completed his epic, *The Ideals of the East*, while living in the house of Surendranath Tagore, and the manuscript was edited by Sister Nivedita, an Irish devotee of Swami Vivekananda. The opening paragraph of this book sums up Okakura Kakuzo's pan-Asian vision:

> Asia is one. The Himalayas divide, only to accentuate two mighty civilizations, the Chinese with its communism of Confucius, and the Indian with its individualism of the Vedas. But not even the snowy barriers can interrupt for one moment that broad expanse of love for the Ultimate and Universal, which is the common thought-inheritance of every Asiatic race, enabling them to produce all the great religions of the world, and distinguishing them from those maritime peoples of the Mediterranean and the Baltic, who love to dwell on the Particular, and to search out the means, not the end, of life.[7]

Rabindranath Tagore was deeply influenced by Vivekananda and Okakura. He was an ardent believer in the Asian renaissance. During his visit to the Netherlands in 1920, his discussions, *inter alia* with the Director of the Colonial Institute in Amsterdam, had for the first time brought to his knowledge the depth and extent of India's civilizational and historical links with Southeast Asia. This information had an electrifying impact on historians, scholars and the general public back in India. The Greater India Society was launched in Calcutta in 1922. Books were written on Indian 'colonies' in the Far East. This led to a great deal of apprehension and misunderstanding in Southeast Asia about India's future intentions as she struggled to free herself from colonial rule. India's intellectuals and scholars, steeped in the thought processes imbibed through the colonially dictated educational curriculum, could not visualize India's glorious pre-colonial past other than in the language of the colonialists.

There was never any colonial relationship between India and Southeast Asia. This region has been described as 'Farther India' by the earliest travellers and map-makers of the first millennium CE. The mariners and traders from India who lived in Southeast Asia had made this region their home. They intermarried locally and continued their trade, with no system of tribute or colonial bondage with India. Rabindranath Tagore put matters in the correct perspective when he spoke at the Greater India Society in Calcutta in July 1927, on the eve of his Southeast Asian tour. He spoke about cultural linkages and fraternal bonding, and the oneness that comes from such ties. Tagore said that:

> The real wealth of India was never kept hidden, like an old deed in an iron safe. The only true expression of India was in all that she gave openly and freely. The surplus of her cultural life, which she scattered everywhere, was the core of her personality. Through our capacity to give our real assets to others we earn the title to call the 'outsider' our own. . . . On the eve of my departure for Java, I pray that my mind be free from all pride and be humble with the realization of the immortal lesson of Truth. The grand message of Fraternity must dawn within us. . . .[8]

Most contemporary scholars do not accept the concept of Indian 'colonies' in Southeast Asia. K.N. Chaudhuri has said 'it is necessary above all to banish the term "Indian colonization" from the vocabulary of social analysis'. Sugata Bose has attributed this concept (Greater India) to 'the scholarship of a strain of colonised, nationalist intellectuals in India who narrated with an arrogant whiff of (sub) imperialism the story of the subcontinent's civilisational gifts to South-east Asia', adding that this has

> obstructed the study of the processes of 'interweaving' that might legitimately lead to an insightful comparative and connective history. . . . In other words, there was a recognized need to distinguish a loftier aspiration of universalism from the haughtier expression of cultural imperialism even though the line between the two became blurred. The universalist current was more creative and generous in its delineation of cultural commonalities and difference.[9]

Contemporaneously with Tagore, as India's freedom movement gathered momentum, several nationalist political leaders were increasingly of the view that Asian countries should join hands in their struggle to rid themselves of Western colonialist rulers. 'They argued that the progress of each country towards freedom could be more rapidly advanced by mutual co-operation than by separate action.'[10] The idea of an Asian federation was mooted to hasten the achievement of independence from colonial rule. Eminent leaders wrote about this, including Mahatma Gandhi (in *Young India* on 14 April 1920), Chittaranjan Das (in *Indian Annual Register*, 1923) and M.A. Ansari (*Indian Quarterly Register*, 1926). Jawaharlal Nehru attended the Congress of Oppressed Nationalities held in Brussels in February 1927, and in his report to the All-India Congress Committee he spoke of a 'very strong desire' for a closer bond among Asian countries.[11] At Calcutta in 1928, the Indian National Congress adopted a resolution on organizing a pan-Asiatic federation meeting in India. This meeting could not be held, but several smaller conferences did take place, such as the All-Asia Education Conference in Benares in December 1930, the All-Asia Women's Conference in Lahore in January 1931, and the long-delayed Pan-Asiatic Labour Congress at Colombo in May 1934. Japan and China, too, had tried their hand at this, with the Pan-Asiatic Congress at Nagasaki in 1926, and the Pan-Asiatic Conference at Shanghai in 1927. Neither of these efforts had yielded any long-term results.

Throughout the 1930s and early 1940s Nehru, through his writings and speeches, kept reverting to the concept of the essential unity of Asia. He even explored the idea of an Asian federation. The Indian National Congress kept itself abreast of developments across Asia, and through resolutions adopted at its annual meetings, 'extended its greetings and support to fellow nationalist movements in China, Turkey, Egypt, Iran, Syria, Iraq, Palestine, Indochina, Ceylon, Burma, Malaya, Indonesia, and the Philippines'.[12]

THE ASIAN RELATIONS CONFERENCE (ARC)

India's interest in closer relations with its Asian neighbours had been intensifying apace with its own sruggle for independence. Public opinion in favour of this had been growing alongside. It is not surprising that the Asian Relations Conference, when it was held in Delhi in March-April 1947, evoked enormous interest. The final plenary session, held at Purana Qila, attracted a gathering of 20,000 people.[13] Pandit Nehru encapsulated the nation's views when he said in his inaugural address:

> During the past two hundred years we have seen the growth of Western imperialisms and of the reduction of large parts of Asia to colonial or semi-colonial status. Much has happened during these years, but perhaps one of the notable consequences of the European domination of Asia has been the isolation of the countries of Asia from one another. India always had contacts and intercourse with her neighbouring countries in the northwest, the northeast, the east and the southeast. With the coming of British rule in India these contacts were broken off and India was almost completely isolated from the rest of Asia. The old land routes almost ceased to function and our window to the outer world looked out on the sea routes which led to England. A similar process affected the other countries of Asia also. Their entire economy was bound up with some European imperialism or other; even culturally they looked towards Europe and not to their own friends and neighbours from whom they had derived so much in the past.
>
> In this Conference and in this work there are no leaders and no followers. All countries of Asia have to meet together on an equal basis in a common task and endeavour. . . . And may I say here that this Conference, and the idea underlying it, is in no way aggressive or against any other continent or country? Ever since news of this Conference went abroad some people in Europe and America have viewed it with doubt, imagining that this was some kind of a Pan-Asian movement directed against Europe or America. We have no designs against anybody; ours is the great design of promoting peace and progress all over the world. For too long we, of Asia, have been petitioners in Western

courts and chancelleries. That story must now belong to the past. We propose to stand on our own feet and to cooperate with all others who are prepared to co-operate with us. We do not intend to be the playthings of others. . . .

We seek no narrow nationalism. Nationalism has a place in each country and should be fostered, but it must not be allowed to become aggressive and come in the way of international development. Asia stretches her hand out in friendship to Europe and America as well as to our suffering brethren in Africa.[14]

Invitations for participation in the Conference were issued to all Asian countries and to Egypt. There were 193 delegates at the ARC from 30 nations, covering the Central Asian republics of the former Soviet Union, Tibet, China, Mongolia, Ceylon, Bhutan, Burma, Nepal, Turkey, Iran, Malaya, Thailand, Vietnam, Philippines and Indonesia. There were 39 observers from these nations, and another 12 institutional representatives (also observers) from the Arab League, UK, USA, USSR, Australia and the UN. The Muslim League (which formed the first government of the soon-to-be-independent Pakistan) boycotted the Conference. The five themes selected for discussion at the Conference were National Movements for Freedom; Racial Problems and Inter-Asian Migration; Economic Development and Social Services; Cultural Problems; and Status of Women and Women's Movements.

Outside South Asia, the Indonesian delegation was the largest, 32 in all, followed by the Malayan delegation with 14 delegates. The Indonesian delegation was flown to Delhi (and back after the Conference) in a chartered aircraft piloted by Congress leader Biju Patnaik, a feat that he accomplished without letting the Dutch colonial authorities get wind of it. The Indonesians formed a representative group, with delegates from youth organizations, women's organizations, students' unions and the peasants' movement, together with individuals who were broadcasters or worked in various ministries. The Malayan delegation, led by Dr Burhanuddin from Kuala Lumpur, included representation from the Chinese, Malay and Indian communities.

The debate and exchange of views at the ARC was amazingly frank, yet cordial and never bitter. Herein lay the greatest significance of the coming together of so many diverse peoples and nationalities. Delegates could state their views unhesitatingly, knowing that they would not be misunderstood, no matter how sensitive the subject of the discussion. They appreciated that 'the Conference was meant to promote understanding of each other's problems and not to go into the internal affairs of any country, and much less to call upon governments of participating countries to give effect to its conclusions, which could only be by legislative action'.[15]

In order to avoid the impression that any participating delegate was being put under pressure through these open exchanges, the Steering Committee of the ARC decided that:

> neither the Conference as a whole nor the individual groups should aim at reaching precise conclusions of the kind that might be embodied in an agreed final resolution and it was the hope of the organisers of the Conference—a hope which was largely fulfilled—that as the discussion in each group proceeded, a general sense of the meeting would emerge. . . . The reports (of each group) did, however, give a balanced summary of the discussion and almost without exception they were adopted by the plenary sessions of the Conference without major amendment.[16]

It is illustrative to go through the discussions in the Roundtable group on Racial Problems and Inter-Asian Migration. This theme, perhaps the most sensitive among those placed before the Conference, is particularly relevant for the post-colonial relations between Malaya and India. The Chairman of this Roundtable group was a delegate from China; and one of the two rapporteurs appointed for this group was the delegate from Malaya, Mohd Salleh Daud.[17] The discussions in this Roundtable, organized under the two sub-themes of Racial Problems and Inter-Asian Migration, were tremendously free and frank.

China, India, Indonesia, Burma, Malaya and Ceylon were among the most active participants in these discussions. It was recognized that most of the problems relating to differences among races and communities in Ceylon, Burma and Malaya were the result of inter-Asian migration in large numbers, primarily from China and India, that had been encouraged, even supported by the colonial power, Britain, with the objective of deriving greater profits from the plantation, mining and other sectors. The numbers involved in this inter-Asian migration were so large that the smaller countries of South and Southeast Asia were in fear of being 'swamped', 'submerged' or 'dominated' by the people of 'the two powerful and populous neighbouring countries, India and China'.[18] The Report of these discussions was succinct when it said:

At the Chairman's request to face the realities of conflict between indigenous and immigrant populations, the delegates proceeded to explore the causes for the hostility and suspicion prevailing in several Asian countries, between the autochthonous inhabitants and recent immigrants. None of the delegates denied that such hostility did exist, and the Vice-Chairman summarised the general view by pointing out that in most cases economic factors were responsible for tension and distrust. People such as the Burmese and the Malays felt that Indians and Chinese exploited them, and used the resources of the country to build up wealth which was finally sent out to the settlers' homeland. The Indians and Chinese, on the other hand, fully conscious of this resentment, were doubtful of the security of their property in Burma or Malaya, and for this very reason tried to transfer profits to India or China. Thus a vicious circle was created which can be broken only by a change of attitude among both parties. The fear of economic submergence on the part of the economically less advanced indigenous populations must be removed, and the newcomers must be assured of full rights of citizenship if they choose to identify themselves with the people of the country. *It was also pointed out that formation of political parties on a communal basis can be an additional cause of racial conflict.*[19]

The Report also contains the Chairman's summary of:

the main principles which should govern the relations of different racial groups in all Asian countries. These principles are complete legal equality of all citizens; complete religious freedom of all citizens; no public social disqualification of any racial group; and equality before the law of persons of foreign origin who have settled in the country.

Representatives of China, India, Ceylon, Indonesia, Burma and several other countries stated that the existing or proposed constitutions of their respective countries did not contain any provision for discrimination based on racial grounds. The consensus of opinion was that equality between all citizens of a country, irrespective of race and creed, should be the rule for all countries. *While condemning unequal treatment, it was hoped that governments would take measures to implement the principle of equality.*[20]

The Report specifically cites 'an Indian delegate (who) pointed out that such countries as India and China should not encourage emigrants to look for help to their home country, but that emigrants permanently settling in a foreign country should be advised to identify themselves with that country'.[21] It was generally felt that 'all foreign settlers in Asian countries who are prepared to comply with the naturalisation laws and who look upon the country of their adoption as their homeland and sole object of their loyalty should be granted full citizenship'.

During the discussion of this Report, a delegate from Azerbaijan said 'we Asian people, meeting here, should make a note in the report that we condemn all theories based on the supremacy of one race over another'.[22] He also called for each country to make statutory provisions against racial discrimination. The Report was adopted by the plenary session. It is instructive to see how such a large and diverse group of nations dealt with the sensitive issues of race and migration with such maturity and sympathetic appreciation of each delegate's concerns and points of view.

Relevant issues resulting from inter-Asian migration also came up in the Roundtable on the first theme, National Movements for Freedom. This group 'was unanimously of the view that non-indigenous minorities resident in any Asian country should support and assist the struggle for that country's freedom. It was necessary to ensure complete unity between all peoples resident in a country'.[23]

Discussions in this Roundtable brought up the idea of a 'neutrality bloc in Asia', put forward by John Thivy from Malaya. John Thivy elaborated on this suggestion, that such a bloc 'would be used both to prevent assistance reaching alien powers in their suppression of freedom struggles in Asia and also to immobilize Asian territory in the event of a world war . . . (that is) to prevent the active use of our manpower, economic resources and military bases by imperial powers dominating subject peoples'.[24] In substance, this idea was quite different from the position of neutrality that countries like Switzerland had followed during the Second World War. This was not an isolationist suggestion in any way: it was aimed at preventing colonial and imperial powers from involving subject-nations, or exploiting their natural resources in wars that these nations had not caused. Thivy's proposal received warm support and was adopted alongside the proposal to push for UN membership for all Asian countries. The only dissenting voice came from the Central Asian Republics of the USSR, who were against the formation of an Asian bloc (shadows of the Cold War!). Thivy's proposal was perhaps an early germination of the thought that later grew into the dynamic non-aligned movement spanning four continents.

There was tremendous appreciation among delegates at the ARC about the vision of India's leaders in conceptualizing and convening this Conference. The head of the Malayan delegation, Dr Burhanuddin said:

> Our presence here today is an expression of the will of the Asian people to unite and find possible ways and means to solve their common problems. To foster friendship and cultural relationship among Asian races was a desideratum of all Asian race. But owing to the domestic conditions prevailing in each of their respective countries Asian solidarity was not possible, and it was only for a great Asian country like India to give a lead towards its achievement.[25]

At the closing Plenary Session on 2 April 1947, Sutan Sjahrir, Prime Minister of Indonesia said:

> We from Indonesia deeply appreciate the reasons which have led to the inauguration of this Conference, namely the desire to see the Asian continent rise to its full stature, not in any spirit of hostility or as a threat to those in other lands, but purely in order to provide Asians the opportunity to plan and execute orderly and coordinated development along humanistic and international lines. . . .
>
> The sentiment which has impelled the races of Asia to struggle for independence is not only based on truth and justice but is also in keeping with the insistent call of progress and absolutely in harmony with the dictates of humanity. But here it is important to bear in mind that that sentiment must be so nurtured that it will not stray from the path of truth, justice, humanity and idealism. For, should we fall prey to careless ways of thought, this selfsame sentiment will turn itself into an instrument of destruction and all our idealistic visions of a brave new world will end. . . .[26]

The ARC adopted just one resolution, relating to establishing the Asian Relations Organisation (ARO) as a permanent organization based in New Delhi. This resolution was moved by the delegate of China, Wen Yuan-ning from the Legislative Yuan in Nanking, at the plenary session on 2 April 1947. The objective of the ARO was to maintain, strengthen and develop the contacts and linkages forged at the ARC. The ARO would promote the study and understanding of Asian problems, and would foster friendly relations and cooperation among the people of Asia and between them and the rest of the world. The ARO would function through a network of affiliated national units, one in each Asian country. These national units were envisaged as being non-governmental in character, with no party affiliations. It was agreed at this plenary session that the next ARC would be held in China in 1949.

The ARO was clearly an idea very close to the heart of Pandit Jawaharlal Nehru. However, it also turned out to be the most contentious proposal before the Conference, one that was debated furiously (albeit informally) and did not find ready acceptance among the delegates. Perhaps in the minds of the delegates, particularly those from Southeast Asia, this idea of a permanent Asian institute located in India linked up with fears of Indian domination. Many delegates must have recalled the 'Greater India' concept that was *au courant* among a section of Indian historians and commentators at that time.

The day before the ARO resolution was moved, Mahatma Gandhi addressed the Asian Relations Conference (he also addressed the closing plenary session on 2 April). The records show that Mahatma Gandhi was warmly welcomed by one and all. The delegate from China (Han Lih-wu from the Ministry of Education in Nanking) described Mahatma Gandhi as 'the spiritual leader of India, the light of Asia and a great man of the world'.[27] The Mahatma was requested to address the plenary session specifically on the proposed permanent Asian Institute. His remarks made clear the extent of the differences of opinion on this issue. Mahatma Gandhi said:

> Some parts of the question of an Asian institute were discussed by Pandit Nehru with me yesterday. . . . I am sorry to have to say that we seem to be fighting. . . . We have so many opinions formed that we do not know how to settle between ourselves in a humane manner. . . .
>
> The representatives of all Asian powers and Asian peoples have come together. Is it in order to wage war against Europe, against America, against non-Asians? I say emphatically 'no'. That is not India's mission and I am free to confess that I would feel extremely sorry if India, having won her independence essentially or rather predominantly through non-violent means, was going to use it for the suppression of other parts of the world—let alone Asian powers—of European powers because they have exploited the different

races inhabiting this vast continent called Asia. I think that would be a sorry thing. You should all go away with the fixed determination that Asia shall live, shall live as free as the other Western nations who flatter themselves into the belief that they are free . . . I just want to say that the idea is sound that such a Conference should be renewed at stated times.[28]

The Asian Relations Conference was the largest of its kind ever organized. The arrangements were impeccable and the participation immense. The edifice of separation among Asian nations and people, carefully constructed during two centuries of colonial domination crumbled away, only to reveal the wide information and knowledge gaps that still stood as barriers dividing Asia. The serious discussions on well-selected themes, combined with the detailed reports prepared by each group, reveal the intense interest among delegates to know more about each other and to share experiences in every sector.

Yet, the success of the ARC was marred and seriously impaired by the fact that the successor conference, scheduled for China in 1949, never took place. China's wariness on moving ahead with any initiative where India enjoyed preeminence was more than evident. This became an important reason for the early failure of what had been a magnificent launch. None the less, for long years, India tried to maintain the façade of Sino-Indian friendship. Scholars have commented that 'the strangest enigma presented by Nehru was that even though he sensed with uncanny perceptivity the real nature of the new China, his actions were contrary to what that awareness required of him'.[29]

Before the ARO could ever become an effective entity, it was finally wound up in 1955. The strong push for a permanent Asian institute had perhaps come too early. The recently renewed contacts among long-separated Asian neighbours should have been given more time to mature into trust, confidence and a deeper friendship. Instead, India's keenness to ensure the longevity of the ARC initiative by setting up the ARO was presented by some as evidence of India's push for domination in post-colonial Asia.

Equally, the widespread interest among academic and intellectual circles in India in the 'Greater India' concept was seen, or perhaps deliberately misrepresented in Southeast Asia as further evidence of independent India's interest in domination of the region. It is well accepted that 'the Indian National Congress never officially supported the revival of the Greater India concept and the idea of Indian overseas expansion'.[30] Pandit Nehru, in his frequent travels to South and Southeast Asia, including Malaya, interacted with the Indians who had settled there. He repeatedly asked them to be loyal to the country they had chosen to settle down in. None the less, every reference in his writings to India's strong historical links with South and Southeast Asia, every expression of interest by him in the well-being and non-discriminatory treatment of Indians living abroad, was unfairly taken by many as either interference in the internal affairs of another country, or as evidence of India's desire for a dominating role in the region. 'The Greater India idea seems, therefore, to have complicated independent India's development of close and amicable relations with its Asian neighbours.'[31]

The two Cold War power blocs, led respectively by the USA and the then USSR, made every effort to ensure that no third bloc emerged. Both blocs viewed the ARC as an incipient third bloc, which needed to be discouraged. Within a few years, as several newly independent countries of Asia became embroiled in disputes and Cold War politics, the spirit with which the ARC had been conceived soon lost relevance for them.

In actual fact, there was a tremendous paucity of direct contact and interaction among nationalist movements as they burgeoned across Asia after the Second World War. This allowed misinformation and misunderstandings to creep in. The ARC and the ARO were valuable efforts to correct this imbalance by creating direct linkages. The effort was, in itself, admirably successful, even though it faltered in the follow-up. Nehru was deeply disappointed with the lack of progress, and the initiative soon lost all momentum. The resultant disappointment within India's post-Independence foreign policy establishment meant that for several decades a much lower priority was attached to regional cooperation arrangements between South and Southeast Asia.

When the spirit of cooperation revived, it was on the broader canvas of the 1955 Asian African Conference in Bandung (Indonesia), which led on to the formation of NAM (Non-Aligned Movement) with its first Summit being held in Cairo in 1961. Such was the negative impact of the failure of the ARO, that India's leaders have continued to staunchly oppose the creation of a secretariat for NAM.

NOTES

1. Timothy Harper, 'Revolt in Malaya: The Indian Connection', in *The Oracle*, Jaunary 2008, p. 37.
2. J.S. Bright (ed.) *Important Speeches of Jawaharlal Nehru:* Volume II: *After Independence: India's Mission at Home and Abroad, 1946-1957*, New Delhi: Indian Printing Works, p. 480.
3. Interview given by Nehru in Allahabad to B. Shiva Rao, correspondent of the *Manchester Guardian* and *The Hindu*, quoted in *Asian Relations: Report of the Proceedings and Documentation of the first Asian Relations Conference New Delhi*, p. 2.
4. Ibid.
5. Ibid., p. 24.
6. T.A. Keenleyside, 'Nationalist Indian Attitudes towards Asia', *Pacific Affairs*, vol. 55, no. 2 (Summer 1982), p. 210.
7. Okakura Kakuzo, *The Ideals of the East*, New York: EP Dutton & Co., 1903, p. 1.
8. Rabindranath Tagore, *Letters from Java: Rabindranath Tagore's Tour of South-East Asia 1927*, tr. Indiradevi Chaudhurani and Supriya Roy, ed. Supriya Roy, Visva-Bharati: Tagore Travelogue Series, p. 17, quoting *Visva-Bharati Quarterly*, May-July 1943 (pp. 1-7).
9. Ibid., p. 18, quoting Sugata Bose, *A Hundred Horizons: The Indian Ocean in the Age of Global Empire*, Delhi: Permanent Black, 2006.
10. Keenleyside, op. cit., p. 216.
11. Ibid., p. 216, fn. 26, 27, 29 and 30.
12. Ibid., p. 217.
13. *Asian Relations*, p. 14.
14. Ibid., pp. 25-9.
15. Ibid., p. 116 (Discussion on the Report of the Roundtable on Racial issues and Inter-Asian migration).
16. Nicholas Mansergh, 'The Asian Conference', *International Affairs* (Royal Institute of International Affairs 1944-), vol. 23, no. 3, July 1947, pp. 297-8. The author was an observer at the Conference (*Asian Relations*, p. 318).
17. *Asian Relations*, op. cit., p. 103.
18. Ibid., p. 114.
19. Ibid.
20. Ibid., pp. 111-12.
21. Ibid., p. 113.

22. Ibid., p. 117.
23. Ibid., p. 93.
24. Ibid., p. 99. Comments made by John Thivy during the discussion of the Roundtable Report, before its adoption in the Plenary session.
25. Ibid., p. 60.
26. Ibid., pp. 271-2.
27. Ibid., p. 198.
28. Ibid., pp. 198-200.
29. Keenleyside, op. cit., p. 226, fn. 85, quoting Patwant Singh in *India and the Future of Asia*, p. 164.
30. Ibid., p. 228.
31. Ibid., p. 229.

16

Malaya Attains Independence: Key Issues of Cooperation

Malaya achieved independence on 31 August 1957, almost exactly ten years after India gained freedom from colonial rule on 15 August 1947. During these ten years, between 1947 and 1957, there was intense interest among the people of India in the independence movements of Malaya, Indonesia, Indo-China and the rest of Southeast Asia. The processes by which these nations were moving towards freedom from colonial rule were closely followed and commented upon in India, inside and outside parliament, in the media and in intellectual circles. The March 1947 Asian Relations Conference had played its role in stimulating this interest because participating delegates from these nations had vividly described, to audiences in India, their respective struggles and aspirations. In January 1949, the Nineteen-Nations Conference on Indonesia was convened in Delhi and in April 1955, the Asian African Conference was held in Bandung, Indonesia.

The Indian nation's interest in the impending independence of Malaya was unique, primarily because of the large number of Malayan Indians struggling for dignity and equality within the larger struggle for Malayan freedom from colonial rule. India's first Prime Minister, Jawaharlal Nehru continued to closely follow developments in Malaya, as he had done before 1947. He frequently visited Malaya and London, where he interacted respectively with Malayan leaders and with the British government on issues concerning the plight of Malayan Indians. His concerns regarding equity for Malayan Indians was as deep as had been Mahatma Gandhi's concerns for the rights of South African Indians who, too, were facing discrimination based on race. 'The Indian government sought to secure equal rights for all Malayan citizens irrespective of their origin, as it was a principle of India's policy, regarding the Indians overseas, that they should not obtain special rights and privileges, but at the same time, they should not be the victims of discrimination.'[1]

Pandit Nehru succinctly spelt out his approach in his speech in the Indian Legislative Assembly, on 4 March 1947, where he stated that

> any representations which the government of India might make in regard to Indians in Malaya would not be to the prejudice of the essential interests of the Malay(an) people themselves, that obviously 'it is our definite policy that we should claim no rights in any country for Indians which go against the rights of the people in that country'.[2]

In 1947, Malayan Indians were close to 6,00,000 or 10.3 per cent of the population of Malaya (including Singapore), a sharp drop from the pre-war 1931 figure of 621,847 or 14.3 per cent of the population.[3] Malayan Indians had substantial investments in Malaya, amounting to US $65.8 million (or Indian Rs. 309.4 million), of which 55 per cent was accounted for by landed interests, and 45 per cent by commercial and financial interests. In addition, monetary remittances to India from Malaya amounted annually to US $2.3 million (Indian Rs. 10 million).[4] These were substantive demographic and economic reasons for the people of newly independent India to follow with keen interest the emerging scenario in Malaya.

In the post-war period, there had been mounting concern in India about Indians in Malaya being 'neglected or victimised by the British Military Administration (BMA)', about Indian intelligentsia being 'arrested wholesale', about Indians 'dying in the streets for want of food and medical attention'.[5] Well-respected journals, such as the *India Quarterly*, published by the ICWA (Indian Council of World Affairs), carried articles giving full details of the adversities being faced by Malayan Indians at the hands of the BMA.[6] The Indian National Congress aggressively followed these developments, with frequent discussions in the Indian Legislative Assembly.

In 1947, the Indian government protested against discriminatory legislation adopted by the British colonial regime in Malaya regarding land-titles and the regime governing debtors and creditors (during the Japanese occupation). These legislations favoured Europeans who had fled Malaya during the Japanese Occupation, but caused huge losses, of up to US $23 million (Indian Rs. 100 million) to Indian mortgagers and creditors.[7] These legislations were held in abeyance for two years, but came into force on 1 October 1949.

The Indian government also pursued issues of discrimination relating to citizenship as promulgated in February 1948. The British government did not relent and the discriminatory provisions remain to this day. Essentially, these laws brought in a distinction between citizenship and nationality. Non-Malays can get citizenship but not nationality, in the sense of being recognized as the subject of the Sultan, in the state where they live.

> The acquisition of federal citizenship did not make the federal citizen a subject of a Malay State (there were nine of them) and entitle him to certain rights and privileges to which a subject of a Sultan of these states was entitled. Indeed, the difficulty of acquiring citizenship made many Indians run the risk of becoming stateless, and of having not even the right to be treated as an alien.[8]

After Independence, the Indian government continued to resist calls to lift the ban on the emigration of unskilled labourers to Malaya, a ban that had been in force since 1938. The Government of India repeatedly emphasized that lifting of the ban must be linked to guarantees regarding the working conditions for Indian labour in Malaya. In April 1949, the then Indian deputy minister of external affairs (B.V. Keskar) visited Kuala Lumpur, where he reiterated that the Government of India does not want 'our people to emigrate to countries without assured decent conditions of service and then to be thrown back to India when they are old and useless'.[9]

During the early years of India's Independence, the Indian government discussed these issues (working conditions for Malayan Indian labour) continuously with the authorities in Malaya and Singapore. The focus remained on ensuring non-discriminatory treatment for Malayan Indians, whether it was the issue of representation of Indians on the various councils of the Federation of Malaya and Singapore, or discriminatory Ordinances, including the ones mentioned above, and the one issued by the government of Malaya in 1953, restricting immigration for purposes of employment, only to those who had 'high professional qualifications' or had a minimum two-year contract with the minimum monthly remuneration of not less than 500 Straits dollars.

None the less, the consistent advice of the Indian government to Malayan Indians was embodied in the words of India's first president, Rajendra Prasad. Addressing Parliament on 31 January 1950, he said that 'India had large numbers of children living abroad, and . . . the government's advice to them had always been "that they should identify themselves with the indigenous people and look upon the country of adoption as their real home"'.[10]

Similarly, during his visit to Singapore in June 1950, Jawaharlal Nehru 'advised the Indians in Malaya to be loyal to the land they lived in and to integrate themselves with other communities'.[11] When Nehru visited Penang in December 1954, he said, while addressing a mass rally of Indians, that 'it was open to them to become Malayan nationals and claim the same rights and privileges as other people. But, he said, "if you decide to become Malayan nationals, then love this country as your own".'[12] Once again, Nehru firmly reiterated the Indian government's policy when he spoke in Parliament in September 1957, saying:

> . . . we have left it to Indians abroad whether they are to continue to remain Indian nationals or to adopt the nationality of whichever country they live in. It is entirely for them to decide. If they remain Indian nationals then all they can claim abroad is favoured alien treatment. They become aliens and they should get as good a treatment as any other aliens get. . . . On the other hand, if they adopt the nationality of the country, then they should be treated as citizens with all the rights of citizenship.[13]

These statements bring out several important aspects of the Indian government's policy on overseas Indians in general and Malayan Indians in particular. The Government of India did not expect or ask for dual citizenship for Malayan Indians. The Government of India's own regulations do not allow dual nationality for Indian citizens. The Indian government did not encourage or expect Malayan Indians, those who had made Malaya their home, to look to India for protection or help at every turn. On the contrary, India encouraged those who had taken citizenship of Malaya to integrate and be loyal to their country of adoption.

From the outset India, as a newly independent nation, was deeply committed to the concept of Asian unity. At the ARC convened at India's initiative in Delhi in March 1947, there had been a free and frank exchange of views among delegates on what Asian unity entailed. India remained sensitive to and perceptive about the apprehensions expressed by delegates from Burma, Malaya and Ceylon about the potential for economic and demographic domination by large Asian countries like China and India once the colonial powers left Asia. India did not want to do anything that could exacerbate these apprehensions, or engender suspicion and distrust of India among the smaller Asian countries, since this would only lead to disunity among Asian nations. In December 1947, while speaking in the Constituent Assembly on the problems of overseas Indians, Nehru recognized that the spread of Indians abroad:

> naturally frightens others who may not have that vitality in them, and they want to protect themselves. Questions then arise of vested interests which India has developed or Indians have developed there. Such questions have arisen, and while on the one hand we are obviously intent on protecting the interests of Indians abroad, on the other hand we cannot protect any vested interests which injure the cause of the country they are in. There is this difficulty. . . .[14]

Accordingly, India did not seek any special privileges for Malayan Indians or for any other group of Indians settled abroad. India's quest has been for equality and non-discriminatory treatment for people of Indian origin living in different corners of the world.

In Malaya, too, India represented vigorously to ensure that Malayan Indian plantation workers, professionals and businessmen (among others) were accorded citizenship alongside all those who were either born and brought up in Malaya, or had spent long years in Malaya. In 1952, with the local elections approaching, the citizenship rules were revised. All those born in the former Crown territories (Penang, Malacca and Singapore) were now regarded as citizens by law. This accorded citizenship automatically to around 2,22,000 Malayan Indians, while another 1,80,000 acquired the right to apply. Together, this covered around 60 per cent of the people of Indian origin living in Malaya.[15] It is most unfortunate that among those entitled and eligible for citizenship, large numbers working and living with their families on plantations deep in the interior of the country, were not registered as residents or citizens, either by their employers or through the good offices of the MIC. The descendants of this group, the stateless Indians in Malaysia, are still suffering untold hardship and ignominy.

The Indian government, working with the British and Malayan authorities, did all they could to provide humanitarian assistance to the Malayan Indians. Sometimes, such efforts were thwarted.

> The Government of the Federation of Malaya passed legislation on 22 December 1949 withdrawing facilities so far given to the Agent of the Government of India in Malaya to inspect work places etc. where Indian labourers are employed. The question as to what extent the functions which the Agent has hitherto been discharging in respect of Indian labourers, can be performed by him in his capacity as Consul, is at present under examination.[16]

In 1952-3, efforts were initiated to constitute a Scholarship Fund in Malaya for the benefit of students of Indian origin for higher studies in the University of Malaya. Towards this end, a Trust was created with funds received by the Indian Relief Committee (created in Malaya during Nehru's visit in 1946) from the British Steam Navigation Company, being the refundable unclaimed balances of quarantine charges lying with them, and India's share of the assets in the Indian National Army and Indian Independence League Funds (these were seized in Malaya soon after the end of the Second World War). This Trust Fund started operations in 1954-5, with the Commissioner of India in Malaya as the principal Trustee. In 1952-3, the Government of Malaya agreed to utilise 'the balances in the Indian Immigration Fund (now estimated to be worth 6 million Straits dollars) for settling Indian labour on land in the Peninsula'.[17] In the following year, two pilot schemes regarding land ownership were prepared by the Government of Malaya to settle Indian labourers. 'The settlers will enjoy full rights over the lands allotted to them but they will not have the right to sell'.[18]

Nehru, as Prime Minister and Minister of External Affairs for India, closely followed these developments. He had been deeply affected by the plight of Malayan Indians, when he visited Malaya immediately after the war, in 1946. He was seriously interested in the positive amelioration in the welfare of Malayan Indians. He knew that the majority of them, born and brought up in Malaya, sought Malayan citizenship, and he wanted equal and non-discriminatory rights for them. Nehru enjoyed an excellent rapport with Tunku Abdul Rahman, who had assumed the Presidency of UMNO in August, 1951. Tunku Abdul Rahman became Chief Minister of Malaya in July 1955, and was independent Malaya's (Malaysia's from 1963 onwards) first Prime Minister, his term extending from August 1957 to September 1970. He is popularly known as *Bapa Kemerdekaan* (Father of Independence) or *Bapa Malaysia* (Father of Malaysia). The British government, Tunku Abdul Rahman and Jawaharlal Nehru remained in close touch as the constitutional talks proceeded towards *Merdeka* or independence for Malaya.

It was under Tunku's leadership that, in 1954, the MIC joined the Alliance (which was renamed Barisan Nasional in 1973). For the first time since its formation in 1946, the MIC moved away from its principle of non-communalism, and abandoned its partnership with the multi-racial IMP (Independence of Malaya Party). This was a huge wrench for the MIC. A significant proportion of Malayan Indians did not support this moving away from the principle of non-communalism. Nonetheless, Nehru welcomed this development. Nehru was well aware of Tunku's views and perspectives on the future directions for a plural and multi-racial Malaya. Accordingly, Nehru perceived the Alliance Party (UMNO, MCA and MIC) as representing the coming together of the three communities in an equal partnership. MIC's joining the Alliance had a tremendously reassuring impact on Nehru, who now felt that the concerns of the Malayan Indians were in safe hands. The British government began the final countdown to *Merdeka* once they were assured that the MIC, too, and not just UMNO and the MCA would, from now on, be part of every decision-making process. The Annual Report of the Ministry of External Affairs for 1955-6, written after MIC had joined the Alliance and Malaya's constitutional talks with the British had been successfully concluded, said 'the Government of India have noted with satisfaction the constitutional progress in Malaya'.[19] In April 1956, India accepted Britain's request to nominate an Indian to the Reid Commission.

This close association between Nehru, the British and Tunku Abdul Rahman influenced Nehru's views on events in Malaya right through the 1950s and beyond. Some months after the communist rebellion started in Malaya in 1948, India's deputy minister for external affairs, upon his return from a visit to Malaya, in May 1949, 'stated at a Press Conference that the troubles in Malaya were "largely a Communist-dominated show", that the Malayan unrest could not be described as a national struggle for liberation, and that he could not describe the insurgents as "anything else but bandits who do not care what or whom they oppose"'.[20] Nehru was even more outspoken in his condemnation of Malayan communist terrorism when he visited Singapore in June, 1950. Speaking at a press conference there on 18 June, he said that Malayan communist terrorism was 'infinitely bad', that this 'cannot and should not be tolerated' and that 'this method of terrorism is degrading to the whole human race and reduces men to the level of beasts'.[21]

Scholars have concluded that

> The Indian government . . . adopted in regard to the rebellion in Malaya an attitude that sharply contrasted with its attitude in regard to the rebellions in Indochina and Indonesia. It also treated British policy in Malaya differently from French and Dutch policies in Indochina and Indonesia. Whereas the French and the Dutch were denounced in the strongest terms, there was no condemnation of the British.[22]

Tunku Abdul Rahman was staunchly anti-communist in his views and policies, and he had Nehru's fullest support on this. Nehru faced and withstood national (in parliament) and international criticism for his support of Malaya (and the British) on several issues, but he did not relent. For Nehru, the overriding factors were his friendship and understanding with Tunku and British leaders, and his concern for the long-term welfare and interests of Malayan Indians.

In the Indian parliament, Nehru faced criticism from members of the Communist Party of India (Hiren Mukherjee) and from non-communists. Veteran Indian parliamentarian N.G. Ranga, then a member of the Congress party, described India's policy with regard to Malaya 'the softest or weakest point' of India's foreign policy. He said:

> What is happening in Malaya is something which should upset many minds. It is true that in Malaya the Communist Party has been playing a role which is

really destructive. It has taken to violent means and violent ways and necessarily its guerrilla [*sic*] has had to be put down by legitimate means including the use of armed forces. But if such steps had been taken by a National Government of Malaya it would have been possible for the rest of the world to appreciate. But when the British Empire has had to take this step, necessarily the position of people like us who have been so closely associated with the Commonwealth becomes very difficult to justify. . . .[23]

The French newspaper, *Le Monde*, wrote trenchantly, expressing its surprise 'that New Delhi denounces French action in Indochina . . . but says nothing about Malaya where the British Expeditionary Corps is endeavouring to suppress for the past eighteen months, a rebellion which is comparable, *mutatis mutandis*, to that of the Vietminh.'[24] The French leader, General Charles de Gaulle, commented 'I cannot understand how Pandit Nehru spoke that way of Indochina and not Malaya and Burma which affect him more closely'.[25]

Pandit Nehru was criticized for not supporting the early withdrawal of Britain's presence from Malaya. Senior Indian parliamentarian, Asoka Mehta, speaking in parliament, queried why India had failed to raise the question of Malaya at the 1954 Colombo Conference, saying that 'while the freedom of Tunisia was asked for . . . the question of Malayan independence and the fact of British occupation forces numbering 130,000 were left shrouded in silence.'[26] Nehru replied in Parliament that 'the Commonwealth link there made the situation of millions of Indians "somewhat easier: while retaining Indian nationality, they can get privileges which they cannot otherwise" '.[27] Nehru's reply revealed his anxiety that key issues relating to citizenship for Malayan Indians be resolved before the British left Malaya.

Well before this debate in the Indian parliament, Nehru was queried about the continuing presence of the British in Malaya (way back in June 1950, during his visit to Singapore). When asked whether Britain should withdraw from Malaya, Nehru said that 'if it must be today, there may be difficulties . . . while Britain remains in this part of the world as a colonial power, it will contribute towards the solution of certain problems. Withdrawal suddenly would result in all manner of difficulties.'[28] The 'all manner of difficulties' referred to by Nehru clearly included the emergence, the previous year, of the communist regime in China. 'As soon as the Chinese communists had won power in China, they started asserting their leadership of the anti-colonial movement in Asia. They also adopted an aggressive attitude in Tibet.'[29] Nehru, supported by public opinion in India, was concerned about the implications for India of the new communist regime in China. In particular, there was 'anxiety to prevent China from helping communist partners in South and South East Asia'.[30] Nehru expressed these concerns directly in a conversation with Norman Cousins, where he admitted that the emergence of Communist China did pose a threat in Southeast Asia.[31]

As the date for Malayan independence neared, it was evident that the newly-independent government led by Tunku Abdul Rahman would be unable, on its own, to resist the ongoing communist insurgency and rebellion, especially in the light of the ideological and material support extended to the communists by the People's Republic of China. In 1957, in order to bolster their capacities for self-defence, the Government of the Federation of Malaya entered into an Agreement on External Defence and Mutual Assistance with the British government. This was known as the AMDA (Anglo-Malayan Defence Agreement), which after 1963, became the Anglo-Malaysian Defence Agreement. Following Britain's decision in 1967, to withdraw its armed forces east of Suez, AMDA was replaced in 1971, by the FPDA (Five Power Defence Arrangements). The FPDA brings together UK, Australia, New Zealand, Singapore and Malaysia through the establishment of an Integrated Air Defence System (IADS), headquartered in Butterworth on the west coast of peninsular Malaysia. Initially restricted to cooperation among the air forces of these five nations, the FPDA, since 2001, provides for an Integrated Area Defence System, by bringing in cooperation among all three branches of the armed forces.

The AMDA concluded in 1957, assured assistance by the UK to Malaya for the external defence of its territory and for the training and development of its armed forces. In exchange, UK received the right to maintain and use bases and facilities, as well as to station its naval, land and air forces in Malaya. Both governments agreed to consult together on the measures to be taken jointly or separately in the event of, or the threat of, an armed attack. In a separate agreement, the government of Malaya declared its determination that 'there shall be no relaxation in the conduct of the Emergency campaign', and requested the governments of UK, Australia and New Zealand to continue to make their forces available for use in emergency operations. As a result, forces from these three countries were stationed in Malaya and took part in the campaign against the ongoing communist rebellion.

In 1956 and 1957, Nehru and the Indian government accepted and publicly supported AMDA. This was the most striking evidence of Nehru's concerns over communist activities in Southeast Asia, combined with his appreciation and understanding of the situation in Malaya which made British defence assistance necessary even after Malayan independence. The Indian government's stance on AMDA stood out in sharp contrast to the staunchly anti-imperial and anti-colonial approach she had been vigorously pursuing in almost every other instance. At the Bandung Conference in April 1955, Nehru had said that 'if we rely on others, whatever great powers they might be, if we look to them for sustenance, then we are weak indeed'.[32] This statement had provoked a major difference of opinion with the Philippine delegate at Bandung. In April 1956, Nehru explained his support for AMDA in an interview to *The Straits Times* where he said:

> Every country has the right to defend itself. A country newly independent, or striving for independence, might very well fear its inability to stand alone, and consequently wish to conclude a defensive alliance. That would be a different matter. An agreement for defence might well be a necessary stage in the evolutionary process of independence.[33]

Neither India nor Malaya can forget their mutually beneficial support and understanding that ensured the emergence of an independent, prosperous and non-communist Malaya, a member of the Commonwealth and later of the Non-Aligned Movement. India particularly appreciated Malaya's consistent stand against joining SEATO (South East Asia Treaty Organisation), despite obvious pressure from the Western powers to do so. India's deputy minister of external affairs, Lakshmi Menon, was quoted as saying that Malaya had done 'the wisest thing in not joining SEATO'.[34]

NOTES

1. Ton That Thien *India and South East Asia, 1947-1960*, Geneva: Libraire Droz, 1963, p. 234.
2. Ibid., p. 236, quoting statement by Pandit Nehru in the Legislative Assembly from *Parliamentary Debates*, 1947, vol. 2, speech made on 4 March, p. 1441.
3. Ibid., p. 226, quoting Federation of Malaya Report, 1955.
4. Ibid., p. 227, quoting B.N. Ganguli, *India's Economic Relations with the Far Eastern and Pacific Countries in the Present Century*, Calcutta: Orient Longmans, 1956, pp. 73-4.
5. Ibid., p. 230.
6. Ibid., quoting *India Quarterly* of January 1946 (article by C. Kondapi on 'Indians Overseas') and May 1946 (article by P. Kondanda Rao on 'Indians Overseas, the Position in Malaya').
7. Ibid., p. 232.
8. Ibid., p. 234, quoting C. Kondapi, *Indians Overseas, 1838-1949*, p. 419.
9. Ibid., p. 235, quoting *The Straits Times*, 27 April 1949.
10. Ibid., p. 236, quoting *Parliamentary Debates*, 1950, vol. 1, pt. 2, 31 January, p. 22.
11. Ibid., p. 239, quoting *The Statesman*, 18 June 1950.
12. Ibid., p. 238, quoting *India News*, 8 January 1955.
13. Ibid., quoting from *India's Foreign Policy*, pp. 128-9.
14. Ibid., quoting Jawaharlal Nehru's speech on 4 December 1947 from *India's Foreign Policy* pp. 127-8.
15. Muzaffar Desmond Tate, *The Malaysian Indians: History, Problems and Future*, p. 108 and fn. 155 (p. 211).
16. Extract (pertaining to Malaya) from the Annual Report of the Ministry of External Affairs, Government of India, 1949-50.
17. Ibid., 1952-3.
18. Ibid., 1953-4.
19. Ibid., 1955-6.
20. Ton That Thien, op. cit., p. 240, quoting from *The Statesman* of 7 May 1949.
21. Ibid., pp. 240-1, quoting *The Statesman* and *The Straits Times*, 19 June 1950.
22. Ibid., p. 241.
23. Ibid., p. 247, quoting *Parliamentary Debates*, Constituent Assembly, 1949, vol. 2, pt. 2, 8 March, p. 1239.
24. Ibid., p. 247, quoting *Le Monde*, 2 November 1949.
25. Ibid., p. 247, quoting *Le Monde*, 19 November 1949. General de Gaulle is referring to a memorandum of the Indian government to

the British government denouncing French policy and the Bao Dai regime in Indochina. This memorandum leaked out in November 1949.

26. Ibid, p. 245, quoting *Parliamentary Debates*, 1954, vol. 7, pt. 2, 2 September, column 3709.
27. Ibid., p. 245, ibid., column 3890.
28. Ibid., p. 245, quoting from *The Statesman* and *The Observer*, 18 June 1950.
29. Ibid., p. 128, including fn. 46, which quotes Chinese leader Liu Shao Chi as saying, in November 1949, in a speech at the World Federation of Trade Unions Congress that: 'The path taken by the Chinese people in defeating imperialism and its lackeys and in founding the People's Republic of China is the path that should be taken by the people of the various colonial and semi-colonial countries in their fight for national independence and people's democracy. . . .'
30. Ibid., p. 128, quoting J.C. Kundra, *Indian Foreign Policy 1947-54*, p. 58.
31. Ibid., p. 130, quoting Norman Cousins, *Talks with Nehru* (Recorded interview), New York: John Day, 1951.
32. Ibid., pp. 245-6. Nehru's statement was quoted by George McT. Kahin in *The Asian African Conference, Bandung, April 1955*, p. 11.
33. Ibid., p. 245, quoted from *The Straits Times*, 20 April 1956.
34. Ibid., p. 249, quoting the *Hindustan Times Weekly* on 9 February 1958.

17

India and Malaysia in the Post-Colonial Era

When Malaya attained independence from colonial rule on 31 August 1957, diplomatic relations between India and Malaya were described as 'cloudless, happy and confident'.[1] Indeed, thanks to the close rapport and understanding between India's first Prime Minister, Jawaharlal Nehru and Malaya's first Prime Minister, Tunku Abdul Rahman, bilateral relations between the two countries were off to a running start.

On the eve of Malaya's independence, on 30 August 1957, in a radio broadcast, Nehru described this as 'a great day, not only for Malaya, but for Asia'.[2] The following day, India was represented by Cabinet Minister S.K. Patil at the Independence Day celebrations in Kuala Lumpur. Speaking in Singapore en route to Kuala Lumpur, Patil congratulated Malaya on 'the statesmanlike way' in which it had settled its problems, adding that it was 'an act of statesmanship' on the part of Great Britain also.[3] The following month, in September 1957, the then Vice-President of India, S. Radhakrishnan, visited Malaya. On 2 September 1957, speaking in parliament in India, Nehru welcomed Malaya's independence with the following words: 'We welcome it because Malaya is a country which has thousands of years of association with India. Even now, if you go to Malaya . . . you will find evidence of India and Indian culture all over the place. And in the past few years also our friendship and cooperation in some matters have grown. . .'[4]

One year later, in December 1958, the then President of India, Rajendra Prasad, visited Malaya. He was the first foreign Head of State to visit the newly-independent Malaya. On this occasion, the Yang di-Pertuan Agong of Malaya, Tuanku Abdul Rahman, Sultan of Negeri Sembilan, said that for countless years 'the soul of India radiated through the history of Malaya'.[5] Malayan Prime Minister Tunku Abdul Rahman was no less lavish in acknowledging Malaya's close links with India. On 8 December 1958, in his speech welcoming the President of India, Tunku said that in its newly won independence, the people of Malaya were 'proud to acknowledge the debt which we and all other freedom-loving people of Asia owe to your great leadership of India'.[6] Tunku went on to say that, although Malaya and India shared many ideals and ideas, the problems which confronted the two countries were different and 'can be best left to each to tackle in its own way by means best suited to conditions and circumstances existing in each of our own countries'.[7] Specifically, in relation to the policies pursued by the two countries in regard to communism, the first prime minister of Malaya said:

> the Indian ideal of democracy allows for active tolerance of all political forces and credo including those practised by the Communists, but we in Malaya can never be neutral because bitter experiences have told us that given a chance communists will destroy our ideal of democracy.[8]

In December 1961, the then Yang di-Pertuan Agong, Tuanku Syed Putra, Sultan of Perlis, visited India on a state visit. This was the first visit to India by the Head of State of Malaya. His warm and genuine expressions of empathy and friendship towards India won the hearts of all in India. Speaking at the banquet held in his honour in New Delhi on 8 December 1961, Tuanku Syed Putra said:

> There is a quality of grandeur and greatness about India which never fails to rouse the respect and admiration of any thoughtful man who cherishes goodwill for mankind. This timeless land has an enduring capacity to awaken questions in an enquiring mind and heart, so much so that throughout the centuries many men have tried to discover without avail the essential element which generates the spirit of India. Even in the short time I have been here I have already felt this sense of inward challenge.
>
> . . . His (Dr Rajendra Prasad's) visit to the Federation of Malaya was . . . historic, because His Excellency was the first Head of State to pay my country the honour of making an official visit. It is most appropriate, therefore, and a circumstance which gives me particular pleasure, that I should make my first journey to another sovereign nation as Head of State to your great country of India.

The ties that link your country and mine are both old and new. The old ties stretch so far back in time and history that it is impossible to say with any precision when the first contacts were made. Certainly it is clear from archaeological discoveries that close links and association between the people of India and Malaya existed more than a thousand years ago. I have no doubt that future finds may well reveal that the cultural and commercial influences of ancient India reached Malayan shores many centuries earlier. Such a revelation surely will not be strange, seeing that India and Malaya are like two arms embracing the same ocean.

But setting aside the undoubted evidence of history, and the questions of commerce and custom, or the presence of many words of Indian origin in the Malayan languages, or the still-living spirit of the *Ramayana* in our songs and stories, there are in modern times even stronger relations and personal ties between our two lands.

Over the years many hundreds of thousands of people from India have gone to Malaya to live or work there either returning to their own country or settling down in Malaya as the land of their adoption, as they have done for some generations past, with the result that today there are many thousands of Indians who are proud to call themselves citizens of the Federation of Malaya.

I would like to take this opportunity to express our appreciation in Malaya of the wisdom and farsightedness of your Government in consistently urging on those of my subjects who come from India, or whose families did so before them, that they should give their loyalty and love, their respect and devotion to Malaya.

I can rightly and fairly say that the Malayans of Indian descent today are making a splendid and constructive contribution to the peace and well-being, the happiness and prosperity of the Federation of Malaya.[9]

There could not have been a more frank yet endearing expression of the key elements in the bilateral relationship between India and Malaya.

COOPERATION IN EDUCATION AND MILITARY TRAINING

The areas of cooperation between Malaya and India that Prime Minister Nehru referred to in his statement in parliament in September 1957, were many and diverse. Outside the traditional and historical sector of trade and commerce, two sectors where cooperation had been acquiring momentum were those of education and military training.

Military cooperation during the colonial period began early in the nineteenth century, when troops of the Madras Native Infantry were deployed by the British for service in Singapore, Malacca and Penang. During the Second World War, units of the British Indian army fought the Japanese in defence of Malaya and Singapore.

In 1932, the IMA (Indian Military Academy), established in Dehradun as the 'Indian Sandhurst', became functional. Soon after this, the tradition began of sending prospective Malayan army officers to IMA for training. Tun Hussein Onn, Prime Minister of Malaya (1976-81) and son of the founder of UMNO, Dato Onn Jaafar, was sent to IMA for training in 1941, while still a teenager. Upon completion of his training, he was absorbed into the Indian Army and served in the Middle East during the Second World War. Another alumnus of the IMA, Tun Ibrahim Ismail, rose to become Chief of Defence Forces in Malaysia, a post he held from 1971 to 1977. Over time, as Malaysia established its own training and defence establishments, training in India for Malaysian armed forces officers became much more selective, focused only on specialized courses.

In the early years after Malayan independence, officers and men of the Malayan armed forces were trained in India. In April 1959, at the request of the Government of Malaya, the Indian government placed the services of Major General Ibrahim Habibullah at the disposal of the Malayan government, as deputy officer commanding the Malayan Army, a post he held for one year.[10]

The tradition of Malaysians receiving training in IMA survives even today. Several generations in the family of the Sultan of Johor have received training in the IMA. In 2003 Tunku Ismail, presently the Crown Prince of Johor, enrolled as a cadet officer in the IMA. He was commissioned in the Jaipur-based 61st Cavalry Regiment of the Indian Army in December 2004, the first member of a Malaysian royal famly to join the Indian armed forces. On 26 January 2007, as a young Captain, he led a unit from the 61st Cavalry Regiment in India's Republic Day Parade, the first foreigner to be accorded this honour.

The sector of Indo-Malayan cooperation that has had perhaps the most widespread impact in Malaya has been that of education. The ISTF (Indian Scholarship Trust Fund) had already started functioning in 1954, to facilitate Malayan Indians in their efforts to obtain higher education. In October 1954, the Selection Committee, chaired by the Indian High Commissioner (then Commissioner) in Kuala Lumpur, awarded the first three ISTF scholarships for studying medicine in India. Far larger in number were the scholarships offered by the Government of India to all Malayan citizens, regardless of race or origin, for graduate and post-graduate studies in India. These scholarships covered a very broad range of fields of study, including medicine and engineering.

> During the 1960s and 1970s, an estimated 30,000 Malaysian students were in Indian institutions of learning. This number has decreased substantially since then. Over 30 per cent of doctors in Malaysia today are Indian-trained. Manipal Medical College alone has over 3000 alumni in Malaysia. (Today) Malaysians account for . . . 10 per cent of the total number of foreign students studying in India. . . .[11]

In the early years of Malaya's independence, India and Malaya cooperated in several sectors of human resource development. In the very first year, 1957, the Malayan government recruited 100 doctors in India to meet their urgent requirements. Qualified Indian professors and teachers were recruited to serve in universities and colleges across Malaya. Malayan technical personnel received training in India under the Colombo Plan and ITEC (Indian Technical and Economic Cooperation) programmes.

MALAYSIA'S FIRST PRIME MINISTER: TUNKU ABDUL RAHMAN

Malaya's first prime minister, Tunku Abdul Rahman, was firm and unwavering in his friendship and understanding towards India. He wrote about this with unreserved frankness in the *Foreign Affairs*, where he said:

> Having experienced the menace of international Communism and overcome it, we are particularly sensitive to its threats elsewhere and have never hesitated to take a positive stand when necessary.
>
> Malaya was among the first to condemn Communist China's invasion of Tibet and the subjugation of that ill-fated nation. Again, when the Communist Chinese pressed on further and treacherously attacked their sympathetic neighbour, India, I was the first to condemn their aggression unreservedly,

as I happened to arrive in Calcutta the day it began; and during my tour of India in that month of October 1962, I exposed the Chinese motives behind aggression. On my return to Singapore in November, I stated that in the event of a declaration of war between India and China, Malaya would give India 'all-out support'. Soon afterwards I launched a public campaign, the 'Save Democracy Fund', which raised more than $1 million to help India defend herself against Chinese aggression.[12]

In this article, Tunku Abdul Rahman was equally frank about the reasons behind the formation of Malaysia in 1963. Here, too, the key motivating factor was the need to resist the onslaught of communism. Tunku said:

. . . Communism remained the prime menace to the peace of Asia. We had successfully overcome the internal threat of Communism in Malaya, but we were only too well aware of its insidious growth in neighbouring areas. I noticed particularly, with growing and grave concern, the increasing influence of Communism in the British territories of Singapore, Sabah, Brunei and Sarawak. The same pattern of Communist exploitation of anticolonial feelings that we had experienced in Malaya, was taking place in those areas. I felt that time was running out, and that the Communist menace had to be swiftly met, otherwise free Malaya would once again be in danger. Therefore, in May 1961, I first announced my hope that the formation of Malaysia would enable the people of these states to achieve the independence they desired and at the same time put an end to colonialism in their part of the world.

. . . For the next two years . . . negotiations took place among leaders of all the states concerned and with the British. With the exception of Brunei, all of the states of Malaya joined Singapore, Sabah and Sarawak in a conviction that Malaysia was their future destiny. The achievement of union in September 1963 was an outstanding testimony to the will and wish of the peoples of the new nation to stand united, to achieve progress and prosperity, and to resist together the Communist bid for power.[13]

It is exceptionally valuable that in this article, Tunku Abdul Rahman explains at length the rationale behind the Constitution of Malaysia. This is unique, since Tunku had, on behalf of Malaya, led the negotiations with the British on the Malayan Constitution. These negotiations continued even after the Reid Commission had given its Report. Several recommendations of the Reid Commission were altered or even rejected. In the *Foreign Affairs* article, Tunku emphasizes that the Malaysian Constitution 'upheld the practice and principles of democracy' and ensured that all Malaysians 'feel they have a part to play and a responsibility to share in the national well-being'. He said that in the Malaysian Constitution:

> . . . all the fundamental freedoms—such as equality, freedom of speech and freedom of association—are protected. One typical section of the Constitution reads, 'All persons are equal before the law and are entitled to the equal protection of the law'. Another states, 'There shall be no discrimination against citizens on the grounds only of religion, race, descent or place of birth in any law'. Although Islam is the official religion of Malaysia, every Malaysian has the right to practice the creed of his own choice.
>
> The constitution also provides for parity among the various racial groups. It was obviously necessary in the general interest to do away with economic and educational handicaps affecting the Malays and other indigenous peoples. By common consent, scholarships and opportunities were made more readily available to the indigenous peoples, the least advanced group economically, to provide an incentive for personal achievement. They were also given easier access into government service. Our aim to establish a system of parity, not only politically but economically, would leave no one out or unable to compete in the forward march of the new Malaysia. The omissions of the past have to be rectified in the cause of future progress.
>
> An American magazine recently stated that Malaysia was a democracy in all respects save one, meaning the 'special privileges for the Malays'. I must point out that although the Constitution provides for a special position for the indigenous peoples at present, it also provides for periodic review of the position when necessary. Ultimately the time will come when it will be possible by legislative action to amend the Constitution because this special position will no longer be needed.[14]

This was precisely the reasoning that had given India's prime minister Nehru such high comfort-levels in welcoming Malaya's emergence as an independent nation. These were also the considerations that went into the formulation of Malaya's foreign policy under its first Prime Minister Tunku Abdul Rahman, who held the foreign affairs portfolio throughout his tenure. In 1957, the ongoing communist insurrection had necessitated the conclusion of the Anglo-Malay Defence Agreement (later renamed the Five Power Defence Agreement or FPDA). Accordingly, Malaya's earliest foreign policy priorities were pro-Western and anti-communist. At the same time, the Tunku was keen to factor in his domestic constituencies, arising from his commitment to a genuinely plural, multi-racial society, combined with pressures emanating within

UMNO and the 'challenge . . . provided by PAS's early search for a pan-Malay/Islamic ideal manifested in its basic anti-colonial stance in matters of foreign policy.'[15]

The Tunku did feel the importance of evolving a 'special relationship' with other Muslim countries, and worked towards instituting a 'Muslim Commonwealth'. In 1956, the soon-to-be prime minister of Malaya directed a delegation of members of the Federal Council to tour Muslim countries 'in order to interest them in the promotion of Islamic brotherhood or failing that, in the study of the possibility of bringing about closer co-operation among Muslim people'.[16]

This focus on highlighting Malaya's (later Malaysia's) Islamic identity through its foreign policy has had two dimensions. In the early years it was perhaps an essential part of the anti-communist struggle, since 'both in terms of ideology and ethnic association, the insurgency was perceived by the largely rural Malay public as a preeminently Chinese attempt to gain control of the state'.[17] By 1956, the focus on Islam had become a significant part of the ruling Alliance/Barisan Nasional Government's strategy for countering the Parti Islam Se-Malaysia (PAS).[18] This group, as the All-Malaya Islamic Association, had been a part of UMNO, but had broken away to form the Pan-Malayan Islamic Party (PMIP) in order to contest the 1955 elections on its own. 'By the 1959 federal elections PAS, under the leadership of Dr Burhanuddin, had made considerable inroads into UMNO's support by appealing to all Malays on religious and communal issues.'[19] So the Tunku's strategy was to counter PAS nationally in the arena of intra-Malay rivalry where the struggle has been for the Malay vote, and internationally through a foreign policy that epitomized 'domestic policy pursued by other means'.[20]

In the late 1950s, there was little support from the Muslim countries for the Tunku's proposal for a 'Muslim Commonwealth'. In Kuala Lumpur, the Malayan Foreign Office preferred 'a completely secular policy in which affective considerations like "Muslim brotherhood" would have no role'.[21] For most of the Tunku's term as Prime Minister, secular considerations did prevail. There was hardly any focus on the 'co-religionist strategy' that would acquire so much prominence under Prime Minister Mahathir. Tunku Abdul

Rahman appreciated that, given Malaya's diverse ethnic, cultural and religious composition, specific and over-riding alignments in foreign policy could prove untenable. He followed each issue on its merits, in keeping with Malaya's national interests. In 1957, speaking in parliament, the Tunku recognized that: 'there would be trouble (from the Malays) if we said anything about the West Irian question, there would be trouble (from the Indians) if we said anything against India and there would be trouble (from Muslims) if we said anything about Pakistan'.[22]

Malaysia supported India in its conflict with Pakistan in 1965. Pakistan broke off diplomatic relations with Malaysia in October 1965 after Malaysia's Permanent Representative at the UN in New York supported India on the issue of Kashmir. 'Despite domestic dissension over the issue and the Malay press's severe criticism of Malaysia's representative at the UN, the Tunku defended the Malaysian position through the observation that despite its status as a Muslim nation, Malaysia's international relations supersede all other considerations.'[23]

At this time, Malaysia was facing a serious existential challenge to its survival as a political entity as a result of its *konfrontasi* with Indonesia (1963-6) over the formation of Malaysia. The Philippines, too, opposed Sabah's merger with Malaysia. India firmly supported Malaysia's stand on the formation of Malaysia. As early as December 1961, just months after the idea of Malaysia had been initially brought out by Tunku Abdul Rahman, India conveyed acquiescence during the State visit of Tuanku Syed Putra. In his banquet speech on 8 December, the then vice-president of India, S. Radhakrishnan said that 'such a State will contribute to the stability of South Eastern Asia and we wish you success. . . .'[24] On 22 February 1963, Prime Minister Jawaharlal Nehru spoke in the Indian parliament (Lok Sabha) on this subject, when he said, in reply to a Calling Attention notice:

> It is proposed to form a Federation of Malaysia which would include Malaya, Singapore, Brunei, Sarawak and North Borneo. This matter was mentioned at the Commonwealth Prime Ministers' Conference which was held in September, 1962. We welcomed the idea of these dependent territories gaining their independence and sovereignty.

> There has been some trouble in Brunei recently, and strong opinions have been expressed for and against the formation of Malaysia.
>
> The Under Secretary of the United Nations has recently visited the area, and the United Nations Secretary-General is taking interest in this problem of orderly and peaceful transfer of power by the United Kingdom authorities. We trust that the efforts of the UN Secretary-General will be successful and the present tension will be removed.[25]

At the Algiers Non-Aligned Conference, in June 1965, India worked hard to ensure Malaysia's acceptance as a member of the Non-Aligned Movement, facing down strong opposition from Indonesia. This was in many ways a turning point for Malaysia, a moving away from her earlier foreign policy focus on relations with the West, a broadening of her foreign policy perspective to encompass the non-aligned nations. Malaysia realized the value of the diplomatic support that Indonesia had been receiving from important non-aligned and Islamic countries, including Egypt and Saudi Arabia. Pakistan, too, had supported Indonesia. Joining the Non-Aligned Movement provided Malaysia the much-needed platform for interacting with these countries, bilaterally and in multilateral fora.

This diversification in Malaysia's foreign policy priorities yielded rich dividends. The *konfrontasi* with Indonesia ended in 1966. Malaysia's diplomatic relations with Pakistan, too, were restored in the same year. Within UMNO, these moves were welcomed as they corresponded to the demands being made by several younger leaders for closer links with non-aligned and Islamic countries. Tunku Abdul Rahman successfully leveraged the growing acceptance of Malaysia among Islamic countries into strengthening Malay support for UMNO *vis-à-vis* PAS within Malaysia. Thus, when the Dewan Ulema (chamber of religious scholars) of PAS (Kelantan) issued a *fatwa* (religious ruling) prohibiting cooperation between Muslims and non-Muslims, and branded UMNO as infidel for doing so, UMNO retaliated by seeking the support of the World Muslim Congress, convened in Kuala Lumpur in 1969. This Congress openly criticized PAS and rejected the *fatwa*, maintaining that such cooperation was 'inevitable if not necessary . . . and was in fact permitted by Islam'.[26]

Side by side, the Tunku remained deeply committed to strengthening the wider process of regional and multi-regional cooperation. In his article in *Foreign Affairs*, Tunku Abdul Rahman described Malaysia as 'a practical working democracy', as a country that had 'made constructive efforts in regional cooperation' and had 'expressed the spirit of Bandung (*panchsheel* or five principles of peaceful coexistence) in the conduct of our foreign policy'.[27] The Tunku added that:

We are very conscious of brotherhood with the Afro-Asian nations. We feel at one with them in campaigning against colonialism, apartheid, disease, hunger and human misery. As far as apartheid is concerned, I have actively condemned this evil violation of human rights. Like our brothers in Afro-Asia we have always stressed the imperative need for a world where laws prevail against racial or religious discrimination. . . . Our special interest in economic progress and development of the region of Southeast Asia is particularly illustrated by the founding of the Association of Southeast Asia (ASA) which I first projected in Manila, in 1960. The founder members—the Philippines, Thailand and Malaya—established ASA in 1961 to promote economic, social and cultural cooperation.[28]

India's bilateral relations with Malaya continued to develop through trade, technical and economic cooperation, and collaboration in key infrastructure and human resource development sectors. Ministerial visits were frequent from both sides, and in October 1966, the then vice-president of India, Zakir Hussain visited Malaysia. Vice-President Zakir Hussain was unstinting in his words of praise for Malaysia's support for India in the 1962 Sino-Indian confrontation, and the 1965 confrontation with Pakistan. At the banquet hosted in his honour on 19 October by Malaysian Prime Minister Tunku Abdul Rahman, Zakir Hussain said:

'You have stood by us in our hour of need and we shall ever cherish that knowledge. The strong support given by you during our difficulties in 1962 and last year and the deep understanding of our problems shown by your Government have carved out a permanent place for Malaysia in the hearts of the people of India'.[29] The following day (at the luncheon hosted by him in honour of the Malaysian PM), Zakir Hussain added that 'your (Tunku Abdul Rahman's) name has become a household word in my country, as that of a true friend of the people of India'.

Each year saw a steady strengthening in the bilateral ties, culminating, in May-June 1968, with the visit to Malaysia by Prime Minister Indira Gandhi, where she was the honoured guest of Prime Minister Tunku Abdul Rahman. Indira Gandhi received a tumultuous welcome, full of warmth and friendship. She addressed a public rally in Kuala Lumpur on 31 May 1968, where she said:

> I have come here twice before with my father. I know what pride he felt at Malaysia's independence and joy at its progress . . . it is another forward step in the awakening and rejuvenation of this ancient continent which has played such an important part in world history. My heart is filled with deep emotion at the friendship which you have shown me since my arrival.
>
> Three great and ancient races have come together in Malaysia. Each has contributed something to the composite culture of this new nation and each in turn has been enriched by the sheltering care of a common citizenship. This is a great tribute to Malaysia, to its leaders and its people. Malaysia and India have traditionally been friends. A thousand years ago there was considerable movement and exchanges between our two countries; then a curtain fell between us. It is now lifted and the nations of Asia are rediscovering one another as kinsmen and neighbours.
>
> Malaysia is a young and dynamic nation which is justifiably proud of its many achievements. . . . They represent freedom, equality, justice, opportunity and enlightenment.
>
> . . . Malaysia and India illustrate mutual co-operation on a footing of equality and to the advantage of both countries. Malaysia and India have much in common. We are multi-racial, multi-lingual and multi-religious. We have been influenced by the impact of Islamic culture and have blended in a happy harmony with other streams to produce a composite culture—an Indian culture in our case and a Malaysian culture in yours. I am glad that all people who made this beautiful country their own are united in the endeavour to build it.[30]

The issues that Indira Gandhi had touched upon with such sensitivity in her address at the public rally were discussed between the two prime ministers as well. The Joint Communique issued on 1 June spelt this out as follows:

> Both Prime Ministers took the opportunity of exchanging views on the continuing efforts for social and economic development in their two countries in both of which people of varied origins and persuasions were living together in harmony. The Prime Minister of India was glad to note that the people of Indian origin in Malaysia, the bulk of whom have become responsible Malaysian citizens, were contributing their best to the progress and prosperity of their

country of adoption as loyal citizens. The Prime Minister of Malaysia expressed the appreciation of his Government at the Indian policy of encouraging people of Indian origin living abroad to identify themselves with the country of their adoption and domicile and to work for its development.[31]

The 'Tunku Era' can, in many ways, be described as the high-water mark of bilateral relations between Malaysia and India. There was complete confidence and trust among the leaders on both sides. There was frank and open appreciation of the historical interaction that had existed for millenia among the people of India and Malaysia. There was ready acceptance of the difficult socio-economic situation in each country, and the need to craft policies that recognized realities and led to social harmony. These long extracts from speeches, articles and joint communiqués between the leaders of Malay(si)a and India, covering the first twelve years of post-*Merdeka* Malaysia, highlight how much Malaysian leaders valued and cherished the pre-colonial interactions between Malaya and India, accepting this as an intrinsic part of contemporary Malaysia's cosmopolitanism, and valuing this contribution to Malaya's culture and language. They accepted the more recent Malaysian Indians as equal citizens, and valued their contribtion to the development of their country of adoption.

MALAYSIAN INDIANS IN POST-COLONIAL MALAYSIA: 13 MAY 1969 AND BEYOND

It is not surprising, then, that the 'Tunku Era' was one of largely fulfilled expectations for Malaysian Indians. During this period, substantial new opportunities came their way. In the words of Muzaffar Desmond Tate:

> This was particularly true for the well-placed few, especially among the professions where a good command of English was indispensable. This was also the case for Indians who in the early years of independence tended to predominate in the civil service, and for whom prospects of rapid promotion suddenly opened up. At the same time, unprecedented opportunities in commerce and business became available to enterprising lower middle-class entrepreneurs. Generally speaking, independence brought a marked increase in the prosperity of the upper and middle-class Indians. The only area in which their enterprise fell short was in their participation in the share market and in big business.

> In addition, for artisans, clerks and other members of the lower middle classes, especially those in the services sector, the early years of independence brought about some upward social mobility and a touch of prosperity, while along with a burgeoning national economy came wider job opportunities.
>
> It was these middle-class beneficiaries of independence who proved to be the mainstay of the MIC (Malayan Indian Congress). . . .[32]

The Tunku and the Alliance Government led by him, recognized the MIC as the sole legitimate representative of and spokesman for Malaysian Indians. This privilege accorded official recognition and formalized the status of Malaysian Indians as the third-largest group in the country after the Malays and the Chinese. This was a tremendous source of patronage for the MIC. Tun V.T. Sambanthan, the then president of the MIC, was made a cabinet minister right after the 1955 elections, a post he held for eighteen years until his retirement. After the 1964 elections, the deputy president of the MIC was also given the post of cabinet minister. Two Malaysian Indians as cabinet ministers was the high-water mark of recognition for the community as a whole.

As president of MIC, Sambanthan was successful in generating support for the party among plantation workers. For the first time large numbers of Tamil estate labourers enrolled as members of the MIC. Sambanthan supported their key interest by promoting Tamil language and culture, and ensuring that Tamil primary schools came up on all estates to cater to the needs of the workers. Among the most serious problems facing rural workers were those of landlessness and unemployment arising from fragmentation and sale of estates by foreign owners during the communist insurgency and in the immediate aftermath of Malayan independence. Initial schemes to settle Malayan Indian plantation workers as farmers of their own landholdings soon dried up. In 1960 the MIC, under Sambanthan's leadership, launched the NLFCS (National Land Finance Cooperative Society Ltd). The central idea was to make the plantation worker 'his own master with his own home by making him a co-owner on a cooperative basis of the estate on which he worked'.[33] With the support of the Alliance Government and the backing of the MIC, the scheme got off to a good start. The NLFCS purchased its first estate in August 1961, and by 1985 owned 12 estates, becoming 'the largest enterprise ever owned by Malaysian labour'.[34] The NLFCS still remains among the largest enterprises ever owned by Malaysian Indians.

Unfortunately, the impact of these developments, including the rapid improvements in the prosperity of urban areas, did not touch the lives of the vast majority of Malaysian Indians working on the plantations and in the estates. Primarily, the severe adversities for Malaysian Indians created by the fragmentation and sub-division of the estates, remained unaddressed. The three-volume Report prepared in 1963 by the government-appointed committee headed by Professor Ungku Abdul Aziz (University of Malaya, Department of Economics)

> came out strongly in favour of immediate government measures to prevent the further subdivision of estates and for action to protect the interests and well-being of the plantation workers directly affected. It refuted the theory that fragmentation of the estates was good for the national economy. To the contrary, it showed that instead of creating a sturdy new breed of Malay(si)an smallholders, it was creating a new class of absentee landlords and urban investors who had no concern for the estate workers and were in effect driving them into destitution. The report also pointed out that, as a result of fragmentation, a wide range of social amenities which had been supported by the former estates were now no longer properly maintained, including estate quarters, health facilities, schools and recreational amenities, causing an inevitable and perceptible decline in living standards.[35]

The Aziz Report recommended strong legislation to stop any further fragmentation of the estates, combined with a government rehabilitation programme to assist the impoverished estate workers who had been retrenched without any reasonable compensation. The government committee endorsed this report. However, the Alliance Government led by Tunku Abdul Rahman, giving in to intense pressure from the European and Chinese representatives of the plantation industry, declined to act upon the recommendations contained in the Aziz Report. This left plantation labour almost exactly where they were before *Merdeka*: entirely at the mercy of plantation owners, absentee or present.

Between 1950 and 1967, about 3,24,931 acres, representing 18 per cent of the total estate acreage in Malaya/Malaysia, were subdivided for sale to mainly Asian owners.[36] The total employment of Indians on rubber-estates fell from 1,48,500 in 1950 to 79,800 in 1971, a fall of 46.2 per cent.[37] The primarily Tamil-speaking estate labourers, now declared redundant, found it almost impossible to find fresh employment because of language difficulties and the paucity of industrial enterprises run by Malaysian Indians. The adherence to Tamil schools on the estates even after the rest of the country had moved on to Malay medium instruction contributed to the plight of these estate labourers and their families. They are unemployable, and, pushed off the estates, had few options other than moving to ghettoes in urban slums and squatter colonies, socially ostracized and separate from the rest of Malaysian society. A scholar's comment on Tamil schools in Malaysia, written in the late 1960s, remains as applicable to the 1930s as it does to the condition of many rural Tamil schools in Malaysia today:

> The remoteness of these single-teacher plantation schools, the absence of post-primary Tamil education, and the lack of opportunity for other than labouring employment, makes education a basically aimless endeavour where only a low level of literacy in the vernacular is achieved.[38]

Merdeka had brought little or no change to the lives of Malaysian Indians working on plantations and living in rural areas. This group remained at the lowest rung of society, beset by poverty, and economic and social deprivation. Tamil became the *lingua franca* of the MIC, but there was deep disappointment, even protests, over the decision to make Malay the sole official language. The majority of Malaysian Indians were strongly in favour of Tamil (and Chinese and English) being declared official languages, alongside Malay as the national language. There was great disenchantment with the MIC over its inability to ensure this, despite its status as one of the three major communal parties. Indeed, 'as much after *Merdeka* as before it, a significant number of Indians found MIC's conversion to communal politics quite unacceptable and refused to be part of it'.[39]

Politically conscious Malay(si)an Indians joined the PMLP (Pan-Malayan Labour Party, the multi-racial political platform for moderate labour leaders), the Perak-based multi-racial PPP (People's Progressive Party, started by the Seenivasagam brothers) and even the Singapore based multi-racial PAP (People's Action Party, which opened branches in Malaysia after 1963, and after

1965, stayed on as the DAP—Democratic Action Party). Despite the MIC's status as the officially recognized voice of Malaysian Indians, despite the tremendous privilege and patronage that this recognition brought with it, 'the MIC never enjoyed the support at any one time of even half the Indians domiciled in Malay(si)a'.[40]

This brings us to the racial riots of 13 May 1969. It has been said that 'the traumatic ethnic riots of 13 May 1969 in Malaysia remain as much a subject of official censorship as the events of 4 June 1989 in China'.[41] Thirty-eight years after the 13 May incident, a Malaysian Chinese academician, Kua Kia Soong, published his assessment, titled *Declassified Documents on the Malaysian Riots of 1969*, based on now-open British documents held at the Public Records Office in Kew Gardens, near London. These documents comprise British diplomatic and intelligence reports of the time 'which suggest that the riots were not spontaneous acts of communal violence, as is constantly alleged by UMNO, but were fanned by Malay elements, with support from the army and police, wanting to discredit the accommodating prime minister and impose a much more rigorous Malay agenda. One British document concluded that the goal was to 'formalise Malay dominance, sideline the Chinese and shelve Tunku'.[42] Another respected Malaysian academic, Syed Husin Ali is quoted as accepting that 'some UMNO figures used the events as an opportunity to sideline the Tunku and set out a pro-Malay agenda', even though he feels that the event 'was not planned as such'.[43]

Ethnic clashes took place in Kuala Lumpur on 13 May 1969, after the general election (10 May) results showed that the ruling Alliance Party had lost its two-thirds majority, while retaining a simple parliamentary majority. The Alliance Party had also lost the states of Penang and Kelantan respectively to the Gerakan Party and to PAS, and was in danger of losing the states of Perak and Selangor as well. The clashes started during 'victory parades' held by the opposition parties, who had received the required permission from the authorities for holding these parades. In an interview granted by the Tunku in Penang in 1972, to Malaysian journalist Raja Petra Kamarudin,[44] the Tunku said:

> . . . when the opposition parties applied for a police permit for a procession to celebrate their success in the results of the general election, I was adamant

against it because the police were convinced that this would lead to trouble. . . . Now, without my knowledge and actually 'behind my back', there were certain political leaders in high positions who were working to force me to step down as PM. . . .

Unfortunately, they were apparently scheming and trying to decide on the best way to force me to resign. The occasion came when the question of the police permit was to be approved . . . when I was in my home in Kedah, I heard over the radio that the permit had been approved.

It seems as if the expected trouble had been anticipated and planned for by Harun and his UMNO Youth. After the humiliating insults hurled by the non-Malays, especially the Chinese, and after the seeming loss of Malay political power to them, they were clearly ready for some retaliatory action.

. . . it really pains me as the Father of Merdeka to have to relive those terrible moments. I have often wondered why God made me live long enough to have witnessed my beloved Malays and Chinese citizens killing each other.[45]

The events of 13 May 1969, continue to reverbrate in the psyche of all those who live in Malaysia today. Parliament was suspended and a national emergency was declared, which remained in force till 1971. An affirmative action programme, the NEP (New Economic Policy) was brought in with the officially declared objective of promoting national unity by eradicating poverty and restructuring Malaysian society. Employment opportunities were to be increased for all Malaysians irrespective of race. Economic imbalances were to be corrected, together with the reduction and eventual elimination of the identification of race with economic function. The specified targets, to be achieved by 1990, included a reduction of the foreign stake in the national economy (to be halved from the 1970 level of 60 per cent), and an increase in the Malay stake 'such that the Malays and other indigenous groups would own and manage at least 30 per cent of the total commercial and industrial activities of the economy in all categories and scales of operation'.[46] The non-Malay Malaysians would benefit by the anticipated rapid increase in economic growth and development of all sectors, which would ensure that there would be no decline in prosperity and well-being for any group.

In reality, however, the impact of the 13 May clashes together with the manner of implementation of the NEP proved to be traumatic for Malaysian Indians, particularly those working on the estates and living in rural areas. 'The NEP was not successful in eradicating poverty in the plantation sector between 1970 and 1990. Because of this failure, the majority of plantation workers, many of whom were Indians, were left out of the mainstream of development'.[47] The State (National Operations Council, NOC, headed by Tun Abdul Razak) now decided to resolve the problem of Malay rural unemployment on a priority basis. In order to achieve this the NOC, in June 1969, extended the application of the work permit system for foreigners that had been introduced under the Employment Restriction Act (1968), to the commercial plantation sector.

This should not have created a problem for Malaysian Indians since they had been living and working on these plantations for decades, and as such, they were eligible for Malaysian citizenship. It was discovered, however, that as many as 80 per cent of those affected by the new regulations were eligible for citizenship, but had failed to apply or receive citizenship, for reasons of remoteness, illiteracy, errors in particulars on documents, lack of marriage certificates, bureaucratic obstruction, or failure to understand the importance of citizenship.[48] The state was unwilling to help. The MIC and the NUPW (National Union of Plantation Workers) bore the brunt of the criticism over their inability and ineffectiveness in helping plantation labourers securing the citizenship for which they were eligible.

As a result, there was enormous disruption on the estates, and 'approximately 60,000 Indians returned to India in fear and uncertainty'.[49] However, since very few Malays came forward to take up the estate jobs that were now available, a large number of Malaysian Indian non-citizens stayed behind on the plantations. They did not receive citizenship, but neither were they sent away. Their work-contribution was sorely needed, and so they continued with temporary permits or without permits. They were now even more isolated and unable to resist exploitative practices. They could no longer be members of trade unions, nor could they vote. They lost mobility and bargaining power. Those without permits were forced into illegal casual employment with very poor remuneration.

As the estates were sub-divided and sold out, erstwhile plantation labourers (legal and illegal residents) gradually moved to urban and semi-urban areas, living in squatter colonies where crime, alcoholism and allied misdemeanours were (and still are) the highest in the country. The Tamil-only schools on the estates meant that these labourers knew no other language, which further isolated them from the rest of society. The decision to retain Tamil as the only medium of instruction in the estate school system even after 1970, when the former English medium schools were obliged to teach in Malay, may have pleased the Tamil cultural nationalists, but it also reinforced communal compartmentalization and prevented integration into a society that would be Malaysian in all aspects. K.A. Neelakandha Aiyer, writing in 1938, accurately foretold what would befall the landless, non-citizen, Malaysian Indian labourers when he said:

> They will form a floating population in the towns occupying lowly positions. . . . This is the general fate of an indigent wage-earning class—a landless proletariat. . . . The stragglers who remain behind in Malaya become the tragic orphans—whom India has well-nigh forgotten and Malaya looks down upon with contempt—as worthless dregs in a prosperous society.[50]

India's leadership was deeply shocked and disturbed by the events of 13 May 1969. Pandit Jawaharlal Nehru had been prescient in anticipating (in 1946) that there could be trouble between the Malays and the Chinese. However, Pandit Nehru could not have envisaged the aftermath of the 13 May race riots, the politicization and manipulation that seems to have mutated the very spirit of *Merdeka,* from equality to superiority and supremacy.

India was careful and measured in its response to the 13 May events. The media and the public were distressed and deeply concerned. The Government of India's response came through a statement made in parliament (Rajya Sabha) on 17 May 1969, by the minister of external affairs, Dinesh Singh, where he said:

> The Government of India are closely watching the current developments in Malaysia. . . . We are sorry that such racial tension should build up in a friendly country which has endeavoured to establish a multi-racial society. Our High Commission in Kuala Lumpur has been in touch with the Malaysian Foreign Office and understands that no Indian nationals have been involved in the recent disturbances. . . . We have every sympathy with the Government and people of Malaysia and are confident that they will be able to resolve their present difficulties and restore racial harmony.[51]

On the face it, little had changed in Malaysia-India relations. There was, however, an undeniable change in atmospherics in the bilateral relationship after 13 May, especially after Prime Minister Tunku Abdul Rahman stepped down. The circumstances under which he was forced to step down made it clear that from then on, race and religion would be increasingly important cards for UMNO. Public opinion in India was, frankly speaking, disenchanted. The Government of India continued its earlier efforts to help the people of Malaysia through economic, trade and investment collaborations and through cooperation in infrastructure and human resource development. Exchanges of high-level visits continued in the 1970s, but slowed down thereafter. For twenty-two years (Indira Gandhi had visited Malaysia in 1968), no Indian prime minister visited Malaysia, till the jinx was broken with Prime Minister V.P. Singh's visit to Kuala Lumpur in 1990. From the Malaysian side, too, there was no return prime ministerial visit (after Indira Gandhi's visit in 1968) for eleven years, till Dato (later Tun) Hussein Onn visited Delhi in January 1979.

It was in the mid-1960s that, after intense negotiations, the UN adopted CERD (Convention on the Elimination on all forms of Racial Discrimination) through the UN General Assembly resolution of December 1965. The Convention came into force in 1969. Malaysia is one of the few countries that has not ratified or accepted this Convention.

BILATERAL VISITS IN THE 1970s

In the 1970s, the most prominent visits were the three exchanged between Malaysia and India at the level of Head of State. In March 1973 President V.V. Giri visited Kuala Lumpur, where he was hosted by the Yang di-Pertuan Agong, Tuanku Abdul Halim, Sultan of Kedah. In December 1974, Tuanku Abdul Halim visited India on a State visit as the guest of President Fakhruddin Ali Ahmed. And in February 1977, President Fakhruddin Ali Ahmed visited Malaysia as the guest of the Yang di-Pertuan Agong, Sultan Yahya Petra of Kelantan. Since 1977, for thirty-five years now, there has been no return visit to India by the Yang di-Pertuan Agong of Malaysia, and as a result, no further exchanges at this level.

It does seem that after the mid-1970s, the warmth and affection that had characterized the bilateral relationship in the years when Tunku Abdul Rahman was at the helm of affairs, now began to wane. An early indicator of this was the changed tenor of the references by Malaysian leaders to the historical links between India and Malaysia.

This change came about gradually. In 1973 and 1974, Tuanku Abdul Halim's public statements in Kuala Lumpur and in Delhi were still full of warmth and special appreciation for the traditional links between the two nations. On 5 March 1973, at the banquet hosted in Kuala Lumpur by Tuanku to welcome the president of India, Tuanku said:

> . . . Your Excellency's presence among us tonight is one of a series of frequent exchanges of visits by the people and leaders of our two countries, visits which go far back into a history of some 1000 years and more. There are many stories of our earlier contacts, some of which have been handed from generation to generation by word of mouth and have become legendary. This is particularly so in my own home state of Kedah. Archaeological traces of these earlier contacts such as the shrines and the other relics of Buddhist and Hindu settlements in the Merbok Estuary in Kedah and the discovery of Sanskrit inscriptions in certain parts of Penang are now considered by scholars to reach well back to the fourth century AD or at least seventh century AD. What these archaeological finds have borne witness to is the fact that in Malaysia, India can find a hidden treasure of some of India's earlier civilization and India's earliest contacts with countries in Southeast Asia. . . . As the late Shri Jawaharlal Nehru, India's beloved Prime Minister once said, India is a close friend who is almost a relation to Malaysia.[52]

Two days later, on 7 March 1973, speaking at the return banquet hosted by President V.V. Giri, Tuanku Abdul Halim referred to the multi-racial composition of Malaysia, adding:

> (Your Excellency) would have also noticed the contribution which our people of Indian origin have made and are making to the progress of this country. Nature has bestowed upon Malaysia enough of its bounties so that there is sufficient opportunity for everyone to seek his own place under the sun, and at the same time to make his contribution to the country's development. Diversity in race and culture has never retarded our progress. Indeed Malaysia's diversity is a source, not of weakness, but of strength and richness, of which we are proud. The correct and positive stand which the Indian government has taken with regard to the people who are of Indian origin in Malaysia, scrupulously

adhering to the principle of non-interference in the internal affairs of other states, is one which we very much appreciate.[53]

This was perhaps the first public acknowledgement and appreciation by the Malaysian leadership of India's quiet, non-aggressive diplomacy after the 13 May racial riots. It is not that India was not concerned. Rather, under the circumstances, India preferred to express these concerns in an understated manner. President Giri in his welcoming speech at this banquet had said:

> Malaysia will not find India wanting to the extent that it is within our capacity, to be of assistance to your people in developing and consolidating their national strength and prosperity. The fact that we each have problems of our own is primarily an indication of our growth and of the process of modernization in our countries. I am confident that in this process, our peoples will always retain their cherished values of tolerance for diversity, respect for human dignity and the brotherhood of man.[54]

However, by February 1977, when President Fakhruddin Ali Ahmed visited Malaysia as the guest of Sultan Yahya Putra of Kelantan, the emphasis on the historical links between Malaysia and India had been toned down considerably. This aspect received only a passing mention in the Sultan's banquet speech on 6 February. Concerns about race-relations retained high priority, and the Sultan said:

> All the development programmes implemented by the government . . . have been aimed at strengthening the unity among our multi-racial society. We are happy to state (that) those people who have come from India to make this country their home, have also contributed towards the objective of the country in achieving unity, prosperity and peace.
>
> . . . we realise that no country can exist on its own. We are dependent on one another. India and Malaysia have long taken the proper initiatives towards maintaining these bilateral relations.[55]

At the same banquet, President Fakhruddin Ali Ahmed, too, had the impoverished Malaysian Indians in mind when he said, after expressing admiration for 'the tremendous economic advance Malaysia has made since independence', that: 'We have also noted that among the principle objectives of the III-Malaysia Plan is the eradication of all disparities and the equitable distribution of national wealth.'[56]

Indian leaders continued to articulate their concerns. In March 1978, Malaysian foreign minister Tengku Ahmad Rithauddeen visited Delhi at the invitation of the then foreign minister, Atal Behari Vajpayee. In his formal dinner speech, the Indian foreign minister said:

> We wish you every success in the implementation of your current Plan whose principal aim, I understand, is not only eradication of poverty but the elimination of disparities, social and regional. . . . Tolerance and secular approach come naturally to your people and it is not surprising that they underly your national policies. They also serve to reassure all of us that in this world of ours, often rocked by pride and prejudice, where vestiges of religious discrimination still haunt us, brotherhood of man will ultimately prevail.[57]

The highlight of Malaysia-India relations in the 1970s was the visit of Malaysia's third Prime Minister Dato (later Tun) Hussein bin Onn in January 1979. This visit, only the second visit by a Malaysian prime minister to India, was taking place seventeen years after the visit by Tunku Abdul Rahman. By this time, the language of Malaysian-Indian relations had changed. The focus on historical links and the contribution of Malaysian Indians had been dispensed with. The relationship was now more fact-oriented rather than emotional bonding. So much so that even the memory of earlier interactions had (and has) become a matter of conjecture and doubt, rather than history.

Dato Hussein bin Onn made sincere and touching references to his stay in India at an important formative stage of his career. He was among the last Malaysian leaders to bring in such warmth and candour on the shared contemporary experiences of Malaysia and India. Dato Hussein bin Onn spoke about his experiences first as a cadet at the IMA in Dehradun, and subsequently as a commissioned officer of the Indian Army. Speaking at the banquet hosted in his honour by Indian Prime Minister Morarji Desai, Dato Hussein bin Onn said:

> It was at the Indian Military Academy in Dehradun at the end of 1941 that I learned to be a soldier. I was only 20 years old then. What had been taught to me at the Academy had made a lasting impression on me. It has been a constant guide and inspiration in my later life. It not only taught me military service but what is more important, it had taught me the art and quality of leadership, loyalty to one's country and responsibility for the welfare and

well-being of those who have given their trust in you. I consider it a great honour to have known some of India's great sons. General Shrinagesh was my Company Commander at the Indian Military Academy; General Thimayya was my Second-in-Command at Agra, and General Raina and I were in the same company and battalion. If I remember with nostalgia my association with the Indian Army, I am proud of it . . . I greatly look forward to a reunion with my old regiment. . . .[58]

Dato Hussein bin Onn did not hesitate in adding that:

India and Malaysia have many things in common . . . both believe in and practice Parliamentary Democracy; many of the provisions of the Malaysian constitution are borrowed from the Indian constitution. The Malaysian Penal Code, Criminal Procedure Code and the Law of Evidence, and the Laws of Contract and Specific Performance are based on the Indian ones. The decisions of the Indian Supreme Court, Courts of Appeal and High Courts still have persuasive authority and in some cases are followed by the Malaysian Courts.[59]

During the 1970s, India's efforts were focused on developing all-round political, economic and cultural relations with Malaysia. In the aftermath of the 13 May racial riots, and in the face of the serious socio-economic difficulties confronting the vast majority of Malaysian Indians, India's best hope was that this group, too, would benefit from any strong upswing in the bilateral relationship. During this decade as many as forty Indo-Malaysian joint ventures were established. In February 1973, after the visit of Tan Sri Ghazali Shafie, Malaysian minister of information to India, cooperation in exchange of news and TV programmes was initiated. In October 1976, India and Malaysia signed a Double Taxation Avoidance Agreement. Regular annual bilateral talks at the foreign secretary level were held, a practice initiated after the visit by Indian foreign minister M.C. Chagla to Kuala Lumpur in May 1967. This greatly facilitated coordination of positions and cooperation in various multilateral forums, including the Non-Aligned Movement, the Commonwealth, the UN and its agencies like UNCTAD and the Commission on Disarmanent. In March 1978, the first Cultural Agreement between Malaysia and India was signed, covering exchanges in the diverse fields of education and research, science and technology, mass media, sports and youth activities. All this culminated, during the visit to India in January 1979, by Dato' Hussein Onn, in the signing of an Economic and

Technical Cooperation Agreement and an Extradition Agreement between the two countries.

These were all unexceptionable and well-intentioned agreements. Unfortunately, however, implementation remained poor. Almost seven years after Dato Hussein Onn's visit, when Malaysian foreign minister Tengku Ahmad Rithauddeen came to India in October 1987, he accepted as much, when he said:

> . . . if in recent times, we have been less close than we might have been, we have all the more reason today to rededicate ourselves to building relations that are closer and firmer than have ever been. The foundations on which our historic relations have been built remain essentially the same. They have not been altered by developments in which our respective perceptions were divergent. Political, economic and even strategic imperatives thrust the regions of South and South-East Asia together, even in spite of ourselves. Therefore, on behalf of my Government, permit me to say that we wish to work together with you to effect the soundest possible relations between our contiguous regions.
>
> . . . our bilateral relations have particularly significant economic aspects. Malaysia is appreciative of the market India has provided for our palm oil, rubber and other commodities. I am very much aware, however, that the present state of our trade relations leaves much to be desired, characterised as it is by a lop-sided imbalance. We are addressing ourselves seriously to correct this unhealthy imbalance in our trading relations. We shall demonstrate indeed, our resolve to establish a mutually beneficial and equitable trading relationship that will stand the test of time.[60]

THE MAHATHIR YEARS

By the late 1980s, in the Mahathir era, Malaysia's foreign policy had evolved enormously from the days of Tunku Abdul Rahman. The Tunku's approach was broad-based, considering each issue on its own merits. He did not want any decision to be seen as specific to just one race or religion. The 13 May 1969 race riots changed all that. In August the same year, the burning of the Al Aqsa Mosque in Jerusalem, one of Islam's holiest sites, led to international outrage. This became the immediate cause for convening the first International Islamic Summit in Rabat (Morocco) in September 1969. Malaysia participated in this Summit. The following month, speaking in the UN General Assembly in October 1969, the Tunku's speech 'certainly gave the impression that Islam was of great significance in Malaysia's foreign policy. . . . The convergence and challenge of international, regional and domestic uncertainties and crises for the first Malay(si)an Administration had, by 1969, indicated the need for a clear shift in foreign policy thinking.'[61] The intra-UMNO pressures for a more Malay-nationalist agenda *ipso facto* led to the Islamization of Malaysian foreign policy, given the central role of religion (Islam) in the Malay identity.

After stepping down as prime minister of Malaysia, the Tunku assumed office as the first secretary general of the OIC (Organisation of the Islamic Conference). Tunku Abdul Rahman perceived the OIC as an institution established 'to complement and not to substitute other fora of international co-operation', functioning as 'a commonwealth of Muslim nations dealing with political matters rather than as a religious body'.[62] Malaysia signed the Islamic Charter of the OIC in 1972. Malaysia's early involvement with the OIC served two objectives. At the national level, this highlighted 'how far Islam in Malaysian foreign policy has been employed towards a domestic political function';[63] and at the international level, it illustrated Malaysia's larger foreign policy strategy of increased and active participation in a broad spectrum of multilateral organizations.

Tun Abdul Razak, Malaysia's second prime minister, accorded high significance to Malaysia's relationship with its neighbours, and to its membership of the Non-Aligned Movement. It was under his stewardship that Malaysia established diplomatic relations with the People's Republic of China in 1974. The same year, Malaysia hosted the Fifth Islamic Conference (OIC Summit), where the prime minister emphasized the importance of 'promoting Islam as a religion of modernization and progress' and the need for 'the evolution of a new system of Islamic education'.[64] Malaysia was among the principal beneficiaries of IDB (Islamic Development Bank) funding and projects. Overall, for Tun Abdul Razak, 'concurrent with the desire to improve Islamic credentials, concern lay with a more even-handed approach. Indeed, in the prime minister's scheme of things, Malaysia's Muslim identity ranked as only a fifth priority in foreign policy, well behind its character as both a Commonwealth and non-aligned nation.'[65]

The first priority, indeed the cornerstone of Malaysia's foreign and security policies, was its membership of ASEAN, and its desire to scrupulously follow the tenets of ASEAN while developing its relations with fellow-members. Malaysia held firm on this under its third prime minister, Tun Hussein Onn. In 1978, Malaysia hosted the second ASEAN Summit in Kuala Lumpur, where the Government was successful in bringing into the Kuala Lumpur Declaration the concept of a Zone of Peace, Freedom and Neutrality in Southeast Asia. Tun Hussein Onn gave great importance to maintaining peace and stability along Malaysia's borders, and good relations with its neighbours, balancing this against mounting pressures (within Malaysia, particularly by PAS) for support to several minority Muslim groups in these countries.

PAS, the Parti Islam Se-Malaysia, earlier known by its English title, the Pan-Malaysian Islamic Party, was a member of the ruling coalition, the Barisan Nasional (BN) from 1973 to 1978. PAS was vociferous in demanding support for minority Muslim populations in neighbouring Thailand and the Philippines, as well as for Islamic causes globally. Tun Hussein Onn resisted the first but developed Malaysia's political, economic, trade and investment links with OIC member countries. 'Leadership, training and attitude of the (first) three Prime Ministers and of the foreign policy elite partly explain this trend, but UMNO's nationalist philosophy above all else meant that if any ideology played a dominant part, it was that of non-alignment.'[66]

All this changed in the early 1980s, after Dato' (now Tun) Dr Mahathir bin Mohamad assumed the prime ministership of Malaysia (July 1981). The parting of the ways between PAS and BN meant that the Malay vote was now split. This key factor played a major role in the Islamization of Malaysia's foreign and national policies. In his struggle to attract the Malay vote away from PAS, Mahathir tried to 'out-Islamise' PAS. The jury is still out on the extent to which Mahathir succeeded in this strategy. What is inescapable is that the efforts to implement policies that would 'out-Islamize PAS' have brought in race and religion as predominant factors affecting every aspect of life in Malaysia. 'The Islamization policy was officially launched in 1983', focused on the need 'to convince the electorate that only UMNO was capable of being both Islamic and moderate without infringing the rights of the non-Muslim communities'.[67] In Malaysia, under Mahathir:

> Islam has constituted a powerful weapon in the struggle for political supremacy. In the face of intensive intra-Malay rivalry, Islam has been used by the Mahathir Administration as a continuing source of political legitimacy and as a shield against external interference in Malay politics. The fear of the emasculation of Malay power through political divisions within the community, in part explains the special concern of Malaysian leaders over the theme of 'unity'.[68]

The most immediate impact of this new focus on the Malay vote within Malaysia was that Mahathir:

> rapidly initiated and articulated a redesign of Malaysian foreign policy priorities, announcing a formal ranking of relations in the order of: (1) ASEAN; (2) Islamic countries; (3) the non-aligned community; and (4) the Commonwealth . . . Malaysia increasingly (but selectively) sought to identify itself with international Muslim issues and as an activist member of the global Islamic community. Both Government and UMNO rhetoric increasingly referred to Malaysia as an Islamic nation and to UMNO itself as the third largest Islamic party in the world.[69]

Within Malaysia, despite fluctuating electoral fortunes, PAS 'always won between 30 per cent and 50 per cent of the Malay vote'.[70] As a result, PAS remained, for UMNO, a challenge and a major irritant. PAS captured two states, Kelantan and Trengganu, in 1959 in the very first post-independence general election. Decades later, when PAS once again ruled Trengganu from 1999 to 2004, 'Trengganu's PAS government forced through unconstitutional legislation adopting *hudud*', and 'went further by providing for the execution of apostates'.[71] Instead of resisting and opposing this trend on constitutional grounds:

> Prodded by the Dr Mahathir-directed federal government, UMNO-ruled states began passing Islamic laws that were almost as harsh. Thus was 'moderate Malaysia' subjected to an ever-escalating 'Islamic policy auction', with mounting implications. From April 2000, various National Front-controlled state legislatures began considering their own laws to stop Muslims from straying religiously. Perlis adopted legislation, prepared in the Prime Minister's Department, which allowed the state's religious authorities to take criminal proceedings against Muslims accused of heresy, deviation or other 'crimes' related to their beliefs. . . . At a special meeting (in Johor), UMNO agreed to introduce full Islamic law, including *hudud*, in the state at an appropriate time.[72]

Prime Minister Mahathir's pronouncements on Malaysia and Islam culminated in September 2001. Just two weeks after he had declared 'all-out support for the United States in the "war on terror"'[73] following the 9/11 destruction of the twin towers at the World Trade Centre in New York, on 29 September 2001, perhaps in a bid to outflank PAS tactically, Mahathir declared Malaysia an 'Islamic State'. He had used this description before, but this time 'he made the announcement at a meeting of *Parti Gerakan Rakyat* Malaysia, an UMNO coalition partner, and called a gathering of all National Front (*Barisan Nasional*) members to endorse the move. He later told parliament that Malaysia was a 'fundamentalist Islamic State'.

Although Mahathir claimed that the leaders of the coalition component parties were 'comfortable' with his concept, his declaration caused an uproar throughout the country, which the mainstream press consciously ignored. Much of the concern was expressed in closed-door meetings or anonymously on the Internet. Senior government officials insisted it was a matter of semantics, that nothing had changed in terms of policy or law, and nor would there be any change. In reality, Mahathir's announcement increased UMNO-PAS friction and made life more problematic for Buddhists, Hindus, Christians, Sikhs and other religious minorities, comprising 40 per cent of the population. The Information Department distributed a booklet, *Malaysia is an Islamic State*, giving four supporting definitions by *ulama*, which the government mistakenly assumed would end the debate. Instead, the publication inflamed the situation by clearly relegating non-Muslims to a secondary position, and eventually was withdrawn.[74]

Mahathir was so absorbed in and involved with Malay politics that he considered the Indian origins of his family to be an unnecessary distraction. Throughout his political career, he claimed a lack of knowledge about his family's Indian origins, which allowed him to maintain a studious silence on this subject. However, neither did he issue a denial when Professor Suresh Narayanan (*Universiti Sains Malaysia*) said the following:

> The list of famous Malabaris . . . cannot be complete without the mention of one Iskandar, who was of Kerala Muslim descent. His son, Mohammed Iskandar, was born of a Malay woman (Siti Hawa). Mohammed Iskandar

eventually left Penang to settle in Kedah, and subsequently acquired fame as an English teacher and as the first headmaster of Alor Star's first English School (now known as Maktab Sultan Abdul Samad). Mohammad Iskandar married a Malay, Wan Tampawan, and the union produced nine children. The youngest, Mahathir bin Mohammad Iskandar, rose to become the fourth Prime Minister of Malaysia.[75]

Mahathir's determined reticence in accepting the Indian origins of his family certainly impacted Malaysia's relations with India during his (Mahathir's) twenty-two year-long prime ministerial tenure. The very special characteristic in Malaysia India relations during the first quarter-century of Malay(si)a's independence had been the effort to carry forward, with understanding and appreciation, the traditional pre-colonial interaction and friendship between the people of both countries. Under Mahathir, what developed was a fairly active and business-like relationship between Malaysia and India, with very little warmth and affection to support and nurture it to its full potential. It is diffiult not to surmise that Mahathir's reluctance to publicly acknowledge his Indian heritage held him back from pushing the bilateral relationship with India more vigorously.

MALAYSIAN INDIANS AND MAHATHIR'S VISION 2020

Mahathir led Malaysia into a period of unprecedented economic development, growth and prosperity. The thirty-year national development blueprint he launched in 1991, popularly known as Mahathir's Vision 2020 project, was indeed a bold and visionary statement, aimed at achieving developed nation status for his country over a period of three decades. Vision 2020 instilled hope and confidence in all citizens, regardless of race or economic status.

Through this blueprint, Mahathir promised his people equity and equitable development, saying that Malaysia would seek development not only in the economic sense, but would seek to be 'fully developed in terms of national unity and social cohesion, in terms of our economy, in terms of social justice, political stability, system of government, quality of life, social and spiritual values, national pride and confidence'.[76] Mahathir emphasized the need for 'establishing a matured, liberal and tolerant society in which Malaysians of all colours and creeds are free to practise and profess their customs, cultures and religious beliefs and yet feel that they belong to one nation'.[77] Mahathir called for 'ensuring an economically just society . . . in which there is a fair and equitable distribution of the wealth of the nation. . . . Such a society cannot be in place so long as there is the identification of race with economic function, and the identification of economic backwardness with race.'[78]

Mahathir's Vision 2020 generated tremendous optimism among Malaysian Indians, who were, by this time (1991), thoroughly disappointed with the implementation of the NEP (New Economic Policy). In the words of the scholar S. Nagarajan:

> . . . the Malay supremacy agenda and ethnic preference policies implemented vigorously from 1971, had a great impact on all strata of the Indian community, though the scale and intensity varied according to the class position of the sub-groups. The New Economic Policy (NEP) and subsequent government development plans emphasised poverty eradication irrespective of ethnicity and the restructuring of society to eliminate the identification of economic functions with ethnic groups as their main goals. In practice, however, restructuring became a one-way process. The government focused on eradicating rural Malay poverty and creating a new Malay capitalist class.[79]

After 1971, the Malaysian Indian share in the administrative services and in other professional, technical and skilled employment had declined substantially. 'The civil service became ethnicized and deeply pro-Malay in implementing policies and dispensing state benefits. Non-Malay citizens often complain that the lower ranking Malay civil servants practise "racial discrimination" in the way they discharge their duties *vis-à-vis* the non-Malays.'[80] The electoral voting process also favoured the Malays. 'Gerrymandering through a "rural weightage" provision has ensured that a rural Malay vote is equivalent to three urban non-Malay votes.'[81]

Unfortunately, the hopes raised by Mahathir's Vision 2020 were soon dashed, at least for Malaysian Indians.

> Paradoxically, the socio-economic situation of Indian Malaysians deteriorated during this period (post-1991) with many in the community increasingly feeling angry, neglected and victimized. . . . Academic and journalistic writings began to refer to the Indians as the 'disenfranchised', the 'marginalized', the

'new underclass' or the 'forgotten community' in Malaysia and the popular media began to stereotype them as violent criminals and gangsters.[82]

Official statistics, including the Ninth Malaysia Plan 2006-10 (published in 2006) show that Malaysian Indians are better off than *bumiputeras,* both in terms of mean monthly gross household incomes and in terms of percentage living below the official poverty line. Malaysian Indians contest these figures, including on the grounds that the *bumiputera* group includes Malays and non-Malays (from Sabah and Sarawak).[83]

What is indisputable is that, among Malaysian Indians, the rapid pace of displacement leading to forced migration from rural to urban areas continued unabated throughout the three decades from 1970 to 2000, an intensification of the similar trend between 1957 and 1971. In 1970, less than 35 per cent of Malaysian Indians lived in urban areas. In 2000, this figure had more than doubled to almost 80 per cent, or 1.34 million in absolute numbers.[84] This may have been an unavoidable consequence of Malaysia's economic transformation, but despite the much-hyped NEP and Vision 2020 'the plight of these displaced people never received serious attention in the national decision-making process and government development plans'.[85] The vast majority of Malaysian Indians, lacking education, skills or any financial support, became slum dwellers in squatter settlements in and around Kuala Lumpur, alienated and marginalized. In addition to economic deprivation there is, among most Malaysian Indians, the mounting 'sense of outrage' over 'cultural and religious marginalization', a very sensitive and contentious issue since this is 'linked to the divisive thoughts of *Ketuanan Melayu* (Malay dominance) and *Ketuanan Islam* (Islamic supremacy)'.[86] In the ultimate analysis, it is this sense of 'deliberate discrimination' that has fuelled anger and discontent.

The process of liberalization and economic reform in India began in 1991, the same year that Mahathir launched his Vision 2020. This was also the year that the then Prime Minister, Narasimha Rao, launched India's 'Look East' policy. By the turn of the millennium, India was being increasingly described as a 'rising power' or 'emerging power', and in sunrise sectors like information technology as an 'IT superpower'. 'Rising India' brought in a new dynamic to the bilateral relationship, with leading Malaysian companies seriously interested in the emerging business opportunities in India, particularly in the infrastructure sectors.

None of this translated into any benefits or increased concern for the most marginalized sector of society in Malaysia: the Malaysian Indians. Conservative groups in Malaysia, imbued with *ketuanan melayu*, went out of their way to emphasize the disconnect between good Malaysia India relations and the impoverished condition of Malaysian Indians as a group. And in India, where expressions of concern about Malaysian Indians were the loudest in the State of Tamil Nadu, most foreign policy experts remain divided on the appropriateness of bringing this issue into the domain of bilateral discussions with Malaysia, lest India be accused of 'interfering in Malaysia's internal affairs'.

Neither in India nor in Malaysia have there been any coherent efforts to appreciate this intrinsic link: that Malaysia India relations can never reach their full potential as long as the elephant in the room (the situation facing Malaysian Indians in Malaysia) is not faced up to, squarely and openly.

NOTES

1. Ton That Thien, *India and South East Asia, 1947-60*, p. 247.
2. Ibid., p. 248, quoting *India News*, 7 September 1957.
3. Ibid., quoting *India News*, 31 August 1957.
4. Ibid., quoting Parliamentary Debates, 1957, vol. 4, pt. 2, 2 September, column 11,329.
5. Ibid., pp. 222-3, quoting *The Hindu*, 7 December 1958.
6. Ibid., p. 248, quoting *The Hindu*, 8 December 1958.
7. Ibid., quoting ibid.
8. Ibid., quoting ibid.
9. *Foreign Affairs Record*, Ministry of External Affairs, Government of India, vol. VII (1961), no. 12 (December), pp. 510-11.
10. That Thien, op. cit., p. 249.
11. Note on 'Education in India' on the website of the High Commission of India, Kuala Lumpur, accessed at http://www.indianhighcommission.com.my/education_ma_in.php on 10 November 2010, p. 1.
12. Tunku Abdul Rahman, 'Malaysia: Key Area in Southeast Asia', *Foreign Affairs*, vol. 43, no. 4, July 1965, pp. 664-5.
13. Ibid., p. 661.

14. Ibid., pp. 661-2.
15. Shanti Nair, *Islam in Malaysian Foreign Policy*, Routledge, 1997, pp. 40-1.
16. Ibid., p. 56 and fn. 3 (pp. 83-4), quoting Ghazali Shafie, 'Elements of Malaysia's Foreign Policy', *Foreign Affairs Malaysia (FAM)*, vol. 2, no. 1, December 1969, pp. 11-14.
17. Ibid., p. 56.
18. PAS, or Parti Islam Se-Malaysia, contested the Malayan General Elections in 1955 under the name Pan-Malayan Islamic Party (PMIP), or, in Malay, Persatuan Islam Sa-Tanah Melayu. This was later changed to PAS.
19. Andaya and Andaya, op. cit., p. 267.
20. Nair, op. cit., p. 8.
21. Ibid., p. 56.
22. Ibid., p. 83, fn. 2.
23. Ibid., p. 57.
24. *Foreign Affairs Record*, Ministry of External Affairs, vol. VII (1961), p. 510.
25. Ibid., vol. IX, no. 2 (February 1963).
26. Ibid., pp. 58-9.
27. Rahman, op. cit., p. 665.
28. Ibid.
29. *Foreign Affairs Record*, Ministry of External Affairs, vol. XII, no. 10, October 1966, p. 253.
30. *The Years of Challenge: Selected Speeches of Indira Gandhi, January 1966 to August 1969*, Publications Division, Ministry of Information and Broadcasting, Government of India.
31. *Foreign Affairs Record*, Ministry of External Affairs, vol. XIV, no. 6, June 1968, p. 136.
32. Tate, op. cit., p. 109.
33. Ibid., p. 121.
34. Ibid.
35. Ibid., p. 119.
36. Stenson, op. cit., p. 203, quoting *General Report 1965-1968*, National Union of Plantation Workers (Petaling Jaya, 1968), pp. 10-11.
37. Stenson, op. cit., p. 204, quoting statistics from Colin Barlow.
38. Ibid., pp. 204-5, quoting S.M. Ponniah 'Multilingual Education: The Disinheritance of a Tamil Worker's Child', *Intisari* 3, no. 4 (1968), p. 64.
39. Tate, op. cit., p. 111.
40. Ibid., pp. 109-10.
41. Philip Bowring, 'May 13: Digging up the Racial Past', *Asia Sentinel*, 17 May 2007 accessed http://www.asiasentinel.com/index.php?

option=com_content&task=view&id=497&Itemid=31 on 15 February 2011.
42. Ibid., p. 1.
43. Ibid., p. 2.
44. This interview was first published in the magazine *Harakah* on 24 September 1999, and later republished in *Malaysia Today* on 11 September 2008, accessed at http://mt.m2day.org/ - The REAL story of May 13 (part 1), on 23 September 2008.
45. Ibid., p. 2.
46. Tate, op. cit., p. 126.
47. Ibid., p. 125, quoting P. Ramasamy, 'The Indian Community in Malaya: A Study of the Economic and Socio-cultural Aspects', 2002.
48. Stenson, op. cit., p. 206.
49. Ibid.
50. Ibid., pp. 206-7, quoting K.A. Neelakandha Aiyer, *Indian Problems in Malaya: A Brief Survey in Relation to Emigration*, Kuala Lumpur: Indian Office, 1938, p. 49.
51. *Foreign Affairs Record*, Ministry of External Affairs, vol. XV, no. 5, May 1969, p. 111.
52. Ibid., vol. XIX, no. 3, March 1973, pp. 119-20.
53. Ibid., p. 123.
54. Ibid., p. 122.
55. Ibid., vol. XXIII, no. 2, February 1977, pp. 31-2.
56. Ibid., p. 30.
57. Ibid., vol. XXIV, no. 3, March 1978, p. 138.
58. Ibid., vol. XXV, no. 1, January 1979, pp. 16-17. The three Generals he has referred to served in later years as Chiefs of Army Staff in the Indian Army: General S.M. Shrinagesh from 1955 to 1957, General K.S. Thimayya from 1957 to 1961 and General T.N. Raina from 1975 to 1978.
59. Ibid., p. 17.
60. *Foreign Affairs Record*, Ministry of External Affairs, vol. XXXI, no. 10, October 1985.
61. Shanti Nair, *Islam in Malaysian Foreign Policy*, pp. 59-60.
62. Ibid., p. 61, quoting the Tunku's speech at the OIC Secretariat's inauguration as published in the *New Straits Times*, 3 December, 1971.
63. Ibid., p. 5.
64. Ibid., p. 61.
65. Ibid.
66. Ibid., p. 66.
67. Ibid., p. 137.
68. Ibid., p. 270.

69. Ibid., p. 80.
70. Barry Wain, *Malysian Maverick*, p. 219.
71. Ibid., p. 233.
72. Ibid.
73. Ibid., p. 234.
74. Ibid.
75. Professor Suresh Narayanan, 'From Malabaris to Malaysians: The Untold Story of Malayalees in Penang', Paper presented on 22 September 2001 at Colloquium on 'Indians in Penang: A Historical Perspective', the Second Colloquium of 'The Penang Story', accessed on 5 August 2010 at http://penangstory.net.my/indian-content-papersuresh.html. The author has also refered to J.V. Morais, *Mahathir: A Profile in Courage*, Petaling Jaya: Eastern Universities Press.
76. 'The Way Forward—Vision 2020', complete text of the Working Paper presented by Mahathir Mohamad at the Malaysian Business Council, p. 1, accessed on 7 March 2012 at http://www.wawasan2020.com/vision/.
77. Ibid., p. 2.
78. Ibid.
79. S. Nagarajan, 'Indians in Malaysia: Towards Vision 2020', Chapter 21, p. 381 in *Rising India and Indian Communities in East Asia*, ed. Kesavapany et al., ISEAS, 2008.
80. Ibid., p. 382.
81. Ibid., p. 380.
82. Ibid., pp. 375-6.
83. Ibid., p. 376.
84. Ibid., p. 378.
85. Ibid., p. 388.
86. Ibid., p. 389.

18

Conclusion: Malaysia and India in the Twenty-first Century

Mahathir's tenure as Prime Minister brought in the twenty-first century, the third consecutive millennium of direct interaction and exchange between Malaysia and India.

Mahathir visited India on at least six occasions during his tenure as Prime Minister of Malaysia: in 1983, 1987, 1993, 1994, 1996 and 2002.[1] Some of these visits were for international conferences, such as in March 1983, for the VII Non-Aligned Summit. His first bilateral visit to India took place almost four years later, in January 1987. Interspersed with Mahathir's visits to India were those by Indian prime ministers to Malaysia: Prime Minister V.P. Singh in 1990, Prime Minister P.V. Narasimha Rao in 1995 and Prime Minister Atal Behari Vajpayee in 2001 and in 2003.

Mahathir's focus on the modernization and economic development of Malaysia found its reflection in the new dimensions that were now added to the bilateral Malaysia India relationship. India provided an important market for Malaysia's commodity exports, primarily palm oil and rubber. When this led to a severe trade imbalance against India, both governments agreed that projects would be allocated, in Malaysia, to Indian companies on a negotiated basis, in sectors such as railways (track rehabilitation, signalling and modernization), engineering goods, power generation and transmission, oil and natural gas, among others.[2] Indian companies like HMT (Hindustan Machine Tools) and IRCON (Indian Railway Construction Company) became active in Malaysia. Science and technology, technical education, computer engineering and software development, human resource development, particularly in the field of medical training: these were the sunrise sectors in the late twentieth century and early twenty-first-century interaction between Malaysia and India.

In December 2002, Mahathir was in Hyderabad, where he visited some of India's most high-profile software companies. Mahathir sought India's cooperation, in his on-going plans for developing Malaysia into an IT-hub through the Multimedia Super Corridor project at Cyberjaya, located near Malaysia's administrative capital of Putrajaya. India's IT professionals were already working in large numbers in Cyberjaya, employed by well-reputed companies. India's prowess in IT was widely talked about and much appreciated across Malaysia by the media and corporate world. There was real potential here for a long-term, win-win collaboration between India and Malaysia.

THE ABDULLAH BADAWI PROMISE

Just three months after Mahathir's 2002 visit to India came a sudden twist, when 270 Indian IT professionals living in Kuala Lumpur were rounded up by the local police in the early hours of Sunday, 9 March 2003, taken to the police station and accorded humiliating treatment, alleging visa irregularities. In Kuala Lumpur and Delhi, strong diplomatic protests were lodged with the Malysian authorities/Malaysian High Commission. There was an international outcry over this incident. Within Malaysia, too, the incident created a furor in the media.

Opposition leader and the then national chairman of the DAP (Democratic Action Party), Lim Kit Siang, issued a statement describing the incident as a set-back to Malaysia's plans for developing a knowledge-economy. He asked Acting Prime Minister Datuk Seri Abdullah Ahmad Badawi to 'give assurance that police and immigration will not spike the national IT plan, to hire the best brains regardless of race and nationality'.[3] Did Lim Kit Siang hit the proverbial nail on the head when he drew a direct link between the mal-treatment of India's IT professionals and domestic inter-race relations between Malays and Malaysian Indians? The message sent out through the intemperate treatment of IT professionals, by the Malay dominated government bureaucracy, seemed to be that Indians doing well in any sector were not to be encouraged, since it could provide the template for similar upward mobility by Malaysian Indians.

Acting Prime Minister Abdullah Badawi did order an investigation and issue an apology over this incident. None the less, this incident irretrievably stymied the robust potential for Indo-Malaysian collaboration in the IT sector.

Datuk Seri (now Tun) Abdullah bin Haji Ahmad Badawi was prime minister of Malaysia for six years, from 2003 to 2009. He visited India in December 2004. In Bangalore, while addressing the Malaysia-India Business Forum, Abdullah Badawi referred to 'a few incidents of backlash against Indian techies in Malaysia', adding that

> in this context, let me assure you that we welcome knowledge workers from India very heartily. I give my word that we'll treat them well. I ask Indians and Malaysians to inform my office immediately if anything untoward happens. . . . We want everything right. We will put it right.[4]

Abdullah Badawi received 'thunderous applause' from the 500-strong audience when he gave these assurances. He was a popular figure in India. During Abdullah Badawi's discussions with Indian Prime Minister Manmohan Singh, both sides agreed to work towards concluding a CECA (Comprehensive Economic Cooperation Agreement) between the two countries. Abdullah Badawi 'stressed that India was a very eligible candidate to join the Security Council, adding that India was "well-placed" to be a member'.[5]

Above all, Abdullah Badawi was admired for his *Islam Hadhari*, or Civilisational Islam proposals, 'his own vehicle for showcasing Malaysia as a moderate Muslim country promoting economic development, progress and harmony'.[6] At the 55th UMNO General Assembly in September 2004, Abdullah Badawi elaborated on *Islam Hadhari* by saying:

> We must reject violence that targets innocent civilians. Similarly, violence that is caused by any party, whether by nations or by militant groups, cannot be accepted nor tolerated. The term *'jihad'* should not be misused and should not be misinterpreted to justify terrorism. Such actions only serve to tarnish the teachings of Islam. Islam does not permit such violence.[7]

Islam Hadhari and the promise held out by Abdullah Badawi's anti-corruption drive resonated so well among the youth of all races that in the March 2004 general elections, the multi-party coalition led by him secured 199 out of 219 parliamentary seats, a 'crushing victory . . . achieved mainly at the expense of PAS, whose representation dropped from 27 seats to 6, while the party (PAS) also lost control of Trengganu and held Kelantan by a thread'.[8]

Unfortunately, however, the great hopes raised by Abdullah Badawi's early pronouncements and by the 2004 electoral victory were soon belied. There were several reasons for this. In the first place:

> . . . neither Abdullah's huge majority nor *Islam Hadhari*'s stress on universal values would arrest the advance of a strict Islamist ideology, which had built up momentum over a couple of decades and taken on a life of its own. Righteous officials in bloated federal and state religious bureaucracies raided homes in the name of moral policing, splitting families where spouses were of different faiths and separating children from their parents. Non-Muslims who sought legal redress were stymied by Dr Mahathir's 1988 constitutional amendment giving *sharia* and civil courts mutually exclusive jurisdiction. Civil courts generally refused to hear cases involving family and Islamic matters, even where non-Muslims were trying to free their wives from rehabilitation centres or recover their children. In what amounted to a rebuke to the Mahathir administration, Judge Abdul Hamid Mohamad said in a ruling in the Federal Court, Malaysia's highest court, that Parliament should act to define jurisdictions clearly, rather than expect the courts to resolve the issue.[9]

Secondly:

> Despite Abdullah's enthusiasm for *Islam Hadhari*, one of whose ten principles is 'protection of the rights of minority groups', he showed little interest in defending religious freedom. . . . He seemed unable to resist pressures to increase the pace and range of Islamisation. All policewomen, regardless of race and religion, were required to wear the traditional *tudung* head-covering for official functions. Mainstream books were banned. . . . When Islamic militants demonstrated against attempts to hold an inter-faith dialogue organised by 'Article 11', a coalition of 13 religious and human rights groups named after the constitutional article that guarantees religious freedom, Abdullah backed the extremists. He shut down 'Article 11' in 2006 in the interests of peace on the streets.[10]

Matters worsened in July 2007, when public furore erupted over the then Deputy Prime Minister Najib Razak's comment that

'Malaysia was an Islamic State and had never been secular'.[11] At first, Prime Minister Abdullah Badawi seemed to contradict Najib's statement by saying that 'Malaysia was neither a theocratic nor a secular state but a parliamentary democracy'.[12] A few weeks later, however, in a written reply in parliament, Prime Minister Badawi said (in August 2007) that 'Malaysia is an Islamic state, ruled based on *Islam Hadhari* which I have introduced'.[13]

THE HINDRAF PHENOMENON

The Hindu Rights Action Force (Hindraf) came into prominence in 2006, when they protested against the spate of demolitions of Hindu temples across Malaysia. Despite their protests, the demolitions continued into 2007. The members of Hindraf, and its political arm, the Human Rights Party Malaysia, are 'drawn primarily (though not exclusively) from the disenfranchised members of the Malaysian underclass. Many . . . came from rubber estates and plantations . . . after five decades of post-colonial development many of them had not seen or enjoyed any of the benefits of independence.'[14] Despite being third and fourth generation Malaysian Indians, many are still without identity cards and passports, and are ineligible to vote. Malaysians of Indian origin remain seriously under-represented in the civil service and armed forces, in the corporate sector and in institutions of higher learning across Malaysia.

The Hindraf protest simultaneously targets substantive issues concerning the miserable socio-economic plight of most Malaysian Indians, and the inability or unwillingness of the MIC to effectively redress these issues, which remain unresolved since *Merdeka* in 1957. The leadership of Hindraf lies primarily with Malaysian Indian lawyers, some of whom are members of opposition parties like the DAP (Democratic Action Party). Hindraf is a broad coalition of around 30 non-governmental grass-roots organizations and associations, whose objectives are to 'defend the language, culture and identity of the Hindu community in Malaysia and to preserve the secular constitution of the country. . . .'[15]

According to the scholar Farish Noor:

> One of the consequences of the Islamization process in Malaysia from the 1980s is the entry of religion into the public domain of mainstream politics.

Malaysia has witnessed the growth and expansion of a parallel religious civil space with more Muslim NGOs and lobby groups coming to the fore. The formation of the Hindu Rights Action Force (Hindraf) marks a new expression of religious-based politics and social mobilisation among Malaysia's minority Hindu community along ethnic-religious lines.[16]

On 31 August 2007, the fiftieth anniversary of Malaysia's independence, the leaders of Hindraf filed

a four trillion dollar lawsuit against the British government on the grounds that, as the head of the Commonwealth, Britain had a responsibility towards its former colonial subjects. The lawsuit claimed $1 million in compensation for every Malaysian of Indian origin living in the country for the 'pain, suffering, humiliation, discrimination and continuous colonization' suffered by them.[17]

Three months later, on 25 November 2007, Hindraf organized what turned out to be one of the largest demonstrations of its kind ever seen in Malaysia, when around 20,000 collected in the centre of Kuala Lumpur, near the British High Commission (where they wanted to submit a petition), and at the Hindu temple at Batu Caves. The demonstrators were carrying posters of Mahatma Gandhi and of the British Queen. There were large-scale arrests, and detention, under Malaysia's infamous ISA (Internal Security Act). In October 2008, the Malaysian government banned Hindraf on the grounds that it was an illegal organization.

Hindraf leader P. Waytha Moorthy travelled to India in November 2007. The Indian government had been watching the situation carefully. Waytha Moorthy could not meet Prime Minister Manmohan Singh, but received strong expressions of concern and support from the then Tamil Nadu Chief Minister Karunanidhi, former Chief Election Commissioner and Member of Parliament, M.S. Gill, and others. The matter was raised in the Indian parliament, and 'both Prime Minister Manmohan Singh and the Foreign Minister expressed their concerns'.[18]

India's defence minister, A.K. Antony, visited Malaysia in January 2008, as part of the ongoing and active, defence cooperation between Malaysia and India. Defence cooperation has been steadily gathering momentum since the bilateral MOU on this subject was signed in 1993, and includes regular meetings of MIDCOM (Malaysia India Defence Cooperation Meeting), participation in joint exercises, and pilot-training as well as technical training for

RMAF (Royal Malaysian Air Force) personnel in India on Sukhoi aircraft.

Antony met Malaysian Prime Minister Abdullah Badawi. He is also said to have discussed the 'ethnic Indian issue' with Mohd. Najib Tun Razak, who was then Malaysia's deputy prime minister and defence minister. Najib later noted that India was 'aware of the political developments in Malaysia'.[19] The day Antony left Kuala Lumpur, the Malaysian government announced a freeze on further recruitment of workers from India, with no further renewal of work permits for those already working in Malaysia. 'The ban was supposed to take effect on 31 December 2007',[20] which seemed to indicate that the decision on this freeze had been taken earlier, with its announcement held up till Antony's departure.

At this very time, Dato' Seri Samy Vellu, the then president of the MIC was in India for the annual *Pravasi Bharatiya Divas* (Overseas Indians' Day) meeting in New Delhi. He called on Prime Minister Manmohan Singh, and later issued a denial of what media reports were describing as a freeze on further recruitments from India by the Malaysian government. Samy Vellu, who stepped down as president of the MIC in December 2010, after being at the helm of this party for 31 long years, had been unable or unwilling to use his power and prestige to significantly ameliorate the adverse socio-economic conditions of Malaysian Indians.

Several conclusions can be drawn from the Hindraf-related sequence of events. The impoverished and discriminatory situation being faced by large numbers of Malaysian Indians is a matter of sensitivity and shame for both the Malaysian and Indian governments. More than one commentator has drawn parallels with apartheid South Africa when describing the grievances of this and other race-defined groups in Malaysia. Sixty years earlier, Pandit Jawaharlal Nehru had followed the condition of Malaysian Indians so intently, precisely to avoid the situation from deteriorating to the extent it has today.

The grievances that Hindraf is trying to highlight are serious and real. It is true that MIC has not been effective in finding solutions on many of these issues. At the same time, MIC's position as the recognized voice of Malaysian Indians, and a member of the ruling

Barisan Nasional (BN) government has to be taken into account by all, including the Government of India.

This conundrum can be solved if one of two things occur. Either the MIC accepts responsibility and agrees to become an active partner in the search for solutions on the full range of issues raised by Hindraf. MIC's credibility is at stake here, and their continued relevance may well depend on their ability to accept these issues as part of their agenda in a real sense. The Malaysian Indian vote is small but significant, as the results of the March 2008 election so aptly illustrated. The UMNO-led BN government can gain immeasurably by taking steps to resolve at least some of the issues being raised by Hindraf, most of which have been festering for decades. Malaysian Indians do not form the majority in any parliamentary constituency, but:

> they could be a critical 'swing vote' in many constituencies. Indians constitute at least 10 per cent of the voters in about 50 of Malaysia's 192 federal parliamentary seats. The highest concentrations are in the states of Selangor, Negri Sembilan, Perlis and Kuala Lumpur. The same ratios can be found in 130 of the 498 state assembly seats.[21]

More recently, Denison Jayasooria, socio-economic analyst and former Human Rights Commissioner with the Human Rights Commission of Malaysia (SUHAKAM), provided valuable insights and details about Malaysian Indians.[22] Malaysian Indians still constitute 8 per cent of Malaysia's population, i.e. almost 2.2 million in a population of close to 27.5 million. Denison Jayasooria describes Malaysian Indians as 'a significant majority. Demographically, there is a concentration of Indians, between 10 and 20 per cent of the population, in 24 districts in seven states and in Kuala Lumpur'. As voters, Malaysian Indians make up 'more than 10 per cent in 54 parliamentary constituencies, which constitute 32.7 per cent of the seats'. In 9 of these 54 constituencies, the percentage of Malaysian Indian voters is well over 20 per cent. At the state level, Malaysian Indian voters 'make up 10 per cent and more in 125 or 28 per cent of the state seats'. In some of the state level constituencies, the percentage of Malaysian Indian voters is significantly higher, such as in 'Buntong—46.2 per cent, Perai—35.8 per cent, Hutan Merlintang—32.1 per cent, Ijok—

31.6 per cent, Bukit Melawati (Selangor)—30.9 per cent, Kota Raja—33 per cent, Jempol—38.6 per cent and Teluk Keman—29.1 per cent'. Denison Jayasooria concludes that Malaysian Indian voters:

> . . . are significant politically, but must convert this to their political advantage. All young Indian Malaysians reaching 21 years of age must register themselves as voters and actively exercise their citizenship rights. . . . There is a need for the Indian Malaysian community to set some basic standards and requirements for potential candidates from their community to secure the community's votes. About 10 to 30 per cent of registered voters is a sizeable group, with a tremendous political significance.

The effectiveness of the Malaysian Indian vote depends on the unity and cohesiveness of the Malaysian Indian community, which is sadly lacking. The Malaysian Indian vote is split between the MIC supporters and those who support one or the other multiracial and/or opposition parties. The 2008 general elections in Malaysia marked a decisive turning point in the move away from the MIC. The opposition victories in states like Selangor, Penang and Kedah has resulted in the emergence of new leaders among Malaysian Indians. Senior positions like the deputy chief minister of Penang and the Speaker of Perak are now, for the first time, held by Malaysian Indians. This represents a great boost for Malaysian Indians, but the MIC has had nothing to do with it. In a democracy, it is essential to be able to exercise the freedom of choice in joining any political party or association. Nonetheless, regardless of political affiliations, Malaysian Indians should unite on issues of common concern, such as education, poverty alleviation and non-discriminatory, equal rights as citizens of Malaysia. Denison Jayasooria points out that 'our problem today is we are extremely divided. While we are in different political parties we must have some common agenda for community advancement'.[23]

The unity of Hindraf itself may have been dented. The Human Rights Party is the political wing of Hindraf. Then there is the MMSP (Malaysian Makkal Sakti Party). This group was launched in October 2009, by none other than Prime Minister Najib, even though this party is not a member of the *Barisan Nasional*. Efforts are afoot to further sub-divide Malaysian Indians by religion and language, through separate meetings with the Sikhs, the Telugus and the Malayalees.

There is another way of looking at this. Malaysian Indians are not the only group in Malaysia that is confronting issues of poverty, lack of access to educational facilities, disenfranchisement and concerns about preservation of linguistic and cultural heritage. Chinese, Malays and Orang Asli are also affected, as are large indigenous communities in the East Malaysian states of Sabah and Sarawak. In addition, across Malaysia, there seems to be a growing clamour, particularly among the younger generation, for moving away from the present race-based system of governance. This is Hindraf's aspiration as well. Perhaps, Hindraf needs to broaden its struggle by inviting people of all races and religions to join in, with the firm belief that what they are seeking is not a zero-sum game, but a win-win situation for all. In the words of the commentator, Raja Petra Kamarudin:

> Though the New Economic Policy (NEP), which was introduced in 1970, was aimed at eventually eradicating poverty 'irrespective of race' and to undertake economic restructuring so as to eliminate the identification of ethnicity, its implementation within the framework of the race-based system of governance has led to a state of affairs where poverty and inequities persist. . . . It is time, therefore, for Hindraf's struggle to include all races and for all races to participate in Hindraf's sruggle.[24]

Denison Jayasooria has expressed similar views in a recent interview to *Free Malaysia Today*, where he says, in support of affirmative action programmes for Malaysian Indians that such programmes should be applicable to:

> . . . all socio-economic groups in the bottom 40 per cent including Malay communities, indigenous communities from Sabah, Sarawak and *Orang Asli*. It should be applied on a needs basis across ethnic groups. While this is the policy since the New Economic Policy, delivery institutions have not aggressively addressed socio-economic disadvantages in a comprehensive way for other minority groups. . . .
>
> In the long term, Malaysians must shift from ethnic, racial and religions' parties towards an approach which is ideologically based towards more inclusive democracy and economic empowerment ensuring all communities have equal opportunities to realize their full potential. Championing from racial, sub-ethnicity and religious framework is divisive and continues to perpetuate disharmony and a compartmentalized approach to nation-building.[25]

The Government of India has preferred to maintain distance from Hindraf. This has seriously detracted from the effectiveness and sincerity with which the Indian government has been pursuing its policy towards overseas Indians. Since 2003, each year on 9 January (the day, in 1915, that Mahatma Gandhi returned to India from South Africa) the Government of India observes *Pravasi Bharatiya Divas*, or Overseas' Indians Day. Expatriate Indians from across the world gather in Delhi or any other Indian city, interacting with each other and with senior Ministers and officials from the Indian government. Does the term 'overseas Indians' include only those who are now economically prosperous and therefore have something to 'give' to their country of origin? When it comes to the issues raised by Hindraf, the Indian government consider these to fall within the purview of 'domestic affairs' or to be an 'internal matter' of the Malaysian government. No such concerns apply when it comes to the well-endowed overseas Indians. Such a differentaiated position on overseas Indians has caused disappointment among Malaysian Indians, and has not in any way enhanced India's global stature.

THE MALAYSIA-INDIA STRATEGIC PARTNERSHIP?

The year 2010 saw the infrastructure of the Malaysia India relationship carried to new heights. Prime Minister Najib visited India in January 2010, covering Delhi and Chennai. The visit was described as the opening of 'a new chapter to forge strategic relationship between the two countries'. During this visit, the prime ministers of Malaysia and India concluded that: 'a long-term and strategic partnership between Malaysia and India could be developed based on historical, cultural and social links, pluralism, open society, shared commitment to democracy and development, and a high degree of commonality of political and economic interests'.[26]

The framework for the India-Malaysia strategic partnership was agreed upon during Prime Minister Manmohan Singh's visit to Kuala Lumpur in October 2010. This document[27] summarized existing interactions and called for a substantive stepping up in key areas, such as biennial foreign office consultations, enhanced defence exchanges and cooperation, including joint collaboration on projects of mutual interest in the defence sector and participation by the Indian defence industry in the soon-to-be established Malaysian Defence and Security Park, establishment of a bilateral joint working group on counter-terrorism, deepening the economic engagement (described as 'the core of the strategic partnership') through the conclusion of 'a high-quality and mutually beneficial Comprehensive Economic Cooperation Agreement (CECA)', expansion of mutual investment, launching the high-level India-Malaysia CEO's Forum, and setting up several working groups and committees, including the Joint ICT Talent Development Consultative Committee, and joint working groups on new and renewable energy, and on higher education. Malaysia announced its decision to issue commercial banking licenses to Indian banks. However, this time Malaysia did not reiterate its support for India's candidature for a permanent seat on the expanded Security Council with quite the same forthrightness as was done during the Abdullah Badawi visit to India in December 2004.

The economic engagement between Malaysia and India is deepening, but present levels are nowhere near realizing their full potential. 'During 2010, India was Malaysia's thirteenth largest import source and eighth largest export destination.'[28] Total bilateral trade reached an all-time high in 2008, when it crossed US $10 billion for the first time, but registered a steep decline in 2009, when it fell to US $7.3 billion, rising again to US $9.38 billion in 2010. Trade figures are essentially driven by Malaysia's exports to India of petroleum products and mineral fuels, palm oil, and machinery and transport equipment. Major items of India's exports to Malaysia are frozen bovine meat and fish, chemicals and chemical products, some machinery/appliances and parts, oilseeds, spices and groundnuts. The balance of trade is heavily skewed in Malaysia's favour. In 2010, India's exports to Malaysia were less than half (US $2.59 billion) its imports from Malaysia (US $6.8 billion).[29]

In the last decade and a half, Malaysian investments in India have risen substantially. By the end of 2010, cumulative Malaysian investments in India stood at US $6 billion, with US $4 billion coming in through the tax saving Mauritius route.[30] FDI (foreign direct investment) from Malaysia to India is primarily focused on roads and highways, telecommunications, oil and gas, power plants, tourism and human resources. In the era of shrinking markets and global recession, almost every large Malaysian company is turning to India (rather than China) for maximizing revenue and profit generation. The list includes public and private sector companies like Petronas, Maxis, Astro All Asia Networks, IJM, Ranhill, Mudajaya, Sunway, UEM, UMW, and Khazanah. Malaysian companies have so far completed 52 construction projects worth US $2.33 billion in India, while 22 projects valued at US $2.3 billion are currently under various stages of implementation.[31]

Indian investments in Malaysia are only now begining to pick up. Currently, there are more than 77 Indian companies, including 70 Indian joint ventures operating in Malaysia. However, cumulative Indian investments in Malaysia over the last 30 years, from 1980 to 2010, are just about US $2.04 billion.[32] Since 2010 several major new projects and joint ventures have been announced, which, as and when they materialize, will significantly boost the Indian presence in Malaysia. India's Reliance group has set up, in Malaysia, one of the largest synthetic textile integrated plants in the world; Mahindra Satyam has moved its Global Solution Centre to Malaysia's Cyberjaya; Wipro has also launched a Global Service Management Centre in Cyberjaya; Biocon has decided to set up its first overseas manufacturing and research facility in Malaysia; the Manipal group has received permission for setting up a multidisciplinary university in Malaysia; and Punj Lloyd is part of a consortium, building a 512 km natural gas pipeline in Sabah in East Malaysia. After a delay of almost a decade, India's public sector railway construction company, IRCON, was recently awarded the Seremban-Gemas railway double-tracking project worth over US $1 billion.

At the G-to-G (government to government) and B-to-B (business or corporate sector) levels, interaction is intensifying between India and Malaysia. There is a mutuality of interest in doing so. The Malaysian corporate sector, in search of new markets and projects for expansion, has found its niche in the infrastructure development and construction sectors in India. Indian corporates, particularly from the IT, higher education, railways and some manufacturing sectors, have responded to the special concessions and facilities being offered by Malaysia.

Despite these positive trends, bilateral efforts to develop this cooperation to its full potential are hampered by unsaid words relating to the 'taboo' areas of discussion between Malaysia and India. The Malaysian government is sensitive about its Achilles heel, viz., the divisive nature of its internal political discourse, which is overtly and covertly driven by issues of race and religion. They do realize, that an 'emerging' and 'rising' India can make it immeasurably more difficult for Malaysia, regionally and globally, should they choose to publicly voice concerns about the miserable plight of Malaysian Indians. The MIC's task is to convince the Indian government to not do so, and instead focus on strengthening the broad contours of the bilateral relationship, with the assurance that ultimately, the benefits of enhanced interaction will percolate down to every level.

On the other hand, both the Malaysian and Indian governments would benefit and grow in stature and popularity if they took a more broad-minded and open approach to the concerns of the Malaysian Indians. The Indian public does have deep misgivings on this issue, which adversely effects their perceptions about and appreciation of Malaysia. It was perhaps in acknowledgement of these concerns that, during his visit to Kuala Lumpur in October 2010, Prime Minister Manmohan Singh announced a contribution of Rs. 5 crores (approx US $1.1 million) to augment the Indian Scholarship Trust Fund. This is the same Fund that was first established in 1946, after Jawaharlal Nehru's visit, to provide assistance to Malaysian Indian students.

In itself, this enhanced contribution is a welcome step. However, many of the Malaysian Indians that Hindraf speaks on behalf of, are in no position to avail of such scholarships. Their problem starts with inadequate primary education (or any other education) facilities, which makes them unemployable and incapable of integrating into Malaysian society at any level. Surely, Malaysia and India can, in discussion, evolve mutually acceptable solutions to meet the needs of Malaysian Indians. If the problem is one of inadequate vernacular schools, India could send trained Tamil teachers to Malaysia in adequate numbers for short-term assignments.

These Tamil teachers could teach English as well, so as to prepare young Malaysian Indians for a fuller and more active participation in society. India has sent teachers and trainers all over the world in response to requests from friendly governments, but somehow with Malaysia, this is considered to be too 'sensitive' a subject, and so is taboo. If Malaysia and India can cooperate in trade, investments, technology and defence, surely it is not beyond their shared ingenuity to evolve a way out of the impasse and ignominy facing a substantial percentage of the 2.2 million Malaysian Indians that constitute around 8 per cent of the overall population of Malaysia.

Prime Ministers Manmohan Singh and Najib Tun Razak addressed a joint press conference in Kuala Lumpur on 27 October 2010. Both prime ministers responded along expected lines to what was almost certainly an expected question from an Indian journalist, on the 'sense of having been left out' and the 'discrimination' being faced by Malaysian Indians. Prime Minister Najib was on the defensive, describing this as 'a purely domestic matter for Malaysia to handle, and we are handling it in a very positive way . . . (this is) not to be discussed bilaterally. . . . ' Prime Minister Manmohan Singh said that:

> . . . like India, Malaysia is a multi-cultural, multi-ethnic entity, it is a democracy and respects fundamental human rights of its citizens, and I am confident that the Malaysian system has the built-in flexibility to tackle any problems of the type that you have mentioned. I have therefore no reason to be apprehensive on that count about the future of the Indian origin community in this great country. . . . [33]

Most certainly, it should never be India's intention to interfere in the domestic affairs of any country, least of all a friendly country like Malaysia, with whom India shares a civilizational heritage. At the same time, any bilateral cooperation with another nation does involve discussions on the nation's internal situation, to a greater or lesser degree. When India sent doctors and teachers to newly-independent Malaya, when India trained officers for Malaysia's armed forces, there was no opprobrium or ulterior motive attached to it. Rather, this was considered as part of a very natural process of helping out a friend in need. So it should be, with the needs of the Malaysian Indian community, particularly in the sectors of education and vocational training.

The strategic partnership between Malaysia and India is being forged on the foundations of shared values of pluralism, open society and democracy. In theory, this is, perhaps, a factually correct statement. In practice, however, it becomes very difficult for the people of India to understand how this can indeed be so, when race and religion are brought into every aspect of daily life and the educational process in Malaysia. There is the requirement to state the student's race and religion on every page of every answer-book submitted by every student throughout Malaysia. There are separate school-leaving examinations, where only students belonging to a specified race and religion are eligible to participate. There are institutions of higher learning (MARA) where only students belonging to a specified race and religion can gain entry. In 1990, when Indian prime minister V.P. Singh gifted to Malaysia a full set of equipment (made by India's public-sector giant, Hindustan Machine Tools or HMT) for a vocational-cum-technical training centre, this centre was segregated and kept apart by the Malaysian government as a MARA institute meant only for the Malays.

The 2011 controversy over the novel *Interlok* (in Bahasa Malaysia) is yet another example of the needless race and religion- based controversies that spring up far too frequently in Malaysia. The inclusion of this novel, as a textbook for Form Five in Malaysian schools, led to vigorous protests by Malaysian Indians because of derogatory references against the community and related factual inaccuracies. The Malaysian government's continuing reluctance, to either delete all such references or withdraw the novel as a textbook, has hurt sensitivities and prolonged the debate over an issue that could and should have been resolved far more expeditiously.

The Federal Government of Malaysia and the MIC have both been either unwilling or unable to stem the disastrous decline in the educational facilities available to the 2.2 million strong community of Malaysian Indians. As a result,

> 80 per cent of the 523 Tamil schools (ethnic minority Malaysian Indian schools) are in dilapidated conditions with almost no sports, recreational, computer, library and other basic facilities accorded to National Schools . . . (these are) still not made fully aided government schools, when primary school education has been made compulsory by law. . . . About 95 per cent of these

> Tamil schools do not have kindergartens unlike 99 per cent in national schools which have the same.
>
> University intake for (Malaysian) Indians reduced from 20 per cent in 1956 and by about 50 per cent from the over 10 per cent quota in 1970 to 5.2 per cent in 2003. . . . If all MARA higher education institutes and overseas scholarships are taken into account the (Malaysian) Indians would actually end up having only about 1 per cent of intake into higher education institutions. . . . Medical seats in the University of Malaya (for Malaysian Indians) was reduced . . . from sixteen seats in 2001 to only one seat in 2003.
>
> About 97 per cent of the civil servants, police and armed forces personnel are from the majority Malay Muslims.[34]

It was certainly in recognition of the dire straits described above that the Indian prime minister announced a contribution of US $1.1 million to the Indian Scholarship Trust Fund in October 2010. The Malaysian government should have welcomed this. Instead of doing so, they displayed such nervousness about this contribution that their national news agency, Bernama, did not even release this information.

Unfortunately, 55 years after *Merdeka*, the issues of race and religion have been thoroughly politicized in Malaysia. The prime consideration for politicians, particularly the leaders of the ruling BN coalition that has been in power almost throughout this period, is neither the substance of the issue being debated nor the welfare and cohesiveness of society: all that matters is the perceived vote-catching ability of a particular statement. The predominant perception seems to be that preserving and strengthening the race and religion based perquisites of the majority community is the only way to ensure that votes are cast in favour of UMNO and BN. Former prime minister, Mahathir, guided Malaysia down this path in order to wean the Malay vote away from the principal opposition party, PAS. The coalition partners, particularly MIC and MCA, have all along appeared helpless in opposing this unshakeable view of UMNO leaders. This has further deepened the fault-lines in society, since this seeming helplessness has alienated large chunks of the Indian and Chinese communities from the ruling BN.

In urban Malaysia, most of the younger generation (across all communities) is not comfortable with this presumption that 'special rights' or *ketuanan melayu* (Malay dominance or Malay supremacy) is the way to go. They are not interested in being divided along racial and/or religious lines any more. In the words of the commentator Raja Petra Kamarudin:

> UMNO must be made to realize that the politics of the future is no more in *Ketuanan Melayu*. UMNO should explain to the Malays—which they refuse to do—that *Ketuanan Melayu* does not exist. What is *Ketuanan Melayu*? . . . If I want to implement *Ketuanan Melayu*, how do I do it? All it is is apartheid isn't it?.[35]

This generation of well-educated Malays (and Chinese and Indians) would much rather have an egalitarian society and a genuine meritocracy, as against the present system of differentiation and rewards based on birth and religious persuasion. Each is confident of holding his/her own on the basis of intrinsic merit rather than inherent right. The increasingly apartheid-like division of society within Malaysia makes them uncomfortable. Many are migrating abroad to live and work elsewhere. Surely, wherever they migrate, they expect respect and equal, non-discriminatory treatment. So how can they deny this to their brethren back in Malaysia?

UMNO essentially banks on the rural vote, which is primarily Malay. The delineation and demarcation of constituencies across Malaysia has been done in such a way that the rural vote receives a higher weightage than the urban vote. However, the rural vote in Malaysia is panning out very differently in the peninsular regions (west Malaysia) and in Sabah and Sarawak (east Malaysia). Although the indigenous communities of Sabah and Sarawak have been given the status of *bumiputera* (sons of the soil), they are increasingly unhappy, both with the lack of control over their natural resources, resulting in their continuing impoverishment; and with the domination exerted by UMNO and the federal authorities over local parties and leaders. Sabah and Sarawak may not remain for too long the BN's 'fixed deposit' or assured vote-bank that it has been, for all these years.

The rural vote in peninsular Malaysia epitomizes the core of the struggle between UMNO and PAS for the Malay vote. PAS is currently a key member of the opposition coalition, together with the DAP (Democratic Action Party, a multi-racial, secular party with Lim Kit Siang as the parliamentary leader, and Malaysian Indian lawyer Karpal Singh as the national chairman) and the PKR (Parti Keadilan Rakyat), led by former Deputy Prime Minister Anwar Ibrahim). The PKR, in 2005, proposed the New Economic Agenda, which envisions a non-racial economic policy, to replace the NEP, which has been almost completely race-based in its implementation.

In the 2008 general elections in Malaysia, this opposition coalition, the Pakatan Rakyat (PR), secured its best results ever, jolting the BN out of its complacency by denying them the much-cherished two-thirds majority in the federal parliament. The opposition coalition also swept five states, and was able to form coalition governments in Kelantan, Kedah, Penang, Perak and Selangor. This has been the most powerful evidence so far of popular disillusionment with the divisive race-based political culture that has been predominant in post-1969 Malaysia.

For a while after the 2008 general elections, it did seem that the message had gone through. Prime Minister Najib Razak, upon assuming office in April 2009, brought in a stong focus on political reform, including through his '1 Malaysia' programme, with its emphasis on ethnic harmony, national unity and efficient governance, including integrity and meritocracy. The New Economic Model and Government Transformation Programme were announced to implement these changes. Prime Minister Najib lifted the ban on two opposition newspapers, and released political figures, detained under the infamous ISA.

Over the last four years, however, the momentum of change has rapidly dissipated, in no small measure because of lack of support within UMNO. As the battle for political supremacy rages, race and religion continue to dominate the discourse. Far from strengthening cohesiveness and social unity, discrimination and segregation are on the rise, leading to even greater concern and dismay among the marginalized Malaysian Indians. Brilliant young students, top scorers in school-leaving examinations, are denied admission to the courses of their choice. There is no transparency in decision-making on such matters, and no recourse to review or appeal.

India finds herself in a bind: how long can she maintain the stance of 'business as usual' in the face of the deteriorating socio-political situation within Malaysia? Malaysia's international image, and most certainly her image within India, is taking a beating. This does not help bilateral relations in any way. Among the mounting clamour, increasing parallels are being drawn between the present situation in Malaysia and the pre-1994 apartheid regime in South Africa. At the same time, there is little doubt that any move away from the present downward spiral has to come from within Malaysia. Like-minded people from the three principal communities in west Malaysia, together with the peoples of Sabah and Sarawak, should collectively mount public pressure to rein in the elements of divisiveness in favour of the pre-1969 social order based on togetherness and shared prosperity. Since Malaysia is a rapidly emerging economy, with a comparatively small population and well-endowed with natural resources, there need be no apprehensions about prosperity being a zero-sum game.

In June 2011, the elections held within PAS (at their annual general assembly or *muktamar*) for senior party posts threw up surprising results. 'The party poll was billed as a contest between the party's conservative *ulama* faction and the professionals (dubbed the Erdogans in a reference to progressive Turkish Prime Minister Recep Tayyip Erdogan).'[36] The Erdogans won handsomely, defeating the conservative faction of PAS, who had been favouring talks with UMNO on Malay unity. The speeches by PAS leadership at this *muktamar* were described as 'refreshing in this racially polarised country'.[37] The PAS president focused on the welfare state that PAS wants to introduce in Malaysia if the PR coalition comes to power. He did not play the race card, quite unlike the fire-and-brimstone speeches on this subject that are routinely heard at UMNO general assemblies.

In August 2012, PAS president Abdul Hadi Awang reiterated this position when he wrote, in *Malaysia Today*, that 'PAS appeals to all Malaysians, especially to Malay Muslims, to rethink their loyalty to UMNO, and to give their mandate to PAS and PR to lead and realize the dream of a welfare state that is just to all'.[38] Some PAS leaders continue to talk about their desire to implement *hudud* and establish an Islamic state in Malaysia, but PAS spiritual leader, Datuk Nik Abdul Aziz Nik Mat explains that 'the party's *hudud* and Islamic state aspirations were not political but religious obligations'.[39] The *Buku Jingga*, or agreed manifesto thrashed out by the component parties of PR has no reference to either hudud or Islamic state. So far, the Pakatan Rakyat is holding firm, despite seemingly deep differences between the secular and socialist DAP and the Islamist PAS.

Malaysia is in election mode, gearing up for the 13th General Elections that must be completed by 27 June 2013 at the very latest. The PR coalition is going all out in its efforts to wrest control of the Federal Government from the multi-party BN, that has been in power since *Merdeka* in 1957. There is a loud clamour of support, across all communities, for the Berish electoral reform movement co-chaired by the well known Malaysian Indian lawyer, Datuk Ambiga Sreenevasan. In August 2012, Hindraf leader P. Waythamoorthy, returned to Malaysia after a 'self-exiled' stay in London of more than four years. He has met PR leaders, and discussed 'forging electoral ties between Hindraf and Pakatan to face Barisan Nasional',[40] but differences persist on seat-sharing and over the contents of the PR Manifesto. At the massive PR rally convened in Kuala Lumpur on 12 January 2013, estimated by some to have attracted over one hundred thousand participants, the principal demand of the PR opposition coalition was for free and fair elections, combined with their promise, if elected, to move away from race-based policies and politics.

Electoral outcomes are difficult to predict, especially because the situation remains fluid and volatile. With the Malay vote evenly (or unevenly) split between UMNO and PAS, the focus is increasingly on the likely voting patterns of the non-Malay *bumiputeras* (from Sabah and Sarawak), the Malaysian Chinese and the Malaysian Indians. Some UMNO politicians in Sabah have left to join the PR. Senior political analyst, Farish A. Noor, has described the 'apparent abandonment of the BN by the non-Malay voters of Malaysia, notably Malaysian Chinese, who seem to have thrown their weight behind the opposition coalition'. Farish Noor adds that 'the BN's age-old formula of ethnic compromise and multi-cultural representation at both Federal and state levels will be severely dented at the coming elections if the current trend does not change, for it implies that the non-Malay component parties of the BN will be vitually wiped out'. He asks the relevant question 'can Malaysia be governed by an overwhelmingly Malay-Muslim government without visible non-Malay support?'[41]

The Indian government is, no doubt keenly observing the unfolding election scenario in Malaysia. India should not hesitate to engage with all sections of society in Malaysia. Much beyond the confines of government-to-government interaction, effective people-to-people diplomacy can help, in persuading all communites to take everyone along in the growth process, rather than turning a deaf ear and a blind eye towards difficulties being faced by large numbers of Malaysian Indians. Branding an entire community as 'gangsters' does not help. Rehabilitating them into the mainstream of social and economic activity can. Jawaharlal Nehru accorded high priority to acquiring first-hand knowledge about the concerns of Malaysian Indians, and then reaching out to all groups in search of solutions, maintaining the best traditions of friendship and mutual benefit between Malaysia and India.

India's twenty-first-century leaders should do the same. In the first half of the twentieth century, the problems facing Malaysian Indians were the result of colonial policies of segregation aimed at 'dividing to rule'. In the twenty-first century, similar arguments are being brought out in order to retain political control and to assure supremacy for one group. Unfortunately, notions of superiority, when repeated incessantly to an unsuspecting and credulous public, tend to ingrain themselves in the psyche. This affects interpersonal relationships and relations between nations. In the words of the author Rajiv Sikri:

> The attitude of the ethnic Malays towards Malaysian citizens of Indian origin . . . seems to regrettably colour Malaysia's attitude towards India. Despite the high level of trade, and the extensive involvement of Malaysian companies in road-building, housing and other infrastructure projects in India and of Indian companies in Malaysia's infrastructure and information technology sectors, India's relations with Malaysia continue to be marked by tension and a degree of mistrust.[42]

Nehru did not hesitate to point out that many of the problems had arisen due to a lack of cohesiveness and social unity among Malaysian Indians themselves. Much of what Jawaharlal Nehru perceived remains unchanged today. The MIC does need to be far more pro-active in overcoming disparities and the socio-economic degradation in the status of the entire community. Instead, they are perceived as being part of the problem, rather than part of the solution. There is a strong sense of alienation between the MIC and large cross-sections of Malaysian Indians, whether the professional elite, urban slum-dwellers or estate labour. This does not augur well either for the MIC or the UMNO-led BN coalition of which MIC is an important member.

The framework for the India-Malaysia strategic partnership recognizes that underpinning the two countries' relationship are vibrant and long-standing people-to-people ties. These long-standing ties weakened considerably under colonial rule. The fifty-five post-*Merdeka* years have not seen enough being done by either side to revive these traditional links to their pre-colonial strength. The inter-twining must strengthen at all levels so that the foundations of Malaysia India friendship and understanding are as strong in the third millennium as they were in the first.

MALAYSIA, ASEAN AND INDIA'S LOOK EAST POLICY

Essentially, India's 'Look East' Policy is bringing about a revival of her pre-colonial multi-dimensional interactions with Southeast Asia. The first stirrings of this revival were seen in the writings of Swami Vivekananda and Rabindranath Tagore in the late nineteenth and early twentieth centuries. Jawaharlal Nehru carried this forward with the convening of the ARC in New Delhi in early 1947. In 1955, the first Afro-Asian Conference was convened in Bandung, Indonesia, which led on to the convening of the first Non-Aligned Countries' Summit in Belgrade in 1961.

The countries of Southeast Asia did not forget the message of the ARC. As early as 1960, Malaysia's first prime minister, Tunku Abdul Rahman, projected ASA (Association of Southeast Asia) to promote economic, social and cultural cooperation among the nations of the region. ASA was established in 1961, with the participation of Malaya, Thailand and the Philippines. A few years later, exactly twenty years after the ARC, ASEAN (Association of South East Asian Nations) came into being with the adoption of the 1967 Bangkok Declaration by Malaysia, Indonesia, Thailand,

Singapore and the Philippines. The guiding principles of ASEAN are an unexceptionable combination of the principles enunciated at the ARC and the principles of *Panchashila*, which were first enunciated in the Joint Declaration between India and China signed in New Delhi in June, 1954.[43] The focus of ASEAN has been to promote the economic, social and cultural development of the region through cooperative programmes, and to safeguard the political and economic stability of the region against big power rivalry. Indira Gandhi, as prime minister of India, strongly supported the evolution of such a 'broad-based regional organization of cooperation, which did not identify itself with any of the super powers' strategic and Cold War oriented interests'.[44] However, since the containment of communism was a strong motive for the coming together of the founding fathers of ASEAN, India did not pursue its interest in this regional grouping.

India preferred a policy of equi-distance between the two Cold War power blocs. As a result, 'India and ASEAN remained "awkward strangers" during the Cold War years and their relationship lacked substance'.[45] India did not join the chorus of criticism in some quarters to the formation of ASEAN. Neither did she take any active steps to develop a positive interaction with this regional grouping.

It is oft quoted, and perhaps not entirely apocryphal, that India was invited to join when ASEAN was formed in 1967, an invitation which was declined. Subsequently, in 1975, when Malaysia invited India to Kuala Lumpur to participate in a dialogue with ASEAN, this, too, was turned down.[46] In May 1980, a meeting between Indian and ASEAN officials took place in Kuala Lumpur, after which a joint statement was issued reflecting agreement on 'a framework for "step-by-step" co-operation between India and 'ASEAN as a group" . . . ., covering economic areas, specifically trade, international economic cooperation, industrial cooperation and scientific and technological cooperation.'[47] The first step in implementation of this joint statement was to be India's participation in the July 1980 ASEAN meeting. This never took place. India accorded formal recognition to Cambodia's Heng Samrin regime, and 'realising that ASEAN would not approve of this action, India's then foreign minister Narasimha Rao avoided participating in the ASEAN meeting in July 1980'.[48] ASEAN also had differences of opinion with

India, over its closeness to the Hanoi government in Vietnam. For the next ten years, there were no further invitations to India for participation in ASEAN meetings.

The decade of the 1990s brought in a sea change in the geopolitics of the relationship between South and Southeast Asia. Externally, the impact of the end of the Cold War and the collapse of the Soviet Union, and internally, the severe financial crisis that faced India in 1991, necessitated the major restructuring of India's foreign and economic policies. Market-driven domestic economic reforms combined with the search abroad for new markets and trading partners led Prime Minister Narasimha Rao to pick up the threads of his earlier interactions with Southeast Asia through his new 'Look East' policy. In short,

> India was forced to explore other options, both regionally and globally, in search of preserving and promoting its economic and strategic interests, and there, the eastern neighbours offered a promising area of engagement. The ASEAN, with Japan, Korea and China put together, constituted economically the most dynamic region, not only in Asia but the whole world. Indian policy could not ignore this region particularly under the new situation when India was in dire need and desperate search for new openings for its 'liberalising economy'.[49]

India's new 'Look East' policy coincided with ASEAN's own 'Look West' policy. By the end of the 1980s, Southeast Asia was once again 'inducing India to have greater involvement with the region. This tendency started towards the end of the eighties as witnessed during the period of the Rajiv Gandhi administration . . . , when a number of ASEAN leaders had consultations with India on the question of resolving the Kampuchean issue'.[50] ASEAN in the 1990s was more than apprehensive about China as a potential security threat, particularly over the volatile situation in the South China Sea, including separate maritime and territorial disputes between China and several members of ASEAN. China's efforts to aggressively develop economic links with Myanmar and the nations of Indo-China, too, did not go unnoticed. It is not surprising, then, that in the 1990s, ASEAN expanded its membership for the first time in almost three decades. Since 1967, just Brunei had joined ASEAN in 1984. In the 1990s, Vietnam became a member in 1995, followed by Laos and Myanmar in 1997 and Cambodia in 1999.

This time, India took the initiative to pursue its proposed interaction with ASEAN. The response was quick and positive, no doubt based on mutually reinforced self-interest and benefit. ASEAN readily embraced India's new role as an emerging regional economic and political power, thanks in no small measure to the success of India's economic reform process.

> The ASEAN . . . have always preferred a multilateral balance of forces in the region in the interest of greater stability and peace. Many of these countries found India a deserving candidate to be involved in this balance, because India had no record of an aggressive or expansionist approach towards this region in the past.[51]

In January 1992, India was accepted by ASEAN as a Sectoral Dialogue Partner. At this stage, only three sectors were identified for this partnership: trade, investment and tourism. These were far fewer, and more restrictive than the sectors that had been agreed upon for India-ASEAN cooperation at the May, 1980 meeting in Kuala Lumpur. None the less, India pursued this cooperation with great seriousness and enthusiasm. In just under four years, at the fifth ASEAN summit in December 1995, India was elevated to the status of a full Dialogue Partner. This enabled India, in 1996, to become a member of the ARF (ASEAN Regional Forum), a unique platform for discussion of security and strategic issues pertinent to this region. It is interesting to note that 'Sectoral Dialogue Partner status was granted by ASEAN to both India and Pakistan at the same time. But soon the ASEAN countries realised that Pakistan had no inclination or potential to get economically engaged with the region'.[52]

The next quantum upgradation in the India-ASEAN interaction took place in 2002, when annual India-ASEAN summit meetings were initiated. Prime Minister Mahathir had secured agreement on annual ASEAN+3 (China, Japan, South Korea) summits as part of what he described as ASEAN's 'Look East' policy, envisioning economic integration of these thirteen nations through an East Asian Economic Caucus. Mahathir firmly resisted India's suggestion to turn these into ASEAN+4 annual summits by including India. Finally, thanks to the support of Singapore and other members of ASEAN, separate India-ASEAN summits were convened. At the very first India-ASEAN summit in Pnom Penh (Cambodia), Prime

Minister Atal Behari Vajpayee offered to conclude a FTA (Free Trade Agreement) with ASEAN, an offer which 'brought credibility to India's seriousness of purpose in engaging with ASEAN'.[53]

The India-ASEAN engagement has grown steadily since then, even though it is still nowhere near realizing its full potential. In 2003, India acceded to the Treaty of Amity and Cooperation in Southeast Asia. The Framework Agreement on Comprehensive Economic Cooperation between India and ASEAN was concluded during the 2003 India-ASEAN summit held in Bali. The CECA envisages concluding a FTA on goods, services and investment between India and ASEAN, encompassing them in the India-ASEAN RTIA (Regional Trade and Investement Area). The FTA on goods has now been concluded, signed in August 2009, after many years of difficult negotiations. This FTA became operational in January 2010.

For many years before he demitted office, Prime Minister Mahathir had been pushing for an EAS (East Asia Summit), as the culmination of his, and ASEAN's Look East policy. For Mahathir, the EAS meant essentially ASEAN + 3 (Japan, China, Korea). This time, too, Mahathir staunchly resisted including India in the EAS. Participation in the EAS became a contentious issue, even a point of discord between India and Malaysia. Malaysia received support on this from China and some other members of ASEAN. Singapore and Japan supported India.

The first EAS took place only in December 2005, more than two years after Mahathir had left office. According to author Rajiv Sikri, who was closely involved in the negotiations with ASEAN nations on this matter:

> India's participation in the first EAS in Kuala Lumpur in 2005 was the logical outcome and a symbol of the success and credibility of India's 'Look East' policy as well as of India's aspirations to be a global player. Arriving at an agreement on India's inclusion in the EAS was not easy. There was no unanimity either within ASEAN or among the ASEAN Plus Three (APT) countries . . . on whether India should be invited to be a part of the EAS from the very beginning. . . . In the end, the consensus, reached with considerable difficulty, was that all sides stood to gain in the long-term by having a more inclusive approach to community building in Asia.[54]

The infrastructure for regional cooperation and interaction between India and Southeast Asia has been strengthened in many different ways over the decade since the India-ASEAN summits first started. The EAS was an important turning point, when India along with Australia and New Zealand, were included as founding members. In 2003, at the second India-ASEAN summit in Bali, the ASEAN-India Joint Declaration for Cooperation to Combat International Terrorism was signed, highlighting the shared concern on crucial security issues, including the joint commitment to 'counter, prevent and suppress all forms of terrorist acts'.[55] In 2007, ASEAN initiated the annual ADMM (ASEAN Defence Ministers' Meeting). Four years later, this group was expanded into the ADMM+8, by including the traditional Plus Three (Japan, China and South Korea) and five other nations, namely India, Australia, New Zealand, Russia and the US. The ADMM+8 convened its first meeting in Vietnam in October 2010. The Delhi Dialogue, initiated in 2009 as an annual exercise in partnership between Indian and ASEAN-linked think-tanks, has emerged as the premier ASEAN-centric platform for discussions on regional and international issues of mutual interest and concern.

These fora have provided the opportunity for India to engage with ASEAN and East Asia in substantive and meaningful ways on security and strategic issues. This new dimension has given greater depth to the more traditional interaction between India and ASEAN on trade, investment and economic cooperation. It has facilitated greater appreciation and understanding of India's perceptions and concerns by the leadership of participating countries. Significantly, the India-ASEAN partnership has, in turn, reinforced and strengthened the bilateral relationships between India and ASEAN countries, including Malaysia.

The year 2012 marked the twentieth anniversary of the commencement, in 1992, of the ASEAN-India relationship. In commemoration, the tenth ASEAN-India Summit was convened in December in New Delhi, for the first time on Indian soil. The Vision Statement agreed upon by the Heads of State and Government participating in this ASEAN-India Commemorative Summit brings out the new depth and maturity that the ASEAN-India partnership has acquired, first and foremost through its elevation to a strategic partnership. The economic dimensions of the partnership were considerably strengthened through the conclusion of the FTA in services and investments, to complement the earlier FTA in goods, as well as the priority given to transport connectivity between ASEAN and India. Maritime cooperation was an area of special focus, including sea piracy, fisheries, maritime security and connectivity, freedom of navigation, and safety of sea lanes of communication for unfettered movement of trade. The Vision Statement emphasizes the need to broaden socio-cultural cooperation, and encourage greater people-to-people interaction in all areas of activity, with the special mention that 'we encourage the study, documentation and dissemination of knowledge about the civilizational links between ASEAN and India'.[56]

Dato Pehin Lim Jock Seng, the Brunei Minister of Foreign Affairs and Trade II, eloquently reflected the sentiments of participants from ASEAN and India when he said:

> . . . how can we embark on a Renaissance of our Golden Age? A Golden Age when we were traders, when there was a free flow of trade, a sharing of education and cultures, and interconnectivity through land and sea despite the odds and challenges of that period. . . .
>
> I believe we need to shift our 'mind-set' to capture our past history, to emphasise that once we were traders, we were neighbours and we were friends. With this mind-set, together, we can continue our journey into the future. . . .
>
> . . . (S)upporting our economic relations is people-to-people contact. We need our people to understand and appreciate our history, our connections and to nurture the understanding required to ensure good relations. One good example of this is through working with our young to instill the appreciation of our close connections and links. It is therefore welcoming to see the Indian Government's commitment to realise a twenty-first century university over the remnants of the ancient University of Nalanda. This is a issue very close to my heart, and I look forward to working with India and other EAS countries to make this goal a reality.[57]

The twenty-first-century contours of India's relations with ASEAN have brought us full circle to the beginnings of this interaction at the dawn of the Common Era. At that time, too, Indian traders interacted as equals and friends all across the region which is today ASEAN, from Myanmar to Vietnam and Thailand to Indonesia. Through these two millennia, different kingdoms and nations rose to prominence and then faded away. What has endured is the people-to-people friendship, mutual understanding and benefit in all interactions, and shared values across borders. The India-ASEAN framework has brought back the memories of our ancient interactions. No nation is bigger than the collective, no one race is superior to any other. Together, we can reap the benefits of socio-economic synergies and complementarities to compete in the globalized world. These are the myriad new (yet old) intertwined strands, which can further enhance and strengthen Malaysia-India linkages and friendship.

NOTES

1. Website of the High Commission of India, Kuala Lumpur, http://www.indianhighcommission.com.my/bilateral.php, accessed on 10 November 2010.
2. 'Malaysia Awards Projects to India', Press Release issued by External Publicity Division (Minstry of External Affairs) in New Delhi on 3 November 1988 on Indo-Malaysian Trade, vol. XXXIV, no. 11, *Foreign Affairs Record*, 1995.
3. 'Roughing up 270 Indians including IT professionals—setback for k-economy', accessed on http://www.dapmalaysia.org/all-archive/English/2003/mar03/lks/lks2170.htm on 9 May 2011.
4. 'Badawi woos Indian techies to Malaysia' report by IANS dated 23 December 2004, carried by Siliconindia News, accessed on 9 May 2011 at http://www.siliconindia.com/shownews/Badawi_woos_Indian_techies_to_Malaysia_-nid-26381.html.
5. 'India Eligible for UN Council Seat: Badawi' by Amit Baruah, carried in *The Hindu* of 22 December 2004, accessed on 9 May 2011 at http://hindu.com/2004/12/22/stories/2004122207341100.htm.
6. Wain, op. cit., p. 235.
7. Johan Saravanamuttu *Malaysia's Foreign Policy: The First Fifty Years: Alignment, Neutralism, Islamism*, Singapore: Institute of South-East Asian Studies (ISEAS), 2010, p. 240 (quoting from Abdullah Ahmad Badawi, *Islam Hadhari: A Model Approach for Development and Progress*, Kuala Lumpur: MPH Group printing Sdn bhd, 2006).
8. Ibid., p. 235.
9. Ibid., p. 236.
10. Ibid.
11. Ibid., p. 237.
12. Ibid.

13. 'Malaysia IS Islamic state (so what?)' by Jeff Ooi, 28 August 2007, accessed on 7 May 2011 at http://asiancorrespondent.com/5794/malaysia-is-islamic-state-so-what/
14. Ibid., p. 7.
15. Ibid., p. 2.
16. Farish A. Noor, 'The Hindu Rights Action Force (HINDRAF) of Malaysia: Communitarianism Across Borders?', Working Paper no. 163 published on 4 July 2008 by S. Rajaratnam School of International Studies (RSIS), Singapore, p. ii.
17. Ibid., p. 3.
18. C.S. Kuppuswamy, 'Malaysia: Whither the Indians?', Paper no. 4212 dated 7 December 2010 carried on the website of SAAG (South Asia Analysis Group), p. 6, accessed on 12 May 2011 at http://www.southasiaanalysis.org/%5Cpapers43%5Cpaper4212.html.
19. 'Abdullah, Antony see Momentum in Defence Ties as Positive Development', by P.S. Suryanarayana, in *The Hindu* on 9 January 2008, accessed on 11 May 2011 at http://www.thehindu.com/todays-paper/tp-international/article1175258.ece.
20. Noor, op. cit., p. 19.
21. Santha Oorjitham, 'Courting the Swing Vote: Indians Now Have More Political Pull', written on 1 September 1999, accessed on 3 June 2011 on http://ris20204.tripod.com/_disc2/00000344.htm.
22. Interview given by Datuk Denison Jayasooria to journalist M. Krishnamoorthy carried by Malaysiakini on 4 October 2011 at www.malaysiakini.com.
23. Denison Jayasooria's 'Reflections at September 11 P.J. Forum', text obtained from Jayasooria.
24. 'How Hindraf and the civil society movements can come together' by Raja Petra Kamaruddin (4 September 2010), accessed on the *Malaysia Today* website on 11 May 2011 at http://malaysia-today.net/mtcolumns/34301.
25. Interview to *Free Malaysia Today* by Denison Jayasooria on 24 September 2011, text obtained from Jayasooria.
26. 'India-Malaysia Relations: Overview', accessed from the website of the Indian High Commission in Kuala Lumpur on 10 November 2010 at http://www.indianhighcommission.com.my/bilateral.php.
27. Joint Statement on the Framework for the India Malaysia Strategic Partnership, accessed on 27 October 2010 at http://meaindia.nic.in/myprint.php?id=519916603&d=27&m=10&y=2010&pg=&flg=1&searchdata1=.
28. Note on 'Economic and Commercial Relations', p. 2, accessed on 3 June 2011 at http://www.indianhighcommission.com.my/ec.php.
29. Ibid., p. 3.

30. Ibid., p. 4.
31. Ibid., p. 5, quoting the Construction Industry Development Board (CIDB) of Malaysia.
32. Ibid., p. 6.
33. 'Indian Press Grills Najib Razak on Discrimination Against Malaysian Indian Poor' YouTube recording of question asked by Vaidyanathan (*Indian Express*), accessed at YouTube http://www.youtube,com/watch?v=Tvk1UNSkGsU on 27 May 2011.
34. C.S. Kuppuswamy 'MALAYSIA: Whither the Indians', Paper number 4212 published on 7 December 2010 by the SAAG, Appendix A (Extracts from a background paper by P. Waytha Moorthy, President Hindraf, presented to the Indian Law Institute in December 2007, accessed at http://www.southasiananalysis.org/55Cpapers43%5Cpaper4212.html on 12 May 2011.
35. Kee Thuan Chye, *March 8: The Day Malaysia Woke Up*, Marshall Cavendish edn., 2008, p. 153, Interview with Raja Petra Kamarudin by Kee Thuan Chye, Andrew Sia and Hariati Azizan.
36. G. Manimaran, 'Ibrahim Ali Calls New PAS Leadership "Anwar's Voice"', carried on 4 June 2011 by *The Malaysian Insider*, accessed on 5 June 2011 at http://www.themalaysian insider.com/Malaysia/article/ibrahim-ali-calls-new-pas-leadership-anwars-voice/.
37. 'Some Lessons from PAS Muktamar', by Guest Columnist, carried on 4 June 2011 by *Malaysia Today*, accessed on 4 June 2011 at http://www.malaysia-today.net/mtcolumns/guest-columnists/40888-some-lessons-from-pas-muktamar.
38. *Malaysia Today*, 9 August 2012, Abdul Hadi Awang (Harakah) 'How UMNO Retards the Advancement of Malays', accessed on 10 August 2012 at http://malaysia-today.net/mtcolumns/guest-columnists/51035-how-...vancement-of-malays?tmpl=component&print=1&layout=default&page=
39. Baradan Kuppuswamy, *The Star*, writing in *Malaysia Today* on 7 August 2012, 'Only Karpal Dares Rock the Boat', p. 3, accessed on 10 August 2012 at http://malaysia-today.net/mtcolumns/guest-columnists/50994-o...es-to-rock-the-boat?tmpl=component&print=1&layout=default&page=
40. *Malaysia Today* web-site report dated 15 September 2012, accessed at malaysia-today.net/mtcolums/newscommentaries/51606-pas-assures-hindraf-better-life-for-indians
41. Farish A. Noor, 'Political Change in Malaysia and Uncertainity in the Future', 10 August 2012, *Malaysia Today*, accessed on 11 August 2012 at http://malaysia-today.net/mtcolumns/from-around-the-blogs/5...sons-from-indonesia?tmpl=component&print=1&layout=default&page=

42. Rajiv Sikri, *Challenge and Strategy: Rethinking India's Foreign Policy*, New Delhi: Sage, 2009, p. 122.
43. The *Panchashila*, or five principles of bilateral relations are mutual respect for sovereignty and territorial integrity; nonaggression; noninterference in the domestic affairs of other states; mutual co-operation; and peaceful coexistence.
44. S.D. Muni, 'India's "Look East" Policy: The Strategic Dimension', ISAS Working Paper no. 121, 1 February 2011, published by the Institute of South Asian Studies (ISAS), Singapore.
45. Tridib Chakraborti, 'Disparate Priorities: Explaining the Penumbra of India's Look East Policy', p. 52 in K. Raja Reddy (ed), *India and ASEAN: Foreign Policy Dimensions from the 21st Century*, New Delhi: New Century Publications, 2005.
46. Rahul Mukherji 'Appraising the Legacy of Bandung: A View from India', ISAS Working Paper no. 11, 8 May 2006, ISAS, Singapore.
47. Muni, op.cit, p. 7, quoting from Kripa Sridharan, *The ASEAN Region in India's Foreign Policy*, USA: Dartmouth Publishing Co. 1996.
48. Ibid., p. 7.
49. Ibid., p. 10.
50. Ibid., p. 11.
51. Ibid., pp. 11-12.
52. Ibid., p. 15.
53. Sikri, op. cit., p. 116.
54. Ibid., p. 117.
55. Text accessed at ASEAN Secretariat web-site, www.aseansec.org/15276.htm on 10t June 2011.
56. Vision Statement: ASEAN-India Commemorative Summit, New Delhi, 20 December 2012, accessed at http://www.mea.giv.in-focus-article.htm?20982/Vision+StatementASEANIndia+Commemorative +Summit
56. Text of the Minister's speech at Delhi Dialogue III (March 2011), obtained from the ICWA (Indian Council of World Affairs), New Delhi.

Epilogue: Back to the Future

In chalking out the future, can India and Malaysia, South and Southeast Asia, draw inspiration from the rich heritage of the past they share? The infrastructure is now in place for the re-emergence of the traditional bonds between South and Southeast Asia. India, Malaysia and ASEAN have put together an impressive architecture of partnerships, trade agreements and projects, which if implemented, could carry their bilateral and regional relationships to new levels of dynamism and mutual benefit. In this, they can count on the support of Singapore and other members of ASEAN, as well the members of BIMSTEC,[1] and most of the members of SAARC[2] as well.

However, the structure in place so far is overly dependent on good relations between bureaucracies and governments. The spontaneity, the freedom and the strength that comes from good people-to-people relations are conspicuous by their absence. The essence of success lies in recognizing that the India Malaysia relationship has traditionally drawn its strength from the interaction among its people. The myriad intertwined strands are the people of India and Malaysia, of South and Southeast Asia. They understood each other because they reached out and knew each other. The colonialists put an end to this, and the post-colonial decades have not yet succeeded in restoring old friendships to their former glory.

All friends and well-wishers of Malaysia fervently hope that intra-Malaysian relations will soon find their equity-based equilibrium. The people of India set particular store by this. They sense the inter-twining between India-Malaysia relations and intra-Malaysian relations. Such sentiments resonate in Malaysia, too: 'A scientist in Malaysia who took part in the study[3] . . . , a researcher at the Human Genome Centre, Universiti Sains Malaysia (USM), hoped, possibly wistfully, that once the new information about common origins filtered down to the people . . . ethnic relations would be improved, and general harmony result.'[4]

Rabindranath Tagore encapsulates these thoughts and yearnings with lyrical beauty and sensitivity in his poem, *To Java*. He composed this poem during his 1927 tour of Southeast Asia. The poem was written in Batavia (Indonesia) on 21 August 1927, directly after his visits to Singapore and Malaya. His words remain as strikingly relevant today as in 1927, when Tagore had just rediscovered for India the antiquity of her links with Southeast Asia:

1

In a dim distant unrecorded age
 we had met, thou and I,—
When my speech became tangled in thine
 and my life in thy life.
The East wind had carried thy beckoning call
 through an unseen path of the air
To a distant sun-lit shore
 fanned by the coconut leaves.
It blended with the conch-shell sound
 that rose in worship at the shrines
 by the sacred waters of the Ganges.
The great God Vishnu spoke to me,
 and spoke Uma, the ten-armed Goddess:
'Make ready thy boat, carry the rites of our worship
 across the unknown sea'.
The Ganges stretched her arm to the eastern ocean
 in a majestic flow of gesture.
From the heavens spoke to me two mighty voices—
 the one that had sung of Rama's glory of sorrow
 and the other of Arjuna's triumphant arm,—
 urging me to bear along the waves
 their epic lines to the eastern islands;
 and the heart of my land murmured to me its hope

that it might build its nest of love
in a far-away land of its dream.

2

The morning came; my boat danced on the dark blue water,
her white sails proud of the favour of a friendly breeze.
She kissed thy shore; a stir ran athwart thy sky,
and the green veil fluttered on the breast of the Nymph of thy woodland.
We met in the shade of the night-fall,
in the dark hours of the earth;
the still evening was touched to its depth
by the blessings of the Seven Holy Stars of Wisdom.
The night waned; and Dawn scattered her prodigal gold
on the path of our meeting
along which two companion souls
combined their journey through ages
among the crowd of gigantic visions.

3

The time wore on, the dark night came upon us,
and we knew not each other.
The seat we shared was buried under the Dust
raised by Time's chariot wheels.
By the receding flood of oblivion I was borne back
to my own lonely shore –
my hands bare, my mind languorous with sleep.
The sea before my house remained dumb
of the mystery of a meeting it had witnessed,
and the garrulous Ganges spoke not to me
of a hidden long track to her other sacred haunt.

4

Thy call reaches me once again
across hundreds of speechless years.

I come to thee, look in thine eyes,
and seem to see there the light of the wonder
at our first meeting in thy forest glade,
of the gladness of a promise
when we tied golden threads of kinship
round each other's wrist.
That ancient token, grown pale,
has not yet slipped off thy right arm,
and our wayfaring path of old
lies strewn with the remnants of my speech.
They help me to retrace my way to the inner chamber of thy life
where still the light is burning that we kindled together
on the forgotten evening of our union.
Remember me, even as I remember thy face,
and recognize in me as thine own
the old that has been lost, to be regained and made new.[5]

NOTES

1. BIMSTEC: Bay of Bengal Initiative for Multi-Sectoral Technical and Economic Cooperation, whose members are Bangladesh, Bhutan, India, Myanmar, Nepal, Sri Lanka and Thailand.
2. SAARC: South Asian Association for Regional Cooperation, whose members are Afghanistan, Bangladesh, Bhutan, India, Maldives, Nepal, Pakistan and Sri Lanka.
3. See Prologue for details of this investigative study: 'Mapping Human Genetic Diversity in Asia'.
4. 'Human Genome Project, Asia', posted on IM Posts on 8 January 2010, accessed at http://www.indonesiamatters.com/7803/genome-genetic-mapping/on 4 March 2011.
5. Translated by Rabindranath Tagore from the original Bengali. The English translation appeared in *The Modern Review* and *Visva-Bharati Quarterly* in October 1927. Rabindranath Tagore, *Letters from Java: Rabindranath Tagore's Tour of South-East Asia 1927*, ed. Supriya Roy, Visva-Bharati, 2010.

Bibliography

BOOKS

Abidin, Mahani Zainal, 2002, *Rewriting the Rules: The Malaysian Crisis Management Model*, Kuala Lumpur: Prentice Hall (Pearson Malaysia).

Ali, Dr Syed Husin, 2008, *The Malays: Their Problems and Future*, Kuala Lumpur: TOP (The Other Press, affiliated to Islamic Book Trust).

Andaya, Barbara Watson and Leonard Y. Andaya, 1982, *A History of Malaysia*, London: Palgrave Macmillan.

Arasaratnam, Sinnappah, 1970, *Indians in Malaysia and Singapore*, Bombay, Kuala Lumpur: Oxford University Press, for the Institute of Race Relations, London.

——, 1986, *Merchants, Companies and Commerce on the Coromandel Coast 1650-1740*, Delhi: Oxford University Press.

——, 1994, *Maritime India in the Seventeenth Century*, Delhi: Oxford University Press.

Asian Relations: Report on the Proceedings and Documentation of the First Asian Relations Conference, New Delhi, March-April, 1947, with an introduction by Professor D. Gopal. First published 1948, in association with Asian Relations Organisation. Second enlarged edn. 2003, Delhi: Authors-press.

Behera, Karuna Sagar, ed., 1999, *Maritime Heritage of India*, Delhi: Aryan Books International.

Bhattacharjee, Arun, 1981, *Greater India*, Delhi: Munshiram Manoharlal.

Bose, Sisir K. and Sugata Bose, eds., 2007, *Chalo Delhi: Writings and Speeches (1943-1945) by Subhas Chandra Bose (Netaji Collected Works*, vol. 12), Kolkata, Delhi: Netaji Research Bureau, and Permanent Black.

Bose, Sugata, 2006, *A Hundred Horizons: The Indian Ocean in the Age of Global Empire*, Cambridge: Harvard University Press.

Bose, Sugata, 2011, *His Majesty's Opponent: Subhas Chandra Bose and India's Struggle Against Empire*, Delhi: Allen Lane (an imprint of Penguin Books).

Bright, J.S. (ed.), *Important Speeches of Jawaharlal Nehru (1946-1957)*, Delhi: Indian Printing Works, for the Ministry of External Affairs.

Chaudhuri, K.N., 1985, *Trade and Civilisation in the Indian Ocean: An Economic History from the Rise of Islam to 1750*, Cambridge: Cambridge Universty Press.

——, 1965, *The English East India Company: The Study of an Early Joint-Stock Company 1600-1640*, London: Frank Cass & Co. Ltd.

Coedes, G., 1968, *The Indianised States of Southeast Asia*, ed. Walter F. Vella, tr. Susan Brown Cowing, Honolulu: East-West Center Press. (First edn. published in Hanoi in 1944 by the Imprimerie d'Extreme-Orient under the title *Histoire Ancienne des Etats Hindouises d'Extreme-orient.*)

——, 1966, *The Making of Southeast Asia*, tr. H.M. Wright, London: Routledge & Kegan Paul.

Curtin, Philip D., 1984, *Cross-Cultural Trade in World History*, Cambridge: Cambridge University Press.

Damodaran, A.K. and U.S. Bajpai, eds., 1990, *Indian Foreign Policy: The Indira Gandhi Years*, New Delhi: Radiant Publishers, issued under the auspices of the Nehru Memorial Museum & Library.

Das, M.N., 1949, *Glimpses of Kalinga History*, Calcutta: Century Publishers.

Datta-Ray, Sunanda K., 2009, *Looking East to Look West: Lee Kuan Yew's Mission to India*, Singapore and Delhi: ISEAS and Penguin (India).

Devahuti, D., 1965, *India and Ancient Malaya: From the Earliest Times to circa AD 1400*, Singapore: Donald Moore for Eastern Universities Press Ltd.

Devare, Sudhir, 2006, *India & Southeast Asia: Towards Security Convergence*, Singapore: ISEAS.

Dubey, Ajay, 2003, *Indian Diaspora: Global Identity*, Kuala Lumpur: GOPIO International.

Feener, R. Michael and Terenjit Sevea eds., 2009, *Islamic Connections: Muslim Societies in South and Southeast Asia*, Singapore: ISEAS.

Ghosh, K.K., 1969, *The Indian National Army: Second Front of the Indian Independence Movement*, Meerut: Meenakshi Prakashan.

Gopal, S. (ed.), 1982, *Selected Works of Jawaharlal Nehru*, Series 1, vols. 8, 9 and 15, New Delhi: Orient Longman, a Project of the Jawaharlal Nehru Memorial Fund.

Gopinath, Aruna, 2007, *Footprints on the Sands of Time: Rasammah Bhupalan, A Life of Purpose*, Kuala Lumpur: Arkib Negara Malaysia.

Hack, Karl and Tobias Rettig, ed., 2006, *Colonial Armies in Southeast Asia*, London: Routledge.

Halim, Tunku, 2003, *A Children's History of Malaysia*, Subang Jaya, Selangor: Pelanduk Publications.

Hall, D.G.E., 1981, *A History of South-East Asia*, 4th edn., London: Macmillan Press Ltd.

Hassan, Ahmad Mustapha, 2007, *The Unmaking of Malaysia: Insider's Reminiscences of UMNO, Razak and Mahathir*, Petaling Jaya, Selangor, Malaysia: SIRD (Strategic Information and Research Development Centre).

Headley, Stephen C., 2004, *Durga's Mosque: Cosmology, Conversion and Community in Central Javanese Islam*, Singapore: ISEAS.

Hng, Hung Yong, 1998, *CEO Malaysia: Strategy in Nation-Building*, Kuala Lumpur: Pelanduk Publications and ASLI (Asian Strategy and Leadership Institute).

Ismail, Yahaya, 2003, *UMNO Politics: Abdullah Badawi's Dilemma*, Kuala Lumpur: Usaha Teguh Sdn Bhd.

Jayasooria, Denison, 2008, *Social Development & Indians in Malaysia: An Agenda for Social Inclusion*, Kuala Lumpur: Yayasan Strategik Sosial (YSS).

Kamarudin, Raja Petra, 2001, *From Prince to Prisoner*, Kuala Lumpur, unknown binding.

Kangle, R.P., tr. and ed., 1965, *The Kautilya Arthasastra*, 3 vols. Delhi: Motilal Banarsidass.

Kee, Thuan Chye, 2008, *March 8: The Day Malaysia Woke Up*, Kuala Lumpur: Marshall Cavendish Editions.

Kennedy, J., 1962, *A History of Malaya: AD 1400 to 1959*, London: Macmillan & Co. Ltd.

Kesavapany, K., A. Mani and P. Ramasamy, eds., 2008, *Rising India and Indian Communities in East Asia*, Singapore: ISEAS.

Kondapi, C., 1951, *Indians Overseas: 1838-1949*, Delhi: Indian Council of World Affairs (ICWA).

Kulke, Hermann, K. Kesavapany, and Vijay Sakhuja, eds., 2009, *Nagapattinam to Suvarnadwipa: Reflections on the Chola Naval Expeditions to Southeast Asia*, Singapore: ISEAS.

Lahiri, Imankalyan, 2009, *Malaysia's Foreign Policy under Mahathir Mohammad*, Delhi: Academic Excellence Publishers.

Lal, Shiv, ed., 1985, *India's Freedom Fighters in South-East Asia,* Delhi: Archives Publishers.

Lapidus, Ira M., 1988, *A History of Islamic Societies*, Cambridge: Cambridge University Press.

Lebra, Joyce Chapman, 2008, *Women Against the Raj: The Rani of Jhansi Regiment*, Singapore: ISEAS.

Lee, Kuan Yew, 2000, *Memoirs: From Third World to First, The Singapore Story (1965-2000)*, Singapore: Singapore Press Holdings and Times Editions.

Mahathir bin Mohamad, 1970, *The Malay Dilemma*, Kuala Lumpur: Times Books International.

——, 2002, *Globalisation and the New Realities (Selected Speeches)*, Putrajaya, Malaysia: Prime Minister's Office.

——, 2000, *The Malaysian Currency Crisis: How and Why it Happened*, Subang Jaya, Malaysia: Pelanduk Publications.

——, 2000, *Reflections on Asia: Articles Written for the Mainichi Daily News of Japan*, Kuala Lumpur: Millennium Books Malaysia.

Majumdar, Asis Kumar, 1982, *South-East Asia in Indian Foreign Policy: A Study of India's Relations with South-East Asian Countries from 1962-1982*, Calcutta: Naya Prokash.

Majumdar, R.C., 1963, *Hindu Colonies in the Far East*, Calcutta: Firma KLM, 1st edn. 1944.

Le May, Reginald, 1962, *The Culture of Southeast Asia: The Heritage of India*, Delhi: The Publications Division, Government of India.

Mahtab, Harekrushna, 1959, *The History of Orissa, Volume I, Up to 1568 AD*, Cuttack: Prajantantra Prachar Samity.

McCrindle, J.W., 1885, *Ancient India as Described by Ptolemy*, being a translation of the chapters which describe India and Central and Eastern Asia in the Treatise on Geography written by Klaudios Ptolemaios, the celebrated Astronomer. Introduction, Commentary and Index by J.W. McCrindle. Ed. Ramchandra Jain with Concult-uruum reference and appendices, New Delhi: Today and Tomorrow's Printers & Publishers.

Means, Gordon P., 2009, *Political Islam in Southeast Asia*, Petaling Jaya, Selangor, Malaysia: SIRD.

Miller, Harry, 1965, *The Story of Malaysia*, London: Faber and Faber.

Mookerji, Radha Kumud, 1962, *Indian Shipping: A History of the Sea-Borne Trade and Maritime Activity of the Indians from the Earliest Times*, 2nd edn., Delhi: Kitab Mahal Private Ltd. (India), 1st edn., 1912, London: Longmans, Green & Co. Ltd.

Musa, M. Bakri, 1999, *The Malay Dilemma Revisited: Race Dynamics in Modern Malaysia*, Gilroy, CA (USA): Merantau Publishers.

Nair, Shanti, 1997, *Islam in Malaysian Foreign Policy*, London and New York: Routledge, under the auspices of the ISEAS, Singapore.

Nair, V.G., ed., 1960, *India and Malaya*, Kuala Lumpur: The Pure Life Society (Swami Satyananda Commemoration Volume).

Navaratnam, Ramon V., 2001, *Malaysia's Economic Recovery: Policy Reforms for Economic Sustainability*, Subang Jaya (Malaysia): Pelanduk Publications.

Noor, Farish A., 2002, *The Other Malaysia: Writings on Malaysia's Subaltern History*, Kuala Lumpur: Silverfish Books.

Noor, Ismail, 2002, *Pak Lah: A Sense of Accountability*, ed. Elina Noor, Kuala Lumpur: Utusan Publications.

Ooi, Kee Beng, 2006, *The Reluctant Politician: Tun Dr Ismail and His Times*, Singapore: ISEAS.

——, 2006, *Era of Transition: Malaysia after Mahathir*, Singapore: ISEAS.

Palanisamy, Muthammal, 2002, *From Shore to Shore*, Selangor, Malaysia: VGV Management Consultant.

Proceedings of the First International Conference Seminar of Tamil Studies, held in Kuala Lumpur in April 1966, vol. 1, published by the International Association of Tamil Research, Department of Indian Studies, University of Malaya, Kuala Lumpur.

Rahim, Lily Zubaidah, 1998, *The Singapore Dilemma: The Political and Educaitonal Marginality of the Malay Community*, New York: Oxford University Press.

Ramachandran, Selvakumaran, 1994, *Indian Plantation Labour in Malaysia*, unknown binding.

Rashid, Rehman, 1993, *A Malaysian Journey*, Kuala Lumpur: Rehman Rashid.

Ray, Himanshu Prabha, 1994, *The Winds of Change: Buddhism and the Maritime Links of Early South Asia*, Delhi: Oxford University Press.

——, 2003, *The Archaeology of Seafaring in Ancient South Asia*, Cambridge: Cambridge University Press.

Ray, Himanshu Prabha and Edward A. Alpers, eds., 2007, *Cross Currents and Community Networks: The History of the Indian Ocean World*, Oxford: Oxford University Press.

Sandhu, Kernail Singh, 1969, *Indians in Malaya: Some Aspects of Their Immigration and Settlement (1786-1957)*, Cambridge: Cambridge University Press.

Sandhu, K.S. and A. Mani, eds, 1993, *Indian Communities in Southeast Asia*, Singapore: ISEAS.

Saravanamuttu, Johan, 2010, *Malaysia's Foreign Policy: The First Fifty Years: Alignment, Neutralism, Islamism*, Singapore: ISEAS.

Sardesai, D.R., 1994, *Southeast Asia: Past and Present*, 3rd edn., Boulder, San Francisco: Westview Press.

Sastri, K.A. Nilakanta, 2001, *Foreign Notices of South India: From Megasthenes to Mahuan*, 3rd edn., Chennai: University of Madras, 1st edn., 1939.

——, 1949, *South Indian Influences in the Far East*, Bombay: Hind Kitabs Limited.

——, 1955, *A History of South India: From Prehistoric Times to the Fall of Vijayanagar*, London: Oxford University Press.

Saw, Swee-Hock and K. Kesavapany, eds., 2006, *Malaysia: Recent Trends and Challenges*, Singapore: ISEAS.

——, 2006, *Singapore-Malaysia Relations Under Abdullah Badawi*, Singapore: ISEAS.

Schoff, W.H., tr. & ed., 1912, *The Periplus of the Erythraean Sea: Travel and Trade in the Indian Ocean by a Merchant of the First Century*, London, Bombay & Calcutta: Longmans, Green and Company.

Sen Gupta, Bhabani, T.T. Poulose and Hemlata Bhatia, 1974, *The Malacca Straits and the Indian Ocean: A Study of the Strategic and Legal Aspects of a Controversial Sea-Lane*, Delhi: Macmillan.

Shaffer, Lynda Norene, 1996, *Maritime Southeast Asia to 1500*, New York: M.E. Sharpe.

Sikri, Rajiv, 2009, *Challenge and Strategy: Rethinking India's Foreign Policy*, Delhi: Sage.

Singh, Gurchan, 1949, *Singa the Lion of Malaysia: Story of the Malayan Resistance Movement*, London: Quality Press.

Smith, Vincent A., 1907, *The Early History of India from 600 BC to the Muhammadan Conquest, including the Invasion of Alexander the Great*, London: Grolier Society.

Singam, S. Durai Raja, 1954, *India and Malaya Through the Ages*, Kuantan (Malaya), unknown binding.

Sridharan, Rear Admiral K., 1982, *A Maritime History of India*, Delhi: Publications Division, Government of India.

Stenson, Michael, 1980, *Class, Race and Colonialism in West Malaysia: The Indian Case*, St Lucia, Queensland, Australia: University of Queensland Press.

Stewart, Ian, 2003, *The Mahathir Legacy: A Nation Divided, A Region at Risk*, St. Leonards, N.S.W.: Allen & Unwin.

Swettenham, Frank, 1906, *British Malaya: An Account of the Origin and Progress of British Influence in Malaya*, London: George Allen & Unwin Ltd.

Tagore, Rabindranath, 2010, *Letters from Java: Rabindranath Tagore's Tour of South-East Asia 1927: Tagore Travelogue Series* (tr. Indiradevi Chaudhurani & Supriya Roy, ed. Supriya Roy), Santiniketan (Paschimbanga): Visva-Bharati University.

Tagore Centenary Volume, 1961, Singapore: Singapore Tagore Centenary Celebration Committee.

Tate, Muzafar Desmond, 2008, *The Malaysian Indians: History, Problems and Future*, Kuala Lumpur: Strategic Information and Research Development Centre.

Thapar, Romila, 1990, *A History of India*, vol. 1, Delhi: Penguin Books.

Ton, That Thien, 1963, *India and South East Asia 1947-1960: A Study of Idnia's Policy Towards the South East Asian Countries*, Geneva: Libraire Droz.

Wain, Barry, 2009, *Malaysian Maverick: Mahathir Mohamad in Turbulent Times*, London: Palgrave Macmillan.

Wales, H.G. Quaritch, 1951, *The Making of Greater India,* London: Bernard Quaritch.

Wang, Gungwu, ed., 1964, *Malaysia: A Survey,* London: Pall Mall Press.

Westerlund, David and Ingvar Svanberg, eds., 1999, *Islam Outside the Arab World,* London: Richmond Curzon Press.

Wheatley, Paul, 1961, *The Golden Khersonese: Studies in the Historical Geography of the Malay Peninsula before AD 1500,* Kuala Lumpur: University of Malaya Press.

Winstedt, Richard, 1961, *The Malays: A Cultural History,* Singapore: Kelly and Walsh (1st edn. 1947).

———, 1948, *Malaya and Its History,* London: Hutchinson's University Library.

———, 1951, *The Malay Magician: Being Shaman, Saiva and Sufi,* Singapore: Oxford University Press.

ARTICLES

Andaya, Leonard Y., 'Orang Asli and the Melayu in the History of the Malay Peninsula', *Journal of the Malaysian Branch of the Royal Asiatic Society* (*JMBRAS*), vol. 75, pt. 1, 2002, pp. 23-47.

Arasaratnam, S., 'Some Notes on the Dutch in Malacca and the Indo-Malayan Trade 1641-1670', *Journal of Southeast Asian History,* vol. 10, no. 3, special issue on International Trade and Politics in Southeast Asia 1500-1800 (December 1969), pp. 480-90.

——, 'Trade and Political Dominion in South India, 1750-1790: Changing British-Indian Relationships', *Modern Asian Studies,* vol. 13, no. 1 (1979), pp. 19-40.

——, 'Indian Society of Malaysia and Its Leaders: Trends in Leadership and Ideology among Malaysian Indians, 1945-60', *Journal of Southeast Asian Studies,* vol. 13, no. 2 (September 1982), pp. 236-51.

Basa, Kishor K., 'Indian Writings on Early History and Archaeology of Southeast Asia: A Historiographical Analysis', *Journal of the Royal Asiatic Society,* Third Series, vol. 8, no. 3, November 1998, pp. 395-410.

Bashiran, Begum Mobarak Ali, 'The Red-Ink Grant: Tracing Legitimacy in History', *University of Malaya Referred Journal,* 2007, accessed on 4 October 2010 at http://umrefjournal.um.edu.my/filebank/published_article/511/2007%20Bashiran%20_%20Malay%20Reservation%20Land.pdf .

Bassett, D.K., 'Changes in the Pattern of Malay Politics, 1629-c. 1655', *Journal of Southeast Asian History,* vol. 10, no. 3, International Trade and Politics in Southeast Asia 1500-1899 December 1969, pp. 429-52.

Bauer, P.T., 'Nationalism and Politics in Malaya', *Foreign Affairs*, vol. 25, no. 3, April 1947, pp. 503-17.

Bhattacharya, Jayati, 'Patriotism and Passion: Resonances of Tagore and Bose in Southeast Asia', paper presented at ISEAS, Singapore Conference on 'An Age in Motion: The Asian Voyages of Rabindranath Tagore', 11-13 May 2010 (under publication).

Bose, Sugata, 'Rabindranath Tagore and Asian Universalism', accessed on 6 October 2010 at http://www.iseas.edu.sg/nsc/documents/conferences/Rabindranath%20Tagore%20and%20Asian%20Universalism.pdf.

Braddell, Roland, 'An Introduction to the Study of Ancient Times in the Malay Peninsula and the Straits of Malacca', *JMBRAS*, vol. XIII, pt. II, 1935, pp. 70-109; vol. XIV, pt. 3, 1936, pp. 10-71; vol. XV, pt. 3, 1937, pp. 64-126; vol. XVII, pt. I, 1939, pp. 146-212.

——, 'Notes on Ancient Times in Malaya', *JMBRAS*, vol. XX, pt. I, pp. 161-186; vol. XX, pt. II, 1947, pp. 1-19; vol. XXII, pt. I, pp. 1-24; vol. XXIII, pt. I, pp. 1-36; vol. XXIII, pt. III, pp. 1-35; vol. XXIV, pt. I, 1951, pp. 1-27.

Briggs, Lawrence Palmer, 'The Origin of the Sailendra Dynasty: Present Status of the Question', *Journal of the American Oriental Society*, vol. 70, no. 2 (April-June 1950), pp. 76-89.

de Bruijn, P.G., 'Trade in the Straits of Malacca in 1785: A Memorandum by P.G. de Bruijn, Governor of Malacca', translated from the Dutch by Brian Harrison, published in *JMBRAS*, vol. XXVI, pt. I, 1953, pp. 56-62.

van Bruinessen, Martin, 'Origins and Development of the Sufi Orders (*tarekat*) in Southeast Asia', *Journal Studies Islamika (Jakarta)*, vol. I, no. I (1994), pp. 1-23.

Callenfels, P.V. van Stein, 'The Founder of Malacca', *JMBRAS*, vol. XV, pt. II, 1937, pp. 160-6.

Chakraborti, Tridib, 'India's Southeast Asia Policy in the 21st Century: Perambulating the Horizon', in Yagama Reddy, ed., *Emerging India in Asia-Pacific*, New Delhi: New Century Publications, 2007, pp. 154-79.

——, 'Disparate Priorities: Explaining the Penumbra of India's Look East Policy', in K. Raja Reddy, ed., *India and ASEAN: Foreign Policy Dimensions from the 21st Century*, New Delhi: New Century Publications, 2005, pp. 52-93.

Chaudhuri, K.N., 'India's Foreign Trade and the Cessation of the East India Company's Trading Activities, 1828-40', *The Economic History Review*, New Series, vol. 19, no. 2 (1966), pp. 345-63.

——, 'The Unity and Disunity of Indian Ocean History from the Rise of

Islam to 1750: The Outline of a Theory and Historical Discourse', *Journal of World History*, vol. 4, no. 1 (Spring 1993), pp. 1-21.

——, 'India's International Economy in the Nineteenth Century: An Historical Survey', *Modern Asian Studies*, vol. 2, no. 1 (1968), pp. 31-50.

——, 'Treasure and Trade Balances: The East India's Company's Export Trade, 1660-1720', *The Economic History Review*, New Series, vol. 21, no. 3 (December 1968), pp. 480-502.

Christian, John L., 'Anglo-French Rivalry in Southeast Asia: Its Historical Geography and Diplomatic Climate', *Geographical Review*, vol. 13, no. 2 (April 1941), pp. 272-82.

Das Gupta, Arun, 'Rabindranath Tagore in Indonesia: An Experiment in Bridge-Building', in *Bijdragen tot de Taal-, Land-en Volkenkunde*, 158 (2002), no. 3, Leiden, 451-77, p. 457, downloaded from http://www.kitlv-journals.nl on 7 October 2010.

Gibson-Hill, C.A., 'The Steamers Employed in Asian Waters, 1819-1839', *JMBRAS,* vol. XXVII, pt. I, 1954, pp 120-62.

Hall, Kenneth R., 'Local and International Trade and Traders in the Straits of Melaka Region: 600-1500', *Journal of the Economic and Social History of the Orient*, vol. 47, no. 2 (2004), pp. 213-60.

Hansard Records of British Parliamentary Debates: Debate on Federation of Malaya Independence Bill on 12 July 1957, pp. 1-43, accessed at http://hansard.millibanksystems.com/commons/1957/jul/12/federation-of-malaya-independence-bill on 18 December 2010.

Harper, Timothy Norman, 'Revolt in Malaya: The Indian Connection', Sisir Kumar Bose Lecture 2007 delivered at the Netaji Research Bureau, Calcutta in January 2007, published in *The Oracle*, January 2008 issue.

Harrison, Tom, 'Gold and Indian Influences in West Borneo', *JMBRAS*, vol. XXII, pt. IV, 1949, pp. 33-110.

Hirschman, Charles, 'The Making of Race in Colonial Malaya: Political Economy and Racial Ideology', *Sociological Forum*, vol. 1, no. 2 (Spring, 1986), pp. 330-61.

——, 'The Meaning and Measurement of Ethnicity in Malaysia: An Analysis of Census Classifications', *The Journal of Asian Studies*, vol. 46, no. 3 (August 1987), pp. 555-82.

Houben, Vincent J.H., 'Southeast Asia and Islam', *Annals of the American Academy of Political and Social Science*, vol. 588, special issue on Islam: Enduring Myths and Changing Realities (July 2003), pp. 149-70.

Hussin, Nordin, 'Trade and Society in the Straits of Melaka: Dutch Melaka and English Penang, 1780-1630', NIAS (Nordic Institute of Asan Studies) Monograph, NUS Press, Singapore, 2007. Accessed at http://www.niaspress.dk/files/excerpts/Nordin-extract.pdf.

Jain, L.C., 'Asian Relations Conference, 1947: India's First Foray in Foreign Affairs', monograph prepared for the Nehru Memorial Museum & Library, New Delhi, December 2009, with Research Associates O.P. Mishra and Shreya Shankar.

Johns, A., 'Aspects of Sufi Thought in India and Indonesia in the First Half of the 17th Century', *JMBRAS*, vol. XXVIII, pt. I, 1955.

Johns, A.H., 'Malay Sufism as Illustrated in an Anonymous Collection of 17th Century Tracts', *JMBRAS*, vol. XXX, pt. 2, 1957.

——, 'Islamization in Southeast Asia: Reflections and Reconsiderations with Special Reference to the Role of Sufism', *Journal of Southeast Asian Studies*, vol. 31, no. 1, June 1993.

Jones, J.P., 'British Rule in India: II', *The North American Review*, vol. 168, no. 509 (April 1899), pp. 463-75.

Sundaram, Jomo Kwame and Ahmed Shabery Cheek, 'The Politics of Malaysia's Islamic Resurgence', *Third World Quarterly*, vol. 10, no. 2, Islam and Politics, April 1988, pp. 843-68.

Kamarudin, Raja Petra, 'The Real Story of May 13 (Parts 1, 2 and 3)', posted on *Malaysia Today* website and accessed at http://mt.m2day.org/2008/index2.php?option=com_content&task=view&id=12512&pop=1&page=0<emid=84 on 23 September 2008.

——, 'Was Merdeka taken or was it given?' posted on *Malaysia Today* website (www.malaysia-today.net) on 8 November 2010.

Keenleyside, T.A., 'Nationalist Indian Attitudes towards Asia: A Troublesome Legacy for Post-Independence Indian Foreign Policy', *Pacific Affairs*, vol. 55, no. 2 (Summer, 1982), pp. 210-30.

Kennedy, B.E., 'Anglo-French Rivalry in Southeast Asia 1763–93: Some Repercussions', *Journal of Southeast Asian Studies*, vol. 4, no. 2 (September 1973), pp. 199-215.

Kim, Khoo Kay, 'Malaysia: Immigration and the Growth of a Plural Society', *JMBRAS*, vol. LXXI, pt. I, 1998.

Kranton, Rachel E. and Anand V. Swamy, 'Contracts, Hold-Up, and Exports: Textiles and Opium in Colonial India', published in December 2006, accessed on 12 July 2010 at http://www.williams.edu/Economics/wp/swamytextileopiumdecember2006final.pdf, pp. 1-36.

Kuppuswamy, C.S., 'MALAYSIA: Whither the Indians', Paper no. 4212, *South Asia Analysis Group (SAAG)*, 7 December 2010.

Lee, Sharon M., 'Female Immigrants and Labour in Colonial Malaya: 1860-1947', *International Migration Review*, vol. 23, no. 2, Summer 1989, pp. 309-31.

Linehan, W., 'A History of Pahang' *JMBRAS*, vol. XIV, pt. II, 1936.

Mahmud, Zaharah, 'The Population of Kedah in the Nineteenth Century', *Journal of Southeast Asian Studies*, vol. 3, no. 2, September 1972, pp. 193-209.

Mansergh, Nicholas, 'The Asian Conference', *International Affairs (Royal Institute of International Affairs 1944-)*, vol. 23, no. 3, July 1947, pp. 295-306.

Marrison, G.E., 'Persian Influence in Malay Life (1280-1650)', *JMBRAS*, vol. XXVIII, pt. I, 1955, pp. 52.

——, 'The Coming of Islam to the East Indies', *JMBRAS*, vol. XXIV, pt. I, 1951.

Marshall, P.J., 'Western Arms in Maritime Asia in the Early Phases of Expansion', *Modern Asan Studies*, vol. 14, no. 1 (1980), pp. 13-28.

Mills, Lennox, 'British Malaya' Part I, *JMBRAS*, vol. I, pt. II, 1925, pp. 1-98; Part II, *JMBRAS*, vol. I, pt. II, 1925, pp. 99-198; Part III, *JMBRAS*, vol. III, pt. II, 1925, pp. 199-338.

Means, Gordon P., '"Special Rights" as a Strategy for Development: The Case of Malaysia', *Comparative Politics* (City University of New York), vol. 5, no. 1, October 1972, pp. 29-61.

——, 'The Role of Islam in the Political Development of Malaysia', *Comparative Politics* (City University of New York), vol. 1, no. 2, January 1969, pp. 264-84.

Milner, Anthony, 'Who Created Malaysia's Plural Society?', *JMBRAS*, vol. 76, pt. II, 2003, pp. 1-24.

Ir Moens, J.L., 'Srivijaya, Yava en Kataha', an abridged translation by RJ de Touche, *JMBRAS*, vol. XVII, 1940.

Morley, J.A.E., 'The Arabs and the Eastern Trade', *JMBRAS*, vol. XXII, pt. I, 1949, pp. 150-76.

Muni, S.D., 'India's "Look East" Policy: The Strategic Dimension', ISAS, Singapore, Working Paper no. 121, 1 February 2011.

Mukerji, Rahul, 'Appraising the Legacy of Bandung: A View from India', ISAS, Singapore, Working Paper no. 11, 8 May 2006.

Noor, Farish A., 'At Home Across the Ocean: The Role of the Indian Muslim Diaspora in the Expansion of Religious Networks in Southeast Asia', paper prepared for the Conference on Counter-Terrorism Strategies for South Asia, organized by the Bangladesh Institute for Peace and Security Studies (BIPSS), Dhaka, 24-5 February 2009.

——, 'From Empire to the War on Terror: The 1915 Indian Sepoy Mutiny in Singapore as a Case Study of the Impact of Profiling of Religious and Ethnic Minorities', paper prepared for S. Rajaratnam School of International Studies (RSIS), Cluster Group 'Transnational Religion in Southeast Asia', Nanyang Technological University, Singapore.

——, 'The Arrival of Islam to Southeast Asia from India: The Second Wave of "Indianisation" Revisited', *Journal of the Society of Indian Ocean Studies*, September 2010, New Delhi.

——, 'From Majapahit to Putrajaya: The *Kris* as a Symptom of Civilisational Development and Decline', *Journal of South East Asian Research*, vol. 8, no. 3, School of Oriental and African Studies, London, November 2000.

——, 'The Hindu Rights Action Force (HINDRAF) of Malaysia: Communitarianism Across Borders?', 4 July 2008, Working Paper no. 163, S. Rajaratnam School of International Studies, Nanyang Technological University, Singapore.

Palmer, J Norman, 'Malaysia 1965: Challenging the Terms of 1957', *Asian Survey*, vol. 6, no. 2, February 1966, pp. 111-18.

Papers presented at Colloquium on 'Indians in Penang: A Historical Perspective' organized in Penang on 22 September 2001 by the Penang Heritage Trust, and co-organized by the Indian Chamber of Commerce and Industry, Penang.

Prakash, Om, 'The Indian Maritime Merchant, 1500-1800', *Journal of the Economic and Social History of the Orient*, vol. 47, no. 3, Special issue: Between the Flux and Facts of Indian History: Papers in Honour of Dirk Kolff (2004), pp. 435-57.

Rabushka, Alvin, 'The Manipulation of Ethnic Politics in Malaya', *Polity*, vol. 2, no. 3 (Palgrave Macmillan Journals), Spring 1970, pp. 345-56.

Rahman, Tunku Abdul, 'Malaysia: Key Area in Southeast Asia', *Foreign Affairs*, vol. 43, no. 4, July 1965, pp. 659-70.

Ramakrishna, Kumar, 'Telling the People the Truth: The Role of Strategic Propaganda in the Malayan Emergency', *JMBRAS*, vol. 75, pt. I, 2002, pp. 49 to 76.

Razaleigh Hamzah, Tengku, 'Race: Time for a New Beginning', speech on Sunday, 9 August 2009 at Melbourne University, Australia, organized by Kelab UMNO Australia Melbourne as part of their Seminar on 'Racial Integration and Its Challenges'.

Reid, Anthony, 'An "Age of Commerce" in Southeast Asian History', *Modern Asian Studies*, vol. 24, no. 1 (February 1990), pp. 1-30.

Rentse, Anker, 'History of Kelantan', *JMBRAS*, vol. XII, pt. II, 1934, pp. 44-61.

van Ronkel, Ph. S., 'A Tamil Malay Manuscript', *Journal of the Straits Branch of the Royal Asiatic Society*, no. 85, 1922.

SCIENCE, weekly journal published by the American Association for the Advancement of Science (AAAS), vol. 326, 11 December 2009, pp. 1470 and 1541-45.

Sen, S.P., 'The Role of Indian Textiles in Southeast Asian Trade in the Seventeenth Century', *Journal of Southeast Asian History*, vol. 3, no. 2, September 1962, pp. 92-110.

Shamsul, A.B., 'A History of an Identity, an Identity of a History: The Idea and Practice of "Malayness" in Malaysia Reconsidered', *Journal of South East Asian Studies*, vol. 32, no. 3, October 2001, pp. 355-66.

Shellabear, William G., 'An Outline of the *Malay Annals* (Shellabear's Romanised edition, Singapore, 1909)', *JMBRAS*, vol. XVI, pt. III, 1938.

Singh, D.S. Ranjit, 'British Proposals for a Dominion of Southeast Asia, 1943-1957', *JMBRAS*, vol. LXXI, pt. I, 1998, pp. 27-40.

Sullivan, Michael, 'Excavations in Kedah and Province Wellesley, 1957', *JMBRAS*, vol. XXXI, pt. I, 1958.

O'Sullivan, W.A., 'The Relations Between Southern India and the Straits Settlements', *Journal of the Straits Branch of the Royal Asiatic Society*, no. 36, 1901.

Suryanarayan, V., 'Malaysian Indian Society in Ferment', paper presented in the International Seminar on India and Asia-Pacific: Convergence and Divergence, held at the Centre for Southeast Asian and Pacific Studies, Sri Venkateswara University, Tirupati, 13 October 2008.

Tarling, Nicholas, 'British Policy in the Malay Peninsula and Archipelago 1824-1871', *JMBRAS*, vol. XXX, pt. III, no. 179, 1957.

——, 'The Superintendence of British Interests in South-East Asian the Nineteenth Century', *Journal of Southeast Asian History*, vol. 7, no. 1 (March 1966), pp. 97-110.

The Indian, back issues from the 1930s, when it was published every Saturday in Kuala Lumpur, accessed in the Library of the National University of Singapore, Singapore

Tibbetts, G.R., 'Early Muslim Traders in South-east Asia', *JMBRAS*, vol. XXX, pt. I, 1957.

Tilak, S.J., ed., 1992, *Netaji Subhas Chandra Bose: A Malaysian Perspective*, Kuala Lumpur: The Netaji Centre.

Turnbull, Constance M., 'Communal Disturbances in the Straits Settlements in 1857', *JMBRAS*, vol. XXXI, pt. I, 1958, pp. 94-144.

Wade, Geoff, 'The Origins and Evolution of Ethnocracy in Malaysia', Asia Research Institute (National University of Singapore) Working Paper Series no. 112, April 2009.

Wales, H.G. Quaritch, 'The Sambas Finds in Relation to the Problems of Indo-Malaysian Art Development', *JMBRAS*, vol. XXII, pt. IV, 1949, pp. 23-32.

——, 'Archaeological Researches on Ancient Indian Colonization in Malaya', conducted by the Greater-India Research Committee representing the Royal Asiatic Society, India Society, and School of Oriental and African Studies, under the patronage of the Governments of Kedah, Perak, and Johore (1937-9), as well as Mrs C.N. Wrentmore (1935-6) and H.H. the late Maharaja Gaekwar of Baroda (1934-5), *JMBRAS*, vol. XVIII, pt. I, 1940.

Wang Gungwu, 'The Nanhai Trade', *JMBRAS*, vol. XXXI, pt. 2, 1959.

——, 'The First Three Rulers of Malacca', *JMBRAS*, vol. 41, pt. 1, 1968, pp. 11-22.

Waythamoorthy, Ponusamy, Text of Claim filed on 30 August 2007 in the High Court of Justice, Queen's Bench Division, London, by Waytha Moorthy Ponnusamy (suing in his personal capacity and as representing and for the benefit of all persons interested in and who are Malaysian citizens of Indian origin) against the Secretary of State for Commonwealth Affairs, pp. 1-29.

Wilkinson, R.J., 'Malay Customs and Beliefs', *JMBRAS*, vol. 30, pt. IV, no. 180.

——, 'Early Indian Influences in Malaysia', *JMBRAS*, vol. XIII, pt. II, 1935, pp. 1-16.

Williams, G.C. Griffith, 'Suggested Origin of the Malay Keris and of the Superstitions Attaching to It', *JMBRAS*, vol. XV, pt. III, 1937, pp. 127-41.

Winstedt, Richard Olaf, 'A History of Malay Literature with a Chapter on Modern Developments by Zaba (Zain al-Abidin bin Ahmad)', *JMBRAS*, vol. XVII, pt. 3, pp. 1-243.

——, 'Kingship and Enthronement in Malaya', *JMBRAS*, vol. XX, pt. I, 1947.

——, 'A History of Selangor', *JMBRAS*, vol. XII, pt. III, October 1934.

——, 'Negri Sembilan: The History, Polity and Beliefs of the Nine States', *JMBRAS*, vol. XII, pt. III, October 1934.

——, 'Kedah Laws', *JMBRAS*, vol. VI, pt. II, 1928, pp. 1-13.

——, 'A History of Johore: 1365-1895 A.D.', *JMBRAS*, vol. X, pt. III, December 1932.

——, 'The Advent of Muhammadanism in the Malay Peninsula and Archipelago', *Journal of the Straits Branch of the Royal Asiatic Society*, no. 77, 1917.

——, 'The Chronicles of Pasai', *JMBRAS*, vol. XVI, pt. II, 1938.

——, 'The Indian Origin of Malay Folk-Tales', *Journal of the Straits Branch of the Royal Asiatic Society*, no. 82, 1920.

——, 'Mother-right among Khasis and Malays', *JMBRAS*, vol. X, pt. I, 1932, pp. 9-13.

——, 'The Founder of Malay Royalty and his Conquest of Saktimuna, the Serpent', *JMBRAS*, vol. IV, 1926, pp. 413-19 .

Winstedt, R.O. and R.J. Wilkinson, 'A History of Perak', *JMBRAS*, vol. XII, pt. I, June 1934, pp. 1-125.

Yang, Anand A., 'Indian Convict Workers in Southeast Asia in the Late 18th and Early 19th Centuries', *Journal of World History* (University of Hawai'i Press), vol. 14, no. 2, June 2003, pp. 179-208.

Index